The First 100 Days of Covid-19

Aleksandar Stojanović · Luisa Scarcella ·
Christina R. Mosalagae
Editors

The First 100 Days of Covid-19

Law and Political Economy of the Global Policy Response

palgrave
macmillan

Editors
Aleksandar Stojanović
New York University
Shanghai, China

Luisa Scarcella
DigiTax Centre
University of Antwerp
Antwerp, Belgium

Christina R. Mosalagae
University of Turin
Turin, Italy

ISBN 978-981-19-6324-7 ISBN 978-981-19-6325-4 (eBook)
https://doi.org/10.1007/978-981-19-6325-4

This Palgrave Macmillan imprint is published by the registered company Springer Nature Singapore Pte Ltd.
The registered company address is: 152 Beach Road, #21-01/04 Gateway East, Singapore 189721, Singapore

Acknowledgements

This collection of essays could not have been completed without the dedication and intellectual contributions of many colleagues, mentors, and friends. Firstly, we would like to thank all the country rapporteurs who participated in the first phase of the *Global Responses to Covid-19: A Law and Economics Comparative Project* by completing questionnaires on Covid-19 policy for their jurisdiction. Your selfless efforts during a precarious time (filled with uncertainty) formed the foundation of our research project and culminated in this book. Moreover, we are especially grateful to those country rapporteurs who became contributors to this book by providing analytical chapters for their jurisdictions. Your commitment and dedication is greatly appreciated. Secondly, we are indebted to the mentors who assisted with the drafting of the questionnaires and provided overall guidance of this research project.

Thirdly, thank you to the Young Scholars Initiative (YSI) of the Institute for New Economic Thinking (INET), the Association for Promotion of Political Economy and Law, the International University College of Turin and Bocconi University for bringing together the young and senior scholars to collaborate on this project.

Lastly, our heartfelt gratitude to Hemapriya Eswanth and Jacob Dreyer for their laborious editorial assistance and patience throughout this process. It goes without saying that the people and institutions listed here bear no responsibility for our own errors, omissions, or opinions.

Contents

Notes on Contributors

Binit Agrawal is a Master's candidate pursuing the European Master's in Law and Economics as an Erasmus Scholar. He graduated with a B.A. LL.B. (Hons.) from the National Law School of India University, Bengaluru in 2021. His research interests include Constitutional Law, Law and Economics, and legal analysis of socio-economic policies. He is also a founding-editor of www.lawschoolpolicyreview.com.

Dashiell Anderson is an incoming Ph.D. candidate in Economics at the University of Leeds. After graduating with degrees in Economics and English from the University of Utah in 2019, he completed an M.A. in Economics from the New School for Social Research. He is most recently completing his LL.M. in Comparative Law, Economics, and Finance at the International University College of Turin. Dash is interested in the history and theory of economic spatiality, economic geography, and economic agglomerations. He is writing his Ph.D. dissertation on how to best differentiate between urban and rural worker exploitation, with a particular emphasis on the spatial history of capital relations and class struggle.

Apilang Apum is currently teaching Economics in JTGMD College, Roing, India. She received a Ph.D. in Economics from Rajiv Gandhi University Itanagar in September 2021. She is also an Executive Member of North Eastern Economics Association and her research interest areas include Development Economics, Labour Economics, and Health Economics.

Zvikomborero Chadambuka is a Visiting Assistant Professor of Law and Fellow in Law, Business and Economics at the Villanova University Charles Widger School of Law. He is also a Non-resident Research Fellow in Law at Yale Law School's Center for Private law. His areas of interest and expertise include property, human rights, comparative law, and law and economics.

Aneesha Chitgupi is a research fellow at the XKDR-Forum-Chennai Mathematical Institute. She received her Ph.D. in 2020 from Institute for Social and Economic Change, Bangalore. Her thesis analysed the economic determinants of India's external stabilization under the balance of payments framework. Her current research interests are public finance, government debt, and liabilities management. She is the coordinator of YSI South Asia Working Group and Alumni member at the Board of Studies for Mount Carmel College, Bangalore.

Wanshu Cong is a post-doctoral fellow at Hong Kong University School of Law. She was a Max Weber fellow at European University Institute (2020–2021). She holds a doctoral degree from McGill University Faculty of Law and an LL.M. from Geneva Academy of International Humanitarian Law and Human Rights. Her research interests include human rights, the intersection of law and technology, and critical legal studies. Her current project looks at transitional data governance from Marxist and postcolonial perspectives.

Luis Cortés is a lawyer with a Bachelor's in Law and Social Sciences from Universidad de Chile. He is a Master's student in Interdisciplinary Latin American Studies, Freie Universität Berlin. His research interests include Regulatory Law, Natural Resources regulation, and Fisheries.

Federica Cristani is a Senior Researcher at the Centre for International Law of the Institute of International Relations in Prague (CZ) and a Visiting Senior Researcher at the Arctic Centre of the University of Lapland (FI). She holds a Ph.D. (with the certificate of Doctor Europaeus) in international law and a degree in law from the University of Verona (IT). She earlier worked as a post-doctoral researcher at the World Trade Institute of the University of Bern (CH), and at the

University of Verona, and has been a visiting scholar in different universities and research centres in Hungary, Slovakia, Germany, Denmark, the United Kingdom, and the United States. She has been adjunct professor in Bologna (IT) and a guest lecturer in Budapest (HU), Bratislava (SK), and Kharkiv (Ukraine). Her main research interests include international economic law, the policies of sub-regional groups in Europe, and international law of cyberspace. She is a Co-Chair of the Coordinating Committee of the Interest Group on International Economic Law of the European Society of International Law (ESIL).

Guo Dongcheng is a graduate student at the China University of Political Science and Law. In Law School, his research field and interests mainly include legal philosophy and sociology of law while the comparative analysis of law and policy is one of his recent areas of study. During the pandemic, in the first quarter of 2020, Guo was part of a team that aimed to compile reports about the legal and financial response to COVID-19 in China.

Osatohanmwen Anastasia Eruaga is an Associate Professor (Research) with the Nigerian Institute of Advanced Legal Studies. She has been involved in extensive legal research and writing in the areas of public international law especially Maritime, Environmental sustainability, and Human Rights Law. Her research interests are Maritime Security, Africa Economic Integration, Environmental Sustainability, and Irregular migration from a maritime perspective. She is currently involved in a research that explores the privatization of maritime security within the Gulf of Guinea.

Leonides Frago, Jr. obtained his B.A. in Political Science from the University of the Philippines-Diliman. He then pursued post-graduate coursework in the M.A. International Relations programme of Beijing Foreign Studies University. His major research interests include political identity and social movements, decentralization and political dynasties, regionalization, and Track II diplomacy.

Elisa Gibellino is a juris doctor with a degree in law obtained from the University of Eastern Piedmont (IT). During the University years she was interested in extracurricular activities as Mediation competitions at the Arbitral Chamber of Milan and International civil rights moot Court. After University she started her Law Practice in order to become a lawyer, in the meantime she obtained two Master's. One in Economy, Finance and Comparative Law at the International University College in Turin and another one in Law of the Internet Technology at Bocconi University with a special interest in Blockchain/Fintech and GDPR. Now she is working in the legal department in a healthcare company in Turin (Piedmont, Italy) as legal and privacy specialist.

Arletta Gorecka is currently a Ph.D. Candidate at the University of Strathclyde. Arletta has worked at various law firms in Scotland and actively supported international, law, and doctoral students. She also acts as a freelance interpreter and provided support for the Vis Moot. Arletta also assists in the delivery of undergraduate and postgraduate modules in the University of Stirling, University of Strathclyde, and Glasgow Caledonian University. She is a Policy Analysis at the Inclusive Competition Forum and Communications, Dissemination and Accessibility Officer at Scottish Law and Innovational Network. Arletta's research interest includes privacy protection, digital economy, goals and enforcement of competition law, and Big Data. Arletta's thesis focuses on the impact of privacy on the EU competition law. She is the author of several articles and chapters in scholarly books about the issues related to competition law and privacy.

Fatemeh Halabisaz is a Ph.D. candidate at the IE Business School in Madrid. She has experience as an economic researcher for the Philippine government, mainly being involved with handling merger and acquisition cases. She has business and economic education from the Philippines, France, and the United Kingdom.

Zita M. Hansungule is a full-time Doctoral candidate working on a thesis that focuses on access to justice for children in South Africa. She worked for the Centre for Child Law, University of Pretoria until 2021 as a project coordinator in its research, monitoring, and evaluation unit. She has a particular interest in child justice, rights of children with disabilities, the care and protection of vulnerable children as well as access to justice for children. She was involved in the Global Study on Children Deprived of Liberty as well as a study on the impact of South Africa's Child Justice Act, commissioned by the Department of Justice and Constitutional Development. She is currently involved in a study on Secure Care Centres in South Africa.

Khensani Hlongwane is currently employed as a Law Researcher at the Labour and the Labour Appeal Court, Johannesburg. Her work includes providing research and editorial assistance on judgements, preparing memorandums and legal opinions concerning labour disputes, and providing updates on recent developments within the law. She holds a Bachelor of Laws degree from the University of Stellenbosch, 2018 and completed her articles of clerkship at Cliffe Dekker Hofmeyr Inc. in 2020. Her areas of interest include employment rights, dispute resolution, and the intersection between human rights and labour law.

Huang Junyue is currently pursuing an LL.M. at Georgetown University Law Center. She has obtained a Bachelor of Laws from Beijing Institute of Technology. During her studies, she tried to explore the theory and application of law in new fields, such as international law in outer space and copyright law under the influence of artificial intelligence. She is also keen to analyse the theories of Weber and Maine on legal rationality and legal formation. She has also studied quantitative history research at Peking University and has a great interest in positive jurisprudence. As a former economics student, she hopes that more economic methods can help prove the practical effect of law and make suggestions for legislation. In this regard, she conducted research on Chinese environmental law with the help of SPSS and AMOS software.

Ádám Kerényi is a Junior Research Fellow at the Institute of World Economics of the Centre for Economic and Regional Studies, where he is a member of the Research Group on European Integration. His research interests include financial stability, innovation, political economy, and public policy, and he studies the effects of digital transformation on legislation at the EU level and in the member states as an external visiting fellow in the Centre for Social Sciences POLECON. He is a member of the World Interdisciplinary Network for Institutional Research (WINIR) and the European Association for Evolutionary Political Economy (EAEPE). He is a working group coordinator at the Institute for New Economic Thinking's Young Scholars Initiative (INET YSI). He is an external lecturer at the University of Szeged and Corvinus University of Budapest, where he was a research assistant to professor János Kornai until his death. He has published articles in Acta Oeconomica, Financial and Economic Review, Economy and Finance, and Public Finance Quarterly.

José Ledesma is a lawyer who holds a Bachelor's in Law and Social Sciences from Universidad de Chile and is a Master's Student in Public

Policy, Universidad de Chile. Research interests: Regulatory Law, Environmental Law, and Mining rent.

Yao Libo has a Bachelor's Degree in Law (2018) and a second Bachelor's Degree in Political Science and Administration (2018) from Tsinghua University. She is working on her Master's degree at Tsinghua Law School. The current focus of her research is on fundamental rights such as privacy right in cyber society. She also has a keen interest in comparative law and law in social theory.

João Victor R. Longi is a Post-Doctoral fellow at the International Postdoctoral Program in New Technologies and Law at the Mediterranea International Center for Human Rights Research (MICHR—Università "Mediterranea" di Reggio Calabria), Italy. Post-Doctor in Legal Studies from Nothern Parana State University, Brazil. Doctors in State Law from University of Sao Paulo, Brazil. Master's in Private Law from Rio de Janeiro State University. Visiting Professor of the Postgraduate Program in Law at Nothern Parana State University. Public Defender of the State of Parana.

Ryan Martinez is a graduate student at the Department of Sociology, University of the Philippines Diliman. He is currently a senior research associate of the Program on Alternative Development of the University of the Philippines Center for Integrative and Development Studies.

Christina R. Mosalagae is currently enrolled as a Ph.D. Candidate in Law and Institutions at the University of Turin. She holds an LL.M. from Cornell University as well as an L.L.M. in Constitutional and Administrative Law from the University of Pretoria; and a Master's in Comparative Law, Economics & Finance from the International University College of Turin (with distinction). Her research interests include: Comparative Law, Constitutional Law, Property Law as well as Law and Political Economy.

Michael W. Müller is currently a postdoctoral researcher at the University of Munich (LMU) Munich. His doctoral dissertation on the law of financial stabilization (summa cum laude) was published with Mohr Siebeck and awarded the LMU Faculty Prize. Michael read law at LMU and holds both Bavarian State Exams, qualifying him for legal practice. Moreover, he obtained an LL.M. from Cambridge University (First Class, Wolfson College Jennings Prize), an M.A. in Philosophy from LMU, and a Diploma in the Law of the European Union from the Academy of European Law, Florence.

Muriuki Muriungi is Partner at Kosgei, Muriuki and Koome Advocates in Nairobi, Kenya and Lecturer at the School of Law, University of Nairobi. He read for a Master of Science in Law and Finance at St. Peter's College, University of Oxford, UK where he was a Standard Bank Africa Chairman Scholar. He also holds a Master of Law in Public Finance and Financial Services Law (LL.M) and a Bachelor of Laws (LL.B) from the University of Nairobi as well as a post-graduate diploma in legal practice from the Kenya School of Law. He is also a doctoral candidate in law researching into the role of central banking in mobilizing climate finance at the University of Nairobi. Muriuki is a member of the global network of the International Network for Sustainable Financial Policy Insights, Research, and Exchange (INSPIRE) currently inquiring into the role of central banks in sustainable finance. His areas of legal practice and research interests reside in the area of sustainable finance, property rights, and financial regulation. Muriuki is widely published in various areas of law including sustainable finance, electoral law, property theory, environmental law, and judicial reforms.

Naomi Musau is an Advocate of the High Court of Kenya and a member of the Law Society of Kenya. She holds a Bachelor of Laws (LL.B.) degree (Hons.) from the University of Nairobi and a Postgraduate Diploma in Law from the Kenya School of Law. She is a member of Young Scholars Initiative (YSI) Finance, Law and Economics Working Group, the Academic Council on United Nations Systems (ACUNS) and Women in Maritime in East and Southern Africa (WOMESA). She has been invited to and participated in various international conferences as a speaker and panellist including the Academic Council on United Nations Systems (ACUNS) Annual Meeting 2019 (Stellenbosch University, South Africa) and the 2020 Afterlives of Development Conference (Ben Gurion University of the Negev, Israel). She has previously researched on Sustainable Development, the Sustainable Blue Economy, and Finance and Law and Economics.

Kelello Nkadimeng currently works for ABSA Group Limited (ABSA) a financial services provider in Johannesburg, South Africa. Her current role at ABSA is Consultant for Regulatory Reporting. Her areas of expertise include banking, regulatory, risk management, compliance, and governance. Kelello holds a BCom Degree, Postgraduate diplomas in Internal Auditing and Insurance & Risk Management. Her current research projects are on: (1) Conduct regulations and the banking industry post COVID-19; and (2) The financial services strategic resilience frameworks. She is affiliated with the Institute of Risk Management of South Africa and the Institute of Internal Auditors South Africa.

Abigail Osiki currently lectures in the Mercantile and Labour Law department at the University of the Western Cape (UWC), South Africa. She is also a research associate at the Centre for Transformative Regulation of Work, UWC, Cape Town. Abigail's research background is in working poverty, sustainable development, and policy reform, with a specific interest in the informal economy in Sub-Saharan Africa. She recently completed a post-doctoral fellowship with the Fairwork Project. She holds a Ph.D. in labour law from the University of Cape Town.

Mariella Pittari is a Ph.D. candidate in Law and Institutions at the University of Turin. Cornell Law School 2018 LL.M.; Master's in Comparative Law, Economics and Finance at the International College of Turin. Alumni at the Institute for US Law in Washington, DC Visiting Scholar at University of Miami Law School. Public Defender in Brazil. Research topics: (1) Political Science and Legal Theory intertwined; (2) Philosophy of Law; (3) Civil Procedure and access to justice in the Age of Technology; (4) State of Exception in Private Law; and (5) the rise of inequality. Currently researching Political Theology and the archeological concepts of Sovereignty.

Alexandre San Martim Portes is a Ph.D. Candidate in Regulation and Global Governance at the Australian National University (School of Regulation and Global Governance—RegNet). He holds a Master's degree in Public Economics, Law, and Politics from Leuphana University (Germany) and a Bachelor's degree in International Relations from the Federal University of Santa Catarina (Brazil). His research interests include trade policy and regulation, intellectual property rights, sustainable development, and international political economy.

Tiago Couto Porto is a Ph.D. candidate in Public Administration and Government at Getulio Vargas Foundation of São Paulo (FGV-SP) and Associate Researcher at the Center for Studies on New Developmentalism at the same institution. Master's degree in economics at University Paris

13Sorbonne Paris Cite, with a period as visiting researcher at the National University of Seoul, South Korea. Major Interests are related to post-Keynesian macroeconomics, technological catch-up strategies, economic development, administration and public sector economics, and political economy.

Vincent Jerald Ramos is a Ph.D. candidate at the DYNAMICS of Demography, Democracy, and Public Policy Research Training Group at the Hertie School Berlin and Humboldt University Berlin. His current research revolves around nonstandard employment and family formation outcomes during periods of crisis.

Sankari Reddy is currently a practising attorney admitted in both Botswana and South Africa and sole director of Sankari Reddy Attorneys based in South Africa. She holds a Bachelor of Commerce degree, and a Bachelor of Laws degree from the University of Pretoria; as well as a Master's in Comparative Law, Economics and Finance (with distinction) from the International University College of Turin; and is currently completing her board exams at the Chartered Governance Institute of Southern Africa. She has also been an entrepreneur for a number of years consulting across Africa in a variety of sectors, such as medical tourism. Her research focus includes ESG, global food law, and international taxation. She is a member of Young Scholars Initiative (YSI) Finance, Law and Economics working group and the Non-Profit Organisation, SABWiL (South African Black Women in Law).

Javiera Rojas holds a Master's in Social Sciences from Universidad de Chile. She is a doctoral researcher at the University of Buenos Aires. Her research interests include agrarian rents, environmental social conflicts, and water disputes in the South American agrarian sector.

Luisa Scarcella is a postdoctoral researcher at the DigiTax Centre of the University of Antwerp (Belgium); and she was recently awarded a Post-doctoral fellowship by the Austrian Academy of Sciences. In 2020, Luisa obtained her Ph.D. with distinction from the Karl-Franzens University of Graz (Austria) with a dissertation focusing on the VAT treatment of cryptocurrencies and in 2015, she graduated in Law from the University of Udine (Italy).

Christopher Pomwene Shafuda is a Lecturer in the School of Management, Governance and Economics at the University of Namibia. His area of research includes public policy, public financial management, welfare, and development economics. He is currently working on informal rules and formal constraints and how they affect individual choices and development processes.

He Simeng is a post-graduate student at Tsinghua Law School, majoring in comparative law. She has a Bachelor's degree in Law from Sun Yat-Sen University and has been an exchange student at the National Tsinghua University in Taiwan. Her interest in the constitutional right on property led her to do projects with the keywords: Chinese traditional contract rule, land regulation, administrative law, and property right, from historical and comparative perspective.

Madhu Sivaraman is a policy research professional and Chevening FCO UK Scholar with 11 years of experience in the domains of industrial policies, urban transport, governance & regulations, and data policies. Madhu is currently working as Policy Manager at LEAD at Krea University handling various evidence-based research initiatives under the MSME vertical. Prior to this, Madhu was a Senior Policy Expert at Ernst & Young LLP advising the State Government of Uttar Pradesh in Khadi and Village Industry Board. Madhu also worked as Director (Research and Projects) at Centre for Public Policy Research (CPPR), a think tank based in Kerala, where he was involved in a multi- disciplinary role engaging in projects and initiatives in urban transport, city governance, livelihood, and education.

Aleksandar Stojanović is an assistant professor of practice in Economics at New York University Shanghai. He holds doctoral degrees in economics (Collegio Carlo Alberto) and law (University of Ghent). His research combines law and political economy, monetary economics, and finance. Currently studies China's cross-border payment system and money markets.

Lauren Sweger-Hollingsworth is a scholar of political economy, with a special focus on the history of thought and environmental ethics. She received a Bachelor of science from Portland State University, majoring in quantitative economics and minoring in mathematics, and a Master's of art from the New School for Social Research in global political economy and finance. She is currently completing additional graduate studies in comparative law, economics, and finance at the International University College of Turin, while also in the applications process for doctoral programmes. As an undergraduate, five of Lauren's working papers were published by her university's library and, upon graduation from the New School, Lauren was selected by the Dean to receive the Outstanding Master of Arts Graduate Award.

Annalisa Tassi is a Ph.D. student at the FAU Erlangen-Nürnberg, Chair of Public Finance. Her main research interests are public economics, labour economics, and European Affairs. She is currently part of a project on VAT.

Javiera Toro is a lawyer who holds a Bachelor's in Law and Social Sciences from Universidad de Chile. Her specialization is in administrative and regulatory Law. Her main research area is social rights. In addition, as an activist and politician, she currently (2022) serves as Minister of National Assets from the government of Gabriel Boric.

Itoro Ubi-Abai obtained his Ph.D. in economics from the Faculty of Social Science, University of Uyo, Nigeria. Itoro serves as a Research Assistant to a Professor of Economics, and performs a supervisory role at the University's Consultancy firm. His areas of expertise are Development Economics, Public Sector Economics, Environmental Economics, Health Economics, and Econometrics. His research interests are contemporary issues in development that include, but not limited to, Public Policy Analysis, Community Welfare Analysis, Climate Change Economic Analysis, Infrastructure Development, and Economic Modelling. He is currently undertaking two research projects aside the Comparative COVID-19 study project. One is investigating the municipal water management and access to water services in Akwa Ibom State, Nigeria. The other is investigating the distribution pattern of food relief materials to households in a Nigerian community since the outbreak of the COVID-19 disease.

Weichen Wang is a Ph.D. researcher at the University of Bath. His research interests include growth theory, automation, and Covid pandemic. He participated in the Extended Problem Solving Workshop (EPSW) under the OECD problem: Effectiveness of Covid policy interventions in different countries and lessons for the future. His research interests include growth theory and automation.

Xinyi Xu studies at the China University of Political Science and Law. She is major in private international law, especially in international commercial arbitration.

An Zhai is currently pursuing an LL.M. at the University College London (specialized in public law). He gained his Bachelor's degree in law from the China University of Political Science and Law, His main academic concerns are public law and political philosophy, with a focus on fundamental rights and judicial review. He is one of the LL.M. editors of the *UCL Journal of Law and Jurisprudence*.

List of Figures

Reinforcement of Economic Inequality and Extra Economic Power—Law and Political Economy of the US Pandemic Policy Response

List of Tables

Global Covid-19 Policy Response Between Law and Political Economy

Aleksandar Stojanović, Luisa Scarcella, and Christina R. Mosalagae

It is probable that in the time to come, historians and commentators will consider the Covid-19 pandemic as one of the defining moments—if not *the* defining moment—of the twenty-first century. Its exceptional importance comes both from the tragic human cost and economic damage that it entailed; as well as from the policy responses that governments around the world mounted to overcome the challenge. States of exception led to the establishment of new types of rules and orders that will affect the lives of generations to come. In that sense, the pandemic is a deeply political event. It is also an event that behind an apparent commonality hides significant diversity. At the onset, societies around the world

A. Stojanović (✉)
New York University in Shanghai, Shanghai, China
e-mail: as14902@nyu.edu

L. Scarcella
University of Antwerp, Antwerpen, Belgium
e-mail: luisa.scarcella@uantwerpen.be

C. R. Mosalagae
University of Turin, Turin, Italy
e-mail: christinarefhilwe.mosalagae@unito.it

A. Stojanović et al. (eds.), *The First 100 Days of Covid-19*,
https://doi.org/10.1007/978-981-19-6325-4_1

were following different albeit interrelated governance models. As the pandemic spread, their institutional environments were affected by significantly different policy choices. As the dangers began to diminish—or the presence of the ever changing virus became the "new normal"—these choices were incorporated into the pre-existing institutional reality in different ways.

This collection of essays is an attempt to account for that diversity to assess the significance that the event of the pandemic might have for societies around the world in the future. In that regard, this book is one among many contributions that have appeared in the recent period. What makes it specific is its synthetic law-and-political-economy approach. Our project started in March 2020, when we gathered a group of friends and colleagues to think about how the legal foundations of policy making will affect and be affected by the specific political economy conditions across different jurisdictions. That conversation led to the creation of a set of questionnaires (we provide here in the Appendix) that addressed the topics we thought were particularly relevant in this regard: (1) state of exception (2) surveillance and compliance (3) legal-financial architecture (4) financial relief for labor (5) financial relief for business and (6) alternative policy proposals made by social movements, activist groups, and civil society. Over one hundred scholars from forty jurisdictions used the framework provided by the questionnaire to evidence the pandemic policy efforts focusing on the interplay between the legal form and that of political-economic conditions existing on the ground during the first 100 days. Their rich and illuminative contributions were published online at http://globalresponsescovid19.com. Once the reports were published, we asked our collaborators to consider: how the law-and-political-economy trajectories across these different policy domains interacted with each other; how the emergency rules invoked were used to surveil and enforce the ongoing limitation of rights and imposition of obligations, while providing economic relief across sectors and social classes; to what extent was this process participatory and solidarity-based, or had it faced resistance, and in what ways had different power formations interacted in the process; and finally, what were the outcomes of this process—in particular in reproducing and exasperating existing inequality and distribution of privileges. The fifteen chapters before you are the outcome of that effort. The rest of this introduction will provide a brief survey of existing comparative literature on the pandemic response policy discussing the specificity of this contribution in that context and a short summary of the chapters.

* * *

Since 2020, the outbreak of the COVID-19 pandemic and the reactions of governments around the world has become a pervasive topic of research. The policy responses to the pandemic crisis have been as diverse as the areas impacted. This diversity is well represented in literature. Among the studies conducted over the past two years, many approached specific areas of inquiry from a global perspective while others offered an overall analysis focusing on a single jurisdiction or region.

Some of the studies are based on empirical databases. These studies mainly, although not exclusively, focus on economic aspects of the pandemic response policy. This is the case of the Oxford COVID-19 Government Response Tracker which continuously updated information on policy measures adopted starting from 1 January 2020 in more than 180 countries related to closure and containment, health and economic policy (Hale et al., 2020). In the Oxford study, policy responses are recorded on ordinal or continuous scales based on 19 policy areas; and its aim is to allow researchers and policymakers to empirically explore the effects of policy responses on the spread of COVID-19 cases and deaths, as well as on economic and social welfare. This dataset has also been used by other scholars complementary to other studies and datasets. This is the case of Kubinec et al. who by combining the Oxford dataset with the CoronaNet COVID-19 Government Response Event Dataset, using a Bayesian time-varying measurement model, presented six new indices that measure the intensity of government responses to COVID-19 within distinct policy domains: social distancing, schools, businesses, health monitoring, health resources and mask wearing from 1 January 2020 to 14 January 2021, for over 180 countries (Kubinec et al., 2021). Another analysis of the economic responses to the COVID-19 pandemic has been published by Elgin et al. who conducted a comprehensive review of different economic policy measures adopted by 166 countries as a response to the COVID-19 pandemic and created a large database including fiscal, monetary, and exchange rate-related measures (Elgin et al., 2020). At the same time, other publications have surveyed the developing and rapidly growing literature on the economic consequences of COVID-19 and the governmental responses, aiming at synthesizing their insights and focusing on aspects related to labor, health, gender, discrimination, and the environment (Brodeur et al., 2021). Another empirically based study, published by Petherick et al. (2021) focuses on the so-called "pandemic fatigue" and examines whether there was a gradual reduction in adherence to protective behaviors against COVID-19 from March through December 2020, as hypothesized based on the fatigue expectations. Similarly to the Oxford database, the geographical scope of this study is quite broad.

A significant number of contributions address the policy process in terms of conditions that affect it and the outcomes it produces. Policy responses to the COVID-19 pandemic have also been analyzed through the lenses of recommendations from standard welfare economics looking at the reasons behind their adoption (Boettke and Powell, 2021). Similarly, the reasons behind the adoption of policies have been the focus of public health researchers (Greer et al., 2020). While the drivers to the adoption of such policies are also present in all the chapters of this book, this is just one of the important components of the content of the book. Another set of studies has looked at specific consequences deriving from governmental responses to the COVID-19 crisis. For instance, one study has investigated the relationship between various economic policy responses to the COVID-19 pandemic (liquidity support, prudential policies, borrower support, asset purchase, and policy rate decisions) and the growth of nonperforming loans (NPLs) in 2020 across 47 economies (Gholipour and Arjomandi, 2021). Other studies have looked at the role played by Central Banks (Mosser, 2020) in relation to their independence (Elgin et al., 2021), or at the measures to restrict exports of medical products adopted by some governments such as China, the European Union and the United States (Hoekman et al., 2020); and non-pharmaceutical interventions (Bo et al., 2020). Moreover, beyond the economic aspects, other studies have addressed surveillance issues arising from measures adopted during the COVID-19 pandemic crisis (Greitens, 2020; Newell, 2021). Analysis of selected topics of interest have also been conducted by authors who have assessed the economic and health costs of COVID-19 and policy responses to COVID-19, looking both at developed and developing countries (Kaplan et al., 2021).

Finally, in terms of geographical representation of research concerning policy responses to the COVID-19 crisis, some authors have focused their analysis on single jurisdictions. This is, for instance, the case of an article analyzing the implications of the COVID-19 economic crisis for macroeconomic policy, and the roles of the State and the Fed and monetary policy in the US economy, in light of the 2008 Financial Crisis (Vernengo and Nabar-Bhaduri, 2020). Attention has also been given to developing countries from a macro-economic policy perspective (Loayza and Pennings, 2020). Furthermore, an edited book titled "COVID-19 in Developing Economies" has also been published in 2020 (Djankov and Panizza, 2020).

* * *

This collection contributes to the existing literature by focusing on the relationship within the set of significant domains of policy response.

A broad law and political economy approach pursued by authors in this volume relates and yet diverges from the existing literature as it combines descriptive statistics with legal analysis across different legal domains and different types of qualitative analysis. In addition it is specific as it considers pandemic-related policy interventions within the existing institutional and policy context, both in developed and developing economies.

The premise of this collection of essays is that prior to the pandemic the mainstream trajectory in policy was defined by either a jurisdiction specific neoliberal trajectory or in some instances a more "statist" approach. When the pandemic occurred states were at varying levels of ill-preparedness to cope with a health crisis of this magnitude and within a specific set of power relations. Consequently, the exceptionality of the pandemic tipped the existing balance in a specific direction. For the purpose of this introduction we can distinguish three themes that run across the different contributions: the deepening of existing inequalities, general economic downturn, and political tensions. It should be noted that all of the contributions display all three of these themes in varying degrees but each contribution emphasizes a specific theme more than the others.

The first theme that was evident from the contributions was that the pandemic deepened existing inequalities, especially in countries that had already been struggling (in varying degrees) with reducing the socio-economic disparities within their societies. The chapters that exemplify this theme most prominently are South Africa and Kenya.

The contribution from South Africa, co-authored by Zita Hansangule, Khensani Hlongwane, Christina R. Mosalagae, Kelello Nkadimeng, and Sankari Reddy, discusses the impact of COVID-19 on existing inequalities in the South African context. In the chapter, inequality is contextualized firstly as a product of South Africa's history, the effect of three centuries of colonialism followed by over four decades of Apartheid (1948–1994) which was a system of legislated segregation, that privileged certain racial groups over others; and secondly as a result of the adoption of neoliberal policies in the fledgling years of the new constitutional democracy from 1994. Moreover, prior to the pandemic, in addition to displaying high levels of inequality based on the Gini coefficient, South Africa was facing high levels of unemployment, stagnant growth, and political tension. Although the South African government was commendably quick to respond to the crisis, the economic and educational losses during the pandemic, as well as a stretched government budget, have only served to entrench socio-economic inequality deeper into South African society, which needs to be urgently addressed for the future.

Similarly, the Kenyan contribution, co-authored by Muriuki Muriungi and Naomi Ngina, assesses Kenya's COVID-19 policy responses with a view to exploring the inequality dimensions of these responses. The chapter finds that the majority of COVID-19 responses exacerbated inequalities, owing to the fact that policymakers overlooked the potential socio-economic impact of the said responses. The chapter further argues that the policy responses, taken together, have partially challenged the dominant neoliberal framework, at least in so far that they involved the state taking a more proactive role. The chapter then advocates for mainstreaming these responses beyond the post-COVID era.

It should be noted that the chapters from the United States, United Kingdom, and Germany also touch on the issue of inequality, with reference to a general increase of inequality in the United States; socio-economic inequalities in the United Kingdom; and the lack of equal burden sharing as a result of the pandemic in the German instance. Notwithstanding, the United Kingdom and Germany displayed the second theme more prominently, while the United States reflected the third theme more prominently.

The second theme, that is perhaps the most pervasive, is the notable concerns regarding an economic downturn experienced by countries across the jurisdictions. More notably, the countries that raise important issues regarding the future of economic policy in a post-pandemic era are the United Kingdom, Hungary, Germany, Namibia, and Zimbabwe.

The contribution from the United Kingdom, authored by Arletta Gorecka, discusses the implication of the COVID-19 pandemic on the

United Kingdom and its economy. The COVID-19 pandemic occurred when the United Kingdom was in the wake of Brexit. This chapter notes the divergence of the pandemic policy from the previous neoliberal approach; and considers pandemic policy in respect of surveillance, data, and marketization. Moreover, this chapter notes areas of concern in respect of economic growth, health, and education. It concludes by summarizing different aspects in the gradual policy shift from neoliberal consideration into more socially oriented policy considerations.

In contrast, the chapter from Hungary, co-authored by Ádám Kerényi and Weichen Wang, argues that economically due to the relatively low level of GDP loss during the pandemic, there was little incentive for the Hungarian government to spend heavily in non-health sectors to save the economy. Nonetheless, the Hungarian context is important to pay attention to in respect of its geo-political position and economic policy decisions post-pandemic.

The contribution from Germany, co-authored by Michael Müller and Annalisa Tassi in collaboration with Niklas Döbbeling and Friederike Hildebrandt, illustrates the tension between the need for swift response and the pressure on public finances. This chapter also illustrated that the economic burden of the pandemic was not equally shared. Therefore, this chapter proposes the development of a new sustainable framework for intervention and burden sharing in a post-pandemic era.

In the same vein, the chapter from Namibia authored by Christopher Shafuda Pomwene predicts that the road to economic recovery will be long and bumpy in light of the ad-hoc policy measures adopted during the pandemic. This chapter argues that the consequences of the extensive use of these unprecedented measures on the economy were not favorable. Furthermore, the emergence of the COVID-19 pandemic threatened the already trailing government efforts to end poverty, inequality, and unemployment.

The contribution from Zimbabwe, authored by Zvikomborero Chadambuka, highlights the impact of pandemic policy on countries with a large informal economy. The implementation of economic restructuring programs promoted by multilateral development agencies during the 1990s created a large informal economy in Zimbabwe. Moreover, the policy measures taken to combat the pandemic had negative effects on businesses, employees, and those working in the informal economy. This chapter focuses on the reality of those in the informal economy and the promulgation of pandemic policy which tended to exclude the informal sector. The COVID-19 policy response also reinforced a growing tendency to allocate resources to politically linked actors through the political system. Therefore, the chapter concludes that pandemic policy largely served to reinforce a politically corrupt variant of neoliberalism while exacerbating the marginalization of the informal sector in Zimbabwe.

Existing at the intersection between two themes in respect of emphasis on the economic downturn and political tensions, the contributions from Italy, India, Nigeria, and the United States share a common thread. The contribution on Italy co-authored by Federica Cristani and Elisa Gibellino provides deeper insight into the experience of the first country in Europe which suffered from the outbreak of the Covid-19 pandemic. This chapter places a special focus on the new concerns regarding surveillance and the right to privacy that the emergency measures created. Moreover, the COVID-19 pandemic had a grave impact on the national economy. Consequently, the second part of the paper is devoted to the analysis of the pre-COVID-19 economic situation and the comparison with the rising protectionism that has characterized the relevant economic measures since the outbreak of the pandemic. Through issues regarding the legality or legitimacy of the implementation of the state of emergency and concerns regarding the invasion of privacy this chapter shows the new image of Italy, a state facing economic pressure and constitutional legitimacy in a post-pandemic era.

The India chapter, co-authored by Apilang Apum, Binit Agrawal, Madhu Sivaraman, and Aneesha Chitgupi, displays similar intersections between an economic downturn and political inaction. This chapter argues that the economic downturn before the pandemic became worse after the pandemic because of slow political action. Moreover, this chapter noted a rise in the encroachment by the central government on the state governments.

Similarly, the chapter on Nigeria, co-authored by Osatohanmwen (Osato) Anastasia Eruaga, Abigail Osiki, and Itoro Ubi-Abai, argues that political stability and socioeconomic development were exacerbated during the pandemic. This chapter also noted that although the government introduced more welfarist policies during the pandemic these policies and strategies failed due to corruption and weak institutions.

The United States chapter co-authored by Aleksandar Stojanović, Lauren Sweger-Hollingsworth, and Dashiell Anderson, shows how the

US policy response resulted in an increase in inequality; and a reinforcement of economic and extra-economic power division. This chapter argues that economic policy was the main US policy tool used by the federal government to tackle the pandemic and it was used in a manner reflective of existing power structures which prioritizes big business and the stock market. Major contradictions plagued the balance of power and representation from democratically elected individuals. Declarations of emergencies within individual States granted excesses of power to governors and the emergency circumstances allowed experts great decision-making powers. State governments partnered with the private sector for surveillance and control measures, often with the State outsourcing the enforcement of these measures to the private sector. The pandemic allowed for an unprecedented rise in the surveillance of private citizens by State, local governments, and employers. Some of these measures continue to persist. This chapter concludes that economic policy was used in a manner reflective of existing power structures, as the existing dominance of the private sector resulted in policy measures that assisted the private sector and the owners of capital before workers, and furthered the power structure already in place.

The third prominent theme that has been identified is the unique challenge to democracy that the pandemic presented. A number of countries saw a steep rise in political power grabbing and usurpation of the democratic process and the weaknesses in their institutional design to both implement pandemic policy and protect the political order.

In the Chile chapter, co-authored by Javiera Rojas, Luis Cortés, José Ledesma, and Javiera Toro, the Covid-19 health crisis occurred while Chile was in the thick of an economic, political, and social crisis that resulted in the 2019 October Revolt mass mobilizations. Sebastian Piñera's administration was under heavy criticism because of his violent response to the mobilizations. However, despite a constituent plebiscite which was agreed upon between the government and opposition parties as a solution for the crisis, the sanitary emergency allowed Piñera's administration to strengthen the character of his own policies. Although the government implemented an economic agenda that subsidized small and medium capitals with funds from the unemployment insurance to avoid mass layoffs, while also injecting liquidity in to companies and giving out focalized relief funds to vulnerable families, the restrictions were used more to control the civil unrest that started in October 2019 and was still active throughout the population. Strict lockdowns were enforced but the measures did not significantly reduce mobility, as the relief packages were limited and most of the population could not work from home.

The Philippines chapter, co-authored by Vincent Jerald Ramos, Fatemeh Halabisaz, Leonides Frago Jr., and Ryan Martinez, illustrates the militarized lockdowns imposed by the Philippines government at the onset of the pandemic as a containment and control measure. More specifically, it analyzes how these lockdowns were shaped by both weak state capacity and an incumbent regime with authoritarian tendencies. This chapter proposes, that moving forward, a pandemic recovery strategy needs to incorporate policies and investments that strengthen state capacity and institutionalize crisis response mechanisms—these would ensure that the Philippines becomes more resilient in the post-pandemic era and beyond.

The chapter on Brazil, co-authored by Tiago Couto Porto, Alexandre San Martim Portes, Mariella Pittari, and João Victor R. Longi, focuses on the impact of the pandemic policy on political, economic, and health issues. This chapter contrasts the response of President Bolsonaro and democratic institutions such as the Supreme Court. By outlining the main policies implemented to tackle the pandemic in Brazil, this chapter explains how the country arrived at the current scenario of "stagflation" with an unprecedented level of unemployment; the resurgence of extreme poverty; instability of the democratic institutions; and accumulation of the number of lives lost to the disease. The chapter concludes that there is no evidence that the current government is using the COVID-19 crisis as a window of opportunity to overcome structural challenges, such as: strengthening democratic institutions; improving the health system (including the health industrial complex); increasing welfare protection coverage; and searching for inclusive and sustainable growth.

The China chapter, co-authored by Aleksandar Stojanović, Wanshu Cong, An Zhai, Libo Yao, Simeng He, Dongcheng Guo, Xinyi Xu, and Junyue Huang, identifies several significant aspects of the ongoing policy transformation in China. In this instance, the process of combating the pandemic allowed for policy justification through a specific type of "state of war" narrative instead of referring to legal rules, especially when those rules were unclear. It has also led to a shift in the utilization of surveillance practices from a national, hierarchical, and visible level to a social, fluid, and less visible level. Unlike in the developed economies in the West, the least significant change has been observed in the domain of economic policy. Instead of a less discriminate liquidity supply approach taken in the West, China's policy makers opted for a set of highly targeted fiscal, monetary, and procurement measures in order to ensure the stability of the financial markets; relieve pressures on the real economy; and secure employment. The measures were rolled out over a very short period of time but they were not as large as in the case of the EU or the United States, and they were retracted significantly faster.

The aim of this project is to account for the first 100 days of pandemic policy across different jurisdictions. Consequently, the essays, to a large extent, are arranged chronologically based on the date that a state of emergency was declared or when the first pandemic policy was issued on that continent. This also shows how the pandemic or fear of the pandemic spread continentally and then to different parts of the world. Beginning with the chapter on China as the first country to record the virus and implement measures, this is in effect ground zero of the pandemic, which is worth observing. The collection ends with the chapter from the United States to juxtapose the position between the two polarizing geopolitical powers of the pandemic period.

References

Bo, Y., Xiaomin, Z., Long, W., Heng, Z., and Bin, C., Why do countries respond differently to COVID-19? A comparative study of Sweden, China, France, and Japan, The American Review of Public Administration, Volume 50, issue 6–7, 762–769 (2020), https://doi.org/10.1177/0275074020942445

Boettke, P., and Powell, B., The political economy of the COVID-19 pandemic, Southern Economic Association, Volume 87, issue 4, 1090–1106 (2021), https://doi.org/10.1002/soej.12488

Brodeur, A., Gray, D., Islam, A., and Bhuiyan, S., A literature review of the economics of COVID-19, Journal of Economic Surveys (2021), https://doi.org/10.1111/joes.12423

Djankov, S., and Panizza, U. (eds), COVID-19 in Developing Economies, CEPR Press (2020).

Elgin, C., Basbug, G., and Yalaman, A., Economic policy responses to a pandemic: Developing the Covid-19 economic stimulus index, Covid Economics Vetted and Real-Time Papers, issue 3 (2020).

Elgin, C., Yalaman, A., Yasar, S., and Basbug, G., Economic policy responses to the COVID-19 pandemic: The role of central bank independence, Economics Letters, Volume 204 (2021), https://doi.org/10.1016/j.econlet.2021.109874

Gholipour, H. F., and Arjomandi, A., Economic policy responses to the COVID-19 pandemic and growth of nonperforming loans, International Review of Finance, 1–16 (2021).

Greer, S. L., King, J., Massard da Fonseca, E., and Peralta-Santos, A., The comparative politics of COVID-19: The need to understand government responses, Global Public Ealth, Volume 15, issue 9, 1413–1416 (2020), https://doi.org/10.1080/17441692.2020.1783340

Greitens, S., Surveillance, Security, and liberal democracy in the post-COVID world, International Organization, Volume 74, issue S1, 169–190 (2020), https://doi.org/10.1017/S0020818320000417

Hale, T., Angrist, N., Kira, B., Petherick, A., and Phillips, T., Variation in government responses to COVID-19, Oxford BSG-WP-2020/032 (2020).

Hoekman, B., Fiorini, M., and Yildirim, A., Export restrictions: A negative-sum policy response to the COVID-19 Crisis (April 2020). Robert Schuman Centre for Advanced Studies Research Paper No. RSCAS 2020/23 (2020).

Kaplan, S., Lefler, J., and Zilberman, D., The political economy of COVID-19, Applied Economic Perspectives and Policy, Volume 44, issue 1, 477–488 (2021), https://doi.org/10.1002/aepp.13164

Kubinec, R., Barceló, J., Goldszmidt, R., Grujic, V., Model, T., Schenk, C., Cheng, C., Hale, T., Hartnett, A. S., and Messerschmidt, L., Statistically validated indices for COVID-19 Public Health Policies, No. rn9xk, SocArXiv, Center for Open Science (2021), https://EconPapers.repec.org/RePEc:osf:socarx:rn9xk

Loayza, N., and Pennings, S. M., Macroeconomic policy in the time of COVID-19: A primer for developing countries, World Bank Research and Policy Briefs No. 147291 (2020).

Makina, A. J., and Layton, A., The global fiscal response to COVID-19: Risks and repercussions, Economic Analysis and Policy, Volume 69, 340–349 (2021), https://doi.org/10.1016/j.eap.2020.12.016

Mosser, P. C. Central bank responses to COVID-19. Business Economics, Volume 55, 191–201 (2020), https://doi.org/10.1057/s11369-020-00189-x

Newell, B. C., Introduction: Surveillance and the COVID-19 pandemic: Views from around the world, Surveillance & Society, Volume 19, issue 1, 81–84 (2021).

Oxford Covid-19 Government Response Tracker, https://www.bsg.ox.ac.uk/research/research-projects/covid-19-government-response-tracker

Petherick, A., Goldszmidt, R., Andrade, E. B., et al, A worldwide assessment of changes in adherence to COVID-19 protective behaviours and hypothesized pandemic fatigue. Nature Human Behaviour, Volume 5, 1145–1160 (2021), https://doi.org/10.1038/s41562-021-01181-x

Vernengo, M., and Nabar-Bhaduri, S., The economic consequences of COVID-19: The great shutdown and the rethinking of economic policy, International Journal of Political Economy, Volume 49, issue 4, 265–277 (2020), https://doi.org/10.1080/08911916.2020.1857589

von Bogdandy, A., and Villarreal, P., International Law on pandemic response: A first stocktaking in light of the coronavirus crisis, Max Planck Institute for Comparative Public Law & International Law (MPIL) Research Paper No. 2020–07 (2020).

Law and Political Economy of China's Early Pandemic Response: Limited Economic Support and Insulation

Aleksandar Stojanović, Wanshu Cong, An Zhai, Yao Libo, He Simeng, Guo Dongcheng, Xinyi Xu, and Huang Junyue

1 Introduction

People's Republic of China was the first country to be hit by the Covid-19 pandemic. The outbreak was officially noticed on the 26 December 2019. Zhang Jixian, director of the Department of Respiratory Medicine at Hubei Xinhua Hospital, reported the emergence of an unidentified type of pneumonia (Gao et al. 2021). Within a month, the Chinese

A. Stojanović (✉)
New York University in Shanghai, Shanghai, China
e-mail: As14902@nyu.edu

W. Cong
Hong Kong University School of Law, Pok Fu Lam, Hong Kong

A. Zhai
University College London, London, UK
e-mail: zhaian2008@126.com

Y. Libo
Tsinghua University, Beijing, China
e-mail: 17888831592@163.com

A. Stojanović et al. (eds.), *The First 100 Days of Covid-19*,
https://doi.org/10.1007/978-981-19-6325-4_2

Communist Party general secretary Xi Jinping warned that China was facing a "grave situation" adopting a set of policies that were to evolve into China's policy response to the pandemic over the next weeks and months (Munroe and Liu 2020). By the end of January 2020 all mainland provinces had launched the so-called Class 1 Responses to Public Health Emergency (Chappell 2020) This arrangement provided government at all levels with significantly extended powers which were deemed necessary to combat the pandemic. Within four months, relying on comparably more radical measures than observed in most of the rest of the world, China's policy makers were able to control the outbreak, so that the death toll of the pandemic stayed under 5000 cases (Ritchie et al. 2021). Until the recent surge in Shanghai, two years later, China appeared to have been almost "Covid free".

Beyond being defined by the objective of containing the pandemic as effectively as possible, China's policy response to the pandemic fits into the wider historical context of China's institutional evolution. In the face of the pandemic, China's policy makers sought to continue and deepen their efforts in constructing a hybrid political-economic system with specifically Chinese characteristics (Boer 2021). On the path of combining and balancing socialist and market arrangements, China has developed legal and regulatory rules to strengthen state institutions. However, the COVID-19 pandemic has revealed various gaps in the operation of the state apparatus (i.e. the relationship between different branches of the government; the relationship between the party, the state, and the legal

H. Simeng
Tsinghua Law School, Beijing, China
e-mail: 295988140@qq.com

G. Dongcheng · X. Xu
China University of Political Science and Law, Beijing, China
e-mail: gdc18672900817@163.com

X. Xu
e-mail: xuxinyi2017@126.com

H. Junyue
Georgetown University Law School, Washington, DC, USA
e-mail: hj040747@163.com

system; and the relationship between local, regional, and national authorities), which propelled the policy makers to continue developing specific legal and regulatory structures to fit China's overall institutional design principles and policy goals. Furthermore, the pandemic has also reinforced a turn towards the "internal sphere", which China's policymakers have already opted for before the pandemic. This turn has involved the focus on internal circulation, domestic consumption, capital controls, debt deleveraging, and equitable rise of welfare standards, as well as attempts in further ideological, political, and informational control.

Since the outbreak of the Covid pandemic, a substantial body of literature examining China's Covid management experience has emerged. One strand of literature studies China's experience from the perspective of public health, examining the efficacy of various measures, such as lockdowns, travel restrictions, and disease monitoring in curbing the coronavirus (Tian et al. 2020; Tangcharoensathien et al. 2021). Another strand of literature looks at China's reaction from the perspective of public policy, particularly highlighting unique features embedded in China's pre-existing administrative structures, such as the "campaign-style" crisis management regime, which helped China mobilize social and human resources (Cai et al. 2022; Mei 2020); the role of individual and community volunteerism (Miao et al. 2021); and the use of social media (Xu et al. 2020; Li et al. 2020). A third body of literature examines the broader social, political, and economic impact of Covid-19 on China (He et al. 2022; Liu 2021a, b; Gao et al. 2021; Liu and Bennett 2020; Yang and Yang 2021). Given the specific disciplinary angles of each strand, no single entry in the current literature attempts to provide comprehensive picture of China's Covid management experience and potential connections between different strands of policy.

This chapter aims to fill the gap in the literature by studying China's policies across institutional domains and analyzing them from a law and political economy perspective. We pay particular attention to China's legal structure, its role in and tension with anti-Covid policies. Our approach allows us to appreciate the specific legal-normative questions that China's Covid-19 management has encountered, which cannot be fully addressed as an efficacy issue in public health. This approach also sheds light on the complex relations between different branches and levels of the government; between the government and the market; and between the government and the individuals/community. Last but not least, the law and political economy approach also allows us to place the Covid-19 pandemic within a longer trajectory of China's social development, which reveals not only disruptions but crucial continuity of China's policy, which is often omitted in the current literature.

We identify several significant aspects of the ongoing policy transformation. In the above mentioned context, the process of combating the pandemic has opened the space for policy justification through a specific type of "state of war" narrative instead of referring to legal rules, especially when those rules are unclear. It has also led to a shift in the utilization of surveillance practices from a national, hierarchical, and visible level to social, fluid, and less visible level. Unlike in the developed economies in the West, the least significant change has been observed in the domain of economic policy where China's policy makers opted for a set of highly targeted fiscal, monetary and procurement measures. The measures were rolled out over a very short period of time but they were not as large as those seen in the developed world, and they were retracted significantly faster.

In this chapter we follow the structure of the questionnaire tracing the policy response across institutional domains. In Sect. 2 we focus on the legal framework around the state of emergency. In Sect. 3 we turn to the issues regarding surveillance and information flows. Section 4 focuses on different aspects of the economic policy such as those related to financial architecture, business, and employee relief. Section 5 concludes.

2 State of Emergency and Its Implementation

As we saw over the course of the initial months of the global spread of the pandemic, policymakers often referred to the exceptional nature of the problem that the jurisdiction was facing in order to empower their decision making to address the pandemic in an appropriate manner. That often included a reference to the statutory provisions on the "state of emergency" that could be found in the constitution and other high level legislative acts. In China, the "state of emergency" provision can be found in articles 67, 80, and 89 of the Constitution PRC, or "state of martial law" in the Martial Law of China. However, these articles were not invoked.

Instead, policy makers invoked the provisions from the legal framework that was specifically designed for the purposes of dealing with public health emergencies. This framework has been established and progressively improved over the two decades before COVID-19, especially following the SARS epidemic in 2003, H1N1 flu in 2009 and H7N9 flu in 2013. The Law on Prevention and Treatment of Infectious Diseases (传染病防治法 hereinafter LPTID) was enacted in 1989, revised in 2004 and 2013. In addition to this special law, measures taken in public health emergencies are also described in the text of the Law on Emergency Responses (突发事件应对法 hereinafter LER), which was promulgated and entered into force in 2007. In addition to these two laws, a wide set of governmental policies, regulations, and emergency plans were designed to respond to public health emergencies, the most significant among them being the National Emergency Plan for Public Health Emergencies (hereinafter NEPPHE) made by the State Council (State Council 2006). Finally, at the local level, emergency plans were made by local executive authorities containing detailed administrative measures to guide their actions under a given set of conditions.[1]

Articles 39–49 of LPTID specify the hierarchy of competences among different levels of authorities, which on its own seems to be clear. For example, article 42 provides that governments above provincial level may arrange manpower and cut down the spreading route of the infectious disease, according to the plans of prevention and control. They may also carry out certain measures by public declaration, after obtaining the central government's permission. The controlling role of the State Council is reflected in such a design. Furthermore, according to articles 43 to 45, the State Council should have decisive power on inter-provincial response measures. In terms of article 43, for example, the State Council is in charge of setting up inter-provincial pandemic areas; ordering a lock down of pandemic areas in large cities, middle cities, across provincial administrative areas and areas which might cause the breakdown of artery traffic or the closure of the state border.

While the hierarchy of general competences in this domain seems coherent, it became clear in the implementation of the policy response, that the legal framework for dealing with the public health emergencies had considerable gaps regarding the specification of who is supposed to do what and under which conditions. Both the LPTID and the LER provide measures for addressing public health emergencies. However, the text of these two laws does not include an explicit clarification of what should be considered as a public health emergency. Although we observe several similar ideas in the text of these two laws related to this concept. However, on their own, they are not sufficient in terms of framing the policy response that was put together against the pandemic. For example, article 19 of the LPTID requires that a system of early-warning should be made and article 20 requires relevant measures according to the plan should be taken after the legal subjects receive "early-warning". However, that does not mean the "early-warning" can be regarded as "public health emergency", for there are several measures that address such an emergency that can be initiated without such an "early-warning". Articles 39 to 49 of the LPTID discuss the response measures. Among them, articles 42, 43, 45, 48, and 49 discuss measures against pandemic of influential diseases and the rest discusses measures that respond to the emergence of individual cases of infectious diseases. Most of these measures can be implemented at the discretion of relevant authorities in the context of a pandemic, while others neces from a higher position in the chain of command. An "early-warning" is not among the necessary pre-conditions. Thus an "early-warning" cannot be regarded as a general state of public health emergency that would initiate a specific set of emergency response measures. While in NEPPHE there are no further statements implying that "early-warning" would lead to any particular response measures, we find several clear provisions on the termination of emergency measures. Essentially, authorities who have adopted the measures are required to terminate them once the situation is under control (Article 47 of the Law on RE, Articles 41–43 of the LPTID). Specific conditions, requirements, and procedures for terminating emergency measures are provided by the National Precautionary Plan for Public Health Emergency (State Council 2006).

This ambivalent and incomplete framework came to be tested as the pandemic emerged, and the above mentioned gaps made the implementation of the policy response significantly more challenging. As commentators pointed out, the emergency responses taken in Hubei and other provinces revealed major shortcomings of the existing legal framework (J. Wang 2020). The lock-down measures in Wuhan, for example, were delivered without warnings or declarations in advance. According to Xianwang Zhou, the then Mayor of Wuhan, he could not issue such declarations or early warnings without authorization from the higher authority (Guancha 2020). Some opinions suggest that the design of the early-warning systems assumed that if the responsible parties knew what they were supposed to do they would do so (J. Wang 2020). The confusion emerged due to the uncertainties in the existing legal framework, such as the conflict between Article 19 of the LPTID and article 43 of the LER regarding who should issue early warnings. As some critics observed, such conflicts also led to selective compliance with the law (Z. J. Wang 2020).

In addition to legal uncertainties, in some cases the legal framework for public health emergencies was practically suspended. Several provinces activated the level-I public health emergency reaction which, according to the Regulation on the Urgent Handling of Public Health Emergencies, should have been activated by the State Council rather than provincial governments (Meng 2020). The incoherence of the law has been criticized by scholars and prompted the government to initiate the process of revision. An amendment of the LPTID has been published based on public comments by the National Health Commission (Nation Health Commission 2020). However, it remains to be seen how concretely the legal framework for public health emergencies will be improved.

Oftentimes, the emergency measures adopted, while lacking legal basis, had been legitimized by a popular slogan of "fighting a people's war" (*China Daily* 2020). This "war" narrative was initially invoked by local governments, first in Shiyan, Hubei.[2] It is important to notice that the narrative was not adopted in the initial central government's anti-covid instructions. The slogan soon became widely invoked by governments of various locales and media (Wang et al. 2021). While the war narrative had been criticized for being inappropriate for regions with only scattered cases, the official media, Xinhua, endorsed this narrative by calling the measures in Wuhan "the Battle Defending Wuhan".

In that context, it becomes clear how, instead of sole reliance on police, medical staff, and other public enforcement bodies, the enforcement of the emergency measures such as movement limitation, health code checks, and others, was executed by a diverse set of actors that were often without specified public institutional roles such as security guards, company employees, and community council members.

Although the pandemic had been under control by mid-2020 and many measures related to the movement of citizens and limitation of economic activity had been withdrawn, Chinese policy makers kept some of the measures, primarily related to surveillance and inter-regional, international travel, in place until today. Despite the emphasis on the balance between surveillance and individual rights by the central government, more severe enforcement measures have been applied by local governments in communities, such as mandatory vaccinations, lock-down quarantines of people in epidemic areas, and severe restrictions on inter-regional traveling (Zhang 2020b). People also faced more frequent legal and extralegal interventions. For example, violations of control measures may be subject not only to criminal penalties but also to sanctions imposed through the national credit system (Luo 2020).[3]

Furthermore, justified by the nationwide zero-case policy, the authorities at all levels kept some of the facilities and bodies formed during the initial wave in place, albeit inactive, in order to be able to call upon them if the occasion arises. The wave of cases in Shanghai in the spring of 2022 is the most stark example of reactivation of the initial measures, such as localized lockdowns and mass testing (Shanghai Municipal Health Commission 2022). The continuation and re-application of such measures, just like their initial adoption, perpetuates significant legal ambiguities that end up being resolved, albeit with significant loss and delay, by discretionary use of power at different levels of the government imposing particularly stringent and encompassing measures. The rigidity and vast character of the measures in turn could be put into question insofar as they fail the requirement of article 27 of the Constitution which stipulates "the principle of simple and efficient administration". The contrast between the law and war narrative shows the limitations of the former that are still to be overcome. However, systematic improvements at the constitutional level are unlikely. Technical and incremental solutions may, however, occur through the revision of specialized laws such as the LPTID.

3 Surveillance and Information Control

In the face of the pandemic, China adopted one of the most pervasive and technically sophisticated surveillance policy responses in the world. Furthermore, many of the surveillance measures adopted during the pandemic were retained even after the health crisis was fought off.

The issue of mass surveillance has not always been controversial in China. Before 2000, due to the vast territory and limits in technology, state supervision was mostly realized through direct citizen supervision. The political movements of the 1950s and 1960s fostered a political culture of citizens' mutual monitoring. Since the 1980s the liberal reform and cultivation of civil society have transformed the image of mutual supervision from a valued societal goal to an undesirable practice (Song and Lin 2018). In the 1982 Constitution, personal dignity, residence, freedom, and privacy of correspondence were protected under chapter II, which addresses "The basic rights and duties of citizens". In the context of changing attitudes and limited economic and technological means, state monitoring penetrated people's lives to a limited extent. Since the late 1990s, state monitoring entered a new stage. With economic reform and the rapid advancement of urbanization, the problems of social and national security have become particularly prominent. Mass surveillance was justified as a necessary means of managing public security. In terms of technology, the boom of domestic surveillance equipment production in the 2000s has enabled the mass use of monitoring tools (Chen et al. 2004). In terms of political justification, a series of incidences of violence and terrorism in 2014 provided an opportunity for the adoption of national surveillance practices (Yu 2014; Zhao 2014), which were incorporated in the Anti-terrorism Law of the People's Republic of China passed in 2015.[4] In 2017, the government officially announced the establishment of the Skynet Project, aimed at real-time monitoring and facial recognition through the utilization of a network of over 20-million public and private street level cameras (Wang 2017). Furthermore, with the rising popularity of the Internet and smartphones since 2010, information on citizens' behavior is also collected by enterprises (Yang 2021).

Measured against this historical background, the pandemic has only intensified the trend towards comprehensive surveillance that already existed in the country. The significance of the pandemic has to do with the pace at which further expansion of mass surveillance occurred; and the development of cooperation between corporate entities and the state. Mega-app providers such as WeChat and Alipay collected citizens' data for the control of their movement. In turn, these mega-apps enabled state monitoring to evolve into a more social, fluid, and invisible form of control which penetrates into citizens' daily lives on a capillary level.

At the outset of the pandemic, the most prominent change in terms of surveillance had to do with the use of digital technologies. As the pandemic emerged local governments and enterprises quickly engaged in significant cooperation (Zhao 2020). The Health code in smartphone applications such as Beijng's JianKangBao which is based on the information on a citizen's ID card, location and tracking history, exposure history and health condition became a requirement for entrance in almost every public space (Sun 2020). The health code is established based on a calculation of the users' virus exposure risk using the information users submitted and the data shared by the health department. This data is further verified using authoritative databases from the departments of health, transportation, communication, and other industrial authorities

(Center For Information Technology 2020). The resulting assignment of the code color based on risk analysis by big data, can further be adjusted by the responsible official staff (Nanchang CDC 2021), allowing for discretionary intervention in the automated decision making. In this process, data that was not traditionally collected by the state such as the consumption and payment information, medical records and employment information became subject to state control. Among them, the location tracking history has received particular attention.

The operation of health code generation exemplifies how surveillance practices shifted from a national, hierarchical and visible level to social, fluid, and less visible level. The prevention of pandemic has shown the diversity in the public private and communal entities that have been mobilized (Zhao and Li 2022). Moreover, it was evident that large-scale implementation of surveillance depends on compliance with grid-based management (Central Committee of the Communist Party of China 2013).[5] As a result, the relationship of control between the citizens and the government has been upgraded to multiple regulatory relationships between officials, non-official staff, and citizens. Not only government departments, but also non-government organizations such as real estate managers or security companies, have acquired power of surveillance and control (JPCMSC 2020). This is even more true of the community members who stood at the forefront of implementing control measures such as the management of visitors, access to public places, traffic patrol, and epidemic prevention education (China Security Association 2020).

The movement of an individual or a group was surveilled through the use of the smartphone code check at different locations by local personnel; and through the online transaction records. The surveillance has also been reinforced through additional infrastructure such as facial recognition in residential buildings and public places such as subways that was developed rapidly following the virus outbreak.

In the context of this novel surveillance reality, it is important to observe the absence of an appropriate response from the legal system and the public. The initial surveillance measures taken during the first months of the pandemic were not accompanied or justified by an explicit legal framework. Instead the law responded after the fact. On 28 May 2020, the Civil Code of the People's Republic of China was passed, in which personal information i.e., personal biometric information and identifiable information are protected under the Personal Rights section (Art. 1034, Civil Code of the People's Republic of China). However, given the nature of the civil code, it regulates the civil relationship between private parties and cannot restrain the power of the government. The Personal Information Protection Law of the People's Republic of China passed in 2021 states in Chapter II that public data controllers are also subject to this legislation, but the enforcement of this chapter remains unclear. Despite such legislative development, legal scholars have expressed concerns for citizen privacy (Jiang 2020; Lao 2021).

Beyond the legal response, public reactions to the rapid development of surveillance measures have been rather scarce due to limitations on the freedom of speech. Although the surveillance measures taken for controlling the pandemic were not designed to regulate speech, such measures ended up going hand in hand with the inhibition of public expression. Information control that already existed before the pandemic due to various internet censorship mechanisms, was reinforced to govern the reaction to the lockdown and surveillance measures that were being taken.

We could see this trend clearly in the way media outlets operated during the pandemic. In China, local newspapers typically treat the issue of liberties and privacy rights by mounting a moderate criticism of local governments' excesses in the enforcement of rules (Jing and Ma 2014). In contrast, in February 2020 one local newspaper in Wuhan asked citizens to "warm the mayor's heart", urging people to reduce their complaints about the inconvenience caused by the controlling measures (Zhang 2020a). This appeal to citizens was eventually criticized by the central government, but such media practice of praising and protecting instead of criticizing the government went on. For example, in border areas such as Ruili, local media seldom published news about local citizens' living, medical, and employment difficulties under the long-lasting lockdown. Instead, it was the retired government officials and media in other regions that spoke on behalf of the silenced people, bringing their testimonies and opinions into the public sphere (Qin 2021). Even though a few media outlets such as Caixin Weekly and IFeng News played a fair role in expressing public opinions, their influence was limited because of the populist "war" narrative mentioned before. In many cases, the silence of official media created a regional information insulation, leaving the people in quarantine areas unnoticed by society.

There are many reasons for the lack of any adequate pushback on the expanding surveillance. The most prominent one being the controlling measures on inadequate speech on social media. For example, the "group chief responsibility system" on a WeChat group chat places an obligation on the managers of a chat group to regulate and stop improper comments by group members (Cyberspace of Administration in China 2017), creating further chilling effects for public expression. In addition to the power exercised by the platforms, traditional legal means have been deployed to repress criticisms rather than to empower the public to express its opinion. The offense of "picking quarrels and provoking troubles" in the Law of the People's Republic of China on Administrative Punishments for Public Security[6] has been used to target not only physical violations of the pandemic control measures but also speech criticizing those measures (a similar practice of repression through the use of the concept of "rumors" in the aforementioned Law was also observed) (Tongzhou District People's Court of Beijing 2020). In this way, not only hate speech or insulting words, but ambiguous complaints concerning the controlling measures taken may fall under the scrutiny of the government.

In general, the surveillance measures taken during the early stage of the pandemic, the justification based on necessity prevailed over considerations of adequacy. Furthermore, many temporary surveillance measures, such as the health-code-related data collection, health-code scanning and temperature measuring in public places, reporting of new-comers and monitoring of focus groups, have become the new normal (Xi'Ji Police 2022). These measures are again justified with a reference to the fact that the pandemic is still ongoing—even if the health emergency has been overcome. Be that as it may, the absence of an adequate public discussion and legal articulation of these measures reinforces an undesirable atmosphere of silence and voluntary use of power.

4 Economic Policy

4.1 Economic Conditions and Policy Before the Pandemic

At the precipice of the pandemic China's economic policy makers faced a specific set of economic challenges. For about four decades, China has been the best-performing economy in the world. However at least since 2010, the phase of the so-called miracle growth ended (Naughon 2018). China faced diminishing supply of cheap labor force inflow, relative saturation of global markets and lower returns on investment in capital. In this context, Chinese policy makers did not follow the policy direction of letting private financial institutions select investment opportunities worthy of their support and stir the economy as was the case when Japan and South Korea faced similar conditions. Instead, they engaged in activist industrial policy based on government spending (see Fig. 1) and central bank support (see Fig. 2). Some of the policies targeted the supply side by supporting "strategic emerging industries", such as industrial automation, internet-based services and green energy. The focus was on research and development as well as on supporting state backed or owned "national champions". Agriculture and demographic growth were also supported. On the demand side, the policy focused primarily on supporting the growing population of domestic middle-class consumers. This direction became even more pronounced as China confronted US-led western policy elites in the trade war. This policy direction is often described as a turn away from the market, but it can alternatively be understood as an attempt at a more active re-design of legal foundations of markets with a case specific treatment of different types of market participants and shifting of roles of different markets within the overall hierarchy and conditionality in creating economic growth. Below is a short survey of economic conditions across the financial architecture, business, and employment as they were before the pandemic.

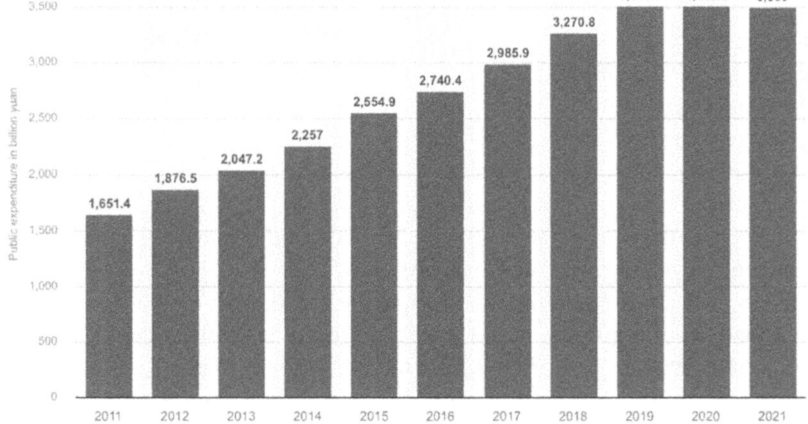

Fig. 1 Government spending (*Source* Statista)

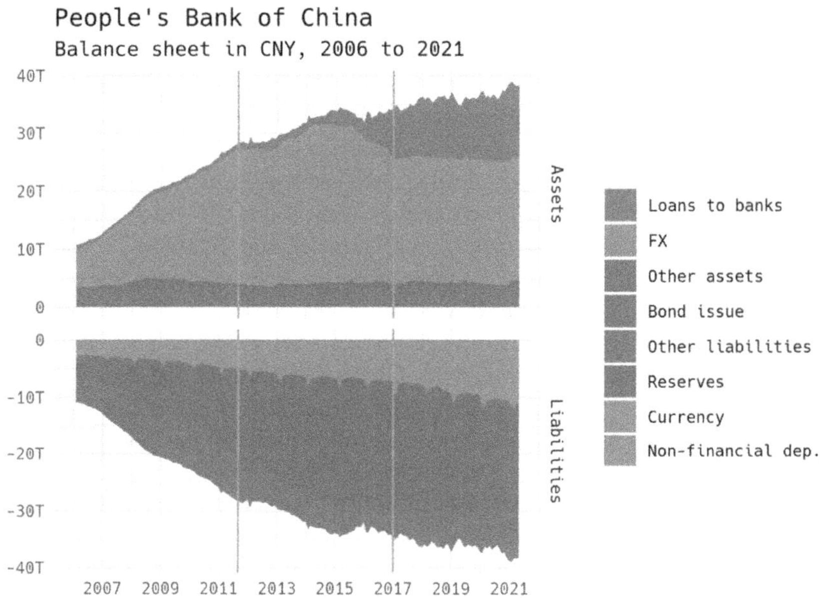

Fig. 2 People's bank of China balance sheet (*Source* Dan Neilsen, https://www.soonparted.co)

In terms of monetary policy and financial architecture it is important to notice that for many decades, interest rates in China were tightly controlled and played almost no role. The People's Bank of China (PBC) used quantitative monetary policy instruments regularly and much more aggressively than any of the developed market economies. In addition, there were large changes in base money, driven by changes in foreign-exchange reserves. Against this background, monetary policy framework has been evolving, following two key themes: migrating from direct control to indirect control; and moving from quantitative regulation to price regulation (Amstad et al. 2020). Furthermore, it is important to mention that since the reform in the 1980s, China's financial system has developed from complete inexistence into a system which today involves a dominant state-owned banking sector and capital markets with diverse financial institutions. Even if China's capital markets have grown to be among the largest in the world, the majority of funding in the financial system comes from the banks (ibid.).

In terms of business conditions in China before the pandemic, there are two specificities that became significant during the pandemic. First is the role and the presence of the State-owned enterprises (SOEs) and small and medium-sized enterprises (SMEs). Since the reforms in the early 1980s China has been moving in the direction of shrinking the SOE presence although that has slowed down in recent years. The 2019 government work report proposed to promote mixed ownership and market-oriented reforms to strengthen SOEs' competitiveness in the fields of electricity, oil and gas, and railways. For SMEs, the Law of Promoting Small and Medium-sized Enterprises enacted in 2002 requires the State Council to make plans and strategies to promote the development of SMEs. Since then, multiple measures were taken to reduce, or exempt SMEs from, various fees, charges, or taxation. These measures were accompanied by detailed policy plans that guided the treatment of the SMEs. Within the central and local budgets special funds were allocated to purchase SME products and services. In order to minimize the difficulties of SMEs accessing finance, articles 14 and 16 of the abovementioned law provided that the PBC and other financial institutions shall provide them with special funding channels and facilitate application process. In 2019, a set of policies on SMEs was enacted with the main purpose of further reducing the financial burden they faced. Specifically, the Ministry of Finance and the State Taxation Administration proposed that taxpayers of small-scale value-added tax with monthly sales of less than 100,000 yuan should be exempted from value-added tax, and the annual taxable income of small and micro enterprises should not exceed 1 million yuan (Ministry of Finance and State Administration of Taxation 2019). In 2019, China Development Bank issued more than 100 billion yuan of loans to small and micro enterprises and industrial poverty alleviation by means of on-lending, and issued a total of 100 billion yuan of special loans for private enterprises, supporting more than 120,000 small and micro enterprises in the process (Xinhua News Agency 2021).

In addition, the government engaged in breaking down the monopolies in the financial and data economy. It initiated legal actions to limit their operations and divide their activities into separate entities (Huang 2020). Promoting employment has been a fundamental policy of China improving people's livelihood (Article 42 of the PRC Constitution). In the last 15 years, the general guiding policy in employment has been focused on "encouraging self-employment, relying on market economy, with the assistant of government" (The State Council Office of the People's Republic of China 2004). Overall, the central government mainly has adopted three approaches to job creation. First, the government boosted investment and domestic consumption by supporting internal circulation to strengthen the economy, in such a manner that growth would lead to the creation of more jobs. Secondly, the government aimed at creating job opportunities through its' support for the SMEs using financial and fiscal subsides. Thirdly, the government has been providing unemployment insurance and subsidies by setting up the Unemployment Insurance Fund. It has also created public employment agencies to help people find jobs under the "Regulations on Unemployment Insurance".

Finally, poverty and lack of education have been identified as one the main obstacles for employment. Since 2011, China's poverty alleviation standard (poverty line) has been raised to 2300 yuan, and by the end of 2011, population under poverty line was about 128 million people, accounting for about 13.4% of the rural population. People of ethnic minorities, women, and people with disabilities in the rural areas are even more likely to be living below the poverty line (Che and Lin 2011). Therefore, the government had included these groups in the "China Rural Poverty Alleviation and Development Program (2011–2020)" (State Council 2011). As for the lack of education, the central government has made effort to raise the education standard across the country and created education facilities for pre-employment and on-the-job training. In this context, the government provided occupational education for vulnerable groups like children of poor families, junior and senior high school graduates who have not yet advanced to higher education, migrant workers, unemployed, transferred workers, and retired soldiers for free. It has also incentivized companies to cooperate with universities to provide additional education and training opportunities.

4.2 *Economic Policy During the Pandemic*

After the outbreak of COVID-19, in order to stabilize the economic conditions, the government immediately launched a series of financial relief measures. This phase lasted about five months. Instead of a less discriminate liquidity supply approach taken in the West, in the first phase China's policy makers launched a set of highly targeted fiscal, monetary, and procurement measures in order to ensure the stability of the financial markets, relieve pressures on the real economy, and secure employment. The measures were rolled out quickly, but they were not as large as in the case of the EU or the United States. After the five months of implementation of relief measures, the government reduced direct assistance to enterprises and maintained other measures, letting the existing institutional structure and markets operate without support.

4.2.1 *Legal Financial Architecture During the Pandemic*

In contrast to the usual focus on preventing "market failure", the Chinese pandemic response policy was more proactive insofar as it was intended to support the banking sector, financial markets, and the real economy as they faced the effects of the pandemic. The policy involved a set of short term, top-down, targeted measures that were worked out further on departmental and local levels.

The main policy documents that enabled this approach are the following: Among the earliest policies related to economic relief, the Circular on Financial Security Policy issued on January 25 (MOF & NHC 2020), which called for governmental financial subsidies for patients, healthcare workers, and medical institutions; the Circular on Securing Epidemic Supplies issued on January 30 (GOSC, Jan. 30, 2020), which required local governments to secure supplies and serve enterprises that produce epidemic supplies; and the Circular on Optimizing Tax Payment Services, which states that taxpayers could apply for an extension of their tax payment service (SAT, Jan. 30, 2020). Later on, the People's Bank of China (PBC), the Ministry of Finance (MOF), the Banking and Insurance Regulatory Commission (CBIRC), the Securities Regulatory Commission (CSRC), and the State Administration of Foreign Exchange (SAFE) released a joint notice, titled "Notice of strength for the financial support of preventing and controlling COVID-19". According to this Notice, China was to adopt a "flexible" national monetary and fiscal policy for the first half of 2020. SAFE also launched a notice for establishing a Green Channel for Foreign Exchange Policy to Support the Prevention and Control of the COVID-19. MOF issued a specific notice to support financially and to Strengthen financial services for the prevention and control of COVID-19.

Based on this framework, the People's Bank of China has taken a series of measures expanding money supply, enhancing the implementation of structural monetary policy, and creating monetary policy tools to directly increase liquidity and reduce the financing cost in specific sectors. The policy response included medium-lending facilities rate cut by 30bps, 7-days Reverse Repo rate cut by 30bps (see Fig. 3); standing lending facilities rate cut by 30bps, loan prime rate cut by 30bps, Excess reserve ratio cut from 0.72–0.35%, three reserve ratio cuts of 150bps in total which released 1.75 trillion RMB, re-lending and re-discount programmes that amounted to 1.8 trillion RMB, the extension of SMEs loans to RMB870 billion and support for SME financing programme at RMB170 billion.[7] These cuts effectively facilitated interbank lending, by pushing the interbank repo rate below 1.7% as can be seen in Fig. 3. We consider specific business-related measures in detail in the next session. In order to set limits to the channels of accessing these relief measures, the Supreme People's Court's "Guiding Opinions on Several Issues Concerning the Proper Trial of Civil Cases related to the COVID-19 (II)", included six articles that addressed financial support during the epidemic.[8] According to the Guiding Opinions, claims of loan repayment acceleration and unilateral termination of the contract made by financial institutions violated the financial support policy. Instead, the court would extend the repayment period according to the principle of fairness for those in need of COVID-19-related hospitalization or quarantine, those who participated in the epidemic prevention and control work, those temporarily lost their income due to the pandemic as well as those liable for disputes related to their housing mortgages, credit card loans, etc. As the pandemic was contained, those short-term financial policies had been gradually retracted, returning to the previously established regime. This was marked by the establishment of the Beijing Stock Exchange on September 3, 2021.

However, these temporary policies did not disappear completely. An element of legal change due to the pandemic that has economic consequences is that the "epidemic" has become one of the legal reasons for "change of circumstances" in civil law. Specifically, the No. 1 Notice of the National Health and Health Commission in 2020 approved by the State Council, stipulated the COVID-19 as one of the Class B infectious diseases, which means that the COVID-19 became a new type of infectious disease in the "Prevention and Control of Infectious Diseases Law", making the COVID-19 a force majeure factor according to Article 180 and Article 533 of the Civil Code.[9] If the purpose of the contract cannot be achieved due to the epidemic, the parties may request to terminate the contract and share the losses according to fair responsibilities.

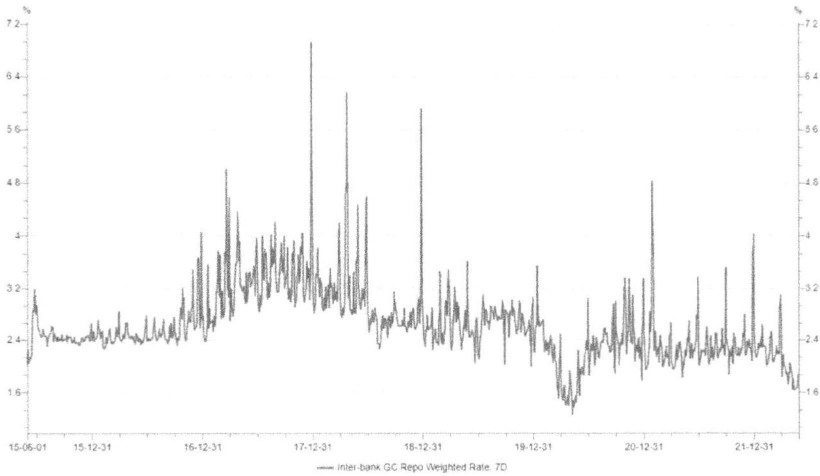

Fig. 3 Interbank lending rate (*Source* Wind)

4.2.2 Business Relief and Protection During the Pandemic

In terms of business relief, the Government's economic support measures targeted individuals, enterprises, public institutions (such as government departments and hospitals), and local financial arrangements (Ministry of Finance and State Administration of Taxation 2021). These measures can be separated into three domains: (1) financial support; (2) tax incentives and relief; and (3) government procurement.

(1) Within the 1.7 trillion RMB expansion, PBC provided 300 billion RMB for lending to maintain the supply chains of products involved in the management of COVID-19, such as critical medical materials and daily necessities. It increased the re-loan and rediscount quota to 500 billion to assist SMEs in resuming production. As SMEs were seriously weakened by the pandemic, the PBC encouraged the medium and small-sized banks to strengthen their support for SMEs. Additionally, another 100 billion re-loans and rediscount quota were set for all groups of enterprises.

The central government's increased credit support allowed local governments to work with financial institutions to promote lower lending rates and to increase credit loans and medium- and long-term loans for SMEs whose development prospects have been affected by COVID-19. The government also introduced a stage-by-stage deferral of payment for the electricity, water, and gas required for the production and operation of

SMEs during the pandemic and enforced the "non-stop supply of arrears" measure during the deferral period. Banks and financial institutions were prohibited from withdrawing, postponing, or stopping loans for enterprises, particularly micro ones, and those in the industries hardest hit by COVID-19, such as wholesale and retail providers, hotels, restaurants, airline operators, and travel agencies.

The general aim of this set of measures was to ensure that the actual financing costs of companies falls below 1.6% and to increase emergency sub-lending funds while reducing emergency sub-lending rate. Local governments also received financial support from the central government, including increasing the proportion of local fiscal funds retained and increasing transfer payments to ease the financial pressure on local governments, especially in relatively underdeveloped regions. As of June 2020, the amount of transfer payments reached 6.28 trillion yuan, an increase of 1.26 trillion yuan over the same period last year. At the same time, fiscal funds were tilted towards areas with severe epidemics (such as Hubei) and the focus of government work (such as environmental protection).

A new portion of central government budget deficit amounting to 1 trillion yuan (RMB) was added, and a special national bond of 1 trillion yuan (RMB) was issued to fight against the epidemic, all 2 trillion yuan of which was transferred to local governments, supporting local governments to fight the epidemic and to give subsidies to companies. In addition, 3.75 trillion yuan (RMB) of new special bonds were arranged for local governments, an increase of 1.6 trillion yuan over the previous year (Ministry of Finance 2021a, b). For the whole year of 2020, the Chinese government invested more than 400 billion yuan in financial resources for COVID-19 prevention, control, and relief (Ministry of Finance 2021a, b).

(2) On 30 January, 2020, the State Administration of Taxation published a policy document titled: "Notice on Optimizing Tax Payment and Payment Services to Cooperate with the Prevention and Control of COVID-19" (State Administration of Taxation 2020b). The document effectively extended the period for paying taxes to fit the needs of epidemic prevention and control. Furthermore, according to the guidance of the central government, all municipalities were to give more tax benefits to SMEs in stages (in Hubei province, these were extended to all enterprises). The policy also paid attention to those SMEs which had faced comparatively better benefits conditions before the epidemic and could restart operation quickly once receiving additional support. For

these SMEs, the government extended social subsidies to 6 months after their resumption of operation.

Overall, four types of tax incentives were put in place. The first type targeted the enterprises, entities (such as hospitals, etc.), or materials related to the epidemic. The government directly exempted or deducted most of their taxes (such as corporate income tax, value-added tax, import tax). From January to November 2020, a total of 65.2 billion yuan (RMB) in tax and fee reductions for enterprises producing anti-epidemic materials (Ministry of Finance 2021a). The second category involved SMEs and privately or individually owned businesses. The government had given these businesses tax relief in areas such as VAT and social insurance contributions to help them reduce costs and get through difficult times. The reduced tax rate was determined by respective local governments. The third category involved the enterprises that are affected by the epidemic more directly, such as the transportation, catering, accommodation, and tourism industries. For example, the maximum carryover period for losses incurred by companies in these difficult industries in 2020 has been extended from 5 to 8 years. A portion of VAT was exempted for them, with a total of 38.2 billion (RMB) in tax exemptions for these industries from January to November 2020 (Ministry of Finance 2021a, b). Finally, the fourth category included public transportation or industries that are highly related to residents' life services. According to the announcement issued by the Ministry of Finance and the General Administration of Taxation in February 2020, taxpayers are exempted from VAT on income derived from the provision of public transportation services, living services, and express delivery and collection services of essential living materials for residents (State Administration of Taxation 2020a, b, c, d). In 2020, tax reductions and exemptions increased by 2.6 trillion yuan (RMB).

(3) Final part of the financial relief policy for business was based on procurement measures. These had two specific targets: the entities involved in pandemic prevention supply chain and the SMEs. The government was involved in procuring large quantities of epidemic prevention materials from domestic suppliers. Firstly, the government subsidized the cost of purchasing epidemic prevention materials for medical institutions, with the local government approving the amount of the subsidy and the central government paying the subsidy (MOF & NHC 2020); and secondly, the government made bulk purchases itself and committed to the overall procurement of all epidemic prevention materials that

companies fail to sell in the market, such as masks and protective clothing (China Government Procurement 2020). On the other hand, it guaranteed that the purchase and sale of supplies are timely through streamlined competition and approval procedures. At the beginning of the epidemic, it opened a "green channel" for the procurement of epidemic prevention materials, exempting them from the procurement procedures stipulated in the government procurement law and eliminating the need for approval for the procurement of imported materials (Ministry of Finance 2020a, b, c, d, e). In addition, it shortened the procurement process by promoting electronic procurement and moving the procurement process online (Ministry of Finance 2020e).

The government also guided budget units at all levels to support SMEs and increase the amount and proportion of procurement from them (Ministry of Industry and Information Technology 2020). In 2020, the contract value awarded to small, medium, and micro enterprises in national government procurement was 2791.80 billion yuan (RMB), accounting for 75.5% of the national government procurement scale (Chinese Government Procurement Website 2021). They have also intensified efforts to clear the accounts owed to SMEs by administrative organizations, institutions, and state-owned enterprises to speed up the completion of clearing arrears without any new overdue arrears being formed. In 2019 and 2020, the government conducted a centralized clearing of arrears within a time limit, and accumulated more than 850 billion yuan in overdue arrears owed by administrative, public institutions and large state-owned enterprises to private enterprises and small and medium-sized enterprises (Guo 2021).

4.2.3 Employment Relief and Protection During the Pandemic

Covid-19 caused severe employment-related problems in 2020. According to the report of the National Bureau of Statistics, in 2020, there were over 11.6 million unemployed people and the unemployment rate in cities was 5.2%, the highest it has been in the past five years. In order to cope with the upcoming unemployment wave as quickly as possible, the central government issued a guiding policy starting from March 2020 to provide relief to both enterprises and employees (State Council of People's Republic of China 2020). The general idea in the early phase of the epidemic was to resume production quickly, minimize layoffs, and raise the unemployment benefits.

According to the "Notice of Properly Handling Labor Relation Issues During the Covid-19 Prevention period" (Ministry of Human Resources and Social Security of the People's Republic of China 2020), during the initial phase of the epidemic in 2020, enterprises had the legal obligation to pay wages even if they stopped working. Furthermore, this policy specified the obligations in the context of a force majeure in the following manner. Firstly, enterprises should not terminate the labor contract with employees who could not work as normal due to the pandemic. Secondly enterprises that stopped operation for less than one wage payment period should pay normal wages. If the operation stopped for more than one wage payment period, the wage would be evaluated on the basis of the type of work that was being performed. Namely, if employees worked normally, they were to be paid not less than the minimum salary as set by the local government. If employees did not work as normal, enterprises were obliged to compensate them with alimony payment. In the context of the pandemic, these rules were combined with other policies. For instance, the General Office of the State Council issued an Opinion, emphasizing the implementation of anti-epidemic measures in workplaces, canteens, and workers' residents to ensure workplaces are non-virus, (The General Office of State Council of People's Republic of China 2020). It also encouraged enterprises to shoulder the social responsibility to maintain the living of employees and reduce prospective layoffs. Apart from the incentives used above, some scholars also proposed that the financial risk of enterprises due to unemployment should fall on the public budget (Sheng 2020).

Beyond these measures there were additional subsidies for the unemployed. The central government announced that individuals whose unemployment insurance had expired or who were unqualified to receive it, could get additional subsidies up to 6 months. In addition, the standard of unemployment insurance was raised by local governments. From March to June in 2020, the temporary subsidies for recipients of unemployment insurance and unemployment benefits increased two times (Ministry of Human Resources and Social Security and Ministry of Finance 2020).

Furthermore, the government also took measures to protect domestic migrant workers. By the end of 2019, domestic migrant workers accounted for nearly 40% of workers in cities (National Bureau of Statistics 2019). As their jobs are more precarious and flexible, these workers enjoy lower levels of social security and employment protection. According to 2017 statistics, only 36.22% of domestic migrant workers were enrolled in the city unemployed insurance programmes (Z. Wang 2020), which means that they were more vulnerable than urban workers to the shock of the pandemic. In this case, the Hunan provincial government adopted several detailed measures to ensure the rights of domestic migrant workers. For example, from March 1, 2020, the newly enrolled domestic migrant workers were required to pay the same insurance premium as city employees, so that both migrant and city workers would be equally insured. Municipal governments also started to encourage domestic migrant workers to enroll in the city unemployment insurance programs (Hunan Provincial Department of Finance 2020).

Finally, strengthening labor protection was identified as another vital effort necessary to support the return of enterprises to production. The government sought to survey and publish information on enterprises' labor demands and promote online supply and demand matching, as well as remote recruitment. Strengthening of local supply and demand matching, was expected to tap the potential of local supply to meet the phased labor demand of enterprises (Ministry of Human Resources and Social Security of PRC 2021).

4.3 Economic Policy Direction in the Aftermath

In 2020 China's domestic product indicators formed a V shape. The spread of COVID-19 in late 2019 and early 2020 posed a great challenge to China's economy. The quarterly GDP data largely shows the impact of the epidemic on the economy (see Fig. 4): in the first quarter, GDP fell sharply to the negative growth level of 6.8%. Public budget revenues fell by 3.9% while public budget expenditures increased by 2.8%. National finance and state-owned capital have filled a part of the economic gap caused by the epidemic. However, the bounce back was quick and most of the relevant macroeconomic indicators were rising already in the second quarter—Fig. 5 shows the recovery of the stock market indices and some evidence of the come back in the sovereign bond market price. In the face of the challenge, China's specific combination of socialist and market arrangements, has showcased a significant degree of resilience and stability. China's economic growth rate of 2.3% surpassed the IMF's initial optimistic prediction. The secondary industry and the tertiary industry are the main forces of economic development, and their added value accounts for 37.8% and 54.5%, respectively, of this growth record. The gross national income was 10,095.1 billion yuan, an increase of 1.9% over the previous year.

In this context, joint stock companies, foreign-related companies, and private companies have all achieved growth in revenue and profit growth, but the growth rate of companies controlled by state-owned capital has declined. Excluding the price factor, the per capita disposable income of

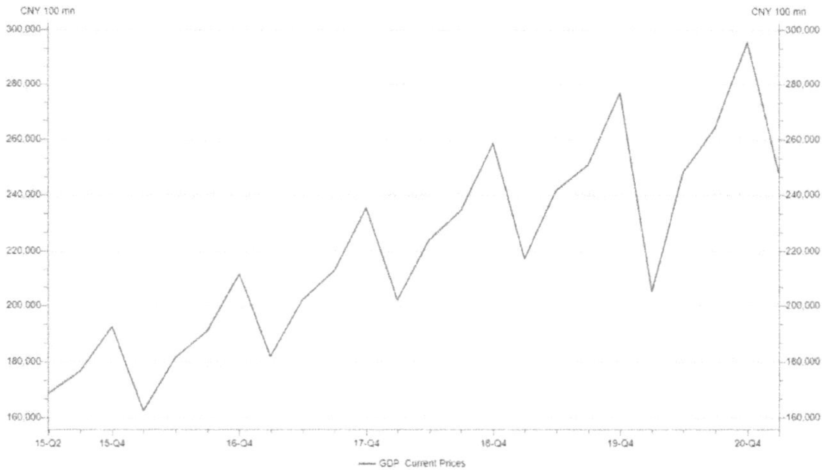

Fig. 4 China's gross domestic product (*Source* Wind)

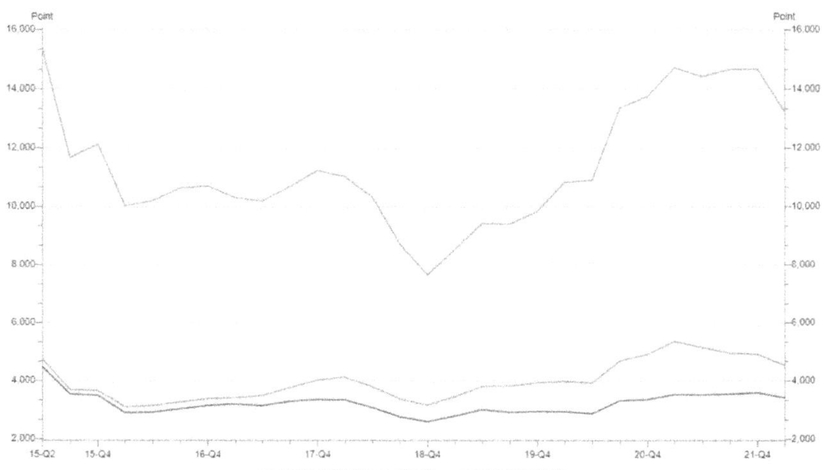

Fig. 5 Stock market performance (*Source* Wind)

residents actually increased by 2.1%; however, the epidemic may also make people's consumption views more conservative. After deducting the price factor, the per capita consumption expenditure of residents fell by 4%.

After the first wave was controlled in the spring of 2020, China's policy makers unwound the pandemic economic response measures and turned to setting longer term economic policy direction. At the beginning of COVID-19, relief measures focused on helping businesses to survive. In April and May, some of the fees and payment obligations were reintroduced (Ministry of Transportation and Communications 2020), while the relief focus shifted to supporting businesses to resume production and operations, such as tax filing extensions for taxpayers in difficulty (SAT 2020).[10] The central government encouraged local governments to provide different types of guarantees for businesses to resume production and operations. For example, local governments were to work with the relevant departments to help enterprises coordinate the return of employees to work, the supply and transportation of materials, and the implement of COVID-19 prevention measures and supply of equipment such as masks, disinfection supplies, and thermometers. Most of the tax benefits lasted until the end of 2020.[11] In February 2021, the process of unwinding the relief measures provoked a reaction from the investors so that interbank rate spiked and PBC representatives in turn decided to slow down with the contraction. The donation tax relief was extended until March 31, 2021, and some other, such as tax deductions for the individually owned business and the film industry were further extended until March 31, 2021 (SAT 2020). Thus, financial subsidies given to those in need did not end in 2020 either, with total funding amounting to 1.7 trillion yuan in 2020 and further increasing to 2.8 trillion yuan in 2021 (MOF 2021).

As the employment conditions started improving, the government turned towards the design of the new employment policy. In that context, the government formulated the 14th five-year plan for promoting employment and set a goal for 2025 (The State council, August, 2021). The plan focused on increasing both quantity and quality in employment. According to the plan, over the next five years, new urban jobs are to increase by 550 million, with the unemployment rate staying within 5.5% limit. Workers would be provided with additional educational opportunities so that the average education period of working-age population would reach 11.3, and more than 55% of the new labor force will have received higher education. As the situation of domestic migrant workers shows, the Covid-19 pandemic has had a greater impact on those who had already been disadvantaged in the job market before the pandemic. Similarly, women were relatively more affected by the epidemic, with slower return to work and higher risks of unemployment. The employment situation of college graduates is severe, and low-skilled workers are more vulnerable to the impact of the epidemic (Qu and Cheng 2020). It remains uncertain to what extent the employment conditions of these disadvantaged groups will improve in the post-Covid era.

Finally, as soon as the pandemic wave was under control, the efforts to redesign the legal foundations of the markets and reshape the hierarchy of the roles different markets play in creating economic growth that were interrupted during the pandemic were continued. This is true of the regulatory pressure on the real estate sector, where companies such as Evergrande have been allowed to default on some of their debt and are in the process of restructuring. It is also true of the digital economy monopolies, where regulators banned the merger of Huya and DouYu on the basis of their relationship with Tencent, an anti-trust case against Meituan, the company behind a large food delivery app has been initiated and Didi, the dominant car hailing company. Furthermore, in November 2021, the Anti-Monopoly Bureau, which was a subdivision under SAMR, was promoted to the deputy ministerial level.

There is no clear evidence that the 14th five-year (2021–2025) plan in 2020 was affected by the Covid-19. However, researchers cite the profound impact of the epidemic on economic conditions faced by diverse stakeholders such as increased economic vulnerability, industry hit, and neglect of safety and health risks (Chen et al. 2020). In that context policy goals related to increasing resilience to risk, developing core technologies and key industries, and addressing climate change are even more important (Yang et al. 2020). The 14th five-year plan has made a tilt towards these areas (Xinhua News Agency 2021). In order to cope with possible threats and external challenges, scientific and technological self-reliance has taken center stage (Smriti 2021). Beyond the measures that go in this direction, the plan has also decided to promote a new credit reporting system. By collecting and analyzing multi-dimensional big data, this system can prompt companies to disclose necessary information and solve the information asymmetry problem between banks and companies (Chu and Chen 2021). High-quality SMEs can obtain more loans more easily by improving their credit scores while the financial risk of banks will be reduced (Zhou et al. 2022).

The limited scope and impact of relief provisioning in confronting the pandemic can be best understood if we compare this intervention to the one mounted to fight the effects of the global financial crisis. At the time, 4 trillion yuan in 2008 provided in order to deal with the crisis made up about 12.5% of China's GDP in 2008, to be spent over 27 months—and this is a conservative account as according to some estimates the total stimulus went up to 9.5 trillion, 27% of the GDP (Yifu and Wang 2021). In 2020, the rescue package of 4 trillion yuan in 2020 is about 4% of the GDP. Pandemic-related support was based on the six guarantees—employment, basic livelihoods, operation of market entities, food and energy security, stable industrial and supply chains, and the normal functioning of primary-level governments, and the six stabilities - stability in employment, financial operations, foreign trade, foreign investment, domestic investment, and expectations. Thus the government's plan this time was much more targeted. This contrasts with 2008 when the 4 trillion were mostly spent on large-scale infrastructure investment, that flooded the economy across sectors. It appears that the consequences of the 2008 liquidity injection—real estate price hikes, unsustainable local government spending, and the rise of shadow banking—were an important concern that policymakers want to avoid in 2020.

5 Conclusion

A good way to begin painting the picture of China's pandemic policy response is to identify it as crisis management by primarily "non-economic" means. As we have seen, the speedy resolution of the problems brought about by the first wave of the pandemic from December 2019 was based on a novel form of cooperation among public, private, and communal bodies to curtail citizen's movement with significant aid of surveillance techniques and data collection. This in turn enabled China's policy makers to use the economic relief measures for a shorter period and to a lesser extent than they would have had to use them otherwise.

This leads to the second important point, which is about the discrepancy in duration as the short term nature of pandemic was reflected in the short term of economic relief measures but not in the short term character of the above mentioned "non-economic" measures. Instead of the pandemic affecting the direction of China's economic policy, it seems that the zero case policy response to the pandemic, in particular in relation to international travel, provided advantageous conditions for pursuance of "internal circulation". As Chinese citizens were disincentivized to leave the country and the internal zero case environment was established, China saw a rise in domestic consumption of goods and services and interprovincial tourism.

What looms large in this use of the pandemic as the occasion to enhance the internal turn is the role of the law. Legal ambiguity and incoherence have plagued the process leading to significant costs and losses. At the same time, this type of legal environment has opened space for "people's war narrative", discretionary executive power, above mentioned involvement of non-public actors in surveillance and enforcement of the policy.

We see the interplay of these elements again in what seems for now to be the 2022 Shanghai pandemic wave (although it might appear to be more). The first 100 days of pandemic response have defined the response that we are seeing now almost to the smallest detail. The usual analysis of the significance of the initial choices made by China's policy makers paints a picture in which policy makers have cornered themselves by their initial choices of vaccine, lockdown, and zero case target and thus lost the opportunity to develop herd immunity of the population for what they pay the price, and will pay even more as they stick to that initial approach. Be that as it may, this type of analysis misses the important point about the way in which the crisis brought about the pandemic has created an opportunity for China's policy makers to push harder in the policy direction set out in the years before. Switching their approach in the current situation, confronting the additional sequences of crisis emergency on the one hand would imply abandoning that course, while despite the high economic and human cost it can be seized as a further opportunity to push in the same direction.

Notes

1. For example the Guangdong Emergency Plans for Public Health Emergencies, 广东省突发公共卫生事件应急预案 2013.8.9.
2. See Zhangwan District, Shiyan city, Hubei, enters the state of war from Feb 13, closing down all buildings. (湖北十堰张湾区 13 日零时起战时管制 所有楼栋封闭管理), People (人民网), http://hb.people.com.cn/n2/2020/0213/c194063-33790226.html, accessed 10 March 2022.
3. "The national credit system" means the National Credit Information Sharing Platform, which records people's behaviours violating certain credit rules. It functions with a punishment mechanism. People listed on

the credit blacklist cannot take high-speed rails or flights for five years, sign up for examination of staff of civil servant and institutions, or get a loan from the bank.

4. Art. 27 of the Anti-terrorism Law of the People's Republic of China passed, 2015.
5. "Grid Management" means to divide jurisdictions of grassroots self-government into grid patterns and connect them into informatization platforms for more precise management and inspection.
6. Art. 26, Law of the People's Republic of China on Administrative Punishments for Public Security, 2005 (amended in 2012).
7. 国家新闻办公室, 2021 年 1 月 15 日: 国新办 2020 年金融统计数据新闻发布会 The State Council Information Office of the People's Republic of China,15th,Jan, 2021: The State Council Information Office held a press conference on financial statistics in 2020, Retrieved from: http://www.scio.gov.cn/xwfbh/xwbfbh/wqfbh/44687/44760/wz44762/Document/1697045/1697045.htm.
8. 最高人民法院, 2020 年 5 月 15 日:《最高人民法院关于依法妥善审理涉新冠肺炎疫情民事案件若干问题的指导意见 (二)》SPC, May 15, 2020: Guiding Opinions on Several Issues Concerning the Proper Trial of Civil Cases related to the COVID-19 (II) Retrieved from: https://www.court.gov.cn/fabu-xiangqing-230181.html.
9. Article 180: "A person who is unable to perform his civil-law obligations due to force majeure bears no civil liability, unless otherwise provided by law. "Force majeure" means objective conditions which are unforeseeable, unavoidable, and insurmountable". Article 533: "After a contract is formed, where a fundamental condition upon which the contract is concluded is significantly changed which are unforeseeable by the parties upon conclusion of the contract and which is not one of the commercial risks, if continuing performance of the contract is obviously unfair to one of the parties, the party that is adversely affected may re-negotiate with the other party; where such an agreement cannot be reached within a reasonable period of time, the parties may request the people's court or an arbitration institution to rectify or rescind the contract.

   The people's court or an arbitration institution shall rectify or rescind the contract in compliance with the principle of fairness, taking into account the actual circumstances of the case".
10. 国家税务总局, 关于明确 2020 年 5 月纳税申报期限有关事项的通知, [State Administration of Taxation (SAT), Notice on matters related to the clarification of the May 2020 tax return deadline]. Retrieved from: http://www.gov.cn/zhengce/zhengceku/2020-04/29/content_5507327.htm.

11. Referring to the Notice of the General Office of the Ministry of Industry and Information Technology on the Key Service Activities of the Public Service System of Small and Medium Enterprises to Help Resumption of Work and Production in 2020 (2020.4.9), the Guidance of the Central COVID-19 Leading Group on Active and Orderly Promotion of Resumption of Work and Production While Effectively Preventing and Controlling the Epidemic (2020.4.7), and the State Council's joint prevention and control mechanism for coping with COVID-19 on Notice on issuing guidelines on measures to prevent and control the epidemic in enterprises and institutions resuming work and production in different risk areas nationwide (2020.4.9).

References

Amstad, M., G. Sun and W. Xiong (2020) *Handbook of China's Financial System*. Princeton: Princeton University Press.

Boer, R. (2021) *Socialism with Chinese Characteristics*. Singapore: Springer.

Cai, C., W. Jiang and N. Tang (2022) 'Campaign-Style Crisis Regime: How China Responded to the Shock of COVID-19', *Policy Studies*, 43(3): 599–619, https://doi.org/10.1080/01442872.2021.1883576.

Center for Information Technology (2020) 'Series of National Standards for Personal Health Information Code FAQ' (《个人健康信息码》系列国家标准问答 (FAQ)), Chinese Electronics Standardization Institute, available at: http://www.cesi.cn/202005/6411.html.

Central Committee of the Communist Party of China (2013) 'Decision of the CCCPC on Some Major Issues Concerning Comprehensively Deepening the Reform' (中共中央关于全面深化改革若干重大问题的决定), available at: http://www.china.org.cn/chinese/2014-01/17/content_31226494_13.htm.

Chen C., W. Xu, Z. Lan and Y. Jiang (2020) 'Study on the Internal and External Environment of China's Development in the 14th Five-Year Plan Period' ("十四五" 时期我国发展内外部环境研究), *Management World* (管理世界), 36(10): 1–14.

China Daily, Tsinghua University and Peking Union Medical College (2020) 'China's Fight Against COVID-19', available at: http://www.chinadaily.com.cn/pdf/2020/Chinas.Fight.Against.COVID-19-0420-final-2.pdf.

China Security Association (2020) 'Zhejiang Security: Guarding the Front Line of Community Prevention and Control' (浙江保安: 守好社区防控第一线),

China Security Association Website, available at: http://www.zgba.org/newsitem/278333040.

Chinese Government Procurement Website (2021) '2020: The National Government Procurement Scale Is 3,697.06 Billion Yuan, an Increase of 11.8% over the Previous Year' (2020 年全国政府采购规模为 36970.6 亿元 较上年增长 11.8%), available at: http://www.ccgp.gov.cn/news/202109/t20210907_16838934.htm.

Chappell, B. (2020) 'Coronavirus Has Now Spread to All Regions of Mainland China', NPR.

Che, Y. and H. Lin (2011) 'Fan Xiaojian, Director of the State Council Poverty Alleviation Office, Explained in Detail the New Standard of 2300 yuan for Poverty Alleviation' (国务院扶贫办主任范小建详解 2300 元扶贫新标准), The Central People's Government of the People's Republic of China, available at: http://www.gov.cn/jrzg/2011-12/02/content_2009471.htm.

Chen, Z., W. Zhang and D. Cai (2004) 'Environmental Factor Analysis of Technological Breakthroughs in China's Digital Monitoring Industry' (中国数字监控行业技术跨越的环境因素分析), *China Security & Protection* (中国安防产品信息), 2004(1): 16–18.

Chu, Q. and Y. Chen (2021) 'Research on the Construction of Digital Transformation of Emerging Financial Services in the Post-Epidemic Era—Taking Credit Industry Chain as an Example' (后疫情时代新兴金融服务数字化转型建设研究——以征信产业链为例), *Modern Finance* (现代金融), 11: 25–27.

Civil Code of the People's Republic of China (2021).

Cyberspace Administration of China (2017) 'Regulations on the Administration of Internet Group Information Services' (互联网群组信息服务管理规定), available at: http://www.cac.gov.cn/2017-09/07/c_1121623889.htm.

Gao, X., Y. Ren and M. Umar (2021) 'To What Extent Does COVID-19 Drive Stock Market Volatility? A Comparison between the U.S. and China', Economic Research-Ekonomska Istraživanja. https://doi.org/10.1080/1331677X.2021.1906730.

General Office of State Council of People's Republic of China (2020) 'Opinions on Implements of Ensuring Employment in Response to the COVID-19' (国务院办公厅关于应对新冠肺炎疫情影响强化稳就业举措的实施意见), available at: http://www.gov.cn/zhengce/content/2020-03/20/content_5493574.htm.

Guancha (2020) 'CCTV Interview Wuhan Mayor: Lockdown Was a Tough Decision as Covid Arrived Unexpectedly' (央视对话武汉市长周先旺实录: 封城是艰难决定, 疫情太突然), Guancha, available at: https://www.guancha.cn/politics/2020_01_28_533402_2.shtml.

Guo J. (2021) 'Ma Shuping: It Is Urgent to Improve the Governance Mechanism for Large Enterprises in Arrears to Small and Medium-Sized Enterprises' (马淑萍: 大企业拖欠中小企业账款的治理机制亟待健全), *China*

Economic Times (中国经济时报), available at: https://www.drc.gov.cn/DocView.aspx?chnid=379&leafid=1338&docid=2904509.

He, A. J., C. Zhang and J. Qian (2022) 'COVID-19 and Social Inequality in China: the Local–Migrant Divide and the Limits of Social Protections in a Pandemic', Policy and Society, 2022. https://doi.org/10.1093/polsoc/puac003.

Huang, Z. (2020) 'China Targets Internet Giants in Antitrust Law Overhaul', Bloomberg, available at: https://www.bloomberg.com/news/articles/2020-01-07/china-targets-internet-giants-in-sweeping-antitrust-law-overhaul?sref=CIpmV6x8

Hunan Provincial Department of Human Resources and Social Security, Department of Finance (2020) '10 Measures of Promoting the secure of Employment, Productions and Post' (湖南省人力资源和社会保障厅湖南省财政厅关于印发《稳企稳岗稳就业十条措施》的通知), available at: http://www.hunan.gov.cn/zqt/zcsd/202002/t20200221_13535512.html.

Jiang, H. Y. (2020) 'On the Protection of Personal Information in the Context of Epidemic: from the Perspective of Proportion Principle' (论疫情下个人信息保护: 以比例原则为视角). *Journal of China University of Political Science and Law* (中国政法大学学报), 4: 184–195.

Jing, M. and D. Ma (2014) 'Why the Local Media Seldom Publish Negative News about Local Community?' (地方媒体本地负面新闻报道的怪象与消解), *XinWen AiHaoZhe* (新闻爱好者), 1: 58–61.

Joint Prevention and Control Mechanism of the State Council (2020) 'Notice on Strengthening Community Work of Preventing and Controlling the Novel Coronavirus Pneumonia' (关于加强新型冠状病毒感染的肺炎疫情社区防控工作的通知), available at: http://www.gov.cn/xinwen/2020-01/26/content_5472235.htm.

Lao, D. Y. (2021) 'Criminal Law Protection of Personal Information in Epidemic Prevention and Control' (疫情防控中个人信息的刑法保护), *Tsinghua Law Review* (清华法律评论), 10(1): 42–56.

Law of the People's Republic of China on Administrative Punishments for Public Security, 2005 (amended in 2012).

Li Y., Y. Chandra and N. Kapucu (2020) 'Crisis Coordination and the Role of Social Media in Response to COVID-19 in Wuhan, China', *The American Review of Public Administration*, 50(6–7): 698–705. https://doi.org/10.1177/0275074020942105.

Liu, K. (2021a) 'COVID-19 and the Chinese Economy: Impacts, Policy Responses and Implications', *International Review of Applied Economics*, 35(2): 308–330. https://doi.org/10.1080/02692171.2021.1876641.

Liu, K. (2021b) 'Deleveraging China', *International Review of Applied Economics*, 35(1): 91–109.

Liu, X. and M. M. Bennett (2020) 'Viral Borders: COVID-19's Effects on Securitization, Surveillance, and Identity in Mainland China and Hong Kong', *Dialogues in Human Geography*, 10(2): 158–163. https://doi.org/10.1177/2043820620933828.

Luo, S. (2020) 'Jiangsu Police Put Legal Sanctions on Injuring Medical Staff' (江苏警方严惩医闹伤医非法行为), Legal Daily (法制日报), available at: http://credit.jiangsu.gov.cn/art/2020/4/13/art_78413_9292753.html, released date 13/04/2020, accessed 5 April 2022.

Mei, Ciqi (2020) 'Policy Style, Consistency and the Effectiveness of the Policy Xix in China's Fight against COVID-19', *Policy and Society*, 39(3): 309–325. https://doi.org/10.1080/14494035.2020.1787627.

Meng, T. (2020) 'The Principle and Construction of Rule of Law in the State of Public Health Emergency—Based on the Research of the Pandemic of Covid-19' (公共卫生紧急状态法治的原理与建构———基于新冠肺炎疫情的研究), *Law Review* (法学评论), 2: 135–147.

Miao, Q., S. Schwarz and G. Schwarz (2021), 'Responding to COVID-19: Community Volunteerism and Coproduction in China', *World Development*, 137. https://doi.org/10.1016/j.worlddev.2020.105128

Ministry of Finance (2020a) 'Notice on Supporting Financial Strengthening Services to Implement the Prevention and Control of COVID-19' (关于支持金融强化服务 做好新型冠状病毒感染肺炎疫情防控工作的通知), available at: http://www.gov.cn/zhengce/zhengceku/2020-02/03/content_5474105.htm.

Ministry of Finance (2020b) 'Notice on Supporting Financial Strengthening Services for the Prevention and Control of COVID-19' (关于支持金融强化服务 做好新型冠状病毒感染肺炎疫情防控工作的通知), available at: http://www.gov.cn/zhengce/zhengceku/2020b-02/03/content_5474105.htm.

Ministry of Finance (2020c) 'Questions and Answers on Government Procurement Policy Measures in the "Questions and Answers on Policy Measures to Support the Prevention and Control of the New Crown Pneumonia Epidemic"' (《财政支持新冠肺炎疫情防控政策措施问答》中的有关政府采购政策措施问答), China Government Procurement (中国政府采购), 4: 13–14.

Ministry of Finance (2020d) 'Urgent Notice on the Organization of the Resumption of Work and Scheduling Arrangements of Key Material Production Enterprises for the Prevention and Control of the Epidemic' (关于疫情防控期间开展政府采购活动有关事项的通知), available at: http://www.gov.cn/zhengce/zhengceku/2020-02/07/content_5475799.htm.

Ministry of Finance (2020e) 'Notice on Facilitating Epidemic Prevention and Control Procurement' (关于疫情防控采购便利化的通知), available at: http://www.ccgp.gov.cn/zcfg/mof/202002/t20200203_13860302.htm.

Ministry of Finance (2021a) 'Ministry of Finance Press Conference on Fiscal Revenue and Expenditure in 2020' (财政部新闻发布会介绍 2020 年财政收支

情况), available at: http://www.gov.cn/xinwen/2021-01/28/content_5583244.htm.

Ministry of Finance (2021b) 'Report on the Implementation of China's Fiscal Policy in 2020' (2020 年中国财政政策执行情况报告), available at: http://www.gov.cn/xinwen/2021-03/06/content_5590913.htm.

Ministry of Finance and National Health Commission (2020) 'Notice on the New Coronavirus Infection Pneumonia Outbreak Prevention and Control Related Funding Security Policy' (关于新型冠状病毒感染肺炎疫情防控有关经费保障政策的通知), available at: http://www.gov.cn/zhengce/zhengceku/2020-01/30/content_5473079.htm.

Ministry of Finance and State Administration of Taxation (2019) 'Notice on Implementing Inclusive Tax Reduction Policy for Small and Micro Enterprises' (关于实施小微企业普惠性税收减免政策的通知), available at: http://www.chinatax.gov.cn/n810341/n810755/c4014090/content.html.

Ministry of Finance and State Administration of Taxation (2021) 'Notice on the Continuation of Relevant Taxation and Fee Policies related to the Covid Epidemic' (关于延续实施应对疫情部分税费优惠政策的公告), available at: http://www.chinatax.gov.cn/chinatax/n359/c5162489/content.html.

Ministry of Human Resources and Social Security (2020), 'Notice of Properly Handling Labor Relation Issues During the Covid-19 Prevention Period' (人力资源社会保障部办公厅关于妥善处理新型冠状病毒感染的肺炎疫情防控期间劳动关系问题的通知), available at: http://www.gov.cn/zhengce/zhengceku/2020-01/27/content_5472508.htm.

Ministry of Human Resources and Social Security and Ministry of Finance (2020) 'Notice on Expanding the Coverage of Unemployment Insurance' (人力资源社会保障部 财政部 关于扩大失业保险保障范围的通知), available at: http://www.mohrss.gov.cn/SYrlzyhshbzb/shehuibaozhang/zcwj/202006/t20200609_375841.html.

Ministry of Human Resources and Social Security, the National Development and Reform Commission, the Ministry of Finance, the Ministry of Commerce, and the State Administration of Market Regulation (2021) 'Opinions on Promoting the High-quality Development of the Human', available at: https://new.qq.com/omn/20211125/20211125A04XWB00.html.

Ministry of Industry and Information Technology (2020) 'Notice on Work Related to Helping Small and Medium Enterprises Resume Work and Production to Tide Over the Difficulties in Response to COVID-19' (工业和信息化部关于应对新型冠状病毒肺炎疫情帮助中小企业复工复产共渡难关有关工作的通知), available at: http://www.gov.cn/zhengce/zhengceku/2020-02/10/content_5476684.htm.

Ministry of Transportation and Communications (2020) 'Announcement on the Resumption of Toll Road Tolls' (交通运输部关于恢复收费公路收费的公

告), available at: http://www.gov.cn/zhengce/zhengceku/2020-04/28/content_5507165.htm

Munroe, T., and R. Liu (2020) 'Xi Says China Faces "Grave Situation" as Virus Death Toll Hits 42', Reuters.

Nanchang Center for Disease Control and Prevention (2021) 'Alert: People from High-Risk Areas to Jiangxi Province Will Be Assigned Red in Health Code' (南昌卫健委紧急提醒!南昌这些人将被赋红黄码!), Jiangxi Daily, available at: https://m.gmw.cn/baijia/2021-07/30/1302443618.html.

National Bureau of Statistics of China (2019). 'Bulletin on the Main Data of the Fourth National Economic Census' (第四次全国经济普查公报), available at: http://www.stats.gov.cn/tjsj/zxfb/201911/t20191119_1710335.html.

National Health Commission (2020) 'Draft of the Revised PRC Law on Prevention and Treatment of Infectious Disease Released for Public Comment' 国家卫生健康委关于《中华人民共和国传染病防治法》(修订草案征求意见稿) 公开征求意见的通知, available at: http://www.nhc.gov.cn/fzs/s3577/202010/330ecbd72c3940408c3e5a49e8651343.shtml.

Naughon B. (2018) *The Chinese Economy: Adaptation and Growth*, The MIT Press.

People (2020) 'Zhangwan District, Shiyan City, Hubei, Enters the State of War from Feb 13, Closing Down All Buildings' (湖北十堰张湾区 13 日零时起战时管制 所有楼栋封闭管理), People (人民网) , available at: http://hb.people.com.cn/n2/2020/0213/c194063-33790226.html, released date 13 February 2020, accessed 10 March 2022.

People's Bank of China, Ministry of Finance, Banking and Insurance Regulatory Commission, Securities Regulatory Commission and State Administration of Foreign Exchange (2020) 'Notice of Strengthening the Financial Support of Preventing and Controlling the COVID-19' (关于进一步强化金融支持防控新型冠状病毒感染肺炎疫情的通知), available at: http://www.gov.cn/zhengce/zhengceku/2020-02/01/content_5473639.htm.

Qin, C. (2021) 'Hear the Voice of Citizens in Ruili, Overcome Difficulties of Pandemic Control and Prevention' (人民热评: 倾听老百姓的呼声, 有助瑞丽渡过难关), People's Daily, available at: http://yn.people.com.cn/n2/2021/1030/c378439-34982166.html.

Qu X. and J. Cheng (2020) 'Impacts of COVID-19 on the Labor Market and Policy Responses' (新冠肺炎疫情对劳动力市场的影响及政策反应), *Journal of Hebei Normal University (Philosophy and Social Sciences)* (河北师范大学学报(哲学社会科学版)), 43(4): 126–133.

Ritchie, H., et al. (2020–2021) 'Coronavirus Pandemic (COVID-19)', Our World in Data.

Shanghai Municipal Health Commission (2022) 'Complete Lockdowns for a New Round of Mass Testing' (新一轮核酸筛查要求封控管理期间人员"

足不出户"), available at: https://wsjkw.sh.gov.cn/xwfb/20220329/5a33e39b7be74e93abd2e14cb321e752.html, released date 29/03/2022, accessed 5 April 2022.

Sheng, F. (2020) 'Study on Risk-Bearing Rule by Performance Obstacle of Employment Contract under the Epidemic Prevention and Control' (疫情防控背景下劳动合同不能履行时的风险负担规则研究), *Journal of Comparative Law* (比较法研究), 2: 40–53.

Smriti, M (2021) 'China's Five-Year Plan Focuses on Scientific Self-Reliance' *Nature*, 591: 353–354.

Song, H. M. and J. G. Lin (2018) 'The "Informers" in the "Scar Literature"' (论"伤痕文学中的告密者形象), Guan Dong Journal (关东学刊), 2018(3): 112–119. https://doi.org/10.19470/j.cnki.cn22-1417/c.2018.03.014.

State Administration of Foreign Exchange (2020) 'Notice of the State Administration of Foreign Exchange on Establishing a Green Channel for Foreign Exchange Policy to Support the Prevention and Control of the COVID-19' (国家外汇管理局关于建立外汇政策绿色通道 支持新型冠状病毒感染的肺炎疫情防控工作的通知)', available at: http://www.safe.gov.cn/safe/2020/0127/15259.html.

State Administration of Taxation (2020a) 'State Administration of Taxation, Notice on optimizing tax payment services to cooperate with the prevention and control of the COVID-19' (国家税务总局关于优化纳税缴费服务配合做好新型冠状病毒感染肺炎疫情防控工作的通知), available at: http://www.gov.cn/zhengce/zhengceku/2020-01/31/content_5473310.htm.

State Administration of Taxation (2020b) 'Notice on Optimizing Tax Payment and Payment Services to Cooperate with the Prevention and Control of COVID-19' (关于优化纳税缴费服务配合做好新型冠状病毒感染肺炎疫情防控工作的通知), available at: http://www.gov.cn/zhengce/zhengceku/2020-01/31/content_5473310.htm

State Administration of Taxation (2020c) 'Announcement on Tax Policies Related to Supporting the Prevention and Control of COVID-19' (关于支持新型冠状病毒感染的肺炎疫情防控有关税收政策的公告), available at: http://www.gov.cn/zhengce/zhengceku/202-02/07/content_5475528.htm.

State Administration of Taxation (2020d) 'Notice on Matters Related to the Clarification of the May 2020 Tax Return Deadline' (国家税务总局关于明确 2020 年 5 月纳税申报期限有关事项的通知), available at: http://www.gov.cn/zhengce/zhengceku/2020-04/29/content_5507327.htm.

State Administration of Taxation and Ministry of Finance (2020) 'Announcement on the Implementation Period of Tax and Fee Policies including Supporting Epidemic Prevention and Control to Ensure Supply' (关于支持疫情防控保供等税费政策实施期限的公告), available at: http://www.gov.cn/zhengce/zhengceku/2020-05/29/content_5515981.htm.

State Council (2006) 'National Emergency Plan for Public Health Emergencies' (国家突发公共卫生事件应急预案), available at: http://www.gov.cn/yjgl/2006-02/26/content_211654.htm.

State Council (2011) 'China Rural Poverty Alleviation and Development Program (2011–2020)' (《中国农村扶贫开发纲要 (2011–2020年) 》), available at: http://www.gov.cn/gongbao/content/2011/content_2020905.htm.

State Council (2021) 'The 14th Five-Year Plan for Promoting Employment' ("十四五"就业促进规划), available at: http://www.gov.cn/zhengce/content/2021-08/27/content_5633714.htm.

State Council Information Office of the People's Republic of China (2004) 'The Current Situation and Guiding Policy of Employment in China' (中国的就业状况和政策), available at: http://www.scio.gov.cn/zfbps/ndhf/2004/Document/307902/307902.htm.

State Council Information Office of the People's Republic of China (2021) 'The State Council Information Office held a press conference on financial statistics in 2020' (2021 年 1 月 15 日: 国新办 2020 年金融统计数据新闻发布会), available at: http://www.scio.gov.cn/xwfbh/xwbfbh/wqfbh/44687/44760/wz44762/Document/1697045/1697045.htm.

Sun, L. (2020) 'Over 9 Million People Have Used Beijing Jian Kang Bao' (北京健康宝已超 900 万人使用), Beijing Daily, available at: http://bj.cri.cn/2020-03-31/b87f1ecb-70c1-502c-48b5-19096a737483.html.

Supreme People's Court (2020) 'Guiding Opinions on Several Issues Concerning the Proper Trial of Civil Cases related to the COVID-19 (II)' (最高人民法院关于依法妥善审理涉新冠肺炎疫情民事案件若干问题的指导意见 (二)), available at: https://www.court.gov.cn/fabu-xiangqing-230181.html.

Tangcharoensathien, V., M.T. Bassett, Q. Meng, and A. Mills (2021) 'Are Overwhelmed Health Systems an Inevitable Consequence of Covid-19? Experiences from China, Thailand, and New York State', *BMJ* 372 (83). https://doi.org/10.1136/bmj.n83.

Tian, H. et al. (2020) 'An Investigation of Transmission Control Measures during the First 50 days of the COVID-19 Epidemic in China', *Science* 368 (6491): 638–642.

Tongzhou District People's Court of Beijing (2020) 'Special Research: Studies on the Legal Application of the Crime of Fabricating and Intentionally Spreading False Information related to epidemic diseases' (编造、故意传播涉疫情虚假信息犯罪法律适用问题研究), The Paper, available at: https://m.thepaper.cn/baijiahao_6779209.

Wang, J. (2020) 'On the Central-Local Power Allocation of the Early-Warning of the Public Health Emergency' (论突发公共卫生事件预警中的央地权限配置), *Contemporary Law Review* (当代法律评论) 3: 54–63.

Wang, S., W. Sheng and M. Zhou (2021) 'Jiangning District Enters the State of War, Testing Over 2 Million People a Day' (江宁全区全员进入战时状态 1 天内完成超 200 万人核酸采样), News of Jiangsu Provincial Committee of the Communist Party of China, available at: http://www.zgjssw.gov.cn/shixianchuanzhen/nanjing/202107/t20210722_7164361.shtml, accessed 28 January 2022.

Wang, J. (2017) 'The 5th Episode of Brilliant China Shows China's "Sky Net Project": The "Eyes" for Protecting People' (《辉煌中国》第五集展示中国 "天网工程": 守护百姓之 "眼"), The Paper, available at: https://www.sohu.com/a/194207136_617374.

Wang, Z. (2020) 'Impact of COVID—19 on China's Employment Protection and Social Security System' (新冠肺炎疫情冲击下的就业保护与社会保障), *Economic Review Journal* (经济纵横), 3: 7–15.

Wang, Z. J. (2020) 'Law in Crisis: A Critical Analysis of the Role of Law in China's Fight Against COVID-19', *Griffith Law Review*, 29(2): 253–227.

Xi'ji Police (2022) 'Epidemic Prevention and Control: 10 Regulations and 30 Measures' (疫情防控十个常态化、30 项防控措施), The Paper, available at: https://www.thepaper.cn/newsDetail_forward_16872031.

Xinhua News Agency (2021) 'The Fourteenth Five-Year Plan for the National Economic and Social Development of the People's Republic of China and the Outline of Long-Term Goals for 2035' (中华人民共和国国民经济和社会发展第十四个五年规划和 2035 年远景目标纲要), available at: http://www.xinhuanet.com/2021-03/13/c_1127205564.htm.

Xu, W., J. Wu and L. Cao (2020) 'COVID-19 Pandemic in China: Context, Experience and Lessons", *Health Policy and Technology*, 9(4): 639–648. https://doi.org/10.1016/j.hlpt.2020.08.006.

Yang B., B. Hu and J. Zhao (2020) 'The Impact of the New Pneumonia Epidemic on the Development of the 14th Five-Year Plan and Its Target Setting (新冠肺炎疫情对制定 "十四五" 规划及其目标设置的影响), *Scitech in China* (科技中国), 11: 41–43.

Yang, J. and C. Yang (2021) 'Economic Policy Uncertainty, COVID-19 Lockdown, and Firm-Level Volatility: Evidence from China', *Pacific-Basin Finance Journal*, 68. https://doi.org/10.1016/j.pacfin.2021.101597

Yang, S. X. (2021) 'Personal Information Should Not Fall Prey to the APPs' (个人信息不是 App 的"唐僧肉"), *Guangming Daily* (光明日报), available at: https://epaper.gmw.cn/gmrb/html/2021-01/25/nw.D110000gmrb_20210125_4-02.htm.

Yifu, L. J. and X. Wang (2021) 'Dual Circulation: A New Structural Economics View of Development', *Journal of Chinese Economic and Business Studies*. https://doi-org.eproxy.lib.hku.hk/10.1080/14765284.2021.1929793.

Yu, Y. (2014) 'The Western Project Xinjiang University Student Volunteers Speak Out Firmly Against Violence and Terrorism' (西部计划新疆大学生志愿者联

合发声——坚决反对暴力恐怖), *People's Daily*, available at: http://politics.people.com.cn/n/2014/0523/c1001-25053528.html.

Zhang, F. (2020) 'Facing the Pandemic, Wuhan Citizens' Hearts Should Be Warmed' ("疫"流而上，最该给武汉市民暖暖心), IFeng News, available from https://ishare.ifeng.com/c/s/v0029UDXd-_NBynqw86yvBmKJLjEB71eXmhPcjHXnhprrBhE__

Zhang, L. (2020) 'Epidemic Prevention and Control Should Not Be Strengthened Without Cause by Local Governments' (疫情防控不能层层加码相互比"硬"). *Legal Daily* (法制日报), available at: http://opinion.people.com.cn/n1/2020/0219/c1003-31593478.html, released date 19/02/2020, accessed 5 April 2022.

Zhao, S. (2020) 'Digital Epidemic Prevention Systems Empowers Epidemic Containment' (数字防疫系统助力疫情防控), *People's Daily*, available at: http://it.people.com.cn/n1/2020/0207/c1009-31576579.html, accessed on 5 April 2022.

Zhao, Y. P. (2014) 'Officials and People of All Ethnic Groups in Xinjiang Strongly Condemn Violent and Terrorist Attacks' (新疆各族干部群众强烈谴责暴恐行为), *People's Daily*, available at: http://cpc.people.com.cn/n/2014/0801/c64387-25381264.html, accessed on 5 April 2022.

Zhao, W. Q. and H. Li (2022) 'The Co-presence of the State and Society: A Study of Social Mobilization Mechanism in Public Health Events' (国家和社会共同在场: 公共卫生事件下社会动员机制研究), *China Health Law* (中国卫生法制), 30(1): 30–35.

Zhou, L., R. Gu, X. Xing and H. Wu (2022) 'Review and Outlook of Frontier Research on Big Data Credit' (大数据征信前沿研究综述与展望), *Credit Reference* (征信), 40(01): 36–44.

Are Militarized Lockdowns the Great Equalizer? Evidence from the Philippines

Vincent Jerald Ramos, Fatemeh Halabisaz, Leonides Frago Jr., and Ryan Martinez

1 Introduction

The Philippines pandemic response was based on a reenactment of the familiar rhetoric that President Rodrigo Duterte employed in his bid for the presidency in the 2016 elections. The representatives of the government vowed to swiftly end the spread of COVID-19 by maintaining peace and order. President Duterte's "strongman" rule and spectacle-driven

V. J. Ramos (✉)
Hertie School Berlin, Berlin, Germany
e-mail: vincent.ramos@hu-berlin.de

Humboldt University Berlin, Berlin, Germany

F. Halabisaz
IE Business School in Madrid, Madrid, Spain
e-mail: fatemeh.halabisaz@student.ie.edu

L. Frago Jr. · R. Martinez
University of the Philippines-Diliman, Quezon, Philippines
e-mail: lcfrago@up.edu.ph

R. Martinez
e-mail: rcmartinez2@up.edu.ph

A. Stojanović et al. (eds.), *The First 100 Days of Covid-19*,
https://doi.org/10.1007/978-981-19-6325-4_3

rhetoric has been widely reported and analyzed by scholars since his assumption into office (Curato 2017). An important asset of the Duterte regime's illiberal democratic order is his commanding presence within the armed forces and law enforcement agencies (Thompson 2017). In the Philippines, the institution responsible for leading the pandemic response policy is the Inter-Agency Task Force for the Management of Emerging Infectious Diseases (IATF-EID) headed by the Secretary of the Department of Health, Francisco Duque III, and composed of the executive branch cabinet and offices. Among others, its primary purposes were to coordinate and decentralize the management of the pandemic; formulate the National Action Plan; and issue resolutions and policies as the situation progressed. However, real power is delegated to the National Task Force Against COVID-19 (NTF) and Joint Task Force COVID-19 Shield which managed the operational side of the pandemic. Correspondingly, this approach entailed entrusting the direct decision making and on-the-ground implementation of regulations to law enforcement and military actors (Tugade 2021a).

A State of Calamity was issued through Proclamation no. 929 series 2020 (Official Gazette 2020a), months after the first detected case of COVID-19 in the country on January 28, 2020. The same proclamation enlisted the ranks of both the Philippine National Police and Armed Force of the Philippines "to ensure peace and order in affected areas, as may be necessary". The public witnessed troops of armed personnel manning the checkpoints in lockdown regions as the imposed month-long Enhanced Community Quarantine (ECQ), the strictest form of the lockdown, took effect on 16 March 2020. Under the IATF-EID Omnibus Guideline (Official Gazette 2020b) issued on 29 April 2020, ECQ "refers to the implementation of temporary measures imposing stringent limitations on movement and transportation of people, strict regulation of operating industries, provisions of food and essential services, and heightened presence of uniformed personnel to enforce community quarantine protocols". These ECQ-level lockdowns were extended, upon the advice of the ex-military generals in the cabinet echoing similar strategies employed in counter-insurgency tactics (Dizon 2020). Moreover, the appointment of former Chief of Staff of the Armed Forces of the Philippines and adviser to the Peace Process Carlito Galvez as overall COVID "Czar" was later rationalized by the executive department (Presidential Communications Operations Office 2020). This appointment is consistent with his preference for appointing military and ex-military officials in key cabinet posts, particularly in crisis situations. President Duterte justified similar choices before by claiming that "the backbone of ...[his] administration is the uniformed personnel of government" (Dizon 2020).

The heavy-handed and militarized response showcased in the Philippines pandemic response prevails because of the reigning culture of impunity at the highest position in the country. Amnesty International Philippines Researcher, Rachel Chhoa-Howard, stated: "This is not an accidental by-product of his administration, but its central feature. Police and other unidentified gunmen know they can kill without consequence. They are taking literally the President's regular incitement to kill, and his promises to protect those who do so – and so should member states at the Human Rights Council" (Amnesty International 2020). Incumbent senator Leila De Lima (2019), a staunch critic and political prisoner of the administration since 2017, called to attention the silent pandemic of "lawfare", which refers to the instrumental weaponization of the legal system against perceived enemy of the state (Nonato 2020). The consequence of lawfare ranges from imprisonment under false charges to extrajudicial killings, as exemplified by the administration's War on Drugs' biased against the poorest population. During the pandemic, aggressive enforcement of lockdown and strict compliance to minimum public health standard has led to the arrest of over 100,000 "quarantine violators" between the period of March 2020 to September 2020. Moreover, the highly controversial "Shoot to kill" pronouncement of President Duterte has raised alarm for international rights monitoring organization, Amnesty International, and was eventually cited in the report of the UN High Commission for Human Rights Michell Bachelet in her assessment of the human rights situation in the Philippines (Tugade 2021b).

In this chapter, we analyze the determinants and the effects of Philippines pandemic policy response. The chapter proceeds as follows: in the next section, we argue that extreme lockdown was consistent with the incumbent administration's strongman leader profile and authoritarian tendencies. Then, we outline the policy responses of the government and discuss some bureaucratic missteps. These lockdowns, we argue, fail to address the inability of the state to accomplish its policy goals, revealing *weak state capacity*, and is exacerbated by a fragile public healthcare system and the absence of established social protection mechanisms that can act as automatic stabilizers during periods of crisis. Finally, we evaluate the effects of lockdowns not only on macroeconomic indicators but also disproportionately on specific sectors and demographic groups, suggesting that these lockdowns are arguably not a "great equalizer".

2 Pre-pandemic Development Trajectory and a Weak State Capacity

In 2016, President Rodrigo Duterte institutionalized his zero to 10-point socioeconomic agenda, which comprised the bulk of what came to be known as "Dutertenomics". Running on a strong commitment against crime and drugs, Dutertenomics underscores peace and order as prerequisites to economic development. Former Socioeconomic Planning Secretary, Ernesto Pernia, at the 2017 World Economic Forum on the Association of Southeast Asian Nations in Cambodia stated: "It's not a 10-point agenda. To remember this, it's a zero-to-10-point agenda, socio-economic agenda and the zero is precisely peace and order" (*Manila Times* 2017). Secretary Pernia added: "President Duterte is addressing that main bedrock of the 10-point economic agenda so that the agenda can materialize. Without his bedrock, then it will be difficult for the economy to thrive and flourish and for the country to prosper" (*Manila Times* 2017). The 10-point socioeconomic agenda covers the priority macroeconomic policy programs of the administration and are composed of the following:

0. Ensuring Peace and Order.
1. Continue and maintain current macroeconomic policies, including fiscal, monetary and trade policies.
2. Institute progressive tax reform and more effective tax collection, indexing taxes to inflation.
3. Increase competitiveness and the ease of doing business. This effort will draw upon successful models used to attract business to local cities.
4. Accelerate annual infrastructure spending to account for 5% of GDP, with Public–Private Partnerships playing a key role.
5. Promote rural and value chain development toward increasing agricultural and rural enterprise productivity and rural tourism.
6. Ensure security of land tenure to encourage investments and address bottlenecks in land management and titling agencies.

7. Invest in human capital development, including health and education systems, and match skills and training to meet the demand of businesses and the private sector.
8. Promote science, technology, and the creative arts to enhance innovation and creative capacity toward self-sustaining, inclusive development.
9. Improve social protection programs, including the government's Conditional Cash Transfer program, to protect the poor against instability and economic shocks.
10. Strengthen implementation of the Responsible Parenthood and Reproductive Health Law to enable especially poor couples to make informed choices on financial and family planning.

Through Executive Order no. 5 issued on October 11, 2016, the 0+10 socioeconomic agenda became institutionalized as part of the 25-year long-term vision of *Ambisyon Natin 2040* and the medium-term Philippine Development Plan (PDP) 2017–2022. The pursuit of the PDP 2017–2022 relies on realizing the administration's effort in securing peace and order as foundations for economic development. As quoted in PDP 2017–2022 "A top priority of the Duterte Administration is the reduction of all forms of criminal laws and illegal drugs. This will be done through a holistic program that involves not only combatting crimes but also the corruption that perpetuate such acts (Chapter 19). The approach will be comprehensive and will include information and education campaigns, community organization and mobilization, and police-community partnerships to ensure public order and safety" (National Economic and Development Authority 2017). The proposed holistic programs on addressing social inequality, criminality, and corruption are immediately overshadowed by the track record of the Duterte administration's threefold war against drugs, corruption, and terrorism.

With regard to the economy, the administration's flagship program "Build, Build, Build" allots 5% of the country's gross domestic product (GDP) towards facilitating infrastructure development and connectivity between major metropolitan areas. According to the PDP 2017–2022 the rationale of the administration's macroeconomic policy is that: "fiscal policy should support a strategic spending program aimed at addressing capacity constraints by investing in infrastructure and encouraging innovation. Monetary and financial policy should continue to support growth through the maintenance of low and stable inflation and financial inclusion. For its part, regulatory policy should promote competition, reduce the set-up costs for new entrants, especially small players, and ensure consumer protection. Finally, social policy needs to expand beyond the current range of services to include social protection for uncovered sectors and disaster risk mitigation, among others, and access to quality healthcare" (NEDA 2017). Despite running on a platform of veering away from its predecessor, the economic policies outline a "business-as-usual" neoliberal economic agenda (IBON Foundation 2016, 2017). Table 1 summarizes select executive orders issued by the Office of the President for the realization 0+10 Socioeconomic Agenda.

To secure the administration's socioeconomic agenda and fulfill the proposals of the Philippine Development Plan by the end of its term, the Philippine government institutionalized the adoption of a "whole-of-government" and "whole-of-nation" approach to facilitate the streamlining of interagency reforms in government processes and involving societal actors in the process of development. The whole-of-government approach is defined by the Organization for Economic Co-operation and Development (OECD) as: "one where a government actively uses formal and/or informal networks across the different agencies within that government to coordinate the design and implementation of the range of interventions that the government's agencies will be making in order to increase the effectiveness of those interventions in achieving the desired objectives" (OCED 2007). Moreover, a whole-of-nation approach refers to a comprehensive approach involving "all organizations in a conflict area to support peace and stability, to reach common goals" (Doyle 2019). Both approaches underscore establishing coordination and structure between administrative, civilian, and security actors in resolving developmental issues and challenges. These approaches defined the Duterte Administration's current strategy in its pandemic management as demonstrated by the Philippines' National Action Plan Against COVID-19.

3 Weak State Capacity

In its broadest understanding, state capacity refers to the ability of a state to execute policies and achieve policy goals (Fukuyama 2004; Dinecco 2017; Norris 2012; Vacarro 2021). While state capacity in developing countries is generally weaker, the Philippines stands out as "on the cusp

Table 1 Summary of pre-pandemic executive orders

	Date published	*Brief description*
Executive Order No. 1 series of 2016	June 30, 2016	Reengineering the Office of the President Towards Greater Responsiveness to the Attainment of Development Goals
Executive Order No. 5 series of 2016	October 11, 2016	Approving and Adopting the Twenty-Five-Year Long Term Vision Entitled Ambisyon Natin 2040 as Guide for Development Planning
Executive Order No. 9 series of 2016	December 1, 2016	Strengthening the Office of the Cabinet Secretary, Enhancing its Powers and Functions, Providing for its Support Staff and for Other Purposes
Philippine Development Plan 2017–2022	January 9, 2017	Designed as the mid-term plan for its strategic counterpart Ambisyon Natin 2040, PDP 2017–2022 outlines the development strategy of the Duterte Administration "0 to 10-point Socioeconomic Agenda" including strategic reforms in government
Executive Order No. 27 series of 2017	June 1, 2017	Directing All Government Agencies And Instrumentalities, Including Local Government Units, To Implement The Philippine Development Plan And Public Investment Program For The Period 2017–2022
Executive Order No. 70 series of 2018	December 4, 2018	Institutionalizing the Whole-of-Nation Approach in Attaining inclusive and Sustainable Peace, Creating a National Task Force to End Local Communist Armed Conflict and Directing the Adoption of a National Peace Framework

(continued)

Table 1 (continued)

	Date published	*Brief description*
Executive Order No. 114 series of 2020	May 6, 2020	Institutionalizing the Balik Probinsya, Bagong Pag-Asa Program as a pillar of Balanced Regional Development, Creating a council Therefor, and for other purposes
Updated Philippine Development Plan 2017–2022	February 5, 2021	The mid-term updated of PDP 2017–2022 released at the onset of the COVID-19 pandemic includes revisions in strategic development with emphasis on recovery and resilience
Executive Order No. 129 series of 2021	April 13, 2021	Creating the Office of the Presidential Adviser on Streamlining of Government Processes, Providing its functions, and for other purposes

Source Official Gazette of the Office of the President

of a weak state" because of the security issues in the southern regions of the Philippines (Rice and Patrick 2008). Indeed, the capacity of a state to achieve its policy goals is hampered under the threat of insurgency and terrorism. In these areas, civilians live in fear and the government faces logistical challenges in implementing development projects. While the "peace and order" focus of the Duterte administration covers the presence of insurgency in the Mindanao region, we argue that weak state capacity is present in the healthcare system and social protection system.

The Philippine Health Insurance Corporation (PhilHealth) is the national health insurance provider and while its mandate is to cover 100% of the population, it has only covered 85% as of August 2020. While this is clearly a massive improvement from a dismal 38% in 2008, the failure to achieve full population coverage at the height of the pandemic is problematic. In terms of hospital capacity, the Philippines in 2014 has an average of 1 hospital bed per 1000 population based on the World Development Indicators, a far cry from the global average of 2.8 beds per 1000 population. Indeed, the lack of hospital beds especially in rural and smaller urban

Table 2 Summary measures of Philippine health care utilization and financing

Measure	*Key findings*
Health insurance coverage	68% of the population has some form of health insurance
PhilHealth coverage	66% in 2017 (38% in 2008); 85% in 2020
Health care treatment	8% of household members visited a health facility for advice or treatment in the 30 days prior to the survey
Hospital care	4% of household members were confined to a hospital or clinic in the 12 months before the survey 50% of persons receiving in-patient care were treated at a public facility
Average cost of treatment	PHP 21,400 (~USD 417) Public: PHP 11,627 (~USD 227) Private: PHP 33,191 (~USD 648)

Source Philippine National Demographic and Health Survey 2017, DOH Press Release 2020

areas poses a threat to the government's ability to swiftly respond to the pandemic (Table 2).

Weak state capacity is reflected not only in the gaps in the health-care system but also in the absence of a robust social protection system. The Philippines' Social Security System (SSS), the main pension fund for Filipino workers in self-employment and in the private sector, has built-in unemployment benefits for its members. According to the SSS, members below 60 years old can apply if they have contributed premiums of at least 3 years and 12 months of it were paid within 18 months before their involuntary separation. It is important to note that the SSS benefit for the unemployed is only a one-time payment of one-month worth of salary. Further, these benefits do not extend to those in vulnerable and informal employment unless they voluntarily contribute. These workers include street vendors, public transportation drivers and conductors, rickshaw bikers, etc. Simply put, they are ineligible to apply for government loans and social insurance programs. A more comprehensive Unemployment Insurance Bill (UIB) that establishes a separate fund from the pension system is pending in Congress.[1] This measure includes provisions to cover the informally employed. Had a UIB system been present, it could have acted as an automatic stabilizer at the onset of the pandemic—it would have diverted resources to unemployed individuals with higher propensities to consume which could have lessened the adverse economic effects of the pandemic.

4 Onset of the Pandemic: Policy Response and Bureaucratic Missteps

4.1 *Militarized Lockdowns*

Primarily to curb the spread of COVID-19, the entire island of Luzon, which includes the capital and its densely populated neighboring regions, was placed under a militarized lockdown on March 15, 2020. Mobility restrictions such as full closure of schools and workplaces, suspension of all forms of mass public transport, and an imposition of an extensive curfew from 8 a.m. to 5 p.m. were all imposed stringently by police and military forces. The President's expansive influence on the legislative branch paved the way for the swift passage of Republic Act 11469 which granted him a wide array of powers to unilaterally impose such mobility restrictions (Tugade 2021a). We argue that this militarized approach in addressing the pandemic follows a recognizable pattern—President Rodrigo Duterte ran and won a campaign promising a swift and unforgiving anti-criminality agenda and his persistent trust in law enforcement agencies shape his form of governance. Table 3 summarizes the highlights of the Philippines' initial response to COVID-19, including other key events that occurred during these periods.

Four years into his administration built on the platform of a relentless war on drugs, President Duterte is facing yet another "war" of his own making, consistent with his "strongman" leadership profile (Curato 2017). This time, it is the "war against *pasaway*", a common Filipino term for anyone who disobeys rules, cannot be put in line, or does not toe the prevailing notion of decorum and order. This is not surprising as the COVID mitigation and management efforts in the Philippines appear to be "securitized" (Atienza et al. 2020; Pitlo 2020; Quijano et al. 2020 as cited in Hapal 2021, p. 226). More specifically, the Philippine government: (1) 'identified an existential threat' in the form of the COVID-19 virus and the disobedient citizens ("pasaways"); (2) legitimized extraordinary and punitive measures to address the pandemic; and (3) successfully employed a populist rhetoric as a legitimizing speech act (Hapal 2021, p. 238).

Pandemics or other "health emergencies create latitude for populists to make a case for the swiftest possible response... offering 'common sense' solutions to complex issues" (Lasco and Curato 2019, p. 3). In the Philippines, this powerful narrative of a war against an enemy both

Table 3 Highlights of the Philippines' pandemic response

2020	*Highlights*
January	The Philippines reports the first case of Coronavirus in the country. The Inter-Agency Task Force for the Management of Emerging Infectious Diseases (IATF-EID) is convened to spearhead its operations. First suspected and confirmed cases of COVID were reported in mid- and end-January, respectively
February	The Department of Health announces the first COVID-19 death in the Philippines on 2 Feb 2020. On the same day, the Philippines imposed an entry ban for travellers from Mainland China and its Special Administrative Regions and an exit ban for Filipinos traveling to China
March	President Rodrigo Duterte declares a State of Calamity through Proclamation No. 929 Deployment of militarized police and army personnel at entry-points in Metro Manila past midnight Republic Act No. 11469 or the *Bayanihan to Heal as One Act* is signed into law, granting emergency powers to the President among others IATF-EID National Action Plan implementing rules released Implementing rules and regulation for the Social Amelioration Program released
April	President Duterte extends the Luzon lockdown to April 30 IATF-EID released Omnibus Guidelines on the Implementation of Community Quarantine
May	ABS-CBN, the largest media conglomerate in the Philippines, closed after Congress denied its renewal of franchise
June	Metro Manila eases into less restrictive General Community Quarantine The Effectiveness of Bayanihan to Heal as One Act expired
July	President Duterte signs the controversial law Republic Act No. 11479, or Anti-terrorism Act of 2020 In a taped televised public address, President Duterte ordered the Philippine National Police to arrest quarantine violators
August	Philippines surpassed Indonesia as most total COVID-19 cases in Southeast Asia

Source Authors' summary based on previous report in Global Response to COVID-19 (2021)

as the unseen virus and unruly citizens, among others, facilitated the often mismatched COVID-19 mitigation priorities and approaches. Lasco (2020) also argues that Duterte's "medical populism" legitimized the granting of his emergency powers. This type of populism simplified the seriousness of the pandemic and dramatized it, at the same time, creating divisions between obedient citizens as "victims" and "elites" such as international bodies like the World Health Organization (WHO) and public intellectuals (academics, health experts, journalists, among others).

Another unique aspect of Duterte's populist rhetoric is its inclusion of China and Chinese interest when appealing to the public, when populists around the world seem to be in unison in painting the Chinese as a scarecrow to their domestic audiences. The Philippine government's relatively pro-China stance figured most prominently in the pandemic response when calls for an entry ban from China, which began in the third week of January 2020, were ignored due to, in the words of the country's Health Secretary, "political and diplomatic repercussions" (Valenzuela 2020). Eventually, the confirmed case of COVID-19 on 2 February 2020, along with concurrent entry bans imposed by its neighboring countries in Southeast Asia, compelled the Philippine government to impose this entry ban immediately. It is not only this missed opportunity to impose stricter border controls much earlier that showed a China-leaning orientation of the government but also its insistence that Philippine Offshore Gaming Operators (POGO) or Chinese casinos continue to operate despite the strictest lockdown level being implemented as cases shot up in the first quarter of the 2020 (Ranada 2020).

In terms of the actual enforcement of these lockdowns, Hapal (2021) argues that the "government's war against COVID-19 is contiguous with its other wars" (p. 227) as evidenced by their usage of the lens and language of the war on drugs. Thus, an overuse of state powers and military muscle encapsulates the Philippine government's approach in managing the pandemic. With the Duterte administration treating "complex issues as mainly law enforcement problems" (De Jesus 2021, p. 3) came harsh, police-centric and draconian measures to the point of mass arrests and harassment targeting dissidents and social workers (Maru 2020). As testament to this crackdown, jeepney drivers protesting their loss of income were arrested (Aspinwall 2020). Additionally, police elements raided a community kitchen and tore down organizers' protest banners demanding food and assistance and this came after arresting the same organizers earlier (Luna 2020).

Against the backdrop of the commander-in-chief giving a "*shoot them dead*" order, over 100,000 quarantine violators were apprehended just half a year into the pandemic (Talabong 2020a, 2020b). In its official pronouncement, the National Police recently stated they will not issue warnings anymore and just proceed to the on-the-spot arrest and inquest of alleged quarantine violators (Bajo 2020). One explanation of this stringent enforcement is the visibility and overrepresentation of military and police officials in the country's IATF-EID. Activating the IATF-EID in January 2020, was the government's first major step in creating the highest body composed of major department ministers to coordinate all pandemic mitigation efforts. Dubbed as the "oddest task force to fight the pandemic, a squad full of soldiers but without a single epidemiologist" (Makabenta 2020), the IATF-EID is a set of uniformed army generals who flanked Duterte when he announced the specific lockdown rules for the first time in March 2020 (Fig. 1).

The optics of this pronouncement is characterized as a dissonance between the "optics of power vs. the voice of science" wherein a specialized task needing the expertise of scientists and intellectuals continues to be impeded by politics (David et al. 2020). Table 4 shows the original composition of the IATF-EID.

In these key leadership positions, 100% are occupied by men, 54% are retired military and police officers, only 18% have medical degrees and experience, no epidemiologists, health economists, nor demographers. Indeed, the lack of diversity in the leadership of the COVID response team in terms of gender, experience, and competence, is notable.

Beyond being just a "shock and awe" (Dizon 2020) tactic, however, this prevalence of military personnel as well as a militarized response to the pandemic is also a continuation of Duterte's overall preference for military and police forces in Cabinet appointments. Generally attributed to his political career limited to local politics, Duterte did not manage

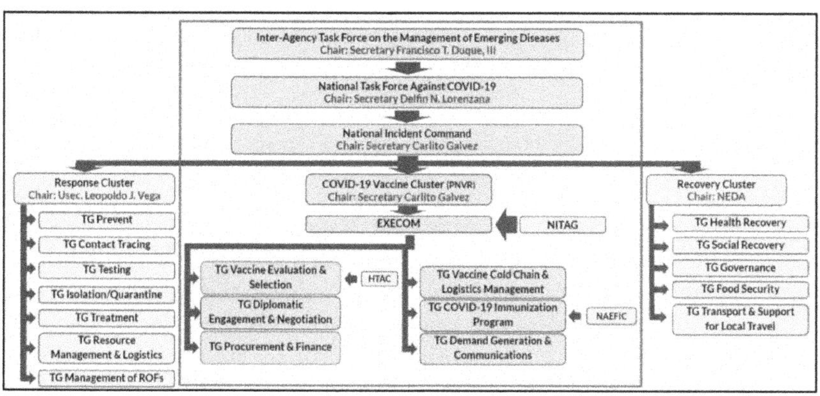

Fig. 1 Organizational chart of the Philippines' COVID response team (*Source* The Philippine National COVID-19 Vaccination Deployment Plan)

Table 4 Composition of the IATF-EID

Position	*Appointee*	*Background*
IATF-EID Chair	Francisco Duque Health Secretary	Medical Doctor, MSc in Pathology
NTF Against COVID-19	Delfin Lorenzana Defense Secretary	Ex-Army General, MBA, Diploma in Strategic Studies
National Incident Command	Carlito Galvez Presidential Adviser on Peace Process	Ex-Army General, Master's in Project Management
Deputy Chief Implementer	Roy Cimatu Environment Secretary	Ex-Army General, Ex-Army Chief of Staff, MBA
Response Cluster and Treatment Czar	Leopoldo Vega Health Undersecretary	Surgeon, MBA
Recovery Cluster	Karl Chua Socioeconomic Planning Secretary	Ph.D. in Economics
Testing Czar	Vicente Dizon Bases Conversion Development Authority Chair	MSc in Applied Development Studies
Contact Tracing Czar	Benjamin Magalong City Mayor	Ex-National Police Director
Isolation Czar	Mark Villar Public Works Secretary	MBA, real estate executive
IATF Member *(Members include all the cabinet secretaries of the President)*	Rolando Bautista Social Welfare Secretary	Ex-Army Chief of Staff
IATF Member	Hermogenes Esperon National Security Adviser	Ex-Army General Ex-Army Chief of Staff

Source Summary table created by the authors based on public records

to assemble "a rich rolodex of nationally respected professionals he knew and trusted enough to place in positions of power" (De Jesus 2021). Thus, throughout his term and well into the delegation of managers and technocrats in a pandemic, the administration continues to be hounded by charges of "recycling corrupt officials" and Duterte's proclivity to woo the military by placing them in high positions across key agencies (Castillo 2021).

From 2016 to 2021, retired military generals have been appointed as Secretaries of Social Welfare and Development, Environment, Interior and Local Government, Defense, and Information and Communication Technologies. Police and military forces are likewise present in other commissions and bureaus, as well as second-level ministerial positions in the Cabinet. It is problematic that appointees are given posts where they have no expertise. For instance, the Secretary of Environment appointed in 2017, Roy Cimatu, is a retired head of the Armed Forces of the Philippines without any degree or experience in environmental policy, in any capacity.

4.2 *Social Assistance*

With regard to fiscal and monetary, several social assistance measures were implemented by the government to mitigate the effects of the pandemic and the ensuing lockdowns. In terms of monetary policy, the Philippine Central Bank (Bangko Sentral ng Pilipinas or BSP) reduced its overnight reverse repurchase (RRP) facility by a total of 175 basis points to 2.25%. Furthermore, it lowered the reserve requirement ratio (RRR) for commercial banks by 200 basis points to 12%. Interest rates on overnight deposit and lending facilities were likewise reduced to 1.75 and 2.75%, respectively. Additionally, the BSP purchased PHP 300 billion (~USD 6.1 billion) worth of government securities and injected an estimated additional liquidity of PHP 220 billion (~USD 4.7 billion) into the economy. The lowering of the reserve ratio as well as the reduction of interest rates are forms of expansionary monetary policy—the central bank intends to inject liquidity into the economy by encouraging banks to lend money (e.g. through loans) and for ordinary consumers to increase spending.

In respect of fiscal policy, the most notable cash grant programs are the Social Amelioration Program (SAP) and the Small Business Wage Subsidy Program (SBWS). Under the first stimulus package passed by Congress, otherwise known as the Bayanihan to Heal as One Act (Republic Act 11469), the Department of Social Welfare and Development (DSWD) was tasked with implementing nationwide social amelioration measures to aid the vulnerable sectors throughout the ECQ period.

The SAP prioritizes 18 million poor Filipino households, including recipients of the government's conditional cash transfer program. Beneficiaries will receive cash or in-kind assistance ranging from PHP 5000–8000 (~USD 100–160), depending on the minimum wage of the region or province. In terms of the Implementing Rules and Regulations of the Social Amelioration Program, the following recipients are specifically targeted: conditional cash transfer beneficiaries; informal economy workers (directly hired or occasional workers); subcontracted workers; home workers; house helpers; public transportation drivers (pedicabs or rickshaw bikes, tricycles, PUVs, TNVS); micro-entrepreneurs and producers; family enterprise owners; sub-minimum wage owners; farmers; employees affected by the no-work, no-pay policy; stranded workers; and other household members belonging to the vulnerable sectors (senior citizens, PWDs, solo parents, etc.).

Through the SBWS, 3.4 million employees in small businesses benefit from a wage subsidy of PHP 5000–8000 (~USD 100–160) per eligible worker affected by the enhanced community quarantine in Luzon and other parts of the country. Of these 3.4 million workers, 2.6 million workers are under employers that are compliant with the Bureau of Internal Revenue (BIR) and SSS regulations and thus can be easily identified and automatically processed for coverage if they are eligible. An additional 800,000 workers whose employers are not fully compliant with the SSS or BIR, are also covered. In this program, the targeted beneficiaries are small businesses whose operations have been affected by the lockdown and thus, were unable to pay the wages of their employees. The amount, which will go directly to the employee, is given on the condition that the business maintains the employment status of the employee and the employee does not resign during the coverage of the support. This program was implemented for two months, until the end of June 2020. Table 5 summarizes the notable measures undertaken by the Philippine Government in order to cushion the shock to people's livelihood especially those of the vulnerable sector.

While these welfare programs were large and unprecedented, implementation constraints were also notable. Firstly, part of the assistance of SAP was in-kind assistance which meant that government units needed to procure food items first, before repackaging and distributing them. Furthermore, the release of cash grants also faced delays due to stringent validation mechanisms imposed by the disbursing government offices (Cervantes 2020). Offering and distributing relief have been burdened by limited funds to sustain the social amelioration program and how the authority to distribute aid was structured. For example, The national list of beneficiaries of DSWD had to be reconciled with the local governments units (LGUs) who have another list. LGUs also submit continuous requests to increase beneficiaries, download more funds, or amend the

Table 5 Summary of Social Amelioration Programs (SAP) in the Philippines for COVID-response

SAP	*Benefiting Sector*	*Benefits*	*Conditions/Eligibility*
Covid-19 Adjustment Measures Program	Formal Workers	~100$ to ~160$	Given regardless if on permanent, probationary, or contractual status
Small Business Wage Subsidy (SBWS)	Formal Workers	~100$ to ~160$	(1) From small business and, (2) did not get paid during the pandemic
TUPAD (Livelihood Assistance) Workers Program	Displaced/Disadvantaged workers	Maximum of 160$	Employment as sanitation workers to disinfect homes/community for a maximum of 10 days
Assistance to Individuals in Crisis Situations (AICS)	Informal workers, vulnerable, indigenous peoples, and those below poverty line	~100$ to ~160$ and food and non-food items (FNFI)	Upon validation of local government, social security workers and National House Targeting System for Poverty Reduction (NHTS-PR)
AKAP for Overseas Filipino Workers (OFWs)	OFWs	One-time 200$	Displaced from jobs due to their host country's lockdown measures
Cash assistance to Rice Farmers	Small-time Farmers	~100$	Planting in less than one-hectare land

Source Authors' summary based on DOLE and DWSD announcements and memoranda eligibility rules (13th Report to the Joint Congressional Committee 2020, p. 2). Moreover, there is a disconnect between the social role of the government to protect the vulnerable workers and its limited recognition of some workers in the gray areas of the law. Sex workers, unregulated jeepney drivers using colorum vehicles and the bulk of workers in the shadow economy all share the common struggle of their "work" not being recognized by the state in its productive value and economic contribution. Finally, it is important to note that the amount of subsidy given to the most vulnerable households (maximum of around 160 USD per household), is even slightly below the national poverty line.

4.3 *Bureaucratic Missteps*

Despite these targeted assistance mechanisms and the swift and stringent imposition of militarized lockdowns, the government has committed a fair share of missteps in its initial COVID response. Most notably, reports about the inefficient management of the finances, emergency powers, and human resources at his disposal threaten the credibility of these policy responses. Despite availability of funds and a streamlined procurement process granted by emergency powers, the government was unable to procure and distribute medical masks at the earliest possible instance. In fact, when asked if the government will give out and address the shortage of masks in January 2020, the Presidential Spokesperson replied "How can we give when there's none?" (Panti 2020).

Popular allies of the President who were caught violating health protocols were also let off the hook (Rhoderos and Santos 2020), in contrast to his tough rhetoric against ordinary citizens. The leader of the President's political party violated quarantine restrictions after testing positive for the virus and the chief of the Philippine National Police also attended a mass gathering for his birthday celebration despite being under lockdown. Both officials were not publicly apprehended. In late February 2020, after Duterte said that he will "slap the virus" (Malasig 2020) in an apparent downplaying of COVID-19's threat, the government began adopting a more serious tone.

When the first Enhanced Community Quarantine (ECQ), the most stringent of all the quarantine levels, was imposed in mid-March 2020, there was notable public unrest. Residents in urban areas started panic buying, while some scrambled to return to their home provinces as quickly as possible, only to be stopped by armed military men who had differing interpretations of the military checkpoint guidelines (Robles 2020).

In terms of key pandemic mitigation measures such as vaccination and testing capacity, the Philippines was also way below the recommended benchmarks. The Health Department admitted that the country was short of 94,000 contact tracers from the WHO-recommended contact tracing ratio of 1:800 people, which should require the Philippines at least 135,000 tracers (Esguerra 2020). The Palace also drew flak for months for its frequently changing policy statements regarding key pandemic strategies such as the necessity of mass testing and testing as a requirement for work (Esguerra 2020), as well as the delineation between the COVID-19 responsibilities of the national and local governments (Rhoderos and Santos 2020). More importantly, vaccine procurement for the country was stalled by the IATF's delay in submitting relevant information for the vaccine indemnification law to Congress, which is required by vaccine manufacturers as additional legal protection (Suzara et al. 2021). This caused the Philippines to lag behind other countries that are also vying for a share of the limited global vaccine supplies. Further, a Senator divulged publicly that the Philippines also missed a deal with Pfizer for 10 million COVID vaccine doses due to the Health Secretary failing to submit a documentary requirement, or the Confidentiality Disclosure Agreement (Gotinga 2020).

5 Effects of COVID-19 Lockdowns: The Great Equalizer?

This section discusses the effects of COVID-19, particularly the effects of extreme lockdowns imposed by the government on two fronts. We first present some overall trends on growth and employment and argue that specific sectors and demographic groups were disproportionately affected. We then proceed with discussing the effects of lockdowns on the youth, arguably among the most heavily affected demographic groups.

5.1 Macroeconomic Trends

While many countries plunged into recessions at the onset of COVID-19, the effect on the Philippines is relatively more pronounced compared to its ASEAN counterparts (Mendoza 2021). Vietnam, which managed the onset of the pandemic somewhat effectively, remained in positive

GDP growth territory. Compared to other middle-income economies in Southeast Asia such as Indonesia, Thailand, and Malaysia, which had experienced GDP contractions of 2, 6, and 6%, respectively, the Philippines experienced the largest contraction at 9.6% (Mendoza 2021). Figure 2 illustrates the annual growth and unemployment rates of the Philippines from 1991 to 2020.

This large adverse effect was likewise notable in the unemployment rate. Figure 3 shows the historically highest unemployment rate in the Philippines in the second quarter of 2020, also the quarter where extreme lockdowns were imposed in various regions. While unemployment trends clearly subsided since that quarter, these are still largely above pre-pandemic levels, suggesting longer-term effects of COVID-19 on the labor market. Indeed, while unemployment patterns are difficult to predict, Furuoka (2012) confirms the presence of unemployment hysteria in 10 countries in the Asia-Pacific region, including the Philippines. Hysteresis suggests that unemployment tends to be path-dependent and that business cycles leave a permanent effect on unemployment.

These adverse effects, however, are not uniformly felt across the population. Using 2021 Labor Force Survey data, Epetia (2021) finds that males, less-educated, and those working in sectors affected by militarized lockdowns have a higher probability of job loss and underemployment. Indeed, the arts, entertainment, and hospitality sector suffered the largest

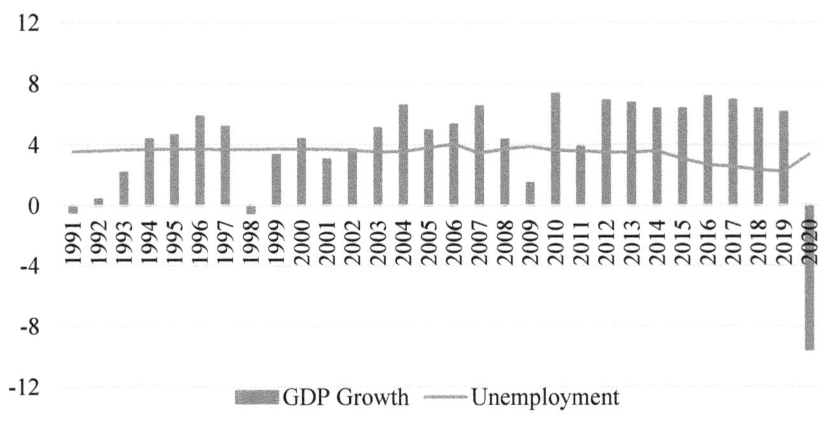

Fig. 2 Growth and Unemployment Time Series of the Philippines, 1991–2020 (*Source* Authors' plot of the World Development Indicators[2])

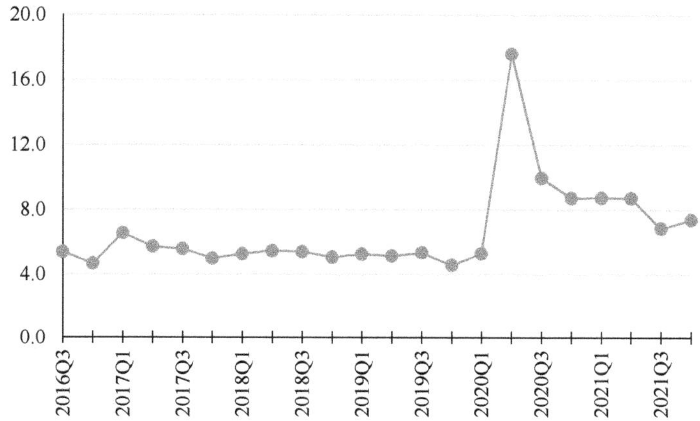

Fig. 3 Quarterly unemployment rate (*Source* Bangko Sentral ng Pilipinas [Central Bank of the Philippines])

year-on-year decline in employment growth at 54.8% in the second quarter of 2020 (Epetia 2021). Due to mobility restrictions that prohibited all unnecessary recreational and leisurely activities, it is unsurprising that this sector suffered the steepest decline.

The National Economic and Development Authority (NEDA) launched three separate surveys in April, which included 389,859 respondents from consumers, individuals from the agricultural sector, and individuals from MSMEs to represent the industry and services sector. According to the responses from the MSMEs, it was found that due to the lockdown and temporary closures, especially of non-essential businesses, close to two-thirds have reported zero sales. Moreover, it was found that 75% of firms that did not operate did not fire employees, which means that they have been absorbing these losses, adding to the burden of revenue loss (NEDA 2020).

In the industry sector, a total loss in revenue was estimated to be 10.03 billion USD for manufacturing, 263.77 million USD for mining and quarrying, and 781 million USD for construction. This is attributed to the fact that 100% of the operations of construction, manufacturing, and mining and quarrying are locked down (not including food-related manufacturing) (NEDA 2020). In total, losses amount to 11 billion USD for industry.

In the services sector, NEDA (2020) reports that 79.7% of retail and wholesale establishments were fully locked down. This translates to 1.78 billion USD in losses. Additionally, the tourism sector is also estimated to have a loss in revenue of 1.24 billion USD from the 60-day interruption on travel due to the community quarantine, as well as the aftermath of the lockdown where people will still be hesitant to travel due to the rising cases of the virus. As for banking services, an estimated amount of 1.16 billion USD of loans is expected to default due to the pandemic. This will come from loans to private companies, as well as both resident and non-resident counterparties. On the other hand, although estimates for transportation services are not yet available, it is expected to be significant because all passenger land and sea transport services were suspended during the ECQ, while many flights abroad and within the country were canceled. In total, estimates of the losses in services amount to 11.73 billion USD (NEDA 2020).

While males have a higher probability of job loss due to COVID-19 (Epetia 2021), looking specifically into the effects of lockdowns paints a different picture. Using a difference-in-differences design with lockdowns considered as a "treatment", Ducanes and Ramos (2021) finds that it is actually women, particularly mothers with minor children, who faced larger job losses, partly due to the increased burden of childcare and house work in lockdown areas. Both papers suggest that social assistance and unemployment insurance mechanisms could have cushioned the effects of these lockdowns and argue that, moving forward, establishing these mechanisms improves household resiliency to economic shocks.

Indeed, insecurity in the labor market translates to vulnerability in living standards. Considering various definitions of vulnerable (usually informal) employment, Ducanes et al. (2021) estimate at least 7.4 million vulnerable households in the Philippines during the peak of these extreme lockdowns. Half of these estimated households live in the major island group of Luzon, which is where these extreme lockdowns were imposed. To cushion these adverse economic effects, the government pursued expansionary monetary and fiscal policy. Inspired by the Keynesian view of "spending your way out of a recession", the Philippines has employed a variety of debt-financed social spending to support the most vulnerable sectors of society and cushion the negative economic impacts of the lockdown.

5.2 *Effects on the Youth*

Preliminary findings show the short-term effects of mass lockdown on youth employment. In particular, a survey by the ILO and UNCF (2020) reveals that 17.4% of youth around the world had ceased working since the crisis began, with 6.9% of them already having lost their jobs, while 10.5% stated that their work hours have now fallen to zero. Moreover, 54% of respondents in the survey expressed that the reason for their job loss was due to either the establishment closing down or because they were let go. In the case of youth workers in temporary contracts, 32.4% lost their work due to the contract ending during the onset of the pandemic. Furthermore, it is important to note that those who have been heavily affected mostly work in customer-facing roles such as clerical work positions, which clearly has been directly affected by social distancing and quarantine measures put in place (ILO 2020). Unsurprisingly, the ILO and UNCF (2020) survey also shows a similar pattern as in previous crises with regard to work hours. According to the survey, 17% of youth have stopped working, while 37% have faced reduction since the crisis began, where a majority of them have faced income losses (ILO and UNCF 2020).

The Philippines is also facing significant headwinds due to the pandemic in terms of employment. The PSA reported a record-breaking unemployment rate of 17.7% or 7.3 million jobs lost due to the pandemic and stringent lockdown measures, as opposed to the unemployment rate of 5.1 the previous year (Teo 2020). The situation is also significantly worse for youth workers specifically, as shown in Table 6.

Table 6 Employment indicators for the youth

Employment indicators	*April 2020*	*April 2019*
Youth population 15–24 years old		
Youth labor force participation rate (%)	32.4	38.8
Youth employment rate (%)	68.4	87.1
Youth underemployment (%)	18.1	11.8
Youth unemployment rate (%)	31.6	12.9
Youth NEET as % of youth population	25.3	18.7
Proportion of youth new entrants to the youth labor force	7	11.2
Youth mean hours of work	31.5	39.9

Source Philippine Statistics Authority (2020)

Most notably, youth employment rate has dropped from 87.1% in April 2019 to 68.4% in April 2020, which was also when the ECQ or the strictest lockdown classification was being observed in the Country (Tomacruz 2020). Conversely, a drastic increase in the youth unemployment rate is also seen, where it increased by 18.7 percentage points to an all-time high of 31.6%. Moreover, the incidence of youth with a NEET or "Not in Education, Employment, or Training" status has also seen a significant increase from 18.7 to 25.3% in April 2020, which means that more Filipino youth than last year are not contributing to the Country's productivity either through employment or increasing their human capital through education and training. It is also important to note that the underemployment rate has increased to 18.1%, an important measure of preference to work additional hours. Clearly, the Philippines is seeing the same negative patterns as observed but in a larger scale than in previous crises, with higher unemployment rates, reduced hours worked, and even more difficulty in finding and securing jobs for youth, especially since many more experienced workers have also lost their jobs and may even be in competition with them for work.

5.3 *Effects on Education and Training*

It is difficult to predict the exact impact of COVID-19 on education from the patterns evident in previous crises. This is because unlike previous crises, the current pandemic has resulted in most schools in 180 countries around the world to close in observance of social distancing (World Bank Group 2020). Still, from observing the impacts from previous crises and deducing from currently available data, it is possible to infer several short-term outcomes for the youth. The most pronounced of which is learning disruption. A recent survey shows that 13% of youth experienced a complete halt in their education and training, while 64% of these youth come from low-to-middle income countries (ILO and UNCF 2020). This is detrimental to the continued growth and learning of these students and further exacerbates the learning crisis—defined as a global crisis involving the widespread waste of talent and human potential largely concerning children and youth in low-income countries—already present before the onset of the crisis (United Nations Educational, Scientific and Cultural Organization 2018). Aside from a decline in learning, a rise in dropouts may also be seen, either because of discouragement in going back to their studies, or because the economic crisis may make it difficult for the student or family to raise funds for continued education (World Bank Group 2020).

Learning inequality has also become apparent at the onset of the current crisis. Students from more disadvantaged households may not have the technology needed for online learning, such as a laptop and access to the Internet, and might not even have the space for it at home (ILO and UNCF 2020). In the Philippines, a "blended learning" scheme, which involves a combination of online learning and the delivery of hard-copy learning materials to households for those who do not have access to the internet, has been in place. Inequality in initial resource allocation therefore affects this since youth from poorer households are less likely to own a laptop or tablet nor have stable internet connection. An internet subscription, alone, will be an impossible cost for many Filipino households, especially since although the country's average internet speed is the slowest, it is also one of the most expensive in Asia (Malindog-Uy 2020).

Another impact of the pandemic on the youth is a more challenging transition from schooling to entering the workforce. As discussed previously, economic crises tend to cause mass unemployment and create an unhealthy job market especially for novel entrants such as new graduates. To illustrate, Cockx (2016) finds that in flexible labor markets, entrants with lower levels of education face penalties during economic downturns, but these only last in the short-term, while for highly educated entrants, although they are less negatively affected, they are penalized for a longer period of time. The same paper likewise finds that it takes about a decade for entrants during economic downturns to catch up to entrants that entered in healthier job markets.

There are many other effects of crises on the well-being of youth such as loneliness and isolation, loss of motivation, and for some, violence and abuse at home which were not explored in this paper. In the case of the Philippine youth, although not explored due to a lack of data, the negative effects could be even more significant. Aside from having the longest and strictest lockdown in the world, mass unemployment, and insufficient government aid to vulnerable groups, the Filipino youth has also been faced with numerous controversies of corruption (most notably that of the Philippine Health Insurance Corporation), the closing of a major broadcast station, and the enactment of the Anti-Terrorism Act, which is argued to have contentious and unconstitutional provisions on detention and surveillance (Tugade 2021b). Mostly, the youth have taken their sentiments and grief on social media through their writing and through "memes", which makes it difficult to quantify how much their well-being has been affected by this outbreak.

6 Conclusion

That COVID-19 lockdowns are the "great equalizer" is perhaps not only an out-of-touch characterization, it is simply an inaccurate depiction of the heterogeneities in their socioeconomic effects. Findings from ongoing and preliminary work on this area suggest a disproportionate effect on certain populations: the youth and women, particularly mothers with minor children. While unprecedented expansionary fiscal spending was undertaken, these efforts were set back by delays and "too little" spending in relative terms. Moving forward, a pandemic recovery strategy needs to incorporate policies and investments for strengthening state capacity and institutionalizing crisis response mechanisms—this ensures that the Philippines is more resilient in the post-pandemic era and beyond.

Notes

1. As of submission of this writing 2021, the consolidated version of House Bills 7028, 7590, and 8229 are passed by the Committee on Labor and Employment but have not been approved by the Plenary.
2. GDP growth is the year-on-year (%) per cent change in real GDP, unemployment is the percentage of the labor force without work but available and willing to work. We use the harmonized ILO estimate.

References

Amnesty International. (2020, September 25). *Philippines: UN Must Intensify Pressure to End Killings as Impunity Reigns.* Retrieved from: https://www.amnesty.org/en/latest/news/2020/09/philippines-un-pressure-end-killings/.

Aspinwall, N. (2020). Jeepney Drivers Face Charges Amid Heightened Protest Crackdown in the Philippines. *The Diplomat.* Retrieved from: https://thediplomat.com/2020/06/jeepney-drivers-face-charges-amid-heightened-protest-crackdown-in-the-philippines/.

Atienza, M. L., Arugay, A. A., & Encinas-Franco, J. (2020). Constitutional Performance Assessment in the Time of a Pandemic: The 1987 Constitution and the Philippines' Covid-19 Response. Stockholm: International Institute for Democracy and Electoral Assistance and University of the Philippines Center for Integrative and Development Studies.

Bajo, A. (2020). PNP Chief Says No More Warnings vs. Violators under Martial Law-Like ECQ. *GMA News Online*. Retrieved from: https://www.gmanetwork.com/news/topstories/nation/734760/pnp-chief-says-no-more-warnings-vs-violators-under-martial-law-like-ecq/story/.

Castillo, M. (2021). *Is the Philippine Government COVID-19 Response Gender-Blind?* NCPAG Working Paper 2021-02.

Cervantes, F. (2020). Stringent Validation Causes Delay in SAP Distribution: DSWD. *Philippine News Agency*.

Cockx, B. (2016). *Do Youths in a Recession Incur Permanent Losses?* IZA World of Labor 2016: 281. https://doi.org/10.15185/izawol.281.

Curato, N. (2017). Politics of Anxiety, Politics of Hope: Penal Populism and Duterte's Rise to Power. *Journal of Current Southeast Asian Affairs* 35(3), 91–109. https://doi.org/10.1177/186810341603500305.

David, G., Rye, R.S., Agbulos, M.P. (2020). *Covid-19 Forecast in the Philippines: NCR, Cebu and Covid-19 Hotspots as of June 25, 2020*. University of the Philippines. Retrieved from: https://www.up.edu.ph/covid-19-forecasts-in-the-philippines-ncr-cebu-and-covid-19-hotspots-as-of-june-25-2020/.

De Jesus, E. (2021). *National Security, Anti-corruption, and Anti-crime Policies in the Duterte Administration*. Retrieved from: https://doi.org/10.2139/ssrn.3888122.

De Lima, L. (2019, November 20). Lawfare: The Silent Pandemic Afflicting the World. *Rappler*. Retrieved from: https://www.rappler.com/voices/thought-leaders/245317-lawfare-silent-pandemic-afflicting-the-world/.

Dinecco, M. (2017). *State Capacity and Economic Development. Present and Past*. Cambridge: Cambridge University Press.

Dizon, N. (2020, July 31). *Duterte and His Generals: A Shock and Awe Response to the Pandemic*. Retrieved from: https://www.rappler.com/newsbreak/in-depth/duterte-shock-and-awe-coronavirus-pandemic-response-generals/.

Doyle, B. (2019). Lessons on Collaboration from Recent Conflicts: The Whole-of Nationa and Whole-of-Government Approaches in Action. *InterAgency Journal* 10(1), 105–122.

Ducanes, G., & Ramos, V. (2021). *COVID-19 Lockdowns, Women's Employment, and the Motherhood Penalty*. Unpublished Working Paper.

Ducanes, G., Daway-Ducanes, S. L., & Tan, E. (2021). Targeting the Highly Vulnerable Households During Strict Lockdowns. *Philippine Review of Economics* 58(1&2), 38–62.

Epetia, M. C. (2021). COVID-19, Job Loss, and Underemployment: Who Is Affected?. *Philippine Review of Economics* 58(1&2), 63–91.

Esguerra, D. (2020). Gov't Targeting to Test 1.5% to 2% of Total PH Population for Coronavirus. Retrieved from: Inquirer.net: Gov't targeting to test 1.5% to 2% of total PH population for coronavirus.

Fukuyama, F. (2004). The Imperative of State-Building. *Journal of Democracy* 15(2), 17–31.

Furuoka, F. (2012). Unemployment Hysteresis in the East Asia-Pacific Region: New Evidence from MADF and SURADF Tests. *Asian-Pacific Economic Literature* 26(2), 133–143.

Global Response to COVID-19. (2021). Reports on the Philippines. Retrieved from: http://globalresponsescovid19.com/.

Gotinga, J. C. (2020, December 17). PH Missed Chance to Get Pfizer Vaccines in January Because of Duque—Lacson. *Rappler.* Retrieved from: https://www.rappler.com/nation/lacson-says-philippines-missed-chance-get-pfizer-vaccines-january-2021-because-duque/.

Hapal. K. (2021). The Philippines' COVID-19 Response: Securitising the Pandemic and Disciplining the Pasaway. *Journal of Current Southeast Asian Affairs* 40(2), 224–244.

IATF-EID. (2020, April 29). *Omnibus Guidelines on the Implementation of Community Quarantine in the Philippines.* Retrieved from: https://www.officialgazette.gov.ph/downloads/2020/05may/20200429-Omnibus-Guidelines-on-the-Implementation-of-Community-Quarantine-in-the-Philippines.pdf.

IATF-EID. (2021, December 14). *Guidelines on the Nationwide Implementation of Alert Level System for COVID-19 Response.* Retrieved from: https://pcoo.gov.ph/wp-content/uploads/2021/12/20211214-IATF-GUIDELINES-RRD.pdf.

IBON Foundation. (2016, May 14). *Duterte's 8-Point Economic Agenda Business as Usual.* Retrieved from: https://www.ibon.org/dutertes-8-point-economic-agenda-business-as-usual/.

IBON Foundation. (2017, June 28). *Rehashed Neoliberal Policies: One Year of Dutertenomics.* Retrieved from: https://www.ibon.org/rehashed-neoliberal-policies-one-year-of-dutertenomics/.

International Labor Organization. (2020). ILO Monitor: COVID-19 and the World of Work [Fourth edition Updated estimates and analysis].

International Labour Organization and United Nations Children's Fund. (2020, June 15). COVID-19 May Push Millions More Children into Child Labour-ILO and UNICEF [Press brief].

Lasco, G. (2020). Medical Populism and the COVID-19 Pandemic. *Global Public Health* 15(10), 1417–1429. https://doi.org/10.1080/17441692.2020.1807581.

Lasco, G., & Curato, N. (2019). Medical Populism. *Social Science & Medicine* 221, 1–8.

Luna, F. (2020, April 6). 'Conducting Dialogue': Cops Raid San Roque Community Kitchens, Tear Protest Materials. *PhilStar.* Retrieved from: https://www.philstar.com/headlines/2020/04/06/2005868/conducting-dialogue-cops-raid-san-roque-community-kitchens-tear-protest-materials.

Makabenta, Y. (2020, May 21). The World's Longest Lockdown, Oddest Task Force vs Covid-19. *The Manila Times.* Retrieved from: https://www.manilatimes.net/2020/05/21/opinion/columnists/topanalysis/the-worlds-longest-lockdown-oddest-task-force-vs-covid-19/726169

Malasig, J. (2020, February 20). From Virus Slapping to Staying United: Duterte's Change of Tone in Addressing COVID-19. *PhilStar.* Retrieved from: https://interaksyon.philstar.com/politics-issues/2020/02/17/162228/from-virus-slapping-staying-united-dutertes-change-of-tone-in-addressing-covid-19/.

Malindog-Uy, A. (2020). "Blended Learning" in Virus-Hit Philippines. *The ASEAN Post.*

Manila Times. (2017, May 29). Zero to 10-Point Agenda. *Manila Times.* Retrieved from: https://www.manilatimes.net/2017/05/29/supplements/zero-10-point-agenda/329787.

Maru, D. (2020). 'F as in Falfak': PH Gov't Getting Failing Marks in Covid-19 Response from These Experts. *ABS-CBN News.* Retrieved from: https://news.abs-cbn.com/news/07/22/20/f-as-in-falfak-ph-govt-gets-failing-marks-in-covid-19-response-from-these-experts.

Mendoza, R. (2021). *The Philippine Economy under the Pandemic: From Asian Tiger to Sick Man Again?* Brookings Institution.

National Economic and Development Authority. (2020). We Recover as One.

National Economic Development Agency. (2017). Philippine Development Plan 2017–2022. https://pdp.neda.gov.ph/philippine-development-plan-2017-2022/.

National Economic Development Agency. (2022). Updated Philippine Development Plan 2017–2022. https://pdp.neda.gov.ph/updated-pdp-2017-2022/.

Nonato, V. (2020, February 24). *'Lawfare': When Legal Processes Are Used to Crack Down on Dissent.* Retrieved from: https://www.onenews.ph/articles/lawfare-when-legal-processes-are-used-to-crack-down-on-dissent.

Norris, P. (2012). *Making Democratic Governance Work: How Regimes Shape Prosperity, Welfare, and Peace.* Cambridge: Cambridge University Press.

Office of the President. (2020, June 22). *13th Report to the Joint Congressional Oversight Committee.* Official Gazette of the Republic of the Philippines. Retrieved from: https://www.officialgazette.gov.ph/2020/06/22/report-to-the-joint-congressional-oversight-committee-june-22-2020/.

Official Gazette. (2020a, March 16). Proclamation No. 929 "Declaring A State of Calamity Throughout the Philippines Due to Corona

Virus Disease 2019". https://www.officialgazette.gov.ph/downloads/2020/03mar/20200316-PROC-929-RRD.pdf.

Official Gazette. (2020b, April 29). *IATF-EID Omnibus Guidelines on the Implementation of Community Quarantine in the Philippines*. https://www.officialgazette.gov.ph/downloads/2020/05may/20200429-Omnibus-Guidelines-on-the-Implementation-of-Community-Quarantine-in-the-Philippines.pdf.

Organisation for Economic Co-operation and Development. (2007). *Whole of Government Approaches to Fragile States*. Retrieved from: https://www.oecd.org/dac/conflict-fragility-resilience/docs/37826256.pdf.

Panti, L. T. (2020). Dizon: Flattening Covid-19 Curve Requires Discipline More Than Anything. *GMA News Online*. Retrieved from: https://www.gmanetwork.com/news/topstories/nation/747125/dizon-flattening-covid-19-curve-requires-discipline-more-than-anything/story/.

Philippine Statistics Authority. (2020). *Employment Situation in April 2020*. Philippine Statistics Authority.

Pitlo, L. B. (2020). Philippines' Covid-19 Response Still Falling Short. *Asia Times*. Retrieved from: https://asiatimes.com/2020/08/philippines-covid-19-response-still-falling-short.

Quijano, N., Fernandez, M., & Pangilinan, A. (2020). Misplaced Priorities, Unnecessary Effects: Collective Suffering and Survival in Pandemic Philippines. *The Asia Pacific Journal* 18, 5(6).

Ranada, P. (2020, July 30). 'Reclassifying' Businesses: Task Force's Way of Reopening Economy Without Changing Quarantine Modes. *Rappler*. Retrieved from: https://www.rappler.com/nation/reclassifying-businesses-task-force-way-reopening-economy-without-change-quarantine-modes/.

Rhoderos, E., & Santos, I. (2020, December 21). *Vera Files Fact Check Yearender: The Two Faces of COVID-19 Lockdown in the Philippines*. Retrieved from: https://verafiles.org/articles/vera-files-fact-check-yearender-two-faces-covid-19-lockdown.

Rice, S., & Patrick, S. (2008). *Index of State Weakness in the Developing World*. Washington, DC: Brookings Institution.

Robles, R. (2020, March 11). Coronavirus: Panic Buying in Manila, Some Flee to Countryside as First Filipino Fatality Confirmed and Cases Rise to 49. *This Week in Asia*. Retrieved from: https://www.scmp.com/week-asia/health-environment/article/3074745/philippines-panic-buying-erupts-metro-manila-after.

Suzara, Z., Abad, L., Punongbayan, J., & Sanders, R. (2021, June 6). *In This Pandemic, Duterte Has His Priorities All Wrong*. Retrieved from: https://www.aljazeera.com/opinions/2021/6/6/dutertes-many-pandemic-failures.

Talabong, R. (2020a, April 21). PNP Begins to Arrest Lockdown Violators Without Warning. *Rappler*. Retrieved from: https://www.rappler.com/nation/258570-pnp-begins-arrest-coronavirus-lockdown-violators-without-warning/.

Talabong, R. (2020b, September 8). Over 100,000 Quarantine Violators Arrested in PH since March. *Rappler*. Retrieved from: https://www.rappler.com/nation/arrested-quarantine-violators-philippines-2020/.

Teo, D. (2020). *Over 7.3 Million Jobs Lost in the Philippines Due to COVID-19*. HRMAsia.

Thompson, G. (2017) Populisms and liberal democracy–business as usual? *Economy and Society*, *46*(1), 43–59. https://doi.org/10.1080/03085147.2017.1307652

Tomacruz, S. (2020). Duterte Extends Luzon Lockdown Until April 30. *Rappler*.

Tugade, R. (2021a). *State of Exception Report on the Philippines. Global Responses to COVID-19*. Retrieved from: http://globalresponsescovid19.com/.

Tugade, R. (2021b). *Surveillance and Compliance Report on the Philippines. Global Responses to COVID-19*. Retrieved from: http://globalresponsescovid19.com/.

UNESCO. (2018). *The Learning Crisis Is Causing a Skills Crisis. Here's Why*. UNESCO.

Vacarro, A. (2021). *Measures of State Capacity: Same Same, but Different?* QoG Working Paper Series 2020: 9.

Valenzuela, S. (2020). "Diplomacy" with China Made the Philippines a Covid-19 Hotspot in Southeast Asia. *Asia Pacific Bulletin* No. 541. East-West Center, Washington, DC.

World Bank Group. (2020). The COVID-19 Pandemic [Shocks to Education and Policy Responses].

First 100 Days of COVID-19 Firefighting: Hits and Misses of the Policy in India

Apilang Apum, Binit Agrawal, Madhu Sivaraman, and Aneesha Chitgupi

1 Introduction

This chapter on India's first 100 days of response to COVID-19 pandemic provides an insight into the immediate response of the State towards combating the pandemic. The Indian government imposed one of the most sudden and stringent lockdowns in the world which had a multifold impact on the lives and livelihood of the people. While it was hailed as a much required step to stem the spread of the virus in the second most populous country with limited resources both medical and financial, the jury is still out on whether it was the most appropriate decision.

The first case of COVID-19 was reported on 30 January 2020, in Kerala, India where the person provided a travel history of train travel

A. Apum
Jomin Tayeng Government Model Degree College Roing, Roing, India
e-mail: apilangapum@gmail.com

B. Agrawal
National Law School of India University, Bengaluru, India
e-mail: binit@alumni.nls.ac.in

A. Stojanović et al. (eds.), *The First 100 Days of Covid-19*,
https://doi.org/10.1007/978-981-19-6325-4_4

between Wuhan and Kunming, China before arrival in India. The State of Kerala having deftly handled the Nipah virus outbreak in the summer of 2018 was quick to respond to the COVID-19 pandemic by enforcing isolation and quarantine; contact tracing for all persons visiting Kerala who had travel history to China; and setting up a 24-h control room to monitor cases. However, the Central Government of India (GoI) took a lax approach towards testing and isolation after China sounded alarm bells in late December 2019 given that there is a considerable diaspora of Indian students in China and a large business community with frequent travels between the two countries. As per the data on COVID-19 in India,[1] the total death toll had crossed 5000 mark with a seven day average of over 200 deaths by 1 June 2020. The total cases of infections increased to over 10,000 by mid June 2020. India suffered a poor recovery rate of less than 80% between March 2020 and April of 2020. By October 2020, it had increased to 98% and remained over that mark even during the second wave which infected India between March 2021 and May 2021.[2]

India has the third highest total number of deaths due to COVID-19 at half a million as of May 2022 behind the United States and Brazil with the United States crossing the one million mark.[3] But when number of deaths per million population is considered, India lies at 151st position in the world behind many developed nations with better healthcare facilities and infrastructure.

The altercations between WHO and GoI on the estimates of the total death toll due to the pandemic during 2020–2021 has highlighted a dire need to scale up birth and death registration system in India. While many experts agree that there could be undercounting of deaths in a large

M. Sivaraman
Department for Promotion of Industry and Internal Trade, Ministry of Commerce, Government of India, New Delhi, India
e-mail: madhus333@gmail.com

A. Chitgupi (✉)
XKDR Forum, Mumbai, India
e-mail: aneeshachitgupi@gmail.com

and populous country like India, yet the WHO estimates of over ten times the official number has not fared well with the Indian authorities.[4] Economists closely working with India's birth and death registry systems have highlighted that the absence of reliable estimates of death data and without the adjustments for sex, age, and location may lead to overestimation of deaths due to pandemic.[5]

The pandemic brought to the fore the limitations of the public as well as the private health care sector in India. The structural adjustment plans adopted by India to tide over the economic crisis of 1990–1991, administered by Bretton Wood Institutions, namely the International Monetary Fund (IMF) and World Bank, led to a decline in public health spending in India by both the Central and the State governments (Mooij and Dev, 2002). Other changes observed in the health care sector upon the adoption of liberalization policies have been the introduction of user fees in government hospitals and liberalization of the pharmaceutical industry and changes to the drug policy in 2002 which led to spiraling of drug prices in the subsequent periods and overall increase in out of pocket health care expenditure (Ghosh, 2011). Studies have found that shifting the responsibility of health coverage from public to private providers has been ineffective in providing access to healthcare and financial protection (Ghosh, 2011; Ghosh and Gupta, 2017). Central government's initiative to provide Universal Health Coverage (UHC) in 2016–2017 and to bring private insurance providers and empanelment of private hospitals suffered from several issues of moral hazard and adverse selection which could exacerbate the problem of inefficiency and inequity in distribution of healthcare services. Not only the healthcare sector but education has also seen a decline in public investment, with the vacuum filled in by the private actors (Kumar, 2011; Tiwana and Singh, 2015).

The 1990s liberalization ushered a new set of policies for the Indian economy with greater participation of private actors; greater integration with the world economy through removal of customs duties; reduction in subsidies; and a general movement towards shrinking the scope and space of the government in economic activities. The withdrawal of government and influx of private capital has resulted in increased labour productivity, rising GDP, yet the growth has been unequal and vulnerable to internal and external crisis (Chandrashekhar, 2010; Chandrashekhar and Ghosh, 2004). While the pitfalls of adopting a neoliberalist regime have provided strong evidence for increasing inequality; reduction in social sector spending; rendering a vast majority of population with no safety net; and greater informalization of the workforce; etc., it is important to mention that government spending comes at a cost which is known as the marginal cost of public funds. For India this is estimated at three rupees meaning for every rupee the Indian government spends, it has to collect three rupees (Shah, 2016). The ineffectiveness of government spending in education (Pritchett and Aiyar, 2014) and healthcare has spurred the demand for private actors (Hammer et. al., 2007). Many now argue that as Indian has chosen the path with greater private capital participation, it is unwise to revert to the drawing board and dismantle the existing system but to invest in developing State capacity, building an efficient and effective government with increased focus on institution building and regulation implementation to channel private participation towards the achievement of public goals.

Given this background, the chapter proceeds to look into the constitutional approach adopted during the pandemic in Sect. 2; Section 3 describes the steps taken for pandemic management. Section 4 discusses the surveillance and compliance techniques adopted. Thereafter, economic policies are enumerated in Sect. 5. Section 6 looks into the alternatives to mainstream responses and conclusion is presented in Sect. 7.

2 Constitutional Approach to Pandemic

2.1 Working of the Federal Structure During COVID-19

Alexandrowicz (1954) surmised India's federal structure as follows: "*Compared with other federations the case of India is sui generis. To promote unity in extremely difficult conditions, she started after gaining independence with a constitution imposed from above. Her central government has considerable powers if compared with the powers of the States…*". Since then the Central government has time and time again displayed that India is at best a quasi-federation, with a strong unitary bent. For instance, when Prof. Alexandrowicz's article was published in 1954, the Indian Union comprised of 18 States and 10 Union territories. By 2014, India had 29 States and 7 Union territories.[6] In 2019, Jammu Kashmir, a major State was broken into two Union territories by the Central government, once again altering India's political map.[7] What this shows is that the ultimate power over the existence of the federal units of the Indian political union lies with the Central government. This stands in contrast with the United

States, where the federation has no right to alter the geographies of the States.

This power imbalance in India had one key valve, which was the collection of revenue. States had the power to collect indirect taxes (for e.g., sales tax), providing them with an independent source of revenue and a certain level of independence. This ability to tax, however, was given up by the States in 2017, through the 101stAmendment to the Constitution of India, which introduced a Goods and Services Tax, to be collected by the Central government and distributed later to the States. In 2020, when the pandemic occurred the States realized the folly they had committed as they had no money. As businesses died down and lockdowns were imposed, the only source of revenue for the States was the money they received from the Central government, with some other smaller sources like property taxes and taxes on alcohol. This State of affairs completely altered India's federal structure and the Central government was able to overpower the federal structure provided in India's Constitution.

2.2 The Federal Structure in the Constitution

The Indian Constitution, as already mentioned, created a quasi-federal structure. The reason behind this was very relevant when the Constitution was implemented back in 1950, but has long been futile. When India gained independence in 1947, it was rocked with communal violence, post-partition enmity, territorial challenges on all fronts, and a general State of instability. Its political future was uncertain and it was widely believed that it was a matter of time before the huge political union crumbled. To tackle such challenges, the union was given a strong arm over the States. Two key Articles of the Constitution are important in this regard.

The first is Article 356. This article allows the Central government to impose an emergency in any State, suspend its government, and take control if it deems that the State is in a situation of unrest (this Article is also referred to as the President's rule as the President becomes the official caretaker of the State). This provision became especially popular during the 70s and 80s: during 1966–1977, it was used a whopping 39 times; and from 1991–1992, it was used 9 times.[8] Its use was restricted only in 1994 after the Supreme Court defined its parameters in its judgement in *SR Bommai v. Union of India*, 1994. Currently, only one erstwhile State, and presently a Union territory, Jammu & Kashmir, continue to remain under the President's Rule. While not put to use during COVID-19, this was a credible threat which kept many State governments under a State of fear (Kamat, 2020).

The second, and more important, is the scheme of power-sharing provided under Part XI (Articles 245–263) of the Constitution, which governs "*Relations between the Union and the States*". Article 246 introduces the concept of three Lists: Union List, State List, and Concurrent List. Each of these lists contains the subjects on which the mentioned federal unit may legislate. The Centre can make laws and govern the matters in the Union List, and the State on the matters in the State List. On the matters in Concurrent List, while both the State and the Centre can make laws, the Centre has been given an upper-hand. The complete lists can be found in the seventh schedule of the Constitution, and enumerate 100 subjects under the Union list, 61 under the State list, and 52 under the concurrent list. Given the large number of subjects, one would imagine that they would be quite comprehensive and cover every possible event. Sadly, the reader would be dismayed: for the Constitution does not mention "disaster", "pandemic", or "public health emergency". The sole reference to 'Public Health' is contained in entry six of the State list. Which raises the question, how did the handling of the COVID-19 pandemic fall into the ambit of the Central government then?

The first option was to resort to entry 97 of the Union List: "*Any other matter not enumerated in List II or List III*". However, there was a better option: the Disaster Management Act, 2005, which is implemented through the National Disaster Management Authority. The statute already contained all the police powers which the Centre needed to impose a command and control mode of governance over the entire country. The law allowed the Centre to usurp most of the powers with the States, and decide every minute aspect of COVID-19, whether it be imposing lockdowns or deciding on the timing of essential shopping. While the act itself provides that the Centre should cooperate with the States in taking decisions, and allow them a fair share of decision-making authority, it is merely recommendatory in nature. One section that trumps every other is Section 35. Section 35 provides the Central government with the power to take all measures it deems necessary and lists almost every area of governance related to a disaster to be under its purview. The law certainly did not envision that a disaster would consume the entirety of the country's governance system for more than a year.

This law has an interesting pedigree as it was legislated under Entry 23 of the Concurrent List: "Social security and social insurance; employment and unemployment". Can this law then be used to impinge on many other subjects, which rightly fall under State's purview (like, public health or public order)? As per the rulings of the Supreme Court of India this cannot happen. In *Waverly Jute Mills v. Raymon* (1962), it held that "specific entries" (like public health under State list) are excluded from and trump any law made under a "general entry" (like entry 23 of the concurrent list). This means that the States could have easily gone to the courts rejecting the Centre's diktats. But they did not. This takes back to what was argued earlier in this section: for one, States have lost financial independence; and for two, Article 356 was the announcement of emergency in the State. So, how far did the Centre actually go in exploiting this political reality of the Indian federation?

2.3 The Federal Structure Under Challenge in 2020

Winston Churchill once said, "Never waste a good crisis".[9] In the last decades, this policy has been put to both positive and negative uses in India. In 1991, a financial crisis was put to use by the Indian government to transform India's economy from a failing one to an emerging one. In 2020, the COVID-19 crisis was used by the Centre to test the limits of its power over States, and it was done rather spectacularly. The Centre's notifications were all-pervasive and one-directional (Agrawal, 2020).The initial lockdowns implemented during the period 24 March to 1 June 2020 were imposed without any consultation with the States, and encompassed many State matters, including State government offices (Entry 41), hospitals (Entry 6), shops and markets (Entry 28), industries (Entry 24), agriculture (Entry 14), alcohol (Entry 8), etc. (Kajol et al., 2020) All of these were purportedly done under a "national importance" justification, which did not have any legal sanction. The Constitution does not provide for any such justification, and the Supreme Court in *Jayant Verma v. Union of India* (2018), had wholly rejected any such justification. The Court held: "*The argument, therefore, that Section 21A is made by Parliament at the national level and is of national importance and must, therefore, prevail over State legislation made within the exclusive subject matters of List II, would again fall foul of the constitutional scheme, in that all the entries of List II would then be subject to Parliamentary law, which is of national importance*".

One of the key flashpoints during this period was that of Centre's new laws on agriculture, which is an area entirely within the State's legislative competence. The Centre, realizing its new gained power over States due to COVID-19, passed a slew of ordinances, completely modifying the agricultural marketing system, which were later also formalized through the farm laws, as they came to be known (Burman, 2020). These laws brought an end to the States' control over agricultural products and allowed big corporates to trade in agricultural goods, which was hitherto prohibited. This was a daring attempt, undertaken without any consultation with States, and in total subversion of their autonomy. In 2021, fearing electoral defeats in key State elections, the Centre took back these laws (Tandon, 2021).

Another major decision that undermined federalism was on display when the Centre choked charitable donation funding to States. India has a law on Corporate Social Responsibility (CSR).[10] Under this law, companies are liable to spend a certain portion of their profits on social work: for instance, donating money to disaster funds to tackle the pandemic. All the States created such funds and were hoping to receive money from the corporations. However, the Central government issued a notice that any funding to State funds would not qualify for CSR exemptions. The only exception was donations to the Prime Minister's (PM) Cares Fund.[11] Moreover, the PM Cares Fund was not a public fund of the Central government, as one might assume. Instead it turned out to be a private fund, headed by key functionaries like the Prime Minister himself. This begs the question why a separate fund for pandemic management was created when India at both the Central government level and State level have constitutionally provided for Relief Funds (Prime Minister's Relief Fund and Chief Ministers' Relief Funds, respectively). Though the audit reports of the PM Cares Fund has been made public,[12] it does not answer the question why such a fund had to be created in the first place. Moreover, the receipts and payments from the PM Cares Fund have generated a greater debate on the deposit of funds and their disbursements with many journalists and activists arguing for greater transparency in the wake of mismatch between receipts, payments, and costs of goods and services that were paid for from the fund.[13]

2.4 *The Centre Eases Its Stand*

Unitary power is a double-edged sword. While you get to take all decisions, you also share all the blame if things go wrong. Centre's surprise announcement of a nation-wide lockdown created havoc and multiple crises piled up on one another. There was the migrants crisis (labourers working away from their homes did not have any transport to get back to their homes); the financial crisis; the unemployment crisis, and the hospitals and essential facilities crisis. Consequently, the Centre came under regular public criticism, leading to a recalibration of the strategy.[14] In later stages of the pandemic, significant power was given back to the States, and the Centre took a step back (Sahoo, 2020). Albeit, by this stage, the overall drift of the management of the pandemic had already been decided and significant damage was done to the public interest.

3 Pandemic Management

3.1 *Phased Approach*

India undertook a three phased approach in the first 100 days based on the necessities required to tackle the initial shocks (NDMA, 2020). The first phase was initiated when news of the spread of COVID-19 among travellers was reported in early January 2020. The government issued advisories making controls on the borders (land, air, and sea) for travelling into India to limit the infection spread (January to early March). At sea, the Directorate General of Shipping mandated Indian ships to have strong quarantine measures and disease outbreak management plans with transit allowed only through official checks. There was a complete stoppage of all international travel followed by the announcement of Vande Bharat Mission to evacuate Indian citizens and including foreign nationals stranded in various countries (Unstarred Question No 139, Rajya Sabha, 2020). The Ministry of Road Transport and Highways issued guidelines for sanitizing bus stations and intensified health inspections at the borders.[15] Simultaneously, information dissemination on COVID-19 ran through various government channels under the direction of the Ministry of Information and Broadcasting to ensure that citizens were aware of the measures and did not panic. These measures were specific government orders which prevailed in the area of concern over a general order which had a wider ramification. The difference in these orders lies in the scope of its application. Specific orders are addressed towards specific areas or institutions and have limited scope of application compared to a general order which applies to a more general audience.

The second phase was a follow-up of the first phase with contact tracing andsocial distancing norms ending in the final phase of strict lockdown across the country. The public who were curiously watching the developments and confused by the situation happening on the ground, did not expect a complete shutdown of activities across the country. As the information of the lockdown got disseminated, concerns were raised on travel and capacities of the people to stay at home. The imposition of strict lockdown implemented on 24 March 2020 with only essential services including healthcare, essential commodities provisioning, and agricultural activities being allowed meant that the government had to ramp up their existing capacities in various layers through a coordinated approach of testing, quarantining, and isolation backed with institutional support for the healthcare professionals at one end. While on the other hand, they had to ensure that essential supplies reached the citizens at their doorsteps. Given that only shops selling essential supplies were allowed to operate, the entire government machinery had to be activated to get the supplies moved from within different regions. The lockdown norms were largely strictly followed by the citizens as it has a legal mandate and the entire machinery was in the streets to ensure its implementation.

The lockdown was extended twice, once on 14 April 2020 and then again on 4 May 2020 which led to large scale disruption of economic activities and stranding of people. It was only by 31 May 2020 that the lockdown measures were eased and businesses were allowed to re-open their shops in unaffected areas. The Third phase or the "Unlock Phase" commenced on 1 June 2020 which aimed at gradual relaxing of the strict measures and guidelines in place. In this phase the Central government imposed strict guidelines against public meetings while mandated work from home for private companies except for essential and emergency services. Full lockdown continued in designated containment zones. The Central government meanwhile took up the mantle to inform and engage while monitoring the social interaction of the citizens including mandatorily wearing masks and other protective gear. Unlike other countries such as the United States where mandatory wearing of masks was questioned and could not be imposed fully, India had seen a higher compliance of mask wearing and social distancing during the period. This was also evidenced from the high demand for masks where the government had to step in. Meanwhile, States like Uttar Pradesh pledged to distribute masks manufactured by government institutions for free to the poor (The Indian Express, 2020).

3.2 Legal Framework for Pandemic Management

India does not have a dedicated and comprehensive National Emergency Response Plan for Public Health Emergencies like China (Muraleedharan et al., 2021). Two other laws were used for emergency management. Firstly, The National Disaster Management Act, 2005 was used to centralize administrative enforcement and to ensure consistency in application of the measure. Secondly, The Essential Commodities Act, 1955 was invoked to curtail movement of goods and ensure control over production and distribution of essentials which primarily included Food and groceries, medicines, etc. Healthcare essentials including masks and PPEs were also included in the list of essentials to provide speedy movement and distribution. This had a positive impact on ensuring sufficient supplies available across mom-and-pop shops (kirana shops) in the country. Also there were the online delivery services which were not curtailed to move around.

Further, as part of the pandemic management, the Central government relied on a colonial law i.e. Epidemic Diseases Act (EDA), 1897 to bestow powers on the executive to impose restrictions on movement and curtail movement of people and goods (James, 2020). Federal States like Kerala went even further by using drone based surveillance to track violators of the restrictions imposed (named Project Eagle) (Nair, 2021a, b). The surveillance measures for restricting and monitoring citizens which were in vogue since the first lockdown was put in place by the executive.

As these regulations restricted movement and confined people to their houses, the government machinery was spent largely to monitor movement of people and goods which were considered "essential". By the end of 100 days, starting from the March 24, 2020 Circular by the Ministry of Home Affairs imposing complete lockdown and Stay at Home Orders, 62 orders were issued for regulating movement and ensuring compliance by the citizens within the country and locally.[16] The lockdown imposed by the Government got rated as the most stringent under the Stringency Index created by the Oxford COVID-19 Government Response Tracker of the University of Oxford. Given the apparatus of the system, it was more convenient for the government to rely on technology to undertake surveillance of its citizens to ensure they do not flout the regulations in place. Hence, the coordination of departments, tracking of activities, and surveillance was done through various digital platforms.

Initially, considered as a step towards ensuring citizen participation in complying with lockdown and curtailing spread of infections, often at times, these measures were reported to be used to curtail freedom of movement of the citizens. As per the powers conferred, the federal police could either levy a fine or arrest citizens who violated the restrictions in place. Across the country, cases due to "disobedience to order duly promulgated by public servants" under Section 188 of the Indian Penal Code (IPC) grew from 29,469 cases in 2019 to 6,12,179 cases in 2020 (NCRB, 2021). The public response to the regulations has been largely supportive despite inconvenience caused due to the restrictions in movement. These norms continued to follow even after the Third Phase (the Unlock Phase) had been announced suggesting that a strong State continued to govern. This has been more prominent in matters related to surveillance which traditionally have been in the control of the State. Surveillance became more of a norm than an exception in this phase. This is discussed further in the next section.

4 Surveillance and Compliance

4.1 *Surveillance Laws*

The Indian government has constantly relied on colonial laws to govern the country especially on matters of law and order. The case also stands true in surveillance where the 137 year old Indian Telegraph Act, 1885 is still being used to intercept communications between individuals and entities. Along with the Information Technology Act, 2000 governing electronic communications; only the government could "legally" undertake surveillance. COVID-19 pandemic brought this "legal" power into the forefront as it was largely used as a tool to monitor and report COVID-19 infected individuals despite issues of privacy and data security. During the pandemic, the State assumed more power and centralized its functions for emergency management, monitoring, and surveillance. Many neoliberalists (Bourne, 2021; Gerbaudo, 2021) opined that this was a return of the big government while The Economist (March 2020) considered it as a requirement for dealing with the pandemic which however needs to recede after pandemic is curtailed.

4.2 *Enforcement and Compliance*

Using the powers conferred under Section 5(2) of the Indian Telegraph Act, the Central government wielded its machinery to intervene in communication. This was designed entirely through digital modes with the full backing of the State. The surveillance took shape in the form of contact tracing and creating alerts based on COVID-19 infected citizen locations and was pioneered through the Arogya Setu Mobile based application which was downloaded by 150 million by end of 2020. It was one of the biggest surveillance app with the highest reach as it was meant to monitor 1.3 billion citizens through their mobile phones with tracking options enabled. In the first 100 days of the pandemic the government used 19 apps (Regina, 2020) to track and trace COVID-19 infections and utilized the support of its citizens to surveil movement and contact points. Thus the surveillance took shape in two ways, one used for identifying and mapping COVID-19 patients and the other to monitor citizens' movement during the government imposed lockdown.

A trajectory of Circulars issued by the Director General of Civil Aviation (DGCA) under the Central government suggests how screening and surveillance transitioned from a monitoring of travellers who had travelled from China (DGCA Order No: 4/1/2020 IR) on 30 January 2020, to its expansion to other countries on 2 March 2020, and eventually leading to total suspension of flights on 23 March 2020 (MHA Order No: 40–3/2020-DM-A[A]). Based on these government advisories, surveillance was undertaken for COVID-19 protocols at all airports in the country. This envisaged tracking and monitoring of international passengers to India and continued even after a year (Circular dated 30 March 2021, DGCA). Meanwhile, The Airports Authority of India (AAI) was in charge of testing and quarantine of all passengers across different States in the country and mandated installation of the Arogya Setu App (State wise Quarantine Regulation, July 2020). Bajpai et al. (July 2020) suggest how a wide spectrum of ICT was used for carrying out surveillance among the citizens and not confined to the air transport passengers.

Public support for the Arogya Setu COVID-19 tracking app was also overwhelming with higher ratings for user acceptance (80%), app usefulness (72.8%), and app features (62.2%) (Kodali et al., 2020). Some (Batra, 2021; Sharma, 2020a, b) did raise concerns on data security, but the overall acceptance backed by the government trust for the App ensured its continued usage. The acceptance of the tracking system ensured that surveillance continued to be used even after the retreat of the first wave of COVID-19 in the country, suggesting how a new paradigm had arisen in the country, that of a surveillance State.

5 Economic Responses to the Pandemic

5.1 *Pre COVID-19 Scenario of Indian Economy*

The Indian economy had already begun to deteriorate before the outbreak of the pandemic due to the contraction in consumption and investment demand from 2017 to 2018. It registered the lowest growth of 3.7% in 2019–2020 since the Global Financial Crisis (GFC) (RBI, 2021). Unlike other countries, the primary drivers of Indian economic growth are consumption and investment demand (Mukhopadhyay, 2021). The pandemic was merely an external shock to this pre-existing condition. GDP growth fell continuously for eight quarters (except for a 0.08% point blip between December 2018 and March 2019). It was 8.2% in March 2018 and had fallen to just 3.1% in March 2020 (Kishore, 2020) just before the lockdown. India was experiencing the highest unemployment rate in 45 years in 2017–2018 as per the Periodic Labor Force Survey (PLFS)-2018 (MoSPI, 2020).

5.2 *Labour Market Scenario*

According to the PLFS, approximately 90% or 419 million of the total 465 million workers are employed in the informal sector, with 95 and 80% in rural and urban areas, respectively. India's unemployment rate in 2019 was 5.8%, according to the annual report of the Periodic Labor Force Survey 2018–2019 (PTI, 2020). The unemployment rate was 8.7% in March 2020, the highest since September 2016. During the lockdown, the situation escalated. The unemployment rate has increased to 23.8% (News18, 2020). The government's hasty announcement of lockdown was a tremendous miscalculation that backfired spectacularly. Before the lockdown, the public was only given a few hours' notices, causing domestic disruption and misery for the vulnerable population, notably migrant laborers. The entire public transportation system was shut down. Millions of migrants were made unemployed, and they were forced to return home with little help from the government. Not only that, but they were stigmatized when they returned home. Approximately 350 million non-migrant workers—self-employed, small-family companies, and casual labor—were badly impacted, in addition to migrant workers (Harris-White, 2020). Such reverse migration added increasing pressure on the demand for work in rural areas.

5.3 *Measures Adopted to Mitigate the Adverse Economic Impact of COVID-19*

Initially, on 26 March 2020, an amount of Rs. 1700 billion (US$ 22.75 billion) was announced as immediate measures by the finance minister under Pradhan Mantri Garib Kalyan Yojana (PMGKY) to provide immediate relief primarily to the distressed migrant workers, farmers, both rural and urban poor and women (Ministry of Finance, 2020a, b). Despite millions of people being laid off due to the imposition of lockdown, this support amounted to only 0.8%of Gross Domestic Product (GDP). After about two months on 12 May 2020, the Central government launched Atmanirbhar Bharat, a second relief package worth Rs. 20,000 billion (US$ 267.59 billion) and accounting for more than 10% of the country's (GDP) (Kumar, 2020). The second relief measures primarily focused on improving business, attracting investments, and strengthening the resolve for "Make in India".

5.3.1 *Support for Labour*

A significant number of 8.7 crore farmers beneficiaries of Pradhan Mantri Kisan Yojana (PMKY) were expected to benefit from PMGKY. PMKY introduced in the year 2018 is a Central government scheme with 100% funding from the government. It provides an income of Rs. 6000 per year to all landholding farmer families. The minimum wage of workers under the Mahatma Gandhi National Rural Employment Guarantee Act (MGNREGA) Scheme was increased to Rs. 202 from Rs. 182 per day which ensured a Rs. 2000 increment to five crore families. MGNREGA is an employment guarantee scheme that provides 100 days of wage employment guaranteed to rural unskilled workers. Later under Atmanirbhar Bharat an additional Rs. 40,000 Crore on 17 May 2020 has been allocated under MGNREGA to address the demand for more work as migrants return home. Although MGNREGA provided social security to the rural unemployed, there was no similar provision for urban unemployment. To aid the senior citizens, the government announced to provide Rs. 1000 per month from April to June 2020.

A total of Rs. 3500 crores under Atmanirbhar scheme has been released to assist migrants, small business owners, street vendors, and the poor. All migrant workers, farmers, poor in rural and urban areas and women were given an immediate relief of 5 kg free rice and 1 kg pulse under the Public Distribution System (PDS) for three months from March 2020–May 2020. PDS began as a mechanism for managing scarcity by distributing food grains at low prices, and run jointly by the Central and federal State governments. To obtain benefits under PDS distribution, one needs to have a Ration Card which is an authorized official document issued by the Government of India. Migrants, including those who were stranded and did not have a ration card, were eligible for a free food grain supply of 5 kg rice and 1 kg pulse for two months in June and July 2020. The PDS beneficiaries are identified by the State government making it difficult for migrant laborers to access subsidized food grains anywhere in the country. To address this issue an ambitious One Nation One Ration Card scheme was launched in August 2019 to allow beneficiaries across India to access PDS. As of August 2020, 24 States and Union territories were integrated under the scheme. This covers 65 crore beneficiaries, or 80% of the population eligible for entitlements under the National Food Security Act. As of June 2020, 74 crore beneficiaries have been covered by disbursement of 120 lakh metric tonnes of food grains (Gupta, 2020).

A large-scale Affordable Rental Housing Complex (ARHC) for migrant workers and the urban poor was to be constructed to provide living facilities at affordable rent under Pradhan Mantri Awas Yojana-Urban (PMAY-U). The PMAY-U seeks to provide housing for all in urban areas by 2022 which will be achieved by converting government-funded housing in the cities into ARHCs through Public–Private Partnerships and through the support of manufacturing units, industries, institutions, and associations to develop ARHCs on their private land and operate them. A total of 20.40 crores Pradhan Mantri Jan Dan Yojana (PMJDY) women account-holders were given ex-gratia of Rs. 500 per month for three months from April to June 2020. PMJDY is a nationwide scheme launched in 2014 to provide financial access to everyone who does not have a bank account. Between April 2020 and June 2020, Rs. 30,705 crore was credited to female PMJDY account holders. Under the Ujjwala Scheme, gas cylinders will be provided to 8 crore families between April 2020 and June 2020. In April 2020, 7.48 crore individuals benefited from the Ujjwala scheme, 4.43 crore beneficiaries were recorded in May 2020 and 1.82 beneficiaries in June 2020. Ujjwala scheme, launched in 2016 aimed to provide Liquified Petroleum Gas connections to women below poverty line.

To assist low wage earners in organized sectors, the central government contributed 12% of the employer's share and 12% of the employee's share through the Employees Provident Fund (EPF). Under EPF scheme an employee is required to contribute 12% of basic wages plus dearness allowance plus retaining allowance towards the scheme and equal contribution is paid by the employer. At the time of retirement, the employee receives a lump sum amount including self and employer's contribution with interest on both, on retirement. It covers every establishment in which 20 or more people are employed and certain organizations are covered, subject to certain conditions and exemptions even if they employ less than 20 persons each. The scheme is managed under the aegis of Employees' Provident Fund Organisation (EPFO). Between March 2020 and August 2020, a total of Rs. 2567 crore was credited to 38.85 lakh eligible employees' EPF accounts via 2.63 lakh establishments. For those who are not covered by PMGKY, the EPF contribution for Business & Workers has been reduced for three months to encourage home take salary. It planned to provide Rs. 6750 crores in liquidity to both employers and employees over the next three months. For those working in an organized sector, a provision was made to withdraw non-refundable 75% Employees Provident Fund or three months' wages for contingency uses.

The State Governments were allowed to use Rs. 31,000 crore Building and Construction Workers Welfare Fund to provide relief to Construction Workers by the Central Government. To ensure protection for frontline COVID-19 warriors, an insurance scheme of Rs. 50 Lakh per health worker was introduced. An amount of Rs. 15,000 crores for health-related measures for containment of COVID-19 includes Rs. 50 Lakh insurance per person for a health profession under PMGKY was allocated in the second relief tranche.

5.3.2 *Support for Businesses*

To counter the effects of the pandemic on businesses, all businesses including Micro, Small, and Medium Enterprises (MSMEs) were provided with collateral-free automatic loans of up to three lakh crore rupees till 31 October 2020. Only the interest rate is to be repaid in a tenor of four-year with a moratorium period of 12 months on principal payment. Under Emergency Credit Line Guarantee Scheme

(ECLGS) provisions were made for MSMEs to borrow up to 20% of their entire outstanding credit as of 29 February 2020, from banks and Non-Banking Financial Companies (NBFCs). Borrowers with up to Rs. 25 crore outstanding and Rs. 100 crore turnover will be eligible for such loans and can avail of the scheme till 31 October 2020. Interest on the loan will be capped and a 100% credit guarantee on principal and interest will be given to banks and NBFCs. The government estimated that the ECLGS will provide a total liquidity of Rs. three lakh crore to 45 lakh businesses.

The government extended equity support of Rs. 50,000 crore for MSMEs through Fund of Funds to provide equity funding for MSMEs with growth potential and viability. Besides, a relief worth Rs. 4000 crore was provided to Credit Guarantee Fund Trust for Micro and Small Enterprises (CGTMSE). CGTMSE will provide partial Credit Guarantee support to Banks. A relief measure of Rs. 1500 crore was allocated for Micro Units Development and Refinance Agency Bank (MUDRA)–Shishu loanees. The limit on collateral-free lending to the 63 lakh women-led Self-Help Groups (SHGs) that help 6.85 crore households has been raised from Rs. 10 to Rs. 20 lakhs. SHGs are self-governing, informal groups of individuals organized for a variety of social and economic reasons to better their living situations (Ministry of Finance, 2020a, b).

The Central government provided an initial working capital of up to Rs. 10,000 to street vendors under the Prime Minister's Atmanirbhar Nidhi (PM SVANidhi) scheme. Under PM SVANidhi, a total of Rs. 5000 crores has been set aside for street vendors to revitalize small businesses. One lakh loan applications out of five lakh have been sanctioned under PM SVANidhi as of 12 August 2020 (Gupta, 2020). The Ministry of Housing and Urban affairs fully funds it, and the implementing agency is the Small Industries Development Bank of India.

Around Rs. 6000 crores in funds was allocated to create employment opportunities in urban, semi-urban, rural, and particularly tribal areas under the Compensatory Afforestation and Planning Authority (CAMPA) It will be used for a variety of purposes, including urban areas, artificial regeneration, assisted natural regeneration, forest management, soil and moisture conservation, forest protection, forest and wildlife-related infrastructure development, wildlife protection and management, and so on. There was, however, no specific package for unemployment benefits.

To protect the workers from salaries or pay reduction, the Ministry of Labour and Employment issued a notification to all the employers of both private and public establishments not to reduce, cut the wages of the workers especially contract workers (Dhingra, 2020). However, due to severe financial crunches, many airlines have reduced the salary of their employees. For instance, regional airlines Turjet, a Hyderabad based company, has reduced the wages of its employees by 50% from 26 June; SpiceJet announced a 30% pay cut for employees for March, etc. Unfortunately, there was no government provision to compensate for the loss of wages.

5.4 *Monetary Measures*

The Reserve Bank of India (RBI) is the central bank of India whose primary function is to manage and govern the financial system of the country. To mitigate the negative economic impacts of COVID-19 RBI held an emergency monetary policy meeting on 27 March 2020 and announced a decisive monetary expansionary policy measure (RBI, 2020). It aimed to increase liquidity, reduce the cost of loans, and encourage lending and regulatory easing. The immediate measures adopted were i) announcing a moratorium of six months on payment of all installments falling due between 1 March 2020 and 31 August 2020 in respect of all term loans and ii) lending institutions were allowed to defer interest payments for three months on any working capital facilities sanctioned in the form of cash credit/overdraft as of 1 March 2020.

The Reverse Repo Rate (RRR), the rate at which banks are paid for depositing cash at the RBI, was reduced from 4.4 to 4% in May 2020. The Repo Rate (RR), which is the rate at which the RBI charges banks for borrowing from it, was cut by 75 basis points to 4.40%. The Marginal Standing Facility (MSF) allows banks to borrow from RBI when their liquidity completely dries up. The limit of MSF was increased from 2 to 3% up to June 2020. It allowed banks to borrow an additional Rs. 137,000 crore of liquidity at a lower MSF rate.

Cash Reserve Ratio (CRR), that is the minimum cash deposits a bank must hold with the RBI was reduced from 4 to 3% in March 2020 for a period of one year. This injected Rs. 13,700 crores of cash into the banking system. To provide relief to the borrowers, a moratorium of three months on a term loan and working capital for all types of loans.

With the mounting cases of COVID-19, investors were worried about bond defaults due to loss of revenue sources. Liquidity and credit risk premiums in the corporate bond market soared as a result. Participation in secondary markets was further hampered by it. Therefore, the RBI announced Targeted Long Term Repo Operations (TLTRO) worth Rs. 1 lakh crores for investment in investment-grade bonds, commercial paper, and non-convertible debentures including those of NBFCs and MFIs to provide adequate liquidity in the corporate market. Further, a Special Liquidity Facility (SLF) of Rs. 50,000 crores was announced for mutual funds to alleviate liquidity pressures.

The borrowing limit for State governments was increased from 3 to 5% of GSDP for 2020–2021. It was expected to offer an additional resource of Rs. 4.28 lakh crore to the States. For seamless continuation of economic activity, Indian public corporations were allowed to list their securities directly in authorized foreign jurisdictions. Private corporations that offer Non-Convertible Debentures (NCDs) on stock exchanges will not be considered listed companies. NCDs are fixed-term debt instruments issued by firms to raise funds for their operations. NCDs, unlike convertible debentures, cannot be converted into the issuing company's equity shares at a later date.

5.5 *Did Fiscal and Monetary Measures Really Mitigate the Adverse Impact of COVID-19?*

Although the government of India announced a big relief measure, the extent of relief measures does not seem to be proportionate to the economic disruption and dislocation caused by the severity of the lockdown. The PMGKY assistance package for the poor and vulnerable was just a reallocation of funds from the existing budgets (Ipchita et al., 2020). In comparison to India, less developed countries such as Indonesia, Pakistan, Vietnam, and Egypt have declared higher stimulus measures as a percentage of GDP, while adopting less stringent measures (Basole and Coutinho, 2020).

The Indian Labour market was the most affected one. As per the Periodic Labour Force Survey (PLFS) quarterly reports for the urban areas, casual labourers were the worst affected during the first and second waves of the pandemic, though the extent of the impact was lower during the second wave. Out of the total casual labourers working during January–March 2020, only 35.3% remained in the same category during the first lockdown period of April–June 2020; nearly 50% were pushed to unemployment and about 10% moved out of the labour force during this period (RBI, 2021).

According to the report of the Standing Committee on Industry chaired by Dr. K. Keshava Rao on the "Impact of COVID-19 Pandemic on MSME Sector and mitigation strategy adopted to counter it" published on 27 July 2021, the stimulus package announced by the government for MSMEs was inadequate and the benefits of the scheme failed to reached the micro and small enterprises. Rather than giving immediate relief by boosting cash flows, the package was more of extending credit facilities and long-term solution. The Committee also noted that barely 50% of the total guarantee amount of Rs. 3 lakh crores has been issued to MSMEs. The scheme that aimed to benefit around 2 lakh MSMEs could only benefit a few MSMEs (Shashank, 2021). Further, the survey conducted by the Consortium of Indian Associations (CIA) revealed that 88% of micro and small industries of over 81,000 self-employed and micro small businesses were yet to receive any stimulus package announced by the government (Deb, 2021).

Even after several regulatory monetary measures, the bank could access only 520 billion rupees out of the emergency credit guaranteed window of 3 trillion rupees (Kugler and Sinha, 2020). Further, COVID-19 exposed the vulnerabilities in the financial system and jeopardized its stability. The Indian security market faces a significant problem as a result of the strict lockdown for several months. It led to acute risk aversion and increased demand for precautionary liquidity by individuals, corporations, and financial agents (*Report on Currency and Finance*, 2021).

According to the data released by the Controller General of Accounts, the corporate tax collection levied on profits fell sharply to 18% in 2020–2021 to a 5 yearlow. It was for the first time that corporate tax collections fell below the personal income tax. This was because of the reduction in tax rates and the economic fallout caused by pandemic (Nair, 2021a, b).

The government failed to anticipate the impending economic disaster prompted by the most severe lockdown. In India, around 40–50 million seasonal migrant workers work on construction sites, in factory production, and in in-service industries. Consequently, as businesses and establishments closed, migrant workers were out of work and were forced to return home. It was also claimed that some persons died while attempting to return home on foot due to the suspensions of buses and trains. While others were trapped in places where they worked. It was extremely difficult for them and their dependent families to survive without work, income, or savings (Shekar and Mansoor, 2021).

The lack of financial sanction for the expansion of testing care or the strengthening of primary Health care centres proved fatal to controlling the spread of the viruses. Further, the government showed little interest in providing funding to nonprofits that worked closely with communities. Osama Manzar writes that the trust deficit between the government and the social sector exacerbated the situation. The massive transfer of funds from Corporate Social Responsibility (CSR) to PM Cares was a huge blow to non-profits that were struggling to retain their employees and organizations that were providing relief on the ground. Some of the catastrophes could have been prevented had the government, civil society, and the private sector collaborated and worked together to combat the effects of COVID-19. Even within the businesses and industry organizations, there was no collaboration among them to better assist their employees. If they had worked together, they could have used their resources to help the mass exodus of migrants from industrial and urban areas return home in a more humane manner (Manzar, 2021).

5.6 Post COVID-19-19 Economic Recovery

Following the most severe lockdown during the first wave of COVID-19, India had one of the world's most severe recessions, with GDP falling by as high as 23.8% in the first quarter of 2020–2021. The economy gradually recovered as the economy opened up, resulting in a GDP annual growth rate of (−) 6.6% in 2020. During the second wave, the impact was significantly reduced. It is expected to be around one-third of the third wave's (RBI Report). Given the pre-COVID-19 Indian economy and the massive economic impact of COVID-19 during that time, the Indian economy is projected to take another 12 years to recover from the pandemic's losses (RBI, 2021).

6 Alternatives to Mainstream Policy Responses

One of the arguments which is often furthered in favour of Indian government's response to COVID-19 is that this was the best it could have done (Deb, 2021). In the absence of adequate funds and given the widespread pre-existing poverty, the government had little elbow room to implement better policies. So, the question is, whether there were alternative responses which the government could have used? There are two points of comparison that we can rely on to answer this question: first, the responses of other similarly placed countries and second, intra-country alternate models implemented at the State level.

6.1 *Responses of Other Similarly Placed Countries*

India made many strategic mistakes in the initial days of the pandemic, which overall ensured that the country became one of the worst affected countries. The folly started with failure to implement a timely travel ban on foreign arrivals, which begun only on 22 March, long after COVID-19 had been declared a pandemic by the WHO.[17] Internally, the government continued to deny the existence of a pandemic and was slow to act. The first ministerial review of the pandemic happened only on 3 March, when the virus had already affected many countries severely.[18] This stands in contrast to Vietnam, which had already set up a national steering committee on 30 January and monitored the progress of the pandemic every two days.[19] The slow reaction of the government meant that the hundreds of millions of citizen who work in places far away from their homes had no time to react, when a sudden, strict, and complete lockdown was imposed on 25 March, after an announcement on the evening of 24 March.

The irrationally short deadline crippled speedy movement of people and resources. This meant that the humanitarian toll of the lockdown were going to be severe, as observed through the migrants crisis and acute lack of access to food and essentials. Further, since people could not swiftly move to safe spaces, they were stuck in crowded spaces, increasing the spread of the virus. Later, as they reached their towns and villages on foot after days of exposure, they brought back the virus, taking COVID-19 deep into the hinterlands of the country. This sudden and ill-measured lockdown was in complete contrast to the norm. For example, Singapore's "Circuit Breaker" approach: the government announced this package of lockdown on 3 April, with a basic set of closures to begin on 7 April, a relatively stringent set of measures on 14 April and complete closure on 21 April. This allowed people the time to ensure that they reached places of safety where they could remain for the coming many months.

The other problem with the complete lockdown was its imposition uniformly across the country which was defined by most commentors as the world's stringiest lockdown (Rukmini, 2020). As explained in the

Sect. 3, the Central government had unilaterally taken over management of the pandemic with little consultation with the federal units. The result was that the tiny villages, small towns, and other unaffected regions went into lockdown at the same time as key metro cities like Delhi and Mumbai, which were the initial hubs of the pandemic. This aggravated the economic impact of the lockdown and left people with no space to move. Neither was this helpful from the view of managing the pandemic, as congestion in the cities significantly increased the number of people affected, who later took the virus back home. This stands in contrast with the approach taken by Vietnam. The country first locked down affected cities (like Son Loi, which went into lockdown on 13 February 2020),[20] and after they had set-up capacities in the key affected hotspots, proceeded with a complete lockdown on 1 April.[21] Given the size of India, this approach would have allowed the government more time to distribute resources and tackle the cases.

The third problem with the national strategy was the absence of a robust fiscal support package from the government for the billion-plus people without employment and income. When the stimulus plan was effected after a week of the lockdown, it lacked a rights-based approach. While the government did make reasonable provisions for ration and LPG, a large number of people were unable to benefit from the same. As mentioned earlier, due to the sudden lockdown, hundreds of millions of workers were stuck in locations away from their homes (Abi-Habib and Yasir, 2020). The consequence was that these people were unable to access government ration of food and fuel, as accessing these benefits required one to have a local ration card (Shrivastava, 2020). The government was nowhere close to implementing the "One Nation, One Ration Card" scheme, which would allow one to access ration anywhere in the country (Katiyar, 2019). These factors were aggravated by the lack of housing and rent protection, leaving millions of migrants homeless and jobless. Furthermore, the total size of fiscal stimulus amounted to just $21 billion, which was merely 0.74% of the GDP and just 7.1% of the total finance package (Sharma, 2020a, b). Lastly, there was a gross lack of income support, which should have been the primary stimulus tool. The small transfers of $6.59 a month made to PMJDY women account holders was not the kind of transfer which can provide a safety net.[22] If one were to consider the World Bank's poverty line of 3.2$, the transfers are enough just for over 2 days. This fiscal stimulus was considerably lower than those of other G20 countries, which averaged to 4.5% of their GDP

(Battersby et. al., 2020). One can contrast, India's response with those of other, much smaller, developing countries. Brazil provided a stimulus of $42 billion (more than double of India's), and Indonesia, a significantly smaller developing country, provided a comparable stimulus of $18 billion.[23] Developed countries naturally had much larger stimulus packages (e.g., Singapore—$25 billion, Australia—$130 billion, etc.).

6.2 *Intra-country Alternate Models Implemented at the State Level*

In addition to strategic errors in imposing lockdown, the government also committed errors in crafting national COVID-19 management policies. The first error was a completely absent testing policy at the union level. This meant that the government could not accurately identify the extent and location of the spread in a timely manner. The State of Kerela offered a much better model in this regard. The State released guidelines to deal with the pandemic on 5 January 2020, much earlier than the first case detection in India. By 20 January, a directive advising all the district authorities had already been sent. Further, by 26 January, it had already released a testing strategy.[24] Hence, the first cases detected in India were from Kerela and the State was the best prepared to deal with the onslaught of the pandemic (WHO, 2020). It had some of the highest testing, detection, and treatment rates. This meant that its fatality rate at 0.5%, was the lowest in the country (which had a fatality rate of 1.5%) (Arun, 2021).

Another error on the part of the government can be noted as its lack of willingness to decentralize the entire COVID-19 management system in its early days. Given that authority was concentrated, the flexibility to respond to local situations was absent. Contrast this with the strategy undertaken by the union territory (semi-State) of Delhi, which was able to significantly bring down its cases in the initial phase of the pandemic. The State appointed Chief Minister's fellow in various hospital clusters to overlook their functioning, accessibility, and availability of resources (Vij, 2020). This had a positive effect on the functioning of the healthcare system. Similar measures could have been taken across the country, with authority being decentralized so that the reaction times and overall effectiveness would have been higher.

7 Conclusion

India did not experience the extreme catastrophe of loss of lives as many European, Latin American countries and the United States did. But India in the hindsight could have managed the initial day of the pandemic better. The complete and stringent lockdown enforced without due notice to the population and without taking States into consideration led to wide spread panic especially among the migrant workers. The fear of unemployment and loss of income made millions of migrant labourers flee the States of their employment. Survey studies have shown a considerable decline in their consumption patterns and increased borrowings especially from the informal sector to stay afloat (Rajan et al., 2022). The centralized stance of the Union government has also been questioned be it with respect to implementation of National Disaster Management Act (2005) and Essential Commodities Act (1955) even when the cases in the country were few and required increased testing and isolation rather than declaration of emergency in the form of national disaster. The success of surveillance and compliance has been phenomenal in India due to the widespread political acceptance of the ruling party. This acquiescence was also observed during the demonetization of Rs. 500 and Rs. 1000 notes in the country in 2016. The economic measures announced during the pandemic provided paltry support to the needy. The insufficient legroom for an expansionary fiscal policy deterred the government from large scale public spending and the policy announcements were forward looking rather than for tackling the immediate crisis. The monetary policy in general suffers from weak transmission, the reduction in interest rates and increased liquidity in the economy benefitted the larger private companies than the smaller ones (RBI, 2022). The post pandemic recovery is poised to be unequal given the disproportionate impact of the pandemic on the households, enterprises and communities.

Notes

1. Data sourced from https://COVID-19-1919tracker.in/.
2. Data sourced from https://www.worldometers.info/coronavirus/country/india/.
3. According to the country ranking provided by worldometers website. https://www.worldometers.info/coronavirus/#countries.

4. https://www.thehindu.com/sci-tech/health/who-estimates-47-million-COVID-19-19-linked-deaths-in-india-10-times-official-count/article65385669.ece.
5. https://www.orfonline.org/research/dont-play-politics-with-COVID-19-death-numbers/.
6. https://www.news18.com/photogallery/india/bifurcation-of-jammu-kashmir-how-the-map-of-india-has-changed-since-2258621-4.html.
7. https://surveyofindia.gov.in/files/POL_MAP_15M_with_watermark.pdf.
8. https://www.livemint.com/Politics/SJ3mETZ7H1cjKNlodkcM8O/How-Presidents-Rule-in-India-has-been-imposed-over-the-year.html.
9. https://realbusiness.co.uk/as-said-by-winston-churchill-never-waste-a-good-crisis.
10. Section 135, Companies Act, 2013.
11. https://www.business-standard.com/article/current-affairs/pm-cares-fund-not-govt-fund-functions-with-transparency-hc-told-121092300557_1.html.
12. https://www.pmcares.gov.in/assets/donation/pdf/Audited_Statement_2020_21.pdf.
13. https://www.moneylife.in/article/pm-cares-funds-2020-21-audit-Statement-fails-to-tally-with-govts-releases-and-rti-replies/66438.html.
14. https://www.hindustantimes.com/columns/covid-19-will-lead-to-a-new-federal-compact/story-2gMpertMOxm9VxLuCXpZuN.html.
15. Ministry of Road Transport and Highways issues accessibility guidelines for bus terminals and bus stops. https://morth.nic.in/sites/default/files/circulars_document/N_3012405_1637043131682.pdf.
16. https://www.mha.gov.in/notifications/circulars-covid-19.
17. https://timesofindia.indiatimes.com/india/govt-bans-all-international-flights-to-india-from-march-22-to-29/articleshow/74720923.cms.
18. https://thewire.in/COVID-19--india-timeline.
19. https://ourworldindata.org/covid-exemplar-vietnam.
20. https://crisis24.garda.com/alerts/2020/02/vietnam-son-loi-vinh-phuc-province-placed-under-quarantine-due-to-coronavirus-february-13-update-7.
21. https://ourworldindata.org/covid-exemplar-vietnam.
22. https://www.ddnews.gov.in/national/govt-transfer-rs-500-women-account-holders-pradhan-mantri-jan-dhan-yojana-june-today.
23. https://www.imf.org/~/media/Files/Publications/fiscal-monitor/2020/April/English/onlineannex11.ashx?la=en.
24. https://dashboard.kerala.gov.in/COVID-19/orders/1588255001.pdf.

References

Abi-Habib, M., and Yasir, S. (2020) India's coronavirus lockdown leaves vast numbers stranded and hungry. The New York Times, 29 March, https://www.nytimes.com/2020/03/29/world/asia/coronavirus-india-migrants.html.

Agrawal, P. (2020) Covid-19 and dwindling Indian Federalism. Economic and Political Weekly 55: 26–27.

Alexandrowicz, C. H. (1954) Is India a Federation? In D. Armitage., & J. Pitts (Eds.), *The law of nations in global history* (Online edn, Oxford Academic, 18 May 2017). https://doi.org/10.1093/acprof:oso/9780198766070.003.0018.

Arun, T. K. (2021) Kerala's COVID-19 management is a model for other states, here's why. MoneyControl, 05 August. https://www.moneycontrol.com/news/opinion/keralas-COVID-19-management-is-a-model-for-other-states-heres-why-7280581.html.

Bajpai, N., Biberman. J., and Wadhwa, M. (2020) ICT Initiatives in India to Combat COVID-19. CSD Working Paper Series: Towards a New Indian Model of Information and Communications Technology-Led Growth and Development.

Basole, A., and Coutinho, J. (2020) The COVID-19 fiscal response and India's standing. The Hindu, July. https://www.thehindu.com/opinion/op-ed/the-covid-19-fiscal-response-and-indias-standing/article32154153.ece.

Batra, V. (2021). In context: Aarogya Setu, data security, and the right to privacy. Institute of Peace and Conflict Studies. April. http://www.ipcs.org/comm_select.php?articleNo=5760.

Battersby, B., Lam, W. R., and Ture, E. (2020). Tracking the $9 trillion global fiscal support to fight COVID-19. IMFBlog, 20 May. https://blogs.imf.org/2020/05/20/tracking-the-9-trillion-global-fiscal-support-to-fight-COVID-19/.

Bourne, R. (2021) The COVID-19 case for bigger government is weak, September. https://www.cato.org/pandemics-policy/covid-19-case-bigger-government-weak#pandemic-preparedness.

Burman, A. (2020). How COVID-19 is changing Indian federalism. https://carnegieindia.org/2020/07/28/how-covid-19-ischanging-indian-federalism-pub-82382.

Chadrashekhar, C. P. (2010). From dirgisme to neoliberalism: Aspects of the political economy of the transition in India. Development and Society 39(1): 29–59.

Chandrasekhar, C. P., and Jayati Ghosh. (2004) The market that failed: Neoliberal economic reforms in India. New Delhi: Leftword Books.

Deb, S. (2021) The curious case of India's success in taming covid-19. LiveMint, 07 February. https://www.livemint.com/opinion/columns/the-curious-case-of-india-s-success-in-taming-COVID-19-11612711676750.html.

Dhingra, S. (2020) Don't cut salaries or fire workers during lockdown—Modi govt issues advisory. The Print, 23 March. https://theprint.in/india/dont-cut-salaries-or-fire-workers-during-lockdown-modi-govt-issues-advisory/386643/.

Gerbaudo, P. (2021) Big government is back. The Foreign Policy, February. https://foreignpolicy.com/2021/02/13/big-government-is-back/.

Ghosh, S. (2011) Catastrophic payments and impoverishment due to out-of-pocket health spending. Economic and Political Weekly 63–70.

Ghosh, S., & Gupta, N. D. (2017) Targeting and effects of Rashtriya Swasthya Bima Yojana on access to care and financial protection. Economic and Political Weekly 52(4): 61–70.

Gupta, S. (2020) Analysis of the Aatma Nirbhar Bharat Abhiyaan. PRS Legislative Research. https://prsindia.org/policy/report-summaries/analysis-aatma-nirbhar-bharat-abhiyaan.

Hammer, J., Aiyar, Y., and Samji, S. (2007) Understanding government failure in Public Health Services. Economic and Political Weekly 42(40): 4049–4057. http://www.jstor.org/stable/40276648.

Harris-White, B. (2020) The Modi Sarkar's Project for India's Informal Economy 20 May, pp. 1–13. https://thewire.in/political-economy/the-modi-sarkars-project-for-indias-informal-economy.

Ipchita, B., Preeti, K., and Sakhthivel, S. (2020) How well is India responding to COVID-19? Brookings, July. https://www.brookings.edu/blog/future-development/2020/07/02/how-well-is-india-responding-to-covid-19/.

James, K. (2020) An overbearing centre: Legal dimensions of India's Covid19 response. Centre for Multilevel Federalism, Institute of Social Sciences. http://www.issin.org/pdf/CMFIndianFederalismPerspectives.pdf.

Kajol et al. (2020) Erosion of fiscal federalism in the times of Covid-19. *The Hindu Business Line*, 25 May. https://www.thehindubusinessline.com/opinion/erosion-of-fiscal-federalism-in-the-times-of-covid-19/article31670568.ece.

Katiyar, P. (2019) One nation, one ration card: Inside food ministry's ambitious scheme to make ration cards portable. The Economic Times, 17 November. https://economictimes.indiatimes.com/news/economy/policy/one-nation-one-ration-card-inside-food-ministrys-ambitious-scheme-to-make-ration-cards-portable/articleshow/72089023.cms?utm_source=contentofinterest&utm_medium=text&utm_campaign=cppst.

Kishore, R. (2020) India's Economy was acing worst-ever deceleration before Covid-19 hit. Hindustan Times, 1 September. https://www.hindustantimes.com/business-news/india-s-economy-was-facing-worst-ever-deceleration-before-covid-19-hit/story-gOJfU86lJ64UPOjLBoypvN.html.

Kodali, P. B., Hense, S., Kopparty, S., Kalapala, G. R., and Haloi, B. (2020) How Indians responded to the Arogya Setu app? Indian Journal of Public Health 64(Supplement): S228–S230. DOI: https://doi.org/10.4103/ijph.IJPH_499_20.

Kugler, M., and Sinha, S. (2020) The impact of COVID-19 and the policy response in India. Brookings, 13 July. https://www.brookings.edu/blog/future-development/2020/07/13/the-impact-of-covid-19-and-the-policy-response-in-india/.

Kumar, R. (2011) Neoliberalism, education and the politics of capital: Searching for possibilities of resistance. Analytical Monthly Review 9(6): 139–152.

Kumar, A. (2020) Summary of announcements: Aatma Nirbhar Bharat Abhiyaan, PRS Legislative Research. https://prsindia.org/policy/report-summaries/summary-announcements-aatma-nirbhar-bharat-abhiyaan.

Manzar, O. (2021) The good, the bad, the uly: What went wrong during India's Covid-19 response. IDR, November. https://idronline.org/article/perspectives/covid-19-how-the-government-social-sector-and-corporates-failed-in-india/.

Ministry of Finance. (2020a) Finance Minister announces Rs 1.70 Lakh Crore relief package under Pradhan Mantri Garib Kalyan Yojana for the poor to help them fight the battle against Corona Virus. Press Information Bureau, 26 March. https://pib.gov.in/PressReleaseIframePage.aspx?PRID=1608345.

Ministry of Finance. (2020b) Fiscal and Monetary Policies to deal with Slowdown due to COVID-19. Press Information Bureau, 20 September. https://pib.gov.in/PressReleasePage.aspx?PRID=1656925#:~:text=On%20May%2012%2020b20%2C%20Government,for%20'Make%20in%20India.

Mooij, J., and Dev, M. (2002) Social sector priorities: An analysis of budgets and expenditures in India in the 1990s. Development Policy Review 22(1): 97–120.

MoSPI. (2020) Periodic labour force survey. https://www.pib.gov.in/PressReleaseIframePage.aspx?PRID=1629366.

Mukhopadhyay, A. (2021) Post-pandemic economic recovery: Seven priorities for India. ORF Occasional Paper, January, pp. 5–6. https://www.orfonline.org/research/post-pandemic-economic-recovery-seven-priorities-india/.

Muraleedharan, M., & Chandak, A. O. (2021) Emerging challenges in the health systems of Kerala India: Qualitative analysis of literature reviews. *Journal of Health Research 36*(2): 242–254. https://doi.org/10.1108/JHR-04-2020-0091.

Nair, D. (2021a) 88 pc micro and small enterprises yet to avail govt.'s COVID stimulus package. SMBSTORY, 24 June. https://yourstory.com/smbstory/micro-small-businesses-government-stimulus-package-covid-msmes/amp.

Nair, R. (2021b) Covid, lower rates push corporate tax collections below personal tax for first time in years. The Print, 2 June. https://theprint.in/economy/covid-lower-rates-push-corporate-tax-collections-below-personal-tax-for-first-time-in-years/669839/.

Nair, M., Sivaraman, M., Solomon, N., Joseph, A. C., and Dharmarajan, D. (2020) A comparative study of Covid-19 outbreak in the Hubei province of China and the Indian State of Kerala, Centre for Public Policy Research Paper, November.

National Disaster Management Authority. (2020) COVID-19 impacts and responses: The Indian Experience, January–May 2020, NDMA, India.

News18. (2020) Unemployment rate rises to 23% Amid Locdown, labour participation & employment rates at all-time low: CMIE. 27 April. https://www.news18.com/news/india/unemployment-rate-rises-to-23-amid-lockdown-labour-participation-employment-rates-at-all-time-low-cmie-2568103.html.

Niranjan, S., and Ghosh, A. K. (2021) The COVID-19 challenge to Indian Federalism. ORF Occasional Paper No. 322, June. Observer Research Foundation.

NCRB. (2021) Crime in India 2021, Statistics Volume 1. *Ministry of Home Affairs*. https://ncrb.gov.in/sites/default/files/CII-2021/CII_2021Volume%201.pdf.

Pritchett, L., and Aiyar, Y. (2014) Value subtraction in public sector production: Accounting versus economic cost of primary schooling in India. Center for Global Development Working Paper 391.

PTI. (2020) India's unemployment rate improved to 5.8 per cent in 2018–19: Govt Data. The Financial Times, 4 June. https://www.financialexpress.com/economy/indias-unemployment-rate-improved-to-5-8-per-cent-in-2018-19-govt-data/1981639/.

Rajan, S. I., Sivadasan, T. M., Jayanth, R. S. S., & Batra, P. (2022) Household pandemic response: The socioeconomic impact of COVID-19 on migrant households in India. Asian Economics Letters 3(2). https://doi.org/10.46557/001c.25382.

RBI. (2020) Statement on developmental and regulatory policies. Press Release, 27 March. https://www.rbi.org.in/SCRIPTS/BS_PressReleaseDisplay.aspx?prid=49582.

RBI. (2021) Report on Currency and Finance-2021. Mumbai: Reserve Bank of India. https://rbidocs.rbi.org.in/rdocs/Publications/PDFs/RCF202122_FULLB5D854DD796948889FF5099C22CD6893.PDF.

Regina, M. (2020) India is using at least 19 apps to track and trace Covid-19, including Aarogya Setu, 16 April. The Print.

Rukmini, S. (2020) India had one of the world's strictest lockdowns. Why are cases still rising?. The Guardian, 04 July. https://www.theguardian.com/commentisfree/2020/jul/04/india-lockdowns-cases-rising.

Shah, A. (2016) Marginal cost of public funds: A valuable tool for thinking about taxation and expenditure in India. The Leap Blog. https://blog.theleapjournal.org/2016/08/marginal-cost-of-public-funds-valuable.html.

Sharma, S. (2020a) Modi's Rs 21 lakh cr special economic package actually costs the govt only this much. Financial Times, 18 May. https://www.financialexpress.com/economy/narendra-modis-rs-21-lakh-cr-special-economic-package-actually-costs-the-govt-only-this-much-nirmala-sitharaman-relief-package/1962288/.

Sharma, U. (2020b) Understanding Aarogya Setu: Navigating privacy during a pandemic proves to be tricky. London School of Economics Blog Series, July. https://blogs.lse.ac.uk/covid19/2020b/07/02/understanding-aarogya-setu-privacy-during-the-pandemic-may-be-compromised/.

Shashank, S. (2021) Standing Committee Report Summary: Impact of COVID-19 Pandemic on MSME Sector. https://prsindia.org/files/policy/policy_committee_reports/SCR_Summary_MSME.pdf.

Shekar, C., and Mansoor, K. (2021) Covid-19: Lockdown impact on informal sector in India, Azim Premji University. https://practiceconnect.azimpremjiuniversity.edu.in/covid-19-lockdown-impact-on-informal-sector-in-india/.

Shrivastava, R. (2020) One nation one ration card, free food schemes falter, marginal beneficiaries covered. India Today, 20 August. https://www.indiatoday.in/india/story/one-nation-one-ration-card-free-food-schemes-falter-marginal-beneficiaries-covered-1713295-2020-08-20.

Tandon, A. (2021) Centre takes back 3 farm laws, Modi announces in address too the nation. The Tribune, 19 November. https://www.tribuneindia.com/news/nation/centre-takes-back-3-farm-laws-modi-announces-in-address-to-the-nation-340216.

The Economist. (2020) The state in the time of Covid-19, 26 March. https://www.economist.com/leaders/2020/03/26/the-state-in-the-time-of-covid-19.

The Indian Express. (2020) UP: Govt may make wearing masks must, will distribute free to poor, 5 April. https://indianexpress.com/article/cities/lucknow/up-govt-may-make-wearing-masks-must-will-distribute-free-to-poor-6347695/.

Tiwana, B. S. & Singh, P. (2015) Nation state, marketisation of social services and uncertainty of livelihood in India. World Review of Political Economy 6(1): 34–57.

Vij, M. (2020) COVID-19 crisis: How Delhi model, if implemented well, can help curb pandemic's spread in rural areas. FirstPost, 17 August, https://www.firstpost.com/health/COVID-19-crisis-how-delhi-model-if-implemented-well-can-help-curb-pandemics-spread-in-rural-areas-8719801.html.

WHO. (2020) Responding to COVID-19–Learnings from Kerala. Feature Stories, 02 July, https://www.who.int/india/news/feature-stories/detail/responding-to-covid-19---learnings-from-kerala.

First 100 Days of Italian COVID-19 Policy: A New Image for Democracy, Security, Education, and the Economy in Italy

Elisa Gibellino and Federica Cristani

1 Introduction

Prior to the pandemic, the image of Italy in the grip of a pandemic always seemed very unlikely. Pandemics or epidemy was something that Italians only visioned in history books and novels.[1] Like all over the world the pandemic hit fast and hard. Italy was the first in Europe which suffered the first impact of the Covid-19. In the first 100 days, there were 90,000 estimated victims and more than half of the Italian population was locked in their houses for 69 days.

Our aim, in this chapter, is to analyze the Italian state of emergency through the lenses of a variety of themes: policy, democracy, economy, security, and education. All of these sectors of Italian life and society were deeply influenced by something completely unexpected.

E. Gibellino
University of Eastern Piedmont, Vercelli, Italy

F. Cristani (✉)
Centre for International Law, Institute of International Relations in Prague, Malá Strana, Czechia
e-mail: cristani@iir.cz

A. Stojanović et al. (eds.), *The First 100 Days of Covid-19*,
https://doi.org/10.1007/978-981-19-6325-4_5

2 The State of Emergency in Italy Before the Pandemic-Age

The idea of State of emergency in the history of Italian State was always linked to the idea of "*exceptional structure to which a territory is temporarily subjected to overcome conditions of social disturbance, through the extension of the powers of the state authorities and the correlative restriction of citizens' freedoms*" (Grasso, 1959).

From the Albertine Statute (1848) through the fascist laws to finally the modern Constitution (*Costituzione della Repubblica italiana*, entered into force on 1 January 1948), the State of emergency was associated with the idea of war or at least to a natural disaster. In every step of the Italian legislation about the State of emergency there has always been a continuous tension between the legislative and the executive power and where, this power, should lie was continually at the center of discussion. With the Albertine Statute[2] it was the king that proclaimed the State of siege. Afterwards, during the fascist dictatorship, all the power was concentrated in the hands of the executive power.

With these examples in mind, the fathers of the Italian Constitution were aware of the necessity to create and enforce precise rules to preserve the legislative power[3] from the inferences of the executive one. The Hon. La Rocca argued about the real necessity of precise rule because: "[...] *silence does not destroy the practice of this power of exceptional gravity, which comes to jeopardize all the rights and freedoms of citizens, and since it cannot be eliminated, since a right of necessity is recognized by all publicists and treatise writers, believes that it is appropriate to regulate it in the Constitution, placing limits and precautions for its implementation*".[4] Of course, there were oppositions to the idea of creating specific rules about the State of emergency, the Hon. Tosatti believed that the case of necessity could be handled through the normal use of the Decree laws[5] and in case of abuse the Government will assume the consequences.[6] In the session of the 14 and 16 October 1947 an article for the regulation of the state of siege was proposed by the Hon. Crispi.[7] In this provision some rights could be limited or suspended in case of necessity but the Parliament and the Senate, even if disbanded, there will be convocated in order to ratify or reject the state of siege. This proposal was not approved. Finally, when the Italian Constitution was enforced, there were no traces of the various proposal for the regulation of the state of emergency. Only

Art. 78 (declaration of state of war) and Art. 16 (there could be limitation to the right of movement for health emergency) are what is left of the discussions.

Only with law 225/1992 Italy finally adopted specific provisions about the state of emergency. With this law and the Code of Civile Protection (D.lgs 1/2018)[8] the State of Emergency was indeed created but, the emergency was only restricted to natural disasters, and there was no space for health emergencies.

2.1 *The State of Emergency During the Pandemic Age*

The previous digression is necessary to understand why Italy struggled to manage the emergency of Sars-CoV-2. The Constitution does not include any reference to health-related emergencies. Emergencies in Italy had been indeed usually caused by natural disasters.[9]

The State of emergency in Italy, in accordance with Art. 5 par. 1 of law 225/1992,[10] is declared in the case of an event of emergency[11] at national level and the Council of Ministry[12] deliberates it. When the State of emergency is declared the first thing that should be done by the Council of Ministers and the Regional Presidents is to determine: the duration of the State of emergency (that could not be longer than twelve [12] months and it cannot be extended for no more than 12 more months[13]); the territorial scope; and how many financial resources must be assigned to face the emergency.[14]

The first measure adopted by the Government to deal with the Corona virus emergency dates back to 31 January 2020, when the only known cases of Covid-19 in Italy was a Chinese couple hospitalized at Spallanzani in Rome. With a resolution of the Council of Ministers, a first State of Emergency was declared for six months, after the first outbreak was identified in Codogno in the province Lodi, Lombardy (North Italy) on 16 February 2020. Following the declaration of the State of Emergency on 21 February 2020, the mandatory quarantine for those who had been in contact with persons who had tested positive for Covid-19 was put in place by the Ministry of Health.

The legislative situation during the State of Emergency was complicated. The first measures that were taken by the Government to face the early stage of the pandemic did not have the validation of the Parliament. In fact, the first announcement was carried out in accordance to the Civil Protection Code (Art. 24), this announcement gave a lot of power to the head of the Civil Protection in order to manage the crisis. The declaration of the state of emergency was taken by the government bypassing the parliament but, the answer to an emergency had to be quick as possible and it was argued that a passage through another body could represent a problem. However, what happened afterwards is the real problem that still now cast doubts on the legality of the first 100 days of COVID-19 in Italy.

Consequently, the management of the emergency in the way the Italian government did led to two major problems: (i) the relationship between regions and the State; and (ii) the legality of the measures taken by the government.

2.2 *The Management of the Emergency or the Solipsism of the Italian Government*

To contrast the emergency, the first acts of the government were neither legislative decree nor decree law but DPCM (President of the Council's Decree). The main question was: why the Government decided to use this "peculiar" legislative instrument?

According to the Code of Civil Protection The Council's President "*Determines the civil protection policies for the promotion and coordination of the activities of the state administrations, central and peripheral, of the regions, metropolitan cities, provinces, municipalities, national and territorial public bodies and any other institution and organization public or private present on the national territory*" (Art. 5, paragraph 1).[15] The Code, also provides that it is always up to the President of the Council of Ministers to adopt directives with which to give "*the guidelines for carrying out, in a coordinated manner, the civil protection activities referred to in Art. 2, in order to ensure their unity in compliance with the peculiarities of the territories*" (Art. 5, paragraph 2).[16] The Government with its first resolution adopted on 31 January 2020 declared a state of emergency for the duration of six months. After a month, a Law decree was issued the 23 February 2020. This law decree was heavily criticized by Sabino Cassese one of the most important and influential Italian constitutional judges. He expressed his disappointment on the management of the emergency by the Government in an interview in which he stressed the fact that the aforementioned law decree was illegitimate because there were no provisions about the duration of the state of emergency and most importantly did not establish the methods for the government to exercise power. In fact, with the law decree of 2 March 2020, no. 9 (*Urgent measures to support families, workers and businesses affected by epidemiological emergency from COVID-19*) the first decree one was almost completely repealed. Nonetheless, the supposed lack of legitimacy of the first period was showed in the continuous use of decrees of the President of the Council of Ministers (*Decreto del Presidente del Consiglio dei ministri* or DPCM).

There is no doubt that the measures were taken with the objective of limiting the spread of the Covid-19 but, the problem is in the instruments used. These types of administrative Acts are, in the Italian legislative body, a secondary source. This means that during the first lockdown some personal freedoms were limited by a secondary source even though Art. 13 of the Constitution clearly states that these kind of rights could be limited only by an Act having force of law, while the DPCM are in fact only administrative measures. With a combined reading of Art. 1 and 3 of the Decree no. 6 of 23 February 2020[17] it is in fact deduced that the President of the Council of Ministers, on a proposal from the Minister of Health, will be able to order measures which include, inter alia, the ban on the removal and suspension of events and school activities. It is necessary to underline how the Decree did not implement these measures, but limited itself to authorizing the Government, in the person of the President of the Council, to do so. In other words, the D.L. constitutes a kind of government "self-delegation". Sabino Cassese also points out that, in accordance with the 1978 law on the National Health Service, the competence to issue most of those acts to deal with the emergency had to be taken by the Minister of Health and not by the Prime Ministero. There was therefore a sort of "appropriation of power" by the executive body. Furthermore, no intervention or participation of others among the three Constitutional Guarantee Bodies, like the Constitutional Court (whose role is to supervise the effective compliance of the law and acts with the Constitution) was envisaged.

It is pretty clear that the aim of the continuous production of DPCM was the centralization of power in the hands of the government, so that all decisions taken to contain the pandemic could be applied harmoniously at national level and quickly. However, the spread of the pandemic has not been uniform. Northern Italy has been more affected than the southern regions.

With the issuance of the law decree no. 19 of 25 March 2020, the regions were expected to participate in the procedure aimed at identifying the measures to contain the infection through the request of their "compulsory opinion". However, this kind of procedure risks completely emptying the meaning of the participation of the regions. Art. 2 (law decree no. 19/2020), reiterates 12 that the measures referred to in Art. 1 are adopted by Decree of the President of the Council of Ministers, requires that the Presidents of the Regions should be consulted in advance, where a specific Region is concerned, or the President of the Conference of Regions and Autonomous Provinces, in the event that the intervention involves the entire national territory. Nonetheless, from how the provision is structured it is clear that the intervention of the regions in the decision-making process can only be understood as a mandatory opinion.

Institutional conflict between regions and government in the management of the crisis, was also a serious issue. At first due to the ambiguous formulation of the Law Decree no. 6 of 23 February 2020 on "Urgent measures for the containment and management of the epidemiological emergency from COVID-19". Art. 2 of the aforementioned Law Decree, in fact attributed the power to take further measures than those specifically indicated in Art. 1. The generality of the provision favored the proliferation of measures issued by the 13 Presidents of the Regions in the form of contingent and urgent ordinances. In many cases, Presidents of the Regions ordered measures restricting the freedoms of citizens in contrast and even more stringent than those of the state. To remedy the situation of uncertainty and the growing spread of the epidemic, the Government intervened with Law Decree no. 19 of March 25, 2020. This time the body of the text of Law Decree no. 19 predetermined the specific areas of competence of the regions and the type of restrictions that can be caused to the freedoms and fundamental rights resulting from the listing of Art. 3, paragraph 1–3, highlights the concrete intention to rationalize and clarify relations between the State and the Regions.

Additionally, the relationship between the Government and the Parliament was unusual, since the law decree no. 19 provides that it will be through DPCMs that the government will issue concrete measures and—from time to time—express restrictive measures and choices on the return to normal. The DCPM, an administrative act, will then graduate reopenings of economic activities which need to be communicated to the Parliamentary chambers only after publication. Every 15 days the Prime

Minister or a delegated Minister report to the Chambers in a specific debate. From the wording of the decree, a relationship between Parliament and Government is created completely *ex-novo*, which, in reality, is specifically governed by the Constitution in the Art. 88. In Art. 88 is expressly stated that Parliament is an expression of the political direction of the State and that the Government must obtain its trust for its formation. Therefore, the Government is directly dependent on the confidence of the Parliament, which has a primary role in the Italian political scene.

During the beginning of the pandemic the role of Parliament was found to be rather marginal and not very incisive. After the end of the lockdown, the Parliament, by resuming its normal activities, converted the decrees issued by the government into law. This conversion into law of the decrees issued during the pandemic was probably done for two reasons: (1) the government was supported by its political majority (2) not converting the decree laws would have led to an institutional crisis in a rather delicate moment.

As it emerged, Italy was one of the European states that suffered the most from the spread of Sars-CoV-2, both in lives lost and a political situation extremely borderline. This discussion still divides peoples and scholars. Some intellectual as Sabino Cassese warned about the danger of the concentration of the power in the hands of few. Others such as Professor Massimo Luciani had an opposite point of view and argued that what the Government did during the pandemic was legitimate (Luciani, 2020).

The truth and the best way to address the state of emergency maybe lie in the middle. Urgent and straight measures were needed, and the involvement of other legislative bodies could have led to a worst aftermath. However, it is pretty obvious that the interweaving between primary sources (i.e. decree law) and secondary sources (i.e. DPCM) had repercussions on the level of constitutional balance, and this disbalanced relationship was clearly visible in the accentuation of the role of the government and the fact that the parliament found itself impeded in its normal situation.

3 Surveillance and Security in Italy

3.1 Pre-COVID-19 Surveillance and Security Mechanism: The Italian Civil Protection System

Italy has always been exposed to a wide range of natural hazards. Accordingly, it has developed a quite robust civil protection system, characterized by an integrated governance mechanism and reliance on volunteer organizations (OECD, 2010a).

The civil protection system in Italy includes several actors at central, regional, provincial, and municipal levels of government, acting in concert with private actors such as volunteer organizations and the scientific research community. The Civil Protection Department, a structure of the Presidency of the Council of Ministers, supervises the execution of emergency measures through the National Civil Protection Service (NCPS)—established with Law no. 225 of 1992—which guarantees the coordination across the different actors (Civil Protection Department, 2022a).

Decree Law no. 59 of 15 May 2012 gave authority to the Council of Ministers to take action upon the outbreak of an extraordinary emergency situation, with the possibility to issue a "Declaration of state of emergency". The duration of the state of emergency—as established by Law no. 119 of 15 October 2013—cannot exceed 180 days and can be extended up to an additional 180 days, with a further decision of the Council of Ministers. During the emergency situation, interventions were implemented through the orders issued by the Head of the Civil Protection Department (Civil Protection Department, 2022b). On the other hand, co-ordination for the whole civil protection system is undertaken by the NCPS, which, among others, defines and implements intervention and action procedures and elaborates the exceptional regulations that are needed to conduct the emergency interventions (OECD, 2010b).

Outside of the state of emergency situation, the daily activities of the Civil Protection Department include monitoring, surveillance, and emergency management for potentially risky events, as well as the development of policies for preparedness and prevention. The new Civil Protection Code issued with Legislative Decree no. 1 of 2 January 2018 has then reinforced the role of the NCPS, by enriching it with new tasks and responsibilities, including the development and organization of national plans for risk scenarios and promotion of activities of risk forecasting and prevention (Civil Protection Department, 2022b).

The civil protection system also works in coordination with the National Fire Brigades, the Armed Forces, the Police Forces, the scientific community, the National Health Service structures, the organized civil protection volunteer service, and the Italian Red Cross.

A key feature of the Italian civil protection system (especially when compared to other national systems), is the highly mobile force of volunteer organizations: "tens of thousands of volunteers could be mobilized to support professionals in emergency response, relief and recovery activities within just a few days" (OECD, 2010a).

However, as a relevant OECD report higlighted, the system "need[ed] to increase damage reduction efforts and better implement prevention policies" (OECD, 2010a). The report also highlighted that emergency management was underveloped in some (more remote) municipalities (OECD, 2010a).

3.2 *Surveillance and Security in a Post Pandemic Age: More Concerns on the Right to Privacy*

Since the declaration of the state of emergency by the Council of Ministers on 31 January 2020 for the COVID-19 pandemic, the Italian government and regional administrations have adopted several emergency measures. In particular, we can identify three phases of the emergency: phase 1, where the complete lockdown on the national territory was progressively introduced; and phase 2 and 3, where such restrictions have been progressively eased. Compliance to such measures has been ensured with a mass informative campaign, coupled with the introduction of specific administrative sanctions in case of non-compliance, as outlined further below.

The government introduced the relevant emergency measures by means of legislative decrees (legislative acts adopted in case of urgency, effective immediately but required to be confirmed by the Parliament in 60 days), which have been implemented by decrees of the President of the council of ministers and orders of the governors of the regions and majors—administrative acts with immediate effect; regions were allowed to adopt more restrictive measures if required by the particular state of emergency (Ramajoli, 2020). The Ministry of Health has issued orders and circulars re-defining the application of the measures, coupled with orders of the Department of Civil Protection. Also the ISS (Istituto Superiore di Sanità–National Institute of Health, the main Italian research institute in public health), has constantly monitored the national emergency situation and advised the government in the different phases (IMF, 2020; Servizio Studi della Camera dei Deputati, 2020b).

In particular, the following measures were adopted: during phase 1 (which started at the end of January, with the declaration of the state of emergency, and lasted until 3 May 2020), progressive lockdown measures, first in the North of Italy, then all over the national territory were introduced, which included restriction of movement across the national territory (and within the regional and municipal territory of residence) and to/from abroad, closure of all schools and universities, closure of all commercial (with exception of groceries and pharmacies), productive, cultural and sports activities. At the regional and municipal level, more restrictive measures were progressively introduced, e.g. in Lombardia (the region with the highest number of cases and deaths at the beginning of the pandemic). Phase 2 (which lasted from 4 May 2020 to 2 June 2020) witnessed a progressive easing of restrictive measures: movement across regions was limited to essential activities related such as work, health issues, or in case of urgency, while movement within the region of residence was allowed to visit close relatives, access public parks (except for playgrounds), practice individual training, attend funerals and access cemeteries, and buy takeaway food, while all schools and universities remained closed. During this period, most primary and secondary productive sectors and most retail shops, businesses, and customer services were allowed to resume their activity, following national COVID-19 safety protocols (e.g. use of thermoscanners). At the regional level, the competent governmental and health authorities adopted ad hoc health security rules for those sectors that were resuming their activities. In phase 3 (which started on 3 June 2020), sports and cultural activities were progressively resumed, traveling across regions in Italy and abroad to/from EU countries were allowed again. At the regional level, regional orders were issued with the aim to limit and control movements between regions. During all three phases, social distancing (1 m) and the use of facemasks, gloves, and sanitary detergent in closed spaces that were accessible to the public (e.g. shops/businesses; public offices; public transport) have always been mandatory.

What has been the reaction to such measures by the society? After the early phase of the emergency, where compliance with emergency rules was quite low, daily press conferences of majors, governors of regions, and the President of the council of ministers (also via social media tools, like Facebook) constantly insisted on the necessity to comply with the emergency rules—supported by the #iorestoacasa ("I stay at home") campaign, promoted by the government (Ministero della Salute, 2020a; Scaramuzzino, 2020). The President of the council of ministries always insisted on the gravity of the situation ("there is no time left [...] we have to give up something for the good of Italy, and we have to do it now", Ministero della salute, 2020d).

On 25 March 2020, the Legislative decree no. 19 was issued, which provided for administrative pecuniary sanctions (between 400 and 3000 EUR) for breach of compliance of the emergency measures included in ministerial decrees, regional and municipal orders. With the introduction of fines for the breach of compliance of the emergency measures, the level of compliance increased, though with few cases of resistances (Ludovico, 2020), as outlined by the regular data compiled by the Ministry of Interior (Ministero dell'Interno, 2020), according to which, by the end of June 2020, on 68,302 controls in Italy, 47 fines were issued (Ministero dell'Interno, 2020). We can recall that in Italy, the Chief of the Department of Civil Protection is in charge of coordinating all emergency measures; he can demand some coordination tasks to the structures of the National service of civil protection (Servizio nazionale della protezione civile), and to public entities and/or private actors—also derogating to the rules of public procurement (Presidenza del Consiglio dei Ministri, 2020). On the other hand, at the local level, the prefects (prefetti)—the State's representatives in the provinces—oversee the compliance with emergency measures, with the support of the local (an eventually military) police force (Servizio Studi della Camera dei Deputati, 2020a). Overall, we can affirm that compliance with the emergency measures has been quite high, as highlighted also by some scientific studies (e.g. Briscese et al., 2020).

Emergency measures were constantly coupled with the constant symptom monitoring of the population: the Ministry of Health activated the National Surveillance System, a monitoring system on epidemiological data, coordinated by ISS (2020a); citizens' health status was also monitored at the regional level—e.g. in Lombardia, with the "LOM Alert" App (Regione Lombardia, 2020c). Moreover, massive test screening was conducted: at the national level, the Department of Civil Protection overseed the distribution and implementation of tests on the national territory (Dipartimento della Protezione Civile, 2020); and at the local level, Regions (which are responsible for health services' delivery) performed nasopharyngeal and serological tests on different rates, even though, particularly at the beginning, experienced a severe lack of testing material and capacity (Fattore et al., 2020).

During the above mentioned three phases, a number of surveillance techniques were progressively implemented: first, a massive use of thermoscanner was introduced in public spaces (e.g. offices, shops, airports, ports, hospitals), and some regions made it mandatory (e.g. Regione Lombardia, 2020a). Second, ad hoctracking mobile application(s) had been developed and implemented, like the "Immuni" App, developed by the Italian company Bending Spoons in coordination with the Ministry of Innovation and Ministry of Health. The App has been free of charge and without any obligation for its use; it uses the Bluetooth technology (Biddle, 2020; Zinzocchi, 2020) to register in an anonymous way the codes from the devices it is close to (Pennisi, 2020b). Moreover, other mobile applications had been developed, e.g. "Protetti" and "SM_COVID19" (NoiOpen Community, 2020; SoftMining, 2020), notwithstanding the concerns of the Italian Data Protection Authority, which has warned against the "proliferation of [...such] initiatives [...], which are hardly compatible with the current legal framework of reference" (Garante per la protezione dei dati personali, 2020b). Mobile surveillance techniques included also the use of cell phones: suffice to briefly recall that in March 2020, Vodafone produced an aggregated and anonymous heat map for Lombardia that visualized population movements (Vodafone, 2020).

Some regions and municipalities also released local mobile applications to monitor the spread of COVID and citizens are invited to cooperate: for example, in Lombardia, citizens could fill in health questionnaire (in anonymous way) through the "AllertaLOM" App, and data were sent to health authorities (Regione Lombardia, 2020c). Another telling example comes from the municipality of Rescaldina (in the province of Milan), where the "1SAFE" App allowed citizens to report situations where the measures were not respected (Comune di Rescaldina, 2020).

The use of mobile applications during the pandemic situation raised some privacy issues. In this respect, based on the favorable opinion from the Data Protection Authority (Garante per la protezione dei dati personali, 2020b), Legislative decree no. 28 of 30 April 2020, which regulates the use of the "Immuni" App, also addresses the relevant privacy issues, in accordance with the existing regulation (Legislative

Decree 101/2018, transposing the EU regulation on data protection): the app is not mandatory (Art. 6[4]) and uses a decentralized system of collecting data in an anonymized way—which does not include personal data including sensitive data (Art. 6[2b]; Ministero dell'Innovazione, 2020). Even though such characteristics helps in preserving the right to privacy, some questions remained still unanswered; for example, Legislative Decree 28/2020 does not specify how many subjects/entities will have access to the data collected by the app; another possible issue concerns the anonymization of data: since anonymized data can be combined with other data to re-identify individuals (Thompson and Warzel, 2019; Harrison, 2020), it would be necessary for the government clearly prohibit the practice of "re-combination" of anonymized data. Art. 6(2d) of Legislative Decree 28/2020 states that the Ministry of Health will ensure that "adequate measures [will be taken] to avoid the risk of re-indentification of the owners of the data that have been pseudonymised"; however, it does not expressly prohibit the re-identification practice, and does not refer to anonymized data. Moreover, the government has not specified which cybersecurity safeguards will be adopted in order to mitigate the risk of security and data breaches (Pennisi, 2020a). Another important question is whether the "Immuni" App will be the only mobile application in Italy or whether it will be operative together with the other mobile applications that have been being developed (and partly implemented). These mobile applications use different data storage systems (for example, the SM_COVID19 allows the use of geo-location data collected through the GPS system, which has been expressly excluded by Art. 6[2c] of Legislative Decree 28/2020); the use of such applications may pose some problems with respect to the right to privacy and data protection of the users. As already recalled, to date, the Data Protection Authority has simply warned against the proliferation of different initiatives similar to the "Immuni" App and it remains to be seen whether the governmental authorities will take some decisions in this respect.

Other privacy concerns have been raised on the way personal data are processed in health care sector, clinical trials, and medical research, or by public and private employers or by schools: the relevant legislative decrees allow the processing of personal data to the extent it is useful to monitor the spread of COVID-19, with the supervision of the Data Protection Authority (Garante per la protezione dei dati personali, 2020a).

4 Challenges to the Italian Economy

4.1 Pre-COVID-19 Situation: Privatization Processes from the 90s

Italy is described as the "third-largest economy in the euro zone [with...] exceptionally high public debt and structural impediments to growth [which] have rendered it vulnerable to scrutiny by financial markets" (CIA, 2022). Italy is the second largest manufacturer in Europe and stands in the top five list of manufacturers in the world (Ministry of Economic Development, 2022).

In Italy, economic development is quite different according to the regions of reference: while northern regions are more developed and host many industries and private companies, southern regions tend to be less-developed, with a higher rate of unemployment. Overall, the strengths of the Italian economy are its metallurgical and engineering industries, along with the chemical sector and textiles, while it generally lacks raw materials and energy sources. Additionally, the services sector, particularly tourism, is also very relevant (Britannica, 2022).

Until the beginning of the 1990s, Italy had a long tradition of state ownership. Then, starting from 1993, a wide privatization program began, which was mainly aimed at fiscal stabilization as a pre-requisite to join the European Monetary Union (Barucci and Pierobon, 2007). The objectives of the privatization program were well explained in a document drafted by a Committee of independent experts appointed by the Ministry of Economy and presented before the Parliament on November 1992, the Green Book on the Participations of State (*Libro Verde sulle Partecipazioni dello Stato*). According to the Green Book, the main objectives of the privatization were (1) to enhance the competitiveness of the economic system, (2) to promote financial development in the market, and (3) to foster the internationalization of the national companies—with the inclusion of foreign investors (Bortolotti, 2005).

The privatization process included several steps. First, the government considered the immediate divestiture of State banks, in order to allow a more competitive financial sector, which would promote economic growth. During this phase, privatized banks tended to develop a set of investment banking services which were used as input in the privatization of nonfinancial firms. Second, the governments opted for public offers of shares, which were moderately underpriced in order to foster the participation of domestic investors. Third, the government introduced golden shares mechanisms in a small number of companies that it considered as being strategic for the national economy; such mechanisms were aimed to maintain (partial) public control in privatized companies, which would in turn allow the preservation of the relevant public interests (Bortolotti, 2005).

This process was implemented through major legislative regulations, which included privatization laws, which established rules, responsibilities, and procedures to regulate the practical implementation of the privatization process (e.g. Law no. 359 of 5 August 1992 and Law no. 474 of 30 July 1994) as well as new competition regulatory framework that would avoid competition distortions and new rules for regulating corporate governance—with the aim to improve the legal protection of minority investors—(e.g. Law 281 of 14 July 1995 and Legislative Decree 58 of 24 February 1998) and new rules for the financial sector (e.g. Law 218 of 30 July 1990) (Bortolotti, 2005).

Nowadays, the private sector is mostly characterized by a multitude of small companies, with businesses with fewer than 50 employees representing more than half of total firms (Barucci and Pierobon, 2007).

4.2 Post COVID-19 Situation: Protectionism on the Rise?

The above mentioned emergency measures adopted by the Italian government had a grave impact on the Italian economy. In order to mitigate the negative effects of the pandemic measures, the government adopted a number of extraordinary containment measures that were aimed to support the national economy.

In particular, the three major regulatory interventions by the Government were the following: (1) Decree Law no. 18 of 17 March 2020 (so-called "*Decreto Cura Italia*"/*Cure Decree*); (2) Decree Law no. 23 of 8 April 2020 (so-called "*Decreto Liquidità*"/*Liquidity Decree*); and (3) Decree Law 19 May 2020 no. 34 (so-called "*Decreto Rilancio*"/*Raise Decree*). The relevant measures that have been adopted included different forms of financial support to companies: Decree Law no. 18 of 17 March 2020 (Cure Decree) provided mainly for financial support measures for small-medium enterpreses (SMEs), which were allowed to ask banks or other financial institutions to postpone/suspend the repayment of loans (until 30 September 2020); Decree Law no. 23 of April 8, 2020 (Liquidity Decree) included measures that facilitated access to credit and tax obligations for businesses. Lastly, Decree Law 19 May 2020 no. 34 (Raise Decree), targeted both families and businesses, with a view to strengthen the Italian economy; in particualr, it foreseed the creraation of special fund, the so-called *Patrimonio Destinato di Rilancio,* amounting to Euro 44 billion and financed by asset provided by the Italian Ministry of Economy and Finance. According to Raise Decree, the resources of the fund should be used to support Italian joint stock companies (including cooperatives and listed companies).

One peculiar feature of the economic measures adopted by the Italian Government has been the tendency to protect the national economic in general and the Italian strategic sectors, in particular. Accordingly, an increasing number of measures have been adopted with a view to strengthen the Italian regime of control on foreign direct investments (FDI) in the country—in order to avoid hostile foreign takeovers of national companies. In this regard, the Italian Government adopted the Decree Law no. 23 on 8 April 2020, which broadens its screening powers over FDI. Then, with Decree Law no. 21 of 15 March 2012 (the so-called "Golden Power Law"), the Italian government reinforced its power to prohibit or impose restrictions/conditions on an investment by foreign persons in certain strategic industries. The main aim of all these measures were well summarized by the then Italian deputy economic minister, who stressed that Italy will not "become someone's shopping territory" (Reuters, 2020).

5 Education

For Italian high school students, 2020 can be considered as a wasted year. On 10 March 2020, the Head of Government decide with a DPCM the closure of all the schools all over the national territory.

All the schools' headmasters were required to guarantee educational continuity through distance learning (Didattica a Distanza, from here DAD). The transition from normal teaching to DAD was not easy and above all homogeneous. Initially some schools did not immediately take action, thinking of a short closure. On 28 March the Ministry of Education allocated approximately 85 million euros in order to allow schools of all levels to equip themselves with platforms to be able to continue lessons, organize training courses for teachers and provide digital tools to less well-off families. On 6 April, a handbook for teachers was issued by the Ministry of Education with instructions on how to give an online lesson to how to support students psychologically.

It has been calculated that since March 2020 about 65 days of regular school have been lost compared to other European countries where school closures took place for only about 27 days.

In addition to the problems deriving from prolonged use of the DAD, the data show that access to distance learning alone was difficult. According to ISTAT, about 3 million children and young people between the ages of 6 and 17 may have had difficulties in distance learning activities due to lack of connectivity or adequate IT tools. The phenomena of "digital poverty" had a terrible outcome. A study by Save the Children measured that the minors that cannot access a good quality connectivity or use IT tools did not reach the minimum skills in literature (42%) mathematics (40.6%) and in science (38.3%) (Save The Children, 2021). This means that the digital poverty has turned into educational and cultural poverty. The degree of preparation has also dropped, about one in four students had a subject to recover at the end of the school year and for 35% of them the number of subjects to be recovered increased compared to the previous year. But this educational poverty is not only seen among school benches. The access to cultural, art, literature experience was seriously impacted. The 67.6% of students between 6 and 17 years old did not go to the theater, the 48.1% did not read a book that wasn't scholastic and the 49.9% did not visit a museum. There have also been problems linked to the psychological sphere of teenagers, a percentage that fluctuates between 22 and 44% turns out to suffer from depression in addition to problems such as tiredness, uncertainty, worry, irritability, anxiety, disorientation, nervousness, and apathy. These types of problems have also arisen also due to the fact that it was impossible for many students to attend to children of their own age. Taking into account that many families only have one child, the isolation was even worse. The school period is one of the most delicate, not only for the acquisition of notions but also for the training of all those other interpersonal skills which unfortunately, with the continuous alternation of school in the presence and distance learning, are unable to train in an appropriate way.

Certainly, the use of digital tools has not only led to inconveniences. As also reported in the Save the Children study, there has been an increase in the management capacity of IT.[18] On the other hand, there has been a worrying trend and problems regarding the ability to discern real life from online life, cases of cyber-bullying have increased and not knowing how to recognize fake news and consequently not developing critical thinking have increased.

The lockdown period has aggravated a number of problems that before, even if they were known, were not so diffused. This situation, in turn, puts us in the conditions of being able to correct the mistakes that have been made. Although the next steps for a strengthening of the school structure have not yet been announced, it is good to note that awareness of the problem has been acquired.

6 Conclusion

The Italian government and local administrations have adopted a series of surveillance measures during the COVID-19 pandemic, ranging from a progressive national lockdown to a progressive easing of the restrictions. The legislative acts, circulars, and orders adopted have resulted in a very fragmented legal framework, in manifold aspects of the society (security, economy, etc.). Though inconsistent messages have come from politicians and experts, citizens have followed the strict emergency rules, as confirmed by the studies that have been undertaken. And indeed, Italy has also been praised at the international level for the measures adopted and enforced (Scevola, 2020).

Overall, after the first 100 days of the pandemic, we see (a) new face(s) of Italy, with manifold challenges, ranging from more concerns on the privacy side when it comes to surveillance and security, and new forms of intervention of the state in the national economy. Additionally, major concerns have come along for democracy and constitutionalism, as the previous paragraphs have illustrated.

It remains to be seen how these challenges will be addressed in the forthcoming months, and to what extent the (new) regulatory framework introduced with the pandemic will be kept in force also beyond the state of emergency.

Notes

1. The Albertine Statue was a sort of "Costitution" promulgate by Carlo Alberto of Savoy in the 1848 and it was used until the promulgation of the actual Italian constitution in 1946.
2. In the Italian law system, the Parliament exercise the power of legislation and it is the expression of the popular will.

3. Report by the Hon. La Rocca Vincenzo of 11 January 1947 at the first Section of the second Subcommittee of the Commission for the Constitution. https://www.nascitacostituzione.it/05appendici/01generali/09/02/index.htm?002.htm&2.
4. Decree laws are the tools of the Government, a Decree law could be in force only for sixty (60) days and it could be renewed only one time, after that the Parliament will convert it in law if not the decree ill decay.
5. Report by the Hon. Tosato Egidio of 11 January 1947 at the first Section of the second Subcommittee of the Commission for the Constitution. https://www.nascitacostituzione.it/05appendici/01generali/09/02/index.htm?002.htm&2.
6. Project of Art. 74-bis of the Constitution, proposed by Hon. Crispo Amerigo in the sessions of 14 and 16 October. https://www.nascitacostituzione.it/05appendici/01generali/09/02/index.htm?002.htm&2.
7. A Legislative Decree in the Italian regulation (Art. 76 Constitutions) is an act having source of law (it is a primary source of law). The Parliament delegates the power to regulate a specific matter to the Government, but it gives also a "frame" made of principles and directive criteria.
8. Italy has dealt with some emergency linked to health issue, for example in 2000 the Bovine Spongifrm Encelphalopathy, or between 1997 and 2005, there were outbreaks of avian flu which struck the northern region of Italy but none of these emergencies never had the gravity or the spread of Sars-CoV-2. Even during the tragedy of Seveso, it was declared as natural disaster rather than a health one, despite the fact that the tragedy has a severe impact on health since its early stages.
9. The text was formally repealed with Art. 48 paragraph 1.a of the Civil Protection Code. But if you look at the text, all the titles of the articles refer to the law of 225/1992. Furthermore, many of the newspapers continue to use law 225 as a reference. Ex. https://tg24.sky.it/politica/approfondimenti/stato-emergenza.
10. Law 225/1992 has provisions for three types of emergencies: type A provides for a direction of interventions at municipal level, the type B at provincial and regional level, type Cat national level.
11. The Council of Ministers is the collegiate executive body of which the Italian Government is composed; it is made up of the President of the Council of Ministers and the Prime Ministers.
12. Art. 24 par. 3 del d. lgs. no. 1/2018.
13. For this purpose, the Council of Ministers allocates an initial sum to carry out the first necessary intervention.
14. Code of Civil Protection (D.lgs 1/2018).
15. Idem 18.
16. Primary source of law as Law, law decree, and legislative decree.
17. The law decree was converted in to law on 5 march 2020.

18. 13-year-old boys and girls who participated in the pilot survey have claimed to be able to independently carry out a series of activities with the tools digital. In particular, 86% of students declare themselves able to copy/move a file or folder; 59.1% to save files on the Cloud; 91.6% send emails; 95% access devices via account and password; 97.4% run/install/update software; 63.8% insert interactive links in a text; 81.4% share the screen during a video call; 79% load and download resources from websites or the school platform, while 41.9% say they do understand how an algorithm works. Additionally, 91.3% say they are able to write a document using Word, 33% perform calculations with Excel, 81% of making a presentation with PowerPoint. 65.4% say they know how to use photo editing software and 61.8 for video and audio editing. 79.7% say they do comment and actively participate in online discussions, even to ask clarifications and indications; 83.4% know how to choose which information to share and finally the 78.3% say they understand safety issues and related laws sharing content created by others.

References

Barucci, E. and Pierobon, F. (2007). Privatizations in Italy: Planning or improvisation? Efficiency gains or rents? Review of economic conditions in Italy 3: 341–369.

Biddle, S. (2020). The inventors of bluetooth say there could be problems using their tech for coronavirus contact tracing. The Intercept, 5 May. https://theintercept.com/2020/05/05/coronavirus-bluetooth-contact-tracing, accessed 13 May 2022.

Bortolotti, B. (2005). Italy's privatization process and its implications for China. FEEM Working Paper No. 118.05, September. https://doi.org/10.2139/ssrn.833265, accessed 13 May 2022.

Briscese, G. et al. (2020). Compliance with COVID-19 social-distancing measures in Italy: The role of expectations and duration. CESifo Working Paper Series 8182. https://ideas.repec.org/p/ces/ceswps/_8182.html, accessed 13 May 2022.

Britannica. (2022). Economy of Italy. https://www.britannica.com/place/Italy/The-arts, accessed 13 May 2022.

CIA. (2022). The World Factbook. Italy. CIA, 7 March. https://www.cia.gov/the-world-factbook/countries/italy/#economy, accessed 13 May 2022.

Civil Protection Department. (2022a). Activities. Protezione Civile. https://www.protezionecivile.gov.it/en/department/activities, accessed 13 May 2022a.

Civil Protection Department. (2022b). Extraordinary and emergency interventions. Protezione Civile. https://www.protezionecivile.gov.it/en/department/meritorious-award/extraordinary-and-emergency-interventions, accessed 13 May 2022.

Comune di Rescaldina. (2020). Attivazione nuova funzionalità App 1SAFE. Rescaldina, 2 March. http://www.rescaldina.org/news/3/7/3268, accessed 13 May 2022.

Fattore, G. et al. (2020). COVID-19 Health Systems Response Monitor (HSRM). Italy. Policy responses for Italy. https://www.covid19healthsystem.org/countries/italy/countrypage.aspx, accessed 13 May 2022.

Garante per la protezione dei dati personali. (2020a). Coronavirus e protezione dei dati: documenti e approfondimenti. GarantePrivacy. https://www.garanteprivacy.it/temi/coronavirus, accessed 13 May 2022.

Garante per la protezione dei dati personali. (2020b). Parere sulla proposta normativa per la previsione di una applicazione volta al tracciamento dei contagi da COVID-19. GarantePrivacy, 29 April, https://www.garanteprivacy.it/home/docweb/-/docweb-display/docweb/9328050, accessed 13 May 2022.

Governo Italiano, Presidenza del Consiglio dei Ministri. (2020). Coronavirus, la normativa. Governo. http://www.governo.it/node/14252, accessed 13 May 2022.

Grasso, P. Giuseppe. (1959). Figure di stato d'assedio negli ordinamenti costituzionali contemporanei. Il Politico 24(2): 327–346.

Harrison, S. (2020). When is anonymous not really anonymous? The Markup, 24 March. https://themarkup.org/ask-the-markup/2020/03/24/when-is-anonymous-not-really-anonymous, accessed 13 May 2022.

International Monetary Fund. (2020). Policy responses to COVID-19. Policy Tracker. Italy. IMF. https://www.imf.org/en/Topics/imf-and-covid19/Policy-Responses-to-COVID-19#I, accessed 13 May 2022.

ISS. (2020a). COVID-19 Integrated Surveillance System. ISS. https://www.epicentro.iss.it/coronavirus/sars-cov-2-sorveglianza, accessed 13 May 2022.

ISS. (2020b). Coronavirus, in uno studio dell'ISS l'effetto delle misure di distanziamento sulla riproducibilità del Sars-Cov-2. ISS, 13 April. https://www.iss.it/primo-piano/-/asset_publisher/o4oGR9qmvUz9/content/coronavirus-in-uno-studio-dell-iss-l-effetto-delle-misure-di-distanziamento-sulla-riproducibilit%25C3%25A0-del-sars-cov-2, accessed 13 May 2022.

Luciani, M. (2020). Il sistema delle fonti del Diritto alla Prova dell'Emergenza. Rivista AIC, 10 April. https://www.rivistaaic.it/it/rivista/ultimi-contributi-pubblicati/massimo-luciani/il-sistema-delle-fonti-del-diritto-alla-prova-dell-emergenza, accessed 13 May 2022.

Ludovico, M. (2020). Coronavirus, le procure: «Difficile punire le autocertificazioni false». Il Sole24ore, 18 March. https://www.ilsole24ore.com/art/coronavirus-procure-difficile-punire-autocertificazioni-false-ADS1HAE, accessed 13 May 2022.

Ministero dell'Innovazione. (2020). Immuni: disponibile il codice sorgente delle app iOS e Android. Innovazione, 25 May. https://innovazione.gov.it/source-code-immuni, accessed 13 May 2022.

Ministero dell'Interno. (2020). Coronavirus, i dati dei servizi di controllo. Interno.https://www.interno.gov.it/it/coronavirus-i-dati-dei-servizi-controllo, accessed 13 May 2022.

Ministero della Salute. (2020b). FAQ. Covid-19, questions and answers. Salute. http://www.salute.gov.it/portale/nuovocoronavirus/dettaglioFaqNuovoCoronavirus.jsp?lingua=english&id=230, accessed 13 May 2022.

Ministero della Salute. (2020c). Covid-19–Sicurezza dei lavoratori. Salute. http://www.salute.gov.it/portale/nuovocoronavirus/dettaglioContenutiNuovoCoronavirus.jsp?lingua=italiano&id=5383&area=nuovoCoronavirus&menu=vuoto, accessed 13 May 2022.

Ministero della Salute. (2020d). Coronavirus, nuovo decreto "#iorestoacasa" estende a tutta Italia limitazioni aree più colpite. Salute, 9 March. http://www.salute.gov.it/portale/news/p3_2_1_1_1.jsp?lingua=italiano&menu=notizie&p=dalministero&id=4184, accessed 13 May 2022.

Minstry of Economic Development. (2022). Economic profile. ICE. https://www.ice.it/en/invest/economic-profile, accessed 13 May 2022.

NoiOpen Community. (2020). Statuto. NoiOpen. https://www.noiopen.it/statuto/

OECD. (2010a). Review of the Italian national civil protection system. OECD, 4 May. https://www.oecd.org/italy/reviewoftheitaliannationalcivilprotectionsystem.htm, accessed 13 May 2022.

OECD. (2010b). Italy 2010b: Review of the Italian National Civil Protection System. Reviews of Risk Management Policies. OECD. https://read.oecd-ilibrary.org/governance/oecd-reviews-of-risk-management-policies-italy-2010b/analysis-of-italy-s-civil-protection-system_9789264082205-4-en#page, accessed 13 May 2022.

Pennisi, M. (2020a). App Immuni, Paola Pisano: L'ho scelta io assieme a Speranza. Pronta entro Maggio. Il Corriere della Sera, 17 May. https://www.corriere.it/tecnologia/20_maggio_17/app-immuni-paola-pisano-l-ho-scelta-io-assieme-speranza-pronta-entro-maggio-2badf3dc-9881-11ea-ba09-20ae073bed63.shtml, accessed 13 May 2022.

Pennisi, M. (2020b). Immuni, al via i test sull'app in tre Regioni. Il Corriere della Sera, 26 May, https://www.corriere.it/tecnologia/20_maggio_26/immuni-via-test-sull-app-tre-regioni-7ec9bd9a-9f1f-11ea-bcda-1b088225c4d4.shtml, accessed 13 May 2022.

Perrone, M. (2020). 15 task force per combattere il virus: ripartenza a rischio caos. Il Sole24ore, 24 June. https://24plus.ilsole24ore.com/art/15-task-force-combattere-virus-ripartenza-rischio-caos-ADMdEyK, accessed 13 May 2022.

Presidenza del Consiglio dei Ministri. Dipartimento della Protezione Civile. (2020). Emergenza Coronavirus: la risposta nazionale. Protezione Civile. http://www.protezionecivile.gov.it/attivita-rischi/rischio-sanitario/emergenze/coronavirus, accessed 13 May 2022.

Ramajoli, M. (2020). Governo, Regioni e Comuni: quale provvedimento prevale durante la ripartenza? Il Sole24ore, 1 May. https://www.ilsole24ore.com/art/governo-regioni-e-comuni-quale-provvedimento-prevale-AD6ZFuN?refresh_ce=1, accessed 13 May 2022.

Regione Lombardia. (2020a). Coronavirus – Ultimi provvedimenti. Regione Lombardia. https://www.regione.lombardia.it/wps/portal/istituzionale/HP/DettaglioRedazionale/servizi-e-informazioni/cittadini/salute-e-prevenzione/prevenzione-e-benessere/red-coronavirusnuoviaggiornamenti, accessed 13 May 2022.

Regione Lombardia. (2020b). Indicazioni sull'utilizzo dei test sierologici. Scheda informativa. Regione Lombardia. https://www.regione.lombardia.it/wps/portal/istituzionale/HP/DettaglioRedazionale/servizi-e-informazioni/cittadini/salute-e-prevenzione/coronavirus/test-sierologici-anticorpi-anti-covid19, accessed 13 May 2022.

Regione Lombardia. (2020c). AllertaLOM: l'app dell'emergenza Covid-19. Regione Lombardia, 16 June. https://www.regione.lombardia.it/wps/portal/istituzionale/HP/DettaglioRedazionale/servizi-e-informazioni/cittadini/salute-e-prevenzione/coronavirus/app-coronavirus/app-coronavirus, accessed 13 May 2022.

Reuters. (2020). Italy to defend 'strategic companies' from foreign takeover'. Reuters, 18 March. https://news.trust.org/item/20200318132807-7e67z, accessed 13 May 2022.

Save the Children. (2021). Una Rilevazione sulla povertà educativa digitale. Save The Children, 7 June. https://www.savethechildren.it/cosa-facciamo/pubblicazioni/una-rilevazione-sulla-poverta-educativa-digitale, accessed 13 May 2022.

Scaramuzzino, M. (2020). #iorestoacasa and Italy Called: Chronicle of a Country that Resists. Italiani.it, 16 March. https://www.italiani.it/en/iorestoacasa-and-italy-called-chronicle-of-a-country-that-resists, accessed 13 May 2022.

Scevola, C. (2020). WHO praises the Italian model in the fight against Coronavirus. Italiani.it, 2 July. https://www.italiani.it/en/who-praises-the-italian-model-in-the-fight-against-coronavirus, accessed 13 May 2022.

Servizio Studi della Camera dei Deputati. (2020a). L'impiego delle forze armate nella fase 1 dell'emergenza COVID-19. Temi Camera, 21

April. https://temi.camera.it/leg18/temi/l-impiego-delle-forze-armate-nell-emergenza-covid-19.html, accessed 13 May 2022.
Servizio Studi della Camera dei Deputati. (2020b). Misure sull'emergenza coronavirus (COVID-19). Quadro generale. Camera, 27 June. https://www.camera.it/temiap/documentazione/temi/pdf/1203754.pdf?_1588279335853, accessed 13 May 2022.
SoftMining. (2020). SM-COVID-19. La prima app italiana di contact tracing. SmCovid19. https://www.smcovid19.org, accessed 13 May 2022.
Thompson, S. A. and Warzel, C. (2019). Twelve million phones, one dataset, zero privacy. New York Times, 19 December. https://www.nytimes.com/interactive/2019/12/19/opinion/location-tracking-cell-phone.html, accessed 13 May 2022.
Vodafone. (2020). Vodafone launches five-point plan to help counter the impacts of the COVID-19 outbreak. Vodafone, 18 March. https://www.vodafone.com/news-and-media/vodafone-group-releases/news/vodafone-launches-five-point-plan-to-help-counter-the-impacts-of-the-covid-19-outbreak, accessed 13 May 2022.
Zinzocchi, R. (2020). Ecco perché Immuni non serve e non funziona. Orwell.live, 16 May. https://www.orwell.live/2020/05/16/ecco-perche-immuni-non-serve-e-non-funziona, accessed 13 May 2022.

First 100 Days of Hungarian COVID-19 Policies

Ádám Kerényi and Weichen Wang

1 Hungary and the Covid Pandemic

1.1 Hungary and Covid Outcomes

In this chapter, we provide an overview of the structural conditions of Hungary, the state of the nation prior to the COVID-19 pandemic together with policy projections made at the time, in order to identify the significance of early pandemic policies and structural conditions. In the second section, we provide a historical narrative of democracy and civil activism in the Hungarian context before and during the initial stages of the pandemic to account for the context in which specific policy decisions were made. In the third section, we provide an account of the shift in surveillance from a state-controlled surveillance. In the fourth section, we consider the shift in economic policy adopted at important

Á. Kerényi (✉)
Hungarian Academy of Sciences Centre of Excellence, Budapest, Hungary
e-mail: kerenyi.adam@eco.u-szeged.hu

W. Wang
University of Bath, Bath, UK
e-mail: ww469@bath.ac.uk

A. Stojanović et al. (eds.), *The First 100 Days of Covid-19*,
https://doi.org/10.1007/978-981-19-6325-4_6

phases of Hungary's post-Communism development concluding with the pandemic. In the fifth section, we focus on the labour policy objectives along this trajectory showing how they increasingly sought to protect and empower labour, although mass unemployment continues to be a significant challenge for the nation. In the sixth and seventh section we consider the historical dynamic related to the significant infrastructural gaps in the health and education sectors, respectively, as it was impacted by the pandemic. Along the previously identified lines, in both of these sectors we observe an impetus from the pandemic which led to a shift in momentum that reinforced socially oriented policies that were put in place prior to the pandemic. Finally, we conclude by summarising different aspects of the gradual shift in policy making.

Hungary is a small country, poor in raw materials, and comprising of a population of only ten million. It is free of civil war, popular uprisings, and terrorism. It has neither become involved in any local wars nor has it been threatened by immediate bankruptcy. So why should we pay attention to what is going on there? As the late Professor Janos Kornai described, the reason is twofold. Firstly, Hungary deserves attention, because as a member of NATO and the European Union, it has begun to turn away from what was perceived as the great achievements of the 1989–1990 transition from dictatorship to democracy, the rule of law, a freely functioning civil society, and pluralism in intellectual life; and started attacking private property and the mechanisms of the free market. Moreover it is doing so in the shadow of increasing geopolitical tensions. Secondly, since Hungary became a member of the European Union CEE and the Baltic group, the country experienced an unprecedented capital inflow of EU-funds. Historically, there have been important checks on the Hungarian government's power even under extraordinary circumstances. In the Hungarian political system, the main actor that engages in the regulatory response to Covid-19 is the National Assembly, under the leadership of Prime Minister Viktor Orbán, whose party (FIDESZ) has had a supermajority (two-thirds) in the National Assembly since 2010 (Kornai 2015). The 4th Orbán-government introduced a constitutional state of exception. In Hungary the State of Emergency and the special mandate of the government have been extended until 30 June 2022.

Compared to other countries, Hungary had a moderate level of excess deaths from January 2020 to March 2021 (Wang et al. 2022). Excess death during the pandemic is mainly made up of direct and indirect deaths caused by Covid. For the case of Hungary, most deaths during the pandemic were caused by people catching Covid-19 and subsequently dying from it directly. A small proportion of death is caused by medical system overload during the pandemic. People who needed surgery or access to the hospital might have died due to the Covid-19 response absorbing the resources that would ordinarily have been available to tend to their medical cases. On the bright side, the Covid pandemic might have saved some lives in Hungary. Social distancing rules and restrictions for combating Covid-19 might have protected some people from catching seasonal flu, decreasing excess mortality. Moreover, many traffic accidents might have been prevented during the lockdowns in Hungary, which again reduced excess death to a small extent.

Economically, Hungary had a moderate to low level of economic losses compared to other countries (Fig. 1). Economic loss is defined as the GDP growth rate adjusted for additional fiscal spending during the pandemic. The average GDP growth rate of Hungary from January 2020 to March 2021 is around 4.8%. Total additional fiscal spending was 9.2% of GDP during the same period; 2.8% of the GDP was spent on health and 6.4% of the GDP was spent in non-health sectors. Hungary spent moderately in non-health sectors. Due to the relatively low level of GDP loss during the pandemic, there was little incentive for the Hungarian government to spend heavily in non-health sectors to save the economy.

1.2 Relevant Structural Conditions for Hungary

For geographical structural conditions, Hungary has seven neighbouring countries which is relatively high compared to other nations. Therefore, border control and testing during the pandemic was crucially important for Hungary, as Covid-19 could spread during the transportation process through the trade of goods. People entering Hungary through borders might also increase infection risks, so tight border controls were in place during the time when Covid cases peaked. Border controls became even more critical when other restrictions are lifted as the population becomes more vulnerable without the restrictions. This is especially true for Hungary as it has many bordering countries, thus bearing higher risks.

For economic and health structural conditions, Hungary had a moderate to high level of tax revenue. Therefore, the government had enough budget to spend. Hungary also had a moderate to high level of government debt. High government debt levels could limit how much

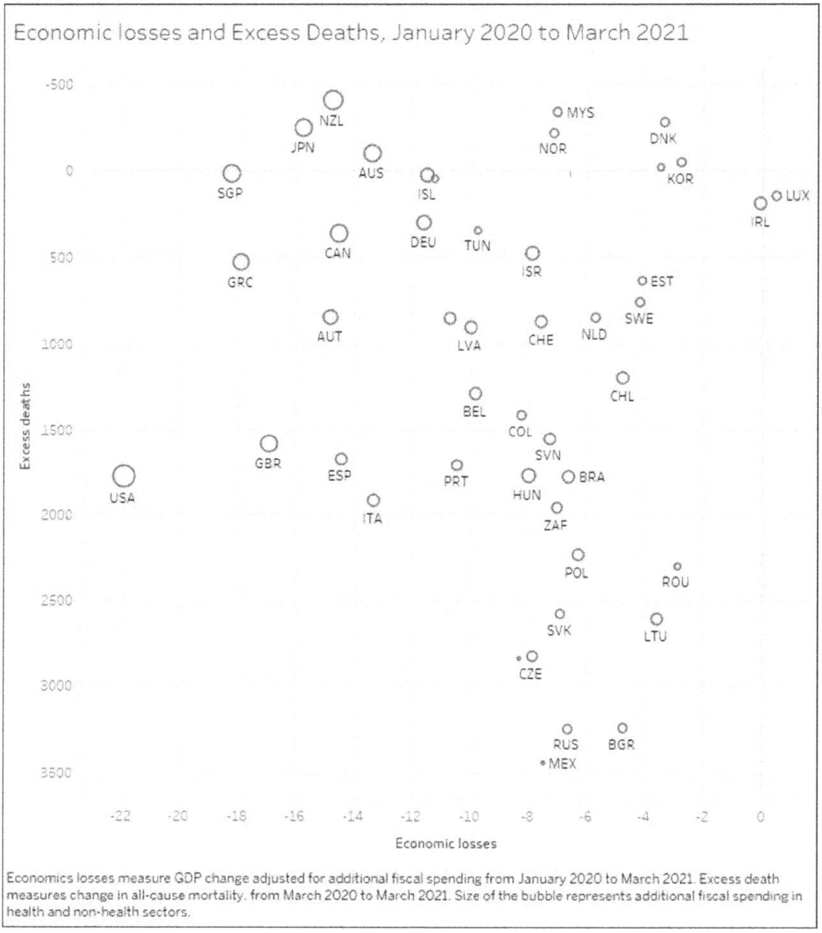

Economics losses measure GDP change adjusted for additional fiscal spending from January 2020 to March 2021. Excess death measures change in all-cause mortality. from March 2020 to March 2021. Size of the bubble represents additional fiscal spending in health and non-health sectors.

Fig. 1 Economic losses and excess mortality, January 2020 to March 2021 (Wang et al. 2022)

a government can spend during the pandemic. In some instances, high government debt might indicate that the government has decent credibility to pay back its debt. Moreover, when government debt is too high, the country might be trapped in a debt crisis such as in the case of Greece. In contrast, Hungary does not have a credibility issue and was not in a debt crisis before the pandemic. Hungary relies heavily on the trade of goods and less on the trade of services. This is a poor structural condition as the trade of goods was severely interrupted during the pandemic, which will directly damage the economy. Moreover, trade of goods might increase transmission risks during the pandemic through logistics and transportation. A strong testing system such as having drive-through testing open to all asymptomatic people could help reduce such risks. Unfortunately, Hungary did not have a high testing capability during the pandemic. Hungary mostly had testing available to people showing Covid-19 symptoms but did not have much open public testing available such as drive-through testing. On the other hand, heavy reliance on the trade of services is a desirable structural condition as more people could work from home and their income would be less affected. For Hungary, this is not the case, thus more people might have an incentive to take on risks by continuing to work in person at their offices as they cannot work at home. This is further proved by looking at the estimated share of jobs that can be done from home before 2020. Hungary has a relatively low share of jobs that can be done from home. Finally, Hungary has a relatively low Gini index, thus the inequality level is relatively low in Hungary.

To better understand the structural issues of Hungary before and after the pandemic in more detail, the article selected several important socioeconomic topics which will be discussed below.

2 Democracy and Civil Activism

2.1 Democracy and Corruption Indicators in Hungary Pre-COVID-19

Hungary was relatively corrupt according to the corruption perception index in 2019 (Transparency International 2022). Corruption is a poor structural condition for the pandemic, as it might reduce the incentive for the government to save lives and the economy. Policy measures and fiscal spending might be over-reported, health performance might be under-reported. However, despite being relatively corrupted, Hungary did not under-report its Covid death judged by the difference between reported Covid death and excess death (Wang et al. 2022).

2.2 Democracy and Legal Challenges in a Post Pandemic Age

The state of danger regime was introduced on 11 March 2020 in response to the coronavirus situation. State of danger is a special form of extraordinary legal regime which can only be introduced and withdrawn by the government. While a state of danger is in force, the government can rule by decree and does not need parliamentary approval. In addition, the Act XII of 2020 on the Containment of the Coronavirus (hereafter: Coronavirus Law) provided the Hungarian government with a *carte blanche* mandate without any sunset clause to suspend the application of Acts of Parliament, derogate from the provisions of Acts, and take other extraordinary measures while the "state of danger" declared on 11 March by government Decree 40/2020 (III. 11.) is in place.

The Coronavirus Law, however, abolished the validity limit, because previously the decrees the government adopted during extraordinary periods were only valid for 15 days. Once expired, the parliament had to extend the validity of these acts, otherwise they automatically became invalid. From 1 April 2020 decrees adopted by the government remained in force only until the government decides to terminate them.

Since the adoption of the coronavirus law, the Hungarian government has been subjected to intensive international criticism. On 31 March 2020 Sophie in't Veld, a Dutch liberal MEP, who chairs the European parliament's rule of law group, said: "*Viktor Orbán has completed his project of killing democracy and the rule of law in Hungary. Clearly, the actions of the Hungarian government are incompatible with EU membership*". Without mentioning Hungary, European Commission President Ursula von der Leyen advised that measures for controlling the pandemic should be "*limited to what is necessary and strictly proportionate*", and "*not at the expense of our fundamental principles and values as set out in the treaties*". (…)The message from Washington was more direct. Eliot L. Engel, the chairman of the US House of Representatives' foreign affairs committee, said Orbán was making "*a blatant power grab in the face of the worst global health crisis in recent history. This legislation marginalises the Hungarian parliament and allows Prime Minister Orbán to rule by decree like a dictator. Such a serious affront to democracy anywhere is outrageous, and particularly within a NATO ally and EU member*" (Rankin 2020). Orbán's supporters argued the law did not give the Hungarian government any more power than similar laws across Europe. They said it was proportionate and could be rescinded at any time by parliament or reviewed by the constitutional court. "*They said there is an unlimited authorisation for the Prime Minister. This is not true, this is fake, this is a lie*" the Minister of Foreign Affairs told Euronews in an interview.

An important check on the government's power during a state of danger has been that the government could issue decrees only on issues specifically delineated in the law on disaster management (Act CXXVIII of 2011), but not on anything else. The Coronavirus Law abolished this constraint. After adopting the Coronavirus Law, the government of Viktor Orbán may regulate any issue it pleases with government decrees, as long as it can come up with an argument to prove that the given measure is somehow related to the coronavirus crisis (Rácz, 2020). According to Article 2(1) of the Coronavirus Law, during the state of danger, the government may, in addition to the extraordinary measures and regulations set forth in the Disaster Management Act, "suspend the application of certain Acts of Parliament, derogate from the provisions of Acts and take other extraordinary measures by means of a decree, in order to guarantee for citizens the safety of life and health, personal safety, the safety of assets and legal certainty, as well as the stability of the national economy". According to Article 2(2), the government may exercise this power "for the purpose of preventing, controlling and eliminating the human epidemic" referred to in Government Decree 40/2020 (III. 11.) on Declaring a State of Danger, and for the purpose of "preventing and averting its harmful effects, to the extent necessary and proportionate to the objective pursued". Thus, the Coronavirus Law first explicitly prescribes the application of the principles of necessity and proportionality. Secondly, the law sets out that the government may exercise its powers for certain, widely formulated purposes related to the state of danger. This very broad framework should serve as a yardstick when reviewing the constitutionality of each government decree (HHC 2020).

3 Surveillance and Security

3.1 Pre-COVID-19 Surveillance and Security

The Covid pandemic is very different from standard social-economic shocks such as financial shocks or wars. Therefore, like many other governments, Hungary did not have much pandemic experience. Due to lack of experience, the Hungarian government also did not have much pandemic surveillance before the pandemic. Lack of pandemic experience and the absence of surveillance left Hungary vulnerable to the unexpected Covid shock.

3.2 Surveillance in a Post Pandemic Age

The Coronavirus Law was adopted by the Hungarian Parliament on 30 March 2020. As of 1 April 2020, the extraordinary powers of Viktor Orbán's government have become de facto unchecked both in terms of duration and content. Duration of the state of danger depended solely on his government (and on the parliament, firmly controlled by him), which can rule with decrees that remain in force until they themselves decide to relinquish this power.

As of July 15, 2020, the government of Hungary introduces entry restrictions. Countries are classified into "red", "yellow", and "green" categories, based on the severity of the COVID situation in each. Hungarian citizens and their relatives can enter Hungary from a "green" country without a health check. A Hungarian citizen coming from a "yellow" or "red" country will be subjected to health checks at the border and must be quarantined for 14 days. An exception to this is if they can credibly show two negative coronavirus tests 48 hours apart in the previous 5 days. A Hungarian citizen coming from a "yellow" country may be released from quarantine after the first negative coronavirus test, but if coming from a "red" country, two negative tests are required. In the case of non-Hungarian citizens, those coming from a "yellow" country can enter under the same conditions as Hungarian citizens, but it is not possible to enter Hungary from a "red" country.

4 Challenges and Constraints on the Hungarian Economy

4.1 Pre-COVID-19 Economic Policy

The 2008–2009global crisis hit the Hungarian economy when it was very vulnerable. Hungary's pre-crisis growth model relied on excessive indebtedness in an unfavourable structure, affecting the state, households (through foreign exchange lending), and companies alike. The country's macroeconomic equilibrium indicators were unfavourable, and in addition to the unsustainably high government debt to GDP, and external debt, Hungary was characterised by a twin deficit, i.e. the simultaneous deficits of public finances and of the current account. In 2010, in addition to the debt crisis, Hungary faced an internal credit crisis, and the unemployment rate also rose to a high level. The macro-financial equilibrium and economic growth entered their respective crises simultaneously. The fiscal turnaround was an essential element of the new growth model. Financial rebalancing was fundamentally conditional on a disciplined budget and a reduction in debt indicators. Economic policy recognised the need to support budgetary revenues with a new tax structure. Between 2010 and 2018, Hungary recorded the sharpest fall in EU member states in the effective personal income tax rate, and, after Latvia, the second sharpest fall in the employer tax wedge. As a result of the new incentives, the domestic labour market has undergone a spectacular transformation. The Hungarian unemployment rate, which exceeded 11% in 2010, decreased to 3.4% by the end of the decade. Debt stocks decreased from historic heights to favourable levels by the end of the decade. Fiscal reforms resulted in a return to budgetary equilibrium from 2012, with gross government debt to GDP ratio falling from above 80% to around 65% by 2019. In 2009, Hungary's net external debt amounted to 54.1% of GDP, its highest debt ratio in 70 years. By the end of the decade, the country's net external debt dropped to around 8% of GDP owing to the economic policy model that sought to maintain equilibrium. Few countries succeeded in reducing public debt simultaneously with the debt of the private sector. Through a significant increase in debt stocks and the sovereign debt crisis in the euro area, the 2008–2009crisis drew attention to the trap of debt-financed growth models. Nevertheless, in the years following the recession, most of the countries saw debt increases or merely rearrangements between the private sector and the state (MNB 2021).

4.2 *Post COVID-19 Economic Prospects*

The Hungarian government has taken effective measures to protect the economy. According to the calculations of the Ministry of Finance, government measures boosted GDP growth by 5.5% in 2020. The government announced the first phase of its three-stage Economy Protection Action Plan on 18 March 2020: reduction of social security contributions, tax cuts, and support for private entrepreneurs as well as moratoria on loan, credit, and lease payments. Hungary has come to an agreement with the European Commission concerning the fact that it may provide state funding with no upper limit to enterprises that realise investment projects in the interests of protecting workplaces. A maximum of half the volume of the investment may be awarded in funding, meaning that in the case of a EUR 1. 6 million foreign investments, an enterprise will be eligible to receive EUR 800 thousand in funding (*Hungary Today* 2020).

The Hungarian Forint (HUF) weakened to historic levels, its exchange rate: 367 HUF/EUR (+8.0% since 28.02.2020)/325 HUF/USD (+5.5% since 28.02.2020) (updated on 14.12.2021). Successful USD and EUR bond issuances on 14 and 15 September 2021, which was the highest international issue amount of Hungary ever, with an oversubscription of 4 times, showed stable investor confidence in Hungary.

Job-related measures included: (i) preserving jobs, (ii) job creation, (iii) protection of priority sectors, and (iv) reduction of the tax burden on employers. The financing of companies and households included: (i) payment moratorium, (ii) interest rate subsidies and guaranteed loans, (iii) State guarantee programme, and (iv) State capital funds and other loan programmes.

Under Article 53 of the Basic Law (the Constitution of Hungary), the government is entitled to issue such decrees to fight the consequences of a natural disaster if a state of danger is formally declared by the government. However, the Constitution itself limits the scope of these decrees for fifteen days, unless the government, based on authorisation by the National Assembly, extends those decrees. Under the Act on the protection against disasters, the content of the decrees is also limited to explicit emergency measures such as restrictions on the movement of citizens. The government had declared a state of danger due to the pandemic on the 11th of March, but on the 30th of March 2020—right after the end of the 15-day time limit of the first emergency measures—the Parliament adopted the Act XII of 2020 on the containment of the coronavirus. The Act had significantly broadened the latitude of the government: the 15-day time frame was de factolifted (the Parliament had given preliminary consent for all future governmental decrees in the Covid-19 state of danger), while the government was entitled to issue state of danger decrees for any regulation topic. Such a decree is only required to be "in order to guarantee that life, health, person, property and rights of the citizens are protected, and to guarantee the stability of the national economy, to the extent necessary and proportionate to the objective pursued".

The Orbán government has adopted 104 state of danger decrees so far, 92 of which were published after the Coronavirus Act. A significant number of the measures are only indirectly linked with the pandemic, such as the fiscal and financial measures to protect the economy, while some of them—like the ones stripping local municipalities (in general or by even naming them) of some of their powers and incomes—were pandemic-related in name only. However, most of the decrees were also not promptly applicable by their nature, so Parliament—which was constantly in session from the beginning of the pandemic—would have been in the position to regulate the wide range of matters in the decrees, from the special rules on judicial proceeding to the limitations of GDPR rights and access to information during the state of danger.

The Minister of Foreign Affairs and Trade issued a decree on 16 April 2020, announcing a new, HUF 50 billion subsidy scheme to improve competitiveness in the face of the coronavirus epidemic. Medium-sized and large enterprises may apply for a subsidy from the HIPA (Hungarian Investment Promotion Agency) for investments worth over EUR 150 thousand—provided that they undertake to maintain existing jobs—if they can prove that their economic difficulties are attributed to the negative impacts of the current pandemic.

The Central Bank of Hungary announced a new version of the Funding for Growth Scheme for micro, small, and medium-sized enterprises providing a total of EUR 4.2 billion (HUF 1500 billion) in funding, and a total of EUR 1.2 billion (HUF 450 billion) for the Bond Funding for Growth Scheme for large enterprises. In addition, through measures aimed at boosting the liquidity of the banking system and other measures, the Central Bank provided HUF 3 thousand billion in fresh funding for the protection of the financial system. In June 2021 the Monetary Council announced a base rate increase cycle to secure price stability. All in all, after 180 bps hike in the base rate (the latest, December rise was 30 bps), the base rate is now 2.40%, while in December the overnight deposit rate was increased by 45 + 80 bps to 2.4% and the overnight and one-week collateralised lending rates were increased by 105 + 30 bps to 4.4%. The one-week deposit rate was raised to 3.6% and functions as the key interest rate. The Hungarian central bank reintroduced its swap facility providing foreign currency liquidity, it provided funds through this instrument for the SME sector with favourable and predictable interest rates to maintain jobs and production capacities and to finance their investments. As a replacement of the FGS and part of its new green instruments strategy, from October 2021 MNB introduced the Green Home Programme for the retail sector with a framework of HUF

200 billion. The loan programme is available for building or buying new flats with at least BB energy efficiency-grade. At its December meeting, the Monetary Council decided to close the Bond Funding for Growth Scheme and its government securities purchase programme. Although occasional and targeted government securities purchases can happen in the future if necessary. The Monetary Council terminated the use of the long-term collateralised lending facility in July 2021. MNB introduces a limited, occasional, and short-term central bank discount Bill that supports the effective sterilisation of liquidity in the financial system. The effectiveness of monetary policy transmission is also facilitated by the modification of the foreign exchange balance ratio (FXBR) regulations by the MNB's Financial Stability Council, which provides more room for banks' activity at the FX swap market.

The Hungarian Development Bank (MFB) and its affiliates (MFB Group) are set to make available to Hungarian businesses a financing package in a total amount of EUR 4.1 billion (HUF 1490 billion) via harmonised loan, capital and guarantee programmes designed to offset the economic impact of the coronavirus epidemic and help relaunch the economy. The programmes come with an 80% state guarantee. The loan programmes can be used to satisfy the short-, mid-, and long-term financing needs of businesses. While the MFB Crisis Loan assists primarily micro and small enterprises (maximum loan amount of EUR 423 thousand (HUF 150 million) at a 2.5% annual interest rate), the MFB Competitiveness Loan Programme is an effective tool primarily for large companies and mid-size companies that are planning to implement major investments. In the framework of the Garantiqa Crisis Guarantee Programme, domestic SMEs and large enterprises can get access to financing in the amount of EUR 141 million (HUF 500 billion) with a 90% government guarantee. The SME Rescue Capital Programme may give a lifeline to struggling SMEs with low capital, while the Startup Rescue Capital Programme may give rapid assistance to successful start-ups that have stalled as a result of the crisis. The Crisis Capital Programme provides financing to distressed strategic companies for purchases and development projects.

When preparing the 2020 budget, the government set a 1% deficit target by anticipating a 4% economic growth and a 2.8% inflation rate, which corresponds to a 1.1% structural deficit. Practically, this would have meant the fulfilment of the medium-term objective established for Hungary. However, the unfolding global coronavirus pandemic is causing significant economic challenges both domestically and internationally, which is expected to result in a deterioration of the budget situation. Since the macroeconomic and fiscal conditions changed as a result of the global pandemic, it is necessary to deviate from the 2020 budget.

The Hungarian government adjusted the accrual deficit target of the 2020 budget from 2.7% of the GDP to 3.8% of the GDP because of the unfavourable economic outlook caused by the COVID-19 pandemic as well as fiscal policy actions intended to mitigate its economic impact. Accordingly, the funding requirement of the central budget increased to HUF 1890 billion. Due to the increased funding requirement and the changed market situation, the Government Debt Management Agency Pte. Ltd. (ÁKK) published the modification of the 2020 financing plan on May 26, 2020. As of July 1, 2020, 60% of the actual 2020 financing plan was completed.

The pandemic-related and economy protection measures implemented by the government affect both the income and expenditure side. In order to provide the resources required for the measures, the government reallocated funds of thousand billion forints from appropriations where savings are expected to occur in the current situation, or where funding may be delayed due to the nature of the given appropriation. The discretionary expenditure items used for the reallocations represent nearly one-third of the central government budget (budgetary organisations, chapter-managed appropriations). It is important to highlight that instead of uniformly cutting specific budget appropriations, a rearrangement took place which, on the one hand, ensures the availability of funds actually necessary within the ministries' budget, and, on the other hand, sets up two funds from the sources released—one for addressing the pandemic situation (Disease Control Fund—DCF) and one for relaunching the economy (Economy Protection Fund—"EPF"). The main source of the Fund for Combatting Pandemic comes from the merger of the Country Protection Fund ("CPF") with total reserves of HUF 378 billion. This is supplemented by the reallocation of 50% of the political parties' subsidy, the newly introduced retail tax, the motor vehicle tax channelled into the central budget from local governments' budget, the contribution of the financial sector and other reallocations. These all resulted in a total funding capacity of HUF 634 billion for the DCF at the time of its founding. The funds released thanks to the savings imposed on ministries are reallocated into the EPF; the combination of these funds and the National Employment Fund give the EPF a total funding capacity of

HUF 1346 billion. Revenues were mostly determined by the processes that commenced prior to the emergence of the pandemic.

On 7 April 2020, the government announced the second phase of the Economy Protection Action Plan. An Epidemic Containment Fund and an EPF were set up and five schemes were launched: job protection, job creation, financing of enterprises, protection of families and pensioners, as well as key sectors' programmes to be implemented in the third phase of the Action Plan. As a result of measures announced so far, the deficit-to-GDP ratio is expected to increase from 1 to 3.8%.

The Hungarian Central Bank unveiled a package of measures to help mitigate the economic fallout of the novel coronavirus outbreak. The measures will be worth 3000 billion forints (EUR 8.3 billion), equalling 6% of GDP. The central bank will make up to 1500 billion forints of cheap and stable financing available to the SME sector in the framework of a programme dubbed Funding for Growth Scheme Go! It will include 500 billion forints that have not been drawn down under the NBH's earlier launched FGS fix programme. FGS Go! will operate with the same conditions as earlier FGS phases: the NBH will continue to provide refinancing loans to banks at 0%, and interest to be paid by SMEs will be capped at 2.5%. Investment loans, including leases, will still be available, but the maximum maturity of refinancing loans will be set at 20 years in order to secure financing for protracted investment projects with a slower payback period.

Measures introduced to mitigate the consequences of the coronavirus pandemic on the Hungarian economy included the exemption of businesses engaged in certain activities (e.g. tourism, catering, entertainment, sport, culture, and passenger transport) between March and June 2020 from the payment of employer payroll taxes in regard to employed persons, while from among the employee payroll contributions, they are only required to pay the minimum amount of healthcare contribution in-kind. Small businesses engaged in specific activities are exempted from the payment of the small business lump-sum tax (KATA) between March and June 2020, and in the case of small business tax (KIVA) subjects, the staff costs paid during this period shall not be included in the calculation of their tax base. The tourism development contribution will not have to be paid in the period between March and June 2020. In the sectors most affected by the crisis, lease contracts regarding non-residential premises may not be terminated and rental fees may not be increased.

Enterprises may request a reduction of their taxes if faced with difficulties because of the pandemic. The amount of such tax reduction may reach HUF 5 million per enterprise. The deadline for submitting the annual reports and related tax statements (corporate tax, local business tax) and paying the taxes was extended from 31 March 2020 to 30 September 2020. The social contribution tax will be cut from 17.5 to 15.5% as of 1 July 2020, while the rate of the small business tax (KIVA) will be lowered from 12 to 11% as of 1 January 2021 (Gov. Decree 47/2020; Gov. Decree 51/2020).

Despite the pandemic, new investments worth more than HUF 3600 billion have been announced since early 2020. Despite the coronavirus, the economy remains resilient to external financial shocks. Despite a temporary increase of the debt ratio, the government is committed to the reduction of public debt. Hungary improved by 5 places in World Competitiveness Ranking 2021 by Swiss-based IMD compared to last year. In addition to achieving the 3rd highest annual progress among all countries, Hungary is the only one that has been able to improve its ranking among Visegrád countries since the financial crisis. An all-time-high 53% of respondents chose competitive tax regime as the best key attractiveness indicator. Economic performance was ranked as 8th best out of 64 economies. As part of it, employment (13.) and international investments (10.) were outstanding.

Budgetary measures, including programmes launched by the Central Bank, reached in total almost 30% of GDP in 2020. Redesigning of budget at all levels: In view of the slower-than-expected recovery in 2020 and the measures taken to protect the economy, the budget deficit was 8.0% of GDP in 2020, which is slightly higher than the average of the EU member states. The budget deficit is expected to be 7.5% of GDP in 2021, based on the budget modification submitted to the Parliament. Use of reserve appropriations was made faster and more flexible. On 3 July 2020, the Hungarian Parliament approved the budget of economic protection. The 2021 budget provides HUF 2550 billion in the EPF for priority programmes, developments, and investments aimed at relaunching the economy, as well as measures related to promotion of employment. Another key pillar of the budget is the Health Insurance and Pandemic Protection Fund (EJEVA), which, in a renewed structure compared to 2020, contains the resources needed for pandemic control and the operation of the health care system in an amount of approximately HUF 3000 billion.

In April 2021, the government submitted amendments to the 2021 budget act that raised the accrual-based deficit target, calculated according to European Union rules, to 7.5% of GDP. The focus of the Bill is to maintain protection against the pandemic and to implement decisions that aim to jump-start the economy. The modification was necessary also because when the 2021 budget act was approved, in July 2020, the expected GDP path was different.

In December 2021, the government decided to postpone certain investments, thus significantly increasing Hungary's financial reserves by a total of HUF 350 billion this year, while reducing public debt.

In the 2022 budget, the government expects a dynamic economic growth of 5.2%, with a deficit target of 5.9% of GDP and public debt of 79.3% of GDP. The most important focus of the budget for 2022 is the relaunch of the economy, while preserving the achievements so far.

Next year not only the two-week—as the budget law stipulated—but also the full 13th-month pension will be paid to retirees.

5 The Labour Market

5.1 *Pre-COVID-19 Unemployment*

In the past decade, Hungary has been a top performer in the EU in terms of increasing employment rate: the employment rate of people aged between 20 and 64 years grew by 12.9% between 2008 and 2018, which is the second best figure among member states. All seven regions of Hungary recorded a double-digit increase, with three regions (Northern Great Plain, Northern Hungary, Southern Great Plain) experiencing a higher than 15% growth in employment.

The employment rate of the 20–64 age group stood at 75.3% in 2019, which means that Hungary managed to achieve the 75% employment rate target defined in the Europe 2020 Strategy. The government aims to further increase the number of employed persons in 2020 by mobilising labour force reserves, that is, primarily by bringing disadvantaged groups including people in public employment, inactive persons and jobseekers, young people, women raising small children and retired persons, back into the labour market. As a result of government measures, the participation rate—following further increase—reached 71.9% in 2018, which took place in parallel with the expansion of employment and the moderation of the unemployment rate to 3.6%. In addition to the increase of employment by 48,000, the number of public workers declined by 46,000 in 2018.

5.2 *The Future of the Hungarian Market*

In announcing the national lockdown measures, the Hungarian government published new regulations and policies to stimulate the economy.

A first wave of fiscal measures was introduced earlier in the epidemic, including, on the revenue side, measures to alleviate the fiscal burden on businesses: (i) employers' social contributions were lifted in the most affected sectors; (ii) the health care contributions were lowered through June 30; (iii) around 80,000 SMEs (mainly in the services sector) were exempt from the small business tax (the payment of the tax by other companies in affected sectors will be deferred until the end of the state of emergency); (iv) the tourism development contributions will be temporarily cancelled; (v) media service providers will be given a tax relief for incurred losses of advertising revenue; and, (vi) procedures for collecting tax arrears will be suspended during the state of emergency. On the spending side, about HUF 245 billion (0.6% of GDP) was reallocated to the healthcare sector.

On April 16, the government introduced three new export support measures through the state-owned Eximbank: (i) EUR 800,000 grant for investments of export companies; (ii) preferential working capital loans, and (iii) a new guarantee and insurance scheme. On April 23, a state-owned development bank MFB launched a HUF 1490 billion package of financial support instruments for companies, consisting of three loan products, two guarantee instruments, and four capital programmes. On May 7, the government announced it will purchase up to HUF 150 billion (0.3% of GDP) of bonds issued by banks in order to support lending during the crisis and to ensure financial stability. Interest-free loans to SMEs will be available from June 12. Half of the programme's budget will be available for investments, while the other 50% is intended to finance liquidity and operations. The highest amount available for investments is HUF 150 million, while asset and liquidity financing loans are capped at HUF 300 million.

The Széchenyi Card Programme designed to support the liquidity of micro, small, and medium-sized enterprises is also going to be modified in order to mitigate the impacts of the coronavirus on SMEs, allocating HUF 2.9 billion for products specifically designed to alleviate the crisis. The measures include several areas. According to the government plans, the economic rescue package's size—including three rounds of measures—will be circa 18–20% of the Hungarian GDP. The measures can be summarised into four aspects. The first aspect is job protection. The state financed 70% of the employees whose full-time jobs were transformed into part-time jobs due to the spread of the Covid-19. The support only applies to firms where the demand fell by 15–50%. People employed in research and development areas will get 40% extra salary support from the government for three months. In this case, full-time employees are also entitled to this support. The second aspect is job creation. In order to create new jobs, the Hungarian government supports new investments, the estimated value of these investments is 450 Billion HUF. The third aspect relates to sectoral subsidies. Supported sectors include government communication, tourism, health care, food processing industry, agriculture, construction sector, transport sector, logistics, creative, and the film industry. The final aspect involves financing for enterprises, the value of favourable credit lines and guarantees is 2.000 Billion HUF (Xin 2020).

In November 2021, the number of registered jobseekers decreased by 18% compared to November 2020. The unemployment rate has remained low during the whole pandemic period. The number of registered jobseekers went below 243 thousand in November 2021. The government has so far helped more than 1.6 million employees. Various subsidy programmes protected 844 thousand jobs. The R&D wage subsidy programme protected 38 thousand jobs, wage subsidies in tourism contributed to retaining more than 180 thousand jobs. More than 78 thousand new jobs have been created through various government programmes. The job creation programme supported 33,655 low educated and young employees. In October 2021, the number of employed persons exceeded 4.67 million while the unemployment rate was 3.8% (EU-27 average: 6.7% in September).

Despite dynamic wage growth, wage adjusted labour productivity is the highest in Hungary among EU countries.

5.3 *Economic Resilience Action Plan in 2020—Immediate and Medium-Term Measures to Create as Many Jobs as the Coronavirus Destroys*

Job-related measures included: (i) preserving jobs, (ii) job creation, (iii) protection of priority sectors, and (iv) reduction of tax burden for employers. To retain jobs, in addition to wage subsidies, the government also supports businesses and employees with taxation instruments and interest-free credit in sectors affected by restrictions (these are detailed in the Taxation and Business development chapters). The enhanced flexibility of labour law rules also serves job retention, enabling modification of the work schedule to the extent necessary and the ordering of working from home or teleworking. To achieve full employment, in the coming years the Recovery and Resilience Facility ("RRF") of the European Union aimed at eliminating negative social and economic consequences of the coronavirus pandemic will finance substantial State public investments, which will ensure continuous orders until Q3 2026 in the construction and renewable energy sectors playing a key role on the labour market, while the implemented infrastructure will create new jobs (GoH 2021).

6 Health Care

6.1 *Pre-COVID-19 Health Care Infrastructure*

The key health indicators of Hungary have been improving in the past decade. Infant mortality fell from 5.3 to 3.4 between 2010 and 2018 for every 1000 live birth, while life expectancy at birth showed a slight increase from 74.38 years to 75.94 years. According to Eurostat data, the number of healthy years expected at birth grew by 3.6 years to 61.1 years. Women are expected to live 4.1 years longer in good health, while the number of healthy years for men grew by 3.2 years. As a consequence of these favourable developments, Hungary has improved its ranking from 23rd to 15th place, approaching the EU average (63.6). Between 2010 and 2018, the per capita health care spending on purchasing power parity increased by 23%, while the number of practising doctors per 10,000 people went up by 20%.

The health of the Hungarian population is not in a good state; despite an increase in both life expectancy at birth and in healthy years in recent years, the figures are still below the EU average. The government aims to promote a healthy lifestyle, ensure the availability of screening to the extent possible, and improve the accessibility and quality of primary care. To fulfil these goals, the boosting of the primary care systems—with a focus on public health—is a central element of the new sectoral strategy (GoH 2021). Hungary did not suffer from the SARS pandemic and not many people died in the H1N1 pandemic. It is reasonable to conclude that Hungary did not have much pandemic experience (for the government and individuals). Hungary has a high level of smoking prevalence which is a poor health structural condition. Hungary also has a high cardiovascular disease death rate, which could result in high excess deaths during the pandemic. This is possible via two channels. First, people who need heart surgery or access to emergency services might struggle during the pandemic, led to a lower survival likelihood. Second, people with heart disease might be less likely to survive if they are infected by Covid-19. Moreover, Hungary has moderate to high level of diabetes prevalence, which is again a poor health structural condition.

6.2 *Health Care Infrastructure in a Post Pandemic Age*

The government of Hungary launched its official webpage and official Facebook page about the novel coronavirus, both on 4 March 2020. The data on the epidemics dynamic and testing are released daily on the government websites.

The Hungarian government's coronavirus response has angered doctors—and created rare tensions within the country's ruling coalition. In early April 2020 the government ordered hospitals to ensure that over 30,000 beds were available in less than a fortnight. That sparked chaos and outrage, as medical staff began calling relatives to take patients home. The Hungarian Medical Chamber, the country's main professional association of doctors, warned the government in a letter that "uncertainty and tension" are growing within the health system. The Hungarian government said that its aim was to ensure that 50% of beds—a total of 32,900—were free by April 19, 2020, and in a later phase raise the number of available beds for coronavirus patients to 39,500. On 22 April 2020, the country's chief medical officer announced that 50% of beds had been freed up. For Hungary's doctors, the order to empty beds created a moral dilemma (Bayer 2020).

Experience related to managing the coronavirus epidemic underscored the vulnerability of the current health care system. As the key element of the new management system, the National Directorate General for Hospitals (NDGH) was established in November 2020 as a central office with a separate budget, also taking over functions of the earlier National Healthcare Service Centre (NHSC). The NDGH is responsible for monitoring the operation of the health care system, laying the groundwork for strategic government decisions relating to its review; in this process it takes part in developing a single and transparent new national health care management system. Within the scope of its diverse functions, it enforces, or—by also providing methodological assistance—procures enforcement of and verifies fulfilment of requirements relating to public functions, and the regular and efficient management of resources.

The financing structure of health institutions will also change. As opposed to current area-based distribution, more flexible, dynamic, case-based financing frameworks will be introduced, which follow patient movements and professional particularities. The projected annual budget is based on the assessment of case numbers of the previous year. In contrast to distribution in the past, the new financing structure is even more adapted to monitoring patient needs and the performance of service providers, enabling payments by the health insurance body based on work actually performed. The reform of the public financing structure adapted to actual health care needs improves the efficiency of allocation, resulting in substantial progress in the sustainable management of institutions carrying out additional functions.

To ensure professional support for enhancing the efficiency of health care financing, in the 2021 period of the technical support instrument of the European Commission, the Ministry of Human Capacities submitted an application entitled "Joint improvement of the efficiency and quality of health care services". The project aims to test the possibility of introducing batch financing methods, integrating several levels of care, and the drawing up of a new concept relating to national (qualitative) management (GoH 2021).

The Hungarian health care system is struggling with enormous challenges relating to human resources; the profession is ageing at a rapid rate, and there is significant outward migration of young and middle-aged physicians. The government is attempting to reverse the negative trend with wage raises, surplus financing of the basic health care system, and by improving the working and living conditions of rural general practitioners. The government has raised physicians' wages in several steps in recent years, which has moderately reduced their outward migration, but continuation of this process is essential. As an encouraging sign, in the 2015 and 2020 age structure, the number of new generation physicians in the 25–29 and 30–34 age groups is increasing. If efforts to keep younger physicians within the health care system are successful, the distribution of age groups may even out in 20–25 years, putting an end to the years-long trend of a shortage of physicians.

Act C of 2020 on health service status ("Health Service Status Act") entered into force on 1 March 2021 to resolve the problem of out-migration of physicians; it provides more transparent employment conditions for physicians entering into a contractual relationship, and an unprecedented wage raise implemented in three phases. The government has planned a budget of HUF 300 billion for implementing the phased wage raise programme. The act regulates in detail the employment of health care workers; under such regulation, health care activities may be carried out by health care providers only within a legal relationship of health service. Workers employed by health care providers operated by the State or local authorities on the effective date of the act, who agreed to the new legal relationship, fall within the scope of the act. The act is applicable to public servants working in both primary care and specialty care. Pursuant to a milestone provision of the act entering into force on 1 January 2021, the provision and acceptance of informal payment constitutes a criminal offence. The elimination of informal payments from the system ensures equal access to health services for all Hungarian citizens.

In a separate decision, the government is providing HUF 96.1 billion in additional funds in 2021 to people working in general medical practices, affecting around 18,400 physicians, dentists, and health care professionals in primary care with a total financing requirement of HUF 96.1 billion in 2021. The wage subsidy will first be paid in early April 2021, retroactively including January 2021; its amount is adjusted to physicians' and health care professionals' pay grades, therefore the amount of subsidies will increase from 1 January 2022 and 1 January 2023 (a wage raise valid from 2022 has been resolved in relation to health care professionals) (GoH 2021).

The Hungarian vaccination campaign was launched on 26 December, when the first vaccine delivery arrived. Vaccination is voluntary and free; vaccination registration is offered on the www.vakcinainfo.gov.hu website. Upon appointment by the Operational Group, the Vaccination Working Group monitors vaccination progress and expected vaccine deliveries. Based on the vaccination programme, the first vaccines for immunity were administered to health workers, followed by residents of retirement homes, the elderly, people with chronic illness under the age of 60, workers employed in law enforcement and critical infrastructure, kindergarten, school and nursery employees, and then the registered population under the age of 60, whose vaccination is still under way. Up to 16 April, Hungary contracted more than 31 million vaccine doses, which is enough for vaccinating 17.6 million people. Among the contracted vaccines, currently 5 types (Pfizer, Moderna, AstraZeneca, Sputnik, and Sinopharm) are available, and the contracted Janssen and Curevac vaccines will also be soon available. On 23 April the number of people receiving at least one dose passed 3.5 million, which was the second highest vaccination rate in the European Union at the time. To keep the vaccination programme on schedule, an online time reservation system was launched on the same day, where all registered and unvaccinated citizens can reserve a place and time for vaccination. As the number of registered people passed 4.3 million in the final week of April, the government launched a promotional campaign to increase their number. With the current vaccination speed, all those citizens who registered were very likely to have received their first vaccination by the first week of May. After 5 million administered vaccines new regulations are to be put in place allowing for much more freedom, among them annulling the obligation to wear a mask in public places.

The digitisation of health care is a key priority in the Hungarian health sector; the government will support this process in the coming period with a number of measures and tenders. The main goal of these digitisation projects is the improvement of efficiency in preventive care, diagnostics and patient care by use of information and communication technologies. During the restrictions introduced in relation to the epidemic, the writing of e-prescriptions—already used on a wide scale last year—and the retrieval of patient data from the Single Health Platform proved to be of significant assistance. In April 2020 the multi-stage drafting of the legislative background of telemedicine care—not requiring the personal presence of patients—commenced. By establishing options for telemedicine, the rate of contact by telecommunications significantly increased during the COVID-19 epidemic. In response to the coronavirus epidemic, the government of Hungary launched the Health Industry Aid Programme with the aim of developing the production of pharmaceutical products and medical devices in Hungary with a HUF 50 billion budget to support the investments and development of Hungarian enterprises.

Based on the decision of the government, the National Coronavirus Vaccine Plant will be established in cooperation between the University of Debrecen and the National Public Health Centre; production of the Hungarian coronavirus vaccine is expected to begin at the end of next year. The National Public Health Centre is establishing the National Security Laboratory with a budget of HUF 12 billion financed by the EU and Hungary. As a unique leading institution in the region, it will have the task of identifying new, hazardous pathogens, to conduct immunological and disease progression research, and to participate in the testing of new vaccines (GoH 2021).

7 Conclusion

The Hungarian Parliament adopted a new Bill which increased the government's powers during the coronavirus pandemic. The Coronavirus Law allowed Viktor Orban's government to extend the state of emergency indefinitely, even if the spread of COVID-19 made it impossible to sit in Parliament. At the time of the first wave of the epidemic, the Coronavirus Law showed well the crisis of the Hungarian state. Through this law it was not the health protection or the economic crisis that followed the epidemic that was better resolved, but the intimidation of dissenting members of society, the looting of local governments and the enrichment of a narrow circle of power. When the Hungarian government announced that it would end the state of emergency and return its special powers to parliament, critics described the move as a political ploy: at the same time as the emergency was lifted, parliament also voted in favour of a draft law on a new, so-called "state of medical emergency". According to this Bill, the government would be able to govern by decree again in such a case, with even less control than before. Both Bills were adopted by Parliament on 16 June 2020. While government officials have trumpeted the government's intention to withdraw the powers on June 20, and demanded apologies from those who criticized Hungary's coronavirus law, an analysis of the new Bill by lawyers from several Hungarian NGOs suggests that it makes possible the declaration of a "state of medical emergency" without parliamentary approval which would grant the government powers similar to those granted by the Coronavirus Law. The Central Bank of Hungary (MNB) declared a moratorium on the installment payment of loans disbursed under the Funding for Growth Scheme (FGS); the MNB also decided to increase the scope of eligible collateral for corporate loans. As a result of these measures, the value of eligible collateral available for central bank operations grew by around 2600 Billion HUF. To sum it up, it can be argued that the Hungarian government and the MNB swiftly took the necessary economic measures to fight against the adverse economic effects of the Covid-19 pandemic. The size of the economic measures seems to be appropriate at this point.

The government responded to the special situation created by the new coronavirus epidemic in 2020 by carrying out a major restructuring of the budget and implementing a wide-ranging package of measures aimed at protecting the population and the economy. The Operational Group Responsible for Containment of the Coronavirus Epidemic was set up at the end of January 2020, is responsible for managing government measures related to the epidemic and for coordinating public bodies.

During 2020 the government introduced restrictions in consideration of epidemiological trends, aimed at protecting the population and preventing overload of the health system, with restrictions on the activity of economic operators to an extent calculated to enable rapid recovery after easing of the epidemic. In the middle of February 2021, the government launched online national consultations on the possible timetable of opening after lifting of restrictions related to the coronavirus epidemic. The majority of respondents (88%) supported a gradual opening. From 8 March 2021, to curb the rising third wave of the epidemic in Europe, the government again ordered tightened protective measures. According to such restrictions, shops were required to remain closed with the exception of shops selling essential goods (grocery stores, pharmacies, petrol stations, drug stores), all services were suspended (except for private health care, social, financial, postal, vehicle servicing services), and kindergartens and primary schools remained closed until 7 April, the end of the spring break. The evening curfew remained in force from 8 p.m. to 5 a.m.; exemption was granted only for documented proof of work. Wearing of masks was mandatory in all streets of residential areas and in public spaces. The government bound the lifting of restrictions to the vaccination rate of the population. The first step of loosening—determined by the government by decree—was 2.5 million vaccinated people. The population reached the required vaccination rate in early April; within the framework of introduced easing measures, the period of the curfew was shortened (from 10 p.m. to 5 a.m.), and shops were allowed to open with a limited number of customers (1 customer per 10 square metres). The opening hours of shops were extended to 9:30 p.m., but catering establishments were still permitted to only offer take-away meals. Kindergartens and lower levels of primary schools reopened on 19 April. Restrictions were to be further lifted after reaching a vaccination rate of 3.5 million, followed by 4 million people. The fixed reopening timetable aimed to enable businesses to plan ahead for the coming period.

References

Bayer, L. (2020) Hungarian doctors question coronavirus response. Politico, 24 April, https://www.politico.eu/article/hungarys-doctors-question-coronavirus-response/, accessed 13 May 2022.

Government of Hungary (GoH). (2021) 2021 National reform programme of Hungary. GoH, April, https://ec.europa.eu/info/sites/default/files/nrp_2021_hungary_en.pdf, accessed 13 May 2022.

Hungarian Helsinki Committee (HHC). (2020) Background note on Act XII of 2020 on the containment of the coronavirus. HHC, 31 March, https://www.helsinki.hu/wp-content/uploads/HHC_background_note_Authorization_Act_31032020.pdf, accessed 13 May 2022.

Hungary Today. (2020) Coronavirus: Govt to launch new programme to support Hungarian businesses. *Hungary Today*, 4 July, https://hungarytoday.hu/coronavirus-govt-to-launch-new-programme-to-support-hungarian-businesses/, accessed 13 May 2022.

Kornai, J. (2015). Hungary's U-Turn. *Capitalism and Society* 10 (1).

Magyar Nemzeti Bank (MNB). (2021) Growth report. MNB, https://www.mnb.hu/letoltes/novjel-2020-eng-digitalis.pdf, accessed 13 May 2022.

Rácz, A. (2020). Hungary's "Coronavirus Law": How Power Becomes Unlimited? Retrieved from: https://icds.ee/en/hungarys-coronavirus-law-how-power-becomes-unlimited/

Rankin, J. (2020) Hungary's emergency law 'incompatible with being in EU', say MEPs group. *The Guardian*, 31 March, https://www.theguardian.com/world/2020/mar/31/hungary-emergency-law-incompatible-with-being-in-eu-say-meps-group-viktor-orban, accessed 13 May 2022.

Transparency International. (2022) Corruption perception index 2019. Transparency International, https://www.transparency.org/en/cpi/2019/index/nzl, accessed 13 May 2022.

Wang W., A. Gurgone, H. Martínez, M. C. Barbieri Goes, E. Gallo, Á. Kerényi, E. M. Turco, C. Coburger, and P. D. S. Andrade. (2022) COVID-19 mortality and economic losses: The role of policies and structural conditions. Paper presented at the Extended Problem Solving Workshop; 23 April 2021, Waterloo, Canada subsequently published as: Wang W., A. Gurgone,

H. Martínez, M. C. Barbieri Goes, E. Gallo, Á. Kerényi, E. M. Turco, C. Coburger, and P. D. S. Andrade. (2022) COVID-19 mortality and economic losses: The role of policies and structural conditions. *Journal of Risk and Financial Management* 2022 (15): 354. https://doi.org/10.3390/jrfm15080354.

Xin, C. (2020) Central and Eastern Europe's responses to the coronavirus pandemic. China-CEE Institute, May, https://china-cee.eu/wp-content/uploads/2020/07/08_pdf_PANDEMIC-final01.pdf, accessed 13 May 2022.

Purchasing Time: The First 100 Days of German COVID-19 Policy

Michael W. Müller and Annalisa Tassi in collaboration with Niklas Döbbeling and Friederike Hildebrandt

1 Introduction

The following chapter analyses the first 100 days of German COVID-19 policy with a specific focus on the legal and economic responses to the immediate outbreak of the Coronavirus and the accompanying public debate. It shows that, while there have been demanding measures against the spread of the virus from the beginning on, first studies suggest a high

The paper is based on reports submitted in August 2020 on the basis of questionnaires drafted by the editors of this volume. The reports are available at http://globalresponsescovid19.com/. Literature that appeared later was occasionally taken into account.

M. W. Müller (✉)
University of Mannheim, Mannheim, Germany
e-mail: m.mueller@uni-mannheim.de

A. Tassi
FAU Erlangen-Nürnberg, Erlangen, Germany
e-mail: annalisa.tassi@fau.de

A. Stojanović et al. (eds.), *The First 100 Days of Covid-19*,
https://doi.org/10.1007/978-981-19-6325-4_7

level of compliance with such measures (Sect. 2). At the same time, significant material support was provided in the form of financial relief for businesses and individuals (Sect. 3). With the crisis further progressing it has, however, been criticized that the relief measures were neither able to fairly distribute the full burdens of the pandemic nor could they be upheld for long without endangering public finances (Sect. 4). All this suggests that Germany, in the early days of the pandemic, was able to purchase time without, however, designing a sustainable framework for intervention and burden-sharing (Sect. 5).

2 COVID-19-Measures, Enforcement, and Surveillance

The German federal system rests on strong competencies on state and communal levels, particularly with regard to the law of emergency management and prevention (Thielbörger, 2021, pp. 95 et seqq.; Hering, 2020, pp. 150 et seqq.). The 2001 German Infection Protection Act (*Infektionsschutzgesetz*, IfSG) entails provisions enabling the state governments and local authorities to take measures to combat the spread of a virus, including curfews, business closures and quarantine orders (Overview for English-speaking readers: Klafki and Kießling, 2020). Already in the first months of the crisis, the IfSG was updated to provide for more specific responses to the specific circumstances of COVID-19 (Klafki, 2020; Kaiser and Hensel, 2021, paras. 14 et seqq.). Regarding concrete enforcement and surveillance measures, decisions have mostly been made by state governments and local authorities. Responses on state levels to some extent have been unified by suggestions and recommendations based on the assessment of a federal institute on medical risk assessment (Robert Koch Institute) and agreed upon between federal and state governments. However, there have been differences between various states regarding enforcement and surveillance techniques (in detail see Kaiser and Hensel, 2021, paras. 54 et seqq.).

All in all, in the early days of the pandemic in Germany, three phases of state reactions could be distinguished: a first, rather short period of recommendations and limited state intervention was soon followed by a phase of strict contact restrictions which then have been gradually relaxed. The following section analyses these three phases (Sect. 2.1) and describes how the transition from the first to the second phase was accompanied by debates about the necessity of mandatory measures (Sect. 2.2).

Enforcement and surveillance have mainly been regarded as a public task (Sect. 2.3), including contact tracing as an important form of restricting the further spread of the virus, particularly when the strict measures of the second phase were loosened (Sect. 2.4).

2.1 Phases of Contact Restrictions

As mentioned above, within the first 100 days of the COVID-19 pandemic (the "first wave" of COVID-19 in Germany), three phases of enforcement measures could be distinguished: during the first, short phase from early to mid-March, the response to the first outbreaks of the COVID-19 in Germany mainly consisted of recommendations (social distancing and hygiene rules), closure of a growing number of public institutions (schools, universities) and leisure facilities, and cancellation of major events. Curfews were only set in place in local communities with a particularly high number of cases (in the following: Phase 1) (Kagermeier, 2020; Golia et al., 2021, pp. 162 et seq.). The second phase was characterized by strict contact restrictions enacted in all states following an agreement between federal and state governments, starting from 22 March 2020. While the terms of these restrictions differed between states, the main characteristics can be described as follows: strict rules of social distancing, closure of public institutions, leisure facilities, restaurants, and shops (except those serving daily needs). In six states (Bavaria, Berlin, Brandenburg, Saarland, Saxony, and Saxony-Anhalt), individuals were allowed to leave their households only for "legitimate reasons" including, however, commuting to work, consulting healthcare professionals, everyday shopping, and exercise in fresh air (in the following: Phase 2) (Schmitt, 2020, p. 1626; Guckelberger, 2020, p. 607; in detail Kaiser and Hensel, 2021, paras. 59 et seqq.). The adherence to social distancing rules and the closure of facilities was consequently monitored (Rebmann et al., 2020). In the third phase, starting from the end of April, the restrictions were slowly relaxed. However, the reopening of public life was accompanied by strict rules regarding hygiene rules in institutions and businesses, contact tracing, and the duty to wear masks in public transportation, restaurants, and shops (in the following: Phase 3). These rules, again, varied among states (Kaiser and Hensel, 2021, para. 58).

2.2 *Compliance*

The strict exit restrictions in Phase 2 were preceded by a short phase of recommendations for social distancing (Fürstenau, 2020). The duty to wear masks was enforced soon after a rather short period of recommendation and voluntary engagement (Gebauer et al., 2020). The Bavarian Minister President Söder referred to an alleged lack of compliance with the voluntary rules to justify the enforcement of strict exit restrictions (Lemkemeyer, 2020). In a press conference on 22 March 2020, Chancellor Angela Merkel reported that the overwhelming majority of the population had complied with the recommendations. To justify the new measures, she mainly referred to an alleged desire of the population for uniform rules (Die Bundeskanzlerin, 2020a). Vivid examples of voluntary engagement included the support and protection of particularly endangered individuals (Piltz, 2020), the introduction of hygiene rules in private businesses (Hoffmeyer, 2020) and many employers' consent to their employees working from home (von Blazekovic, 2020). In the society, concerns were raised against strict exit and contact restrictions regarding their consequences, e.g., for business owners, families, children, and individuals with psychological problems (Entringer et al., 2020; Huang, 2020; Huebener et al., 2020; Müller et al., 2020). Starting from April a growing number of people demonstrated against the restrictions, with some demonstrations, however, being led by conspiracy theorists and right-wing ideologists (Deutschlandfunk, 2020). The overall number of reported violations of restrictions was low, with a number of minor violations of social distancing rules particularly in cities (Frigelj, 2020). Mandatory measures were accompanied by public statements of leading policymakers on federal and state levels, referring mainly to the need to protect the most vulnerable groups of society and to prevent an overburdening of the healthcare system. In addition, there were media conferences informing on all developments on a regular, at times daily, basis (Fäßler, 2020).

2.3 *Enforcement*

According to the German Law on Combatting Infectious Diseases, violations of mandatory measures can be punished as criminal or administrative offences, depending on the degree of the respective violation (Kunst, 2020b). Fees have been imposed mainly upon individuals violating the restrictions by illegally opening restaurants or leisure facilities or meeting up in groups (Schmidt, 2020). In a small number of cases, individuals were arrested for continued violation of restrictions (Litschko, 2020). The enforcement policies varied significantly among states: from about 19 fines per 100,000 inhabitants in Berlin to 281 fines per 100,000 inhabitants in Bavaria until June 2020 (Kaiser and Hensel, 2021, para. 95 with further references). Only occasionally, have there been incidents of individuals reporting allegedly illegal behaviour to public authorities (Stutte, 2020). While there has been public criticism of major companies not implementing hygiene related arrangements (Frese, 2020), labour inspection took place only occasionally. The inspections were not made more frequent during the crisis and this has been criticized (Zeit Online, 2020). Only in special cases, additional inspections have been reported. In one case, a serious misconduct in a slaughterhouse led to the infection of above 1400 workers in a single factory. The factory could reopen only upon inspection (Manager Magazin, 2020).

2.4 Contact Tracing

Contact tracing was carried out mainly in two ways: Firstly, under the German Law of Combatting Infectious Diseases, public health authorities (*Gesundheitsämter*) are entitled to question individuals who were infected or had contact to infected persons. When questioned, individuals are obliged to report on their contact with infected persons. The health authorities may also require medical examinations of contact persons (Kunst, 2020a). Secondly, with exit restrictions being relaxed, owners of restaurants and leisure facilities were obliged to keep lists of individuals visiting their premises and to make those lists available upon request by state authorities (Härting, 2020). Symptom monitoring was mainly carried out in test stations (Gensing and Grill, 2020). However, the use of telemedicine was encouraged in order to help individuals distinguish COVID-19 symptoms from other illnesses. In particular, employees were temporarily allowed to rely on medical certificates on illness issued via telemedicine. Quarantine controls were carried out by public health authorities mainly via telephone control (Wiring and Schüngel, 2020). The extent of testing was continuously increased throughout the crisis with allocation criteria being modified over time (Gensing and Grill,

2020; Kühling and Schildbach, 2020). Thereafter, in June 2020, a tracing app was launched. Following public debate on privacy rights (see Kühling and Schildbach, 2020; Hamann, 2020), the use of the app has only been introduced on a voluntary basis (Rzepka, 2020).

Contact tracing and quarantine control have been carried out by public health authorities. In order to deal with the large number of cases, the personnel capacities of those authorities have been enlarged through secondments of officers from other authorities (Baars et al., 2020) and by hiring students as short-term assistants (Becker et al., 2020). The testing stations have been run or supervised by healthcare professionals and health authorities. In some cases, private parties have been engaged in organizing the tests and guaranteeing security of the test stations (Töngi, 2020). Private companies have been involved in the process of developing the voluntary tracing app (Klöckner, 2020). Also, as owners of restaurants and other facilities could be held liable for hygiene rules being observed in their premises, they were, to some extent, obliged to monitor the behaviour of their customers (Rosendorff and Meier, 2020). Besides this, no involvement of private actors in the enforcement of rules has been reported.

3 Preserving the Economic Structure

As part of the European Monetary Union (EMU), the monetary policy of Germany is directly under the control of the European Central Bank (ECB), while the federal government, the governments of the 16 states, and the local authorities affect fiscal and tax policy (Seitz, 2000). In order to confront the upcoming crisis, on 25 March 2020 the German parliament declared that the country was facing exceptional circumstances, thus allowing the government to issue more than 0.35% of nominal GDP in public debt.[1] In the second quarter of 2020, the forecast was that 156 billion Euro would be issued in public debt, which amounts to 4.5% of the GDP (EU Independent Fiscal Institutions, 2020).

This section presents the main policies targeting businesses, workers, and other groups, put in place to preserve the economic structure of the country, while safeguarding stakeholders' health. The section starts by describing the ECB and government's interventions (Sect. 3.1) and continues by describing business relief (Sect. 3.2) through taxation during the pandemic (Sect. 3.2.1), special subsidies (Sect. 3.2.2), and liquidity measures (Sect. 3.2.3) in more detail. Policies targeting employees

(Sect. 3.3), private households and the unemployed (Sect. 3.4), and measures aiming at safeguarding health in the workplace (Sect. 3.5) are the focus of the following subsections.

3.1 Financial Sources for Policy Intervention

After the debt-issuance decision by the parliament, policymakers were not particularly concerned about unfavourable borrowing conditions from the financial market, as Germany had not accumulated public debt for six years and could rely on a solid budget. Most of the new debt has a 20-year maturity or less, starting from 2023 (Süddeutsche Zeitung, 2020b).

Moreover, in March 2020 the European Central Bank (ECB) already announced its intention to support Member States by expanding its purchasing programmes. For example, the ECB has launched the temporary pandemic emergency purchase programme (PEPP), with a ceiling of 750 billion Euro (Deutsche Bundesbank, 2020). The Governing Council of the ECB has increased the envelope of the PEPP to 1350 billion Euro on 4 June 2020. The PEPP has been extended at least until the end of June 2021 (ECB, n.d.). The ECB has also eased the conditions of the third series of targeted longer-term refinancing operations (TLTRO-III) to support the provision of credits to the private sector (companies and households). The interest rates, on the other hand, have remained unchanged (Deutsche Bundesbank, 2020).

As of the end of May 2020, the ECB has bought 46,749 million Euro of German public sector securities, which makes up around one quarter of all PEPP purchases. These public sector securities have a weighted average maturity of about 3 years (ECB, n.d.). The ECB has also bought German corporate bonds (ECB, 2020). Additionally, the ECB holds 35,384 million Euro in commercial paper, but there is no further information on the distribution of such securities across Member States (ECB, n.d.).

The resources collected from the financial market would be used to finance the Economic Stabilisation Fund and to provide liquidity to people and companies. Individuals and companies have been granted liquidity in the form of grants, subsidies, publicly- backed loans, and guarantees. While these measures (for employees, self-employed, SMEs, and large companies) are discussed in more detail below, it is worth mentioning that the amounts made available and the risk assumption by the state-owned investment bank (KfW) vary with business size and seniority.

The 16 German states or the KfW and the regular banks have mostly managed the (online) applications to grants and benefits (BMF, n.d.). The applications have been simplified via reduced or ex-post checks in order to promptly provide liquidity. The need for simplification and promptness came with a toll, though. Many states have reported cases of fraud through fake websites, emails trying to extort sensitive data, and users falsifying their data in order to receive the grants. This has led to a slowdown and even to a temporary stop of the application procedures (Süddeutsche Zeitung, 2020a).

3.2 *Business Relief*

The German economy is export oriented, heavily reliant on the manufacturing sector, with automobile industry being the most prominent example (Grund et al., 2020). Moreover, 99.5% of all German businesses are SMEs (*Mittelständler*) (BMF, 2020b) and such smaller enterprises employ around 60% of the workforce (BMWE, n.d.). Before the spread of COVID-19 (last quarter of 2019), the German economy was already experiencing a period of zero growth in terms of GDP, with exports and automobile industry being the hardest hit by the slowdown (Inman and Wearden, 2020). It seems therefore relevant to discuss whether policy-makers have differently targeted businesses of different sizes or active in different sectors.

3.2.1 *Taxation*

This subsection discusses how taxation was temporarily adjusted to support businesses in distress. The federal government, together with state governments, has implemented a package of tax relief measures for self-employed and companies. Among others, tax relief measures have been adopted for the value added tax (VAT) and special bonuses. In order to reward hard-working employees, bonuses of up to 1500 Euro paid between March and December 2020 were tax-free (BMF, 2020a).

VAT on catering and restaurants was lowered from 19 to 7% (excluding beverages) from July 2020 to June 2021 (BMF, 2020c). The government has also decided to postpone the payment of VAT by publicly- owned companies until the end of 2022, granting them two more years to adapt their infrastructures. Merging companies or those changing their juridical form have more time to adapt to the taxation system (BMF, 2020c).

Another tax-relief measure regards short-time work, which was already in place before the pandemic. Until the end 2020, however, the receipt of short-time work salary of up to 80% of the net salary was to be untaxed, which was not the case beforehand (BMF, 2020c). The short-time work scheme was publicly subsidized in order to give employers enough incentives to keep their workforce. The employers were responsible for applying for the subsidies (BMF, n.d.).

Companies, which due to liquidity constraints were not able to pay their taxes (income, corporate, VAT), could apply for an extension of the payments, during which no interest would be charged. Such applicants had to demonstrate to the tax authority that they were directly affected by the crisis. The charges for late payments (i.e., for overdue taxes) were dropped until the end of 2020. This was valid for income tax, VAT, energy tax, air traffic tax, insurance tax, and corporate tax (BMF, 2020d).

Companies and self-employed could adjust the amount of their income and corporate tax advance payments if they expected their revenues to deviate from their previous predictions. In this case, companies and self-employed simply had to contact the tax authority and they could also apply for a reimbursement. Moreover, small enterprises and self-employed might apply for a liquidity-help in the form of a flat-rate reimbursement of taxes paid in 2019 and advance payments for the year 2020. The reimbursement occurred whenever the applicant could demonstrate to be incurring a loss during the fiscal year 2020, due to the pandemic. All the application periods mentioned above ran until the end of December 2020 (BMF, 2020d).

3.2.2 Special Subsidies

This subsection presents special subsidies related to Lufthansa and electric cars. Except for these two cases, policymakers had focused on the size of firms rather than the sector in which they operated, when designing relief measures. The decision of rescuing Lufthansa, for example, was based on the fact that the company was financially and operationally sound before the crisis (vulnerability criterion). The future prospects of the company were good and the government decided to support Lufthansa with a package of around 9 billion Euro in equity and debt. The package had been granted under the commitment that Lufthansa would achieve predetermined sustainability goals such as the renewal of its fleet (BMF and

BMWE, 2020). Another targeted measure was the increase of the e-car premiums, to boost demand for more environmentally- friendly cars. These premiums were subsidies by the federal government and by the producer to reduce the total cost borne by the buyer. The government-subsidized share doubled as of July 2020 and until the end of 2020 (Süddeutsche Zeitung, 2020c). Except for the case of Lufthansa and the e-car premiums, the other measures presented here did not typically entail climate or environmental targets.

3.2.3 Liquidity

This subsection presents the measures implemented to provide liquidity to companies, such as eased access to loans and grants for the self-employed. Starting from the first announcements in mid-March 2020, the German federal and state governments have begun rolling out policies under the Economic Stabilisation Fund to rescue businesses in financial distress. The Economic Stabilisation Fund, as active from the 30 March 2020, had a scope of around 800 billion Euro (Jennen, 2020). In addition to this, the German liquidity programme via the state-owned investment bank (KfW) initially had a scope of 465 billion Euro, which became unlimited (Grund et al., 2020).

As of June 2020, the government had taken no direct measure to prevent distress sales of domestic businesses via foreign direct investment (FDI). Although an indirect way of protecting domestic companies, was relaxing the bankruptcy procedure, thus lowering the incentives for distress sales. For the time being, companies experiencing cash-flow difficulties due to COVID-19 do not have to declare bankruptcy (BMF, n.d.).

Companies could apply for two different types of loans based on their seniority (i.e., years of activity). Loans could be of maximum 100 million Euro and could be used to cover acquisition and operating costs. Start-ups could additionally decide to opt out of the KfW's risk assumption thus obtaining longer time to maturity and adjustable interest rates (BMF, n.d.).

Some programmes were available to all companies, regardless of their size, like the KfW special loan programme (*Sonderprogramm*). The aim was to provide companies with liquidity for investment and operating costs in a quick and uncomplicated manner. The KfW offered loans with low interest rates and a simplified financing procedure. The programme was open to all enterprises, which were not under financial distress until the end of December 2019 (BMF, n.d.).

The main programme targeting large companies was the Economic Stabilisation Fund.[2] The package included guarantees (400 billion Euro), loans through the KfW (100 billion Euro), and equity stakes (100 billion Euro) (Jennen, 2020). The Fund was provisionally established until the end of 2021. Conditionality may apply to companies, for example with respect to the dividend or to the compensation policies (see BMF [n.d.] for details). Small and medium enterprises (SMEs) could have been granted access to the programme if they were key to the German economic infrastructure (Fincompare, 2020). The KfW also offered fast loans (*KfW-Schnellkredite*) to medium and large enterprises, which are 100% guaranteed by the KfW (BMF, n.d.).

The programmes targeting SMEs and self-employed were the immediate assistance programme (*Soforthilfen*) and the basic income support. The *Soforthilfen* are grants to self-employed and companies employing up to 10 people in full-time equivalents (FTEs). The applicants could receive up to 15,000 Euro for three months. The only requirement was proving that the business was not in financial distress before the end of December 2019, i.e., before the pandemic (BMF, n.d.). These grants do not have to be paid back. Self-employed people could also apply for basic income support in order to cover their housing and living expenses. To quickly ensure liquidity, these benefits should be handed out without the need of disclosing the financial situation, which would be nonetheless tested at a later point in time (BMF, n.d.). However, this apparent ease has been criticized by unions because of the heavy bureaucratic procedure (Ver.di, 2020b).

Some of the federal states and cities offered additional support to self-employed, especially artists, with lump-sum transfers between 400 Euro and 3000 Euro. These one-time payments did not seem sufficient to cover expenses in the medium run and they did not apply to all self-employed (Kiel, 2020: 15).

3.3 *Employees*

In order to prevent massive dismissals, the government has eased access to the short-time-work scheme during the pandemic. The replacement rate has also been increased for employees affected for longer periods (BMAS, 2020a).[3] For employees whose working hours are reduced by 50% or more, the replacement rate was increased to 70% (or 77% for parents) as of the fourth month of short-time work and to 80% (or 87% for parents) as of the seventh month. This scheme was planned to be in place between 1 March 2020 and the end of December 2020 (BMAS, 2020b).

Employees are further protected as follows: If an employee is quarantined or written ill according to the Infection Protection Act (*Infektionsschutzgesetz*) payments of wages have to continue up to six weeks. Other categories of employees are not so well protected from precarious working conditions: temporary agency workers, people with a *Minijob*, informal workers, etc.[4] Temporary agency workers fall under the short-term work scheme, but are not protected from being terminated within the framework of their contracts. Temporary agencies said that they suffered on average 90–100% loss of clients and almost 50% terminated contracts of employees, while 75% applied for the short-term work scheme (iGZ, 2020). *Minijob* contracts can be terminated within the normal notice of four weeks and are not covered by the short-time working scheme (Knappschaft Bahn, 2020). *Minijobs* often represent an additional source of income for students, parents and pensioners. These groups are already more likely to live under precarious conditions. Still, there have not been specific measures that compensate for the loss of *Minijobs* during the pandemic.

A solution has been proposed to support students. The Federal Ministry for Research and Education offered an interest-free support credit for students that suffer economic losses. German students can apply from May 2020, foreign students from June 2020. Furthermore, the requirements for the state support programme for students (*BAFöG*), that normally demands a certain amount of achievements per semester, have been lowered. Additionally, since June 16 students in acute distress can apply for an allowance up to 500 Euro for May, June, and July 2020 (BMBF, 2020). These measures have been criticized as insufficient to replace *Minijobs* and other forms of income, as well as the assumption that all students will be able to repay credits in the near future after the pandemic (Stendera, 2020: 9f.).

The effect of the pandemic on the informally employed has not been researched yet, even though the shadow economy is estimated to be worth 11% of the German GDP (Enste, 2017, p. 7). The majority of informal sectors were affected strongly by the contact limitations and businesses in such sectors applied for the short-time work, but this could only apply to formal employees (see Hammerschmid et al., 2020). The informal sectors were additionally affected by the closing of national borders, as some informal workers are non-German citizens, e.g., from other European countries.[5]

3.4 *Protecting (Unemployed) Households*

The government also introduced other measures targeting the unemployed and other vulnerable groups. For example, the conditions to apply for basic security benefits were eased, with two aims to[6] (i) allow access for larger groups of the population; and (ii) streamline the approval procedures. Unemployment benefits were extended by three months between 1 May 2020 and 31 December 2020 (BMAS, 2020d).

Social security benefits or other monetary transfers cover Germans and EU citizens who used to work in Germany (EU-Gleichbehandlungsstelle, 2020). Between March and September 2020 only labor income was considered for the provision of social security benefits, while capital ownership was disregarded (up to 60,000 Euro). This was supposed to give access to the benefits particularly to self-employed, who may own some business capital (BMAS, 2020c, 2020f).

Government policies have also targeted parents. Low-income parents could receive an additional support of up to 185 Euro a month without an assessment of means and property. This support scheme did not apply for unemployed parents, which has been criticized (Mängel, 2020). Furthermore, employed parents that lost earnings because of the closure of childcare facilities could receive additional compensation. Pregnant employees received the full maternity leave payments, even if they fell under the short-term work scheme (BMFSFJ, 2020).

Finally, the Federal Ministry of Justice and Consumer Protection has proposed and passed a regulation on the protection of tenants. Housing contracts could not be cancelled from April 2020 to July 2020 in case of missing rental payment by the tenant. If the tenant's income was affected by the pandemic, she would have had time until the end of June 2022 to pay back the missing rents. Private households with mortgages (or loans) could also postpone the installment payments in case their income has been negatively impacted by the crisis (BMJV, n.d.). For further discussion, see Zehner (2020), Ekkenga and Schirrmacher (2020), and Mahdi and Rosner (2020).

3.5 *Safeguarding Workers' Health*

The rather comprehensive package of liquidity responses has been put into existence in order to contain the negative effects of a simultaneous demand and supply shock in the economy. Beyond the financial support, quick interventions were necessary to ensure that production and essential services could be carried out, while containing the spread of the virus.

The Federal Ministry of Labour and Social Affairs published the "SARS-CoV-2 Occupational Safety and Health Standard", which applies to every workplace, i.e., employers are deemed liable for the implementation of such health and safety measures (BMAS, 2020e). The Federal Institute for Occupational Safety and Health and other entities are then responsible for adapting the general guidelines to specific cases (i.e., hair salons, gyms, etc.).

The main measures included in the guideline are home-office (which should be practised whenever possible), shifts (in order to work in small teams and easily respect distances), ventilation, and the use of personal protective equipment (PPE) and disinfectants (BMAS, 2020h). Workers with customer contact were protected by transparent plastic covers (dpa, 2020) or through a reorganization of processes (e.g., passengers were not allowed to enter buses next to the driver [rbb24, 2020]).

Businesses had to provide for their own supplies, there was no centralized support (BMAS, 2020h). All the costs incurred because of the pandemic may be financed through the loan programmes discussed above, if they fall into the category of operating costs. Otherwise, there are no extra subventions specifically targeting safety- or health-related expenditures.

One of the major challenges soon after the outbreak of the pandemic was that Germany experienced a shortage of disinfectants and masks. This led to a heavily criticized and promptly cancelled export ban of these products. Industrial networks abroad have been quickly exploited to import these products, but ministers have recognized the priority of moving medical production back inland (Wiedmann-Schmidt et al., 2020). Governmental decrees have also allowed the use of other raw materials for PPE, so that pharmacies and pharmaceutical industries could produce them by themselves (Bambauer, 2020). The textile industry started producing and selling their own masks and some breweries started donating alcohol or producing their own disinfectants (Korinth, 2020; Reinartz, 2020; Neuscheler, 2020).

Social consumption (such as indoor sport, cultural, and leisure activities) was the most heavily hit by the restrictions as these activities remained in many cases still closed or restricted as of June 2020.

4 A Moderate Public Debate, Its Reasons and Development

The previous sections have shown that in Germany rather strict restrictions of personal and economic freedoms were accompanied by a broad variety of relief programmes for businesses and employees. Besides the perceived necessity of the measures and the involvement of both renowned experts and interest groups in the political and public debate (Sect. 4.1), this combination might have been a major reason for an—in general—very moderate public debate in these early days. Only occasionally interventions have been significantly criticized or challenged. However, first traces of later discussions became visible: There have been demonstrations against too far-reaching restrictions of personal freedoms (Sect. 4.2); privacy concerns with regard to surveillance measures (Sect. 4.3); discussions about the fairness of burden-sharing in the pandemic (Sect. 4.4); and doubts that the relief programmes could be upheld in the long run without seriously endangering public finances (Sect. 4.5).

4.1 Expertocracy

From early on, national and state governments have consulted with both the Robert Koch Institute and independent experts on strategies of combatting the pandemic (Deutscher Bundestag, 2020). There have been early studies on the spread of the virus in areas with a particularly high number of cases (Streeck et al., 2020). There have also been studies carried out on the effectiveness of a duty to wear masks (Mitze et al., 2020). More general studies on the effectiveness and the efficacy of the measures have been started. A first assessment has shown a high effectiveness of school closures during the crisis (Dehning et al., 2020). Other studies have discussed the economic and social consequences of the restrictions showing, e.g., that young parents (Huebener et al., 2020; Müller et al. 2020) and people suffering from loneliness (Entringer et al., 2020, pp. 18 et seq.) have been affected particularly badly. While some of these studies were highly disputed (Auster and Linnhoff, 2020), the involvement of experts into the public debate can be seen as an important factor of keeping the overall discourse on a rational level and helping decision makers in balancing the various interests involved. Already at that time, however, traces of the later intensified debate on the role of experts (on this debate see Münkler, 2021) were visible.

Since the beginning of the pandemic, unions have been involved in conversations with the government about the economic effects of the pandemic (Die Bundeskanzlerin, 2020b), as well as later regarding specific issues as the support for the car industry (Bundesregierung, 2020) and the discussions around the rescue package for the airline Lufthansa and the possible dismissals of employees. In 2019, 5.9 million German workers (employees, self-employed, as well as students) were union members (DGB, 2020). Unions have been involved in the negotiations and consultations for the social security measures,[7] and they have been publishing critical evaluations of the situation (see DGB, 2020). Also, the increase of short-time work allowances to up to 80% was demanded by the unions (DGB, 2020) and later fulfilled by the government.

4.2 Criticism and Judicial Review

Also, from early on, some of the restrictions (see Sect. 2) have been challenged before administrative and constitutional courts. Some decisions led to major corrections of the restrictions, mainly in view of proportionality (Hering, 2020, pp. 155 et seqq.). For example, the Federal Constitutional Court declared exit restrictions unconstitutional which contained a blanket ban on religious service (BVerfG Beschl. v. 29.4.2020—1 BvQ 44/20, COVuR 2020, 92). It further stated that authorities are obliged to assess the individual circumstances before intervening in the fundamental right of freedom of assembly (BVerfG, Beschl. v. 15.4.2020—1 BvR 828/20, NJW 2020, 1426). When more nuanced restrictions were implemented from late April 2020 on (the “third phase” of contact restrictions, cf. Sect. 2.1), courts have paid close attention to ensure that those measures were implemented in a non-discriminatory manner and have declared unjustified differentiations, for example regarding different sorts or sizes of facilities, unconstitutional (VGH München Beschl. v. 27.4.2020—20 NE 20.793, BeckRS 2020, 6630; OVG Lüneburg Beschl. v. 14.5.2020—13 MN 165/20, BeckRS 2020, 8506; VGH München, Beschl. v. 19.06.2020—20 NE 20.1127).

In 2021, courts have published their final decisions on the early day interventions. While again some measures have been overruled as being unnecessary or overly restrictive (see in particular Bayerischer Verwaltungsgerichtshof, Beschluss v. 4.10.2021—20 N 20.767 on exit restrictions), most measures have been seen as justified under the German constitution given the speed of the dissemination and the uncertainties at the time of the outbreak (Bundesverfassungsgericht, Beschluss des Ersten Senats vom 19.11.2021—1 BvR 781/21 et al.; from the early scholarly debate, see in particular Kämmerer and Jischkowski, 2020, p. 352; Hase, 2020, p. 701).

With the pandemic further progressing, there have been serious demonstrations, including incidents of violent protests and criminal offences, from a group of individuals referring to themselves as *Querdenker* (a concept that translates best as "out-of-the-box thinkers"). While the targets of these protests changed over time—including questioning the existence of the Coronavirus and thus the overall necessity of state measures, challenging individual measures such as exit restrictions and the closure of public facilities, as well as concerns against vaccination—its early traces can be seen in demonstrations and protests starting from the first introduction of preventive measures (Deutschlandfunk, 2020).

4.3 Privacy Concerns

While the general debate has been very moderate in the beginning, the development of surveillance and contact tracing tools have been accompanied by privacy concerns from early on. For example, a tracing app was implemented only on a voluntary level (Rzepka, 2020) following an intense scholarly debate on privacy concerns regarding a tracing app (Kühling and Schildbach, 2020; Hamann, 2020). These privacy concerns have also been voiced with regard to the duty of restaurant owners and other facilities to keep lists of customers. It became known that police authorities made use of those lists in order to investigate unrelated offences (Sikora, 2020). Privacy issues with regard to modern technology in Germany are mainly governed by the Regulation (EU) 2016/679 of the European Parliament and of the Council of 27 April 2016 on the protection of natural persons with regard to the processing of personal data and on the free movement of such data, and repealing Directive 95/46/EC (General Data Protection Regulation) and the Directive (EU) 2016/680 of the European Parliament and of the Council of 27 April

2016 on the protection of natural persons with regard to the processing of personal data by competent authorities for the purposes of the prevention, investigation, detection or prosecution of criminal offences or the execution of criminal penalties, and on the free movement of such data, and repealing Council Framework Decision 2008/977/JHA which has been implemented into German law. Both frameworks in general limit the use of personal data to the original purpose of the processing (Sikora, 2020). The ongoing privacy debate may have been a major factor for contact tracing losing its role as a major tool of prevention in the further development of the pandemic. With vaccination being available, obligations to trace contacts were often replaced by entry regulations allowing access only for individuals that have been vaccinated or tested.

4.4 *Fairness of Burden-Sharing*

It is a general problem of distributional justice that benefits and reliefs granted to some are challenged as unfair by others. Therefore, it does not come as a surprise that relief programmes have been accompanied by debate and criticism. E.g., increased e-car premiums have been criticized as a measure that mainly boosts demand for foreign cars, as foreign car manufacturers supply 75% of the car models to which the premium can apply (Süddeutsche Zeitung, 2020c). Another criticism related to the fact that the subsidies are tax-financed and that a similar policy, the scrappage premium of 2009, only had marginal economic effects (Boerner, 2020). The public debate further revolved around the influence and bargaining power of the automotive industry, which might lead to an unjustified preferential treatment of this industry (Heuser and Nienhaus, 2020).

One concern, however, is of a more general nature: As many relief programmes specifically targeted the economy, it is to be feared that other sectors, working class individuals, and families might not receive fair compensation for the burdens they had to bear during the pandemic. Also, it was argued that the policies were not targeting unemployed individuals or people receiving social assistance have not been affected by the measures. Some criticism has been raised concerning the lack of measures specifically targeting the poor, as could be an increase of the basic security benefits (Fried, 2020). The access to the benefits also required a valid settlement or residence permit (Bundesagentur für Arbeit, n.d.), implying that undocumented migrants cannot benefit from them.

Since the beginning of the crisis, nurses and caregivers have complained about their working conditions. Their complaints were mostly directed towards politicians and not towards single employers. The complaints were twofold. In the beginning of the crisis PPE was becoming rare, which raised employees' concerns to get infected. Moreover, complaints about the organization and small salaries were reiterated (Szymanowski, 2020). Studies showed that workers in essential jobs receive hourly wages below the average hourly wage (Koebe et al., 2020, p. 3). With regard to this question, there have also been several smaller bottom-up initiatives. An example is the initiative "*Statt Blumen*" (Instead of Flowers), a campaign that emphasizes that gender-equality and equal pay for women in essential jobs should be supported instead of just gifting them flowers (Röders-Arnold and Starken, 2020).

From early on, the closure of schools and childcare facilities have been seen as over-proportionally affecting women. At the same time many women are working in sectors with higher health risks (e.g. health sector, care, food services, and retail) (Hammerschmid et al., 2020). The debates have been and are ongoing throughout the pandemic. All this shows that there will be a long way to go until a fair distribution of burdens is reached (see also Klauck et al., 2021, p. 745; Kersten and Rixen, 2021, ch. VII.1).

4.5 *Public Finance*

As many of the discussed programmes have been state-financed, a growing concern has centred around the question to what extent public finances can be strained during this time. While the government justified the far-reaching expenditures as temporary countercyclical measures, economists have warned that the crisis should not be taken as "an excuse" for unlimited public expenditures and low tax rates (Bofinger et al., 2020). Also, public expenditures should not be treated as a substitute for private demand (on the debate Bofinger et al., 2020).

In the early days of the crisis, the government was confident that there should not be a major concern that Germany might not be able to repay the debt incurred for fighting the pandemic. Once the economy would have recovered—the argument went—federal and state governments should be able to work on budget consolidation, with tax rates adjustments and so forth (Süddeutsche Zeitung, 2020b). Also, some economists were quite confident that the government could still issue 30-year bonds at favourable conditions (Süddeutsche Zeitung, 2020b).

The political opposition even expressed the wish of issuing debt with longer maturity (Funk, 2020). From early on, however, there were critical comments on the large amount of debt incurred, as compared to previous crises (Streck, 2020).

Later the question how to finance the costs of the pandemic—besides other expenditures, e.g., for social security benefits and the fight against climate change—has become a major debate in the election campaign and the government negotiations (Korioth and Müller, 2021, p. 960).

5 Conclusion

First assessments of Germany's early COVID-19 policy have regarded the governmental approach as "comparatively mild" (Golia et al., 2021, p. 163) and reported that "[d]uring the first wave, Germany was widely considered a poster-child for its approach in tackling the pandemic" (Thielbörger, 2021, p. 94). It is, indeed, remarkable that the restrictions and enforcement measures in the early days of the pandemic have been widely agreed upon in the political system and broadly accepted by the population. Our analysis suggests the economic response as a major reason for this acceptance: the German government has implemented several measures to pump liquidity into the supply side of the economy. At the same time, however, we have shown that such measures have been criticized for being neither comprehensive nor sustainable in the longer run. Also, it became visible that some of the later debates have already been foreshadowed in the early days of the pandemic (see also Thielbörger, 2021, p. 94). At least, however, the German government was able to purchase time which is not the worst response in the immediate outbreak of an international crisis. The longer the pandemic endures, it becomes more and more important to find an appropriate balance between personal freedoms and measures preventing the further spread of the virus. Also, the fair distribution of the economic burdens resulting from the pandemic is subject to future discussions. Moreover, a major societal task lies in not getting used to the leading role of the state in servicing general interest and deciding on individual lifestyle and risk assessment.

Acknowledgements The authors of this paper thank Niklas Döbbeling and Friederike Hildebrandt for the permission to draw on their report on "Employee relief and protection of work". We thank William Dean, Tom Ruppenthal, Tim Sennewald, and Talitha du Toit for helpful research assistance.

Notes

1. Since 2016, the structural federal deficit must not exceed 0.35% of the GDP by law. This rule is called "debt brake" (*Schuldenbremse*). The interested reader could refer to Truger and Will (2013), among others.
2. Large companies are defined as those with more than 249 employees, a balance sheet of more than 43 million Euro, and annual revenues of more than 50 million Euro (Fincompare, 2020).
3. For an employer to apply for this programme the share of employees facing a cut in working time (of at least 10%) was lowered from one third to a tenth of the staff (BMAS, 2020a).
4. Temporary agency is a subcontracted labour scheme characterized by employment by an agency, but working for another company. People with a Minijob work for up to 10 h per week and do not pay social security benefits.
5. The situation of foreign workers both formally and informally employed during the pandemics has been heavily discussed and criticized in the public debate. Better protection for them has been demanded by unions (Ver.di, 2020a) different associations (AbL, 2020), and the churches (Bönte, 2020).
6. The aim of these basic security benefits is to provide a "decent subsistence level". A single person receives 432 Euro for cost of living and 344 Euro for accommodation, which increases if the person has kids (BMAS, 2020g).
7. The first package of measures for Social Protection was passed by the government rather quickly only three days after its announcement (BMAS, 2020a; Deutscher Bundestag, 2020) The second package of measures for Social Protection was discussed and commented on by representatives of the Federation of German Trade Unions (DGB), German Employers Association (BCDA), Federation of Welfare Associations in Germany (Deutscher Paritätischer Wohlfahrtsverband), German Caritas Association (Deutscher Caritasverband), the Opposition and other surveyors in the committee on employment and social affairs (Deutscher Bundestag, 2020).

References

AbL (Arbeitsgemeinschaft bäuerliche Landwirtschaft e.V.). (2020). AbL Niedersachsen: Breites Bündnis fordert sofortige Schutzmaßnahmen für Arbeitsmigranten, April 3. https://www.abl-ev.de/apendix/news/details/?tx_ttnews%5Btt_news%5D=3117&cHash=b67160e747a378864a603b0ad66af2b1, accessed 16 May 2022.

Auster, O., and Linnhoff, C. (2020). SARS-CoV-2-Infektionen: Diskussion um Heinsberg-Studie. ÄrzteZeitung, April 13. https://www.aerztezeitung.de/Nachrichten/SARS-CoV-2-Infektionen-Diskussion-um-Heinsberg-Studie-408544.html, accessed 16 May 2022.

Baars, C., Grill, M., and Kempmann, A. (2020). Viele Ämter bleiben hinter Vorgaben. Tagesschau, May 14. https://www.tagesschau.de/investigativ/ndr-wdr/corona-gesundheitsaemter-103.html, accessed 16 May 2022.

Bambauer, A. (2020). Allgemeinverfügung zur Zulassung 2-Propanol-haltiger Biozidprodukte zur hygienischen Händedesinfektion aufgrund einer Gefahr für die öffentliche Gesundheit. Bundesamt für Arbeitsschutz und Arbeitsmedizin, March 4. https://www.bvmed.de/download/allgemeinverfuegung-2-propanol-haltige-biozidprodukte.pdf, accessed 16 May 2022.

Becker, K. B., Soldt, R., and Steppat, T. (2020). Die Virenjäger kämpfen am Telefon. Frankfurter Allgemeine Zeitung, May 4. https://www.faz.net/aktuell/politik/inland/studenten-helfen-als-containment-scouts-im-gesundheitsamt-16750156.html, accessed 16 May 2022.

Blazekovic, J. von. (2020). Der Siegeszug des Homeoffice. Frankfurter Allgemeine Zeitung, July 13. https://www.faz.net/aktuell/karriere-hochschule/buero-co/der-siegeszug-des-homeoffice-16859055.html, accessed 16 May 2022.

BMAS. (2020a). Gesetz zu befristeten krisenbedingten Verbesserung der Regelungen für das Kurzarbeitergeld, Bundesgesetzblatt 493 Teil I. https://www.bmas.de/SharedDocs/Downloads/DE/PDF-Meldungen/2020a/kurzarbeit-wird-erleichtert-gesetzentwurf-de-bundestags.pdf?__blob=publicationFile&v=8, accessed 16 May 2022.

BMAS. (2020b). Questions and answers relating to short-time work (Kurzarbeit) and skills development. https://www.bmas.de/DE/Corona/sozialschutz-paket.html, accessed 16 May 2022.

BMAS. (2020c). Sozialschutz-Pakete, Abfederung sozialer und wirtschaftlichen Folgen aufgrund der Corona-Pandemie. https://www.bmas.de/DE/Schwerpunkte/Informationen-Corona/Sozialschutz-Paket/sozialschutz-paket-artikel.html, accessed 16 May 2022.

BMAS. (2020d). Antworten zur Grundsicherung für Arbeitsuchende/Sozialschutz-Paket (SGB II) Häufige Fragen zum erleichterten Zugang zur Grundsicherung für Arbeitsuchende infolge des Coronavirus SARS-CoV-2 (Sozialschutz-Paket), Vereinfachte Vermögensprüfung aufgrund § 67 Abs. 2 SGB II. https://www.bmas.de/DE/Schwerpunkte/Informationen-Corona/Fragen-und-Antworten/Fragen-und-Anworten-zugang-sgb2/faq-zugang-sgb2.html;jsessionid=31A104B2763B97022B08245B64368035, accessed 16 May 2022.

BMAS. (2020e). Arbeitsschutz und Arbeitsschutzstandard während Corona. https://www.bmas.de/DE/Schwerpunkte/Informationen-Corona/Arbeitsschutz/arbeitsschutz.html, accessed 16 May 2022.

BMAS. (2020f). Häufige Fragen zum erleichterten Zugang zur Grundsicherung für Arbeitsuchende infolge des Coronavirus SARS-CoV-2 (Sozialschutz-Paket), Vereinfachte Vermögensprüfung aufgrund § 67 Abs. 2 SGB II. https://www.bmas.de/DE/Schwerpunkte/Informationen-Corona/Fragen-und-Antworten/Fragen-und-Anworten-zugang-sgb2/faq-zugang-sgb2.html;jsessionid=31A104B2763B97022B08245B64368035, accessed 16 May 2022.

BMAS. (2020g). Leistungen zur Sicherung des Lebensunterhalts. https://www.bmas.de/DE/Themen/Arbeitsmarkt/Grundsicherung/Leistungen-zur-Sicherung-des-Lebensunterhalts/2-teaser-artikelseite-arbeitslosengeld-2-sozialgeld.html, accessed 16 May 2022.

BMAS. (2020h). SARS-CoV-2 Occupational Safety and Health Standard. https://www.bmas.de/SharedDocs/Downloads/DE/PDF-Schwerpunkte/sars-cov-2-arbeitsschutzstandard-en.pdf?__blob=publicationFile&v=2, accessed 16 May 2022.

BMBF. (2020). Zuschuss für Studierende in akuter Notlage kann ab Dienstag beantragt werden, Pressemitteilung: 078/2020. https://www.bmbf.de/de/zuschuss-fuer-studierende-in-akuter-notlage-kann-ab-dienstag-beantragt-werden-11820.html, accessed 16 May 2022.

BMF. (n.d.). For Jobs and the Economy: Immediate Assistance Programme and Economic Stabilisation Fund. https://www.bundesfinanzministerium.de/Content/EN/Standardartikel/Topics/Priority-Issues/Corona/2020-04-01-immediate-assistance-programme-economic-stabilisation-fund.html, accessed 16 May 2022.

BMF. (2020a). Sonderzahlungen jetzt steuerfrei. https://www.bundesfinanzministerium.de/Content/DE/Pressemitteilungen/Finanzpolitik/2020a/04/2020-04-03-GPM-Bonuszahlungen.html, accessed 16 May 2022.

BMF. (2020b). Gemeinsame Pressemitteilung: Bundesregierung beschließt weitergehenden KfW-Schnellkredit für den Mittelstand. https://www.bundesfinanzministerium.de/Content/DE/Pressemitteilungen/Finanzpolitik/2020b/04/2020-04-06-gemeinsame-pm-bmf-bmwi-kfw.html, accessed 16 May 2022.

BMF. (2020c). Gezielte Unterstützung in der Corona-Krise: Schnelle Umsetzung steuerlicher Hilfen für Gastronomie und Beschäftigte in Kurzarbeit. https://www.bundesfinanzministerium.de/Content/DE/Pressemitteilungen/Finanzpolitik/2020c/05/2020-05-06-Hilfen-Gastronomie.html, accessed 16 May 2022.

BMF. (2020d). Steuerliche Hilfen für Unternehmen und Beschäftigte. https://www.bundesfinanzministerium.de/Content/DE/Standardartikel/Themen/Schlaglichter/Corona-Schutzschild/2020d-03-19-steuerliche-Massnahmen.html, accessed 16 May 2022.
BMF and BMWE. (2020). The Federal Government Agrees on Financial Support Package for Lufthansa. https://www.bmwi.de/Redaktion/EN/Pressemitteilungen/2020/20200525-the-federal-government-agrees-on-financial-support-package-for-lufthansa.html, accessed 16 May 2022.
BMFSFJ. (2020). Corona-Pandemie Finanzielle Unterstützung, https://www.bmfsfj.de/bmfsfj/themen/corona-pandemie/finanzielle-unterstuetzung, accessed 16 May 2022.
BMJV. (n.d.). Kündigungsschutz für Mieter und wichtige Zahlungsaufschübe für Verbraucher und Kleinstgewerbetreibende, https://www.bmjv.de/DE/Themen/FokusThemen/Corona/Miete/Corona_Miete_node.html, accessed 16 May 2022.
BMWE. (n.d.). The German Mittelstand: Facts and figures about German SMEs. https://www.bmwi.de/Redaktion/EN/Publikationen/wirtschaftsmotor-mittelstand-zahlen-und-fakten-zu-den-deutschen-kmu.pdf?__blob=publicationFile&v=1, accessed 16 May 2022.
Boerner, S. (2020). Lessons from the pandemic for the conservative welfare state. Social Europe, June 2. https://www.socialeurope.eu/lessons-from-the-pandemic-for-the-conservative-welfare-state, accessed 16 May 2022.
Bofinger, P., Dullien, S., Felbermayr, G., Fuest, C., Hüther, M., Südekum, J., and Weder di Mauro, B. (2020). Wirtschaftliche Implikationen der Corona-Krise und wirtschaftspolitische Maßnahmen. Wirtschaftsdienst 4: 259–265.
Bönte, M. (2020). Kossen verurteilt den Umgang mit Arbeitsmigranten in der Corona-Krise. Kirche + Leben Netz, March 28. https://www.kirche-und-leben.de/artikel/kossen-verurteilt-den-umgang-mit-arbeitsmigranten-in-der-corona-krise, accessed 16 May 2022.
Bundesagentur für Arbeit. (n.d.). Hartz IV. https://www.arbeitsagentur.de/lexikon/hartz-4, accessed 16 May 2022.
Bundesregierung (2020). Gespräch mit Vertretern der Automobilindustrie und Gewerkschaften, Pressemitteilung 150, 5 May. [Press release]. https://www.bundesregierung.de/breg-de/aktuelles/gespraech-mit-vertretern-der-automobilindustrie-und-gewerkschaften-1750498, accessed 16 May 2022.
Dehning, J., Zierenberg, J., Spitzner, F. P., Wibral, M., Pinheiro Neto, J., Wilczek, M., and Priesemann, V. (2020). Inferring Change Points in the Spread of COVID-19 Reveals the Effectiveness of Interventions. Science 369(6500). https://science.sciencemag.org/content/369/6500/eabb9789.full, accessed 16 May 2022.
Dettmer, M., Knobbe, M., Sauga, M., Traufetter, G., and Wiedmann-Schmidt, W. (2020). Die Bundesregierung will den starken Staat, Spiegel Online,

18 May. https://www.spiegel.de/politik/deutschland/innere-sicherheit-arbeitsmarkt-industriepolitik-die-bundesregierung-will-den-starken-staat-a-00000000-0002-0001-0000-000170923495, accessed 16 May 2022.

Deutsche Bundesbank. (2020). Monthly Report: May 2020, 72(5). https://www.bundesbank.de/resource/blob/832786/f6fefe4a9d4885c42f4bcd993bc50b2e/mL/2020-05-monatsbericht-data.pdf, accessed 16 May 2022.

Deutscher Bundestag. (2020). Antwort der Bundesregierung auf die Kleine Anfrage der Abgeordneten Doris Achelwilm u.a., Geschlechtergerechtes Entscheidungsmanagement zur Bewältigung der Coronakrise. 27 May. BT-Drs. 19/19525, 8.

Deutschlandfunk. (2020). Corona-Demonstrationen: Positionen und Protagonisten, March 8. https://www.deutschlandfunk.de/covid-19-pandemie-corona-demonstrationen-positionen-und.2897.de.html?dram:article_id=476457, accessed 16 May 2022.

DGB. (2020). Folgen der Corona-Pandemie, Maßnahmen gegen Corona-Folgen: Wo noch mehr kommen muss, March 22. https://www.dgb.de/themen/++co++9c486f32-6c17-11ea-8667-52540088cada, accessed 16 May 2022.

Die Bundeskanzlerin. (2020a). Pressekonferenz von Bundeskanzlerin Merkel zu der Besprechung mit den Regierungschefinnen und Regierungschefs der Länder zum Coronavirus, [Press Release]. 22 March. https://www.bundeskanzler.de/bk-de/aktuelles/pressekonferenz-von-bundeskanzlerin-merkel-zu-der-besprechung-mit-den-regierungschefinnen-und-regierungschefs-der-laender-zum-coronavirus-1733286, accessed 16 May 2022.

Die Bundeskanzlerin. (2020b). Gespräch von Bundeskanzlerin Merkel mit Wirtschaftsverbänden und Gewerkschaften zu den wirtschaftlichen Folgen des Corona-Virus am 24. April 2020. [Press release]. https://www.bundeskanzlerin.de/bkin-de/aktuelles/gespraech-von-bundeskanzlerin-merkel-mit-wirtschaftsverbaenden-und-gewerkschaften-zu-den-wirtschaftlichen-folgen-des-corona-virus-am-24-april-2020-1746830, accessed 16 May 2022.

dpa. (2020). Supermärkte und Discounter: Scheiben sollen Kassierer schützen. ZDF. 21 March. https://www.zdf.de/nachrichten/wirtschaft/supermaerkte-und-discounter-scheiben-sollen-kassierer-schuetzen-100.html, accessed 16 May 2022.

ECB. (2020). CSPP PEPP Corporate Bond Holdings. https://www.ecb.europa.eu/mopo/pdf/CSPP_PEPP_corporate_bond_holdings_20200612.csv?859aaa1c28ec1967f150b83767da29e0, accessed 16 May 2022.

ECB. (n.d.). Pandemic Emergency Purchase Programme (PEPP). https://www.ecb.europa.eu/mopo/implement/pepp/html/index.en.html, accessed 16 May 2022.

Ekkenga, J., and Schirrmacher, C. (2020). Auswirkungen der COVID-19-Katastrophe auf die Zahlungspflichten gewerblicher Mieter und Pächter. Neue Zeitschrift für Miet- und Wohnungsrecht 410.

Enste, D. (2017). Schwarzarbeit und Schattenwirtschaft- Argumente und Fakten zur nicht angemeldeten Erwerbstätigkeit in Deutschland und Europa. Köln, Germany: Institut der deutschen Wirtschaft. IW Report 2017 no. 9.

Entringer, T., Kroeger, H., Schupp, J., Kuehen, S., Liebig, S., Goebel, J., Grabka, M. M., Graeber, D., Kroh, M., Schroeder, C., Seebauer, J., and Zinn, S. (2020). Psychische Krise durch Covid-19? Sorgen sinken, Einsamkeit steigt, Lebenszufriedenheit bleibt stabil. Berlin, Germany. Deutsches Institut für Wirtschaftsforschung. SOEPpapers no. 1087. https://www.diw.de/documents/publikationen/73/diw_01.c.791307.de/diw_sp1087.pdf, accessed 16 May 2022.

EU Independent Fiscal Institutions. (2020). European Fiscal Monitor Special Update. https://www.euifis.eu/download/european_fiscal_monitor_special_update_may.pdf, accessed 16 May 2022.

EU-Gleichbehandlungsstelle. (2020). EU Bürger, Arbeitslosigkeit. https://www.eu-gleichbehandlungsstelle.de/eugs-de/eu-buerger/infothek/sozialleistungen/arbeitslosigkeit/arbeitslosigkeit-367398#tar-2, accessed 16 May 2022.

Fäßler, H.-R. (2020). Man kann und muss mit den Bürgern über alles reden. Cicero, 8 May. https://www.cicero.de/innenpolitik/informationsmanagement-bundesregierung-seuchen-kommunikation, accessed 16 May 2022

Fincompare. (2022). Corona-Krise: Wirtschaftsstabilitätsfonds WSF—Welche Betriebe profitieren. Fincompare, 2 April. https://fincompare.de/wirtschaftsstabilitaetsfonds-welche-betriebe-profitieren, accessed 16 May 2022.

Frese, A. (2020). Tönnies droht zum zweiten Ischgl zu werden. Der Tagesspiegel, 22 June. https://www.tagesspiegel.de/wirtschaft/die-kritik-an-der-fleischindustrie-waechst-toennies-droht-zum-zweiten-ischgl-zu-werden/25939576.html, accessed 16 May 2022.

Fried, N. (2020). Für alle etwas dabei. Süddeutsche Zeitung, 4 June. https://www.sueddeutsche.de/politik/wirtschaftshilfe-fuer-alle-etwas-dabei-1.4927496, accessed 16 May 2022.

Frigelj, K. (2020). So häufig verstoßen die Deutschen gegen die Corona-Regeln. Welt, 11 April. https://www.welt.de/politik/deutschland/article207189479/Corona-So-haeufig-verstossen-die-Deutschen-gegen-die-Regeln.html, accessed 16 May 2022.

Funk, A. (2020). Wie der Staat die Schulden des Corona-Rettungspakets wieder abbauen will. Der Tagesspiegel, 23 March. https://www.tagesspiegel.de/wirtschaft/ausnahmeregelung-der-schuldenbremse-wie-der-staat-die-schulden-des-corona-rettungspakets-wieder-abbauen-will/25681804.html, accessed 16 May 2022.

Fürstenau, M. (2020). Kommentar: Deutschland, schau nach Bayern! Deutsche Welle, 21 March. https://www.dw.com/de/kommentar-deutschland-schau-nach-bayern/a-52873244, accessed 16 May 2022.

Gebauer, M., Lehmann, T., Medick, V., and Teevs, C. (2020). Deutschland maskiert sich. Spiegel Online, 20 April. https://www.spiegel.de/politik/deutschland/corona-krise-in-deutschland-bundesweite-maskenpflicht-wird-wahrscheinlicher-a-d02ee09f-8202-45af-82b9-b6b5fe348c5f, accessed 16 May 2022.

Gensing, P., and Grill, M. (2020). 40 Prozent mehr Tests in Deutschland. Tagesschau, 6 May. https://www.tagesschau.de/investigativ/corona-tests-rki-101.html, accessed 16 May 2022

Golia, A., Hering, L., Moser, C., and Sparks, T. (2021). Constitutions and Contagion—European Constitutional Systems and the COVID-19 Pandemic. Zeitschrift für ausländisches öffentliches Recht und Völkerrecht 81: 147–234.

Grund, S., Guttenberg, L., and Odendahl, C. (2020). Sharing the Fiscal Burden of the Crisis: A Pandemic Solidarity Instrument for the EU. In: A. Bénassy-Quéré and B. Weder di Mauro (eds.) Europe in the Time of Covid-19, pp. 173–186.

Guckelberger, A. (2020). Ausgangsbeschränkungen und Kontaktverbote anlässlich der Corona-Pandemie. Neue Zeitschrift für Verwaltungsrecht 607.

Hamann, C. (2020). "Zwangstracking"—Ein rechtliches No-Go? Recht und Politik 56(2): 133–138.

Hammerschmid, A., Schmieder, J., and Wrohlich, K. (2020). Frauen in Corona-Krise stärker am Arbeitsmarkt betroffen als Männer. Berlin, Germany: Deutsches Institut für Wirtschaftsforschung. DIW-Aktuell no. 42.

Härting, N. (2020). Vorratsdatenspeicherung in der Gastronomie: Kein Essen ohne Kontaktdaten? CR-online.de Blog, 5 May. https://www.cr-online.de/blog/2020/05/10/vorratsdatenspeicherung-in-der-gastronomie-kein-essen-ohne-kontaktdaten/h, accessed 16 May 2022.

Hase, F. (2020). Corona-Krise und Verfassungsdiskurs. Juristenzeitung 14(8): 697–704.

Hering, L. (2020). COVID-19 and Constitutional Law: The Case of Germany. In J. M. Serna de la Garza (ed.), Covid-19 and Constitutional Law. Mexico City: Universidad Nacional Autónoma de México, Instituto de Investigaciones Jurídicas, pp. 149–156.

Heuser, U. J., and Nienhaus, L. (2020). Mein Feind und Helfer. Die Zeit, 7 April. https://www.zeit.de/2020/16/staatliche-unterstuetzung-coronavirus-kredite-missbrauch-spekulation, accessed 16 May 2022.

Hoffmeyer, M. (2020). Riesiges Regelwerk. Süddeutsche Zeitung, 3 July. https://www.sueddeutsche.de/karriere/corona-hygienekonzepte-riesiges-regelwerk-1.4954557, accessed 16 May 2022.

Huang, S. (2020). Wie Corona soziale Ungleichheiten aufdeckt und verschärft. Berlin, Germany: Deutsches Institut für Wirtschaftsforschung. DIW Wochenbericht 29/2020, p. 524.

Huebener, M., Spieß, K., Siegel, N. A., and Wagner, G. (2020). Wohlbefinden von Familien in Zeiten von Corona: Eltern mit jungen Kindern am stärksten beeinträchtigt. Berlin, Germany: Deutsches Institut für Wirtschaftsforschung. DIW Wochenbericht 30/31/2020, pp. 528–537.

iGZ—Interessenverband Dt. Zeitarbeitsunternehmen e.V. (2020). Zeitarbeit in der Corona-Krise: Ein Drittel der Unternehmen hält Corona-Krise für "existenzgefährdend". 15 April. https://www.presseportal.de/pm/70553/4572042, accessed 16 May 2022.

Inman, P., and Wearden, G. (2020). German economy flatlines after spending and exports slowdown. GDP growth at 0% for final quarter of 2019 with no upturn forecast in the short term. The Guardian, 14 February. https://www.theguardian.com/world/2020/feb/14/german-economy-flatlines-after-spending-and-exports-slowdown, accessed 16 May 2022.

Jennen, B. (2020). Germany Unleashes $800 Billion Package to Cushion Virus Blow. Bloomberg, 23 March. https://www.bloomberg.com/news/articles/2020-03-23/germany-approves-800-billion-package-to-counter-virus-impact, accessed 16 May 2022.

Kagermeier, E. (2020). Erst die Ausgangssperre, dann die Schuldzuweisungen. Zeit Online, 19 March. https://www.zeit.de/gesellschaft/zeitgeschehen/2020-03/mitterteich-ausgangssperre-coronavirus-quarantaene-ansteckungsgefahr-deutschland, accessed 16 May 2022.

Kaiser, A.-B., and Hensel, R. (2021). Federal Republic of Germany: Legal Response to Covid-19. In: J. King and O. Ferraz (eds.), The Oxford Compendium of National Legal Responses to Covid-19, April. https://oxcon.ouplaw.com/view/https://doi.org/10.1093/law-occ19/law-occ19-e2?rskey=sTnZ8w&result=8&prd=OCC19, accessed 16 May 2022.

Kämmerer, J. A., and Jischkowski, L. (2020). Grundrechtsschutz in der Pandemie—Der „Corona-Lockdown" im Visier der Verfassungs- und Verwaltungsgerichtsbarkeit. GesundheitsRecht (GesR) 19 (6): 341–353.

Kersten, J., and Rixen, S. (2021). Der Verfassungsstaat in der Corona-Krise. München: C. H. Beck. Edited volume, 2nd edition.

Kiel, F. (2020). Ohne Lobby: Selbstständige in der Coronakrise. Blätter für deutsche und internationale Politik 65: 13.

Klafki, A. (2020). Neue Rechtsgrundlagen im Kampf gegen Covid-19. Der Gesetzesentwurf zum Schutz der Bevölkerung bei einer epidemischen Lage von nationaler Tragweite. Verfassungsblog—On Matters Constitutional, 25 March. https://verfassungsblog.de/neue-rechtsgrundlagen-im-kampf-gegen-covid-19/, accessed 16 May 2022.

Klafki, A., and Kießling, A. (2020). Fighting COVID 19—Legal Powers and Risks: Germany. Verfassungsblog—On Matters Constitutional, 20 March. https://verfassungsblog.de/fighting-covid-19-legal-powers-and-risks-germany/, accessed 16 May 2022.

Klauck, D., Müller, M. W., and Riedner, L. (2021). Finanzielle Folgen der Covid-19-Pandemie für Staat und Gesellschaft. Juristische Schulung (JuS) 8: 739–745.

Klöckner, J. (2020). Entwicklung der Warn-App hat 20 Millionen Euro gekostet. Handelsblatt, 11 June. https://www.handelsblatt.com/politik/deutschland/corona-entwicklung-der-warn-app-hat-20-millionen-euro-gekostet/25907216.html?ticket=ST-11276318-Q1sznJQdc4tI0wSCKTqb-ap4, accessed 16 May 2022.

Knappschaft Bahn. (2020). Corona: Erheblicher Rückgang bei den Minijobs. Knappschaft Bahn, 12 May. https://www.kbs.de/SharedDocs/Presse/Pressemitteilungen/MJZ/2020/12_05.html?nn=943904, accessed 16 May 2022.

Koebe, J., Samtleben, C., Schrenker, A., and Zucco, A. (2020). Systemrelevant, aber dennoch kaum anerkannt: Entlohnung unverzichtbarer Berufe in der Corona-Krise unterdurchschnittlich. Deutsches Institut für Wirtschaftsforschung Berlin—Aktuell 48, 29 June. https://www.diw.de/de/diw_01.c.792754.de/publikationen/diw_aktuell/2020_0048/systemrelevant__aber_dennoch_kaum_anerkannt__entlohnung_unverzichtbarer_berufe_in_der_corona-krise_unterdurchschnittlich.html, accessed 16 May 2022.

Korinth, S. (2020). Engpässe: Dessoushersteller produziert jetzt Atemschutzmasken. Schwäbische, 20 March. https://www.schwaebische.de/landkreis/landkreis-sigmaringen/zollernalb_artikel,-engpaesse-dessoushersteller-produziert-jetzt-atemschutzmasken-_arid,11202914.html, accessed 16 May 2022.

Korioth, S., and Müller, M. W. (2021). Die Konjunkturkomponente der Schuldenbremse — Spielräume und Grenzen. Wirtschaftsdienst 101 (12): 960–963.

Kühling, J. and Schildbach, R. (2020). Corona-Apps—Daten- und Grundrechtsschutz in Krisenzeiten. Neue Juristische Wochenschrift (NJW) 22: 1545–1550.

Kunst, K. (2020a). Reform des Infektionsschutzgesetzes: mehr Eingriffsrechte zur Eindämmung von Corona. Haufe, 3 April. https://www.haufe.de/recht/weitere-rechtsgebiete/strafrecht-oeffentl-recht/moegliche-behoerden massnahmen-zur-eindaemmung-des-coronavirus_204_510706.html, accessed 16 May 2022.

Kunst, K. (2020b). Infektionsschutzgesetz—Maßnahmen zur Corona-Abwehr und Sanktionen. Haufe, 15 May. https://www.haufe.de/recht/weitere-rechtsgebiete/strafrecht-oeffentl-recht/sanktionen-bei-verstoessen-gegen-das-infektionsschutzgesetz_204_512206.html, accessed 16 May 2022.

Lemkemeyer, S. (2020). Söder prescht mit Ausgangsbeschränkungen in Bayern vor. Der Tagesspiegel, 20 March. https://www.tagesspiegel.de/wirtschaft/anti-corona-massnahmen-der-bundeslaender-soeder-prescht-mit-ausgangsbeschraenkungen-in-bayern-vor/25665542.html, accessed 16 May 2022.

Litschko, K. (2020). Corona-Verstoß? Ab in Haft!. taz, 9 April. https://taz.de/Verordnungen-gegen-Pandemie/!5677824/, accessed 16 May 2022.

Mahdi, F., and Rosner, M. (2020). Kündigung trotz COVID-19-Kündigungsbeschränkung bei unterbliebenem Wiederauffüllen der vom Vermieter „gezogenen" Mietsicherheit? Zur Reichweite von Art. EGBGB Artikel 240 § EGBGB Artikel 240 § 2 EGBGB im Gewerberaummietrecht. Neue Zeitschrift für Miet- und Wohnungsrecht (NZM) 9: 416–423.

Manager Magazin. (2020). Zwangspause bei Tönnies aufgehoben. Manager Magazin, 17 July. https://www.manager-magazin.de/unternehmen/toennies-werk-in-rheda-wiedenbrueck-startet-probelauf-bei-zerlegung-schlachtung-unterbrochen-a-50fb5b0b-d384-46e0-92a8-54ac51789f74, accessed 16 May 2022.

Mängel, A. (2020). Corona: Die ignorierten Armen. Blätter für deutsche und internationale Politik 65 (6): 9–12.

Mitze, T. (2020). Masken tragen offenbar deutlich zur Eindämmung der Corona-Pandemie bei [Press release]. 8 June. https://www.uni-mainz.de/presse/aktuell/11532_DEU_HTML.php, accessed 16 May 2022.

Müller, K.-U., Samtleben, C., Schmieder, J., and Wrohlich, K. (2020). Corona-Krise erschwert Vereinbarkeit von Beruf und Familie vor allem für Mütter—Erwerbstätige Eltern sollten entlastet werden. DIW Wochenbericht 19: 332–340.

Münkler, L. (2021). »Nothing else matters«. Wem Gehör schenken in der »Corona-Krise«? Jahrbuch des öffentlichen Rechts der Gegenwart. Neue Folge 69 (1): 535–553.

Neuscheler, T. (2020). Jägermeister liefert Alkohol für Desinfektionsmittel. Frankfurter Allgemeine Zeitung (FAZ), 23 March. https://www.faz.net/aktuell/wirtschaft/corona-jaegermeister-liefert-alkohol-fuer-desinfektionsmittel-16692757.html, accessed 16 May 2022.

Piltz, C. (2020). Die lieben Nachbarn. Spiegel Online, 19 March. https://www.spiegel.de/panorama/gesellschaft/coronavirus-solidaritaet-in-zeiten-von-corona-die-lieben-nachbarn-a-8f44f39d-f8c8-4002-9f2f-7b47a3c5a39c, accessed 16 May 2022.

rbb24. (2020). Busfahrer in Berlin verkaufen keine Tickets mehr—und Fahrgäste müssen hinten einsteigen, March 11. https://www.rbb24.de/panorama/thema/2020/coronavirus/beitraege/bus-berlin-bvg-busfahrer-coronavirus-corona-nahverkehr.html, accessed 16 May 2022.

Rebmann, S., Soldt, R., and Truscheit, K. (2020). Auf Corona-Streife mit der Polizei. Frankfurter Allgemeine Zeitung (FAZ), 14 April. https://www.faz.net/aktuell/gesellschaft/gesundheit/coronavirus/einsatz-in-der-pandemie-auf-corona-streife-mit-der-polizei-16721877.html, accessed 16 May 2022.

Reinartz, P. (2020). Coronakrise—Frechener Gin-Destillerie steigt auf Desinfektionsmittel um. Kölner Stadt Anzeiger, 20 March. https://www.ksta.de/region/rhein-erft/frechen/coronakrise-frechener-gin-destillerie-steigt-auf-desinfektionsmittel-um—36446246, accessed 16 May 2022.

Röders-Arnold, C., and Starken, L. S. (2020). „Gesuch Gleichberechtigung #stattblumen“. https://www.gleichberechtigung-statt-blumen.de/, accessed 16 May 2022.

Rosendorff, K. and Meier, F. (2020). Corona-Krise in Frankfurt: Gäste müssen Daten im Restaurant angeben—Ohne Name kein Essen. Frankfurter Rundschau, 28 May. https://www.fr.de/frankfurt/frankfurt-am-main-ort28687/corona-frankfurt-daten-restaurant-angeben-ohne-name-kein-essen-13778845.html, accessed 16 May 2022.

Rzepka, D. (2020). Chaos Computer Club lobt deutsche Corona-App. ZDF, 16 June. https://www.zdf.de/nachrichten/politik/corona-app-launch-100.html, accessed 16 May 2022.

Schmidt, T. J. (2020). Corona-Verstöße: Frankfurter sind Bußgeld-Spitzenreiter. Frankfurter Neue Presse, 17 June. https://www.fnp.de/frankfurt/corona-verstoesse-frankfurter-sind-bussgeld-spitzenreiter-13801792.html, accessed 16 May 2022.

Schmitt, F. (2020). Die Verfassungswidrigkeit der landesweiten Ausgangsverbote. Neue Juristische Wochenschrift (NJW) 23: 1626–1631.

Seitz, H. (2000). Fiscal Policy, Deficits and Politics of Subnational Governments: The Case of the German Laender. Public Choice, 102 (3/4): 183–218.

Sikora, J. (2020). Bitte woher haben Sie meine Handynummer? Die Nutzung personenbezogener Daten aus Corona-Kontaktlisten zur Strafverfolgung. Junge Wissenschaft im öffentlichen Recht, Blog 103, 21 July. https://www.juwiss.de/103-2020/, accessed 16 May 2022.

Stendera, P. (2020). Studieren auf Pump: Corona und die akademische Spaltung. Blätter für deutsche und internationale Politik 65 (8): 9–13.

Streck, R. (2020). Wir werden auch die Corona-Schulden nicht zurückzahlen!. Telepolis, 24 May. https://www.heise.de/tp/features/Wir-werden-auch-die-Corona-Schulden-nicht-zurueckzahlen-4727599.html?seite=all, accessed 16 May 2022.

Streeck, H., Schulte, B., Kümmerer, B. M., Richter, E., Höller, T., Fuhrmann, C., Bartok, E., Dolscheid, R., Berger, M., Wessendorf, L., Eschbach-Bludau, M., Kellings, A., Schwaiger, A., Coenen, M., Hoffmann, P., Stoffel-Wagner, B., Nöthen, M. M., Eis-Hübinger, A.-M., Exner, M., Schmithausen, R. M.,

Schmid M., and Hartmann, G. (2020). Infection fatality rate of SARS-CoV-2 infection in a German community with a super-spreading event. Nature Communications 11, 17 November. https://www.nature.com/articles/s41467-020-19509-y, accessed 16 May 2022.

Stutte, H. (2020). Blockwart-Boom: Macht Corona uns zu Denunzianten? Frankfurter Rundschau, 6 April. https://www.fr.de/panorama/blockwart-boom-13641319.html, accessed 16 May 2022.

Süddeutsche Zeitung. (2020a). Anträge auf Corona-Soforthilfen wieder möglich, April 17. https://www.sueddeutsche.de/wirtschaft/wirtschaftspolitik-duesseldorf-antraege-auf-corona-soforthilfen-wieder-moeglich-dpa.urn-newsml-dpa-com-20090101-200417-99-738387, accessed 16 May 2022.

Süddeutsche Zeitung. (2020b). Bund plant Rekordschulden von 218, 5 Milliarden Euro, June 15. https://www.sueddeutsche.de/wirtschaft/haushalt-bund-plant-rekordschulden-von-218-5-milliarden-euro-dpa.urn-newsml-dpa-com-20090101-200615-99-432599, accessed 16 May 2022.

Süddeutsche Zeitung. (2020c). Bundesregierung will Prämie für E-Autos erhöhen, June 4. https://www.sueddeutsche.de/wirtschaft/auto-bundesregierung-will-praemie-fuer-e-autos-erhoehen-dpa.urn-newsml-dpa-com-20090101-200604-99-307010, accessed 16 May 2022.

Szymanowski, G. (2020). Corona-Krise: Pflegekräfte fordern mehr als Applaus. Deutsche Welle, 2 April. https://www.dw.com/de/corona-krise-pflegekr%C3%A4fte-fordern-mehr-als-applaus/a-52983411, accessed 16 May 2022.

Thielbörger, P. (2021). Germany—Federalism in Action. In: M. C. Kettemann, and K. Lachmayer (eds.) Pandemocracy in Europe—Power, Parliaments and People in Times of COVID-19. Oxford and New York: Hart, pp. 91–116.

Töngi, C. (2020). Kein Boom für private Sicherheitsdienste in der Corona-Krise. Badische Neueste Nachrichten, 11 April. https://bnn.de/karlsruhe/waehrend-der-fluechtlingskrise-erlebten-private-sicherheitsdienste-einen-boom-doch-damals-lief-vieles-anders-als-heute, accessed 16 May 2022.

Truger, A., and Will, H. (2013). The German "Debt Brake": A Shining Example for European Fiscal Policy? Revue de l'OFCE, N° 127 (1): 153–188.

Ver.di. (2020a). Corona wirft Scheinwerferlicht auf ausbeuterische Branchen. https://arbeitsmarkt-und-sozialpolitik.verdi.de/ueber-uns/nachrichten/++co++6f958f16-d8a4-11ea-b816-001a4a160119, accessed 16 May 2022.

Ver.di. (2020b). Corona- FAQ für Solo-Selbstständige https://selbststaendige.verdi.de/beratung/corona-infopool/++co++aa8e1eea-6896-11ea-bfc7-001a4a160100, accessed 16 May 2022.

Wiring, R., and Schüngel, J. (2020). COVID-19: Immerhin ein Schub für die Telemedizin. CMS Deutschland bloggt, 21 April. https://www.cmshs-bloggt.de/life-sciences-healthcare/covid-19-telemedizin-videosprechstunde/, accessed 16 May 2022.

Zehner, D. (2020). Mietrechtliche Neuregelungen in Zeiten der Coronakrise. Juristische Arbeitsblätter (JA) 7: 488–493.

Zeit Online. (2020). Zahl der Arbeitsschutzkontrollen in Betrieben sinkt weiter. Zeit Online, 4 May. https://www.zeit.de/arbeit/2020-05/arbeitsschutz-kontrollen-betriebe-sicherheit-gesundheitsschutz, accessed 16 May 2022.

COVID-19 Crisis in the United Kingdom: The First 100 Days of the Unknown

Arletta Gorecka

1 Introduction

The United Kingdom (UK) is a unique jurisdiction with a partially codified constitution. Therefore, it is theorised as a political constitution premised on the Westminster government model (Murkens, 2017). This model conceives democracy in procedural, but not substantive term. Furthermore, the United Kingdom has three different legal regimes: one each for England and Wales, one for Scotland, and one for Northern Ireland. Despite this, there are four shared fundamental British values: democracy, rule of law, respect and tolerance, and individual liberty. Decisions of the United Kingdom government must reflect these values. This includes deciding to declare a national state of disaster in the light of the COVID-19 pandemic, resulting in a national lockdown and other restrictions on social and economic interactions.

The first case of the novel coronavirus (COVID-19) in the United Kingdom was confirmed on 31 January 2020. On 23 March 2020, the United Kingdom's Prime Minister announced the enforcement of the

A. Gorecka (✉)
University of Strathclyde, Glasgow, UK
e-mail: arletta.gorecka@strath.ac.uk

A. Stojanović et al. (eds.), *The First 100 Days of Covid-19*,
https://doi.org/10.1007/978-981-19-6325-4_8

tightened measures aimed at mitigating the spread of COVID-19 with the nation placing a restriction on the freedom of movement (lockdown), for a reviewable period of three weeks. The United Kingdom Government adopted several measures to protect the United Kingdom's economy during the outbreak of the COVID-19, which aims at economical sustaining industries. The GDP is fed by four main sectors: services (79%), production (15%), construction (6%), and agriculture (0.7%), (ONS, 2022). According to the OECD (2020), the anticipated fall of the GDP by 14% is due to pandemic safety measures.

The COVID-19 pandemic occurred when the United Kingdom was vulnerable; as it was still recovering from its exit from the European Union and attempting to resolve several ongoing issues over the devolved nations, especially Scotland and Northern Ireland. Both countries voted to remain in the EU during the 2016 referendum. When the pandemic hit in 2020, there were no significant differences in approaches between the United Kingdom government and the governments of Scotland, and Northern Ireland. In March 2020, the United Kingdom entered a nationwide lockdown. By mid-March, certain discrepancies in the approaches had been noted. This chapter aims to present an overview of the United Kingdom before the COVID-19 pandemic together with policy projections made at the time. As will be noted, the policy contrasted with a neoliberal approach in several ways; specifically, I consider the approach concerning surveillance, data, and marketisation. Thereafter, I highlight the areas of policy that are most prominent for the United Kingdom context: economic grown, health, and education. The main focus is on identifying how the limits of political autonomy, neoliberal logic, and inequalities have been further exacerbated by the COVID-19 pandemic.

This chapter is structured as follows: In Sect. 2, I discuss the state of exception. This narrative is important to account for the context in which specific decisions were made. Essentially, the United Kingdom consists of four countries: Scotland, England, Northern Ireland, and Wales. Health is a devolved power in the United Kingdom. In this respect, countries such as Scotland have a responsibility for their health policies. Although the narrative of this chapter aims to assess the COVID crisis through the UK-wide lens, occasionally references to policies made in individual UK nations will be made.[1] In Sect. 3, I consider the shift in surveillance. This section will specifically compare the different approaches adopted in the UK nations. The emphasis will be placed on the approach adopted by Scotland. Section 4, I consider the economic shift taken by the United

Kingdom to support the economy during the COVID-19 crisis. I will consider how the United Kingdom has had to make an ideological leap than most to meet the challenges of the COVID pandemic. Initially, from an initial look, I try to discern two sources of the new policy-making wave. One is based on social democracy and the other is based on the "new economics" wave, still based on neoliberalism. The "new economic" wave has been characterised by sudden changes, diminishing the economic austerity measures. It has been characterised by technological developments. This section provides a potential trajectory of the economy after the COVID pandemic. In Sects. 6 and 7, I will provide the analysis of the health and education systems, respectively, as they were impacted by the pandemic. The health and educational system have been politically debated prior to the pandemic (and was in the Brexit focus), with the UK government trying to introduce changes allowing to improve such system. As it will be discussed later, the UK economics, together with such structural problems shaped past COVID outcomes (economic and health outcomes). I will conclude by summarising different aspects in the gradual policy shift from neoliberal consideration into more socially oriented policy considerations.

2 The United Kingdom: State of Nations and COVID Pandemic

The United Kingdom's political system is based on a parliamentary democracy that functions under a constitutional monarchy. Exclusive powers, powers to implement and enforce law lay with the Government. The Government, monitored and scrutinised by Parliament, could propose any new law.

Before the 2008 financial crisis, the United Kingdom government was governed by a simple set of rules. The neoliberal macroeconomic approach policy was characterised by low inflation, deregulation of product markets, and capital flows liberalisation (Grimshaw, 2012). Following the 2008 financial crisis, the United Kingdom faced a period of vulnerability. The crisis was, to an extent, a product of the United Kingdom's model of capitalism, which was centralised around a vulnerable structural condition for the 2008 financial crisis, but potentially saved lives during the pandemic, as many people can work at home. The United Kingdom faced a period of recession and continued to be gripped by political austerity. Firstly, the United Kingdom entered the recession with a strongly neoliberal socio-economic model. The New Labour government modified the United Kingdom neoliberal approach by strengthening the commitment to public service provisions. That government continued through the recession and introduced measures supporting the United Kingdom market and economy. The New Labour government introduced the national minimum wage and opted in several EU directives. This was a major step in ensuring a flexible labour market in the context of the financial crisis. The United Kingdom experienced a shift in approach in the role of the state, and its approach to introduce policy incentives to reduce poverty effects as the aftermath of the recession. Poverty is a poor structural condition during the pandemic, as low-income workers have more incentive to work during the pandemic to survive, thus increase infection risks. Therefore, the policy here might have helped to an extent. Essentially, this created further difficulty in distinguishing the role of the United Kingdom macroeconomic policy as opposed to political ideology during the austerity crisis. Neoliberalism was seen as a cause of slow recovery and recession. Undoubtedly, it was witnessing a renaissance in the United Kingdom with voices and opinions from free-market economics (Grimshaw, 2012). The slow economic recovery continued in the post-financial crisis governments, with the Conservative-Liberal Democrat coalition rule (2010–2015) and the Conservative government (2015–2020). The United Kingdom's exit from the EU marked a steep-change in policy making. However, the United Kingdom is still recovering from the Brexit process, attempting to resolve several ongoing issues over the devolved nations, especially Scotland and Northern Ireland. Although Brexit and Scottish independence referendums have been seen as a vital point for development of economic policy, it is beyond the scope of this chapter to address those factors. Importantly, both of these countries voted to remain in the EU during the 2016 referendum. Furthermore, in 2014, Scotland had its independence referendum, won narrowly by the "No" side. The United Kingdom's political arena is characterised by the right-wing Conservative government ruling in London, and the devoted administration led (usually) by the centre-left government.

The COVID-19 pandemic only furthered the economic uncertainty, introducing major changes for policymakers, trying to protect the United Kingdom economy during the lockdown and its future prompt recovery. Lockdown itself is a policy: policymakers introduced lockdowns to protect the United Kingdom economy (and most importantly to save lives).

Certainly, several such debates demonstrated the need for a permanent increase in the intervention of government. There was some evidence that official lockdown exacerbated the economic impact, at least in the short term. There is clearly a trade-off in COVID policy design. Increasing COVID restrictions will have a negative economic impact in the short run. However, to reduce excessive economic cost, the government must lift up restrictions again, the problem of structural conditions (e.g. poverty) will kick in once more. Davies (2020) pointed out that the pandemic sped up social and economic changes that had already existed. However, the problem of the pandemic is compounded by unknowns. Notably, Knight (1921) distinguished between "uncertainty" and "risk". In the conditions of "uncertainty", society could not know the possible outcomes and their potential probabilities. On the other hand, "risk" relates to problems where society understands the range of possible outcomes. Essentially, applying this to the United Kingdom scenario, it remains difficult to identify the counterfactual, or what could have potentially happened if the government had not acted at all.

The COVID-19 crisis introduced several unknowns. These include excess mortality and reported death, which could be linked to the COVID-19, and those that could have been avoided by government intervention if the health service carried out treatment for conditions unrelated to COVID-19. Deaths due to the collapse of medical system. This is linked to health structural conditions such as how many people need surgery or access to hospital during the pandemic. It also depends on past COVID outcomes, the United Kingdom suffered from high COVID deaths and fast rising new cases, which reduced the supply of medical services (non-COVID) during the pandemic. This is also linked to the NHS system in the United Kingdom. Assessing these uncertainties impose a danger that policy would focus too much on the most easily identifiable victims.

3 Surveillance and Compliance

3.1 Surveillance Prior to COVID-19 Pandemic

This section offers an overview of the United Kingdom surveillance regime. There are two main forms of surveillance: overt and covert surveillance of persons (Home Office, 2014). The use of technology for surveillance has become increasingly pervasive in public places

(Mortenson et al., 2013). The same could be said for its application in health and care settings (Desai, 2009). There is a long history of surveillance, yet the new technical development introduced more options in this respect. These include cameras, monitors, sends, and web-based technologies. This wide array of technologies corresponds to Desai noting that there was no single body that could collect and monitor all information.

The debate on surveillance is categorised into inter alia the following areas of research factors: technical discourse, discourse on rights, and managerial discourse. These factors highlight benefits for introducing better information about high-risk behaviour (Mortenson et al., 2013, p. 2). The United Kingdom regime of practices sits under the umbrella of the European Convention on Human Rights (ECHR) and the Human Rights Act 1998 (HRA). The United Kingdom legal framework for legal interception and storage of communication data is based on the Regulation of Investigatory Powers Act 2000 and a few other pieces of legislation. The Data Retention and Investigatory Power Act 2014 deals with the retention of certain communications data.

The ethical implications of surveillance remain complex and under-researched. The aspects of ethics remained one of the most prominent themes in the literature. Alistair et al., (2010) noted that the practical and ethical implications of surveillance interventions remained unknown. This theme is linked to privacy. Privacy is protected by Article 7 of the European Charter of Rights which indicates that: "everyone has the right to respect for his or her private of family-like, home and communication". The right to privacy is further protected by Article 8 of the Charter, which further enshrined the data protection by protecting "private and family life, his home, and his correspondence". At the United Kingdom national level, privacy is protected in Article 8(1) of the HRA, which gives individuals the right to respect their private and family life. Essentially, the use of surveillance further introduces the question of the consent and moral acceptability of any technological intervention. Data protection has been further expanded by the 1995 Directive, and with the new EU-wide GDPR in 2018. With this wide protection, the EU is recognising data protection as a part of the wide regulatory framework that strongly protects the EU citizens and their interests. The issue of the right to privacy remains complex.

Overall, the United Kingdom research on surveillance has been limited. Therefore, it is a necessity to understand surveillance from different perspectives. Alistair et al., (2010) highlighted several perspectives: "that of the institution, the resident; and the care relation". This suggests that the implementation of surveillance technology could introduce unintended consequences, with the technology being socially transformative. This could be both negative and positive. However, the area of use of surveillance remains debated with its effectiveness and impacts, methods, or different circumstances question.

3.2 Surveillance During Pandemic: Data and Marketisation

With the beginning of the COVID, the need to control the movement of the United Kingdom residents emerged. It led to the development of a state-based surveillance model. By mid-March, the United Kingdom had abandoned the manual contact tracing model, and had invited Big Tech firms, including Palantir to join their forces in establishing a contract-tracing app. Subsequently, the English public health service data unit, NHSX,[2] began its preparation for a contract-tracing app, amid Johnsons' techno-determinist claim that the United Kingdom could digitise our way out of pandemic. In May 2020, when the United Kingdom was on the pathway out of lockdown, the divergence between the United Kingdom-wide and the United Kingdom nations approaches have been noted. This was particularly evident with the Test, Trace, Isolate Support policy. Essentially, this policy signalled to launch the contact tracing scheme, foregrounding manual contact tracing.[3] Instead, they aimed to supplement the existing manual contract tracing by a "web-based" digital tool, which was not an application (app). Interestingly, in the COVID-19 context, data was only produced by contact tracing and apps, even if they constituted the focus of significant debate. The data released by the government were only a restrain about COVID-19 infection level and only vitally informed political debates. Such a situation presents a complex picture of the tension between politics and the economy at the United Kingdom level (Daly, 2021).

The UK approach to the contract tracing and the app are the most prominent examples of the divergence between the UK central government and the UK nations on the COVID-19 data policy. Essentially, there has not been a UK-wide contact tracing since each UK nation was responsible for its system. Since May 2020, Scotland has set up its contract tracing system, which was building in the capacity of the public healthcare service. On the contrary, England outsourced the NHS and opted to hire private companies to launch its contact tracing and app. Scotland, in the beginning, expressed reservations towards the NHSX app and the lack of consultation with the devolved administrations (Daly, 2021). However, the Scottish government changed its decision in August and announced the launch of a contract racing app, adopted on the Republic of Ireland's model, and developed by Irish company Nearform (Daly, 2021). Northern Ireland also adopted this model, making more sense given the geographical reasons. On the contrary, the Scottish decision to adopt Northern Ireland's model was political. Nevertheless, on the closer examination of the Republic of Ireland's app, the app is reasonably more privacy-oriented through the adoption of the Google-Apple app protocol. Furthermore, the app has a decentralised design and has a record of functioning well. This cannot be said about the NHSX app (Daly, 2021).

The choice behind the app varied between political and geographical choices. Essentially, Scotland opted for the Republic of Ireland's model due to political reasons. Yet, the need to comply with the Google-Apple protocol to establish functioning apps does limit political entitles' digital sovereignty. The Google-Apple protocol is known as promoting measures of privacy protectionism, which the UK Government's NHSX app lacks. However, the need to adopt this protocol for the successful functioning of the app could only reinforce Big Tech firm power.

On the adoption of the app, the Scottish government acted more transparently about its contract tracking app, compared to its counterparts in respect of the NHS app. According to a series of investigations carried out by openDemocracy in 2020 (Daly, 2021), Big Tech firms provided the UK government with the necessary digital infrastructure for the COVID-19 pandemic management. The Scottish government does not have a flawless approach to governmental transparency, due to the pandemic outbreak, the Scottish government relaxed freedom of information (FoI). This allows for the governmental agencies to extend their deadlines for responding to the FoI requests. In the same spectre, the access to public data and information has been extended beyond FoI. The COVID-19 data gathered allowed us to know who was infected and who and where died from the virus. Essentially, this allowed us to understand whether certain groups have been more impacted by the virus. In England, Black and Minority Ethics (BAME) backgrounds have been more prone to infection and death from COVID-19. This was grounded in the socio-economic circumstances, pre-existing health problems and structural racism. To compare, Scotland has a significant population of South Asian minorities. There was a piece of evidence to suggest that, in spring 2020, the community was more exposed to the virus. The evidence was proven in July 2020 when the National Records of Scotland published a study on ethnicity and COVID-19 finding that the South Asian minority were nearly as twice as likely to die of COVID-19 (Woods, 2020). At the same time, the Coalition for Racial Equality and Rights raised concerns about the lack of data available on the real impact of COVID-19 on the ethnic minority (Haria, 2020). This finding corresponds with the findings UK-wide.

About contact tracing, the Scottish government followed a less privatised and neoliberal approach to England. In England, these functions have been outsourced to a private company. Yet, marketisation and privatisation have obfuscated what kind of data is available to the UK public. Like in the UK and other western countries, the elders and disabled citizens were the most impacted by COVID-19 and remained most residents dying from the disease. One of the most prominent examples is the Home Farm care home, located in the Isle of Skye, where ten residents die because of the COVID-19. On the other hand, the marketised universities brought students back to campuses at the start of the new academic year. In September 2020, the UK students returned to their university accommodations.

Essentially, the approach adopted by the UK-nations varied significantly. For instance, Scotland opted for a contract training that remains in the public health service, rather than being outsourced to private companies, like England. Yet, the worst excesses of the UK's government digitalised COVID-19 response. Things have not been perfect in all the UK nations. There have been substantive limits of political autonomy and neoliberal logic. Data is still likely to be seen as a power both from a political and economic stance.

4 UK Economics: Challenges and Constraints

4.1 Pre-COVID-19 Economic Policy: General Overview of Economic Landscape in the UK

As it was mentioned above, the United Kingdom economy was hit hard by the 2008 financial crisis. The United Kingdom also witnessed a period of underinvestment between 2010 and 2018; and had the lowest average annual gross capital formation of all G7 countries. The latest threat to the United Kingdom economy was seen by the EU referendum. Brexit involved dramatic adjustment costs to the United Kingdom economy. Such costs were not yet fully understood, despite several attempts to estimate them (Blackaby, 2018). The early suggestion forecasted the economic output to be smaller than it would have been if the United Kingdom had remained in the EU (Blackaby, 2018). Essentially, the UK economy held up well in the earliest months. However, the economy slowed down from early 2017 (PWC, 2018). Such a slowdown continued into early 2018. However, there was certainly evidence of a growing GDP in the second quarter of 2018. The slow-growing GDP continued in 2019, as Brexit-related uncertainties speeded up. In October 2019, the EU and UK agreed on a withdrawal declaration. Such declaration has now been transposed into the law.

Essentially, the Government elections only carried out one message: "get Brexit done" and "unleash the potential of our whole country" (Conservative Party Manifesto, 2019). In fact, I am not arguing that Brexit should be labelled as economic policy. Yet, Brexit is unquestionably an event that impacted on the development of economic policy in the UK. Any later commitment has been now interpreted as a promise to improve the UK living standards by "levelling up" incomes and opportunities that contributed to leaving the EU. The economic impact of Brexit is still in question. Notwithstanding, its impact had consequences on macroeconomic policy in the UK. It has been noted that Brexit reduced openness associated with lower economic output. However, since the withdrawal agreement has become law, the UK government (2018b) summarised the potential beneficial effects of the Brexit agreement:

> In the long run, theory and evidence suggest that international trade increases output and raises living standards through four key channels:
>
> (a) Domestic specialisation allows each country to put more resources into what it does best, leading to higher productivity and real wages;
> (b) Greater variety of inputs and products for businesses and consumers, with increased competition and lower prices leads to (1) more efficient production for businesses; (2) increased consumer choice;
> (c) Access to new markets allows firms to scale their production up, leading to efficiency gains where there are increasing returns to scale;

(d) Exposure to competition leads demand to shift away from the least competitive firms while the most competitive (and productive) firms gain opportunities to expand into new markets. (p. 5)

Such effect is still measured and has been to a certain extent already recognized (Hope, 2019). However, the earliest post-Brexit economic evidence introduced several further unknowns and a possible lack of understanding of its long-turn impacts. Consumer spending remained relatively resilient despite the slowdown in the post-Brexit UK's growth. Business investment continued to shrink as a result of Brexit, as the economic uncertainty become more acute. Essentially, this has a huge impact on invent and stock building due to the plans for a potential no-deal Brexit. On the other hand, the job market generally remained strong, with unemployment down to its lowest rate since the mid-1970s (PWC, 2018). This evidence only furthered the understanding that the scarcity of workers finally lent them some bargains power, fed through increased real wage growth.

4.2 *Post-COVID-19 Economic Policy: How the COVID Crisis Will End for the UK?*

The UK introduced a number of economic policies, during the pandemic. They included: Coronavirus Job Retention Scheme (JRS)—grant support which aims to cover up to 80% of the "usual monthly wage costs" (up to £2,500), excluding fees, bonuses, and commissions; Coronavirus Statutory Sick Pay Rebate Scheme ("CSSPRS") for small or medium sized businesses; Deferral of VAT payments; Deferral of Income Tax payments; Competition Market Authority Guidelines aimed at relaxing competition rules for "essential businesses"; Time to Pay arrangements for other taxes; Business rates for hospitality, leisure, holiday, retail, and nursery businesses (and grants for retail, hospitality, and leisure businesses).

In addition, employers are not obliged to top up the remaining further 20%. As or 10 June, it is impossible to send new employees on furlough scheme. The scheme is set to function: from 1 March 2020 to 30 June 2020: 80% of the basic salary up to £2500 is covered. From 1 July to 31 July 2020: government continues paying up to 80% of the basic salary up to £2500; however, the furloughed employee could work part time. From 1 August 2020 to 31 August 2020: government continues to pay the 80% of the basic salary up to £2500, however employer is required to cover the NICs and pensions payment. From 1 September 2020 to 30 September 2020, the government will pay 70% of the basic monthly salary up to f £2,187.50, with a minimum contribution of 10% and NICs and pension contribution covered by an employer. From 1 October 2020 to 31 October 2020, the government would cover only 60% of the basic monthly wage up to £1,875, an employer would be required to contribute minimum of 20% of the wage and pay furloughed employees' NICs and pension contribution.

Several points should be analysed about the future of the UK economy. The key question remains if the current degree of state intervention was justified. As mentioned above, the UK government reached a highly exceptional decision to shut down a large part of the market economy to save the lives of the UK's residents. This action provided a rationale for such an exceptional policy response that aims to protect jobs and businesses. The additional support offered to businesses amounted to cheap loans and job subsidies. This is a good example of the government trying to prevent a temporary economic shock from becoming a prolonged economic depression.

However, the support measures, such as additional fiscal spending during the pandemic, were not an omnipotent approach. There were transaction costs of several good businesses going bankrupt due to the government's order to close the economy. Booth (2020) suggested that it could be inefficient if good businesses go bust and then re-enter the market or have their place at the market taken by other businesses when the crisis ends. Essentially, the moral hazard argument could be inapplicable here, as the COVID crisis is not an event that most businesses have been expected to insure against. The COVID-oriented intervention should be a call for the state to play a greater part in normal times as well.

Yet, the new economic measures are designed to only be temporary. At some point, the restrictions to protect public health would be lifted and the normal functioning of the market will be resumed. Essentially, even the classical liberal sympathisers believed that governmental intervention has always been expected to play part in the healthy functioning of the market. The public health issues should not be entirely left to markets. UK spent heavily in health aimed to release the pressure for NHS during the pandemic. However, lack of supply in medical workers, hospital beds, and COVID-related equipment cannot catch up with the rising demand. There is clearly a diminishing return effect in health spending here. The UK government spending in non-health gives people more incentive to stay at home instead of taking on excessive risks, which includes the funding for the COVID-19 vaccine. Townley (2009) argued that non-efficiency economic goals must be considered within the competition legal framework, as "jurisdiction may not have the legal capacity to achieve the ends by other means". (p. 39). Societal deliberations are labelled as "non-economic interests", and often, there are no powers to pursue these objectives. The risk of several deaths from coronavirus is a textbook example that serious negative externalities could be only dealt with by collective actions. However, the COVID-related deaths were not the only issue. It is disputed whether (for example) competition law could assist any public interest agreements, which include sustainability, as competition law assessment does not generally focus on consumer welfare. This might originate to the EU legal foundation; certain matters are solely within the Member States' exclusive competence. This is approved by the Chicken of Tomorrow case (2014), where the competitive spectre of sustainability depends heavily on how the national competition authorises and the EU Commission value the sustainability and balance this against competition law. Above all, free-market capitalism and COVID-oriented issues furthered the deepening conflicts in the intervention of economic and its interlinked social deliberations.

Furthermore, many questioned if the COVID-19 crisis brought a sudden end to globalisation. This argument is highly unlikely. There is a broad understanding that freer trade has brought high social and economic benefits in the UK. Certainly, there are critics of globalisation. Yet, it is far from obvious that the coronavirus crisis introduced any new concern for globalisation. It has been suggested that the delocalisation of products corresponded with the UK's shortages of basic medical equipment. However, the COVID crisis overwhelmed the UK supply chain even if any goods or services were supplied locally. It could be inadvisable to undermine the international trade benefits as this might reduce any future pandemic costs.

Lastly, how would our "new normal" eventually look like? Perhaps, this question is widely echoed across the UK. It is assumed that the "new normal" would remarkably mirror the pre-COVID crisis normality. The social distancing practicalities could remain to introduce long-lasting impacts in some sectors, including hospitality and leisure. The UK residents could be reluctant to go out, eat out or travel abroad. Nevertheless, consumer tastes are unlikely to change significantly, since most UK's residents would prefer to return to enjoy services they enjoyed before the crisis (Kohli et al., 2020). At the time of the writing, the UK still faced the COVID measures, requiring people to practise social distancing. Essentially, the UK Chancellor would prefer to respond to this crisis with a greater emergency budget. This might be a great stimulus package to tackle the problems of frictional unemployment. However, the gradual easing of the lockdown and a recovery in business and consumer confidence could be a significant factor to kick-start the economy, without the need for any further state intervention.

5 UK Economy and Health

5.1 Pre-COVID-19 Health Care

In the UK, the national health service (NHS) is the government-funded medical and health care service that everyone in the UK can use without incurring any cost. NHS is a tax-funded service, preforming well in the UK economy.

NHS is committed to meeting governmental transparency on how the funds are spend. In 2020/2021, the Department for Health and Social Care (governing the NHS in England) (The King's Fund, 2022) spent £192 billions for the NHS. This budget is used to fund a wide range of health and care services in England. Approximately, £2.5 billions were spent on the administration costs, such as the NHS payroll. The remains money is disturbed to meet the costs associated with the medical supply and health spending, including one's ability to visit a GP out-of-charge.

Health is a devolved power in the UK. In this respect, the politics and policy debates of the UK four systems are distinct, with their leaders having the autonomy to pursue different values with different success (Greer, 2008). The autonomy and diversity originate from the 1998 legislations, giving Scotland, Northern Ireland, and Wales greater power over public health and health services. Thus, autonomy is not subject to any law of the shared values. The UK states receive block grants, not related to need but could be spending as the UK states choose. Essentially, the UK political system encourages policy divergence (Greer, 2008). Divergence of labour markets, equity, and consequences for standards have always existed in the UK. The UK nations have always had distinctive histories and influences.

Scotland's trajectory has been established in its history. The underlying politics of Scottish health care has long had a high status: medical leaders are closely connected with the policy. This area is still home to a dense concentration of academics and professional leaders, who advise the Scottish government. Consequently, the medical-political landscape values professionalism and professionals. On the other hand, the Welsh health policy appears to be the most radical and innovative. Unlike the English and Scottish approaches, the Welsh health policy focus on improving the health sector, rather than the NHS. The overall strategy of localism changed in 2003, during the reorganisation of the NHS Wales. The change quickly focused on the politicisation of the health policy. Essentially, this made the Welsh public health agenda erode back to campaigns about a healthy lifestyle. The current Welsh approach is similar to the Scottish model. Northern Ireland's devolution model has not functioned the same as elsewhere, due to politics. Yet, the approach to public health policy has remained stable. In the end, health systems are difficult to be changed, with the NHS system never being a single legal unity. The directions of the public health systems are, unquestionably, heading in a different direction, with the COVID-19 pandemic putting pressure on the system.

5.2 *The Future of the UK's Health Care*

The COVID-19 pandemic unquestionably is the biggest challenge the health system has ever faced. Essentially, it is necessary to learn the lessons from this experience, whether from the rapid progress achieved through digitalisation or inequalities brought into focus. The future of health care should not be built to prepare for possible future waves. Foremost, the health care system should ensure a positive change and renewal benefiting in health and wellbeing for everyone.

The outbreak of the virus has demonstrated the UK health and care systems at their greatest. Health and care workers responded with dedication and skills, rapidly developing new manners of delivering services safely. Furthermore, hospitals offered each other mutual support and aid, while other local services worked together to support communities. This crisis underlined public support for the NHS. However, the events during the outbreak of the virus also exposed issues, somehow exacerbating existing shortcomings. Firstly, the COVID-19 pandemic demonstrated the weaknesses in a social care system, which has been underfunded for a long time. Essentially, this section was neglected by the government at the start of the pandemic. This resulted in tragic consequences for the staff, families, and service users, and in an unacceptable number of deaths of both healthcare workers and patients. This evidence demonstrated that social care is in desperate need of reform and investment. The potential reform would unquestionably aim to further the spending costs or reshape the known administrative structure of the healthcare system. Furthermore, several years of fragmented policies and poor workforce planning resulted in the crisis across both health and social care systems. The system has been touched by the disproportionate death toll on staff from an ethnic minority background. Research demonstrated that such excess death could have been explained by the gene, provably preventing to respond to the virus properly (UKRI, 2021). Furthermore, the funding squeeze, which was the result of the 2008 crisis, already made the functioning of the NHS service worse. The NHS entered the crisis already stretched to the limits. The lockdown has only deepened the social and economic consequences of the crisis.

The health and care system is exposed to significant challenges of restoring their services, not only in the hospital but also in social care, primary care, community-based services, and mental health. One of the greatest challenges remains to maintain the vaccination success, as well as the need to prepare for the potential new waves of COVID-19. Additionally, it remains difficult to deliver routine care while COVID-19 remains a risk. Despite the less visible in national data, demand pressure will extend to primary, and elderly care, mental care and community services. Such services still need to deal with the effects of the pandemic, including needs steaming from the virus and prolonged stay at the intensive care unit. The King's Fund's research (2021a) into the experience of recovery from other disasters found that support for mental health is essentially the most successful way for recovery. Aspects relating to the elderly care are also significant here. The pandemic has disproportionately affected elderly people living in the care home, which accounted for an estimable 30% of all deaths (Collateral Global, 2021). The main reason why care homes were seriously affected by the virus relates to the vulnerability of their residents, affected by their age, and underlying conditions.

Consequently, there are two greatest priorities for renewal. Neoliberal policies have again come under scrutiny since the UK Government have been adopting austerity measures to decrease its budget expenditure. According to Karamessini (2012), the neoliberal offensive has been a distributive effect on social cohesion. Mladenov (2015) argues that the important element of neoliberalism is to ensure the welfare dimension of the state, ensuring the optimal functioning of the markets. At large, this understanding could be translated into more expensive, less controlled, and lower quality healthcare services. This is a classic debate between lassies faire and government intervention, in the context of public good provision. Yet, the question in the post-COVID world remains how to identify the correct pathways through which neoliberal reforms could affect access to healthcare. As mentioned above, the pandemic introduced several perils impacting the population. Essentially, I propose that two pathways affect access to healthcare. The first angle concerns the policies directly or indirectly affect healthcare. The second angle concerns the policies affecting socioeconomic determinants. In order to avoid reconceptualizing healthcare as a private good, rather than a public good, these two angles consider a hybrid approach to address any reform needs. Overall, increased healthcare needs due to the COVID-19 with the presence of negative effects of neoliberal policies could further lead to increased varies to healthcare access for the population.

Since any health inequalities are typically aggrieved by neoliberal policies, which furthers societal inequalities and makes accessing the same level of health care by various social groups difficult, future UK political commitment together with public understanding of the COVID-19 effects are necessary to address the need to reform healthcare, potentially introducing more spending in the healthcare finding, as well as introducing plans to minimise the healthcare's hardship. Reforming the healthcare is a difficult incentive, as it remains difficult for the government provide high-quality healthcare services to all people, when there is a limited budget. The post-COVID-19 healthcare sector in the UK could embed three spheres for needs for reform and renewal. Firstly, the UK health service is facing inequalities in population health. Secondly, it is necessary to consider and embed the digital changes. The digital incentives might allow to introduce further innovation in the healthcare sector, involving plans of creating a closely integrated system. This plan could have potentially included various options on how to access the essential healthcare systems either via home, or community centre rather than the hospital. Lastly, the reform of social care is of utmost importance. Looking beyond the immediate issues of restoring the NHS services, the experience brought pandemic offered a unique opportunity to reconsider the focus of the UK health system. The approach for renewal should be delivered through coordinated actions across the NHS.

Firstly, COVID-19 exposed the deepening health inequalities that existed in the UK. Before the pandemic, there was a certain improvement in life expectancy amongst the social groups. However, the health inequalities between the richest and the poorest were still widening. The data suggests that men living in the least deprived areas could expect to live 9.4 years longer than those in the most deprived areas; for women, this difference was 7.4 years (ONS, 2019). This gap keeps increasing. The aftermath of the COVID-19 pandemic only furthered this growing gap. The virus has taken a disproportionate toll on the poorest health facing groups. In particular, the structural disadvantage was experienced by ethnic minority groups who were at the greatest risk of contracting and dying from the virus (UKRI, 2021). Consequently, the economic and social impacts of the virus are still worsening these inequalities. This is a call to renew the public policy to improve the population's health and combat the entrenching inequalities. To address any inequalities, the government should respond by addressing socio-economic drivers of healthcare system. At first, the step could include ambitious steps to improve health and reduce any inequalities. The government could achieve this by developing a strategy on addressing health inequalities, by being bolder in using all available resources, including tax and regulation. It is thought the funds distribution that often countries reduce the social inequality gap. The strategies in combat inequality often ignore the generation need: we need to have the collective investment in areas of health, education, and employment to improve the society outcome. Again, spending is not cost free, there is always an opportunity cost. Excessive spending could also result in an increase in national debt, which might lead to potential default or must be repaid by future households. The reduction of inequalities should remain the central focus of such regulations.

Secondly, as we live in the age of digitalisation, the COVID-19 pandemic furthered the need for accelerating digital changes. Within the weeks of the pandemic, almost three-quarters of general practitioner (GP) appointments were conducted via video (The King's Fund, 2021b), and nearly half of all consultations were conducted via telephone (NHS, 2020). The NHS has never witnessed a similar increased and rapid widespread channel shift. Such a shift was only possible by clinical and support staff rapidly changing the way they worked and sharing learning and good practice along the way. This technical and technological focus enabled the delivery of care. Such achievements stand in contrast to the poor record of the digital shift noticed in England, including the over-centralised decision-making process and insufficient investment in such infrastructure. Essentially, such factors only hampered the process for too long. This process has been also mirrored in the digitalisation of social care, which has been contained in the past by lack of funding.

By looking at the present issues and development, the task of the national bodies is substantially to learn lessons from the COVID-19 pandemic experience. The digital legacy of the pandemic needs to be durable: it needs to be built on public consent and support of health and care staff in their roles. Such rapid development could be a cornerstone of future digital change. Unquestionably, this includes the need to understand the impact of this innovative environment, as well as the development of necessary tools with transparency and involvement from pubic and health staff. Such tools should prevent the widening of health inequalities. Importantly, this chapter argues that most medical services must be done in hospitals. In terms of technology, the latest technology allows personal devices to monitor some simple health indicators of individuals. The data is then analysed using various methods or could be handed to doctors. For the post-pandemic reality, innovation should be seen as the most important aspect, taking for in developing new medicines, studying diseases, etc. For COVID, the most important innovation must be vaccination development or finding cures to COVID. All things mentioned above require spending or market incentives.

Thirdly, there is a huge importance for improving the social care system. The scale of deaths recorded at care homes from COVID-19 is a national tragedy. Between March and mid-June 2020, approximately more than 19,000 care home residents died from COVID-19 (ONS, 2020). A further 16,000 care home residents lost their lives to COVID-19 between November 2020 and early February 2021 (ONS, 2021). Despite any effort of staff, it remained difficult to keep staff and care home residents relatively safe, particularly at the early stages of the COVID-19 pandemic. Essentially, several factors contributed to this, inclining challenges in obtaining PPE (PPE refers to personal protective equipment) and financial support. This only furthered the already existing crisis caused by the austerity measures. The social system care has been not adequately supported for many years before the pandemic outbreak. A possible positive vision of social care could be foremost achieved by the government urgently addressing the funding pressures (ADASS, 2021). This could further prevent the deterioration of experience and outcomes for people in need of social care support. Such wider reform should introduce proposals for longer-term investment, creating fairer systems. Any proposal needs to recognise that the problem of social care is not the funding, but also lack of adequate quality and fragmentation of the NHS.

To achieve the aforementioned factors, the renewal of the health and social care system should not rely on past mistakes. The 2019 Conservative Party manifesto made the NHS a key priority, promising to resolve any pitfalls of the sector. Essentially, this message is achievable through the tailored approach of public services working together with local communities by putting the welfare of the workforce at the key point of the agenda. Such action requires the involvement of local, regional, and national authorities. Making progress requires political involvement, not only to push the contentious long-term social care reform but to renew the existing framework learning from the furthering perils of the pandemic.

6 Education

6.1 Pre-COVID-19 Education Era

In the UK policy perception, education, skills, and learning are considered as a universal solution to a vast array of socio-economic problems. This has been officially endorsed in 1997 by the Labour government, which aimed to establish a "knowledge-driven economy" (DTI, 1998). Essentially, the UK educational system is a devolved matter. It means that each of the UK countries has a separate system. The UK Government is responsible for England, the Welsh Government is responsible for Wales, while the Scottish Government and the Northern Ireland, Executive are responsible for Scotland and Northern Ireland, respectively. According to the OECD, the overall knowledge and skills of British pupils rank in 13th place in reading, mathematics, and science.

In each UK country, there are five stages of education: early years, primary, secondary, further education, and higher education. Full-time education is compulsory for all children between the age of 5 and 16. In England, compulsory education has been extended to 18 for those born on or before 1 September 1997. The National Circular provides a framework of education in England and Wales for children between the ages of 5 and 18. The Scottish equivalent is the Curriculum for Excellence programme, while in Northern Ireland the governing body is known as the Common Curriculum.

UK education is also exposed to the crisis of reform. In 2018, the Guardian commended that successful schools tend to choose pupils from wealthy backgrounds. Students from a deprived background and challenging students are often concentrated in schools that do less in the inspection. Furthermore, children from prosperous backgrounds tend to study at outstanding schools, compared to disadvantaged children that are likely to be in an inadequate educational institution (*The Guardian*, 2018). However, this inequality gap is closing with more students from all social backgrounds studying in good or outstanding schools (GOV.UK, 2015). Yet, the problem remains ongoing. In 2016, the report conducted by the Equality and Human Rights Commission concluded that racial inequality remains to exist in the UK educational system. In 2021, the further report indicated that students from poor backgrounds, eligible for free school meals, tend to do less well at the overall figure of pupils (*The Guardian*, 2021).

To this date, the UK policy continues to picture the edition as an emerging part of the knowledge economy. However, little evidence suggests that the existing UK economy disregarded neo-Fordism and hierarchal low-trust management from its educational system.

6.2 The Future of Education in the UK

Low-skill jobs are vulnerable during the pandemic as many of them cannot be carried out at home. People with low level of education are most likely working in these occupations. Therefore, to better prepare for the next pandemic, automation of low-skill jobs might be a solution. Also, government should help push more people into high-skill jobs, this is achieved through education. The UK faced significant challenges to improve the education system. Even if a large proportion of young people go to university, there are still many people with low basic skills (Musset and Field, 2013). Several weaknesses hinder efforts to reduce inequality (Bagaria et al., 2013). The UK investment in education has always been vital to improve economic performance.

The COVID-19 pandemic is certainly characterised by a swift move into digital educational resources. During the COVID-19 pandemic, network usage has increased around the world. Most of the operators experienced a growth in the traffic volume of around 100%, as the networks, of enterprise and education networks moved to the consumer broadband networks. The biggest challenge for the existing broadband consumer network is the pandemic It was characterised by a rapid increase of the traffic distribution: traffic, which was previously distributed among education, public WiFi networks, or enterprises, has been combined into single network access with a fixed consumer broadband network. As a result, the changes were initiated in the traffic composition, which bought challenges for networks internationally (Sandvine, p. 5). The report of Sandvine demonstrated that the traffic has grown almost by 40% between 1 February and 19 April 2020 (Sandvine, p. 5). This is a staggering increase in the volume. The increase in the volume occurred during the date when the broadband was utilised by students and adults at work. The use of the internet is said to be increased by a larger demand from the end-users' side, which was witnessed on an increased volume of downstream video streaming, conferencing, or game downloading, mixed with upstream video conferencing, use of social media and messaging platforms. To ensure non-discriminatory internet access, in March 2018, the UK Government introduced a broadband Universal Service Order, which ensures that individuals have a right to request a broadband connection with a download speed of at least 10 Mbit/s, and upload speed of—1 Mbit/s. Due to the COVID-19 pandemic, the USO has been temporarily paused, while the BT is now starting to raise awareness to eligible consumers. Furthermore, the Department for Education announced their intent to introduce a package to support learning for vulnerable children (Get help with technology during coronavirus [COVID-19], 2020). The initiative offered the access to Microsoft 365, Oak Academy, Google Education and BBC Bitesize without any financial costs.

However, the post-COVID-19 education approach introduces several perils of socio-economic inequalities. There is a substantial gap in education achievement between people from various socio-economic groups. Such a gap is evident from the beginning of education and continues to its end (Feinstein, 2003; Hansen and Hawkes, 2009). Even if we have evidence to suggest that early years education is important, it needs to be reinforced with capital investment as learning is cumulative. COVID-19 pandemic implications have been widely documented (Andrew et al., 2020).

The study of Elliot Major et al. (2020) demonstrated that during the lockdown almost 74% of private school students benefited from full school days. It was almost twice the proportion of state school students. By the common deliberation, full school days are improving the quality of learning. Full day school is not only improving the educational abilities of the students, but also allows students to develop their interpersonal skills. Around a quarter of students had no formal tutoring during the lockdown. Also, Andrew et al. (2020) suggested that during the first lockdown children from higher-income households were more likely to benefit from online schooling and spend more time studying. So far, the evidence suggests that the inequality gap only furthered during the lockdown. The data also suggest that policy intervention as delivering laptops to disadvantaged students could have been more effective during the closure of schools when carried out as promptly as possible. Essentially, the disadvantaged students came from poor backgrounds and/or various ethnic groups. However, even if such help was provided, Montacute and Cullinane (2021) noted that students, returning to school upon the lockdown measures lift, reported a lower standard of work.

A variety of socio-economic inequalities could arise or deepen as a direct result of the COVID-19 crisis. Students are facing difficulties in the admission process when accessing higher education. Because prediction grades are no longer accurate in evaluating the abilities of students, many higher educational institutions increased their admission requirements. Meanwhile, many students delayed their application due to COVID, resulted in excessive competition. These are short-run issues, nevertheless very important. Furthermore, higher rates of unemployment could increase income inequality, making it even more difficult for students to face education during the pandemic. Based on this, students are less likely to access education due to their parents being unemployed, and the high unemployment rate will make students more difficult to find jobs after graduation. In the longer run, the implications of the pandemic mean less teaching staff, as the staff was directly affected by COVID infection, and lower educational achievement. These factors would hit the students from poorer backgrounds harder. Younger generations could see fewer labour market opportunities and disturbing education. Such prospects will be mirrored for gender, ethnic and regional inequalities. Essentially, inequalities are the driving trend of the COVID-19 pandemic. There might be changes in consumer preferences, the number of people working from home and other major shocks. Having that difficult financial pattern would only make it harder for the young generation to successfully progress into the labour markets.

7 Conclusion

This chapter assessed the outcome of the COVID-19 pandemic on the UK's economy. It highlighted the changes before and after the pandemic, considering the aspects relating to the economy, health, surveillance, and education. It will be some time before the real extent of the COVID-19 impact is clear. The present evidence is disturbing.

Essentially, the UK's approach to the pandemic could be pictured as "humanitarian" and "political". The former focused on the human strategy during the pandemic, including the lost lives and grieving. However, the approach to making sure that the virus does not discriminate reminded us that the pandemic was difficult to be fully controlled. The latter approach took us in a different direction, which highlighted the problems of this chapter. The political approach questioned why certain groups tended to suffer more from the pandemic, as well as drew attention to the UK's success in tacking the virus. In short, the political approach considered how the pre-existing political factors were linked and furthered by the COVID-19 pandemic.

On that account, the failure of British neoliberalism seemed worse than in the over. In particular, the Conservative, party ruling the UK, needed to make a greater ideological leap to meet most of the challenges introduced by the COVID-19 pandemic. This drastic overhaul of economic policy should remind us of two elements. Firstly, the political and media enforcers regarded as a common-sense approach could be regarded as an extreme movement, as the political decisions were often taken without its strong reasoning on the scientific approaches. Secondly, the acknowledgement that the system would fail would not replace the present problems. We need to ignite the change necessary to boost up the post-COVID-19 UK's economy.

Notes

1. UK constitution allows for devolution which refers to the transfer of certain powers for the central UK government to nations and regions within

the UK. Policies relating to COVID-19 were both passed by the UK government and each government or assembly of the UK nations.
2. The term NHS refers to the National Health Service. The NHSX refers to the digitalised national health service.
3. Manual contact trading at large referred to asking a COVID infected person to remember who they have been in contract with; the person could have identified only the people they know.

References

ADASS. (2021) ADASS Budget Survey. https://www.adass.org.uk/adass-budget-survey-2020, accessed 16 December 2021.

Alistair R., Niemeijer Brenda J. M., Frederiks Ingrid I., Riphagen Johan, Legemaate Jan A., Eefsting Cees M. P. M., Hertogh. (2010) Ethical and practical concerns of surveillance technologies in residential care for people with dementia or intellectual disabilities: An overview of the literature. International Psychogeriatrics 22(7): 1129–1142. https://doi.org/10.1017/S1041610210000037

Andrew, A., Cattan, S., Costa Dias, M., et al. (2020) Family Time Use and Home Learning during the COVID-19 Lockdown. Institute for Fiscal Studies (IFS), Report R178, https://www.ifs.org.uk/publications/15038, accessed 16 December 2021.

Bagaria, N., Bottini, N., and Coelho, M. (2013) Human Capital and Growth: A Focus on Primary and Secondary Education in the UK. In: T. Besley and J. Van Reenen (eds.), Investing for Prosperity: A Manifesto for Growth. London: LSE Academic Publishing.

Blackaby, D. (2018) The UK Economy and Brexit. In: Y. K. Dwivedi (ed.), Emerging Markets from a Multidisciplinary Perspective. Springer International Publishing.

Booth, P. (2020) How Should We Pay for All this Extra Government Spending. IEA blog, 2 April. https://iea.org.uk/how-should-we-pay-for-all-this-extra-government-spending/, accessed 20 December 2021.

Collateral Global. (2021) Report 6: Effects of COVID-19 in Care Homes—A Mixed Methods Review, https://collateralglobal.org/article/effects-of-covid-19-in-care-homes, accessed 10 December 2021.

Conservative Party Manifesto. (2019) https://assets-global.website-files.com/5da42e2cae7ebd3f8bde353c/5dda924905da587992a064ba_Conservative%202019%20Manifesto.pdf

Daly, A., Milan, S., Treré, E., dand Masiero, S. (eds.), (2021) COVID-19 data on the fringes : The Scottish story. In: COVID-19 From the Margins. Amsterdam University of Applied Sciences Institute of Network Cultures, Amsterdam, pp. 135–140.

Davies, S. (2020) Pandemics and the consequences of COVID-19. Economic Affairs 40(2): 131–137. https://doi.org/10.1111/ecaf.12415
Desai, K. (2009) The New Stars of CCTV: What is the Purpose of Monitoring Patients in Communal Areas of Psychiatric Wards, Bedrooms and Seclusion Rooms? Diversity in Health and Care 6: 45–53.
DTI. (1998) Our Competitive Future: Building the Knowledge-driven Economy. London: HMSO Cm 4176.
Feinstein, F. (2003) Inequality in the Early Cognitive Development of British Children in the 1970 Cohort. Economica, 70: 73–97.
GOV.UK. (2015) Record Number of Pupils in "Good" or "Outstanding" Schools. https://www.gov.uk/government/news/record-number-of-pupils-in-good-or-outstanding-schools, accessed 17 December 2021.
GOV.UK. (2018) EU Exit: Long-Term Economic Analysis Technical Reference Paper. https://assets.publishing.service.gov.uk/government/uploads/system/uploads/attachment_data/file/759763/28_November_EU_Exit_Long-Term_Economic_Analysis_Technical_Reference_Paper.PDF, accessed 17 December 2021.
Greer, S. L. (2008) Devolution and Divergence in UK Health Policies. British Medical Bulletin 337: 2616.
Grimshaw, J. M., Eccles, M. P., Lavis, J. N. et al. (2012) Knowledge translation of research findings. Implementation Science 7: 50. https://doi.org/10.1186/1748-5908-7-50
Hansen, K., and Hawkes, D. (2009) Early Childcare and Child Development. Journal of Social Policy 38: 211–239.
Haria, J. (2020) COVID-19 and ethnicity in Scotland: Where's the data? [Online] Available at: https://www.crer.scot/post/2020/06/22/covid-19-and-ethnicity-in-scotland-wheres-the-data, accessed 16 July 2021.
Home Office. (2014) Draft Code of Practice. London: Home Office.
Hope, M. (2019) The Economic Impact of Brexit on London. GLA Economics. https://www.london.gov.uk/sites/default/files/brexit-analysis-final.pdf, accessed 17 December 2021.
Imperial Business Insights. (2021) Does COVID-19 Mean the End for Globalization? https://www.forbes.com/sites/imperialinsights/2021/01/08/does-covid-19-mean-the-end-for-globalization/?sh=20128c60671e, accessed 15 December 2021.
Karamessini, M. (2012) Sovereign Debt Crisis: An Opportunity to Complete the Neoliberal Project and Dismantle the Greek Employment Model. In: S. Lehndorff (ed.), A Triumph of Failed Ideas: European Models of Capitalism in the Crisis. Brussels: ETUI.
Knight, F. H. (1921) Risk, Uncertainty and Profit. University of Illinois at Urbana-Champaign's Academy for Entrepreneurial Leadership Historical

Research Reference in Entrepreneurship, Available at SSRN: https://ssrn.com/abstract=1496192

Kohli S., Timelin B., et al. (2020) How COVID-19 is Changing Consumer Behavior—Now and Forever. https://www.mckinsey.com/~/media/mckinsey/industries/retail/our%20insights/how%20covid%2019%20is%20changing%20consumer%20behavior%20now%20and%20forever/how-covid-19-is-changing-consumer-behaviornow-and-forever.pdf, accessed 14 December 2021.

Major Elliot, L., Eyles, A., and Machin, S. (2020) Generation COVID: Emerging Work and Education Inequalities. Centre for Economic Performance (CEP), COVID-19 Analysis, Paper No. 011, https://cep.lse.ac.uk/pubs/download/cepcovid-19-011.pdf, accessed 19 December 2021.

Mladenov, T. (2015) Neoliberalism, postsocialism', disability. Disability & Society 30(3): 445–459.

Montacute, R., and Cullinane, C. (2021) Learning in Lockdown. Sutton Trust Research Brief, January 2021. https://www.suttontrust.com/wp-content/uploads/2021/01/Learning-in-Lockdown.pdf, accessed 17 December 2021.

Mortenson, W. B., Sixsmith, A., and Woolrych, R. (2013) The Powers of Observation: Theoretical Perspectives on Surveillance Technologies and Older People. Ageing & Society 1–19.

Murkens, J. E. K. (2017) Democracy as the Legitimating Condition in the UK Constitution. LSE Law, Society and Economy Working Papers 8/2017. http://eprints.lse.ac.uk/87551/1/Murkens_Legitimating%20Condition_Author.pdf, accessed 12 December 2021.

Musset, P., and Field, S. (2013), A Skills beyond School Review of England. Paris: OECD Publishing.

NHS Digital. (2020) Appointments in General Practice May 2020. https://digital.nhs.uk/data-and-information/publications/statistical/appointments-in-general-practice/may-2020, accessed 17 December 2021.

OECD. (2020) United Kingdom: Economic Outlook 2020b. https://www.oecd-ilibrary.org/sites/38369400-en/index.html?itemId=/content/component/38369400-en, accessed 16 December 2021.

ONS. (2019) UK health indicators: 2019 to 2020. https://www.ons.gov.uk/releases/healthindicatorsfortheunitedkingdom2019to2020

ONS. (2020) Child Poverty and Education Outcomes by Ethnicity. https://www.ons.gov.uk/economy/nationalaccounts/uksectoraccounts/compendium/economicreview/february2020/childpovertyandeducationoutcomesbyethnicity, accessed 17 December 2021.

ONS. (2021) Deaths Involving COVID-19 in the Care Sector. England and Wales: Office for National Statistics. https://www.ons.gov.uk/peoplepopulationandcommunity/birthsdeathsandmarriages/deaths/articles/deathsinvolvingcovid19inthecaresectorenglandandwales/deathsoccurringupto12june2020andregisteredupto20june2020provisional#deaths-of-recipients-of-domiciliary-care-in-england, accessed 17 December 2021.
ONS. (2022) ONS website, statistical bulletin.
PWC. (2018) UK Economic Outlook. https://www.pwc.co.uk/economic-services/ukeo/ukeo-july18-full-report.pdf, accessed 17 December 2021.
The Guardian. (2018) Coalition Education Reforms "Fuelled Inequality in Schools". https://www.theguardian.com/education/2018/jun/30/coalition-education-reform-academies-fuelling-inequality, accessed 17 December 2021.
The Guardian. (2021) Tory MPs Accused of Adding Fuel to "Culture War" in Education Report. https://www.theguardian.com/education/2021/jun/21/tory-mps-accused-of-adding-fuel-to-culture-war-in-education-report, accessed 17 December 2021.
The King's Fund. (2021a) COVID-19 Recovery and Resilience: What Can Health and Care Learn from Other Disasters? https://features.kingsfund.org.uk/2021a/02/covid-19-recovery-resilience-health-care/?_ga=2.105860675.1788489819.1639931566-1434252453.1639931566#group-Mental-health-and-wellbeing-D7xtjmALyH, accessed 17 December 2021.
The King's Fund. (2021b) The Road to Renewal: Five Priorities for Health and Care. The King's Fund. http://www.kingsfund.org.uk/publications/covid-19-road-renewal-health-and-care#pitfalls, accessed 17 December 2021b.
The King's Fund. (2022) Key Facts and Figures about the NHS. https://www.kingsfund.org.uk/audio-video/key-facts-figures-nhs, accessed 10 December 2021.
Townley, C. (2009) Article 81 EC and Public Policy. Oxford: Hart Publishing.
UKRI. (2021) Ethnicity and COVID-19. https://www.ukri.org/news-and-events/tackling-the-impact-of-covid-19/understanding-coronavirus-covid-19-and-epidemics/covid-19-and-ethnicity/, accessed 12 December 2021.

Nigeria's Political, Economic, and Social Dynamics in a Pandemic Era

Osatohanmwen Anastasia Eruaga, Abigail Osiki, and Itoro Ubi-Abai

1 Introduction

Nigeria as a sovereign entity recognises the obligation of the government to protect the interests of its citizens. The idea of the Nigerian government as a provider and protector of the interests of its people as evidenced in the preamble of the Constitution of the Federal Republic of Nigeria, 1999 (as amended) (1999 Constitution) which hinges on the principles of freedom, equality, justice, and consolidation of unity in diversity (1999 Constitution, Preamble). The objectives of these principles are to ensure the security of citizens while facilitating developments which serve the society. However, since its independence on 1 October 1960, Nigeria has experimented with various political systems, ideologies, economic policies,

O. A. Eruaga (✉)
Nigerian Institute of Advanced Legal Studies, Abuja, Nigeria
e-mail: o.eruaga@nials.edu.ng

A. Osiki
University of Western Cape, Cape Town, South Africa

I. Ubi-Abai
University of Uyo, Uyo, Nigeria

A. Stojanović et al. (eds.), *The First 100 Days of Covid-19*,
https://doi.org/10.1007/978-981-19-6325-4_9

and cultural paradigms (Adebanwi and Obadare, 2010). The multicultural and religiously diverse nature of the country, coupled with the experiences of a three-year civil war and long periods of military rule have shaped the country's struggle to attaining an equitable, fair and just democratic state. These have contributed to political instability and socio-economic developmental challenges in the country which were exacerbated during the COVID-19 pandemic.

The actions of the Nigerian government towards the protection of its citizens underwent detailed scrutiny and circumspection in the advent of the coronavirus pandemic in March 2021. As the country experienced a steady increase in the number of confirmed cases within a few weeks, the government introduced several broad categories of containment measures including mobility and social gathering restrictions; economic palliatives; and hygiene-related practices in public spaces (COVID-19 Regulations, 2020; Chukwu, 2020; Kelvin-Alerechi, 2020; Obayomi, 2020). To ensure these measures were implemented, the government provided several basic structures and facilities necessary for the country to function efficiently with the COVID-19 era. Furthermore, the Presidential Task Force (PTF) for the Control of Coronavirus COVID-19 was established on 9 March 2020 as the overarching structure to coordinate the country's efforts to contain the spread and mitigate the impact of the COVID-19 virus in Nigeria (PTF, 2020; NCDC, 2020).

Against this backdrop, this chapter examines Nigeria's policy responses to the pandemic and their impact on Nigeria's political and socio-economic development. The chapter argues that government's intervention was not restricted to only the formulation of policies but included practical welfare strategies to facilitate the provision of basic utilities which are key for social-economic development of Nigerians. This was a shift from the existing neoliberal governance model to a more welfarist model. However, these policies and strategies failed due to certain prevailing factors such as corruption and weak institutions.

This chapter is divided into six broad parts. Section 2 provides a brief overview of democracy and activism in Nigeria both before the pandemic and during the first three months of pandemic, i.e. from 27 March to 30 June 2021. Section 3 explores security and surveillance in Nigeria. A key point that emerges is the persistent brutality and violation of human rights of Nigerian citizens by state actors. Section 4 provides a critical analysis of Nigeria's economic policies from independence till the pandemic. The main argument in this section is that most of these policies were inappropriate for the socio-economic context of the country. As a result, the country continues to experience poor economic growth and rising poverty levels. This leads to Sect. 5 where the labour market challenges of Nigeria are examined. It describes how government's labour policies are underlined by neoliberal principles which do not consider the realities in the Nigerian labour market. The implication is that there is persistent informality and majority of the workforce have limited labour and social protections, if any. Section 6 considers how Nigeria's health sector was impacted by the pandemic. This chapter concludes by noting the continuous governance deficit and urges urgent action on the part of policymakers to avoid the looming socio-economic crisis in the country.

2 Democracy and Activism

Nigeria is a federation comprised of more than 250 ethnic groups, 36 autonomous states, and the Federal Capital Territory (The 1999 Constitution, section 2(2)). Nigeria adopted federalism as the mode of governance in 1950. The country's federalism denotes a division and vesting of law-making authority between the central government and the state units (The 1999 Constitution, sections 4 and 5; Babalola, 2013).

2.1 Democracy in Pre-Pandemic Nigeria

Shortly after gaining independence from British colonial masters, Nigeria's federalism suffered deep challenges that severely stagnated socio-economic development. Intense tribal loyalties and sectional interests culminated in the country going into the trenches of a military dictatorship, barely six years after independence. Military rule lasted till 1999, with intervals of civil rule between 1979 and 1983. Importantly, military rule in Nigeria was characterised by the suspension of the Constitution and the gradual degeneration into suppressive regimes where human rights abuses were prevalent. Successive military heads became increasingly hegemonic, leading to the commission of heinous political crimes (Amuwo, 2001).

With the transition into democracy in 1999, the country was expected to experience economic growth and increase in human development. The newly elected democratic President Olusegun Obasanjo in his acceptance speech highlighted the provision of infrastructure, job creation, poverty alleviation among others as priority issues to be addressed (Obasanjo, 1999). However, this speech turned out to be a mere political statement and did not translate to any actions by the government. Almost twenty-three years into this democratic dispensation which began in 1999, the scale of Nigeria's developmental failure remains on a downward spiral. The country continues to grapple with rising levels of poverty, socio-cultural conflicts, inequality, increasing unemployment rate, mounting insecurity, and poor economic growth among other developmental challenges.

At the heart of Nigeria's many developmental problems is corruption (Akinwumi-Othman, 2017), a phenomenon that several scholars assert predates the Nigerian post-colonial setting (Aluko, 2002; Ajayi and Ojo, 2014; Bolu, 2016). Indeed, corruption is argued to be completely institutionalized, perhaps more than democracy in the country (Aluko, 2002; Ajayi and Ojo, 2014). For example, Nigeria ranked 149 out of 180 countries surveyed with regard to the prevalence of corruption in 2020 (Transparency International, 2020). To address this menace, several anti-corruption laws and institutions have been enacted and established by various administrations. These include Economic and Financial Crimes Commission (EFCC) Establishment Act 2004; Independent Corrupt Practices and Other Related Offences Act 2000; Advance Fee Fraud and Other Related Offences Act 2006; and Money Laundering (Prohibition) (Amendment) Act 2012. However, the impact of these laws remains minimal.

A key factor that has facilitated this endemic corruption is the country's weak public institutions. In principle, the 1999 Constitution makes provisions for the organs of state and other democratic institutions to serve as checks against corrupt practices within the government and in the private sector (1999 Constitution, sections 85–88; 143 and Fifth schedule). However, in practice, the executive arm of government dominates and manipulates all other arms using tactics such as budgetary controls, fund allocations, promotion and appointment into political offices. Furthermore, this is aggravated by the fact that many employees of public institutions are themselves beneficiaries of the corrupt system (Adeyeri, 2010). Overall, the direct consequences of this corrupt system are retarded social development, economic stagnancy, discouraged foreign investments and reduced resources available for infrastructural development, public service, and poverty alleviation programmes (Page, 2018; Ogbeidi, 2012: 18; Mohammed, 2013).

In this regard, Nigeria's over 500,000 registered and unregistered civil societies have had to play a critical role in the entrenchment of democracy, good governance and eradication of corruption since the return to democratic government (CSO 2019 Sustainability Index, 190; Ukase and Audu, 2015; Orji, 2004). Through activities such as staging of protest marches, provision of platforms for public enlightenment and public debates on issues surrounding the formulation and implementation of government obligations and restraining the abuse of state power through court orders, these organisations have been at the centre of agitations to entrench accountability and good governance in the country. However, their effectiveness is increasingly being undermined by the government use of state agencies to stifle oppositions or criticism. For example, in the period leading up to the general elections in 2019, governments, at both the federal and state levels, restricted civic space by arresting and detaining individuals, especially journalists who expressed views critical of the government. Additionally, two state governments (Borno and Akwa Ibom) in 2019, introduced new stringent requirements for civil society organisations (CSOs) to operate within the state. In the same year, the Federal Government reintroduced several bills such as the CSO Regulatory Commission Bill, Hate Speech Bill, and the Social Media Bill, which if passed would have allowed the government to further stifle critical views and constrain constitutionally guaranteed freedom of expression.

2.2 *Democracy and Legal Challenges in a Pandemic Age*

Pursuant to the powers under sections 2 to 4 of the Quarantine Act of 1926 (the Quarantine Act), the government issued the COVID-19 Regulations 2020 (the Regulations). The Regulations gave the government wide powers to restrict or prohibit movements within Nigeria. Places identified as the infected areas—Lagos, Federal Capital Territory, and Ogun state, were immediately placed on lockdown on 29 March 2019 for an initial period of 14 days which was subsequently extended due to the rise in the number of infected persons (COVID-19 Regulations, 2020). Similarly, in accordance with section 8 of the Quarantine Act and in response to the pandemic in their jurisdictions, the respective state governments implemented mitigation measures within their jurisdiction. These measures included total lockdowns, prohibition of interstate travel, ban on social and religious gatherings, maintenance of social distance, closure of schools, dusk to dawn curfew and the temporary shutdown of open markets.

Initially, there were no legal challenges to these mitigation measures. However, several individuals and CSOs raised concerns that the mitigation measures would infringe on human rights and civil liberties and undermine the socio-economic foundations of survival and resilience structures of the country's most vulnerable (Soludo, 2020). Several incidents indicated that these concerns were not farfetched. Government at the federal and state levels used these measures to undermine critical political institutions and silence critics and journalists (Media Foundation for West Africa, 2020). For instance, on 8 May 2020, during the lockdown, the governor of Rivers State ordered the demolition of two hotels in the State as a punitive measure for violating the ban on hotel operations (Godwin, 2020). These hospitality establishments were in Eleme Local Government Area which was not among the two local government areas where lockdown measures were enforced (Ukpong, 2020). Assertions exist that the executive order to demolish these establishments was politically motivated. Another example of fostering political interests of the incumbent government could also be gleaned from the occurrence of ruling party campaign flag offs involving thousands of supporters in Edo and Ondo state (Akinwale, 2020) while restrictions on social gatherings were still subsisting. There were also records of inhumane treatment by government security forces in the bid to enforce the movement restriction measures. Apart from undermining the fundamental rights of Nigerians, these violations had several implications. For example, the indiscriminate detention of citizens for minor offences increased the risks of the spread of the virus; the arrest of journalists undermined public discourse and extortion put further pressure on the already uncertain income of many informal workers (Onuoha et al., 2021).

Section 45 of the 1999 Constitution validates laws which limit the enjoyment of the fundamental rights to freedom of religion, peaceful assembly, association, and movement in the interest of public health, among other certain circumstances. However, there must be a balance between protecting public health and respecting the rights of the populace (OHCHR, 2020; Cianciardo, 2010). Fortunately, CSOs reacted strongly to the human rights abuses by security agents. Organisations such as the International Centre for Investigative Reporting (ICIR), the CLEEN Foundation, Socio-Economic Rights and Accountability Project (SERAP), among other CSOs used the multi prong approach of data collection and analysis, public awareness, and mobilisation to launch spirited advocacy efforts (Kanu, 2020; Azu, 2020; Nnaemeka, 2020; Ojewale, 2020; Azu, 2020; Ewepu, 2020). One of the things achieved from this was the formulation of Guidelines for Policing during COVID-19 emergency by the Nigerian Police Force. However, this had little impact as members of the Nigerian Police Force who continued to violate the human rights of citizens leading to nationwide protests against police brutality for about three weeks in October 2020 (Iwuoha and Aniche, 2021).

The absence of connecting competence with performance is a feature of weak public institutions, this is also reflected in the implementation of government policies and directives as evidenced by various events occurring within the period under review. Most of the mapped out multi-sector or cross-dimensional strategies of the respective government levels were either not implemented or were improperly implemented. An instance of such underperformance could be gleaned from the handling of inmates within the correctional facilities. Correctional facilities and custodial centres in Nigeria are overpopulated and poorly maintained. The 240 institutions with a capacity of about 50,000 people were at roughly 146% occupancy level at the beginning of the pandemic. Preventing rapid spread, therefore necessitated decongestion of these facilities. In March 2020, the Federal Government approved the release of inmates convicted for or standing trial for minor or petty offences and those whose terms were almost over. These categories were estimated to be over 75% of persons in Nigeria's custodial facilities. However, there was poor and slow-paced implementation of the policy, with only 15 out of the 36 states releasing a limited number of prisoners, not less than eight weeks after the initiative was announced (*The Vanguard*, 2020). Executing government obligation requires a high level of managerial skills to avoid diminishing returns with compliance or growing non-compliance. Although failure to commence immediate implementation did not have direct pandemic effect on health, it however heightened security threats by triggering protests within the correctional facilities that led to the death of 5 inmates and injury of some officials (Alabi, 2020). Another example of a failure to implement commitments, is the failure of the federal and state governments to timeously implement the payment of salaries, hazard allowances, and provision of personal protective equipment (PPEs) for healthcare professionals

3 Surveillance and Security

As a federation, the central government, and the states in Nigeria share the responsibility of ensuring the security of its citizens, as its primary purpose (1999 Constitution, section 14). This obligation to provide security of citizens is fulfilled through an architecture comprising of several security agencies enforcing law and order. These security agencies are established by the 1999 Constitution and their respective statutory instruments. The security agencies include the Nigeria Police the State Security Services, Nigerian Immigration Services, the Nigerian Customs, Nigerian Civil Security, and Civil Defence (Afolabi, 2017). The fundamental rights of citizens, embodied in Chapter VI of the 1999 Constitution, serves as the yardstick to determine the extent of adherence to the primary obligation of ensuring security of citizens.

3.1 Security in Nigeria Pre-Pandemic Era

The Nigeria Police Force is the principal law enforcement agency, established in 1820, as part of the British colonial governance structure. The Force comprising of 36 state commands grouped into 12 zones is essentially responsible for preserving law and order through the prevention and detection of crime; apprehension of offenders; protection of property as well as the enforcement of all laws and regulations without prejudice to the enabling laws of other security agencies (Police Act, 2010, Section 4). The duties bestowed on the members of the Police Force include powers of arrest, search, and detention of person or property as well as the use of force in certain situations. For decades, the Nigeria Police has battled with the challenge of underfunding to acquire appropriate infrastructure and equipment to carry out its functions. Similarly, remuneration is abysmal for the over 400,000 members of the Force (Ayitogo, 2020). The allocation of N403 billion to the Nigerian Police Force in the 2020 budget, is the highest it has been allocated in the last 5 years (PLAC, 2020). This however amounts to only 22.3% of the security budget for the year. Further analysis of the budget reveals that recurrent expenditure including remuneration, makes up 96.4% of the budget for police formations and command. Capital expenditure at 3.6% of the budget is significantly low, considering the limited facilities. The challenge of underfunding has greatly inhibited the performance of the Nigeria Police Force, leading to inefficiency due to poorly trained and ill-equipped personnel. This has contributed to the escalating insecurity in the country. Consequently, it has become common for the military, an arm of the Nigerian Armed Forces, ordinarily responsible for defence of the Nigerian territory from external aggression, to be deployed to handle perceived instances of breakdown of law and order, even in democratic dispensations (1999 Constitution, section 217(2)).

Despite the constitutional obligations to protect the rights of citizens, which are also spelt out in respective laws establishing security agencies, security forces have been known to continuously infringe on these rights through widespread extrajudicial killing, use of lethal force to suppress civil unrest, torture,, and illegal arrests (Madubuike-Ekwe and Obayemi, 2018). For example, the Special Anti-Robbery Squad (SARS), a unit of the Nigerian police tasked with tackling crimes of violence and kidnapping is known to be involved in cases of extortion, torture, and ill-treatment of persons as a routine and systemic part of their investigation (Amnesty International, 2020). The inhumane ways the police carry out their duties is connected to the colonial-linked perception of the police as a tool of the State to keep citizens in check. This is further compounded by the "warrior-mindset" learned within Nigeria's prolonged military era (Alemika, 1993; Okukpon and Eruaga, 2021). The eight successful coups that brought about 29 years of military rule suspended the Constitution, creating room for the repression of citizens' rights. Additionally, corruption and poor welfare packages leave police officers open to political manipulation for the benefit of persons with financial strength. The use of armed forces even during the democratic dispensation in instances of civil unrest also raises incidents of inhumane treatment and excessive use of force. Members of the Nigerian Armed Forces are known to arbitrarily arrest and detain persons, torture and engage in the deprivation of life of persons under the pretext of restoring law and order (Human Rights Watch, 2019). Consequently, citizens generally perceive security operatives as adversaries.

Notably, while the state is saddled with the responsibility of security of citizens within its municipalities, the governors of the respective states have no control over the Police and other security agencies established by federal law (1999 Constitution, s214). These security apparatuses are wholly controlled by the federal government. State governments are thus unable to take immediate actions in situations of security emergencies without the federal government's approval. There have been agitations, especially by state governors for the creation of state-controlled security apparatuses. This move has been met with severe resistance on the grounds that the governors may employ the state-controlled operatives for their personal benefits.

Nigeria has faced series of internal security challenges that threaten the existence of the country; some of which still linger. From the mid-2000s, activists (known as militants), claiming to represent citizens' interests in the Niger-Delta region agitated for a greater share of the Country's oil revenue. These armed activists engaged in the large-scale vandalisation of oil pipelines, kidnapping of expatriate workers and conducting of acts of piracy and armed robbery against ships. These crimes and violent acts ravaged the Nigerian upstream petroleum sector, causing the country to suffer huge losses in revenue. The security agencies were unable to effectively curtail the internal security threat. The Federal Government eventually initiated the Presidential Amnesty Programme to address the violent conflicts in the region and threats they portend for the Nigerian state.

Furthermore, Jihadist violence spreading across the northeast of the country continues to be Nigeria's most contemporary pressing security threat. Since 2015, violent attacks linked to the Muslim sect Boko Haram and its offshoot, the Islamic State in West Africa (ISWA), have ravaged the Northeast. The violence has caused over 350,000 deaths and forcefully displaced millions from their homes (Sanni, 2021). Both groups have proven impermeable by Nigerian security operatives (Newton, 2021). In August 2019, the military withdrew from areas of conflict into consolidated camps (Carsten, 2019), leaving more than 220,000 people without protection. In this fragile security situation, United Nations Office for the Coordination of Humanitarian Affairs (OCHA) reported that more than 7 million people were in urgent need of assistance, 1.8 million people were internally displaced, and 823,000 people were inaccessible to humanitarian actors (OCHA, 2019). Attacks have also adversely affected trade routes and grain cultivation in the North, contributing to a spike in the price of food grown in the Northern states.

Another significant security challenge is the protracted disputes between predominantly Fulani herders and farmers across Nigeria over land, water, and grazing routes (Newton, 2021). These clashes have become increasingly deadly since 2017 as global climate change and the resultant increasing desertification manifestations in the Northern part of Nigeria located in the Sahel region which has forced herders to travel further down south. The presence of the herders in the south are characterised by intrusion into farmlands, destruction of economic crops as well as deadly attacks. Benue State has recorded the deadliest attacks. The reoccurring conflict between herdsmen and farmers as a disruption of the food supply chain has become a major challenge to food security in Nigeria (Idowu, 2016).

Moreover, apart from brutality by security forces, there has also been a level of repression of the constitutional right of free speech. The right of citizens to constructively criticise government action is paramount to democracy and overall national security interest. The government frequently engages in surveillance and stifling the public utterances of known critics, political opponents, and journalists. The provisions of the Cybercrime Act enacted in 2015 has been used to further stifle free speech online under the guise of classifying online criticism as offences such as cyber-stalking and bullying (Adegborowa, 2021).

3.2 *Surveillance and Security in a Pandemic Era*

In line with the concept of human security as a "public good" (Ersel, 2017) the advent of the COVID-19 pandemic created the push for the federal government to initiate containment measures precipitated by the World Health Organisation (WHO). In March 2020, WHO urged governments to take urgent and aggressive action to stop the spread of the COVID-19 virus (Human Rights Watch, 2020). The Nigeria Centre for Disease Control (NCDC) through the National Emergency Operations Centre (EOC) and the Ministry of Health at federal and state levels led the public health response in Nigeria with oversight of the Presidential Task Force on COVID-19. Flowing from the ripple effect of the measures on all sectors of the Nigerian polity, several other government-related bodies were involved in response activities. For instance, agencies connected with points of entry (PoEs) into Nigeria were mandated to assist the Port Health facilities to boost response to the pandemic. Similarly, the National Emergency Management Agency (NEMA) supported by the Federal Ministry of Humanitarian, Disaster Management and Social Development (FMHDS), Federal Ministry of Agriculture and Rural Development (FMARD), and State Emergency Management Agency (SEMA) coordinated stakeholders towards effective national and local level developmental response to the health event. Based on the country's "test-treat-trace" strategy (NCDC, 2020, State surveillance), the responsible agencies utilised several basic surveillance techniques such as case identification and contact tracing through oral as well as documentary investigation; use of thermal scanners to detect abnormal body temperature; as well as targeted testing for the detection and control of the virus.

Adherence to the measures set up by the government remained essential to ensuring public health and safety. Enforcement surveillance teams were created at both federal and state levels. Although the composition of the enforcement surveillance team varied across the respective states, the Nigerian Police, Nigerian Army and the Civil Defence were among the most visible security institutions that remained an essential part of the surveillance framework. The enforcement surveillance teams adopted several general strategies to enable compliance. The most common across the states and the federal capital was physical monitoring in the form of patrols to disperse public gatherings. "Stop and question" tactics were also applied in the course of these patrol to people in transit, especially within curfew hours to ensure that these persons were within the class of persons authorised to be moved. Teams engaged in sealing up of businesses and places of worship, arresting persons as well as impounding vehicles perceived to be in violation of the extant lockdown directives and restrictions on gathering protocols. Defaulters were frequently arraigned for prosecution in Mobile Courts set up explicitly for this purpose (Izuora, 2020; Adediran, 2020).

Enforcement officers in the process of implementing compliance overtly carried out human rights violations with minimal consequences (Aborisade, 2021; Okukpon and Eruaga, 2021). There were more deaths due to brutality by the enforcement officers than from the virus itself (Okukpon and Eruaga, 2021) According to the National Human Rights Commission some of the major forms of human rights violations recorded included extra-judicial killings, violation of the right to freedom of movement, unlawful arrest and detention, seizure/confiscation of properties, discrimination, torture, sexual and gender-based violence, and extortion (Odigbo et al., 2020; Onuoha et al., 2021). The victims of these violations included essential workers such as health workers and journalists (Onuoha et al., 2021). Furthermore, between 31 March 2020 and 4 May 2020, there were 209 recorded incidents associated with the enforcement of the lockdown (National Human Rights Commission [NHRC], 2020a, 2020b). However, this can be argued to be an inaccurate picture of the human rights violation in Nigeria at this time. In addition to the culture of underreporting crime in the country, the lockdown was further extended till 4 June 2020. The latter time frame was not captured in the reports (Ayodele and Aderinto, 2016; Eze et al., 2019; CLEEN, 2011).

With monitoring and enforcement in place, the fear of sanctions shadowed initial adherence to lockdown measures. However, a few weeks into the implementation of the mandatory lockdown and restriction measures citizens began to display resistance (Adediran, 2020). Increased non-compliance by the citizenry was triggered by reasons not limited to poor living conditions, limited water, sanitation and hygiene (WASH) facilities (*BBC News*, 2020), financial challenges arising from diminished trade prospects and the uneven distribution and access to the promised palliatives due to the country's vulnerable and poor people (Ezeah, 2020; Onyeji, 2020; Njoku et al., 2020; Social Action, 2020). From a social interaction needs perspective, citizens found the imposition of mobility restrictions as a cultural shock to the communal lifestyle typical of Africans (Agulanna, 2010). Subsequently, monitoring and enforcement of the lockdown measures on the part of the government in several locations waned greatly, even when these measures had not been lifted.

4 The Nigerian Economy

4.1 *Pre-COVID 19 Economic Status and Policies: The March to Neoliberalism in Nigeria*

Nigeria's pre-COVID-19 economic status and policy progressively shifted from a relatively welfare state at the time of independence to an ad-hoc welfare state before settling as a full-blown free market economy (Ekanade, 2014). In this regard, the government transcended from active participation in all sectors of the economy to performing a mainly regulatory role. Following Nigeria's independence in 1960, the government took an active role in resource allocation and production activities aimed at fostering economic development, and presumably—shared prosperity. Notably, Nigeria's expenditure during this period was underlined by welfarist ethos with the government concentrating on the provision of public infrastructures to foster industrialisation, creation of employment opportunities and the subsidisation of essential commodities and social amenities (Egharevba, 2008).

The welfarist outlook of government was largely enabled by the sale of crude oil which provided unprecedented revenue for government expenditure. However, by the early 1980s, it became apparent that this welfare-statist system was not sustainable. This was because of dysfunctional market regulations, import substitution, high commodity dependence, misuse of public funds combined with political instability, corruption, and the fall of crude oil prices in the late 1970s (Fosu and Gafa, 2020; Saitoti, 2003). To sustain its expenditure, the government embarked on imprudent foreign borrowing which laid the basis for Nigeria's debt crisis and compounded the economic challenges of the country (Akinboye, 2010).

The first serious attempt to examine the role of the state in economic development post-independence was in 1981 when the Shehu Shagari regime appointed a presidential commission of inquiry to examine the role of public enterprises. This commission advocated for an increased role of the private sector in administering partially owned-government organisations. In the meantime, to address the visible downward trend in the economy, the Shehu Shagari administration introduced the Economic Stabilisation Act in April 1982. The Act contained austerity measures largely targeting Nigeria's excessive level of imports, emphasised fiscal discipline, reduction in state expenditure on social and welfare services, restrictions on borrowing to the private sector and other lending regulations. However, the implementation of this Act did not yield significant results. For example, the restriction on imports affected manufacturing industries who responded by closing down or laying off workers. Furthermore, the wage freeze in many public institutions and the embargo placed on employment into the public sector had severe implications such as the expansion of the informal economy and the increase of the national unemployment rate from 4.3 to 6.4% (Anochie and Duru, 2015; Owosekun, 1985; Njoku and Okezie, 2011).

Subsequently, the government approached the International Monetary Fund (IMF) for extension of the loan facility. However, the conditions attached to this loan would have far-reaching effects on the socio-economic and political system of Nigeria. These conditions included privatisation, a curb on government spending; trade liberalisation, withdrawal of subsidies on social services, and introduction of sales tax, among others (Owosekun, 1985: 212). This loan agreement was not finalised before that government was overthrown. The successive government agreed on the need for fundamental economic reform in Nigeria but refused the neoliberal policies of the IMF. This resulted in the boycott of Nigeria as international financial institutions insisted that Nigeria had to agree to IMF's conditions before fresh capital injections into the country could be authorised. Consequently, the government introduced a comprehensive package of austerity measures which unfortunately had colossal implications for Nigeria's national development. The negative impact on local industries led to retrenchment of many workers. The measures also led to high inflation, severe deterioration of social amenities and decline in real wages. For the first time, poverty and unemployment became a developmental challenge in the country.

By mid-1986, the Nigerian government began implementation of the neoliberal policy, called the Structural Adjustment Policy (SAP). This was a World Bank/IMF model implemented in many developing countries, aimed at strengthening market forces through privatisation, deregulation and liberalisation while rolling back the State's involvement in the economy (Bangura, 1987). The immediate consequences of this included disbanding of public enterprises, drastic reduction in industrial capacity utilisation, high production costs as a result of the high exchange rate of the naira with other foreign currencies and decay of public infrastructure (Ekanade, 2014). For example, Nigeria's industrial capacity utilisation, which was 70%, dropped to 38.2% within a year of the implementation of this policy (Chete et al., 2014). Unfortunately, the country has not attained the pre-SAP level of industrial capacity utilisation till date. By 1999, the Nigerian economy was marked by low GDP, galloping inflation, high unemployment, falling per capita income, an energy crisis and declining industrial capacity (Okonjo-Iweala and Osafo-Kwaako, 2007). The various governments following the restoration to democracy in Nigeria have continued to adopt privatisation policies justified by the need to reposition the government to concentrate resources on its core functions and responsibilities while enforcing rules and policies so that the market can work efficiently. The Bureau of Public Enterprise was created in 1999 as the key driver of the government's economic reform programme. A key challenge to the privatisation agenda is the problem of corruption which erodes transparency and accountability in the process of divesting previous government control and encouraging public–private partnerships as an alternative source of infrastructure financing.

The current government led by President Muhammed Buhari, as part of its election campaign, promised to improve the social security safety net of citizens with low income. In line with the promise, the government established programmes such as conditional cash transfer, feeding children at primary school level, installation of solar panels in selected markets to improve power generation for small and medium scale enterprises. These welfarist inclined schemes have suffered certain setbacks due to lack of accountability and corruption. For instance, some states in the southern part of Nigeria in 2020, complained that they had yet to benefit significantly almost three years after the schemes commenced (Igoni, 2020).

The pre-COVID Nigerian state before 1985, embraced planned and balanced economic development through systematic development plans. The adopted pathway to economic development in Nigeria has from all ramifications taken a neoliberal outlook. Macroeconomic indicators, unemployment rates, and trend in Foreign Direct Investment inflows as shown in Table 1, mirrors the status of the Nigerian economy.

Although the continued implementation of neoliberal associated policies might have facilitated economic growth, they have also squeezed public funding to the extent that the essential functions of the government including intervention in the labour market and provision of social welfare have been jeopardised (Bolarinwa, 2012).

Table 1 Summary of Nigeria's economy highlighting gross domestic product, unemployment rate, and foreign direct investment

Year	*Gross domestic product (₦,billion)*	*Unemployment rate (%)*	*Inflation rate (%)*	*Foreign direct investment ($, billion)*
1981	19,549.56	–	9.97	−0.79
1990	29,462.73	–	7.36	0.59
2000	25,169.54	–	6.93	1.14
2010	54,612.26	5.092	13.72	6.04
2020	70,014.37	33.3	11.4	2.35

Sources CBN Statistical Bulletin (2022), World Bank (2022), and NBS (2021)

4.2 *The Nigerian Economy in a Pandemic Era and the Future*

As a country heavily dependent on revenue from oil exports, the already weak national economy was severely affected by the global drop in oil prices during the outbreak. Formal and informal sectors witnessed increased economic vulnerability associated with the negative effects of the global drop in oil prices following the outbreak as well as of movement restrictions and social distancing measure. According to joint research by the United Nations Development Program and the National Bureau of Statistics, 43% of the enterprises sampled experienced a decline in the work force—with around 20% of workers in the surveyed enterprises losing their jobs during this period (UNDP and NBS, 2021).

The government in recognition of the adverse effect of movement restriction on the socio-economic well-being of its citizens introduced palliatives both at the federal and state levels (COVID-19 Regulations, 2020; Chukwu, 2020; Kelvin-Alerechi, 2020; Obayomi, 2020). Economic controls were in the form of interventions applicable to individuals and businesses (COVID-19 Regulations, 2020). The funding challenge faced by the federal and state governments during the pandemic led to a Public–Private-Partnership initiative when the federal government collaborated with the Coalition Alliance Against COVID-19 (CACOVID), comprising the Central Bank of Nigeria and the Deposit Money Banks as well as key stakeholders in the private sector in 2020 (CBN, 2020a). Notably, the Government began to: (i) harmonise exchange rates; (ii) initiated reforms to eliminate gasoline subsidies; (iii) adjusted electricity tariffs to more cost-reflective levels; (iv) cut non-essential spending; and (v) enhanced debt management as well as increased transparency in the public sector, especially for oil and gas operations (World Bank, 2021b).

Furthermore, the additional mitigation measures introduced included approved distribution of relief materials; two months conditional cash transfer (CCT); three-month suspension of repayment of bank loans; and food rations to the most vulnerable and internally displaced persons (COVID-19 Regulations, 2020, Section 5). The welfarist scheme established by the government to improve the social security net of the low-income citizens was grossly abused during the pandemic. The pandemic provided an avenue for the perpetuation of corruption. For instance, the government claimed that the feeding programme for primary school children continued, despite the imposed total lockdown; economic palliatives for the vulnerable and low-income earners were purchased, stored in undisclosed warehouses but not distributed (Amusan and Samuel, 2010; Okon, 2020).

Nonetheless, Nigeria's economy faces promising prospects despite the challenges faced as a result of the COVID-19 pandemic. The World Bank predicted that the Nigerian economy will grow at 2.5% in 2022 citing the rebound to higher oil prices as well as accelerated growth in some sectors of the economy (*Premium Times*, 2022). It is expected that the growth in total output would have a positive multiplier effect on other macroeconomic variables. However, uncertainty looms as the Federal Government postponed the plan to eliminate fuel subsidy to 18 months and determined the official exchange rate to about $1/₦415, while the parallel market reflects an exchange rate based on the forces of demand and supply, moves outrightly opposed by the International Monetary Fund (IMF) to propel economic growth (Nairametrics, 2022).

Moreover, with a vibrant population, it is expected that the Nigerian economy is set to bounce back from an economic status that is threatened by the COVID-19 pandemic to one that is resilient. But the challenge of corruption and financial indiscipline remain significant determinants to achieving economic development.

5 The Nigerian Labour Market

5.1 Nigeria's Labour Market

In the first two decades after its independence, Nigeria was one of the fastest-growing population globally, accounting for one in five Sub-Saharan people. As of 1970, Nigeria boasted of an estimated population of 55.98 million and growing at nearly 3% annually between 1973 and 1980 (World Bank, 2017b) and approximately 25% annual real GDP growth. The demographic trends had the potential to position the country for increased productive potentials through labour force participation and correspondingly labour supply, and by extension, raising economic support ratio. However, the Nigerian labour market was severely impacted by socio-economic conditions as a result of the implementation of neoliberal policies. To cope, as previously mentioned, firms had to either scale down production costs, engage in job outsourcing or close completely. At the same time, because of the promotion of the private sector as the main driver of the economy, the public sector also experienced contraction. Consequently, there was a sharp decline in employment opportunities, leaving many workers without jobs or access to new opportunities. Almost four decades later, neoliberal policies such as the Poverty Alleviation Programme (PAP) and the National Economic Empowerment and Development Strategy (NEEDS), among others, remain a part of the economic landscape of Nigeria.

The significant outcome has been that those without formal jobs had to turn to the informal economy to make a living.[1] Since then, the informal economy has emerged as an integral part of the Nigerian economy, serving an essential role of employment generation and source of income for Nigerians. This has led to the continued expansion of the informal economy. Correspondingly, research suggests that 93% of all employment in Nigeria is informal (ILO, 2018a). This expansion is part of the series of survival strategies adopted by Nigerians to weather the negative implications of the realities of the economic crisis, SAP and other austerity measures (Meagher and Yinusa, 1991). However, jobs created in the informal economy are characterised by low incomes, low productivity, insecure working conditions, and lack of access to social protection, among others (Osiki, 2018). The vulnerability of jobs in the informal economy is made worse because they are often unprotected by labour and social protection regulations.

Simultaneous with the expansion of the informal economy is the increase in poverty levels in the country (Aderounmu et al., 2021).[2] For example, the poverty profile of Nigeria has persistently increased since the start of the implementation of neoliberal economic policies from 27% in 1980 to 40% of Nigerians living below the international poverty line of $1.90 per person per day (Egharevba, 2011; National Bureau of Statistics, 2019; World Bank, 2021b). Indeed, Nigeria since 2018 has been infamously recognised as the poverty capital of the world (Uzoho, 2021). With 93.9 million people currently living below the poverty line, Nigeria has maintained this infamous position in close proximity with India which in 2021 was considered as the poverty capital. Yet, Nigeria's GDP amounted to 514 billion US dollars in 2021 and records the highest gross domestic product in Africa (Kamer, 2022). Considering the depth of Nigeria's adoption of the free market-friendly reforms of privatisation, deregulation and liberalisation, the government's efforts towards addressing poverty and inequality can be described as superficial at best.

While, Nigeria has experienced relatively improved macro-economic performance, particularly in the last decade pre-COVID. As highlighted in the previous section, the implementation of austerity measures has not translated to employment generation and poverty reduction (Bolarinwa, 2012; Igwe et al., 2016). Furthermore, years of piecemeal poverty alleviation programmes developed by the government have proven ineffective and had little impact in addressing the country's developmental challenges (Okosun et al., 2010). Besides this, national employment policies and strategies to generate productive employment have been formulated (Evoh and Agu, 2016; ILO, 2018b). Yet it remains unclear the extent to which these policies/strategies have created decent and sustainable jobs, with the unemployment rate at 23.1% in 2018 and increasing poverty levels (NBS, 2018; Ojima, 2019; Evoh and Agu, 2015).

Indeed, labour market policies remain largely underpinned by neoliberal principles. An example is the National Minimum Wage Act (NMA) 2019. Besides the political intrigues leading to the enactment of this law, the Federal Government did not initially consider it necessary to increase the minimum wage because of the country's poor economic growth (Opone and Kelikwuma, 2021). Nonetheless, after tripartite consultations the minimum wage was harmonised to N30,000 for workers. In terms of section 3, NMA 2019, every employer is expected to pay the above sum per month to every worker under the employer's establishment. However, this law in section 3(1) excludes part-time and piece-rate workers. It further states that the obligation to pay the national minimum wage applies to only establishments with at least twenty-five employees. As a result, the Act effectively excludes a significant proportion of the Nigerian labour force who are either in non-standard forms of work arrangements, or in the informal economy. In addition, the National Minimum Wage Act is a federal legislation that ought to operate throughout the federation. Still, the states have vehemently opposed its implementation in their respective states based on their alleged inability to accommodate the minimum wage as ascribed by the Act. Besides these, for workers who fall within the law's scope of application, implementation remains a key challenge as Nigeria lacks the resources to monitor the enforcement of labour standards (Adedeji et al., 2016; Adewumi and Adenugba, 2010).

5.2 *The Future of the Nigerian Labour Market*

Subsequent to the COVID-19 Emergency Regulations, businesses and work that could be conducted remotely continued from home. While, apart from workers deemed essential, those whose businesses or work could not be undertaken effectively remotely were forced to shut down temporarily, and their workers were directed to stay home with either full pay, reduced salaries, or no pay (Okunbor, 2020). In some extreme cases, many workers were laid off. Official statistics show that during the second quarter of 2020—which was the peak of the strictest lockdown measure, the unemployment rate increased to 27.1%, while underemployment increased to 28.6% (NBS, 2020). Similarly, research by World Bank shows that 56% of Nigerians with jobs before the pandemic stopped working (World Bank, 2021a; Contreras-Gonzalez et al., 2020). However, the workers in the informal economy who are the majority in the Nigerian labour force were the most affected by the lockdown measures. The majority of these workers comprising of informal waged employees, the self-employed in various informal sectors, casual workers, among others for whom work is a valuable means to gain daily sustenance, were particularly vulnerable to the sudden stoppage of economic activities (ILO, 2020).

In trying to sustain livelihoods and the economy, the government established the Economic Sustainability Committee to develop strategies to reform the economy during the pandemic (Economic Sustainability Committee, 2020). Within this context, the government introduced fiscal stimulus and expansionary monetary policies to facilitate the viability of businesses during containment. The monetary policies included an extension of a one-year moratorium on principal intervention loans; interest rate was reduced to 5% for one year; credit support was extended to the healthcare industry; various incentives to encourage longer-tenured credit facilities to individuals, households, and businesses (CBN, 2020b; PWC, 2020). The fiscal policies included an injection of 50 billion Naira credit facility to support households and enterprises whose livelihood were adversely impacted by the pandemic; 100 billion credit support to the health sector; and allocation of stabilisation funds to States (CBN, 2020b; PWC, 2020; NSIA, 2020). For the credit facilities to individuals and enterprises, the government deemed specific sectors vulnerable. These included value chain activities; the hospitality sector; healthcare sector, airlines, trading, and manufacturing/value addition sectors.

Similarly, to facilitate the protection of jobs, particularly in the private sector, the House of Representatives, on 24 March 2020, passed the Emergency Economic Stimulus Bill. The Bill, among others, aimed to provide temporary relief to companies and individuals by mitigating the financial consequences of the slowdown of economic activities caused by the pandemic. Furthermore, it sought to protect the employment status of Nigerians who would otherwise have become unemployed. In terms of the scope of application, unregistered businesses or employers were excluded from the benefits of this Bill. This, in essence, means informal enterprises or employers—who by virtue of their characteristics are mainly unregistered and the self-employed are not covered by this Bill. This Bill disregarded the realities of Nigeria, whereas previously mentioned, about 93% of all employment in Nigeria is informal (ILO, 2018a). However, this Bill was not passed by the Senate nor assented by the President of Nigeria (Ejiogu et al., 2020).

Nonetheless, workers in the public sector continued to enjoy the complete payment of monthly wages despite their inactivity. Furthermore, workers in the public health sector received additional incentives such as three months special COVID-19 allowance, payment of 50% of net salary as hazard allowance and a 40% increase on consolidated salaries were provided (Odiase, 2020). On the other hand, most employees in the private sector did not enjoy this benefit since the law which would have made this possible was never enacted. Consequently, most workers in Nigeria were left without any protection of their employment status.

Besides the above, a significant gap in the COVID-19 mitigation measures instituted by the government is the lack of specific policy targeted at the informal economy. For many of these workers, pre-existing vulnerabilities were exacerbated by policy responses to the COVID-19 pandemic, which made it impossible for informal workers to earn their livelihoods. As a result, the survival of these workers and their families—who in many instances are already living at the edge of various degrees of poverty—was threatened (Olurounbi, 2020). Notably, while the virus itself may not have been discriminatory, existing socio-economic inequalities meant that the impact of the virus and the various containment measures were significantly worse for informal workers, particularly women and youth (Abubakar et al., 2021; Alon et al., 2020; Gottlieb, 2020). This situation is made worse because Nigeria lacks a national social welfare programme, leaving citizens without welfare relief to cope with the socio-economic effects of the pandemic (Ozili, 2020). Indeed, while there is no updated poverty profile for Nigeria, economic simulations already suggest that more than 10.9 million Nigerians could be pushed into monetary poverty in 2022 by the economic effects of the pandemic (Irwin et al., 2021; Lain and Vishwanath, 2020). The pandemic has revealed the limitations of Nigeria's existing labour policy framework. Now, more than ever, there is need for the development of policies centred on the realities in the Nigerian labour market and the provision of decent work for all.

6 Health Care

6.1 *The Nigerian Healthcare Framework Pre-COVID*

The Nigerian health care system exists as a collaborative structure of multiple health care providers within the public and private sphere operating at federal, state, and local government levels. Studies reveal that the country's healthcare system is plagued with systemic weaknesses in its implementation in absolute terms and relative to other developing countries (Adeyi, 2016; Fullman et al., 2018). Nigeria ranked poorly based on the World Bank's Universal Health Coverage Service Coverage Index in 2017 (World Bank, 2017a).

Significant factors accounting for the poor health care system include rapid population growth, inadequate funding, mismanagement as well as socio-economic determinants of health such as access to education, availability of food, infrastructure, and the environment (Adeyi, 2016). The sources of financing for the Nigerian public healthcare system are general budgetary allocation, out-of-pocket payments, social health insurance, private voluntary health insurance, community-based health insurance, and donor funding. Budgetary allocation to the health care sector has persistently been abysmally low. In the annual federal budgets for 2018 and 2019, the health care sector accounted for only 3.6 and 4.5% of the total annual budget of 2018 and 2019, respectively (Aworinde, 2020; Adekoya et al., 2018). This low funding was despite Nigeria's pledge under the *2001 Abuja Declaration* to allocate at least 15% of her annual budget to improve the health sector (African Union, 2001). State governments are expected to commit some of their consolidated funding towards establishing and running primary healthcare centres, but funding at this level is also minimal. Financing of the health sector is also adversely affected by weak financial management that manifests in the form of mismanagement and corruption (Adeyi, 2016). Drug malpractices, absenteeism, bribes (informal payments), and embezzlement of money are also prominent in the health care system. Although several private actors exist in the healthcare matrix, these providers are usually not readily affordable to a majority of the Nigerian populace who ordinarily live below the poverty line.

The Nigerian Government established the National Health Insurance Scheme (NHIS) to attain equity in health service delivery. This scheme was established in 1999 after several previous attempts to implement various healthcare coverage reforms. Years into its implementation after its eventual launch in 2005, the vulnerable people identified to enjoy free and exempt mechanisms under the scheme still essentially pay to access health care. The plan covers only about 10% of the total population and is largely restricted to urban areas. In addition, the scheme is majorly accepted in government establishments where there is a lack of drugs and quality health care services. Private healthcare providers are unwilling to key into the scheme or have pulled out of the scheme mainly due to late payment by HMOs and running the scheme at a loss (Campbell et al., 2014).

The poor reward system for health care workers and the resultant industrial actions by health workers have also contributed to the steady decline of the system. There have been alarmingly increased incidents of mass relocation of health care workers outside of Nigeria due to the poor salary and decay in the health care sector. Consequently, although the government through the Minister of Health, promised to address these concerns, the case of previously unfulfilled promises concerning the same issues means the healthcare workers lack confidence in the government.

6.2 *Healthcare Development in a Pandemic Era and the Future of Equal Access to Healthcare*

The emergence of the COVID-19 pandemic in Nigeria created disruptions in health service delivery. The pandemic exposed the dilapidated state of the Nigerian health care system. Most hospitals and health care centres, especially those owned by the government were not prepared to respond to the COVID-19 outbreak. The travel ban instituted by several countries following the outbreak created a scenario where the derelict system threatened citizens, irrespective of social class. This, in turn, triggered some levels of positive health-related responses by the government in the form of setting up isolation centres in almost all 36 states and the Federal Capital Territory; provision of medical supplies; renovation of some hospitals, and setting up testing laboratories around the country (Aregbeshola and Folayan, 2021). Following these improvements, infected citizens using the government facilities during the first pandemic wave enjoyed the absence of user fees at the point of care (Healthwise, 2020). However, the policy of testing only sick persons coupled with the stigma associated with the disease meant that many people sought private health care for infections (Healthnews.ng, 2020). This translated to a substantial financial burden, especially since national health insurance packages for less than 5% of the population covered (Aregbeshola and Khan, 2018) does not include funding for COVID-19 management (Aregbeshola and Folayan, 2021).

In the wake of the pandemic, the health care sector witnessed investment from other private and international organizations (Toluwani, 2020; Aregbeshola and Folayan, 2021). Nigeria projected that it would need US$330 million to control its COVID-19 pandemic. However, it raised more than US$560.52 million, of which more than 90% came from the private sector and the donor/philanthropist community (Aregbeshola and Folayan, 2021). Unfortunately, the pooled COVID-19 fund is mainly being expended on the pandemic's temporary public health and clinical care measures. Very little has been invested in strengthening the health care system beyond the pandemic. As such, the prospects of a positive trajectory in health care beyond the pandemic remain minimal.

During the pandemic, healthcare workers as frontline workers are severely affected by the decline in the health care system. They grappled with the challenges associated with inadequacies of relevant supplies, including PPEs to protect themselves and tackle the virus. The challenges of inadequate PPEs, unpaid COVID-19 hazard allowances and other poor welfare issues, compelled resident doctors in Nigeria to embark on a national strike in June 2020. However, Nigeria's health care ranking on the World Health Organisation's (WHO) health system has improved from 187 out of 191 rankings two decades ago to 163 out of 191 countries. This improvement is arguably attributed to the increase in the health consciousness of most Nigerians, mainly because of technological advancement, rather than improvement in other non-human attributes of the healthcare system (Muanya and Ozioma, 2021).

7 Concluding Remarks

The Nigerian State has experienced fluctuations in the political, economic, and social spheres since its policy directions tilted toward neoliberalism. These fluctuations, greatly influenced by endemic corruption, weak institutions, lack of accountability and transparency in governance, have had profound impacts on democracy and civil activism, surveillance and security, health care, and the economy in general before and during the COVID-19 pandemic era, as highlighted in this chapter. In the absence of appropriate policy measures that address gaps, Nigeria may continue to experience retarded socio-economic and political development. Consequently, it is imperative that Nigeria's institutional frameworks be strengthened to ensure effective accountability, transparency in governance, obedience to the rule of law, adherence to societal customs and norms that shape positive economic behaviour and socio-economic activity. Related to this is the formulation and implementation of sound macroeconomic policies which take into consideration the realities of the Nigerian society.

Notes

1. Informal job refers to jobs which in law or in practice are not subject to national labour legislation, income taxation, social protection, or entitlement to certain employment benefits.
2. Arguably, while not all informal workers are poor, there is an income and poverty risk hierarchy in the informal economy with women being at the lowest level.

References

Aborisade, R. (2021) Accounts of Unlawful Use of Force and Misconduct of the Nigerian Police in the Enforcement of COVID-19 Measures. Journal of Police and Criminal Psychology, https://doi.org/10.1007/s11896-021-09431-4, accessed 04 January 2022.

Abubakar, I., et al. (2021) Lessons from Co-production of Evidence and Policy in Nigeria's COVID-19 Response. BMJ Global Health 6(3).

Adebanwi, W., and Obadare, E. (2010) Introducing Nigeria at Fifty: The Nation in Narration. Journal of Contemporary African Studies 28(4): pp. 379–405.

Adedeji, G. A., et al. (2016) Ergonomic Evaluation and Labour Inspection in Cluster-sawmill in Port Harcourt, Nigeria. Pro Ligno 12(2): pp. 38–50.

Adediran, I. (2020) Lockdown: 202 Street Joggers Bag Community Service, Fines in Lagos, *Premium Times*, 9 April, https://www.premiumtimesng.com/coronavirus/386945-lockdown-202-street-joggers-bag-community-service-fines-in-lagos.html, accessed 02 June 2021.

Adegborowa, E. (2021) Criminalisation of Freedom of Expression Nigerian Tribune 7 December, https://tribuneonlineng.com/criminalisation-of-freedom-of-expression-2/, accessed 4 December 2022.

Adekoya, F., et al. (2018) Analysts Unveil Highs, Lows of 2019 Budget. *The Guardian Newspaper*, 21 December, https://guardian.ng/news/analysts-unveil-highs-lows-of-2019-budget/, accessed 7 December 2022.

Aderounmu, B., et al. (2021) Poverty Drivers and Nigeria's Development: Implications for Policy Intervention. Cogent Arts & Humanities 8(1). https://doi.org/10.1080/23311983.2021.1927495.

Adewumi, F., and Adenugba, A. (2010) The State of Workers Rights in Nigeria: An Examination of the Banking, Oil and Gas and Telecommunication Sectors. Lagos: Friedrich-Ebert-Stiftung.

Adeyeri, O. (2010) Federalism and the Challenges of Nation-Building in Nigeria. International Journal of Research in Arts and Social Sciences 2: pp. 23–38.

Adeyi, O. (2016) Health System in Nigeria: From Underperformance to Measured Optimism, Health Systems & Reform, 2(4): pp. 285–289, DOI: https://doi.org/10.1080/23288604.2016.1224023.

Afolabi, M. (2017) Nigeria's Major Internal Security Agencies and their Statutory Roles. In L. N. Asiegbu, M. B. Afolabi, and D. O. Bodunde (Eds.), Unending Frontiers in Intelligence and Security Studies. Ado—Ekiti: Intelligence and Security Studies Programme, Afe Babalola University: pp. 225–268.

Agulanna, C. (2010) Community and Human Well-Being in an African Culture rames. Journal of the Humanities & Social Sciences 14(3): pp. 288–289, https://kirj.ee/public/trames_pdf/2010/issue_3/trames-2010-3-282-297.pdf, accessed 5 December 2022.

Ajayi, A. T., and Ojo, E. O. (2014) Democracy in Nigeria: Practice, Problems and Prospects. Journal of Developing Country Studies 4(2): pp. 107–125.

Akinboye, S. O. (2010) Africa's Debt Crisis: Perspectives on Nigeria's Escape from External Debt Trap. Journal of Global Initiatives: Policy, Pedagogy, Perspective 1(2): pp. 79–94.

Akinwale, A. (2020) APC Violated Protocols in Edo Campaign, Says PGF DG. *This Day*, 11 August, https://www.thisdaylive.com/index.php/2020/08/11/apc-violated-protocols-in-edo-campaign-says-pgf-dg/, accessed 17 May 2022.

Akinwunmi-Othman, M. N. (2017) Globalisation and Africa's Transition to Constitutional Rule: Socio-Political Developments in Nigeria. Springer.

Alabi, M. (2020) How Nigerian Security Operatives Killed Five Prison Inmates during Riot. *Premium Times*, 4 April, https://www.premiumtimesng.com/news/headlines/385878-how-nigerian-security-operatives-killed-five-prison-inmates-during-riot.html, accessed 16 May 2022.

Alemika, E. (1993) Colonialism, State and Policing in Nigeria. Crime Law and Social Change 187, pp. 202–211.

Alon, T., et al. (2020) How Should Policy Responses to the COVID-19 Pandemic Differ in the Developing World? National Bureau of Economic Research, No. w27273.

Aluko, M. A. O. (2002) The Political Institutionalization of Corruption and its Impact on Political Culture and Behaviours in Nigeria. Nordic Journal of African Studies 11(3): pp. 396–401.

Amnesty International. (2020) Time to End Impunity: Torture and Other Violations by Special Anti-Robbery Squad (SARS). Abuja: Amnesty International Nigeria, https://www.amnesty.org/download/Documents/AFR4495052020ENGLISH.PDF, accessed 02 June 2021.

Amusan, L. and Samuel, C. A. (2010) The COVID-19 Pandemic and the Crisis of Lockdowns in Nigeria: The Household Food Security Perspective. Africa's Public Service Delivery & Performance Review 9(1) https://apsdpr.org/index.php/apsdpr/article/view/484/803, accessed 17 January 2022.

Amuwo, K. (2001) Introduction. Transition as Democratic Regression. In Nigeria during the Abacha Years (1993–1998). In K. Amuwo, D. C. Bach, and Y. Lebeau (Eds.) The Domestic and International Politics of Democratization. Ibadan: IFRA-Nigeria. pp. 1–56.

Anochie, U. C., and Duru, E. E. (2015) Stabilisation Measures and Management of the Economy: The Case of Nigeria. International Journal of Development and Economic Sustainability 3(3): pp. 1–12.

Aregbeshola, B. S., and Folayan, M. O. (2021). Nigeria's Financing of Healthcare during the COVID-19 Pandemic: Challenges and Recommendations. World Medical & Health Policy, advance online publication. https://doi.org/10.1002/wmh3.484.

Aregbeshola, B. S., and Khan, S. M. (2018). Predictors of Enrolment in the National Health Insurance Scheme among Women of Reproductive Age in Nigeria. International Journal of Health Policy and Management 7(11): pp. 1015–1023.

Aworinde, T. (2020) COVID-19 Exposes Nigeria's Wobbling Healthcare System. *The Punch Newspaper*, 10 May, https://healthwise.punchng.com/covid-19-exposes-nigerias-wobbling-healthcare-system/, accessed 5 December 2022.

Ayitogo, N. (2020) #EndSARS Analysis: Poor Remuneration and its Contribution to Excesses of Nigerian Police Officers. *Premium Times*, 1 November, https://www.premiumtimesng.com/news/headlines/424019-endsars-analysis-poor-remuneration-and-its-contribution-to-excesses-of-nigerian-police-officers.html, accessed 15 January 2022.

Ayodele, J. O. and Aderinto, A. A. (2016) Socio-cultural Conditions of Victims and their Crime Reporting Practices in Lagos, Nigeria. African Journal of Criminology and Justice Studies 9(1): pp. 207–242.

Azu, J. C. (2020) COVID-19: Uproar over Restrictions, Human Rights, *Daily Trust*, https://www.dailytrust.com.ng/covid-19-uproar-over-restictions-human-rights.html, accessed 28 December 2021.

Babalola, D. (2013) The Origins of Nigerian Federalism: The Rikerian Theory and Beyond Federal Governance 8 (3): pp. 43–54.

Bangura, Y. (1987) The IMF/World Bank conditionality and Nigeria's structural adjustment programme. *Seminar Proceedings from the Scandinavian Institute of African Studies (Sweden)*, accessed 5 December 2022.

BBC News. (2020) Lagos Lockdown over Coronavirus: How Will My Children Survive? 30 March, https://www.bbc.com/news/world-africa-52093343, accessed 2 February 2022.

Bolarinwa, M. (2012) The Challenge of Job Creation in Nigeria: Some Policies are More Equal than the Others. Paper Presented at the NISER Research Seminar Series, 10 July, https://ngfrepository.org.ng:8443/bitstream/123456789/493/1/THE%20CHALLENGE%20OF%20JOB%20CREATION%20IN%20NIGERIA%3B%20SOME%20POLICIES%20ARE%20MORE%20EQUAL%20THE%20OTHERS%20-%20MICHAEL%20KAYODE%20BOLARINWA%20NISER.pdf, accessed 10 January 2022.

Bolu, I. (2016) The Anti-Corruption Legal Framework and Its Effect on Nigeria's Development, https://www.mondaq.com/nigeria/white-collar-crime-anti-corruption-fraud/490434/the-anti-corruption-legal-framework-and-its-effect-on-nigerias-development, accessed 5 December 2022.

Campbell, P. C., et al. (2014) National Health Insurance Scheme: How Receptive are the Private Healthcare Practitioners in a Local Government Area of Lagos State. Nigerian Medical Journal 55(6): pp. 512–516.

Carsten, P. (2019) Islamic State Fills the Void in Nigeria as Soldiers Retreat to 'Super Camps'. *Reuters*, 16 September, https://www.reuters.com/article/us-nigeria-security-insurgency-idUSKBN1W10FU, accessed 16 May 2022.

CBN Statistical Bulletin. (2022) https://www.cbn.gov.ng/documents/Statbulletin.asp, accessed 7 December 2022.

Central Bank of Nigeria (CBN). (2020a) Press Conference on Activities by CACOVID, 30 November, https://www.cbn.gov.ng/Out/2020a/CCD/CACOVID%20press%20conference%20FINAL.pdf, accessed 15 May 2022.

Central Bank of Nigeria (CBN). (2020b) Circular to Deposit Money Banks and the General Public: CBN Policy Measures in Response to COVID-19

Outbreak and Spillovers, 16 March, https://www.cbn.gov.ng/out/2020b/fprd/cbn%20policy%20measures%20in%20response%20to%20covid-19%20outbreak%20and%20spillovers.pdf, accessed 15 May 2022.

Chete, L. N., et al. (2014) Industrial Development and Growth in Nigeria: Lessons and Challenges. World Institute for Development Economics Research, Advance Online Publication January, https://doi.org/10.35188/UNU-WIDER/2014/740-0.

Chukwu, I. (2020) Palliatives: What Other States May Learn from Rivers' Model. *This Day*, *Business Day*, 19 April, https://businessday.ng/lead-story/article/palliatives-what-other-states-may-learn-from-rivers-model/.

Cianciardo, J. (2010) The Principle of Proportionality: The Challenges of Human Rights. Journal of Civil Law Studies 3(1): pp. 177–186.

Cleen. (2011) Criminal Victimisation, Safety and Policing in Nigeria. Lagos: CLEEN Foundation.

Contreras-Gonzalez, I., et al. (2020) The Labour Market Impacts of COVID-19 in Four African Countries (April to October 2020): Evidence from LSMS-Supported High-Frequency Phone Surveys on COVID-19 Living Standards Measurement Study. Washington DC: World Bank Group.

COVID-19 Regulations. (2020) https://covid19.ncdc.gov.ng/media/archives/COVID-19_REGULATIONS_2020_20200330214102_KOhShnx.pdf, accessed 22 December 2021.

Economic Sustainability Committee. (2020) Bouncing Back: Nigeria Economic Sustainability Plan, Federal Government of Nigeria, 9 July, https://nesp.gov.ng/wp-content/uploads/2020/09/Nigeria-Economic-Sustainability-Plan.pdf, accessed 13 January 2022.

Egharevba, M. (2011) Labour Market and the Poverty Globalisation in the Nigerian Informal Economy. In I. P. Onyeonoru, et al. (Eds.), Perspectives on Nigerian Labour Market and the Global Economy. Illorin: Michael Imoudu National Institute for Labour Studies, pp. 121–145.

Egharevba, M. E. (2008) Neo-liberal Socio-economic Policy and Human Development in the Informal Sector of Lagos State. PhD Thesis, Covenant University, Ogun State, Nigeria.

Ejiogu, A., Obiora, O., and Ejiogu, C. (2020) Nigerian Budgetary Response to the COVID-19 Pandemic and its Shrinking Fiscal Space: Financial Sustainability, Employment, Social Inequality and Business Implications. Journal of Public Budgeting, Accounting & Financial Management, pp. 919–928.

Ekanade, O. V. (2014) The Dynamics of Forced Neoliberalism in Nigeria Since the 1980s. Journal of Retracing Africa 1(1): pp. 1–24.

Ersel, H. (2017) Putting Human Security at the Heart of Public Policy Making, October 10, https://theforum.erf.org.eg/2017/10/08/putting-human-security-heart-public-policy-making/#:~:text=In%20public%20economics%2C%20national%20security,example%20of%20a%20public%20good.&text=Government%20strategies%20that%20overemphasise%20national,as%20a%20composite%20public%20good.

Evoh, C. J., and Agu, U. O. (2015) Employment Mapping, Institutional Assessment and Coordination Mechanism Study: The Case of Nigeria. Nigeria: International Labour Organisation.

Evoh, C. J., and Agu, U. O. (2016) The National Employment Policy (NEP) Of Nigeria: A Review, https://docplayer.net/58212754-The-national-employment-policy-nep-of-nigeria-a-review.html, accessed 12 January 2022.

Ewepu, G. (2020) Action Aid Calls for CSOs Inclusion to Stop Spread of COVID-19, *The Vanguard*, 3 April. https://www.vanguardngr.com/2020/04/actionaid-calls-for-csos-inclusion-to-stop-spread-of-covid-19/, accessed 15 January 2022.

Eze, V., et al. (2019) Investigating the Impact of Crime Reporting on Crime Control in Gwagwalada Area Council Abuja North Central Nigeria. Library Philosophy and Practice pp. 1–18.

Ezeah, P. (2020) Chaotic Distribution of CODIV-19 Pandemic Lockdown Palliatives in Abuja, Nigeria. King's Global Health Institute, https://www.kcl.ac.uk/kghi/news/peter-nigeria, accessed 4 December 2022.

Fosu, A. K., and Gafa, D. W. (2020) Economic Neoliberalism and African Development. In M. Tribe (Ed.), Economic Neoliberalism and International Development. London: Routledge.

Fullman, N., et al. (2018) Measuring Performance on the Healthcare Access and Quality Index for 195 Countries and Territories and Selected Subnational Locations: A Systematic Analysis from the Global Burden of Disease Study 2016. The Lancet 391: pp. 2236–2271.

Godwin, A. (2020) Wike Demolishes Two Hotels in Rivers for Flouting Executive Order. *The Guardian*, May 2020, https://guardian.ng/news/wike-demolishes-two-hotels-in-rivers-for-flouting-executive-order/, accessed 13 February 2022.

Gottlieb, J. (2020) Identity, Resilience, and Risk in the Informal Sector: Differential Effects of COVID-19 in Lagos, Nigeria. The Takeaway Policy Briefs from the Mosbacher Institute for Trade, Economics and Public Policy 11(10), August.

Healthnews.ng. (2020). Nigeria's COVID-19 Response Threatened by Social Stigma, http://www.healthnews.ng/nigerias-covid-19-response-threatened-by-social-stigma/, accessed 22 December 2021.

Healthwise. (2020) COVID-19 Tests in 61 Laboratories Free, Says NCDC, https://healthwise.punchng.com/covid-19-tests-in-61-laboratories-free-says-ncdc/, accessed 5 December 2022.

Human Rights Watch. (2019) They Didn't Know if I Was Alive or Dead: Military Detention of Children for Suspected Boko Haram Involvement in Northeast Nigeria, https://www.hrw.org/sites/default/files/report_pdf/nigeria0919_web.pdf, accessed 20 December 2021.

Human Rights Watch. (2020) Human Rights Dimensions of COVID-19 Response, March 19, https://reliefweb.int/sites/reliefweb.int/files/resources/Human%20Rights%20Dimensions%20of%20COVID-19%20Response.pdf, accessed 20 December 2021.

Idowu, S. (2016) Farmers-Herdsmen Conflict and Its Implication on Food Security in Kwara State, Nigeria, *JPSD* 2(1): pp. 158–174.

Igoni, D. (2020). We Deserve School Feeding, Cash Transfer Programme—Diri. *The Punch*, June 25, https://punchng.com/we-deserve-school-feeding-cash-transfer-programme-diri/, accessed 12 January 2022.

Igwe, S. C., et al. (2016) Impact of External Debt-induced Structural Adjustment Policies on Salient Aspects of the Nigerian Economy. Canadian Social Science 12 (12): pp. 42–47.

International Labour Organisation (ILO). (2018a) Women and Men in the Informal Economy: A Statistical Picture. Geneva: International Labour Organisation.

International Labour Organisation (ILO). (2018b) Decent Work Country Programme II (2015–2018b), https://www.ilo.org/wcmsp5/groups/public/---ed_mas/---program/documents/genericdocument/wcms_561063.pdf, accessed 15 May 2022.

International Labour Organisation (ILO). (2020) COVID-19 Crisis and the Informal Economy: Immediate Responses and Policy Challenges. *ILO Brief*, May, https://www.ilo.org/global/topics/employment-promotion/informal-economy/publications/WCMS_743623/lang--en/index.htm, accessed 15 May 2022.

Irwin, A., et al. (2021) Using Data to Combat the Ongoing Crisis, and the Next in Nigeria (January), https://blogs.worldbank.org/opendata/using-data-combat-ongoing-crisis-and-next-nigeria, accessed 15 May 2022.

Iwuoha, V. C., and Aniche, E. T. (2021) Protests and Blood on the Streets: Repressive State, Police Brutality and# EndSARS Protest in Nigeria. Security Journal, https://doi.org/10.1057/s41284-021-00316-z, accessed 17 May 2022.

Izuora, R. (2020) Anambra State Impose N10,000 for Facemask Violation. *Oriental News*, 26 June, https://orientalnewsng.com/anambra-state-imposes-n10000-fine-for-face-mask-violations/, accessed 03 January 2022.

Kamer, L. (2022) GDP of African countries 2021, by Country, https://www.statista.com/statistics/1120999/gdp-of-african-countries-by-country/#:~:text=Nigeria's%20GDP%20amounted%20to%20514,second%2Dhighest%20on%20the%20continent, accessed 17 May 2022.

Kanu, D. (2020) COVID-19 Lockdown: Right Groups Caution FG on Abuse Of Citizens' Rights, *The Sun*, 4 April https://www.sunnewsonline.com/covid-19-lockdown-right-groups-caution-fg-on-abuse-of-citizens-rights/, accessed 17 May 2022.

Kelvin-Alerechi, E. (2020) Rivers Govt Distributes Palliative to Riverine Community. *Premium Times*, 14 May, https://www.premiumtimesng.com/regional/south-south-regional/392753-rivers-govt distributes-palliative-to-riverine-community.html, accessed 7 January 2022.

Lain, J., and Vishwanath, T. (2020) COVID-19 and Welfare in Nigeria: New Evidence for Policy World Bank Poverty Team, October, https://pubdocs.worldbank.org/en/961791611161231868/pdf/COVID-19-and-Welfare-in-Nigeria-New-Evidence-for-Policy-October-2020.pdf, accessed 19 January 2022.

Madubuike-Ekwe N. J., and Obayemi, O. K. (2018) Assessment of the Role of the Nigerian Police Force in the Promotion and Protection of Human Rights in Nigeria. Annual Survey of International & Comparative Law 23:19.

Meagher, K., and Yinusa M. (1991) Limits to Labour Absorption: Conceptual and Historical Background to Adjustment in Nigeria's Urban Informal Sector. United Nations Research Institute for Social Development (UNRISD) *Discussion Papers*, https://digitallibrary.un.org/record/226334?ln=en.

Media Foundation for West Africa. (2020) Media and COVID-19 in West Africa: The Case of Nigeria, https://www.mfwa.org/publication/media-and-covid-19-in-west-africa-the-case-of-nigeria/, accessed 7 December 2022.

Mohammed, U. (2013) Corruption in Nigeria: A Challenge to Sustainable Development in the Fourth Republic. European Scientific Journal 9(4): pp. 125–135.

Muanya, C., and Ozioma, C. (2021) Nigeria Improves on WHO Health System Ranking, Says ACPN. *The Guardian Newspaper*, 26 November, https://guardian.ng/news/nigeria-improves-on-who-health-system-ranking-says-acpn/, accessed 7 December 2022.

Nairametrics. (2022) IMF Urges Nigeria to Abandon Official Exchange Rate, Fuel Subsidy, https://nairametrics.com/2022/02/08/imf-urges-cbn-fg-to-abandon-the-official-exchange-and-fuel-subsidy/, accessed 12 February 2022.

National Bureau of Statistics. (2019) 2019 Poverty and Inequality in Nigeria, https://nigerianstat.gov.ng/elibrary/read/1092#:~:text=In%20Nigeria%2040.1%20percent%20of,considered%20poor%20by%20national%20standards, accessed 7 December 2022.

National Human Rights Commission (NHRC). (2020a) Report on Human Rights Violations Following the Implementation of COVID-19 Regulations 2020a and Directives Issued by Federal and State Government from 31st March to 13th April 2020, https://www.nigeriarights.gov.ng/publications/119-report-on-human-rights-violations-following-the-implementation-of-covid-19-regulations-2020-and-directives-issued-by-federal-and-state-governments-from-31st-march-to-13th-april-2020.html, accessed 15 January 2022.

National Human Rights Commission (NHRC). (2020b) Report of Alleged Human Rights Violations Recorded Between 13th April to 4th May, 2020b Following the Extension of the Lockdown Period, https://www.nigeriarights.gov.ng/files/publications/SECOND-EXECUTIVE-SUMMARY-OF-COVID-19-VIOLATIONS.pdf, accessed 18 January 2022.

NBS. (2018). Labour Force Statistics: Unemployment and Underemployment Report (Q4-2017-Q2018): 4, https://nigerianstat.gov.ng/download/856, accessed 15 May 2022.

NBS. (2020) Labour Force Statistics: Unemployment and Underemployment Report: Abridged Labour Force Survey under COVID-19 (Q2 2020): 18, https://www.nigerianstat.gov.ng/pdfuploads/Q2_2020_Unemployment_Report.pdf, accessed 22 February, 2022.

NBS. (2021) Labour Force Statistics: Unemployment and Underemployment Report (Q4 2020), https://nigerianstat.gov.ng/elibrary/read/1238, accessed 5 December 2022.

Newton, T. (2021) A Country on the Brink: Nigeria's Unravelling Security Crisis, The Organisation of World Peace, 28 July, https://theowp.org/reports/a-country-on-the-brink-nigerias-unravelling-security-crisis/, accessed 23 January 2022.

Nigeria Centre for Disease Control (NCDC). (2020) Public Health Advisory to Nigerians on Coronavirus Disease, 1 July, https://covid19.ncdc.gov.ng/advisory/, accessed 2 March 2022.

Nigeria Sovereign Investment Authority (NSIA). (2020) Nigerian Government to Withdraw US$150 million from the Stabilisation Fund (SF) of the Sovereign Wealth Fund (SWF) to Contain Emerging Fiscal Risks. Press Release, 8 April.

Njoku, A. C., and Okezie A. I. (2011) Unemployment and Nigerian Economic growth (1985–2009). Mediterranean Journal of Social Sciences 2(6): p. 23.

Njoku, L., et al. (2020) Why Controversy over FG's COVID-19 Palliatives Persists. *The Guardian*, 26 April, https://guardian.ng/news/why-controversy-over-fgs-covid-19-palliatives-persists/, accessed 12 January 2022.

Nnaemeka, W. (2020) COVID-19: UN Warns Governments Against Violation of Human Rights Nigeria. *The Whistler*, 23 April, https://thewhistler.ng/covid-19-unwarns-governments-against-violation-of-human-rights/, accessed 18 January 2022.

Obasanjo, O. (1999) President Obasanjo's Inaugural Address to the Nation, 29 May, https://www.dawodu.com/obas1.htm, accessed 19 January 2022.

Obayomi, W. (2020) COVID-19 Tax Measures—LIRS Extends Filing Deadline for Annual Returns, 26 March, https://home.kpmg/ng/en/home/insights/2020/03/covid-19-tax-measures---lirs-extends-filing-deadline-for-annual-.html.

OCHA. (2019). Nigeria Humanitarian Response Strategy 2019–2021 (January 2019–December 2021), https://reliefweb.int/report/nigeria/nigeria-humanitarian-response-strategy-2019-2021-january-2019-december-2021-december, accessed 18 January 2022.

Odiase, P. O. (2020) COVID-19 and Labour Law: Nigeria. Italian Labour Law eJournal 13(1): p. 3.

Odigbo, B., et al. (2020) COVID-19 Lockdown Controls and Human Rights Abuses: The Social Marketing Implications. Emerald Open Research 2: p. 45.

Ogbeidi, M. M. (2012) Political Leadership and Corruption in Nigeria since 1960: A Socio-economic Analysis. Journal of Nigeria studies 1(2): p. 20.

OHCHR. (2020) COVID-19: States Should not Abuse Emergency Measures to Suppress Human Rights—UN Experts, 16 March, https://www.ohchr.org/en/press-releases/2020/03/covid-19-states-should-not-abuse-emergency-measures-suppress-human-rights-un, accessed 19 January 2022.

Ojewale, O. (2020) Rights-based Approach to Pandemic Policing in Nigeria. *TheCable*, 14 April, https://www.thecable.ng/rights-based-approach-to-pandemic-policing-in-nigeria, accessed 15 May 2022.

Ojima, D. (2019) Unemployment and Economic Development in Nigeria (1980–2017). *Advances in Social Sciences Research Journal* 6(1), https://doi.org/10.14738/assrj.61.5827.

Okon D. (2020) Lamentation Still Trails Lagos, FG's Palliative Package as Middlemen Hijack Programme. *Business Day*, 19 April, https://businessday.ng/features/article/lamentation-still-trails-lagos-fgs-palliative-package-as-middlemen-hijack-programme/, accessed 20 January 2022.

Okonjo-Iweala, N. and Osafo-Kwaako, P. (2007) Nigeria's Economic Reforms: Progress and Challenges. Brookings Global Economy and Development Working Paper 6.

Okosun, I., et al. (2010). Poverty Alleviation and Employment Scenario in Nigeria: A Review. *Insight on Africa* 2(1): pp. 67–78.

Okukpon, I. and Eruaga, O. (2021). Police Brutality and Human Right Violations in the COVID-19 Era through the Lens of Selected African Countries. ELTE Law Journal 2: pp. 32–35.

Okunbor, K. O. (2020) Arik Air Cuts Workers' Salaries by 80 Percent, *The Nation*, 25 April https://thenationonlineng.net/arik-air-cuts-workers-salaries-by-80-percent/, accessed 19 January 2022.

Olurounbi, R. (2020), Nigeria: Pandemic to Poverty in the Post-COVID Future, *The Africa Report*, 13 July, https://www.theafricareport.com/33300/pandemic-to-poverty-nigeria-in-the-post-covid-future/, accessed 15 January 2022.

Onuoha, F. C., Ezirim, G. E., and Onuh, P. A. (2021) Extortionate Policing and the Futility of COVID-19 Pandemic Nationwide Lockdown in Nigeria: Insights from the South East Zone. African Security Review 30(4): pp. 451–472.

Onyeji, E. (2020) Coronavirus: Group Assists Poor, Vulnerable Citizens During Lockdown. *Premium Times*, 4 May, https://www.premiumtimesng.com/coronavirus/394369-coronavirus-group-assists-poor-vulnerable-citizens-during-lockdown.html, accessed 7 December 2022.

Opone, P. O., and Kelikwuma, K. (2021) Analysing the Politics of Nigeria's 2019 National Minimum Wage: Towards a Public Policy. The Indian Journal of Labour Economics 64(4): pp. 1135–1149.

Organisation of African Unity (African Union). (2001) Abuja Declaration on HIV/AIDS, Tuberculosis and Other Related Infectious Diseases OAU/SPS/ABUJA/3, https://au.int/sites/default/files/pages/32904-file-2001_abuja_declaration.pdf, accessed 5 December 2022.

Orji, N. (2004). Civil Society and Reduction in Africa. Journal of Political and Administrative Studies 1(1).

Osiki, A. E. (2018) The Interdependence of Human Rights: A Case Study with Recommendations for Law Reform to Promote Decent Work in the Informal Economy and Street Vending Sector in Nigeria. Unpublished PhD Thesis, University of Cape Town.

Owosekun, A. A. (1985) A Case Study of Stabilization Measures in Nigeria. Africa Development/Afrique et Développement 10 (1/2): pp. 208–216.

Ozili, P. K. (2020) COVID-19 Pandemic and Economic Crisis: The Nigerian Experience and Structural Causes. Journal of Economic and Administrative Sciences 37(4): pp. 401–418.

Page, M. T. (2018) A new Taxonomy for Corruption in Nigeria. Carnegie Endowment for International Peace, https://carnegieendowment.org/2018/07/17/new-taxonomy-for-corruption-in-nigeria-pub-76811, accessed 20 January 2022.

Police Act. (2010) Cap. (P19) Laws of the Federation of Nigeria 2004, ss 3, 9 and 143.

Policy and Legal Advocacy Centre (PLAC). (2020) Analysis of 2020 Appropriation for the Nigeria Police Force, https://placng.org/i/wp-content/uploads/2020/03/Analysis-of-Police-Bill-Factsheet-1.pdf, accessed 4 December 2022.

Premium Times. (2022) Nigeria's Economy to Grow 2.5% in 2022-World Bank, https://www.premiumtimesng.com/news/top-news/505393-nigerias-economy-to-grow-2-5-in-2022-world-bank.html#:~:text=The%20Nigerian%20economy%20is%20expected,the%20World%20Bank%20has%20said.&text=%E2%80%9CNew%20threats%20from%20COVID%2D19,economies%2C%E2%80%9D%20the%20report%20said, accessed 15 May 2022.

Presidential Task Force (PTF). (2020) Government Palliatives, https://statehouse.gov.ng/covid19/government-palliatives/, accessed 20 January 2022.

Price Water Coopers (PwC). (2020) Government's COVID-19 Response Measures, https://www.pwc.com/ng/en/covid-19/government-covid-19-response-measures.html, accessed 20 January 2022.

Saitoti, G. (2003) Reflections on African development. Journal of Third World Studies 20(2): pp. 13–29.

Sanni, K. (2021) Boko Haram: 350,000 Dead in Nigeria—UN, *Premium Times*, 28 June, https://www.premiumtimesng.com/news/headlines/470476-insurgency-has-killed-almost-350000-in-north-east-undp.html, accessed 20 January 2022.

Social Action. (2020) Rivers State CSO/Media COVID-19 Situation Room Lament Federal Government Neglects of States in The South-South, http://saction.org/rivers-state-csomedia-covid-19-situation-room-lament-federal-government-neglects-of-states-in-the-south-south/, accessed 5 December 2022.

Soludo, C. (2020) COVID-19: Can Africa Afford Lockdowns? *Premium Times*, 24 April, https://opinion.premiumtimesng.com/2020/04/24/covid-19-can-africa-afford-lockdowns-by-chukwuma-charles-soludo/, accessed 17 January 2022.

Toluwani, O. (2020) Opinion: COVID-19 is a Game-Changer for Health Financing in Nigeria, 10 June, https://www.devex.com/news/opinion-covid-19-is-a-game-changer-for-health-financing-in-nigeria-97117, accessed 19 January 2022.

Transparency International. (2020) Corruption Perceptions Index 2020, https://www.transparency.org/en/cpi/2020/index/nga.

Ukase, P., and Audu, B. (2015) The Role of Civil Society in the Fight Against Corruption in Nigeria's Fourth Republic: Problems, Prospects and the way Forward. European Scientific Journal 11(2): p. 172.

Ukpong, C. (2020) Hotel Demolition: "We've Done No Wrong"—Wike. *Premium Times*, 11 May, https://www.premiumtimesng.com/coronavirus/392306-hotel-demolition-weve-done-no-wrong-wike.html, accessed 16 May 2022.

United Nations Development programme (UNDP) and National Bureau of Statistics (NBS). (2021). The Impact of COVID-19 on Business Enterprises in Nigeria, https://www.ng.undp.org/content/nigeria/en/home/library/mdg/the-impact-of-covid-19-on-business-enterprises-in-nigeria.html, accessed 15 May 2022.

United Nations Industrial Development Organization. (1985). Industrial Development Review Series, Nigeria. https://open.unido.org/api/documents/4810091/download/NIGERIA.%20INDUSTRIAL%20DEVELOPMENT%20REVIEW%20SERIES%20(15462.en), accessed 19 January 2022.

Uzoho, P. (2021) Report: Nigeria Still Poverty Capital of the World, *This Day*, September 6, https://www.thisdaylive.com/index.php/2021/09/06/report-nigeria-still-poverty-capital-of-the-world/, accessed 17 May 2022.

The Vanguard. (2020) COVID-19: Lawyers Alert threatens legal action over poor, slow pace of prison decongestion, 28 April, https://www.vanguardngr.com/2020/04/covid-19-lawyers-alert-threatens-legal-action-over-poor-slow-pace-of-prison-decongestion/, accessed 29 January 2022.

World Bank. (2017a) UHC Service Coverage Index: Nigeria https://www.who.int/data/gho, accessed 17 May 2022.

World Bank. (2017b) World Development Indicators 2017. Washington, DC, https://openknowledge.worldbank.org/handle/10986/26447.

World Bank. (2021a) Poverty & Equity Brief Nigeria, Africa Western & Central, https://databank.worldbank.org/data/download/poverty/987B9C90-CB9F-4D93-AE8C-750588BF00QA/AM2020/Global_POVEQ_NGA.pdf, accessed 13 June 2021.

World Bank. (2021b) The World Bank in Nigeria: Overview, https://www.worldbank.org/en/country/nigeria/overview, accessed 17 May 2022.

World Bank. (2022) World Development Indicator, https://data.worldbank.org/country/NG, accessed 7 December 2022.

Inequality Dimensions of Kenya's Responses to COVID-19

Muriuki Muriungi and Naomi Musau

1 Introduction

The World Health Organisation (WHO) declared COVID-19 a global pandemic on 11 March 2020. About a year later, Kenya had registered over 100,000 COVID-19 cases and nearly 2000 deaths from the virus (Worldometer 2021). The fast and extensive spread of the virus forced governments worldwide to take various measures, some of them unprecedented, to contain the pandemic. Admittedly, while some of the responses were legitimate and justified measures directed at containing the pandemic, other responses such as night curfews were neither borne of science nor defensible and justifiable. They ostensibly seemed to be aimed at dealing with crime associated with economic difficulties wrought by the pandemic. Most of the policy measures taken in response to

M. Muriungi (✉)
University of Embu, Nairobi, Kenya
e-mail: titomurk@gmail.com

KMK Africa Law Advocates, Nairobi, Kenya

N. Musau
IKM Advocates (DLA Piper Africa), Nairobi, Kenya

A. Stojanović et al. (eds.), *The First 100 Days of Covid-19*,
https://doi.org/10.1007/978-981-19-6325-4_10

COVID-19 particularly in developing countries such as Kenya exacerbated extant inequalities. There were deepening economic inequalities across gender, social, economic, and political classes with profound and pronounced consequences on the vulnerable. A large part of this resultant phenomenon was a result of the failure to undertake a socio-economic impact of the said COVID-19 responses before their imposition.

Kenya was no exception to the foregoing phenomenon especially given its high levels of informality in the economy, lack of robust welfare programmes, and high unemployment and poverty rates. The COVID-19 pandemic was both a public health emergency and an economic crisis, which prompted various policy responses in Kenya. The pandemic altered, reordered, and reconfigured the economic and political order, with pronounced consequences particularly on the vulnerable. The pandemic responses also potentially redefined and raised questions about the role of the state within a neoliberal economic paradigm that has long defined state-market relations. Thus, an assessment of the consequences of COVID-19 responses on the citizenry's various classes, particularly on the equality front, is essential.

This chapter assesses Kenya's COVID-19 policy responses with a view to exploring the dynamics of inequality of these responses. It highlights the pernicious effects of the various COVID-19 responses during the pandemic, particularly on the vulnerable, tracing the same to the structuring of the economy and failure to undertake a socio-economic impact assessment of the responses. The chapter argues that the policy responses, taken together, partially challenged the neoliberal framework, at least in so far that they involved a more active role on the part of the state. The chapter then calls for reassertion and mainstreaming of these responses beyond the post-COVID era.

This chapter is structured as follows: Sect. 1 deals with the introduction, Sect. 2 is an overview of Kenya's socio-economic context in the pre-COVID era. Section 3 discusses the impacts of various COVID-19 policy responses through an equality lens and Sect. 4 concludes the chapter.

2 Kenya's Political and Socio-Economic Context in the Pre-Pandemic Era

Kenya was one of the fastest growing economies in the African continent before the onset of the COVID-19 pandemic, registering an average growth rate of 5.9% of Gross Domestic Product (GDP) from 2010 to 2018 (USAID 2019). The country had achieved a lower-middle income country status and it still serves as the key entry point into the larger East African region (USAID 2019). The agriculture sector constitutes the backbone of the country's economy contributing up to 33% of GDP and employing more than 40% of the population, and 70% of the rural population (USAID 2019). Nearly two-thirds of the country's total population was living in poverty, making slightly above 3 dollars on a daily basis. The national Gini Coefficient, which measures the distribution of income across the entire population of a particular area thereby serving as a useful marker of inequality, stood at 0.404 in 2015/2016 indicating high levels of inequality (KNBS 2020a). In 2019, Kenya registered an economic growth rate of 5.4% with public debt standing at 61% of the GDP. The economy was projected to grow by about 6.2% in 2020 but the pandemic led to a drastic fall to about −0.1% negative growth rate (Onsomu et al. 2021). As of 2019, the number of persons working in the informal sector grew by 5.4% to around 15.1 million people, indicating the high informality levels in the labour market (KNBS 2020b).

In the education sector, Kenya had made progress achieving a near parity between boys and girls in terms of school enrolment (Presidency 2015). There have also been various pro-poor measures in education instituted by government including: provision of free primary education and subsidized secondary education; school feeding programmes; health and deworming programmes for students; secondary school bursary funds for poor students; higher education loans to needy students attending tertiary institutions; support to special needs education; enhanced budgetary support for early childhood education, among others (KNBS 2020a). With respect to the health sector, Kenya does not have a comprehensive health insurance scheme for all. However, there have been efforts to roll out universal health coverage (UHC) albeit with little success. Only about 11% of Kenyans are covered by the national insurance scheme (Ouma et al. 2020). The vast majority of informal sector workers who constitute the majority of the population have no medical insurance cover. Public health facilities are ill-resourced in terms of personnel, yet they serve a large part of the public. The health sector is underfunded averaging around 6% of the total budget, against the ideal 15% of the annual budget as set by the Abuja Declaration (Oneko 2020).

Government's investment in social policy and social protection measures has been limited and rather market centric. The structural adjustment policies that accompanied the neoliberal economic era led to a retreat of the state in provision of various public goods such as health and education (Mkandawire 2001). Accordingly, these essential public goods were, to a significant extent, left to the markets which meant that only those with the requisite economic power would be able to acquire them. This notwithstanding, Kenya has instituted some social protection measures comprising of cash transfer schemes mainly with the support of development partners. For instance, there is the nationwide cash transfer scheme targeting elderly persons above the age of 70 under a national safety net programme known as *Inua Jamii*.

3 COVID-19 Responses and Their Implications

3.1 Civil and Political Liberties

The declaration of COVID-19 as a formidable epidemic disease in Kenya enabled the government to invoke the Public Order Act, Cap 56 and the Public Health Act, Cap 242, which operate in extraordinary times to limit fundamental rights and freedoms (Kagwe 2020). While the Kenyan government did not declare a state of emergency, the invocation of these laws created a state of exception and influenced the kind and character of regulatory measures taken by the government (Kenya Law 2020). These measures included night curfew, lockdowns, quarantines, restrictions on travel/movement, a ban on public gatherings, and closure of schools and restaurants. The restrictions imposed by the Kenyan government in response to the pandemic, particularly within the first six months of the pandemic, were among the strictest measures among various countries (University of Oxford 2021). They had the effect of seriously limiting fundamental freedoms and liberties, with the state through its agents, especially the police, taking an increasingly prominent role. This was evident, particularly in the enforcement of the night curfew, quarantine, and lockdown measures where the state used police officers to forcefully ensure compliance among the citizenry (Kimari 2020). There were multiple accounts of police brutality during this period in a bid to ensure compliance with state directives (OHCHR 2020). For instance, over 100 people were killed by the police within the first months of the pandemic, as police officers sought to forcefully enforce the COVID-19 measures, especially the night curfew (Kiruga 2020).

The shift in approach to law and order or security-oriented approach in COVID-19 responses was a step toward a militarized state where liberties are severely limited under the guise of maintaining public order and public health. An argument may well be made that the night curfew served no useful purpose in dealing with the pandemic, at least from a scientific approach, given that the same did not apply during the day. The difficulties in enforcing the various COVID-19 measures during the night may partly explain the imposition of the night curfew (Luesby 2021). However, an argument may also be made that the demands on law enforcement during the night are significantly reduced due to reduced human activity during the night. The more likely explanation for the night curfew and lockdown measures may have been the need to contain crime given the economic difficulties that the pandemic had wreaked.

The COVID-19 responses had profound impacts on citizens' liberties, freedoms, and security, which reinforced and deepened socio-economic inequalities. To illustrate, persons infected and affected by the virus were unable to work either due to ill health or simply because they had to take care of their sick loved ones. In effect, the pandemic significantly reduced the number of a person's ability to work, thereby increasing the income dependency ratio in a country with a high-income dependency ratio.

The COVID-19 responses were both self-imposed and government-imposed. Owing to aversion behaviour, some citizens wary of catching the COVID-19 virus opted to stay at home and away from public places and places of work (Moore 2020). This had a direct deleterious effect on freedom of assembly and association and their participation in the labour market and other forms of public life. Other COVID-19 responses were government-imposed, partly motivated by the aversion behaviour of some citizens, the need to contain the pandemic, the need to avoid overwhelming the fragile health systems and to reduce incidences of crime. In particular, upon confirmation of the first COVID-19 case in Kenya (Ministry of Health 2020), the Kenyan government imposed a number of restrictions, namely: banning entry of foreigners through the Kenyan airspace, working at home mandates, and lockdown and quarantine measures, which in effect limited on the freedom of association and movement. In particular, a curfew and travel ban were simultaneously announced on 15 March 2020; all bars and restaurants except for restaurant takeaway services were closed effective 22 March 2020 while on 6 April 2020, movement into and out of Nairobi was suspended for 21 days. These measures had far reaching consequences.

3.2 *Fiscal, Economic, and Monetary Responses*

Prior to COVID-19, Kenya's economy had been on a steady growth curve. According to the World Bank, Kenya's growth from 2015 to 2019 was at an average of 4.7% with significant efforts to reduce poverty and inequality (The World Bank 2021). According to the World Bank (2021), the COVID-19 pandemic disrupted various sectors resulting in a ripple negative effect on the economy. The negative effect on the economy is demonstrated by the African Development Bank's report on Kenya's economic outlook which indicated that Kenya's public debt to GDP surged from 61% in 2019 to 72% in 2020. Furthermore, various countries, including Kenya, imposed lockdown measures to contain the spread of COVID-19. These measures impeded international transport, trade and tourism and negatively affected the economy.

The Government of Kenya, directly and through its various agencies and institutions, imposed several fiscal, economic, and monetary policies to cushion the vulnerable and stimulate growth given the contraction of the economy in light of the COVID-19 pandemic. One of the immediate fiscal policies introduced by the Central Bank of Kenya (CBK) was the elimination of all transfer charges between mobile money wallets and banks as well as increasing mobile money transaction limits while eliminating monthly total transaction limits which encouraged contactless payments. CBK also directed various banks to review loan extension requests from their customers for up to one year, with the banks bearing the costs of extension and restructuring of loans. CBK also lowered the Cash Reserve Ration (CRR) to 4.25% to provide additional liquidity to the commercial banks and the Central Bank Rate (CBR) was lowered to 7% from 7.25% to enable commercial banks to lower their loan interest rates and encourage borrowing. Furthermore, the government paid at least $130 Million of the verified pending bills to increase liquidity in businesses.

On 6 April 2020 and in subsequent presidential addresses, the President of Kenya announced various enhanced relief measures in response to the COVID-19 Pandemic including specific tax relief measures (His Excellency President Uhuru Kenyatta 2020). The tax relief measures included a 100% tax waiver for those earning less than Kshs 24,000 per month, reduced VAT rate from 16 to 14% and reduced corporate income tax resident rates from 30 to 25%. The government also directed the

Kenya Revenue Authority to immediately make payments of processed VAT refund claims to ensure liquidity of taxpayers during the pandemic.

Aside from the tax relief measures, one of the significant fiscal responses was the cash transfer and stimulus packages targeting the community's vulnerable groups, including the elderly, the youth, and people living with disabilities. The government also provided a stimulus package on a work for pay basis to artists, actors, and musicians who were involved in producing awareness content during the pandemic. Indeed, the fiscal and monetary policies and measures shifted the economic dynamics in the market, with the government taking a prominent role in providing relief measures to mitigate the high cost of living during the pandemic.

The ban on international travel caused huge disruption to the tourism sector, which ranks as Kenya's largest foreign exchange earner. A significant portion of citizens, particularly in coastal regions, depend on this sector. Besides the obvious economic loss to hotels and the government in the form of reduced revenue, low-income persons working in the tourism industry suffered a complete or near-complete loss of livelihood (Muragu et al. 2021). According to Obulutsa (2022), the tourism sector shed close to 1.2 million jobs as a result of the pandemic.

The horticultural sector and the wider agricultural sector also bore the brunt of the ban on international travel given the reduced demand for cut flowers and other agricultural products (Mbabazi 2020). Horticultural and agricultural exports dropped by over 60% resulting in loss of thousands of jobs and incomes for workers in horticultural farms and farmers who grow various crops and produce for the export market (Mbabazi 2020). Accordingly, restriction of international travel, while meant to reduce the spread of the virus, especially at the onset of the pandemic, resulted in untold suffering to many persons dependent on the tourism economy for livelihood and certainly exacerbated income inequalities.

The restriction in the public transport sector that required public transport vehicles to only carry half their capacity also had an adverse economic impact on owners of the vehicles and passengers (Okadia 2021). Persons using public transport in Kenya are the majority comprising of low income and middle-income earners, given the high cost of purchasing and maintaining a private vehicle. The requirement for public service vehicles (PSVs) to carry half capacity led to an increase in fares charged on passengers to make up for the reduced income. The increase in fares was also exacerbated by the rise in international crude oil prices due to disruption of international supply chains leading to a rise in fuel costs. As a result, the middle- and low-income earners were adversely affected by the increased cost of living.

The cash transfer and stimulus packages issued to the vulnerable groups were instrumental in cushioning the target groups against the effects of the pandemic. However, while cash is easy to administer and may offer the much-needed freedom to recipients to choose what to acquire with the money, cash transfers serve to distract from broad-based policy responses (Ouma 2021). In addition, the amounts disbursed in the cash transfers were barely adequate and as they only benefited a small proportion of the needy (Ouma 2021).

Whereas the fiscal and monetary relief measures can be seen as nationalistic and state-driven, they were predominantly funded through loans, significantly increasing Kenya's external debt. In light of the effects of the pandemic and the loans received by Kenya to combat the COVID-19 crisis, the International Monetary Fund (IMF) raised Kenya's debt distress risk from moderate to high (Miriri 2020). According to the African Development Bank, Kenya's Public Debt ratio increased significantly during the pandemic. Furthermore, while, these loans have a grace period before the repayment period commences, the taxpayer who was meant to be cushioned from the economic effects of the pandemic will have to bear the brunt of loan repayment aside from other existing loans that Kenya is repaying. In the end, the economic effects of the pandemic will still be felt in the years to come as Kenya repays her external debts.

3.3 Employment and Labour

The Kenyan employment sector is governed by various laws including the Constitution of Kenya, the Employment Act, the Occupational Health and Safety Act, the Employment and Labour Relations Court Act, and the Labour Relations Act, among others. Kenya also applies international labour standards, having ratified several International Labour Organisation (ILO) Conventions among other international and regional agreements (Danish Trade Union Development Agency 2020). Government statistics indicate that Kenya's employment sector comprises of over 80% employees in the informal sector (Kenya Labour Market Information System 2022). Furthermore, the number of unemployed youths has steadily increased over the years to 38.9% of young persons between 18 and 34 years (Alushula 2020). Job creation has slowed down prior to the COVID-19 pandemic and consequently, the numbers of unemployed Kenya increased significantly as a result of the COVID-19 pandemic.

The Government of Kenya introduced various measures targeting the labour market in response to the COVID-19 pandemic. These measures included the tax relief measures introduced to benefit the employees, employers and the self-employed by easing their tax burden. Furthermore, the Government encouraged employers to implement work from home strategies to reduce the risks of infection (Birir 2020). Government workers over the age of 58 years were required to take leave or work from home to alleviate the risk of infection. Additionally, vulnerable groups, the elderly and the severely disabled, received cash transfers to cushion them from the effects of the pandemic.

The restriction of movement and public gathering resulted in massive loss of revenue streams for workers in the informal sector and those in the creatives industry who depended on income from public gatherings such as concerts. On 6 April 2020, the President of Kenya issued a directive to the Sports, Art, and Social Development Fund to avail Kenya Shillings 100 Million to cushion embers of the creatives industry from the effects of the COVID-19 Pandemic. Following this directive, the Government provided a stimulus package for members of the creative industry through the work for pay programme to create a source of income (Permanent Presidential Music Commission 2020). The work for pay programme involved members of the creative industry producing various artistic expressions geared towards sensitization on COVID-19 in exchange for being paid a given amount (Ilado 2020).

Another significant COVID-19 response by the Government was the enhancement of social protection measures in the form of public works programmes that sought to cushion unemployed youths (Doyle and Ikutwa 2021). Through the then Ministry of Labour and Social Protection in collaboration with county governments and non-state actors, the Government of Kenya offered significant support in the form of cash, food, and medical supplies, especially in informal settlements (Doyle and Ikutwa 2021). The public works programme dubbed "Kazi Kwa Vijana programme" was targeted toward vulnerable but able-bodied youths living in informal settlements who provided manual labour for various government projects for payment.

The government's employment and protection of work responses created significant inequalities, with workers in the informal sector being more vulnerable during the pandemic. First, the lockdown and curfew measures imposed by the government resulted in a loss of revenue streams, especially in urban areas with 24-h economies. Secondly, some of the critical measures, such as social distancing in public transport, led to price hikes increasing the cost of living significantly in urban areas such as Nairobi (Gikandi 2020). These factors increased the inequality between the informal sector and the formal sector. The government's role in bridging the inequality gaps between the formal and informal sector through strategic measures was largely passive, and as a consequence, the gap significantly increased during the pandemic.

Workers in the informal sector lost sources of livelihood, and food security became a critical issue for those living in slum areas. The government handouts and cash transfers were marred by allegations of corruption, with the most vulnerable in the society suffering from loss of livelihoods (Wasike 2021). Furthermore, most of the workers in the informal sector did not fall under the targeted tax brackets and could only have benefited from the Value Added Tax (VAT) reduced rate which was not significant.

In a bid to stay afloat, various companies declared redundancies and either laid off staff or shut down completely (Wafula 2020). The government ban on public gatherings and the closure of bars and restaurants also negatively impacted the hospitality and creative industries (Chacha et al. 2021). The restrictions on movement and ban on public gatherings caused supply chain disruptions, preventing small-scale businesspeople from obtaining supplies for onward selling. Where they did, they bought them at higher prices due to the supply shortages. In addition, these measures exacerbated food insecurity given that most people purchase their food supplies in the open-air markets, which sell fresh farm produce at an affordable price. While the government issued stimulus packages to soften the impact of a loss of revenue, the packages were targeting specific groups, and consequently, a number of people were left out. The interventions adopted by the government for the protection of work were not as aggressive, and as a consequence, decisions on whether to lay off workers were left to employers.

The Kenyan government did not enforce any subsidy or tax incentives geared towards encouraging employers to retain employees during the pandemic, as was the case in some European countries (OECD 2020). Further, some of the surveillance interventions like curfews and lockdowns contributed significantly to the loss of income for various households. This is because the sustainability of those interventions at an individual level depends on the level of financial cushioning available to an individual. As a result, interventions such as working remotely, social distancing, and lockdowns were not beneficial, especially to the informal sector, which depended on daily livelihood income to survive. As a matter of fact, these interventions only widened the gap between those in the informal sector and those in the formal sector and significantly increased the poverty rate in the country.

The work from home mandates imposed by the government only favoured civil servants and those working in white-collar jobs in the private sector. These mandates were not directed toward the blue-collar workers and informal economy workers who constitute the majority of Kenyan workers, up to 83% of the total workforce in the country as of 2019 (Gikandi 2020). Informal workers do not have the luxury of working from home, given that the nature of their work almost invariably requires their physical presence. Even were if they were to fall sick from the virus, they would have had to go out to seek work, given the fact that they do not have the luxury of paid sick leave, as is the case with most formal sector workers. Further, most informal sector workers do not enjoy any form of health insurance (KNBS 2020a), leaving them exposed to further impoverishment if their relatives or themselves fall sick and have to pay out-of-pocket medical expenses.

For these reasons, the COVID-19 responses in the employment sector were largely one-sided favouring the formal employment sector while leaving the informal sector vulnerable to both the risk of infection and increased poverty levels. On another front and given the work from home mandates, some employers released their employees who would work in their homes as house helps for fear of those employees spreading the virus to them (Schmidt 2020). In a sense, therefore, these measures worked doubly to the disadvantage of the economically vulnerable (Quaife et al. 2020). Consequently, the poverty and inequality gaps increased significantly during the COVID-19 pandemic.

3.4 Health

Kenya has been striving to achieve universal health coverage (UHC) whose aim is ensuring access to healthcare for everyone without financial constraints and access to well-managed, financed, and responsive healthcare systems (Moses et al. 2021). To this end, Kenya has adopted various strategies with the President of Kenya pledging to make sure that all

Kenyans can access quality health services (World Health Organization Africa 2018). These strategies include removal of use fees in four counties' public healthcare centres. Prior to the COVID-19 pandemic, the Kenyan healthcare sector was faced with a myriad of challenges including corruption in the public healthcare centres, the fight against persistent diseases such as Malaria, frequent strikes and disproportionate ratio of healthcare workers vis a vis the general population (Ouma et al. 2020). These gaps proved to be risk areas at the onset of the pandemic and the Government had to step in and upgrade the public healthcare facilities to have the capacity to handle COVID-19 infections (Barasa et al. 2020).

From the onset of the pandemic, the government moved to upgrade various facilities so as to enhance capacity to deal with a surge of infections during the pandemic. With an increase in the number of positive cases, patients, and their contacts 1 were quarantined at their own cost. Initially, most insurance companies refused to cover the cost of COVID-19 treatment (CGTN 2020). Furthermore, the country was thrown into a frenzy with members of the public hoarding items, thereby causing an artificial rise in prices of masks and sanitisers and other essential supplies, which hurt the vulnerable the most (Herbling 2021).

The government through the Public Health (COVID-19 Restriction of Movement of Persons and Related Measures) Rules 2020 required all users of public or private transport to wear protective masks. This requirement supplemented the presidential directive on wearing of masks and keeping social distance. Contravening this directive was an offence and the national security organs carried out arrests of such persons (Achuka 2020). Workplaces also adopted policies geared towards ensuring employees maintain social distancing in workplaces, observe hygiene procedures and wear masks. Several buildings and workplaces introduced contactless temperature checks at entry points as a measure of minimizing infection by flagging people with high body temperatures.

The pandemic revealed the massive gaps existing in the healthcare system and infrastructure both at the national and county levels (Mohiddin and Temmerman 2020). Further, misinformation also fed into the public frenzy with a lot of stigma associated with the COVID-19 pandemic. In March 2020, nurses at the Mbagathi hospital went on strike after two more cases were confirmed in Kenya. The nurses cited lack of training and stated that they felt unsafe and unprepared to handle infected persons. On 4 May, the Kenya National Union of Nurses (KNUN) issued the government with a 14 day notice threatening to down their tools on 18 May if their demand for harmonization of risk allowances during the pandemic was not met. This was based on claims that the Ministry of Health was only supporting a section of the health workers. Allegations of healthcare professionals being mishandled was also raised. The strike was suspended for 21 days after the government agreed to hold discussions with the health workers on their demands. The Kenya Health Professional Society also issued a seven-day industrial strike notice. The grounds for the strike were improved compensation and protection of healthcare workers who were responding to the pandemic.

Private enterprises provided masks and sanitisers at a high cost. While at the same time, the government made efforts to procure and distribute masks and sanitisers to the public, the effect was not far-reaching (Gathara 2021). The government also took charge of burying those who succumbed to the virus with strict burial guidelines and restricted access. As the pandemic continued to spread, the private sector also took an active role and monetized the health services given to COVID-19 patients, including the initial COVID-19 vaccines (Gathara 2021). On the other hand, the government ensured that the vaccine was available to everyone, with the number of those vaccinated increasing steadily over the past year (Bhalla 2021). The demand for healthcare services has continued to increase, and lobby groups have called for the government to take a significant role in healthcare delivery to avert the high cost of accessing healthcare services from private institutions (Bhalla 2021). The cost of COVID-19 care was also very expensive increasing the inequalities between the rich who could afford private healthcare facilities and equipment and the poor who solely depended on poorly equipped public hospitals.

3.5 Education

The closure of schools for a significant period through the year 2020 meant that children were at home for a longer period than would be the case, with attendant consequences (Mlaba 2021). In particular, the school closures disproportionately negatively affected the disadvantaged children who could not afford personal tutors teaching them at home or whose parents and guardians are uneducated and therefore unable to assist them in their learning. This is especially important given that the closure of schools extended for a considerable period of time from 16 March 2020 to the partial opening on 19 October 2020 and the final school opening on 4 January 2021 (Abuya 2022). Accordingly, the closure of learning institutions served to deepen and reinforce educational inequalities across economic and social classes (Parsitau and Jepkemei 2020).

Further, there were widening inequalities along gender lines, with women and girls being more disadvantaged than men and boys (PMA 2021). This is largely on account of the gendered nature of various roles and responsibilities in Kenyan society. By being at home as opposed to being at school for a long period, female parents and female members of households took over the additional burden of care adding to their "time poverty", which left even less time to engage in gainful or paid work (Republic of Kenya and United Nations 2020). This is a result of the fact that women tend to be caregivers within a household in charge of various household chores including cooking, nursing, and managing the home-which work is unremunerated for the most part (Republic of Kenya and United Nations 2020). Even where the same is remunerated, say in the case of employed house helps, the pay for this kind of work is usually notably low, occasionally going below the set minimum wage. In addition, again, owing to gendered roles in society, girls took on additional responsibilities within the home, leaving them little time for studying relative to boys, certainly laying the foundation for differential educational performance.

There were various reported cases of child labour, early marriage, and sexual-based violence against girls and women during the pandemic owing to the closure of schools since girls were at home for an extended period of time in close association with their male counterparts (Ganju et al. 2021). This was manifested in high cases of unwanted and teenage pregnancies that were reported relative to other times (Zulaika et al. 2022). The hospitality sector was also disproportionately affected by the measures taken in response to the pandemic relative to other sectors, thereby disproportionately affecting women negatively. This is because the proportion of sfemalesfemales is higher in the hospitality sector compared to males.

There was also a widespread adoption of remote learning across primary schools, high schools, and tertiary institutions, which depended on digital technologies and the internet (OECD 2020). Students would only access this remote learning if they possessed smartphones or computers and reliable internet access and had the ability to operate in the online environment (Jelimo 2020). Again, poor students could neither access these digital gadgets nor could they afford internet, with some having challenges operating the gadgets and operating within an online environment. Put differently, the shift into remote learning which is digitally powered only served to "leave poor students behind" in terms of education, thereby reinforcing the existent inequalities. The government appeared to support this shift in learning, oblivious to the fact that a significant section of learners would be severely disadvantaged.

Children benefiting from school feeding programmes whereby learners are provided with meals at school also lost this benefit following the closure of schools (Borkowski et al. 2021). Given that this coincided with drought and locust invasion (Kairu 2021), poor children particularly from the marginalized areas of the country, suffered immensely from this official government response of school closure without providing alternative means (Ramthun 2021).

3.6 Access to Justice

The National Council on Administration of Justice (NCAJ) issued a number of directives on 15 March 2020 in light of the pandemic, namely: general scaling down of activities in the courts; suspension of all court sittings save for urgent matters; suspension of foreign travel for Judiciary staff; cancellation of all workshops, colloquia and training till further notice; reduction in number of judicial officers (judges and magistrates) physically present in the courts; video conference hearings as much as possible, adoption of technology in filing of cases and delivery of judgements; and suspension of execution proceedings for a two weeks' period (NCAJ 2020). The Judiciary was thus constrained to availing minimal essential services in the circumstances. Accordingly, many people faced difficulties accessing justice or the court system on account of these restrictions.

As a result, the digitization of court processes resulted in an increased rate of disposal of cases (Muhindi 2021). On the other hand, it also limited access to justice only to those able to access the digital platforms. The digitization of the court process may have increased inequality, especially against those in low-income households who could not access the electronic gadgets required to attend virtual court sessions.

4 Conclusion

This chapter has assessed the Kenyan government's policy responses to the COVID-19 pandemic. The assessment has revealed that most of the policy responses were modelled on the extant neoliberal framework, with a few detours toward state intervention largely through social protection interventions and fiscal and monetary policies. For the most part, the COVID-19 policy responses overlooked the existent inequalities among the different socio-economic classes, including gender, with the inevitable consequence of widening the gulf between the rich and the poor on the one hand and men and women on the other hand. While the state interventions in the form of social protection and fiscal and monetary policies provided much needed relief, they did not go far enough. This notwithstanding, the utility and effectiveness of these state interventions highlight the policy propositions that governments ought to pursue during a pandemic, and even in the post-pandemic era.

References

Abuya, B.A. (2022). *Deeper divide: What Kenya's pandemic school closures left in their wake*. [online] The Conversation. Available at: https://theconversation.com/deeper-divide-what-kenyas-pandemic-school-closures-left-in-their-wake-176098 [Accessed 28 Mar. 2022].

Achuka, V. (2020). *You face arrest you for not wearing a face mask in public*. [online] Nation. Available at: https://nation.africa/kenya/news/you-face-arrest-you-for-not-wearing-a-face-mask-in-public-285946 [Accessed 28 Mar. 2022].

Alushula, P. (2020). *Census: 39pc of Kenya youth are unemployed*. [online] Business Daily. Available at: https://www.businessdailyafrica.com/bd/economy/census-39pc-of-kenya-youth-are-unemployed-2281430.

Barasa, E.W., Ouma, P.O. and Okiro, E.A. (2020). Assessing the hospital surge capacity of the Kenyan health system in the face of the COVID-19 pandemic. *PLOS ONE*, 15(7), p. e0236308. https://doi.org/10.1371/journal.pone.0236308.

Bhalla, N. (2021). 'Pricing out the poor': Fears over COVID-19 vaccine access as Kenya lets in private sector. [online] Reuters. 25 Mar. Available at: https://www.reuters.com/article/us-health-coronavirus-kenya-vaccine-idUSKBN2BH2Q9.

Birir, C. (2020). *Working from home: How to cope amid Covid-19 pandemic.* [online] The Standard. Available at: https://www.standardmedia.co.ke/business/work-life/article/2001370376/covid-19-the-challenges-of-working-from-home [Accessed 28 Mar. 2022].

Borkowski, A., Santiago, J., Correa, O., Bundy, D., Burbano, C., Hayashi, C., Lloyd-Evans, E., Neitzel, J. and Reuge, N. (2021). *COVID-19: Missing more than a classroom the impact of school closures on children's nutrition.* [online] Available at: https://www.unicef-irc.org/publications/pdf/COVID-19_Missing_More_Than_a_Classroom_The_impact_of_school_closures_on_childrens_nutrition.pdf.

CGTN (2020). *Kenya's COVID-19 patients left with hefty bills after hospitalisation.* [online] newsaf.cgtn.com. Available at: https://newsaf.cgtn.com/news/2020-12-15/Kenya-s-COVID-19-patients-left-with-hefty-bills-after-hospitalisation-We4S9qGrmg/index.html [Accessed 14 Feb. 2022].

Chacha, P., Kirui, B. and Wiedemann, V. (2021). *The short-term impact of the COVID-19 shock on employment in formal firms in Kenya.* [online] PEDL. Available at: https://pedl.cepr.org/publications/short-term-impact-covid-19-shock-employment-formal-firms-kenya [Accessed 14 Feb. 2022].

Danish Trade Union Development Agency (2020). *Labour Market Profile 2020, Kenya.* [online] Available at: https://www.ulandssekretariatet.dk/wp-content/uploads/2020/03/Kenya_lmp_2020.pdf.

Doyle, A. and Ikutwa, N. (2021). *Towards shock-responsive social protection: lessons from the COVID-19 response in Kenya Research report Alexandra Doyle with support from Nivea Ikutwa About Maintains.* [online] Available at: https://socialprotection.org/sites/default/files/publications_files/Maintains%20COVID-19%20SRSP%20responses%20-%20Kenya%20case%20study%20-%20final_0.pdf [Accessed 28 Mar. 2022].

Ganju, C.K., Dana Schmidt, and Erin (2021). *What do we know about the effects of COVID-19 on girls' return to school?* [online] Brookings. Available at: https://www.brookings.edu/blog/education-plus-development/2021/09/22/what-do-we-know-about-the-effects-of-covid-19-on-girls-return-to-school/.

Gathara, P. (2021). *What is going on with Kenya's COVID-19 vaccine drive?* [online] www.aljazeera.com. Available at: https://www.aljazeera.com/opinions/2021/4/3/what-is-going-wrong-with-kenyas-covid-19-vaccine-drive.

Gikandi, L. (2020). COVID-19 and vulnerable, hardworking Kenyans: Why it's time for a strong social protection plan. [online] https://doi.org/10.21201/2020.6591.

Herbling, D. (2021). Kenyans Hoard oxygen cylinders, starving hospitals of gas. *Bloomberg.com.* [online] 30 Mar. Available at: https://www.bloomberg.com/news/articles/2021-03-30/kenyans-hoard-oxygen-cylinders-starving-hospitals-of-the-gas.

His Excellency President Uhuru Kenyatta (2020). *Presidential address on enhanced measures in response to the covid-19 pandemic*. [online] Kenya Law. Available at: http://www.kenyalaw.org/kl/fileadmin/pdfdownloads/presidential-address-6th-April-2020.pdf.

Ilado, L. (2020). *Kenyan govt rolls out COVID-19 relief fund for artists*. [online] Music In Africa. Available at: https://www.musicinafrica.net/magazine/kenyan-govt-rolls-out-covid-19-relief-fund-artists [Accessed 28 Mar. 2022].

Jelimo, C. (2020). *Impact of Covid-19 on the right to education in Kenya*. [online] Right to Education Initiative. Available at: https://www.right-to-education.org/blog/impact-covid-19-right-education-kenya.

Kagwe, M. (2020). *Legal Notice No. 37 of 2020*. [online] Available at: http://www.parliament.go.ke/sites/default/files/2020-04/LN.%2037%20Public%20Health%20%28Declaration%20of%20Formidable%20Epidemic%20Disease%29%20Order%2C%202020.pdf [Accessed 11 Feb. 2022].

Kairu, P. (2021). *Hunger looms amid new locust invasion, Covid, drought and floods*. [online] The East African. Available at: https://www.theeastafrican.co.ke/tea/news/east-africa/hunger-looms-amid-new-locust-invasion-covid-3513172 [Accessed 28 Mar. 2022].

Kenya Labour Market Information System (2022). *Labour Demand | Key Labour Market Indicators | Employment in the Informal Sector*. [online] Kenya Labour Market Information System. Available at: https://www.labourmarket.go.ke/demand/indicator/ [Accessed 28 Mar. 2022].

Kenya Law (2020). *Public Legal Information on Kenya's Response to COVID-19 | Kenya Law*. [online] www.kenyalaw.org. Available at: http://kenyalaw.org/kenyalawblog/kenyas-response-to-covid-19/.

Kimari, B. (2020). *Policing the Covid-19 Crisis in Kenya—Policy Options for management of public health emergencies*. [online] Available at: https://www.chrips.or.ke/wp-content/uploads/2020/05/Policy-Brief-1-May-2020-Policing-the-COVID-19-Crisis-in-Kenya.pdf [Accessed 11 Feb. 2022].

Kiruga, M. (2020). *Nairobi's fight against Coronavirus gets violent*. [online] The Africa Report.com. Available at: https://www.theafricareport.com/25634/nairobi-fight-against-coronavirus-gets-violent/ [Accessed 12 Feb. 2022].

KNBS (2020a). *Economic Survey 2020*. [online] Kenya National Bureau of Statistics. Available at: https://www.knbs.or.ke/?wpdmpro=economic-survey-2020.

KNBS (2020b). *Inequality trends and diagnostics in Kenya 2020 | A Joint Report of the Kenya National Bureau of Statistics on Multidimensional Inequality |*. [online] Available at: https://www.knbs.or.ke/wp-content/uploads/2021/07/Inequality-Trends-and-Diagnostics-in-Kenya-Report.pdf [Accessed 8 Oct. 2021].

KNBS (2020c). *Quarterly Labour Force Report, Forth Quarter 2019*. [online] Kenya National Bureau of Statistics. Available at: https://www.knbs.or.ke/?wpdmpro=quarterly-labour-force-report-forth-quarter-2019.

Luesby, J. (2021). *Lift Kenya's Covid-19 curfew now*. [online] Business Daily. Available at: https://www.businessdailyafrica.com/bd/opinion-analysis/columnists/lift-kenya-s-covid-19-curfew-now-3581192.

Mbabazi, E. (2020). *Horticulture sector loses KSh8 billion to COVID-19*. [online] Kenyan Wallstreet. Available at: https://kenyanwallstreet.com/horticulture-sector-loses-ksh8-billion-to-covid-19/.

Ministry of Health (2020). *First case of coronavirus disease confirmed in Kenya—Ministry of Health*. [online] www.health.go.ke. Available at: https://www.health.go.ke/first-case-of-coronavirus-disease-confirmed-in-kenya/.

Miriri, D. (2020). UPDATE 2-IMF raises Kenya's risk of debt distress to high from moderate. *Reuters*. [online] 12 May. Available at: https://www.reuters.com/article/health-coronavirus-kenya-debt-idUSL8N2CU3F5 [Accessed 29 Mar. 2022].

Mkandawire, T. (2001). *Social policy in a development context Thandika Mkandawire*. [online] Available at: https://www.files.ethz.ch/isn/102709/7.pdf.

Mlaba, K. (2021). *Thousands of children in Kenya failed to return to school this week*. [online] Global Citizen. Available at: https://www.globalcitizen.org/en/content/children-missing-out-on-school-kenya-covid/.

Mohiddin, A. and Temmerman, M. (2020). *COVID-19 exposes weaknesses in Kenya's healthcare system. And what can be done*. [online] The Conversation. Available at: https://theconversation.com/covid-19-exposes-weaknesses-in-kenyas-healthcare-system-and-what-can-be-done-143356.

Moore, D. (2020). *'We fear, but have to work': Isolation not an option for the poor of Nairobi*. [online] the Guardian. Available at: https://www.theguardian.com/global-development/2020/mar/27/we-fear-but-have-to-work-isolation-not-an-option-for-the-poor-of-nairobi-coronavirus.

Moses, M.W., Korir, J., Zeng, W., Musiega, A., Oyasi, J., Lu, R., Chuma, J. and Giorgio, L.D. (2021). Performance assessment of the county healthcare systems in Kenya: A mixed-methods analysis. *BMJ Global Health*, [online] 6(6), p. e004707. https://doi.org/10.1136/bmjgh-2020-004707.

Muhindi, S. (2021). *Access to justice amid the Covid-19 pandemic*. [online] The Star. Available at: https://www.the-star.co.ke/news/big-read/2021-12-07-access-to-justice-amid-the-covid-19-pandemic/ [Accessed 14 Feb. 2022].

Muragu, M.M., Nyadera, I.N. and Mbugua, C.W. (2021). Gearing up for the new normal: Kenya's tourism sector before and after the COVID-19 pandemic. *Journal of Policy Research in Tourism, Leisure and Events*, pp. 1–18. https://doi.org/10.1080/19407963.2021.1903020.

NCAJ (2020). *Statement on justice sector operations in the wake of the COVID-19 pandemic—National Council on the Administration of Justice*. [online] www.ncaj.go.ke. Available at: https://www.ncaj.go.ke/statement-on-justice-sector-operations-in-the-wake-of-the-covid-19-pandemic/ [Accessed 28 Mar. 2022].

Obulutsa, G. (2022). Kenyan tourism begins recovery from pandemic slump as locals fuel travel. *Reuters*. [online] 19 Jan. Available at: https://www.reuters.com/world/africa/kenyan-tourism-begins-recovery-pandemic-slump-locals-fuel-travel-2022-01-19/ [Accessed 29 Mar. 2022].

OECD (2020). *The impact of COVID-19 on student equity and inclusion: Supporting vulnerable students during school closures and school re-openings*. [online] OECD. Available at: https://www.oecd.org/coronavirus/policy-responses/the-impact-of-covid-19-on-student-equity-and-inclusion-supporting-vulnerable-students-during-school-closures-and-school-re-openings-d593b5c8/.

OHCHR (2020). *Kenya: Monitoring Human Rights impacts of Covid-19 in informal settlements*. [online] Office of the High Commissioner on Human Rights. Available at: https://www.ohchr.org/Documents/Countries/KE/15april-6may-OHCHR-SJCWG.pdf [Accessed 12 Feb. 2022].

Okadia, F. (2021). *The delusion that was and is COVID 19 measures in the Matatu Sector*. [online] IEA Kenya. Available at: https://ieakenya.or.ke/blog/the-delusion-that-was-and-is-covid-19-measures-in-the-matatu-sector/ [Accessed 12 Feb. 2022].

Oneko, S. (2020). *Health budgets: Will the pandemic change Kenya's priorities? | DW | 11.06.2020*. [online] DW.COM. Available at: https://www.dw.com/en/health-budgets-will-the-pandemic-change-kenyas-priorities/a-53779046.

Onsomu, E., Munga, B. and Nyabaro, V. (2021). *The impact of COVID-19 on industries without smokestacks in Kenya The case of horticulture, ICT, and tourism sectors*. [online] Available at: https://www.brookings.edu/wp-content/uploads/2021/07/21.07.27-Kenya-Covid-Update.pdf.

Ouma, M. (2021). *Kenya's Social Policy Response to Covid-19: Tax Cuts, Cash Transfers and Public Works*. [online] *SSOAR*, Bremen: Universität Bremen, SFB 1342 Globale Entwicklungsdynamiken von Sozialpolitik / CRC 1342 Global Dynamics of Social Policy. Available at: https://www.ssoar.info/ssoar/handle/document/73167 [Accessed 28 Mar. 2022].

Ouma, P.N., Masai, A.N. and Nyadera, I.N. (2020). Health coverage and what Kenya can learn from the COVID-19 pandemic. *Journal of Global Health*, 10(2). https://doi.org/10.7189/jogh.10.020362.

Parsitau, D.S. and Jepkemei, E. (2020). *How school closures during COVID-19 further marginalize vulnerable children in Kenya*. [online] Brookings. Available at: https://www.brookings.edu/blog/education-plus-development/2020/05/06/how-school-closures-during-covid-19-further-marginalize-vulnerable-children-in-kenya/.

Permanent Presidential Music Commission (2020). *Stimulus Programme for Musicians and Dancers*. [online] ppmc.go.ke. Available at: https://ppmc.go.ke/index.php/page/work-for-pay [Accessed 28 Mar. 2022].

PMA (2021). *Study reveals stark gendered social and economic impacts of COVID-19 for youth in Kenya | PMA Data*. [online] www.pmadata.org. Available at: https://www.pmadata.org/news/study-reveals-stark-gendered-social-and-economic-impacts-covid-19-youth-kenya-0.

Presidency (2015). *Kenya has achieved gender parity in schools, says First Lady | The Presidency*. [online] President.go.ke. Available at: https://www.president.go.ke/2015/08/07/kenya-has-achieved-gender-parity-in-schools-says-first-lady/ [Accessed 28 Mar. 2022].

Quaife, M., van Zandvoort, K., Gimma, A., Shah, K., McCreesh, N., Prem, K., Barasa, E., Mwanga, D., Kangwana, B., Pinchoff, J., Edmunds, W.J., Jarvis, C.I. and Austrian, K. (2020). The impact of COVID-19 control measures on social contacts and transmission in Kenyan informal settlements. *BMC Medicine*, 18(1). https://doi.org/10.1186/s12916-020-01779-4.

Ramthun, J. (2021). *Triple Threat: Helping Kenya Protect Against Floods, Locusts, and COVID | NASA Applied Sciences*. [online] appliedsciences.nasa.gov. Available at: https://appliedsciences.nasa.gov/our-impact/news/triple-threat-helping-kenya-protect-against-floods-locusts-and-covid [Accessed 28 Mar. 2022].

Republic of Kenya and United Nations (2020). *An Assessment of the Gendered Effects of the COVID-19 Pandemic on Households*. [online] reliefweb. Available at: https://reliefweb.int/sites/reliefweb.int/files/resources/covid-19_gender_assessment_kenya_1.pdf [Accessed 12 Feb. 2022].

Schmidt, M. (2020). *'Life On These Stones Is Very Hard' – House Helps in Covid-19 Nairobi*. [online] Developing Economics. Available at: https://developingeconomics.org/2020/11/13/life-on-these-stones-is-very-hard-house-helps-in-covid-19-nairobi/ [Accessed 28 Mar. 2022].

The World Bank (2021). *The World Bank in Kenya*. [online] World Bank. Available at: https://www.worldbank.org/en/country/kenya/overview#1.

University of Oxford (2021). *COVID-19: Government Response Stringency Index*. [online] Our World in Data. Available at: https://ourworldindata.org/grapher/covid-stringency-index?tab=chart&year=latest&country=~KEN®ion=Africa.

USAID (2019). *Economic Growth and Trade | Kenya | U.S. Agency for International Development*. [online] Usaid.gov. Available at: https://www.usaid.gov/kenya/economic-growth-and-trade.

Wafula, P. (2020). *Over one million rendered jobless in Kenya as Covid-19 takes toll on businesses*. [online] The East African. Available at: https://www.theeastafrican.co.ke/tea/business/over-one-million-rendered-jobless-in-kenya-as-covid-19-takes-toll-on-businesses-1442672.

Wasike, A. (2021). *Irregularities mar Kenya's COVID-19 cash transfer program: HRW*. [online] www.aa.com.tr. Available at: https://www.aa.com.tr/en/africa/irregularities-mar-kenyas-covid-19-cash-transfer-program-hrw/2310385 [Accessed 14 Feb. 2022].

World Health Organization Africa (2018). *Building Health: Kenya's move to universal health coverage*. [online] WHO | Regional Office for Africa. Available at: https://www.afro.who.int/news/building-health-kenyas-move-universal-health-coverage.

Worldometer (2021). *Kenya Coronavirus: 31,015 Cases and 506 Deaths—Worldometer*. [online] www.worldometers.info. Available at: https://www.worldometers.info/coronavirus/country/kenya/.

Zulaika, G., Bulbarelli, M., Nyothach, E., Eijk, A. van, Mason, L., Fwaya, E., Obor, D., Kwaro, D., Wang, D., Mehta, S.D. and Phillips-Howard, P.A. (2022). Impact of COVID-19 lockdowns on adolescent pregnancy and school dropout among secondary schoolgirls in Kenya. *BMJ Global Health*, [online] 7(1), p. e007666. https://doi.org/10.1136/bmjgh-2021-007666.

Reinforcing Inequality: First 100 Days of South African COVID-19 Policy

Zita M. Hansungule, Khensani Hlongwane, Christina R. Mosalagae, Kelello Nkadimeng, and Sankari Reddy

1 Introduction

South Africa's constitutional democracy is founded on the values of human dignity; non-racism; non-sexism; supremacy of the Constitution and the rule of law; and universal adult suffrage. The Bill of Rights not only has vertical application but also horizontal application (Section 8 of the Constitution of the Republic of South Africa 1996). Therefore,

Z. M. Hansungule (✉)
University of Pretoria, Pretoria, South Africa

K. Hlongwane
Labour Appeal Court, Johannesburg, South Africa

C. R. Mosalagae
University of Turin, Turin, Italy

K. Nkadimeng
ABSA Group Limited, Johannesburg, South Africa

S. Reddy
Pan African Investment and Research Services (Pty) Ltd, Sandton, South Africa

A. Stojanović et al. (eds.), *The First 100 Days of Covid-19*,
https://doi.org/10.1007/978-981-19-6325-4_11

decisions made and actions taken by the state that impact citizens and residents of South Africa must find their basis on these values. This includes the decision to declare a national state of disaster in the light of COVID-19 pandemic that resulted in a nationwide lockdown and other related restrictions on people's movements, social interactions, and economic transactions.

In this chapter, we provide an overview of the state of the nation prior to the COVID-19 pandemic together with policy projections made at the time, in order to identify the significance of the early pandemic policy. In this regard, we argue that post-Apartheid (post-1994) socio-economic governance was characterised by a neoliberal policy approach, that swept through most developing nations from the 1980s onwards, with some socially orientated policies that were characteristic of the desire to redress the injustices of the past that are rife in South African history (Narsiah 2002). Moreover, we argue that the unprecedented measures that were taken in response to the COVID-19 pandemic stand in contrast with a neoliberal approach in several ways. Specifically, we consider pandemic policy issued during the initial shock wave between March 2020 and June 2020. Thereafter, we highlight the areas of policy that are most pertinent to the South African context: economic growth, employment, health, and education. Our main focus is on identifying the ways in which the level of inequality within the nation that had been growing during the neoliberal period has been further exacerbated by the COVID-19 pandemic, despite the pro-social measures taken in response to the pandemic. Between 1996 and 2015, South Africa's Gini Coefficient, as a measure of inequality, increased from 0.61 to 0.63 (Amnesty International 2020: 17); and it is expected that inequality will significantly increase in the post-COVID-19 period (NIDS-CRAM Wave 2 Synthesis Findings 2020: 3, 5). This increase in inequality will have important policy implications for the future of South Africa. Therefore, we argue that although the pandemic measures that were taken preserved human life and improved health infrastructure, the pandemic heightened the urgency to address the rampant inequality within the nation by expanding on the socially oriented policies taken during the pandemic on a deeper institutional level.

The remainder of this chapter is structured as follows: In the second section, we provide a historical narrative of democracy and civil activism in the South African context before and during the initial stage of the pandemic, in order to account for the context in which specific policy decisions were made. In the third section, we provide an account of the shift in surveillance from a state-controlled surveillance during Apartheid to surveillance largely controlled by private security prior to COVID-19. However, we argue that the state took back the lead role in mass surveillance due to the COVID-19 pandemic. In the fourth section, we consider the shift in economic policy adopted at important phases of South Africa's post-Apartheid development concluding with the pandemic. We show how the socially oriented characteristics of the neoliberal policy before the pandemic (Narsiah 2002) started to gain new importance as the crisis developed. In the fifth section, we focus on the labour policy objectives along this trajectory showing how they increasingly sought to protect and empower labour. Although mass unemployment continues to be a significant challenge for the nation. In the sixth and seventh section we consider the historical dynamics related to the significant infrastructural gaps in the health and education sectors, respectively, as these sectors were severely impacted by the pandemic. We conclude by summarising different aspects of the gradual shift in policy making from a neoliberal approach toward more socially oriented policy decisions. As we shall try to show, already prior to the pandemic, it was becoming clear that this shift was necessary to bridge the significant inequality in the nation. Due to the massive disruption of COVID-19 on the National Development Goals this became hard to ignore. However, we conclude that the state's capacity to shift policy goals will inevitably be a challenge in light of the issues, in the various sectors identified, which are simultaneously competing for the state's attention.

2 Democracy and Civil Activism

2.1 State of the Nation Pre-COVID-19

Historically, inequality has been a dominant narrative in South Africa, weaved in large part by South Africa's experience of "*settler violence, economic oppression and apartheid racism*" (Ngcukaitobi 2018). The occupation and colonisation of South Africa was characterized by the often violent nature in which land was dispossessed from the indigenous people by Europeans who: "monopolized their grasp on the raw materials in South Africa and soon began to change the hierarchy of land ownership. This would later feed into racial policies that were written into legislation regarding land ownership, distribution of land,

and white minority rule" (Piotrowski 2019). The indigenous people were then placed on smaller and disproportionate sizes of land and oppressed through slavery and forced labour (Piotrowski 2019).

South Africa was first occupied by the Dutch from 1652 to 1795 (Oliver and Oliver 2017) and thereafter occupation and colonisation by Great Britain occurred from 1795 to 1803 and 1806 to 1961 (Oliver and Oliver 2017). South Africa became a Union with a white led government in 1910 but was still a self-governing territory of the British empire until 1961 (Oliver and Oliver 2017). In 1948, after the end of the Second World War, the Afrikaner National Party won national elections, marking the beginning of Apartheid from 1948 to 1994 (Oliver and Oliver 2017). Apartheid was a legislated system of racial segregation characterised by discriminatory treatment along racial lines that entrenched legal, economic, and spatial inequality (McLachlan 2018). The Apartheid regime continued to oppress the black majority of the country through the denial of the right to vote or to own land. Furthermore, black people were restricted from moving freely within the country, in terms of Pass laws (discussed later in this chapter), among other race-based laws (McLachlan 2018).

It is argued that since the advent of a constitutional democracy in 1994, there have been significant strides made in the strengthening of South Africa's democracy (Southall 2000). This has been achieved through successful democratic elections, the continued deliberation and grappling with issues such as political diversity, and the testing of constitutional rights in courts of law (Southall 2000). However, deepening levels of inequality; increasingly high unemployment rates, levels of violence, including gender-based violence (World Bank 2022; Statistics South Africa 2021a; Deutsche Gesellschaft für Internationale Zusammenarbeit [GIZ] 2014) challenge this view and make it clear that not all public policies serve the poor, disadvantaged and vulnerable of society (Southall 2000; Nattrass and Seekings 2001). Ngcukaitobi eloquently describes the doubts and disappointments expressed, by many, of the strides made since the advent of a constitutional democracy in South Africa: "*despite the admiration of the world, many of the promises contained in the Constitution remain a hollow hope. Millions continue to starve, while a fortunate few enjoy the wealth of the country. Does South Africa really belong to all? In this climate of economic exclusion, and social and political marginalisation, where the winners take all, some question whether the constitutional framework was in fact the correct response to colonialism and apartheid*"

(Ngcukaitobi 2018). Persistent patterns of exclusion from the economy have retained the legacy of Apartheid through subtle practices of racism. (Friedman 2021; Msimang 2021).

It is also clear that much remains for South Africa's democracy to address rights violations and for duty bearers to be held accountable for fulfilling their constitutional mandates. In this regard, civil society and opposition political parties have begun to play a critical role in the strengthening of South Africa's democracy. As one of the commentators states, civil society has become the "*last line of defence fighting on behalf of ordinary citizens against out-of-control corruption, public service delivery failure and abuse of power by elected public representatives*" (Gumede 2018). South Africa's civil-society make-up has become diverse, dynamic, and assertive. In the post-Apartheid period, it persisted in holding the government accountable, fighting corruption, and supporting democracy and democratic institutions (Gumede 2018). Additionally, opposition political parties have been able to provide institutional space as alternatives to the ruling party, facilitate debate on political issues and public policy as well as carry out oversight (Mottiar 2015).

2.2 Democracy and Legal Challenges in a Post Pandemic Age

South Africa's response to the COVID-19 pandemic was developed in terms of the Disaster Management Act, 57 of 2002 (the Act). The Act, in section 27(1), gives the Minister of Co-operative Governance and Traditional Affairs (the Minister) the power to declare a national state of disaster. Section 27(2) of the Act also gives the Minister the power, after consulting with responsible Cabinet members/ministers, to make regulations, issue directions, or authorise the issuing of directions for the purpose of assisting and protecting the public; providing relief to the public; protecting property; preventing or combatting disruption; or dealing with the destruction and other effects of the disaster.

On 15 March 2020, the Minister declared, in terms of Government Gazette number 43096, a national state of disaster due to the magnitude and severity of the COVID-19 pandemic (Government Gazette [Vol. 313, No. 43096] 2020). A national state of disaster lapses 3 months after it has been declared. The Minister has the power to extend the state of disaster by notice in the Government Gazette for one month at a time before it lapses. The Act is noticeably silent on how often these extensions can occur.

The Act further provides, in section 26, that it is the primary responsibility of the National Executive, which is Cabinet, to coordinate and manage the disaster. The Cabinet must deal with the national disaster in terms of existing legislation and contingency arrangements as augmented by regulations or directions issued in terms of the Act. A number of directions and regulations were written up by members of Cabinet on issues related to, inter alia, restrictions on movement in relation to entry into the country, limitations of gatherings, restrictions on the leaving of personal residences, and limitations on the selling of goods. A risk-adjusted strategy was also developed to manage the manner in which different sectors of the economy will be opened up based on a tracking of the impact of the COVID-19 pandemic on South Africa. In response, there have been court challenges against the manner in which the state of disaster was implemented. A few are highlighted here.

On 2 June 2020, the High Court in Pretoria handed down judgement in *De Beer and Others v Minister of Cooperative Governance and Traditional Affairs* [2020] ZAGPPHC 184. The Court found that the declaration of the national state of disaster in response to COVID-19 was rational, however regulations promulgated in respect of alert levels 4 and 3 were declared unconstitutional as they were not rationally connected to the objectives of slowing down the infection of COVID-19, or limiting its spread. Furthermore, in *Mohamed and Others v President of the Republic of South Africa and Others* [2020] ZAGPPHC 120; [2020] 2 All SA 844 (GP); 2020 (7) BCLR 865 (GP), in which judgement was handed down on 30 April 2020, the Pretoria High Court had to determine whether regulations that limited public gatherings were overbroad, excessive and unconstitutional in as far as they unjustifiably limited movement of persons between residences and places of worship. The High Court dismissed the application on the basis that the restrictions were justifiable and if regard was had to the sacrifices that have had to be made by South Africa and its residents, the applicants could not ask that exceptions of the nature sought be made. Other court actions were brought to challenge the ban on sale of tobacco products (African News Agency 2020), sale of alcohol (BusinessTech 2020a), the reopening of schools (Dan Meyer 2020), relief aid allocations (Democratic Alliance 2020).

A number of rights have been affected by the declaration of State of National Disaster and resultant imposition of a national lockdown that limited various rights and freedoms. These include equal access to basic education through the closure of schools, as will be addressed later in this chapter; the right to freedom of trade, occupation, and profession through the restrictions on movement and specifically informal trade that can only be conducted in person; the rights to food and social security which were hampered by the inability of a significant portion of the population to afford food and support their livelihoods without employment. It is important to point out that the rights to food and social security, and similar socio-economic rights, are justiciable and enforceable rights in South Africa. The South African Constitutional Court has noted that such rights can be protected through judicial protection that prevents the State from acting in a manner that would infringe on socio-economic rights directly (Currie and De Waal 2013). The State's alleged dereliction of its positive duties to take steps to fulfill the realisation of socio-economic rights sets in motion the judiciary's job to determine if reasonable legislative and other measures have been taken to achieve the progressive realisation of the socio-economic rights in question within the available resources (Currie and De Waal 2013).

Moreover, the limitation of rights and freedoms impacted the right to life, equality, and human dignity of the poorest and vulnerable members of society. Social justice actors (civil society organisations and social justice activists) made use of platforms such as the courts, social media, protests, strikes, and lobbying to put pressure on government duty bearers to address challenges and barriers arising from COVID-19 and the measures put in place to limit its spread and impact. Highlighted below are some pressing issues that were raised by social justice actors.

Increased poverty and food insecurity as a result of the economic impact of the imposition of a nationwide lockdown, with its accompanying restrictions on work, proved to be devastating to South African households. It was noted that: "*South Africa already has very high rates of poverty, unemployment and inequality, and the effects of lockdown on work and earnings threaten to exacerbate all these dynamics. More people will become poor, and the depth of poverty will be greater. More people will go hungry*" (Hall 2020). In order to mitigate the economic impact on largely vulnerable households, several civil society organisations called on the President and the government to temporarily increase the amount of social assistance grants provided to such households (Children's Institute 2020). In April 2020, President Cyril Ramaphosa announced temporary economic and social relief measures that included increases to social assistance grants such as the child support grant (beneficiaries would receive an additional R300 in May 2020 and an additional R500 from June 2020 to the grant valued at R450 as at the end of 2020 and then R460 from April 2020), the disability grant and old age grant (beneficiaries would receive an additional R250 from May 2020) as well as the introduction of a special Social Relief of Distress grant, valued at R350, to be paid to qualifying unemployed persons (President Cyril Ramaphosa 2020). The value of the Social Relief of Distress grant, in particular, was the subject of criticism that highlighted the fact that it was well below the food poverty line and would not meet the nutritional requirements of a single person and that a larger grant would effectively reduce hunger and poverty for all affected (C19 People's Coalition 2020b).

Furthermore, as early as April 2020, a number of civil society organisations expressed concerns on the lack of measures put in place to protect mining-affected communities and workers from COVID-19 as "gold, gold refinery, coal and essential mining" were classified as essential services that would continue during the national lockdown (Mining Affected Communities United in Action [MACUA] and 10 organisations 2020). The organisations highlighted the fact that mining communities and workers were particularly vulnerable due to factors such as limited or no access to piped water and the prevalence of underlying respiratory illnesses due to air pollution from mining activities (MACUA and 10 organisations 2020). The matter was escalated to the Labour Court of South Africa which, on 1 May 2020, handed down a court order in favour of AMCU. It ordered that the requested guidelines in terms of section 9(3) and 49(6) of the Mine Health and Safety Act, 1996 (MHSA), be developed; and that experts, trade unions, employer organisations, MACUA, and other interested parties should all be consulted before the guidelines are published and made available to the public.

Social justice actors also called for a moratorium on evictions in light of the COVID-19 pandemic (Ndifuna Ukwazi and 26 organisations 2020). They noted that people facing evictions experienced an added layer of vulnerability due to exposure to the health risks posed by COVID-19 and being left homeless (Ndifuna Ukwazi and 26 organisations 2020). Also, concern was raised about the adverse effect that restricting the operations of the informal economy would have on the lives of millions of people who work in and depend on the informal sector. When the national lockdown was instituted informal food traders were not considered an essential service and therefore not allowed to trade, they lost all income almost immediately, and fresh produce that had not been sold or eaten (Wegerif 2020). Many people lost convenient access to food and had to travel long distances and face greater risks of contracting COVID-19 to get food (Wegerif 2020). Government, facing heavy criticism, revised the lockdown regulations to allow some informal food traders to operate (Rafapa 2020).

In addition, it is of significance to point out that the "C19 People's Coalition", is an alliance of over 300 social movements, trade unions, community organisations, and NGOs committed to ensuring that the South African government's response to the COVID-19 virus is effective, just, equitable, and meets the needs of the most marginal members of society (C19 People's Coalition 2020a, b). The coalition developed and endorsed a Programme of Action that guided their work and expressed their commitment to realising a response to the pandemic that is rooted in equity and solidarity (C19 People's Coalition 2020a).

Thus, we can see the vigilant role of civil activism in ensuring that pandemic policy was aimed at serving the most vulnerable members of society through more pro-poor policy decisions which were sensitive to the particular plight of South Africans in the scenarios discussed above. It is acknowledged that advocacy and lobbying goals were achieved—as there were many shortcomings of the government pandemic policy that remained—but it is clear that the continued role of social activism in policy making will play a significant role in determining the direction that post pandemic policy will take.

3 Surveillance and Security

3.1 Pre-COVID-19 Surveillance and Security

One of the significant aspects of Apartheid legislation was the restriction of movement. Particularly, black South Africans over the 16 years of age (primarily men) were required to carry "pass books" in terms of the Pass Laws Act of 1952. The pass books identified a person's race and allowed or denied them access into racially exclusive zones. Moreover, during the Apartheid period, maintaining the "separate, but equal" social order was sustained by significant surveillance practices through labour intensive state-policing activities (Frankel 1979). Consequently, in the post-Apartheid age, as a break from the discriminatory limitations on movement and the intensive state surveillance that accompanied it, freedom of movement was constitutionally enshrined as a fundamental right that needed to be guaranteed to all citizens. Against this background, surveillance in post-Apartheid South Africa carries historical baggage which could perhaps explain the lack of explicit state surveillance until the COVID-19 pandemic. Although there were significant incidents of state surveillance by the Former President Jacob Zuma that were revealed during the Zondo Commission these were more covert than explicit (Thamm 2021).

With regard to security measures like policing intended to protect the population from crime, we observed that black poverty was the basis for unfair discrimination. As Killander observed in the context of municipal by-laws related to homelessness, the criminalisation of poverty, in the South African context, has a racial complexion (Killander 2019). On 14 December 2018, in the landmark decision of *Social Justice Coalition and Others v Minister of Police and Others* [2018] ZAWCHC 181; 2019 (4) SA 82 (WCC), it was declared that the system employed by the South African Police Service to determine the allocation of police human resources, in so far as it has been shown to be the case in the Western Cape Province, unfairly discriminates against black and poor people on the basis of race and poverty. The report showed that: "*as of 2018, there were 58.78 million people and 192 277 police officers in the country, which is a 1:305 ratio(3), however the ratio favoured higher income areas*". This case revealed that prior to the lockdown across the country there was unequal, indeed lack of security in rural, denser areas of South Africa. The involvement of the South African National Defence Force ("SANDF") has primarily been against external forces, in peacekeeping missions and the fight against piracy (Heleta 2017). Internal military deployment has been isolated to certain areas where gang wars in townships became uncontrollable (Harrisberg and Moloney 2019).

In contrast, not only did higher income households have more access to state policing services over the poor, higher income households could also afford additional private security. The Private Security Industry Regulatory Authority has stated that South Africa has one of the world's biggest private security industries, with more than 9000 registered companies and 450,000 active guards, which numbers exceed the human resource capacity of the South African Police Service (SAPS) (Basimanyane and Gandhi 2019). This additional service for policing and movement controls, supplements the already unequal police presence favouring higher income areas (Ewinyu and Mtshali 2020). This inequity is particularly noticeable as higher income areas also engage in access controls for privately owned property, excluding lower income persons from access to certain wealthier, more protected areas of the country.

Thus, in post-Apartheid South Africa private security companies not only provide exclusive security services to higher income neighbourhoods but also engage in patrol and surveillance measures. Previously, during Apartheid, black people were routinely stopped by state police forces when entering white only neighbourhoods. In post-Apartheid South Africa private security for enclosed neighbourhoods (neighbourhoods that have been cordoned off with access gates) routinely allow or deny people access to certain neighbourhoods, in some instances, people are requested to present a form of identification like a driver's licence and provide an account for their presence in the neighbourhood (Landman 2004). Through this we have observed that although the Apartheid laws that resulted in state surveillance have been diminished, black poverty has become the new basis for surveillance. Essentially, although black people are now no longer oppressed by Apartheid laws, the lack of any redistribution of wealth puts them in a dire economic position that is approached as a source of potential crime against civil laws. Moreover, one of the tenets of neoliberalism is a strong focus on enforcing property rights and making individuals responsible for their economic success in an increasingly competitive world, without taking into consideration the historical facts that created the present conditions of inequality (Schneider 2003). This approach condemns those who are unable to meet the exacting standards of neoliberalism and creates the justification for the criminalisation of black poverty. As previously alluded to, the enclosure of historically white neighbourhoods as a response to the crime rate in the country, in effect limits the freedom of movement of the poor and marginalised population of the country through the use of private security guards, check points, and cameras, thus reinforcing a post-Apartheid style of surveillance through private security. Therefore, pre-pandemic surveillance was no longer exclusively state-based but securitisation and surveillance became more distributed at the private security level. Moreover, surveillance at the private security level was based on socio-economic status, which inevitably has a racial due to the fact that it is the black majority that has been historically disadvantaged resulting in the criminalisation of poverty and race.

3.2 Surveillance in a Post Pandemic Age

The pandemic marked a shift from covert to explicit state surveillance for the first time in post-Apartheid South Africa. Section 14 of the Constitution provides the right to privacy: "Everyone has the right to privacy, which includes the right not to have—(a) their person or home searched; (b) their property searched; (c) their possessions seized; or (d) the privacy of their communications infringed". Furthermore, the Protection of Personal Information Act 4 of 2013 ("POPI"), which commenced on 1 July 2020, with only certain sections in full force and effect, is also applicable. POPI statutorily establishes an Information Regulator which is intended to, amongst other things, prevent abuses by the State of personal information. CCTV surveillance (including drones and body-cams) is not regulated currently and is used extensively in public spaces and private spaces (Basimanyane and Gandhi 2019). Private companies are also able to purchase the public footage to deepen their service offering to higher income persons, including licence plate recognition technology and additional features, such as recognition of individuals' identity (Swart 2020).

The main communication surveillance law is the Regulation of Interception of Communications and Provision of Communication-Related Information Act 70 of 2002 (RICA) which together with the National Strategic Intelligence Act 39 of 1994 (NSIA) and POPI govern the use, collection, and interception of electronic communication. RICA allows for the interception of communication in certain instances however any authorisation must be in writing by a judge and is only valid for three months. Abuse of the interception of communication is inevitable where the SAPS is the largest user of RICA information and the owner of the information is never notified (Privacy International 2021).

The case of *AmaBhungane Centre for Investigative Journalism NPC and Another v Minister of Justice and Correctional Services and Others; Minister of Police v AmaBhungane Centre for Investigative Journalism NPC and Others* [2021] ZACC 3; 2021 (4) BCLR 349 (CC); 2021 (3) SA 246 (CC) (4 February 2021) was instituted prior to the outbreak of COVID-19 in South Africa, having been decided upon on 16 September 2019 and confirmed by the Constitutional Court on 4 February 2021. It was found that the practice of secret, unregulated mass surveillance is unlawful. It was not necessary for the Court to decide whether a law permitting bulk interception would be constitutionally compliant, as it concluded that there was no such law to begin with. This will be contrasted to the situation post-COVID where bulk surveillance was deemed necessary. In the sections below we describe pandemic policy on this issue.

On 15 March 2020, a 21-day national lockdown was promulgated which would commence on 26 March under level 5. Additionally, gatherings of more than 100 people were prohibited (Government Gazette [Vol. 318, No. 43107] 2020). The government implemented a five-tier alert level system, and as the lockdown levels ascended the restrictions would ease. Under Level 5, amongst other things, a curfew of 9 pm to 4am was imposed; all schools and businesses were closed; people were confined to their homes (except to seek essential services) (Government Gazette [Vol. 398, No. 43148] 2020). Under Level 4, an expanded list of businesses which were permitted to open was published and the curfew was amended to 8 pm–5am. Under Level 3, the curfew was lifted, only to be re-imposed on 12 July due to the strain on hospitals (Bax 2020). The above-mentioned measures were largely self-regulated. However, roadblocks set up by the SAPS and the SANDF served as "checkpoints" and citizens had to demonstrate compliance. Under Level 3 and 4, employers were obligated to regulate their employees in the workplace and issue permits for movement. Department of Health inspectors were tasked with enforcing these requirements.

However, surveillance and movement control efforts were severely frustrated due to the fact that around 60% of South Africans live in overpopulated informal settlements comprising cramped shacks without access to basic amenities (Ntshidi and Mahlakoana 2020). A number of people living in informal settlements were classified as essential workers from the outset and relied on overcrowded taxis to travel to work. Observing social distancing and confinement to one's home was largely impossible in such circumstances and resultantly an increased police and military presence was noted in lower income areas (Trippe 2020) to monitor movements of the poorer population (contrary to the lack of police presence pre-lockdown); and police brutality was a serious issue with allegations in some cases of citizen deaths, which are the subject of ongoing investigation (Nombembe 2021). In some instances, the courts have taken swift action to uphold the rule of law in these instances, placing members of the SANDF on suspension (*Khosa and others vs. Minister of Defence and others* 2020). However, there may be instances of abuse that have gone unreported.

On 18 March 2020, the Minister specifically directed that all citizens must submit to the authority of healthcare professionals/enforcement officers and that no person can refuse a medical examination, prophylaxis, treatment, isolation, and quarantine. Transgressors would be placed in isolation or quarantine for a period of 48 hours pending a warrant being issued by a magistrate, on application by an enforcement officer for the medical examination (Government Gazette [Vol. 318, No. 43107] 2020).

To that end, over 28,000 fieldworkers in the public and private health sector were called upon to commence active manual case finding and Community Screening and Testing from 7 April 2020 ("CST") (Department of Health 2020; David and Mash 2020). At the time of writing, almost 20 million citizens had been screened in strategic areas or "hotspot areas" as identified by local authorities (The South African Government, 8 July 2020). Focus was on Persons Under Investigation ("PUI") who were: (1) Symptomatic individuals seeking testing; (2) Hospitalised individuals subjected to tests; (3) People in high-risk occupations; (4) People in outbreak settings; and (5) Strategic areas identified by the local authorities (The National Institute for Communicable Diseases 2020). However, this mass physical testing was discontinued on 17 May 2020 as a result of pressure on the government to take a more targeted approach, due to the shortage of testing kits; and the inability to effectively isolate PUI's, because of the lack of spatial infrastructure of informal housing structures (Green 2020). The practical reality of this initiative is that the poor, crowded areas in South Africa constituting the "hotspots" (Africa Research Bulletin, 1 July 2020) were forcefully infiltrated and its inhabitants subjected to mandatory testing for fear of prosecution.

Following the declaration of the national state of disaster, contact tracing and tracking (Government Gazette [Vol 480, No. 43258] 2020) performed by electronic means and through information mandatorily submitted by the public and private sectors (both individually and institutionally); maintenance of a central information database by the Department of Health (Government Gazette [Vol 446, No. 43199] 2020); issuing of movement permits; symptom monitoring through questionnaires, attendance forms and thermal scanners; quarantine control; and ongoing development of apps using GPS systems such as CoviID (Krige 2020), were amongst the surveillance measures that were applied.

Monetizing the personal data of citizens has been a practice present for decades among South African Electronic Communications Service

Providers (which includes private cellular network providers) which have been enriched through the processing and storing of client data. For example, in 2018 South Africa had 65.8 million mobile cellular data subscriptions, which number is larger than its population size (ICASA, 19 March 2019). The resultant control wielded by Electronic Service Providers over the population led the Minister of Communications and Digital Technologies, on 26 March 2020, to issue directions obliging licensed Electronic Communications Service Providers (which includes private cellular network providers) to provide location-based services and access to their databases in support of tracking and tracing efforts of PUI's (Government Gazette [Vol. 417, No. 43164] 2020; Information Regulator, 3 April 2020). This directive was withdrawn on 8 May 2020 however (Government Gazette [Vol. 516, No. 43299] 2020). Notwithstanding, the Department of Health has set up a "COVID-19 Tracing Database" consisting of the information obtained from all receiving parties. Furthermore, Smartphone app development efforts continue to be spear-headed through governmental partnerships with institutions such as the University of Cape Town (University of Cape Town 2020).

The pre-COVID climate where secret bulk surveillance was facilitated through RICA and NSIA (Ongeso and Dyer 2021; Privacy International 2021) and later found unconstitutional can be contrasted to the post-pandemic setting where due to security measures for the alleged protection of the population (Lim 2020), as opposed to simply State surveillance, bulk surveillance was once again initiated and carried out by the State primarily targeting residents of lower income areas, due to their locality in hotspots—black poverty again forming the basis for surveillance.

4 Challenges and Constraints on the South African Economy

4.1 Pre-COVID-19 Economic Policy

The end of Apartheid in 1994 was an important moment in the history of South Africa not only politically but also economically. The newly elected democratic government led by the African National Congress (ANC) inherited a significant government debt from the previous regime that had faced international trade sanctions from the late 1980s, as well as deeply entrenched racial-based inequality (Williams and Taylor 2000: 27).

Initially the ANC government had adopted the more socialist-orientated Reconstruction and Development Programme (RDP) (Narsiah 2002: 1); but by June 1996, this was abandoned for the Growth, Employment and Redistribution (GEAR) strategy which was based on neoliberal economic principles: "the key policies being deficit reduction, low inflation, trade liberalization, privatization, tax cuts, and deregulation" (Schneider 2003: 43). At a critical moment of history the ANC government adopted neoliberal economic policy which was touted as the only way to boost economic growth (Schneider 2003: 37); and accepted the notion that the mechanisms of free markets and competition would inevitably level out the deep inequality in the country (Schneider 2003: 26). Although the economic policies adopted by the ANC government over the past two and half decades have to some extent pulled some South Africans above the poverty line and created a new black middle class (Mattes 2015); the redistributive efficacy of neoliberal policy has been severely lacking.

Schneider observed that one of the critical flaws of applying neoliberal policy to developing nations or emerging markets like South Africa was that it did not account for the manner in which free markets would entrench the existing socioeconomic inequality between the economic elites and the poor: "*By ignoring the social costs of inequality, in particular the instability created by an economy which does not effectively serve the majority of the population, neoliberal economists abstract from reality and ignore the economic benefits that could stem from developing an economy from the bottom up*" (Schneider 2003: 25).

After the failure of the GEAR policy the ANC government adopted the Accelerated Shared Growth Initiative for South Africa (AsgiSA) in 2006 with the hope that job creation would accelerate economic growth and reduce poverty by half, through the state taking a more active role in the economy (Mwipikeni 2019: 86). However, the AsgiSA policy also failed to meet its ambitious goals and the government subsequently adopted the National Development Path in 2010 with the goal of reducing unemployment by 10% by 2030. This was followed by the National Development Plan (NDP) in 2013 which sought to eliminate poverty and inequality (Mwipikeni 2019: 87). Thus, in 2019, prior to COVID-19, the government was faced with the shortcomings of the National Development Plan in reaching its target, among other economic challenges which will be considered below.

4.2 *Post COVID-19 Economic Prospects*

South Africa is one of the most stable economies in the African continent. It is a middle-income country, emerging market with a rich supply of natural resources. South Africa's real GDP growth projections pre-COVID for 2020 have been lowered further in November and December 2019, with estimates by the International Monetary Fund (IMF), South African National Treasury, and the South African Reserve Bank (SARB) ranging between 0.5 and 1%, all below the 0.8% achieved in December 2019 (STATSSA 2020a). South African economic policies, which are focused on controlling inflation and attaining a budget surplus, have been somewhat efficient as the inflation rate pre-COVID was around 4.2% (IMF 2020). South Africa's economy has been traditionally rooted in the primary sectors. Among the key sectors that contribute to the gross domestic product and keep the economic engine running are manufacturing, wholesale and retail trade, financial services, transport, mining, agriculture, and tourism. The services sector employs 72.3% of the workforce and represents 61.2% of the country's GDP as of December 2019 (STATSSA 2020a). The major sectors of the economy are finance, real estate and business services, followed by general government services. According to the department of statistics of South Africa, tourism contributed 2.8% to South Africa's GDP, which amounted to R139 billion in 2019 (STATSSA 2020a).

According to Valodia and Francis, when South Africa entered its 100 days of lockdown effective from Midnight March 26 2020: "the political message was that South Africans were all in it together. However, it was clear that while society had been united politically to fight COVID-19, there are extreme and persistent economic and social inequalities" (Valodia and Francis 2020).

The state went into alert level 5 of lockdown, which confined everyone to their home for 3 months, April 2020 to June 2020, and cost the South African economy a reported negative growth balance of 8.0% with an estimated five-year GDP recovery from COVID-19 (STATSSA 2020a). The impact of the simulated COVID-19 pandemic has been quite harsh on the economy, depicting a 30 per cent decline in GDP at market prices. The economy was simultaneously affected by a supply and a demand shock as evidenced by the shortage of medical masks and ethanol alcohol used for alcohol-based sanitizers (IMF 2020; PA SARB 2020).

To alleviate the economic burden, the Government issued a number of policies but for our purposes we will consider only six of these. Firstly, the government assisted companies and workers facing distress through the Unemployment Insurance Fund (UIF) and special programmes from the Industrial Development Corporation. Secondly, additional funds were made available for the healthcare sector's response to COVID-19. Thirdly, workers with an income below a R6500 threshold received a small tax subsidy for four months, and the most vulnerable families received temporarily higher social grant amounts. Fourthly, an official loan guarantee scheme was introduced to provide bank loans, guaranteed by the government, to eligible businesses to assist them during the pandemic with operational expenses. Fifthly, the revenue administration accelerated reimbursements and tax credits, allowing Small Medium Enterprises to defer certain tax liabilities, and issued a list of essential goods for a full rebate of customs duty and import value added tax exemption. Lastly, a four-month skills development levy tax holiday was also implemented (IDC 2020; STATSSA 2020b).

On 20 March 2020, the South African Reserve Bank (SARB) announced measures to ease liquidity conditions by: (1) increasing the number of repo auctions to two to provide intraday liquidity support to clearing banks at the policy rate; (2) reducing the upper and lower limits of the standing facility to lend at the repo rate and borrow at 200 basis below the repo rate; and (3) raising the size of the main weekly refinancing operations as needed. On 23 March 2020, the government announced the launch of a unified approach to enable banks to provide debt relief to borrowers. On 25 March 2020, the SARB announced further measures to ease liquidity strains observed in funding markets. The programme aims to purchase government securities in the secondary market across the entire yield curve and extend the main refinancing instrument maturities from 3 to 12 months. On 26 March 2020, the SARB issued guidelines on modalities to provide debt relief to bank customers (PA SARB 2020). Furthermore, on 19 March and 27 March 2020, the Department of Trade and Industry (DTI) introduced regulations against price gouging and export control measures on essential goods, respectively. The government also outlined measures for COVID-19 emergency procurement including the specifications of the health essentials and the maximum prices for the personal protective equipment (Patel 2020; Dlamini-Zuma 2020).

At the time of writing, the Government, through the National Treasury, said it was exploring all funding avenues to finance all COVID-19-related programmes and measures aimed at addressing the pandemic. The funding avenues will include the government exploring funding from international financial institutions. Nonetheless, the government has reiterated its commitment to implement structural economic reforms to address the weak economic growth, constrained fiscus and ailing state-owned companies (Department of National Treasury 2020).

According to the Prestige Credit Group: "The ANC-led government's plan in the aftermath of the COVID-19 crisis is based on the aggressive implementation of the Economic Reconstruction and Recovery Plan, 2020, which aims to stimulate equitable and inclusive growth. At the heart of the plan is mobilising investment, creating new jobs, supporting existing ones and accelerating industrialisation" (Prestige Credit Group 2021).

The COVID-19 pandemic and measures taken to address its spread have had a substantial negative impact on economic growth and government's fiscal position. The Pre-existing fiscal position was precarious, and there is a need to ensure that whatever is done does not harm South Africa's long-run fiscal sustainability (Department of National Treasury 2020).

South Africa's response to the COVID-19 outbreak has been one of the most responsive in the region. However, the effects of the crisis are clearly visible. Government debt has increased to 82.8% of GDP in 2021, up from an already high level in June 2020 (78.8%) and is expected to rise in January 2022 (85.7%) (IMF 2020). The difficulties of public companies (such as the state-owned power company Eskom) are compounded by private company operational closure due to the hard lockdown. Although the government is investing in aid programmes, the financial situation of the companies represents a risk to public finances. In addition, the country's budget deficit reached 9.1% by 30 June 2020 (STASSA, Report No.: 03-10-19).

5 The Labour Market

5.1 *Pre-COVID-19 Unemployment*

Neoliberal reform of the labour market is characterised by the abandonment of a minimum wage, weakened labour protection in order to attract investors and the proliferation of precarious forms of flexible short-term contracts with little or no benefits (Harvey 2005). In the initial post-Apartheid period, in addition to adopting a number of neoliberal policies, the South African government also signed a number of bilateral investment treaties in order to attract investors which placed workers in a precarious position (Masipa 2018).

Although South Africa's economic policy is characterised by an early neoliberal period as a response to the social and economic inequality experienced by South African citizens during Apartheid, the need to address income inequality resulted in the contemplation and eventual development of social relief measures through social protection cash transfers to vulnerable persons aimed at "protect[ing] individuals from the impact of shocks (e.g. market shocks, political unrest, flooding, crop disease, drought) while supporting the accumulation of human, productive and financial assets (Winchester et al. 2021). The first democratically elected government introduced extensive legislative reform intended to address income inequality, promote the employment of persons previously discriminated against under the Apartheid regime and to provide protection for all employees against future unemployment through the introduction of an unemployment insurance fund. Despite these efforts, the unemployment rate was reported at 29.1% in 2019, whilst half of the population was reported to be living below the upper bound poverty line.

South Africa's growing unemployment rate and in particular, the widening inequality gap between rich and poor South Africans has remained a long-standing feature of the South African economy due to inter alia large slow economic growth; inequalities in access to economic power, property, and opportunities and dysfunctional social structures and high levels of crime (Geffen 2018). These problems persisted long before the COVID-19 pandemic was first reported but worsened by the introduction of strict and restrictive regulations prohibiting the movement of citizens, which has had a disproportionate impact on vulnerable persons and those employed in the informal sector.

Prior to the COVID-19 pandemic, the South African government introduced several social assistance and security initiatives, intended to provide financial assistance to the most vulnerable persons within the country, in line with its obligations as set out in the Constitution of the Republic of South Africa, 1996. Such social assistance, as administered by the South African Social Security Agency (SASSA), included the provision of grants and financial aid to inter alia children and their caregivers, persons with disabilities, the elderly (ranging from a value of R445 (24,75 USD) to R1 860 (103.45 USD) per month during the 2020/2021 budget year) and war veterans (valued at an estimated R1 880 p/m during the 2020/2021 budget year [approximately 104.57 USD as at 1 April 2020]) (Department of Social Development 2020). Comparatively, the food poverty line is at a value of R585 (32.54 USD) per person, per month in April 2020 prices, whilst the upper bound poverty line is at an amount of R1 268 (70.53 USD) per person, per month in April 2020 prices. Although the national poverty lines are not used in the determination of the value of the social grants at a national level, these figures provide us with a better understanding of the dire straits under which recipients of social assistance live under. As of March 2020, a reported 18 million people were receiving social assistance from the South African government (Orlandi 2021). Whereas the aforementioned social assistance is aimed primarily that those persons who may not be unable to be formally employed, whether due to their age or ability; the Unemployment Insurance Fund (UIF) was created in 2001 to limit the financial burden of possible future unemployment or extended leave periods due to illness or such employees who are on maternity leave by mandating employees and their employers to contribute 1% of each employee's monthly salary (a maximum of R148.72 per person, approximately 10 USD) to the fund as insurance for possible future unemployment. However, as both the UIF and the social security programme limit the category of persons eligible for economic relief through its qualifying criteria, a subsect of people, particularly those between the ages of 18–59, do not qualify for short term social relief of distress benefits or disability grants and accordingly are left without social assistance.

Further legislative and regulatory reform was introduced to address the discrepancies in access to wealth and economic prosperity that existed between men and women, as well as such discrepancies between those socially classified under different "racial" categories. To limit this differentiation within the formal sector and to engage the private sector in addressing economic inequality, the Broad-Based Black Economic

Empowerment Act 53 of 2003 ("B-BBEE") was promulgated to, among other things, increase the effective participation of black people in the economy, achieve substantial change in the racial composition of ownership and management structures and in skilled occupation of existing and new enterprises employment, increase the extent to which black women own and manage existing and new enterprises and to promote access to finance for black economic empowerment. Although not primarily intended as a means to intervene in the South African labour market, B-BBEE is not an isolated policy but rather one that works hand in hand with the South African labour laws to transform the structure of the economy and the workplace (Francis and Valodia 2021). Notwithstanding its objectives, B-BBEE has been marred with criticism and controversy since its inception, The main criticism of B-BBEE is its failure to create meaningful and effective structural changes in the economy as it provided "enhanced opportunities for black individuals (rather than groups) to improve their position via affirmative action. This is done by allocating extra resources created by higher economic growth, rather than by redistributing existing resources" (Ponte et al. 2007; Francis and Valodia 2021). However, in their criticism of B-BBEE, Ponte has observed that as B-BBEE is applied within the context of neoliberal economic policy "it can only take specific forms and achieve limited results. The failure to deliver meaningful change in areas that need it most (land, skills development, employment) and where it would be most feasible (fisheries...) are testimony to this" (Ponte et al. 2007).

Employees in the informal sector, particularly farm labourers and those providing domestic and housekeeping services, have been highlighted as vulnerable persons by the South African government and efforts had been made in the past to improve their economic and working conditions, including the introduction of the national minimum wage and various sectoral determinations aimed at regulating the remuneration of such categories of employees.

Despite the promulgation of a suite of legislation geared towards addressing social and economic inequality, approximately half of South Africa's adult population (being 49.2%) was living below the upper-bound poverty line (STATSSA 2014/2015), being R992 (approximately $69) per person per month between 2014 and 2015. From these statistics, two things were evident, black African persons and women continued to represent the majority of people living below the poverty line, and that the Limpopo and Eastern Cape provinces, traditionally agricultural and mining dominated economies, had the highest headcount of poverty-stricken individuals in the country (STATSSA 2014/2015). Where reform was intended to aid the most vulnerable people within the country, the gap in access to employment opportunities and economic participation grew further and in 2019, the unemployment rate was at a reported 29.1% of the population.

Another legislative endeavour (and break with neoliberal policy) that occurred is the adoption of the national minimum wage. After a significantly long period of debate and the active role of the Congress of South African Trade Unions (COSATU), the National Minimum Wage Act 9 of 2018, was passed into law in December 2018; and in January 2019 the minimum wage was determined as R20 per hour and R3500 ($244,55) per month as set out in section 4 of the Act which states that "*every worker is entitled to payment of a wage in an amount no less than the national minimum wage*". In ensuring compliance with the terms of National Minimum Wage Act, the National Minimum Wage Commission was created to, among other functions, investigate the impact of the national minimum wage on the economy, investigate instances of income differentials within the labour market and to advise the Minister of Labour on matters relating to conditions of employment. The provisions of the National Minimum Wage Act form a part of every employees' contracts of employment and an employer's failure to comply with the terms of the Act may give rise to a claim of unfair labour practices and a referral of the dispute being referred to the relevant labour tribunal or the Labour Court.

Prior to the pandemic, labour policy was in theory geared toward curbing the significant unemployment in the country while also ensuring those in the labour market were adequately protected against future unemployment or labour exploitation. Policies include the expanded public works programme and the Presidential Jobs Summit: Framework Agreement produced with the intention of creating an estimated 275,000 jobs annually. However, unemployment persisted as identified by the Minister of Employment and Labour due to low economic growth, limited skills acquisition, and training for the people between the ages of 15 and 34 years old and rapid changes in the labour market fuelled by digitisation and automation (Writer 2020). Despite these policies, particularly those geared towards addressing youth unemployment, those between the ages of 15 to 34 years old, who accounted for 42.8% of the total number of unemployed persons in the country (STATSSA 2022). Additionally, South Africa started cancelling or not renewing its bilateral investment treaties specifically with global North countries; and implementing local legislation for the adjudication of investment disputes to allow for context specific dispute resolution with investors that was sensitive to South African conditions (Department of Trade and Industry BIT Review 2009).

5.2 *The Future of the South African Labour Market*

In announcing the national lockdown measures, the South African government published new regulations to the Disaster Management Act no. 57 of 2002 limiting the movement of people within the country to two categories of persons: (1) those persons who obtained essential goods and services; and (2) those who were employed as "essential service workers" as defined in the Labour Relations Act No. 66 of 1995 ("LRA"). In terms of section 213 of the LRA, read together with the regulations to the Disaster Management Act, essential service workers included those persons: employed in the health sector; emergency personnel; the South African police services; parliamentary services; the financial sector; telecommunication; and food production and supply. The limited definition of what constituted essential service workers coupled with an inability to tender their employment services remotely meant that a portion of employees were rendered unable to work for the duration of the level five lockdown period, being 35 days. Where employees were not able to take their annual leave entitlement for the 35 days or such entitlement had been exhausted, employers had no option other than to reduce their employees' salaries and in certain instances, downsize their organisations.

To mitigate against possible job losses, the Department of Employment and Labour, introduced the Temporary Employer/Employee Relief Scheme benefit ("TERS"), aimed at providing financial relief to employees who, due to the COVID-19 pandemic, received reduced salaries and wages, experienced a reduction of their working hours or had been quarantined for ten days due to a suspected or confirmed infection by SARS CoV-2.

In making provision of the employee relief measures as set out above, the Department of Employment and Labour introduced a set of qualifying criteria to be adhered to in order to receive the TERS benefits.

The qualifying criteria, did not place an emphasis on economically vulnerable workers, instead it was limited to all persons who: (1) constituted an "employee" as defined in the LRA; (2) were registered to work in South Africa; (3) had been impacted by the COVID-19 pandemic; and (4) were not receiving any additional social benefit or employee relief measure at the time the application was made.

Although the qualifying criteria is minimal, accessibility to TERS benefits was hindered by South Africa's Labour laws, which have a narrow definition for the term "employee". "Employee" is defined in section 213 of the LRA as: "*any person, excluding independent contractors who works for another person or who assists in conducting the business of an employer*". Therefore, self-employed individuals, freelancers, and those engaged in the gig economy did not fall within this definition, and accordingly did not qualify for the TERS benefits. It was estimated that approximately 45% of South African workers were not eligible for the TERS benefits under its (then) qualifying criteria, read together with the provisions of the LRA (Bassier et al. 2022). Such persons who were disqualified from the TERS benefits would have to apply to SASSA for financial aid or apply for the newly introduced Social Relief of Distress Grant (colloquially referred to as the "Covid-19 grant"), an amount of R350 (approximately 24.47 USD) per month per unemployed persons. Comparatively, the Upper bound poverty line as of April 2019 was valued at R1227 whilst the food poverty line was R561, which meant that recipients of the unemployment grant were not able to afford the purchase enough food to meet their minimum required daily energy intake nor were they able to afford non-food items.

Additionally, the rollout of the TERS benefits were not without problem. Employees who were eligible for TERS benefits experienced delays or problems in receiving their funds where some employees received short pay or no payments at all whilst foreign nationals who were legally employed to work in South Africa did not receive their TERS benefits because their passport numbers were not recognised by the TERS online application system (Business Insider 2020).

Despite the provision of employee relief benefits, the slow transition from total lockdown practices to partially relaxed lockdown rules meant that an estimated 2.9 million jobs had been lost from February 2020 to April 2020, of which 67% were women (Casale and Shepherd 2021) resulting in an overall increase in the unemployment rate. Further, the National Income Dynamics Study, Coronavirus Rapid Mobile Survey

(NIDS-CRAM), an independent and broadly represented panel survey, reported that when considering the rate of job losses between persons employed in the formal sector compared to those employed in the informal sector, the rate of job losses was higher amongst informally employed persons (Benhura and Magejo 2020).

At the onset of the COVID-19 pandemic and the subsequent lockdown regulations in South Africa, the TERS benefit had been intended as a temporary measure to assist employees for a limited period of three months. However, by May 2020, although many sectors had resumed operations, it was clear that the impact of the pandemic would have long-lasting consequences on the South African Labour market. To address this, the UIF, as endorsed by the National Economic Development and Labour Council had proposed that the TERS benefits be extended until 15 March 2021 and that the categories of employees eligible to receive TERS benefits be extended to include those employed in sectors still affected by lockdown regulations, including the hospitality and liquor industry, employees with comorbidities and employees who are over the age of 60 years old and who could not be reasonably accommodated at work.

In conjunction with extended TERS benefits, a measured reduction and easing of lockdown restrictions have been introduced by the South African government to ensure that more people were able to return to work and for the economy to return to its pre-COVID-19 position. However, as reported, the unemployment rate grew to a rate of 32.5% in 2020 (Statistics South Africa 2021) by quarter 4 (October to December 2020), the highest rate recorded since 2008. In contrast, NIDS-CRAM has indicated that there has been a small but promising upswing in the number of persons actively employed in the country as early as June 2020, due in part to the easing of lockdown restrictions allowing more persons to return to their places of work together with the slow re-employment of persons who were rendered unemployed during the initial months of the pandemic.

With the intended rollout of vaccinations during 2021 to the greater South African population, and further reductions in lockdown restrictions, including the lifting of bans on the manufacturing and sale of liquor and the relaxation of restrictions on curfews, many remain hopeful that a return to normalcy, pre the COVID-19 pandemic will be achieved soon, resulting in a decreased unemployment rate.

The promulgation of restrictive regulations following the announcement of the first positive case of COVID-19 in South Africa exacerbated the problems in the South African labour market, resulting in an increase in the unemployment rate despite early government interventions through amended social assistance programmes and the introduction of COVID-19 relief fund benefits to employees. The pandemic resulted in mass job losses across the country, particularly affecting vulnerable persons and those employed in the informal sector. Although slight economic recovery has been reported, where the real gross domestic product grew by 6,3% in the fourth quarter of 2020 (STATSSA 2021), the impact of COVID-19 on the South African labour market shall be experienced for many years to come, particularly by those who were unable to access such COVID-19 relief schemes due to the restrictive qualifying criteria.

6 Health Care

6.1 Pre-COVID-19 Health Care Infrastructure

The inequities in the South African healthcare system are inherited from the fragmented Apartheid structuring of society. The National Department of Health, as mandated by the Constitution and the National Health Act 61 of 2003, has grappled with addressing these inequities to date (Maphumulo and Bhengu 2019), with the public facilities lacking the basic tenets for proper healthcare service delivery, primarily to the lower income population (Investec 2020). In contrast, the private healthcare sector continues to thrive in South Africa providing healthcare for consumers that can afford private healthcare, thus commodifying healthcare and making it accessible to higher income households.

In 2019, 84% of an estimated population of 55.5 million was dependent on public healthcare and a very small minority of around 16% of the population are attended to by private healthcare facilities as members of medical aid schemes (Maphumulo and Bhengu 2019). The Department of Health found that 50% of the total healthcare expenditure and 80% of medical specialists are attributable to 16% of the population who belong to medical aid and the remainder of the population were reliant on the under-resourced public healthcare sector (Maphumulo and Bhengu 2019). This status quo persists to date.

Free, universal healthcare is a priority for the South African government (Maphumulo and Bhengu 2019) and at the time of writing, the government was in the middle of finalising public comments on the National Health Insurance Bill which was published at the end of 2019 (BusinessTech 2020b). The NHI Bill has been met with much opposition, causing a long delay in its ultimate implementation (Toyana and Auriacmbe 2013). In terms of the NHI Bill, the government is aiming to implement the National Health Insurance over a 14-year period commencing from 2012 (Child 2011). The NHI would constitute one of the largest policy changes since independence (Ngcuka 2019). However, additional resources will be required if the NHI is to meet the needs of all South Africans equally and to retain the expertise of healthcare professionals in the country; and as at the time of writing the country was not adequately resourced in every respect but particularly in terms of numbers of healthcare workers (Discovery Health Medical Scheme 2019; Investec 2020) available to provide healthcare services to the public at large. It has been noted that health problems in South Africa are worsened by inequitable distribution of the active and available health professionals between the private and public sectors (Maphumulo and Bhengu 2019). 32.65% of the total population resides in rural areas (Macrotrends 2022), with 42% of SA's public healthcare system operating therein but only 15% of doctors and 20% of nurses stationed therein (Investec 2020).

The major issues in public healthcare facilities are: (1) overcrowding, due to influx of people to the cities and undocumented migrants; (2) poor facilities management; (3) corruption in procurement and expenditure; (4) hygiene and infection control shortcomings; (5) extended waiting time or turning away of patients; (6) shortage of expertise, medication, and equipment; (7) poor recordkeeping which can result in misdiagnosis; (8) unskilled leadership and lack of governance (Investec 2020); and (9) a lack of basic healthcare infrastructure in rural communities such as piped water (Maphumulo and Bhengu 2019; Investec 2020).

The government has attempted many interventions, however pre-COVID-19, it was clear that public healthcare facilities were unable or failing to meet basic standards of care (National Department of Health 2012). Public loss of confidence and trust in the public healthcare system was prevalent (Maphumulo and Bhengu 2019) and South African scholars have described the healthcare system in South Africa as ruined and in serious need of repair (Maphumulo and Bhengu 2019; Koelble and Siddle 2014). Many believed that the South African government has not done sufficient work to ensure equitable distribution of resources across public and private healthcare facilities, which would entail a re-distribution from private to the public (Maphumulo and Bhengu 2019).

6.2 Health Care Infrastructure in a Post Pandemic Age

In an address by President Ramaphosa on May 24, 2020, he stated:

> As a result of the measures we imposed – and the sacrifices you made – we have managed to slow the rate of infection and prevent our health facilities from being overwhelmed. We have used the time during the lockdown to build up an extensive public health response and prepare our health system for the anticipated surge in infections.

This claim is doubtful and not meaningfully verifiable, as no clear evidence that the public healthcare infrastructure goals had been met prior to removal of the hard lockdown were readily available. South Africa went into this early lockdown to allegedly ramp up and prepare the healthcare system to cope with the South African population (Valodia et al. 2020; Investec 2020) by attempting to procure hospital beds (estimated between 25,000 and 35,000), and increasing equipment and staffing (Cowan 2020). Negotiations between private and public sector to increase bed capacity seems to have had failings nationally, only being marginally successful in the Western Cape (BusinessTech 2020b). Experts foresaw that ICU beds would run out by July 2020 and that public sector patients would have to be moved to private hospitals, with field hospitals being built to increase capacity (Investec 2020).

It is unclear whether any additional beds were in fact added to the existing capacity, which was 2300 in both public and private (Maphumulo and Bhengu 2019). Public facilities also failed to provide accurate health data resulting in skewed reporting numbers to authorities.

Media reported that there was a backlog in public laboratories of approximately 100,000 tests and 10 days lag, with the intent to ramp up capacity to 30,000 tests per day which goal was not reached (Cowan 2020) due global supply issue of testing and extraction kits. The private sector however accounted for 57% of testing conducted nationally, despite almost 60,000 community health workers being mobilised to attend to door-to-door screening in rural areas—it is reported that only 21% of the population was reached, equating to 12 million screenings (Investec 2020).

As at September 2020, information on ventilator shortage could not be established in any healthcare facilities despite there having been shortcomings in the order and delivery of the same (Cowan 2020; Investec 2020) with 20,000 deemed to be required and only 3216 available country-wide. Data collection systems and reporting remained an issue throughout the lockdown period (Cowan 2020) with delays, withholding of information and underreporting by public facilities hindering the true view of the country's response and capabilities during the lockdown period. (Cowan 2020).

COVID-19 has accelerated teachings around staffing, health and safety and health products which according to the Department of Health, "will help boost the implementation of the NHI" (Discovery Health Medical Scheme 2019). The impact of COVID on NHI rollout, scheduled for 2025 is unclear, however the President seems committed to its implementation (BusinessTech 2020b). Due to the economic downturn caused by the lockdown and closure of many businesses resulting in the loss of many jobs, there will be significant challenges to raising additional revenue through taxes in order to create revenue to fund the NHI system (Discovery Health Medical Scheme 2019). Despite the pandemic, the National Department of Health has registered in excess of 45 million NHS beneficiaries exceeding their target of 40 million and that a total of 3059 public healthcare facilities implemented the Health Patient Registration System (HPRS) (BusinessTech 2020c).

7 Education

7.1 Unequal Education in South Africa

The education system in South Africa is managed by the Department of Basic Education for primary and high school education; and the Department of Higher Education for tertiary education. According to section 29(1) of the Constitution: "Everyone has the right—(a) to a basic education, including adult basic education; and (b) to further education, which the state, through reasonable measures, must make progressively available and accessible". Prior to the pandemic both spheres had experienced serious challenges in fulfilling its constitutional mandate.

In respect of basic education, the Constitution provides that the right to basic education is an immediately realisable right without an internal qualifier for progressive realisation (Mtwesi 2013). In this regard, the government, in part provides access to basic education through no-fee schools as part of its constitutional duty of providing access to education (Simbo 2018). Moreover, since the transition to democracy there has been slow but meaningful improvement in the education system (Gustafsson and Nuga 2020). However, the quality of education has been criticised as below par (Amnesty International 2020: 22). A report by Amnesty International described the education system as "broken and unequal" and described the significant infrastructural challenges and lack of resources faced by schools in the country. In contrast private schools which are only accessible to higher income households have increased in South Africa. This has created a market for the commodification of education where parents can select curriculums that would allow their children a competitive advantage in the marketplace. Moreover, this has widened the education and skills gap between children in no fee schools and private schools.

The second component of the State's constitutional duty is progressive realisation of providing further education. In this respect, tertiary education in the country is subsidised to some extent by the government but students need to pay significant tuition fees or obtain a scholarship in order to obtain tertiary education (Commission of Inquiry into Higher Education and Training 2017). Consequently, universities across the country experienced significant student protests regarding exorbitant universities that made access to higher education unobtainable for the vast majority of the country (Mavunga 2019: 81). Student protests resulted in campuses being closed or disrupted for a significant part of 2016–2018 (Mutekwe 2017: 142). In response, the government began investigating the possibility of providing free higher education or further subsidies for tertiary education on a scale for the poor (Commission of Inquiry into Higher Education and Training 2017). This process was still ongoing when the pandemic occurred creating further strain on government spending.

7.2 *The Future of Education in South Africa*

During the pandemic schools and university campuses were closed to avoid the spread of the virus. However, these closures had a detrimental impact on the already strained education system. Firstly, it was estimated that 40% of school days were lost for most children in 2020 (NIDS-CRAM Wave 2 Synthesis Report 2020: 5). However, Gustafsson and Nuga argued that the number of school days lost does not accurately capture the learning losses and proposed that the number of days should be adjusted by a further 25% to capture learning losses meaning that learners were actually 50 days behind on learning at the end of 2020 (Gustafsson and Nuga 2020). This will have a significant impact on post school education and the labour market if learners are unable to catch up the lost learning (Gustafsson and Nuga 2020). Secondly, not only was the option of online lessons accessible to the wealthier population demographic who had access to a computer and data at home; but it was also estimated that children who fit within the wealthier demographic were twice as likely to attend school despite their grade being closed (NIDS-CRAM Wave 2 Synthesis Report 2020: 5). Thus, lockdown significantly increased the educational inequality in the country between the wealthy and the poor.

Furthermore, the closure of schools also had an impact on hunger in the country because children could no longer access meals from school during the school closures (NIDS-CRAM Wave 3 Synthesis Report 2021: 5). According to Gustafsson and Nuga (2020: 3): "*After successes over twenty years in reducing, though not eliminating, child hunger, two factors relating to the pandemic have undone this trend: income losses in households, and interruptions in access to meals at schools. The reductions in hunger over the longer term are likely to have contributed to educational improvements and, conversely, the COVID-19 nutrition shock could exacerbate learning losses. Tackling child hunger that has arisen as a result of the pandemic is arguably South Africa's most pressing social policy challenge currently*". Therefore, as a matter of priority in basic education policy, is the need to address child hunger. With regard to education policy in general, lost learning time needs to be recovered so that learners do not fall behind and avoid spillover effects into tertiary education and access to the labour market.

As evident in other sectors discussed above, the COVID-19 pandemic revealed and exacerbated the deep inequality in South African education.

Moreover, this indicates that closing the inequality gap in a post pandemic age will continue to be challenging when the government's budget is split in so many directions that require urgent attention. The downward turn in the economy will also cause slow growth in these inequalities going forward.

8 Conclusion

The COVID-19 pandemic has made it painfully clear that inequality is entrenched in the fabric of South African society. Moreover, it is clear that the socioeconomic inequality faced by millions of poor, vulnerable and marginalised members of society has grown during the pandemic and will continue to grow in the post pandemic period (Graham 2020) (York 2020). In this chapter, we identified the impact of the pandemic on the areas of: democratic governance and social activism; surveillance and security; economic policy; the labour market; health infrastructure; and the education sector. This chapter contributes to the discussion on the potential post-pandemic policy trajectories in each of these sectors by focusing on specific policies prior to the pandemic and during the first one hundred days of pandemic policy. We concluded that the downward socio-economic trajectory across these sectors will continue unless drastic action is taken to decisively address these inequalities. There is a need for the State to adopt pro-poor and human rights-based budgeting to make available "the maximum possible resources available for promoting, respecting protecting and fulfilling fundamental human rights" (Budget Justice Coalition 2021). These measures may include: greater regulation of private and state surveillance; the provision of basic services such as clean water, electricity, and sanitation that must be of a quality that promotes people's dignity (Graham 2020); addressing the vulnerabilities experienced by low-wage, casual, and informal workers (Graham 2020); the implementation of universal or basic income grant (Blacksash 2021); improving public health care; and addressing the learning losses that have disproportionately affected the poor. The South African economy is currently in a precarious economic position, the decisions that will be taken, in light of the pandemic, have the potential to either alleviate some of the deep inequalities in the country or entrench them deeper into the fabric of society.

References

African News Agency. (2020) Supreme Court grants FITA leave to appeal lockdown tobacco ban judgment. 15 August, https://www.iol.co.za/news/politics/supreme-court-grants-fita-leave-to-appeal-lockdown-tobacco-ban-judgment-38e7196b-8129-4ea8-ba79-3a10fd3b3563.

AmaBhungane Centre for Investigative Journalism NPC and Another v Minister of Justice and Correctional Services and Others; Minister of Police v AmaBhungane Centre for Investigative Journalism NPC and Others [2021] ZACC 3.

Amnesty International (2020) Broken and unequal: The state of education in South Africa. London, UK: Amnesty International Ltd. Index: AFR 53/1705/2020.

Basimanyane, D. & Gandhi, D. (2019) Striking a balance between CCTV surveillance and the digital right to privacy in South Africa. Cape Town, South Africa: African Policing Civilian Oversight Forum (APCOF). Research Paper 27.

Bassier, I., Budlender, J. & Goldman, M. (2022). Social distress and (some) relief: Estimating the impact of pandemic job loss on poverty in South Africa. United Nations University World Institute for Development Economics Research. Working Paper 2022/80.

Bax, P. (2020) Trauma wards fill up in South Africa after alcohol ban is lifted. Bloomberg. 10 June, https://www.bloomberg.com/news/articles/2020-06-10/traumawards-fill-up-in-south-africa-after-alcohol-ban-is-lifted, accessed 31 July 2020.

Benhura, M. & Magejo, P. (2020) Differences between formal and informal workers' outcomes during the COVID-19 crisis lockdown in South Africa. Johannesburg, South Africa: The University of the Witwatersrand. National Income Dynamics Study—Coronavirus Rapid Mobile Survey (NIDS-CRAM). Wave 2: 30 September 2020.

Blacksash. (2021) Basic Income Support for 18 to 59 Now! June 2021, http://www.blacksash.org.za/images/campaigns/basicincomesupport/0547_Blacksash_BIS_A4_Factsheet_-_June2021.pdf, accessed 18 February 2022.

Broad Based Black Economic Empowerment Act 53 of 2003.

Budget Justice Coalition. (2021) Submission by the Budget Justice Coalition to the Select and Standing Committees on Finance on the 2021 Budget. March 2021, https://budgetjusticesa.org/assets/downloads/2021BudgetFinanceSubmission.pdf, accessed 18 February 2022.

Business Insider SA (2020) UIF Covid-19 payout trouble: These are the most common problems holding back the cash. 11 May, https://www.businessinsider.co.za/how-to-avoid-uif-problems-2020-5, accessed 31 July 2020.

BusinessTech. (2020a) Government prepares for move to South Africa's new NHI—but there's a hitch. 3 September, https://businesstech.co.za/news/government/430934/government-prepares-for-move-to-south-africas-new-nhi-but-theres-a-hitch/ accessed 31 July 2020a.

BusinessTech. (2020b) Government has already registered over 45 million South Africans to its NHI database. 19 November, https://businesstech.co.za/news/government/449795/government-has-already-registered-over-45-mil lion-south-africans-to-its-nhi-database/ accessed 31 July 2020.

BusinessTech (2020c) Why young people can't find work in South Africa. 18 September, https://businesstech.co.za/news/business/433474/why-young-people-cant-find-work-in-south-africa-minister/, accessed 27 March 2022.

Business Tech Staff Writer. (2020) Former shoprite CEO joins court battle against South Africa's alcohol sales ban. Business Tech. 7 August, https://businesstech.co.za/news/business/423746/former-shoprite-ceo-wades-into-court-battle-against-south-africasalcohol-sales-ban/ accessed 31 July 2020.

C19 People's Coalition. (2020a) A Programme of Action in the time of Covid-19. https://c19peoplescoalition.org.za/poa/, accessed 18 February 2022.

C19 People's Coalition. (2020b) Covid-19 Relief Grant falls short of promised reprieve. Media Statement. 19 May, https://c19peoplescoalition.org.za/relief grantfallsshort/ accessed 18 February 2022.

Child, K. (2011) National Health Insurance: A dummy's guide. The Mail & Guardian. 12 August, https://mg.co.za/article/2011-08-12-national-health-insurance-a-dummys-guide/, accessed 15 July 2020.

Casale, D. & Shepherd, D. (2021) The Gendered Effects of the Covid-19 Crisis and Ongoing Lockdown in South Africa: Evidence from NIDS-CRAM Waves 1–3. Johannesburg, South Africa: The University of the Witwatersrand. National Income Dynamics Study—Coronavirus Rapid Mobile Survey (NIDS-CRAM). Wave 3: 17 February 2021.

Children's Institute, University of Cape Town and 29 organisations. (2020) Letter to President Cyril Ramaphosa: Increase the CSG to protect families against starvation. 3 April.

Commission of Inquiry into Higher Education and Training. (2017) Report of the Commission of Enquiry into Higher Education and Training to the President of South Africa. Pretoria, South Africa: Commission of Inquiry into Higher Education and Training, https://www.thepresidency.gov.za/sites/def ault/files/Commission%20of%20Inquiry%20into%20Higher%20Education% 20Report.pdf.

Cowan, K. (2020) Auditing SA's public health response to Covid-19—here's how we did. News24. 17 September, https://www.nicd.ac.za/wp-content/uploads/2020/09/Auditing-SAs-public-health-response-to-Covid-19-heres-how-we-did.pdf.

Currie, I. & De Waal, J. (eds) (2013) The Bill of Rights Handbook. Cape Town: Juta & Co Ltd.

David, N. & Mash, R. (2020) Community-based screening and testing for Coronavirus in Cape Town, South Africa: Short report. African Journal of Primary Health Care & Family Medicine 12(1), https://phcfm.org/index.php/phcfm/article/view/2499/3856.

De Groot, J. & Lemanski, C. (2020) COVID-19 responses: infrastructure inequality and privileged capacity to transform everyday life in South Africa. Environment and Urbanisation 33(1): 255–272.

Democratic Alliance. (2020) A lockdown extension will create an economic disaster. Press Release. 9 April, https://www.da.org.za/2020/04/a-lockdown-extensionwill-create-an-economic-disaster, access 31 July 2020

Department of Health. (2020) COVID—19 Screening campaign, 26 April, http://www.health.gov.za/covid-19-screening-campaign/, accessed 31 July 2020.

Department of Social Development. (2020) Minister Lindiwe Zulu welcomes increase in Social Grants. Media Statement. 27 February, https://www.gov.za/speeches/increase-social-grants-27-feb-2020-0000, accessed 31 July 2020.

Department of Trade and Industry, General Notice, Notice 961 of 2009, Staatskoerant 7 Julie 2009 No. 32386.

Department of National Treasury. (2020) Economic Measures for COVID-19. Department of National Treasury. Media Statement: 28 April, http://www.treasury.gov.za/comm_media/press/2020/20200428_COVID_Economic_Response_final.pdf, accessed 31 July 2020.

The South African Judiciary, Magisterial District of Tshwane Central, Tshwane North and Tshwane East. (2020) Determination of admission of guilt fines in respect of offences in terms of the Disaster Management Regulations, 2020, https://www.judiciary.org.za/images/Determinations/Gauteng_Province/Determination_of_Admission_of_Guilt_Fines_in_Respect_of_Offences_Committed_in_Terms_of_the_Disaster_Management_Act_Regulations_2020.pdf, accessed 15 July 2020.

Deutsche Gesellschaft für Internationale Zusammenarbeit (GIZ) GmbH. (2014) Building Safer Communities through systemic approaches to violence prevention: Book 1. Pretoria, South Africa: Deutsche Gesellschaft für Internationale Zusammenarbeit (GIZ) GmbH, https://www.saferspaces.org.za/uploads/files/VCP_Toolkit_Book1_web.pdf, accessed 18 February 2022.

Discovery Health Medical Scheme. (2019) Understanding the National Health Insurance (NHI) Bill. November 2019, https://www.discovery.co.za/corporate/health-nhi-the-role-of-medical-schemes, accessed 31 July 2020.

Dlamini-Zuma N. (2020) Disaster Management Act: Declaration of a state of disaster. Government Gazette No. 43096. Pretoria: Department of Cooperative Governance and Traditional Affairs. 15 March, https://www.gov.za/sites/default/files/gcis_document/202003/43096gon313.pdf, accessed 31 July 2020.

Ewinyu, A.K. & Mtshali, H. (2020) Policing and protection in SA: Are we all equal under lockdown? The Daily Maverick. 8 June, https://www.dailymaverick.co.za/article/2020-06-08-policing-and-protection-in-sa-are-we-all-equal-under-lockdown/, accessed 31 July 2020.

Francis, D. & Valodia, I. (2021) Black Economic Empowerment: A Review of the Literature. SCIS Working Paper no. 21, online publication September 2021, https://www.wits.ac.za/media/wits-university/faculties-and-schools/commerce-law-and-management/research-entities/scis/documents/BEE%20A%20Review%20of%20the%20Literature_%202021.pdf.

Frankel, P. (1979) The politics of passes: Control and change in South Africa. The Journal of Modern African Studies 17(2): 199–217.

Friedman, S. (2021) Prisoners of the Past South African Democracy and the Legacy of Minority Rule. Johannesburg, South Africa: WITS University Press.

Geffen, N. (2018) Review of a History of Inequality in South Africa 1652—2002 by Sampie Terreblance, https://www.ekon.sun.ac.za/sampieterreblanche/wp-content/uploads/2018/05/Nathan-Geffen-n.d.-c2003.-Review-of-Terreblanches-Inequality-book.pdf.

Government Gazette (Vol 313, No. 43096). (2020) Disaster Management Act, 2002, Declaration of a National State of Disaster, 15 March 2020, https://www.gov.za/sites/default/files/gcis_document/202003/43096gon313.pdf, 24 August 2020.

Government Gazette (Vol 318, No. 43107). (2020) Disaster Management Act, 2002, Regulations issued in terms of Section 27 (2) of the Disaster Management Act, 2002, 18 March 2020, https://www.gov.za/sites/default/files/gcis_document/202003/43107gon318.pdf.

Government Gazette (Vol 398, No. 43148). (2020) Disaster Management Act, 2002, Regulations issued in terms of Section 27 (2) of the Disaster Management Act, 2002, 25 March 2020, https://www.gov.za/sites/default/files/gcis_document/202003/4314825-3cogta.pdf.

Government Gazette (Vol 417, No. 43164). (2020) Disaster Management Act, 2002, Electronic Communications, Postal and Broadcasting Directions issued under Regulation 10(8) of the Regulations made under the Disaster Management Act, 2002 (Act No. 57 of 2002), 26 March, https://www.gov.za/sites/default/files/gcis_document/202003/43168regl1067gon419.pdf.

Government Gazette (Vol 446, No. 43199). (2020) Disaster Management Act, 2002, Regulations issued in terms of Section 27 (2), 2

April, https://www.gov.za/sites/default/files/gcis_document/202004/43199rgl1078-gon446.pdf.
Government Gazette (Vol 480, No. 43258). (2020) Disaster Management Act, 2002, Regulations issued in terms of Section 27 (2) of the Disaster Management Act, 2002, 29 April, https://www.gov.za/sites/default/files/gcis_document/202004/43258rgl1098gon480s.pdf.
Government Gazette (Vol 516, No. 43299). (2020) Amendment of Electronic Communications, Postal and Broadcasting Directions Issued Under Regulation 10(8) of The Regulations Made Under The Disaster Management Act, 2002 (Act No. 57 of 2002) 8 May, https://www.gov.za/sites/default/files/gcis_document/202006/43299gon516.pdf.
Government Gazette (Vol 657, No. 43116). (2020) Consumer and Customer Protection and National Management Regulations and Directions. 19 March 2020, http://www.thedtic.gov.za/wp-content/uploads/43116.pdf.
Graham, L. (2020) Pandemic underscores gross inequalities in South Africa, and the need to fix them. The Conversation, 5April, https://theconversation.com/pandemic-underscores-gross-inequalities-in-south-africa-and-the-need-to-fix-them-135070.
Green, A. (2020, April 27). COVID-19: Is SA's testing criteria too restrictive? Spotlight. https://www.spotlightnsp.co.za/2020/04/24/covid-19-is-sas-testing-criteria-too-restrictive/, accessed 31 July 2020
Gumede, W. (2018) How civil society has strengthened democracy in South Africa. Democracy Works Foundation: Policy Brief 32, https://democracyworks.org.za/policy-brief-32-how-civil-society-can-strengthen-the-capacity-of-south-africas-parliament/, accessed 31 July 2020.
Gustafsson, M. & Nuga, C. (2020) How is the COVID-19 pandemic affecting educational quality in South Africa? Evidence to date and future Risks. Insight Briefs. 15 July, https://cramsurvey.org/wp-content/uploads/2020/07/Gustafsson.-Nuga.-How-is-the-COVID-19-pandemic-affecting-educational-quality-in-South-Africa_-1.pdf, accessed 31 July 2020.
Hall, K. (2020) Covid-19 info brief: Social grant increases are an immediate and feasible route to protecting children and their families. Cape Town, South African: The Children's Institute. Information Brief.
Harrisberg, K. & Moloney, A. (2019) This country uses 450,000 private security guards to tackle crime. World Economic Forum. 28 October, https://www.weforum.org/agenda/2019/10/how-south-africas-cities-fighting-crime/, accessed 31 July 2020.
Harvey, D. (2005) A Brief History of Neoliberalism. Oxford: Oxford University Press.

Heleta, S. (2017) South Africa's army is in steady decline and nothing's being done to fix it. The Conversation. 5 April, https://theconversation.com/south-africas-army-is-in-steady-decline-and-nothings-being-done-to-fix-it-74712#:~:text=The%20South%20African%20constitution%20says,has%20about%2080%2C000%20active%20personnel.

ICASA. (2019) The State of the ICT sector Report in South Africa. Pretoria, South Africa: Independent Communications Authority of South Africa. Research Report March 2019.

Industrial Development Corporation. (2020) Economic overview: Recent developments in the global and South African economies. Johannesburg, South Africa: Industrial Development Corporation, https://www.idc.co.za/wp-content/uploads/2020/07/IDC-RI-publication-Economic-Overview-External-release-June-2020.pdf.

Information Regulator. (2020) Guidance Note On The Processing Of Personal Information In The Management And Containment Of Covid-19 Pandemic In Terms Of The Protection Of Personal Information Act 4 Of 2013 (POPIA). 3 April, https://www.justice.gov.za/inforeg/docs/InfoRegSA-GuidanceNote-PPI-Covid19-20200403.pdf.

International Monetary Fund. African Dept. (2020) IMF Executive Board Concludes 2019 Article IV Consultation with South Africa. Press Release. 30 January, https://www.imf.org/en/Publications/CR/Issues/2020/01/29/South-Africa-2019-Article-IV-Consultation-Press-Release-and-Staff-Report-and-Statement-by-49003, accessed 31 July 2020.

Investec. (2020) Is SA's healthcare system prepared for Covid-19. Focus Insights. 8 June, https://www.investec.com/en_za/focus/beyond-wealth/is-south-africas-healthcare-system-prepared-for-covid-19.html, accessed 31 July 2020.

John Wiley & Sons Ltd. (2020) Social and Cultural. Africa Research Bulletin 22819, 1 July, https://onlinelibrary.wiley.com/doi/pdf/10.1111/j.1467-825X.2020.09585.x, accessed 31 July 2020.

Khosa v Minister of Defence and Military Defence and Military Veterans [2020] ZAGPPHC 147.

Killander, M. (2019) Criminalising homelessness and survival strategies through municipal by-laws: Colonial legacy and constitutionality. South African Journal on Human Rights 35(1): 70–93.

Koelble, T.A. & Siddle, A. (2014) Institutional complexity and unanticipated consequences: The failure of decentralization in South Africa. Democratization 21(6): 1117–1133.

Krige, N. (2020) CoviID: new app to avoid future lockdowns. University of Cape Town News. 27 March, https://www.news.uct.ac.za/article/-2020-03-27-coviid-new-app-to-avoid-future-lockdowns.

Landman, K. (2004) Gated Communities in South Africa: Comparison of Four Case Studies in Gauteng. Pretoria, South Africa: CSIR Building and Construction Technology.

Lim, W. (2020) Assessing the implications of digital contact tracing for COVID-19 for human rights and the rule of law in South Africa. African Human Rights Law Journal 20(2): 540–557.

Macrotrends. (2022) South Africa Rural Population 1960–2022. https://www.macrotrends.net/countries/ZAF/south-africa/rural-population#:~:text=South%20Africa%20rural%20population%20for,a%200.13%25%20decline%20from%202017, accessed 18 February 2022.

Maphumulo, W.T. & Bhengu, BR. (2019) Challenges of quality improvement in the healthcare of South Africa post-apartheid: A critical review. Curationis 42(1). Published online 29 May 2019, https://www.ncbi.nlm.nih.gov/pmc/articles/PMC6556866/.

Masipa, T.S. (2018) The relationship between foreign direct investment and economic growth in South Africa: Vector error correction analysis. Acta Commercii 18(1). Published online 31 May 2018, https://doi.org/10.4102/ac.v18i1.466.

Mattes, R. (2015) South Africa's emerging black middle class: A harbinger of political change? Journal of International Development 27(5): 665–692.

Mavunga, G. (2019) #FeesMustFall Protests in South Africa: A Critical Realist Analysis of Selected Newspaper Articles. Journal of Student Affairs in Africa 7(1): 81–99.

McLachlan, J.N. (2018) The history of the occupation of land in the cape colony and its effect on land law and constitutionally mandated land reform. LLD thesis, University of Pretoria, Pretoria, South Africa.

Mehlwana, L. (2020) The battle against stigma in Eastern Cape. Daily Maverick. 8 May, https://www.dailymaverick.co.za/article/2020-05-08-the-battle-against-stigma-in-easterncape/.

Meyer, D. (2020) Maimane submits second court bid to prevent school reopening. The South African. 15 June, https://www.thesouthafrican.com/news/mmusi-maimane-one-sa-movement-school-reopening-education-16-june-2020/.

Mining Affected Communities United in Action (MACUA) and 10 organisations. (2020) Letter to President Cyril Ramaphosa and Minister Gwede Mantashe: Civil society writes to President Cyril Ramaphosa and Minister Gwede Mantashe on measures to protect mining-affected communities and workers from coronavirus. Open letter. 14 April, https://www.wits.ac.za/news/sources/cals-news/2020/open-letter-on-mining-communities-and-coronavirus.html, accessed 31 July 2020.

Mkhize, Z. (2020) Update to Parliament on Coronavirus COVID-19 pandemic. Speech/update to Parliament. Cape Town, 8 July.

Mottiar, S. (2015) The Democratic Alliance and the Role of Opposition Parties in South Africa. Journal of African Elections 14(1): 106–123.

Mohamed and Others v President of the Republic of South Africa and Others [2020] ZAGPPHC 120.

Msimang, S. (2021) How Apartheid Endures: The Betrayal of South Africa. Foreign Affairs 100(6): 184–189.

Mtwesi, A. (2013) The Right to Basic Education. Helen Suzman Foundation Briefs, 25 April, https://hsf.org.za/publications/hsf-briefs/the-right-to-basic-education, accessed 31 July 2020.

Mutekwe, E. (2017) Unmasking the Ramifications of the Fees-Must-Fall Conundrum in Higher Education Institutions in South Africa: A Critical Perspective. Perspectives in Education 35(2): 142–154.

Mwipikeni, P. (2019) Ubuntu, rights, and neoliberalism in South Africa. International Journal of African Renaissance Studies 14(2): 81–102.

Narsiah, S. (2002) Neoliberalism and privatisation in South Africa. GeoJournal 57(1/2): 29–38.

National Department of Health. (2012) The National Health Care Facilities Baseline Audit: National Summary Report. Pretoria, South Africa: National Department of Health.

National Institute for Communicable Diseases. (2020) COVID-19 testing summary (Week 26). NICD Covid-19 Testing Summary, 27 June, https://www.nicd.ac.za/wp-content/uploads/2020/07/NICDCOVID-19-Testing-Summary_-Week-26-2020.pdf, accessed 31 July 2020.

Nattrass, N. & Seekings, J. (2001) Democracy and distribution in high unequal economies: The case of South Africa. The Journal of Modern African Studies 39(3): 471–498.

Ndifuna Ukwazi and 26 organisations. (2020) Letter to the presidency and members of cabinet: Urgent moratorium on evictions leading to displacement and homelessness during the declared state of national disaster in light of COVID-19.

Ngatane, N. (2020) COVID-19 has huge impact on poor citizens, says Ramaphosa in May Day message. EWN Eyewitness News. 3 May, https://ewn.co.za/2020/05/01/covid-19-hashuge-impact-on-poor-citizens-says-ramaphosa-in-may-day-message.

Ngcuka, O. (2019) South Africa puts initial universal healthcare cost at $17 billion. Reuters. 8 August, https://www.reuters.com/article/us-safrica-health-idUSKCN1UY1R2.

Ngcukaitobi, T. (2018) The Land is Ours: South Africa's First Black Lawyers and the Birth of Constitutionalism. Cape Town: Penguin Books.

Nkanjeni, U. (2020) We will be over the worst by October/November: Prof Salim Abdool Karim on Covid-19 infections. SowetanLIVE. 22 July. https://www.sowetanlive.co.za/news/south-africa/2020-07-22-we-will-be-over-the-worst-by-octobernovember-profsalim-abdool-karim-on-covid-19-infections/.

Nombembe, P. (2021) 49 cases of police brutality at start of lockdown being probed by Ipid. TimesLIVE. 6 March, https://www.timeslive.co.za/news/south-africa/2021-03-06-49-cases-of-police-brutality-at-start-of-lockdown-being-probed-by-ipid/

Ntshidi, E. & Mahlakoana, T. (2020) Alexandra, Zandspruit residents go about life as usual despite lockdown. EWN Eyewitness News. 27 March, https://ewn.co.za/2020/03/27/alexandra-zandspruit-residents-go-about-life-as-usual-despite-lockdown.

Ongeso, J.P. & Dyer, L. (2021) South Africa: Constitutional Court Upholds Declaration of Invalidity of Rica. Mondaq. 8 February, https://www.mondaq.com/southafrica/constitutional-administrative-law/1034108/constitutional-court-upholds-declaration-of-invalidity-of-rica.

Orlandi, N. (2021) Social grant performance as at end March 20/21. Parliamentary Budget Office Report. 1 March, https://www.parliament.gov.za/storage/app/media/PBO/National_Development_Plan_Analysis/2021/june/03-06-2021/May_2021_Social_Grant_fact_sheet.pdf.

Oliver, E. & Oliver, W.H. (2017) The Colonisation of South Africa: A unique case. HTS Teologiese Studies/Theological Studies 73(3): 1–8.

Patel, E. (2020). Minister Ebhrahim Patel: Government's intervention measures on Coronavirus. 24 March 2020. https://www.gov.za/speeches/minister-ebrahim-patel-government%E2%80%99s-intervention-measures-coronavirus-24-mar-2020-0000, accessed 12 December 2022.

Piotrowski, A. (2019) Colonialism, Apartheid, and Democracy: South Africa's Historical Implications on the Land Reform Debate. Journal of Interdisciplinary Undergraduate Research 11(4): 53–71.

Ponte, S., Roberts, S. & van Sittert, L. (2007) 'Black Economic Empowerment' Business and the State in South Africa. Development and Change 38(5): 933–955.

Prestige Credit Group. (2021) South Africa: Economic and Political Outline. Website post. 3 March, https://prestigecredit.co.za/south-africa-economic-and-political-outline/.

Privacy International. (2021) South African Constitutional Court declares bulk surveillance powers unlawful. Privacy International. 4 February, https://privacyinternational.org/news-analysis/4416/south-african-constitutional-court-declares-bulk-surveillance-powers-unlawful.

Protection of Personal Information Act No. 4 of 2013.

Prudential Authority, South African Reserve Bank. (2020) Matters relating to the application of International Financial Reporting Standard (IFRS) 9 in response

to the Coronavirus pandemic (Covid-19). Pretoria, South Africa: Prudential Authority, South African Reserve Bank. Report No.: 15/8/2 G3/2020.
Rafapa, M. (2020) Lockdown: Street vendor says she can now feed family of 17 under relaxed regulations. News24. 6 April, https://www.news24.com/news24/SouthAfrica/News/lockdown-street-vendor-says-she-can-now-feed-family-of-17-underrelaxed-regulations-20200406.
Ramaphosa, C. (2020) Additional Coronavirus (COVID-19) economic social relief measure. Presidential Address to the Nation. Pretoria, 21 April.
Regulation of Interception of Communications and Provision of Communication-Related Information Act 70 of 2002 (RICA).
Saba, A. (2018) Has BEE been a dismissal failure. Mail & Guardian, 31 August, https://mg.co.za/article/2018-08-31-00-has-bee-been-a-dismal-failure/.
Schneider, G. (2003) Neoliberalism and economic justice in South Africa: Revisiting the debate on economic apartheid. Review of Social Economy 61(1): 23–50.
Simbo, C. (2018) A Hexagon Right: The Six Dimensions of the South African Right for Basic Education. Obiter 39(1): 126–151.
Social Justice Coalition and Others v Minister of Police and Others [2018] ZAWCHC 181.
South African Government. COVID-19/Novel Coronavirus 2020. South African Government. https://www.gov.za/Coronavirus.
South African Government News Agency. (2021) Health system boosted to respond to COVID-19. South African Government News Agency. 24 February, https://www.sanews.gov.za/south-africa/health-system-boosted-respond-covid-19.
Southall, R. (2000) The state of democracy in South Africa. Journal of Commonwealth & Comparative Politics 38(3): 147–170.
Spaull, N. et al. (2020a) NIDS-CRAM Wave 1 Synthesis Report: Observations and Findings. Johannesburg, South Africa: University of the Witwatersrand. NIDS-CRAM Wave 1 Synthesis Report.
Spaull, N. et al. (2020b) NIDS-CRAM Wave 2 Synthesis Findings. Johannesburg, South Africa: University of the Witwatersrand. NIDS-CRAM Wave 2 Synthesis Report.
Spaull, N., Daniels, R. et al. (2021) NIDS-CRAM Wave 3 Synthesis. Johannesburg, South Africa: University of the Witwatersrand. NIDS-CRAM Wave 3 Synthesis Report.
Statistics South Africa. (2014/2015) Men, Women and Children: Findings of the Living Cibdutuibs Survey 2014/15. Pretoria, South Africa: Statistics South Africa. Report number 03-10-02 2014/15.
Statistics South Africa. (2019) Inequality trends in South Africa: A multidimensional diagnostic of inequality. Pretoria, South Africa: Statistics South Africa. Report No.: 03-10-19.

Statistics South Africa. (2020a) Business impact survey of the COVID-19 pandemic in South Africa. 2020. Pretoria, South Africa: Statistics South Africa.
Statistics South Africa. (2020b) Results from wave 2 survey on the impact of the COVID-19 pandemic on employment and income in South Africa. Pretoria, South Africa: Statistics South Africa.
Statistics South Africa. (2021a) Quarterly Labour Force Survey—Quarter 4: 2020. Pretoria, South Africa: Statistics South Africa.
Statistics South Africa. (2021b) More People Participate in the South African Labour Market in the 4th quarter of 2020. Pretoria, South Africa: Statistics South Africa.
Statistics South Africa. (2021c) Gross domestic product - Fourth Quarter 2020. Pretoria, South Africa: Statistics South Africa.
Statistics South Africa. (2021d) Quarterly Labour Force Survey - Quarter 3: 2021. Pretoria, South Africa: Statistics South Africa.
Statistics South Africa (STATSSA). (2022, 3,29). Quarterly Labour Force Survey—Quarter 4: 2021. http://www.statssa.gov.za/publications/P0211/P02114thQuarter2021.pdf, accessed 13 December 2022.
Super, G. (2013) Governing through Crime in South Africa: The Politics of Race and Class in Neoliberalizing Regimes. Dorchester: Ashgate.
Swart, H. (2020) Video surveillance in Southern Africa, Case studies of security camera systems in the region. Pretoria, South Africa: The Media and Democracy Project. Report, May 2020.
Thamm, M. (2021) Zuma's Spy State: A decade of unfettered surveillance, secrets, lies and lootings propped up by a private army of spies. Daily Maverick, 30 January, https://www.dailymaverick.co.za/article/2021-01-30-zumas-spy-state-a-decade-of-unfettered-surveillance-secrets-lies-and-lootings-propped-up-by-a-private-army-of-spies/.
The Constitution of the Republic of South Africa, 1996.
The Disaster Management Act 57 of 2002.
The National Strategic Intelligence Act 39 of 1994 (NSIA).
Toyana, M. & Auriacmbe C.J. (2013) Considerations for the implementation of the National Health Insurance: Health worker shortages. Administratio Publica 22: 62–219.
Trippe, K. (2020) Pandemic Policing: South Africa's most vulnerable face a sharp increase in police-related brutality. Atlantic Council's Africa Center, 24 June, https://www.atlanticcouncil.org/blogs/africasource/pandemic-policing-south-africas-most-vulnerable-face-a-sharp-increase-in-police-related-brutality/.
University of Cape Town. (2020) Special COVID-19 app to screen SA's workforce. Press release, 29 May, https://www.news.uct.ac.za/article/-2020-05-29-specialcovid-19-app-to-screen-sas-workforce, access 31 July 2020.

Valodia, I., and Francis, D. (2020) South Africa Needs to Mitigate the Worst of its Inequalities in Tracking Coronavirus. The Conversation, 5 April, https://theconversation.com/south-africa-needs-to-mitigate-the-worst-of-its-inequalities-in-tackling-coronavirus-135564.

Valodia, I., Van Den Heever, A., Allais, L., Veller, M., & Venter, F. (2020) South Africa's COVID-19 strategy needs updating: here's why and how. WITS University, 16 May, https://www.wits.ac.za/news/latest-news/opinion/2020/2020-05/south-africas-covid-19-strategy-needs-updating-heres-why-and-how.html.

Wegerif, (2020) "Informal" food traders and food security: experiences from the Covid-19 response in South Africa. Springer, 7 July, https://link.springer.com/article/10.1007/s12571-020-01078-z.

Williams, P., & Taylor, I. (2000) Neoliberalism and the political economy of the 'New' South Africa, New Political Economy 5(1): 21–40.

Winchester, MS. (2021) "It's not enough": Local experiences of social grants, economic precarity, and health inequity in Mpumalanga, South Africa. Wellbeing, Space and Society 2: 1–8.

World Bank. (2022) Inequality in Southern Africa: An Assessment of the Southern African Customs Union. Washington, United States of America; World Bank.

York, G. (2020) COVID-19 exposes the fault line of inequality in South Africa. The Globe and Mail, 5 July, https://www.theglobeandmail.com/world/article-covid-19-exposes-the-fault-lines-of-inequality-in-south-africa/.

A Bumpy and Gloomy Road Ahead: An Analysis of Covid-19 Response in Namibia

Christopher Pomwene Shafuda

1 Introduction

The Namibian economy has gone through several stages of discrimination between the white settlers and the black inhabitants. During Apartheid rule, for example, black Namibians lost political, economic, and social rights through a series of laws and regulations governing almost every aspect of their lives (Bauer, 2001). As a result, after gaining independence, the independent Government inherited an economy of highly skewed income distribution with resourceful minorities, while most of the country's population was in absolute poverty. Income inequality in Namibia was extreme, as was inequity in the access to primary economic resources, education, and healthcare. To correct the errors of the colonial leadership, the new Government put more stress on improving equality and quality of life for every Namibian. As a result, the Namibian economy has gone through some government policy interventions and reforms since the 1990s.

C. P. Shafuda (✉)
University of Namibia, Rundu, Namibia
e-mail: poshafuda@gmail.com

A. Stojanović et al. (eds.), *The First 100 Days of Covid-19*,
https://doi.org/10.1007/978-981-19-6325-4_12

The Government of independent Namibia intervened in different sectors of the economy to ensure that all Namibian people enjoyed the same benefits irrespective of their race, colour, or tribe. Furthermore, reforms in other sectors of the economy were adopted to reduce the inter-racial differences in the country. These reforms aimed to achieve high and sustained economic growth, create employment opportunities for all Namibians, and reduce poverty and inequality among the Namibian people (National Planning Commission, 1995). Although interventions were made to address the mistakes of the past governments, not all were efficient. Challenges of unemployment, inequality, and poverty remained high even before the emergence of COVID-19 in the country.

The emergence of the COVID-19 pandemic threatened the already trailing government efforts to end poverty, inequality and unemployment as authorities have used ad-hoc policy measures during the pandemic, such as lockdowns and mass quarantines, to slow its transmission. However, the consequences of the widespread use of these unprecedented measures are not clearly understood. This chapter, therefore, aims to contribute to the understanding of the economic and social consequences of COVID-19. The chapter looked at the history of pandemics and Neoclassical economic theory, COVID-19 policy responses, and their social and economic consequences in Namibia.

2 Pandemics and Neoclassical Economic Theory

Diseases and illnesses have been troubling humanity since the earliest days. However, it was not until the marked shift to agrarian communities that the scale and spread of diseases increased significantly (Dobson and Carper, 1996). Trade between communities has increased interactions between humans and animals and facilitated the transmission of zoonotic pathogens that accelerate such epidemics (Piret and Boivin, 2021). The words epidemic and pandemic have been in existence in social and medical contexts since the seventeenth century (Morens et al., 2009). Epidemic, endemic, outbreak, and pandemic words are used to express how frequent and geographically the extent a disease is now compared to previously. These terms are not solely used to describe infections but also to describe non-infectious conditions such as cancer and hypertension (Grennan, 2019; Sampath et al., 2021). Although these terms are somehow not familiar in the neoclassical theories, neoclassical theoretical concepts are at the core of modern health economics (Hodgson, 2007).

In neoclassical economics, health is defined broadly to include longevity and illness-free days in a given year, and it is both demanded and produced by consumers (Grossman, 1972). The neoclassical theory sees human beings as individualistic beings who want to maximise their utility. Therefore, it logically follows that humans desire health because it generates utilities. According to the theory, utility is generated from health in two ways. First, ill-health is painful; hence, it is a source of disutility. Health goes into the individual utility function directly and positively influences welfare. Second, health is viewed as human capital. Good health means more sick-free days available for an individual. Thus, people can go to the market and produce income and leisure that generate utility on these sick-free days. Therefore, health is a consumer good and a human capital, an investment suitable for the household production function (Jiang, 2009). However, Eichenbaum et al. (2020) claim that the neoclassical model does not rationalize the positive comovement of consumption and investment observed in recessions associated with an epidemic and infectious diseases.

In the neoclassical models, age, income, healthcare, education, environmental, and lifestyle factors are classified as health determinants (Henderson, 2005). An individual begins with a stock of health, which depends on the individual's genetic factors. However, as an individual's age increases, the health stock depreciates. The depreciation rate depends on the rest of the determinants mentioned above (Santerre and Neun, 2007). Healthcare, for example, restores an individual health stock. The neoclassical theory defines health care as a composite of "myriad goods and services that maintain, improve, or restore a person's physical or mental well-being" (Santerre and Neun, P24). Hence, healthcare, like other commodities, is produced and distributed in the marketplace.

With both health and health care defined, we can now detect the relationship between healthcare and utility and the relationship between health/healthcare, investment and consumption, and eventually economic growth. An extensive microeconomic literature examines the effects of varying health determinants on health outcomes themselves, human capital attributes that are contingent on health outcomes, and economic growth. For example, Weil (2007) and Bloom et al. (2004) find that countries with better population health experience faster economic growth. Goenka et al. (2014) study the economic impact of infectious diseases by integrating epidemiological dynamics into a neoclassical growth model and establish that there are multiple steady states, and the local dynamics of the model are fully characterised. At the same time, the interaction of the disease and economic variables is non-linear and can be non-monotonic.

Studies about infectious diseases show that diseases negatively impact the labour force, productivity, and economic growth (Acemoglu and Johnson 2007; Weil, 2007; Ashraf et al., 2008; Agénor, 2015). Chou et al. (2004), Hai et al. (2004), and Siu and Wong (2004) showed that the 2003 SARS outbreak had a significant gross domestic product decline in the service and manufacturing sectors. Acemoglu and Johnson (2007) pointed out that affectation in low-income countries is higher than in high-income countries. Hence, countries with a high initial capital level after a high-impact shock will recover faster. Infectious diseases will directly increase the health costs of residents, hinder the accumulation of human capital, reduce labour time, and ultimately harm economic growth in the long term (Almond, 2006). Therefore, using the variable of labour supply as an intermediary can link the dynamic spread of infectious disease with the fluctuation of the macroeconomy (Goenka and Liu, 2012; Augier and Yaly, 2013). From this literature, we can expect that Namibia, a small economy with a history of commodity-led growth, will likely be hard hit by the COVID-19 pandemic.

3 Country Profile and State of the Nation Pre- COVID-19 Era

Namibia is a small open economy with rich mineral resources like diamonds, uranium, zinc, gold, copper, and natural gas, to mention a few. In 2009 the country was reclassified as an upper middle income by the United Nations Development Programme (UNDP). It is situated in the bottom South-West part of the African continent. Being under the control of South Africa as its 5th province for about 75 years from 1915 to 1990, the country has a very close economic linkage with the South African economy. Thus, the structure of Namibia's economy was highly characterised by the colonial legacy of South Africa until the late 1980s. Before South African control, Namibia was a German colony for over 30 years, and thus previously, it was referred to as Germany South-West Africa.

The country comprises of about 2.54 million people as per 2020 World Bank estimates. With over 842 thousand square kilometres in size, Namibia has the second-lowest population density of any sovereign country, after Mongolia (UN, 2009). Namibia is largely a desert, ranchland with a long coastline on the South of Atlantic; it lies northwest of South Africa, bordering Angola to the North and Botswana to the east. The Caprivi Strip, which stretches off Namibia's northeast edge, extends the country's borders to connect Namibia to Zambia and later Zimbabwe. The country experiences dry to hot desert conditions with limited and erratic rainfall, making it the driest country in Sub-Saharan Africa (Shadbolt, 2012).

Namibia has been a member of the Southern African Customs Union (SACU) since 1990, which provides for free movement of goods between the members consisting of Botswana, Lesotho, Namibia, South Africa, and Eswatini. Duties are levied in a common external tariff on goods originating outside the Union, and no duties or quantitative restrictions apply to intra-SACU trade. SACU is responsible for collecting all the customs and duties and distributing them to all the member countries on a certain agreed formula. Customs revenue is pooled and shared in a negotiated revenue sharing formula.

Namibia introduced its own currency, the Namibian Dollar (N$), in 1993. But, the Namibian dollar was pegged on par (1:1) with the South African currency unit (Rand), which is also accepted as legal tender in Namibia. Namibia is also a member of the Common Monetary Area (CMA) with South Africa, Lesotho, and Eswatini, dating back to the pre-independence period (Sherbourne, 2016). While the CMA is not a full monetary union with a common central bank and common pool of reserves, the South African Rand is the de facto common currency and is legal tender throughout the CMA, and the central banks within the smaller CMA members essentially shadow the South African Reserve Bank interest rates (Nchake et al., 2018). Hence, monetary policies throughout the CMA are mostly influenced by the South African Reserve Bank.

Under a common monetary regime, Namibia has little freedom on monetary policy instruments. Thus, the burden of safeguarding macroeconomic stability in Namibia falls mainly on fiscal policy, interventions, and structural reforms. Hence, fiscal policy and regulatory framework are crucial for the nation's growth and development. However, the country enjoys a slightly flexible monetary policy and has the autonomy to fix interest rates and repo rates. Nevertheless, interest rates in Namibia have mostly moved very closely in line with the South African rates and vice versa.

The Namibian economy has pursued free-market economic principles since 1990, when the country gained its independence, to promote commercial development, create jobs, and bring disadvantaged Namibians into the mainstream economy. The economy experienced an average annual growth of 4.4% between 1991 and 2015 (World Bank, 2020). However, it fell into recession in 2016 and has since struggled to recover, and COVID-19 has made it even worse. Namibia is one of a few countries in sub-Saharan Africa with state provision of cash transfers to needy population groups (Levine et al., 2009). However, in the face of the generous public spending on social programmes, extreme socio-economic conditions inherited from when the country was under apartheid persist. Despite the economy having achieved notable progress in reducing poverty, it is still widespread. Poverty eradicating policies are moving at a sluggish pace. Inequality has been high but falling, while unemployment keeps rising, particularly affecting women and youth. (Jauch, 2015; Chiripanhura, 2018). At the same time, housing and household food security has been a major challenge (Humavindu and Stage, 2013; The World Bank, 2017).

Housing, education, and healthcare were some of the priority areas of development identified by the Government at independence. Hence provisions are made on the Constitution to push for housing, education, and healthcare agendas. However, even in its most progressive interpretation, the Namibian Constitution does not have any provision for the right to health care for any person in Namibia. The right to housing is encompassed in the Namibian Constitution under Article 95, which calls for the promotion of the welfare of the people. Article 20 makes provision that all Namibian persons shall have the right to education—as a result, primary education is enforced in Namibia.

4 The Emergence of COVID-19 in Namibia

The COVID-19 pandemic in Namibia started with a hastily arranged press conference on a Saturday morning, 14 March 2020, with the Minister of Health and Social Services when two Romanian tourists tested positive for the virus on the previous day. This set the beginning of a regular series of briefings, first with the Minister of health, then the President, who later declared COVID-19 as a state of emergency, with effect from 17 March 2020, under Article 26(1) of the Namibian Constitution, recite together with Section 30(3) of the Disaster Risk Management

Act, 2012 (Act No. 10 of 2012), and further introduced measures such as the closure of borders to non-residents and suspension of gatherings. The President proclaimed a state of emergency and later detailed a series/stages of lockdowns, starting with two regions and extending to the whole country. Stage one regulations cease economic activities in the country. Businesses, offices (excluding essential services/businesses; those that were only selling food and medical items as well as those that were providing other essential services), and schools were shut, national borders were closed, and consumption and sale of alcohol and tobacco products was prohibited. Wearing of masks in public places was enforced.

Responding to the declaration of the State of Emergency, the Government proclaimed regulations and measures to support the economy and Namibian individuals who were economically affected by COVID-19 and also provided support for impacted businesses. The Namibian Government and the Central Bank then announced the first phase of the Economic Stimulus measures to address urgent funding needs in the health sector, mitigate the impact of COVID-19 on the economy and support livelihoods at the household level. The "Economic Stimulus and Relief Package: Impact of COVID-19 on the Economy and Households" announced by the Ministry of Finance and "Policy and Regulatory Changes in Response to the Impact by COVID-19 on the Banking Industry" by the Bank of Namibia.

The measures announced by the Ministry of Finance were: wage subsidy for the hardest-hit sectors; accelerated repayment of overdue and undisputed VAT refunds. Other measures included accelerated payment of overdue and undisputed invoices for goods and services provided to Government; Non-agricultural small business loan scheme and agricultural business loan scheme. The Ministry also announced the tax-back loan scheme for non-mining corporates as well as relaxation of labour regulations; and granting of the policy relief to borrowers by Development Bank of Namibia (DBN[1]) and Agricultural Bank of Namibia (AgriBank[2]) in the form of a capital repayment moratorium where a holiday is allowed on the principal amount for a period ranging between six (6) months, but not exceeding two years (24 months) (Ministry of Finance, 2020a, b, c). The Central Bank announced measures such as Loan payment moratorium, Liquidity relief measures, Capital conservation buffer, and Concentration risk limit/single borrower limit. Also, the Central Bank cut the Repo rate by 250 basis points, with further cuts expected in August 2020 (Bank of Namibia, 2020a, b).

The measures announced by the Bank of Namibia to directly support individuals as well as small and medium-sized enterprises (SMEs) and corporations to manage the impact of the COVID-19 outbreak through the banking system were Loan payment moratorium.

There were no conditions attached to the measures and packages adopted to support economic activities and economically sustaining companies. All Namibian registered companies were allowed to apply for the reliefs and available packages for their operational activities. However, for some supports like the Tax-back loan scheme, companies were required to be in good standing with the tax authorities. While to apply for a wage subsidy, a company was required to be up to date with their previous social security contributions.

5 Post-COVID-19 Pandemic Era

5.1 *Surveillances and Security*

Namibia has been a multiparty democracy, with normative values enshrined in a liberal constitution that protects civil rights and liberties (BTI Report, 2018). The country has a number of laws on the statute books that enable or have a significant bearing on surveillance in some form or other, whether as part of evidence gathering in criminal matters or telecommunications interception for anti-terrorism purposes. These laws include: Criminal Procedure Act 51 of 1977, Protection of Information Act 84 of 1982, Police Act 19 of 1990, Namibia Central Intelligence Service Act 10 of 1997, Communications Act of 8 2009 and Prevention and Combating of Terrorist and Proliferation Activities Act of 2014 (Links, 2019). However, Namibia does not have adequate oversight mechanisms to enable legitimate, proportionate and necessary surveillance in the digital age (Mare, 2019).

The national police force of Namibia, the Namibian Police Force (NAMPOL), was established by the Namibian Constitution and enacted by an Act of Parliament. It replaced the South West African Police as the national police force of the country in 1990 when the country gained its independence. NAMPOL aims and functions are to preserve Namibian internal security; to ensure law and order; prevent, detect, and investigate crime; and protect life and property. To carry out its function effectively, NAMPOL is being assisted by municipality and city policing and community policing such as men and women network in the villages and townships as well as Neighborhood Watch and Working Groups. However, public access to municipality and city policing is skewed towards the city of Windhoek and larger towns such as Swakopmund and Walvis Bay. Hence there is inequality in such policing. For instance, Windhoek City Police indicated that the capital had installed high-resolution surveillance cameras across the city to fight crime (Links, 2019). High-resolution surveillance cameras can also be found in Swakopmund and Walvis Bay. At the same time, poor municipalities such as Rundu and Oshakati, for example, have none, and neither do they have municipality police units. The Constitution also established an Ombudsman whose mandate is to investigate complaints of violation of human rights, abuse of power and unfair or harsh treatment of an inhabitant of Namibia (Walters, 2010).

During the State of emergency's proclamation, surveillance, and security were intensified. Military personnel were deployed to help the police keep law and order during lockdowns. Due to the lockdown, crime rates, road accidents and rape decreased significantly (Brandt, 2020; Newaka, 2020). Hospitals reported fewer admissions due to alcohol-related violence but shot up in the first day the alcohol sales ban was lifted again (Newaka, 2020; Oliveira et al., 2020). Although the State of emergency is already a violation of some of the fundamental rights of the Namibian people, the office of the Ombudsman received reports of police mistreatment of COVID-19 detainees. Furthermore, the denial of visitation rights during the COVID-19 State of emergency was also brought to the Ombudsman. There were also two reports of Namibian Military members beating suspects. Additionally, images showing Namibian Police officers beating detained illegal immigrants were released online by local newspapers (US Embassy, 2020).

Section one of the Article 26, State of Emergency State of National Defence and Martial Law, of the Namibian Constitution grants permission the President to make regulations that have an effect on restricting some human rights where such restrictions are "reasonably justifiable" and "have the purpose of dealing with the situation which has given rise to the emergency". Some of the regulations enacted by the President prohibited employers, for reasons related to COVID-19, from dismissing employees, terminating contracts of employment, forcing employees to take unpaid leave or annual leave, and reducing the remuneration of employees (Mutandwa, 2020).

Two organisations representing Namibian employers launched a High Court case against the President, the government and trade unions to suspend parts of the Labour Act number 11 of 2007 during Namibia's COVID-19 State of emergency declared unconstitutional (Menges, 2020a, b, May). In the proclamations, the President suspended some provisions of some laws—including the Labour Act number 11 of 2007. The proclamations stipulate that during the COVID-19 lockdown, employers may not dismiss any of their employees due to the impact of the COVID-19 pandemic on their businesses. Due to the pandemic, they also may not force employees to take unpaid or annual leave. And they may not reduce the wages/salaries of any employee for reasons related to COVID-19 (Menges, 2020a, b, May). The Court indeed found the COVID-19 dismissals ban unconstitutional (Menges, 2020a, b, June).

In respect of COVID-19 surveillance, Namibia adopted the first edition of the Regional Strategy for Integrated Diseases Surveillance and Response technical guidelines of 2002 in 2003 and started with systematic implementation about ten years ago. Technical guidelines have provided valuable guidance for surveillance, outbreak detection, investigation, response and reporting in Namibia. However, the country has been confronted with some challenges, including a shortage of human capital, high staff attrition rates of surveillance focal persons, while some health facilities are hard-to-reach (WHO, 2021). The country adopted the same techniques of integrated disease surveillance and responses for the COVID-19 pandemic—some of the quick responses were screening at all points of entry and making wearing masks mandatory. All Namibians returning from high-risk areas were to go under required quarantine for 14 days, and the Government covered all costs. All schools (public and private) were closed for a month, and large gatherings were prohibited.

Soon after the President declared a state of emergency which introduced measures such as the closure of all borders, suspension of gatherings and related economic resolutions, the Ministry of Health and Social Services established an emergency response team, operating 24/7. The team aimed to intensify the surveillance of COVID-19 in the country, especially at the borders of Namibia. A COVID-19 communication hotline was established on 15 March 2020 and is hosted by the Ministry of Health and the Centre for Disease Control of Namibia (CDC). The hotline serves to assist in answering general inquiries from the public by assisting persons seeking guidance from the Ministry on issues related to COVID-19 and/or reporting possible symptoms or cases of COVID-19.

With the establishment of an Emergency Response team, the Ministry strengthened the surveillance in monitoring the situation of COVID-19 in the country. The response team operates 24 h Monday to Sunday (Ministry of Health and Social Services, 2020). The Government further strengthened its communication to the public via various platforms, such as the COVID-19 communication centre operated by Namibia Broadcast Corporation and Ministry of Health and Social Services social media accounts, to mitigate fear and panic caused by misinformation, especially from social media (Ministry of Health and Social Services, 2020).

5.2 *Social Safety Net and Financial Framework*

Namibia has a variety of legislations that provide for social protection in the country. It has several social protection measures, including housing and living expenses allowances for vulnerable groups, means-tested cash transfers, food-for-work programmes, and free access to primary healthcare and basic education (Chiripanhura1 and Niño-Zarazúa, 2013). The need for social protection in the country arises from the realization that high inequality limits some households to opportunities in the economy (Chiripanhura1 and Niño-Zarazúa, 2013). According to the 2010 Income and Expenditure Survey, the Namibian social safety net includes the old age grant/pensions, child maintenance grant for orphan and vulnerable children under 19 years of age, disability grant to all the disabled adults under the age of 60, foster care, war veterans, and drought relief assistance.

The Old Age Pension, sometimes referred to as Basic Social Grant, is a universal and unconditional cash transfer to Namibians aged 60 years and above to prevent poverty among the beneficiaries and reduce inequality among Namibians. Old Age Pension in Namibia dates back to the pre-independence period, whereas, from 1973, all citizens of Namibia could be eligible to receive the social grant (Subbarao, 1998; Devereux, 2001; Levine et al., 2009). The main qualifying criteria have remained age (60 years and above) and citizenship—the beneficiary must be a citizen of Namibia, have permanent residence; and reside in Namibia. At independence, white Namibians' social pension income was seven times higher than their black counterparts (Devereux, 2001). According to the colonial administration, it occupied the lowest echelons of the social hierarchy. The Government, however, opted to freeze the top level while adjusting the lower levels upwards. In 1994, all social pension income was equalised at N$120.

Although Namibia is one of the few African countries with a well structured social safety net, it is still faced with a number of social issues as the part of the population does not have access to some of the necessities. Hence, the battle against COVID-19 requires access to basic services and needs such as housing, sanitation, potable water, food, and other amenities that have remained neglected and has widened inequality in Namibia (Marenga and Amupanda, 2021).

The State of Emergency COVID-19 suspended the provisions of Section 9(2) of the State Finance Act, 1991 (Act No. 31 of 1991). The suspension empowers the Minister of finance to authorise the withdrawal of an amount of money exceeding 3% of the total amount appropriated by the current Appropriation Act for the period from 9 April 2020 to 30 June 2020 in order to defray expenditure on services of a special nature as contemplated in Section 9(1)(b)(ii) of the said Act (Centre for Human Right, 2020). Therefore, the Minister of Finance announced some social safety measures during the State of emergency in the form of access to free portable water in the informal settlements, providing food and shelter to the homelessness and relief package, in the form of grants, for the business entities and households. The Minister of finance announced the COVID-19 Economic Stimulus and Relief Package for the business and households directed at formal and informal businesses in sectors that are directly or indirectly affected by the lockdown measures and other external and internal demand supply-side shocks.

The relief package targeted all Namibians of 18 to 59 years of age who lost income due to the COVID-19 outbreak. It also targeted individuals who are unemployed, taking into consideration that the effects of COVID-19 and related public health protective measures weakened the means of support and subsistence income across the country. The grant excludes employed persons who have not experienced a reduction in wages and persons receiving any form of state social grants and Government support such as Disability Grant, Old Age Basic Income Grant, and Namibia Students Financial Assistance. Applicants for the grant were required to have a valid Namibian ID number.

Applications for emergency income grants were submitted through mobile phones by sending an SMS to a toll-free number and following a set of clear and simple instructions. Applicants did not necessarily need to use their own mobile phones, but they did need to provide a mobile number where they were comfortable to receive the token of the money. The Government said that the application process took "less than five minutes". After the approval of the application, the applicant would receive a token from the Bank they selected in the application process. The token would be for one of the following e-money products offered by the respective banks: e-wallet, blue-wallets, or easy-wallets. The token could then be redeemed using the cardless services at that Bank's ATM or can be used to transact directly via the various value-added services provided by the various wallets. There was no need for an applicant to a bank account (Ministry of Finance, 2020b).

The Government also offered tax reliefs and wage subsidies to all Namibian registered businesses (Ministry of Finance, 2020b). According to the Ministry of Finance (2020a) the types of tax relief which were adopted are the following:

i. Tax-back loan scheme for tax-paying non-mining corporates who are cashflow constraint: To provide reliefs to such businesses, they can borrow an amount equal to 1/12th of their tax payment in the previous tax year, to be repaid after one year. The interest rate will be concessional, below prime, on the back of the Government guarantee, capped at N$470.00 million. Applications will be made via commercial banks.
ii. Tax-back loan scheme for tax-paying employees and self-employed individuals who have lost income or are experiencing difficulties due to COVID-19 outbreak, Those individuals can borrow an amount equal to 1/12th of their tax payment in the previous tax be repaid after one year. The interest rate will be concessional, below prime, on the back of a Government guarantee. The total guarantee is capped at the maximum of N$1.1 billion, based on the PAYE tax register and the potential loan size. In collaboration with the banking institutions, the Government may institute statutory and administrative measures to enhance compliance with loan conditions.
iii. Acceleration the repayment of overdue and undisputed VAT refunds: The Government immediately speed up such repayments to enhance the cash flow of enterprises paying VAT. The total amount of the refunds to be settled within one week of the implementation of these measures stands about N$3.0 billion.

Some businesses and individuals could not honour their monthly insurances contributions because of COVID-19. Hence, The Namibia Financial Institutions Supervisory Authority (NAMFISA) requested that financial institutions in the insurance industry provide premium holiday relief with the possibility for extension in the event the State of Emergency is prolonged, whilst ensuring that clients are covered 100% during the period determined by the insurers (Namibia Financial Institutions Supervisory Authority, 2020). In the event that a claim occurs during or after the period, the outstanding premiums should be deducted from the claim amount.

NAMFISA further directed medical aid (insurance) funds to allow members to downgrade benefit options anytime during the State of Emergency. Members of medical aid schemes are usually are only permitted to change options at the beginning of the year. This enabled the affected members to downgrade to more affordable benefit options. The medical aid providers were also directed to not discontinue the benefits of members who are in sectors that are severely impacted, such as tourism and are not able to honour their monthly contribution and to provide *ex-gratia* allowance/benefits to all COVID-19-related claims where a member benefits relating to laboratory tests, consultations, and hospitalization or any other COVID-19-related treatment is or will be depleted (See NAMFISA, 2020).

The Monetary Policy Committee (MPC) of the Bank of Namibia cut the Repo rate by 250 basis points from 6.25% in February 2020 to 4.0% in June 2020 to mitigate the anticipated impact of COVID-19 and support domestic economic activity. The Bank of Namibia also introduced regulatory and policy relief measures to directly support individuals, small and medium-sized enterprises (SMEs), and corporations to manage the impact of the COVID-19 outbreak through the banking system. Regulatory and policy measures include loan payment moratorium: In respect of customers of banking institutions, banks can grant loan payment moratorium/payment holidays whereby the holiday in respect of loan payment (which include principal and interest) is allowed for a period ranging from six (6) months up to 24 months (two years) based on a thorough assessment of economic and financial difficulties experienced by individual borrowers. Banking institutions should apply such holidays in a transparent fair and equitable manner (Bank of Namibia, 2020a, b).

To assist banking institutions in instituting adequate support measures to individuals, small and medium-sized enterprises (SMEs) and corporations, the Bank of Namibia decided on the following regulatory and policy relief measures: (i) Liquidity relief measures, The Bank decided to relax the Determination on Liquidity Risk Management whereby banking institutions are required to ensure that their cash inflows match the cash outflows expected within the 0–7 days. The limit has been relaxed such that the expected outflows may exceed the inflows, but not more than the excess liquidity above their regulatory limit. (ii) Capital conservation buffer, The Bank reduced the capital conservation buffer rate to 0% for at least 24 months to support banking institutions to supply credit to the economy. The capital conservation buffer will enable banking institutions to use the capital they have built up during good times, to use during times of distress. The release of the buffer is to allow banking institutions to boost an already distressed economy by lending to the most vulnerable economic sectors. (iii) Concentration risk limit/single borrower limit, The Bank postponed the effective date of implementation of the 25% single borrower limit and concentration risk limit to allow banking institutions a wider scope to lend.

Bank of Namibia strongly requested that the local banks give payment holidays. Individuals and businesses affected by COVID-19 can apply for capital and interest deferment up to NAD 2.5 million from the local Banks. They can postpone payments for three to six months on loan facilities such as vehicle, asset and mortgage finance, and overdrafts—however, no regulation compiling the landlord to reduce or give their clients payment holiday.

Also, as a relief measure to assist start-up businesses, StartUp Namibia, in partnership with the Ministry of Industrialisation and Trade and with funding from the German Government, availed the COVID-19 StartUp Grant Fund amounting to 3 million Namibian dollars. The grant was meant to help small businesses that met the specified criteria to receive a direct supplement to pay wages and other fixed costs and offset the decline in revenue during and after the lockdown (German Embassy Windhoek, 2020a, b).

As a member of the CMA, Namibia measures/economic relief packages could only be funded through loans and savings. The Government used the funds from borrowing within the local market and savings from the Emergency Fund, while the rest of the funds were made available through budget shifting and saving techniques. The Government also received donations from local businesses and individuals and also from the international community such as the US and EU member countries. The Bank of Namibia is not participating in financial market trading. However, it has made a provision for the Government to draw an overdraft of not more than NAD 3 billion at a below-market interest rate (Bank of Namibia, 2019). The debt accumulated by the Government during the COVID-19 is being held in local currency.

5.3 *Employment and Labour Market*

Namibia has one of the most comprehensive social protection systems in Africa (Schade et al., 2019). Since independence, the Government has spent on average 13% of GDP on social protection, while over 5% of its GDP on average is spent on education alone (De and Shafuda, 2020). Despite massive spending on education, the Namibian Government has failed to solve the challenge of income inequality and unemployment. Employment performance has deteriorated since the 1980s. Before independence, unemployment can be attributed to the war of independence, which destroyed infrastructure and destabilized the economy (Sunde and Akanbi, 2016). Although there were mild declines in unemployment in the early 1990s, the rate has kept increasing ever since to reach a maximum of 37.6% in 2008, after which it started to decline (Sunde and Akanbi, 2016). In 2015, 28% of the labour force was unemployed and rose again to 33% in 2019 (De and Shafuda, 2020). Hence, COVID-19 has just added oil to an already burning flame.

Unlike South Africa, its neighbouring country, Namibia does not have an unemployment insurance fund which usually pays up to 60% of one's salary/wages for up to 9 months, provided that they were retrenched through no fault of their own (Nuyo, 2020). Instead, Namibia administers all its employees' issues through its Social Security Commission, and wealthier employees opt for private unemployment insurance through private insurances. According to the Social Security Act 34 of 1994 read with the Employees Compensation Act of 30 of 1941, the Social Security Commission of Namibia is responsible for administering a national pension fund, employee's compensation fund, maternity leave, and a sick and death benefit fund (Social Security Commission, 2020). Therefore, the stimulus package announced by the Minister of finance was administered through the SSC to assist the most severely affected employees.

In anticipation of employees losing their job due to COVID-19, The Labour Act provisions were suspended in proclamations issued by President Hage Geingob. The proclamations stipulated that during Namibia's COVID-19 lockdown period, which started on 28 March, employers may not dismiss any of their employees, reduce their pay or force them to take leave because of the impact COVID-19 pandemic has on the employers' business (Menges, 2020a, b). However, The High Court's judgement, in the matter of ..., found the proclamation unconstitutional. The Judgement upholds the principle of legality and thereby the rule of law by requesting the President to follow constitutional and legal procedures in responding to COVID-19. The Court's assertion that restrictions of rights in terms of emergencies must be interpreted strictly and narrowly also sends a strong message to the executive to be cautious of overreaching in the name COVID-19 response measures.

The Government, therefore, had to rely only on the economic stimulus package to mitigate the loss of jobs. Thus, The Ministry of Finance availed N$400 million. At the same time, the Social Security Commission contributed N$253 million to provide employers and employees relief programmes to ensure that the employment sector is not too hard hit by the Covid-19 pandemic (Deloite, 2020). Namibia has a Salary Protection and National Employment Scheme for Covid-19 designed in Section 37 of the Social Security Act No. 34 of 1994. This scheme's primary purpose is to persuade employers to retrench their staff and support employees who have lost their employment due to the Covid-19 pandemic. This scheme offers employers an Employer Wage Subsidy Program and offers employees an Affected Employees Program.

The Employer Wage Subsidy Program is accessible to employers in critical industries such as tourism, hospitality, construction, and aviation. Employers can apply to the SSC for a wage subsidy to remunerate their employees through the Employer Wage Subsidy Program. Other employers in the services and entertainment sectors, retailers (non-food), domestic and garden workers, farming, manufacturing, and transport would be contacted directly by the SSC to apply for wage subsidies. However, it has a condition that the employer agrees not to retrench their staff for at least three months, not reduce their staff salaries by more than 50% and should be a good standing member of the SSC. Furthermore, in certain instances, sectors not mentioned above can also apply to the SCC for wage subsidies provided they are paid up members of the

SSC and must prove that their incomes were affected by the COVID-19 pandemic.

Namibia does not regularly produce employment or unemployment statistics, and a Namibian Labour Force Survey is conducted every two years, with the last one taking place in 2018. However, at the official inauguration of the Labour Commissioner's new offices, Labour Minister Utoni Nujoma revealed that 8881 employees had been dismissed by the two quarters between April and September 2020. Data released later by the Ministry showed that 12,198 people were retrenched by 896 employers between 1 January to 15 December 2020. According to released data, 8803 Namibians had lost their jobs due to economic reasons, while 2842 had been retrenched due to COVID-19-related reasons IPPR (2020), where most jobs lost due to COVID-19 are in the tourism and hospitality industry.

5.4 *Education and Healthcare*

The colonial Government was not interested in developing and extending economic benefits to the natives, as is evident in the rest of Africa (Rodney, 1972). According to Jauch, Edwards, and Cupido (2009), the German and South African colonial administrations are the root cause of social and economic distresses that broadened the inequality gap in post-independent Namibia. However, since the arrival of independence, no significant achievement has been made in narrowing this gap, as most Namibians remain destitute. Several policies and legislative interventions put in place to narrow the inequality ratios had very little success has been recorded, owing to blatant implementation gaps (Sepúlveda, 2012; Marenga and Amupanda, 2021).

At the time of independence, Namibia inherited an education and healthcare system characterised by major disparities in opportunities and facilities among different sections of the Namibian community. The provision of healthcare, education, and training was skewed in racial and regional terms and was largely a privilege of the few (Wallace and Kinahan, 2011). The Government of independent Namibia vide new macroeconomic policies, gave more stress on education, healthcare, and other social security measures to attain faster economic growth and reduce inequality (Sherbourne, 2016). Expenditures on human resource development (on education, healthcare and social welfare, and protection schemes) have been expanded. Conversely, new taxes and tax rates were introduced to enhance the expenditure capability.

Educational reform particularly basic education became one of Namibia's top priorities after independence. In 1990, Namibia's Education Ministry set itself five goals: (1) Improved and equitable access to education, (2) Improved quality in the education system, (3) Enhancement of democratic participation in the education system, (4) Improved efficiency in the education system, and (5) Promotion of life-long learning (Zaaruka et al., 2001). To achieve these goals, the allocation to the Ministry of education was increased from 18.3% of total expenditure between 1985 and 1989 to an average of 23.5% in 1990 through 1994. This is quite a sizeable amount compared to that of most low middle-income countries that only spend 12.8% of their national budgets on an average on education, according to the World Development Report (1993). In recent years, about 26% of total Government expenditure is incurred on education (De and Shafuda, 2020). However, despite these massive budgetary injections into the sector and growth of literacy rate, enrolment at tertiary education (higher level of education) is quite poor.

According to Article 20 of the Constitution and Education Act 16 of 2001 of Namibia, primary education is compulsory for all Namibian children, and it is provided free of charge in all government schools. However, there is a vibrant private sector presence at pre-primary, primary, secondary, and tertiary levels of education where education is not free (Chiripanhura and Niño-Zarazúa, 2013). The Act further states that children shall not be allowed to leave school until they have completed their primary education or have attained the age of 16 years (Article 20, Section 3) (Legal Assistant Centre, 1998). Although not compulsory like primary education, secondary education is also provided free in all government schools. However, parents were expected to contribute to the school development fund (SDF) and pay the other private costs of education like purchasing study material (Ministry of Education, 2011). However, in 2013 contribution to SDF and other private costs in all government schools at the primary level was scraped, and that was extended further to the secondary level in 2015, rendering basic education in Namibia totally free (Shafuda, 2020).

The proclamation of the State of Emergency required that all schools, early development childhood centres, and tertiary institutions be closed and attendance prohibited. Schools were to reopen in a phased manner necessitating the grades with higher priorities and workload to open first. However, due to lack of infrastructure, the reopening of schools was delayed at most government schools. Infrastructures at these schools were not adequate to accommodate COVID-19 regulations. Hence, schools were forced to shift to online teaching mode. Although the Namibian Government acknowledged the significant role that information and communications technology, or technologies (ICT) can play as the country moves towards a knowledge-based society aspired to in Vision 2030 and its development plans, COVID-19 has exposed the Namibian basic education system's preparedness to embrace ICT. Some schools in the villages do not even have electricity, while some do not have network coverage and internet connectivity. Hence teachers had to come up with innovative ways to ensure that the education has reached their pupils. For example, teachers in some remote villages developed study manuals that they distribute to students on a weekly basis. Teachers used text messaging services (short message services [SMS]) to contact the learners' parents to inform them to pick up the study manuals.

However, the Government also tried to meet the teachers halfway to make things easier. The Ministry of Education, Arts and Culture (MoEAC) ended the second term early and introduced a winter break, the MoEAC, parents, and children closely monitoring the daily case counts (CDC Namibia, 2021). The face-to-face classes for 11 and 12 students of grades resumed on 03 June 2020, while primary and pre-primary schools in Namibia reopened under strict health guidelines 07 July 2020, after COVID-19 shutdowns, students must comply with safety and hygiene measures by wearing masks and conducting social distancing. Further, the Ministry allocated 29.8 million Namibian dollars towards purchasing COVID-19 protective equipment.

Tertiary education remained online. However, students reported experiencing challenges when attempting to access the e-learning platform (Kaisara and Bwalya, 2021) due to the unusually high volume of user traffic on the e-learning platform. Furthermore, internet network coverage is poor in most areas in Namibia (Taruvinga et al., 2020) which could have contributed to accessibility challenges. Also, the challenges of data costs impeded students' ability to access the university e-learning platform. Costs have been identified as a major factor impeding successful e-learning implementation in developing countries (Kibuku et al., 2020), including in Namibia (Ilonga et al., 2020).

Independent Namibia did not just attach importance to education but also to health services. Before gaining independence from South Africa in

1990, Namibia's healthcare system reflected a traditional medical model, which focused mainly on hospital-based and curative services (Christians, 2020). Health services were generally poor, and also, inequity in access to health services was high. The Ministry of Health and Social Services is the custodian and provider of public health services in Namibia. It operates a four-tiered health system, consisting of primary healthcare sites, district hospitals, intermediate hospitals, and a referral hospital.

The current health services model in Namibia are twofold: private health services, mostly serving 18% of the population with medical insurance, and public health services, serving the remaining 82%. This, in part, is due to the country's income inequality. Furthermore, 24% of the Namibian population lives outside a 10 km radius of a healthcare facility. On average, there are about 5780 people per PHC clinic and 58,825 people per district hospital in rural areas, as per 2017 statistics. Hospitals, however, suffer from overcrowding and long wait times, as a large number of people bypass clinics and health centres closer to home and go directly to hospitals that are perceived to offer a higher quality of care (Namibia Ministry of Health and Social Services, 2017).

The budget allocated to the Ministry of Health has been relatively large since independence. Healthcare service is one of Namibia's most prioritized human development and social welfare measures. After education, safety and security, the Government attached the third most important priority to healthcare services in its domain of activities. Healthcare accounted for 10.5% of total government expenditure at independence (1990–1995) and increased to 13.4% during 2015–2016. Although the Government gave health the third most important priority of its activities, the mortality rate increased significantly between 1995 and 2004, and the life expectancy decreased sharply during the same period due to the emergence of the HIV pandemic other communicable diseases, including Malaria during the 1990s. (De and Shafuda, 2020). Also, the newly independent country suffered from a lack of expertise in different areas from the 1990s till early 2000. Hence, the healthcare sector also suffered from a sudden deficiency of medical experts. The first medical school in independent Namibia was established in 2011. Thus, it was not until 2016 that Namibia began to enjoy the services of its first locally trained medical expertise.

Primary healthcare is subsidised to ensure that many households have access to medical care. Yet, some households face challenges raising the required user fees, even though they may be relatively small. In both the education and health sectors, there are complaints from households about the declining quality of services in the public health and education sectors resulting in those that can afford to go to the private sector preferring to do so. This creates two tiers in both the education and health sectors, with the state sector being the poorer sector. The discrepancies translate into labour market outcomes which perpetuate rather than eliminate inequality.

5.5 *Housing and Homelessness*

Neo-classical propose a withdrawal of the State from the market based on the idea that markets would achieve a balance through their own doing (Harvey, 2007). In the realm of housing, policies based on capital subsidies primarily aimed at benefiting the private sector were developed for the developing countries with American influence and support (Gilbert, 2002). The aim was mainly to secure public support despite the general neoliberal turn that economic thinking was making at the time. The World Bank report titled "Housing: Enabling Markets to Grow" marked a key turn in this sequence (World Bank, 1993). The report laid out commercial-based approaches to housing and assigned the State the clear role of "enabler". Both neoliberalism and its associated housing policies were later exported to various parts of the world (Brenner et al., 2010), including South Africa in the 1990s (Gilbert, 2000). In the 1990s, Mabogunje (1990, 1994) observed how each approach to housing represented a downgrading of the State's role relative to the former period until the present when this is limited to simply providing and managing infrastructure in Sub-Saharan Africa. While debates on 'neoliberalism" abound, the term is here only raised as a way to frame the transition of the role of the State, particularly in the delivery of social services, including housing (Delgado, 2019).

The colonial discrimination on the provision of goods and services and development between rural and urban areas created significant urban housing challenges in independent Namibia (Marenga and Amupanda, 2021). There is an alarmingly high number of informal dwellings due largely to people relocating to towns and cities from rural areas in search of better services and jobs. According to Lennon (2018), 20% of the population lives in the slums in Namibia. By 2016, the rate of shacks to brick houses rose to 4:1 in Namibia. The informal settlements that have arisen out of people's need for housing contributed to a lack of potable water, electricity, or toilet facilities. This lack of resources increases the population's susceptibility to diseases such as cholera, polio, and Hepatitis E diseases. In addition, shack fires are common occurrences, often resulting in loss of life. Homeless people in Namibia usually take refuge in unused city buildings, on park benches, abandoned houses, and under bridges.

In the age of COVID-19 State of emergency, the Government has rounded up hundreds of Namibia's homeless people (Herestofa, 2021). Additionally, the Government provides tent shelters for homeless people and encourages them to seclude themselves to prevent the spread of the virus. Moreover, concerns over sanitation have arisen, especially as certain members of the population have tuberculosis (TB). Food is provided by churches, but it is not enough. The beds are reportedly too close together to comply with social distancing (Borgen Project, 2020).

6 Conclusion

The Namibia economy has been in an economic downturn since 2016. The COVID-19 pandemic has amplified the challenges of an already struggling economic environment. The declaration of COVID-19 as a state of emergency and the series of lockdown proclamations by the President of Namibia affected the economy badly and pushed it further to the bitter end of the stick. Sectors such as hospitality, aviation, healthcare, education, tourism, and hotel and accommodation were amongst those most severely affected (Harambee Prosperity Plan, 2020). The COVID-19 State of emergency declaration resulted in significant financial distress for business entities of all shapes and sizes. While some signs have already manifested through the liquidations of various private and public entities, it is expected that the worse is still to come.

The Government and the Central Bank announced several policies and regulatory changes to stimulate the economy and address funding needs in the health and education sector, to mitigate the impact of COVID-19 on the economy, and support livelihoods at the household level, poverty and inequality are expected to widen. State of emergency policies and regulatory framework benefited many low-class individual members of society. However, these policies failed to help the individuals who fall in the low- middle-class member of society—leaving them to lose their jobs, while self-employed people have to close their businesses. The COVID-19 policies and regulations also failed to sustain medium and big enterprises, especially those in the most affected sectors, like the hospitality and transport sectors. Some businesses have closed down, some have retrenched more than half of their employee base, while some are still on the verge of filing for bankruptcy.

COVID-19 will not only impact unemployment, poverty, and inequality but it is also expected to put relentless upward pressure on government expenditure. Namibia's legislation and regulations pertaining to businesses in financial distress can play a vital role in reducing the economic scarring expected during these hard times. However, it is a bumpy and gloomy road to economic recovery. There is a need for radical measures if the country is to get to its glory days in the next few years. The economy needs a financial booster to improve education and healthcare infrastructures and create employment.

Nonetheless, with the currency pack and the CMA agreement, Namibia can not run its monetary policy independently. Hence, the country mainly relays on fiscal policies to push for economic recovery. However, the Namibian Government does not have fiscal space, meaning it is not in a position to spend. The Government has no money, while the debt to GDP is already high, making it difficult to borrow. Bringing about sustained and inclusive growth amid fiscal consolidation is the Government's huge challenge. The austerity measures adopted since 2016 failed to deliver the expected outcome. Nevertheless, if the Government does not respond, efforts made to reduce poverty and inequality over 29 years before COVID-19 will be undone due rise in unemployment and financial distress caused by COVID-19. Therefore, the Government should consider other recovery measures while getting rid of austerity.

The potential of the green hydrogen project and the recent oil discovery at the country's southern onshore deliver some hope for the economy. However, these long-term projects can take some time to deliver the expected results. The economy needs urgent solutions to push the economic recovery in the short term. Hence, improving resource mobilisation and eliminating inefficiencies in the public sector to increase productivity is one of the short-term solutions. Furthermore, the economy needs to attract foreign direct investment, especially in the agricultural and tourism sectors, which employ many people. There is also an urgent need to reform the state-owned enterprises to minimise their dependence on government revenue. Instead, SOEs should generate revenue for the Government rather than look up to government bailouts. Reforms should also be carried out to other government urgencies such as municipalities, town councils' and village councils. Government urgencies should avoid being an obstacle to the growth processes. Domestic demand mechanisms such as increasing production and export are also recommended. Increase investments in infrastructure development to boost employment. Also, there is a need to increase investments in ICT and digital infrastructure to reduce costs.

Notes

1. DBN is a government-owned development bank in Namibia with the mandate to promote and finance development activities in those sectors of the economy which support development and the welfare of the citizens of the country.
2. Agribank is a government-Owned Enterprise with the mandate to promote the growth and development of agricultural sector in Namibia through affordable and innovative financing.

References

Acemoglu, D. and Johnson, S. (2007) Disease and development: the effect of life expectancy on economic growth. Journal of political Economy 115(6): 925–985.

Agénor, P. (2015) Public capital, health persistence and poverty traps. Journal of Economics 115(2): 103–131.

Almond, D. (2006) Is the 1918 influenza pandemic over? Long-term effects of in utero influenza exposure in the post-1940 US population. Journal of Political Economy 114(4): 672–712.

Ashraf, Q. H., Lester, A. and Weil, D. N. (2008) When does improving health raise GDP? NBER Macroeconomics Annual 23(1):157–204.

Augier, L. and Yaly, A. (2013) Economic growth and disease in the OLG model: the HIV/AIDS case. Economic Model 33: 471–481. https://doi.org/10.1016/j.econmod.2013.04.033

Bank of Namibia. (2019) Bank of Namibia 2019 Annual report. https://www.bon.com.na/CMSTemplates/Bon/Files/bon.com.na/3a/3af2b4ce-c0f2-4e99-9d68-dc64a7c1ecb4.pdf

Bank of Namibia. (2020a) Monetary Policy Statements. https://www.bon.com.na/Bank/Monetary-Policy/Monetary-Policy-Statements/2020a-Monetary-Policy-Statements.aspx, Accessed 13 July 2020.

Bank of Namibia. (2020b) Policy and Regulatory Changes by BoN in Response to the Impact by COVID-19. https://www.bon.com.na/CMSTemplates/Bon/Files/bon.com.na/46/46e61cb3-b3d9-479d-8b27-7e23d9fc9082.pdf, Accessed 13 July 2020.

Bauer, G. (2001) Namibia in the first decade of independence: how democratic? Journal of Southern African Studies 27(1): 33–55. Retrieved from www.jstor.org/stable/823289

Bloom, D. E., Canning, D. and Sevilla, J. (2004) The effect of health on economic growth: a production function approach. World Development 32(1): 1–13.

Borgen Project. (2020) Homelessness in Namibia. https://borgenproject.org/homelessness-in-namibia/#:~:text=In%20Namibia%2C%20there%20is%20an,water%2C%20electricity%20or%20toilet%20facilities

Brandt, E. (2020, 20 May) COVID-19 profiteers unmasked … commission has clear evidence of price exploitation. New Era (in en-ZA). https://neweralive.na/posts/COVID-19-profiteers-unmasked-commission-has-clear-evidence-of-price-exploitation, Accessed 03 July 2020.

Brenner, N., Peck, J. and Theodore, N. (2010) Variegated neoliberalization: geographies, modalities, pathways. Global Networks 10(2):182–222.

BTI. (2018) Country Report: Namibia. https://bti-project.org/content/en/downloads/reports/country_report_2018_NAM.pdf, Accessed 14 July 2020.

Centre for Human Right. (2020) A. Nature and description of emergency COVID-19 measures. https://www.chr.up.ac.za/covid19-database/namibia, Accessed 13 September 2020.

CDC Namibia. (2021) Keeping Learners in School in Namibia: An Outbreak Investigation of COVID-19 in Schools. https://na.usembassy.gov/understanding-covid-outbreaks-in-namibian-schools/, Accessed 11 July 2020.

Chiripanhura, B. M. (2018) Housing in Namibia: The challenges and prospects for adequate future provision (ILMI Working paper No. 7). Windhoek, Namibia: Namibia University of Science and Technology.

Chiripanhura, B. M. and Niño-Zarazúa, M. (2013) Social safety nets in Namibia: structure, effectiveness and the possibility for a universal cash transfer scheme. Social Safety Nets in Namibia: assessing current programmes and future options. Bank of Namibia 15th Annual Symposium, pp 13–43. https://www.bon.com.na/CMSTemplates/Bon/Files/bon.com.na/0f/0fa7f5ba-5585-4471-9511-1a42811bd0d1.pdf, Accessed 13 July 2020.

Chou, J., Kuo, N. and Peng, S. (2004) Potential impacts of the Sars outbreak on Taiwan's economy. Asian Economic Papers 3(1): 84–99.

Christians F. (2020) Country profile – primary healthcare and family medicine in Namibia. African Journal of Primary Health Care & Family Medicine 12(1): 1–3. https://doi.org/10.4102/phcfm.v12i1.2242

De, U. K. and Shafuda, C. P. (2020) Changing public policy on expenditure in Namibia after independence and its impact on healthcare and education. International Journal of Public Policy 15(5–6): 358–379. https://doi.org/10.1504/IJPP.2020.113708

Delgado, G. (2019) Land and housing practices in Namibia: cases of access to land rights and production of housing in Windhoek, Oshakati and Gobabis. Engineering and the Built Environment, School of Architecture, Planning and Geomatics. Retrieved from http://hdl.handle.net/11427/31363, Accessed 13 July 2020.

Deloite. (2020) COVID-19 Pandemic: SSC Economic Stimulus Package Announced. https://www2.deloitte.com/za/en/namibia/pages/tax/articles/COVID-19-Announcement-of-SSC-economic-stimulus-package-by-the-SSC-Tax-Alert.html, Accessed 1 July 2020.

Devereux, S. (2001) Social Pensions in Namibia and South Africa. IDS Discussion Paper 379, Institute of Development Studies.

Dobson A. P. and Carper E. R. (1996) Infectious diseases and human population history: throughout history the establishment of disease has been a side effect of the growth of civilisation. Bioscience 46: 115–126.

Eichenbaum, M. S., Rebelo, S. and Trabandt, M. (2020) Epidemics in the neoclassical and new Keynesian models (No. w27430). National Bureau of Economic Research.

German Embasy Windhoek. (2020a) COVID-19 StartUp Grant to provide relief to Namibian start-ups. https://windhuk.diplo.de/na-en/aktuelles/-/2282190, Accessed 09 September 2020.

German Embasy Windhoek. (2020b) StartUp Namibia launches #StartUpSurvivalGrant. https://windhuk.diplo.de/na-en/aktuelles/-/2380496, Accessed 09 September 2020.

Gilbert, A. (2000) What might South Africa have learned about housing subsidies from Chile? South African Geographical Journal 82(1):21–29.

Gilbert, A. (2002) Power, ideology and the Washington consensus: the development and spread of Chilean housing policy. Housing Studies 17(2): 305–324.

Goenka, A, and Liu, L. (2012) Infectious diseases and endogenous fluctuations. Econ Theory 50: 125–149. https://doi.org/10.1007/s00199-010-0553-y

Goenka, A., Liu, L. and Nguyen, M. H. (2014) Infectious diseases and economic growth. Journal of Mathematical Economics 50: 34–53, S0304406813000967. https://doi.org/10.1016/j.jmateco.2013.10.004

Government of Namibia, Ministry of Finance. (2020a) Frequently Asked Questions about the Emergency Income Grant of the Economic Stimulus and Relief Package. https://mof.gov.na/documents/35641/89902/FQA+Emergency+Income+Grant.pdf/cd1b50d2-ef25-d3c6-e4e8-d6e2297ec9a4, Accessed 03 July 2020.

Government of Namibia, Ministry of Finance. (2020b) Launch Statement: Emergency Income Grant of the Economic Stimulus and Relief Package. https://mof.gov.na/documents/35641/36580/Launch+Statement+EIG+of+the+COVID-19+Economic+Stimulus+Package.pdf.pdf/1c4c320b-efae-72f4-6cb6-2942923fdc12, Accessed 13 July 2020.

Government of Namibia, Ministry of Finance. (2020c) MEDIA STATEMENT Economic Stimulus and Relief Package: Impact of COVID-19 on the Economy and Households. https://mof.gov.na/documents/35641/36580/Phase+1+VF+Stimulus+and+Relief+Package%2C+Republic+of+Namibia.pdf/9a2314de-4b39-00a1-b8bd-4ffcfe1f20d3, Accessed 03 July 2020.

Grennan, D. (2019) What is a Pandemic? JAMA 321(9): 910–919. https://doi.org/10.1001/jama.2019.0700

Grossman, M. (1972) On the concept of health capital and the demand for health. Journal of Political Economy 80:223–255.

Hai, W., Zhao, Z., Wang, J. and Hou, Z. (2004) The short-term impact of Sars on the chinese economy. Asian Economic Papers 3(1): 57–61.

Harambee Prosperity Plan. (2020) Activity 2: Augment Namibia's business rescue legislative frameworks, to limit economic scarring. https://hppii.gov.na/activities/activity-2-augment-namibias-business-rescue-legislative-frameworks-to-limit-economic-scarring/, Accessed 20 October 2020.

Harvey, D. (2007) A Brief History of Neoliberalism. Oxford: Oxford University Press.

Henderson, J. (2005) Health Economics & Policy. New York: Thomson.

Herestofa, L. (2021) The Legislative Plan to Fight Gender-Based Violence in Namibia. https://borgenproject.org/tag/namibias-government/, Accessed 20 October 2020.

Hodgson, G. M. (2007) An institutional and evolutionary perspective on health economics. Cambridge Journal of Economics 32(2): 235–256.

Humavindu, M. N. and Stage, J. (2013) Key Sectors of the Namibian Economy. Economic Structures 2: 1. https://doi.org/10.1186/2193-2409-2-1

Ilonga, A., Ashipala, D. O. and Tomas, N. (2020) Challenges experienced by students studying through Open and Distance Learning at a Higher Education Institution in Namibia: implications for strategic planning. International Journal of Higher Education 9(4): 116–127. https://doi.org/10.5430/ijhe.v9n4p116

IPPR (2020). Namibia Quarterly Economic Review Q4 2020. https://ippr.org.na/wp-content/uploads/2021/02/Namibia-QER-Q4-2020_Final.pdf, Accessed 20 October 2020.

Jauch, H. (2015) The rise and fall of the basic income grant campaign: lessons from Namibia. Global Labour Journal 6(3): 336–351. https://doi.org/10.15173/glj.v6i3.2367

Jauch, H., Edwards, L. and Cupido, B. (2009) A rich country with poor people: Inequality in Namibia. Labour Resource and Research Institute.

Jiang, X. (2009) A critique of neoclassical theory of health care consumption. Doctoral dissertation, University of Denver, Colorado.

Kaisara, G. and Bwalya, K. J. (2021) Investigating the E-learning challenges faced by students during COVID-19 in Namibia. International Journal of Higher Education 10(1): 308–318.

Kibuku, R. N., Ochieng, D. O. and Wausi, A. N. (2020) e-Learning challenges faced by universities in Kenya: a literature review. The Electronic Journal of e-Learning 18(2): 150–161. https://doi.org/10.34190/EJEL.20.18.2.004

Legal Assistant Centre. (1998) The Constitution of the Republic of Namibia. http://www.lac.org.na/Pdf/namcon.pdf

Lennon, J. (2018). How Namibia's housing shortage became a humanitarian crisis. https://jade-lennon.medium.com/how-namibias-housing-shortage-became-a-humanitarian-crisis-eef05ba14b9b, Accessed 20 October 2020.

Levine, S., van der Berg, S. and Yu, D. (2009) Measuring the impact of social cash transfers on poverty and inequality in Namibia. In Conference on Policies for Reducing Inequality in the Developing World (September, 2009), Stellenbosch Economic Working Papers: 25/09. https://core.ac.uk/download/pdf/6313029.pdf

Links, F. (2019) Spying on Speech. Democracy Report, Special Briefing No.28, June 2019. Retrieved on 7 May 2019 from https://ippr.org.na/wp-content/uploads/2019/06/IPPR-surveilance-web.pdf, Accessed 20 October 2020.

Mabogunje, A. L. (1990) Urban planning and the post-colonial State in Africa: a research overview. African Studies Review 33(02): 121–203.

Mabogunje, A. L. (1994) Overview of Research Priorities in Africa. In Africa. R. Stren, Ed. Urban Research in the Developing World. Toronto: University of Toronto. 21–45.

Mare, A. (2019) Communication Surveillance in Namibia: An Exploratory Study. Media Policy and Democracy Project.

Marenga, R. and Amupanda, J. S. (2021) The coronavirus and social justice in Namibia. Politikon 48(2): 206–225.

Menges, W. (2020a). Namibia: COVID-19 Dismissals Ban Unconstitutional. from https://allafrica.com/stories/202006230522.html, Accessed 28 June 2020.

Menges, W. (2020b, May). Bosses fight job cut ban. The Namibian Newspaper, https://www.namibian.com.na/200982/archive-read/Bosses-fight-job-cut-ban, Accessed 28 June 2020.

Ministry of Education. (2011) Free Primary Education in Namibia: Current Context. Windhoek: GRN Publication. https://www.unicef.org/namibia/na.MoE_2011_Oct_Free_Primary_Education_print_final.pdf

Ministry of Health and Social Services-Namibia. (2020) Statement by honorable minister dr. Kalumbi Shangula, on the COVID-19 situation in namibia. https://www.facebook.com/MoHSSNamibia/photos/a.500006330672375/574750056531335/?type=3, Accessed 7 August 2020.

Morens, D. M., Folkers, G. K. and Fauci, A. S. (2009) What is a pandemic?. The Journal of infectious diseases *200*(7): 1018-1021.

Mutandwa, V. (2020) COVID-19 and Africa Symposium: Lockdowns, the Right to Work and the Rule of Law in Namibia. http://opiniojuris.org/2020/12/08/lockdowns-the-right-to-work-and-the-rule-of-law-in-nambia/, Accessed 28 September 2020.

Namibia Financial Institutions Supervisory Authority. (2020) Namfisa's Response to The Impact of COVID-19 on the Non-Bank Financial Institutions (NBFIs) Sector. http://www.finconet.org/Media_release-NAMFISA_response_COVID-19.pdf, Accessed 13 July 2020.

Namibia Ministry of Health and Social Services-Namibia. (2017) Namibia 2014/15 Health Accounts Report [homepage on the Internet]. Windhoek. Available from: https://www.afro.who.int/sites/default/files/2017-10/Namibia%20Health%20Accounts%20Report%202014-2015%20-%20final%202017.09.07.pdf, Accessed 28 June 2020.

National Planning Commission, Government of Namibia. (1995). National Development Plan 1 (NDP-1). Retrieved from: https://www.npc.gov.na/?page_id=208, Accessed 04 July 2020.

Nchake, M. A., Edwards, L. and Rankin, N. (2018) Closer monetary union and product market integration in emerging economies: evidence from the Common Monetary Area in Southern Africa. International Review of Economics & Finance 54: 154–164.

Newaka, T. (2020, 5 June). Crime decreases during lockdown. The Namibian. p. 3. https://www.namibian.com.na/201434/archive-read/%EF%BB%BFFewer-rapes-more-drugs-during-lockdown, Accessed 28 June 2020.

Nuyo, T. (2020) Namibia Unemployment Insurance Fund. Retrieved from https://www.namibian.com.na/167182/archive-read/Namibia-Unemployment-Insurance-Fund, Accessed 30 June 2020.

Oliveira, Y., Ngatjiheue, C. and Hartmann, A. (5 June 2020). "Mayhem returns after booze ban lift". The Namibian. p. 3. Retrieved from: https://web.archive.org/web/20200607081850/https://www.namibian.com.na/91593/read/Mayhem-returns-after-booze-ban-lift, Accessed 7 June 2020.

Piret, J. and Boivin, G. (2021) Pandemics throughout history. Frontiers in Microbiology 11: 6317–6336. https://doi.org/10.3389/fmicb.2020.631736

Rodney, W. (1972) How Europe Underdeveloped Africa. London: Bogle-L'Ouverture Publications.

Sampath, S., Khedr, A., Qamar, S., Tekin, A., Singh, R., Green, R. and Kashyap, R. (2021) Pandemics throughout the history. Cureus 13(9). https://doi.org/10.7759/cureus.18136

Santerre, R. E. and Neun, S. P. (2007) Health Economics: Theories. Insights, and Industry Studies, 4th ed., Mason: Cengage Learning.

Schade, K., La, J. & Pick, A. (2019) Financing social protection in Namibia. https://www.oecd.org/countries/namibia/SPSR_Namibia.pdf, Accessed 1 June 2020.

Sepúlveda, M. (2012) Unacceptable Inequalities Persist 20 Years after Independence – UN Poverty Expert. https://reliefweb.int/report/namibia/%E2%80%9Cunacceptable-inequalities-persist-20-years-after-independence%E2%80%9D-%E2%80%93-un-poverty-expert, Accessed 08 October 2020.

Shadbolt, P. (2012). Namibia country profile: Moving on from a difficult past. CNN Tue October 23, 2012. https://edition.cnn.com/2012/10/23/world/africa/namibia-eye-on-country-profile/index.html

Shafuda, C. (2020). Policy induced public expenditure thrust on education and related outcome in Namibia after independence. International Journal of Economic Development 13(2): 95–121.

Sherbourne, R., (2016). Guide to the Namibian Economy. 16th ed. Windhoek: IPPR publication.

Social Security Commission. (2020). About Social Security Commission. Retrieved from http://www.ssc.org.na/about.html, Accessed 30 June 2020.

Subbarao, K. (1998) Namibia's Social Safety Net: Issues and Options for Reform. Policy Research Working Paper 1996. World Bank: Washington DC.

Siu, A. and Wong, R. (2004) Economic impact of Sars: The case of Hong Kong. Asian Economic Papers 3(1): 62–83.

Sunde, T. and Akanbi, O. A. (2016). Sources of unemployment in Namibia: an application of the structural VAR approach. International Journal of Sustainable Economy 8(2): 125–143.

Taruvinga, A., Chikohora, E., Jere, N. and van den Dool, R. (2020). Integrated mobile veld fire detection and notification system for rural communities: a case of South Africa, Zimbabwe and Namibia. International Journal of Environmental Science and Development 11(2): 94–98. https://doi.org/10.18178/ijesd.2020.11.2.1232

The World Bank. (1993) Housing: enabling markets to work. (11820). The World Bank. Available: http://documents.worldbank.org/curated/en/1993/04/1561159/housing-enablingmarkets-work, Accessed 03 September 2020.

The World Bank. (2017) Does Fiscal Policy Benefit the Poor and Reduce Inequality in Namibia? https://documents1.worldbank.org/curated/en/991551497258273367/pdf/116029-WP-P148652-PUBLIC-NamibiaCEQReport.pdf, Accessed 04 October 2020.

The World Bank. (2020) Namibia overview. https://www.worldbank.org/en/country/namibia/overview#1, Accessed 04 October 2020.
UN. (2009) Population Division of the Department of Economic and Social Affairs of the United Nations Secretariat: World Population Prospects: The 2008 Revision (PDF). New York: United Nations.
US Embasy. (2020) Country Reports on Human Rights Practices for 2020: Namibia 2020 Human Rights Report. https://na.usembassy.gov/wp-content/uploads/sites/132/NAMIBIA-2020-HUMAN-RIGHTS-REPORT.pdf, Accessed 04 October 2020.
Wallace, M. and Kinahan, J. (2011) A History of Namibia: from the Beginning to 1990. New York City: Colombia University Press
Walters, J. (2010) The protection and promotion of human rights in Namibia: the constitutional mandate of the Ombudsman. https://www.kas.de/c/document_library/get_file?uuid=11ac0afe-65d7-745c-3a7a-e4b11adf1dd4&groupId=252038, Accessed 04 July 2020.
Weil, D. N. (2007) Accounting for the effect of health on economic growth. The Quarterly Journal of Economics, 122(3): 1265–1306.
WHO. (2021) Strengthening Integrated Disease Surveillance and Response (IDSR) capacities in Namibia. https://www.afro.who.int/news/strengthening-integrated-disease-surveillance-and-response-idsr-capacities-namibia, Accessed 04 October 2020.
Zaaruka, B, Biwa, B. and Kalenga, P. (2001). "Public Expenditure Management in Namibia Health and Education Sectors – Preliminary Analysis," BON Working Paper No.1/02.

The Informal Economy and the First 100 days of the Pandemic Policy in Zimbabwe

Zvikomborero Chadambuka

1 Introduction

This chapter discusses the policy measures put in place to deal with the pandemic in Zimbabwe. It focuses on the fate of those in the informal economy and the extent to which their concerns were considered in the promulgation and implementation of policy measures relating to the pandemic and the post-pandemic period.

Socioeconomic policy in immediate post-colonial (post-1980) Zimbabwe featured a strong government with an active agenda that sought to undo the injustices of the colonial period. At the beginning of the 1990s, Zimbabwe changed course and signed on to a neoliberal policy agenda by implementing the economic restructuring programmes pushed by the multilateral development agencies (Brett and Winter, 2003). This entailed reducing the public sector and opening up the country's markets to international trade and investment, a consequence of which was the emergence of a huge informal economy (Narula, 2020; Vainio, 2012). A large informal economy persists in the country to

Z. Chadambuka (✉)
Villanova University Charles Widger School of Law, Villanova, PA, USA

A. Stojanović et al. (eds.), *The First 100 Days of Covid-19*,
https://doi.org/10.1007/978-981-19-6325-4_13

date. Huge unbudgeted-for payments to political allies by the ruling regime, involvement in the war in the Democratic Republic of Congo, and the chaotic manner of the land reform program—all of which occurred around the beginning of the millennium—began a political and economic crisis dominated by economic contraction and hyperinflation (Brett and Winter, 2003). The economic stagnation has continued for the last 20 years, save for a brief period of growth between 2009 and 2013 (World Bank data, 2020). This brief respite came during a unity government formed after the disputed 2008 elections and upon the introduction of a multi-currency system in 2009 after the collapse of the Zimbabwe dollar. Anemic growth and stagnation reemerged from 2013—when the unity government came to an end—up till the reintroduction of the Zimbabwe dollar and outlawing of the use of other currencies in 2019, which precipitated a return to economic contraction; hyperinflation had also returned by the beginning of 2020 when the pandemic struck (World Bank data, 2020). The annualized inflation rate was 676.39, 765.57, 785.55, and 737.26% for the months of March, April, May, and June 2020, respectively (ZIMSTAT, 2020). Understanding this hyperinflationary context facilitates a realistic assessment of the substantive effects of the measures taken to protect against economic difficulties during the pandemic.

On 21 March 2020, the first positive case of COVID-19 was confirmed in Zimbabwe, with the first death occurring on 23 March 2020 (Ndebele, 2020). In response, the government of Zimbabwe imposed a three-week national lockdown period beginning on 30 March 2020. By this time, three positive cases had been recorded, with one fatality. However, cases were rising exponentially in neighboring South Africa, with which Zimbabwe has many trade and travel links. On Sunday 19 April 2020, the lockdown was extended by two weeks with restrictions slightly loosened. From 4 May 2020, the country entered into a less restrictive phase in which formal businesses were allowed to open if they tested their employees for COVID-19 and took measures such as social distancing. As of 28 June 2020, there were 567 positive tests with 6 fatalities.

The pandemic and the policy measures taken to combat it such as the national lockdown had negative effects on businesses, employees, informal economy actors, and the general populace. Due to the chronic economic challenges which have afflicted Zimbabwe for the last two decades, most Zimbabweans survive through activities in the informal sector. A 2014 survey by Zimbabwe's statistical agency ZIMSTAT found that 94.5% of the Zimbabwean workforce was working in the informal sector (Economist Intelligence Unit, 2015; ZIMSTAT, 2019). The 2019 ZIMSTAT survey found that 75.6% of the workforce was employed in the informal economy (ZIMSTAT, 2019). Medina and Schneider (2017)in an IMF working paper estimated in 2018 that Zimbabwe had the second largest informal sector in the world as measured by contribution to GDP at 60.6% of GDP, second only to Bolivia's 62.3% of GDP. Yet the various policies employed by the government of Zimbabwe in response to the pandemic have featured relatively few protections for those who make a living in the informal sector. This is notwithstanding that the restrictions placed on economic activity in seeking to deal with the pandemic have disproportionately impacted this group.

This chapter seeks to explore the effects of the pandemic and the policy measures employed to deal with it on the general populace during the first 100 days of the pandemic's emergence in Zimbabwe. Particular attention is paid to the implications for those who operate in the informal economy. The chapter proceeds as follows. The next section features a discussion of surveillance and compliance in relation to pandemic restrictions in Zimbabwe. The third section assesses democracy and civil activism in Zimbabwe before and during the initial stages of the pandemic. Section four discusses economic policy and the means deployed to seek to mitigate the economic effects of the pandemic and its associated restrictions; effects on business are also discussed in this section. In the fifth section, effects on employees and their livelihoods are discussed, as are matters relating to social movements and their responses to the pandemic. Section six concludes. The discussion generally shows the continuing predominance of the neoliberal laissez-faire economic approach to resource allocation introduced by the economic restructuring programmes of the 1990s, and that this approach continues to exclude the informal economy. This neoliberal laissez-faire approach is now supplemented by a growing tendency to allocate resources to private actors through the political system. The latter serves as a counterpart as well as a facilitator of—and perhaps just as a synonym for—the endemic corruption throughout the country. That latter element has been strengthened under the policies taken in response to COVID-19. Neoliberal law's tendency to purport to privilege "neutral" markets while being, in reality, politically driven to support a powerful and connected minority finds its craven zenith in Zimbabwe's COVID-19 policy.

2 Surveillance and Compliance

On 17 March 2020, the president of Zimbabwe declared COVID-19 a national disaster in terms of the Civil Protection Act. This was followed by the issuing of the Public Health (COVID-19 Prevention, Containment) Regulations, 2020 (principal regulations). These regulations were issued by the Minister of Health and Child Welfare in terms of Sect. 68 of the Public Health Act, a provision which clothes the Minister with powers to make regulations in the event of the occurrence or threatened outbreak of any formidable epidemic disease. The principal regulations were the primary regulatory measure used to address the pandemic.

Limitations introduced by regulation included a national lockdown, movement restrictions, social distancing requirements, a ban on gatherings, face mask requirements in public places, and quarantining for international travelers. Under the provisions relating to the lockdown, movement was—with a few exceptions—restricted to a five-kilometer radius from one's residence, and only for a specific purpose. The ability to fit within the exceptions for purposes of engaging in economic activity turned on being classified as an essential service. Emergence from the initial lockdown thus proceeded largely by expanding the number of economic sectors identified as essential services. The sectors and entities falling under this classification continually expanded from the end of the first phase of lockdown. Under the initial lockdown phase, the classification covered medical and other rescue services, limited transport services, electricity supply, water supply, sewerage and sanitary services, food, fuel and coal, banking, IT services, and state security services. That was later expanded to include all courts, funerals, agriculture, and some education. Manufacturers—both formal and informal—were declared essential services on 21 April. Other *formal* industrial and commercial sector businesses were declared essential services on 4 May, although they were required to test their employees for COVID-19 before they could resume business.

The limitations introduced by the regulations were backed by the threat of criminal sanctions. Publishing or communicating false news about any public officer, official or enforcement officer with the effect of prejudicing the state's enforcement of the national lockdown rendered one liable for prosecution under Section 31 of the criminal code, a provision which criminalizes publishing or communicating false statements prejudicial to the state. Breach of the prohibition on gatherings attracted imprisonment or a fine not exceeding level 12 (fine not exceeding USD 2000.00), or both. Failure to comply with lockdown restrictions by those who did not fall under the category of essential services was punishable by a fine not exceeding level 13 (fine not exceeding USD 3000.00) or imprisonment for a period not exceeding one year, or both. There was also a prohibition on hoarding of medical supplies needed to combat COVID-19; any person suspected of hoarding could have their home searched and such goods seized upon issuance of a warrant from the courts allowing such search and seizure. Formal commercial and industrial businesses, which were required to test their employees for COVID-19 before resuming work, were obliged to allow enforcement officers to access their premises to check if those businesses had complied with the testing requirement. Failure to comply with the testing requirement rendered the businesses guilty of an offence punishable by a fine or imprisonment not exceeding one year, or both.

The limitations employed were also coupled with some surveillance techniques. These surveillance techniques included an immediate case notification system, contact tracing, participatory surveillance through self-reporting of symptoms to local authorities, and collection of electronic health records at many ports of entry. Broader measures included knowledge, attitudes, and practices (KAP) surveys, mortality surveillance through daily recording of the number of deaths caused by COVID-19, sentinel surveillance using the existing Global Influenza Surveillance and Response Systems, and the use of call center systems/telephone hotlines (Karombo, 23 April 2020).

The Ministry of Health and Child Care had formal control in respect of ensuring compliance with the measures adopted, with the aid of enforcement officers including the police and the army, and local authorities. There was strict enforcement of these measures. Multiple checkpoints were set up and numerous arrests were made under the regulations. It was reported that by the end of May 2020, over 40,000 people had been arrested for allegedly flouting lockdown regulations (ZPP, May 2020). On 19 July 2020, it was reported that the number of people arrested for allegedly violating the regulations had now reached 100,000 (BBC, 2020, July 19). There was concern that the deployment of the army and its involvement in civilian affairs could lead to the assault and torture of citizens (Forum, 16 June 2020). There were cases of overreach in the use of enforcement powers as enforcement officers were accused of perpetrating violence on suspected lockdown violators (Mavhunga, 2020a, b).

As the high numbers of arrests suggest, the populace showed some unwillingness to comply with the principal regulations. The obligation for employers providing essential services to conduct mandatory testing for their staff members before opening also created challenges. Testing was to be carried out at the employer's cost, causing many businesses to fail to comply as they were already struggling under the burden of low business due to the pandemic and its associated restrictions. Members of the public who, under the regulations, were detained in quarantine centers often objected to the conditions at these centers, describing them as inhumane, lacking proper sanitation and offering poor-quality diets; this led to some citizens escaping from these centers (Mutsaka, 2020).

There was particularly strong resistance to the restrictions on movement. Sporadic demonstrations occurred against the lockdown, especially in Harare's high density population centers. Movement restrictions had especially harsh effects on informal economy actors, who constitute the majority of the population; for such actors, economic inactivity spelt financial doom. Informal economy actors were not classified as belonging to essential services as defined by the principal regulation, thus rendering economic activity by those in the informal sector unlawful. Informal sector players were therefore behind some substantial resistance against the tough-law, small government approach to COVID-19 policy. The informal sector mobilized against the discrimination against them in COVID-19 policy and enforcement. They formed and mobilized associations such as the Zimbabwe Chamber for Informal Workers, the Zimbabwe Chamber of Informal Economy Association, and the Bulawayo Vendors and Traders Association. These associations engaged in advocacy and litigation to fight perceived unfair treatment of the informal sector. Such entities highlighted significant issues that could otherwise have been buried in the more general discourse on pandemic control; for example, the Bulawayo Vendors and Traders Association issued a statement highlighting the particularly woeful plight of vendors and informal traders with disabilities due to the restrictions on the informal economy under pandemic regulation (Forum, 28 May 2020).

Informal sector associations also spearheaded legal challenges in Zimbabwe's high court, although many of these were unsuccessful. The most notable of these cases is *Zimbabwe Chamber for Informal Workers and Ors v the Minister of Health and Child Welfare and Ors* HH

334/2020. The applicants in this matter approached the court seeking an amendment to the principal regulation as it sought to turn urban transport into a public monopoly under the state-owned Zimbabwe United Passenger Company (Private) Limited (ZUPCO). They alleged that the creation of a ZUPCO monopoly infringed bus and other transport operators' constitutional right to freedom of trade and occupation. The applicants argued that the law should allow the operation of registered transporters and other operators to ferry passengers on their licensed routes subject to compliance with relevant lockdown conditions such as social distancing, temperature checks and use of sanitizers. They also noted that ZUPCO had only 160 buses, thereby making it impossible for it to meet the demand for transport. The applicants also argued that the regulations, by opening up the formal sector while continuing to outlaw economic activity in the informal sector, engaged in unjustifiable discrimination and that this discrimination served no legitimate public purpose. The court dismissed the application, holding that re-opening the informal sector could have had the possible effect of fueling the spread of COVID-19 since it would be more difficult to monitor the lockdown rules in the informal sector than it would be in the formal sector. More generally, the court decided that the measures taken by the government were rationally connected to a legitimate purpose.

It must be noted that it is unclear why it was deemed imperative, from a public interest perspective, to create a public transport monopoly. What was notable, however, is that companies linked to senior politicians and government officials were alleged to have been awarded contracts to procure government buses at patently exorbitant prices, creating a corruption controversy (The Independent, 2020). The monopolization of the urban transport sector also made social distancing much tougher as ZUPCO was unable to meet the public transport demand. This led to long transport queues, and consequently, subjection to long hours of exposure as people waited for buses, coupled with a failure to observe social distancing among queues of long-suffering, patience-depleted commuters. It was similarly difficult to practice social distancing as economic hardships and basic food shortages created a need for constant social interactions in order to obtain the basic necessities of life.

3 Democracy and Civil Activism

Some choices made around pandemic policy and the enforcement of such policy created doubt as to whether such policy measures were based on public health concerns or were driven by ulterior motives. The government was in the process of amending 27 sections of the Constitution of Zimbabwe; these were constitutional provisions (in the Constitution promulgated recently, in 2013) that the general law should have been aligned with, but never was due to central government resistance. The constitutional amendment bill had gone for its first reading in the parliament (the parliament consists of the senate and the house of assembly) before COVID-19 struck. The amendment bill faced resistance from civil society organizations, activists, and lawyers. There was also ongoing political fallout from a bitterly disputed 2018 national election, which manifested in disputes between the ruling party and the opposition as well as intra-party disputes. Thus, the political climate in Zimbabwe was tense just before the pandemic. Some specifics of pandemic policy in this setting support the suggestion that much pandemic policy was deployed as a means to seek political advantage. The fact that the Supreme Court chose the second day of the very first lockdown to hand down a judgment that dramatically fractured the political opposition— this is the judgment in *Movement for Democratic Change and Ors v Mashavira and Ors SC 56/2020*—also strengthens the suspicion that much initial COVID-19 policy was motivated by political considerations rather than public health considerations. The political system became increasingly polarized with pandemic-justified restrictive measures facilitating an increase in arrests of figures of the political opposition and journalists, with muted engagement between civil sector organizations and the government, punctuated by the occasional attempt at judicial redress (Forum, 2020, June 6). The socio-economic difficulties brought by the pandemic and the policies introduced to deal with the pandemic combined with political tension to result in public demonstrations. One demonstration against hunger and price hikes during the national lockdown was held in the high-density suburb of Warren Park and led by members of the opposition and activists, including opposition legislator Joana Mamombe and two activists named Cecilia Chimbiri and Netsai Marova. On the 13th of May, the three activists were allegedly abducted, tortured, and assaulted before being dumped by the side of a road. The three women were then arrested for communicating falsehoods for recounting their allegations of abduction and abuse. Restrictions also meant that political engagement by the citizenry was difficult, especially in a poor country where internet costs are high and internet penetration is not very high. Thus, the troublesome elements of neoliberalism's nightwatchman state were here in full vogue.

The decisions made relating to COVID-19 had minimal input from the parliament or local authorities. The national executive had near-complete control of the response to COVID-19. Local authorities merely attended to the implementation of central government policy within their jurisdictions. The other elected bodies were ineffective in probing or holding the executive accountable for COVID-19 policy. The parliament was not fully active as there was a fear of contracting and spreading the virus. However, the parliament did not resort to the use of technology to conduct its business. There was also a political impasse within the parliament as a result of the aforementioned COVID-19 judgment in *Movement for Democratic Change and Ors v Mashavira and Ors SC 56/2020* which sought to address the legitimacy and legality of the opposition presidential candidate's rise to power and which ultimately fractured the opposition. The (alternative) candidate empowered by the judgment went on a spree of recalling members of the senate and house of assembly who were aligned to her rival (and constituted the vast bulk of opposition parliamentarians). This left numerous vacant parliamentary seats and effectively absorbed parliament in that intrigue and, more generally, hamstrung parliament from carrying out its role (NewZimbabwe, 2020; Karombo, 2020a, b). At law, by-elections were supposed to be held to replace all the vacant parliamentary positions, but that was not done as it was alleged that doing so would have exacerbated the spread of COVID-19 (Economist Intelligence Unit, 2020). Yet public hearings to amend the Constitution went ahead. An application to stop the hearings on the bases that such hearings could exacerbate the spread of COVID-19 and that participation would be limited for fear of COVID-19 was dismissed by the courts (Forum, 10 June 2020; Forum, 16 June 2020). This decision to take important political decisions under limited public participation excluded from participation the poor and those whose movement was otherwise particularly restricted. The end result for informal economy actors was that they bore both the weight of pandemic restrictions and the burden of exclusion from democratic discourse.

4 The Economy and Business

Three features typified the Zimbabwean economic policy response to COVID-19. First was a tendency to resort to the usual channels—particularly financial sector channels—in distributing resources. These channels were set up in the heady neo-liberalism era of economic structural adjustment in Zimbabwe when the current banking structure was put in place. Second was a tendency to direct government resources to politically linked or politically supportive market players; this tendency was particularly marked as it determined the few departures from standard channels. Finally, there was a tendency to diminish the government's role in the actual response, and so to palm the costs and responsibility for the response off onto the private sector; this "smaller-government" tendency was facilitated by a focus on forcing formality on informal economy actors in order to palm off more of the costs of the pandemic response on them. The result of this was a policy response that exacerbated the difficulties imposed upon the poor by the pandemic.

The Reserve Bank of Zimbabwe (RBZ) was particularly active in the response to the COVID-19 pandemic. At the end of March, the RBZ allowed the use of foreign currency in domestic transactions. This came barely a year after its outlawing of such use led to a precipitous fall in the parallel market value of the Zimbabwean dollar from 1:1 to 1:39 by 30 March 2020 (when the national lockdown first began) and to 1:105 with the USD by 27 June 2020. The move to the Zimbabwean dollar thus amounted to a massive confiscation of value from the populace; suspicions that facilitation of such confiscation was the motive for the move can only have been deepened by the quick, poorly reasoned, and somewhat uncertain return to the multi-currency regime. This substantial return to dollarization was asserted to be necessary in order to make it easier for the public to conduct business during the pandemic. The explanation was widely panned as being pretextual as nothing about the pandemic justified the return to dollarization (ZimEye, 2020). The RBZ also suspended the floating exchange rate system in favor of a fixed exchange rate system, asserting this to have been done to ensure greater price certainty. They, however, reverted to a market-based system based on a centralized and restricted currency auction system in June. This pretextual use of COVID-19 to enable value confiscation and the creation of currency policy inconsistency enable the capture of value by those with policymaking power.

On 26 March 2020, the RBZ increased the Medium-Term Bank Accommodation (MBA) facility for supporting productive sector activities by ZW$1 billion to ZW$2.5 billion, with the additional amount targeted at financing the 2020 winter wheat planting program. On 1 May 2020, the MBA facility was further increased to ZW$3 billion, with a pledge to raise an additional ZW$2 billion from the market through money supply-neutral financial instruments. The interest rate on the facility was also reduced from 15 to 10% per annum while banks that access the MBA facility were encouraged to on-lend at interest rates not exceeding 20%. On 26 March 2020, the RBZ reduced the statutory reserve ratio from 5 to 4.5% in order to free some funds to the banks to enhance their lending activities. They further reduced the statutory reserve ratio from 4.5 to 2.5% with effect from 8 June 2020. The RBZ also reduced the bank's policy rate from 35 to 25% on 30 March with the expectation that banks would also follow suit and adjust their lending rates to meet the requirements of their customers who were being adversely affected by the pandemic. On 1 May 2020, the bank policy rate was further reduced to 15%. It was then increased from 15% back to 35% on June 26 as the RBZ asserted that it had become concerned about speculative borrowing in the hyperinflationary environment. Surprisingly, these concerns did not lead to the interest rate on the MBA facility also being increased notwithstanding that parity of reasoning ought to have counseled a similar course in terms of the MBA facility rate. The concern is that speculative opportunities were being opened for selected persons; this is an especially relevant concern given the RBZ's hyper-politicized quasi-fiscal inflationary history which is intertwined with funding for agriculture (Muñoz, 2007). Given inflation, those lending rates are so low that they created massive windfall benefits for those who were allowed access to them. There is a long history of non-repayment of government-provided agricultural loans by persons who are never openly identified and appear to continue to receive further agricultural loans notwithstanding the non-repayment of prior loans (Chimhangwa, 2020).

All these measures entailed using the same old channels of delivering resources as were in place before the pandemic. The RBZ used the formal banking system to deliver its economic benefits. That would suggest that only those within the formal sector got any of that relief. Given that Zimbabwe has high socio-economic inequality, distribution through the usual bank channels probably exacerbated the country's pre-existing inequalities. The monetary policy measures provided benefits to the usual people who have access to formal banking. These are likely to be large, formal, and well-connected entities. The inequality-increasing implications of this tendency to employ standard channels for resource distribution are likely to be exacerbated by the fact that hyperinflation meant that real interest rates had in any case been negative for a while, turning any RBZ money creation activity into a mere non-productive trough to which access was already very difficult and appeared to be largely determined by political and personal connections. There seemed to be little meaningful policy motivation to lowering of an already negative real interest rate when demand for those funds was already very high, especially in the absence of any alternative transparent principle of distribution.

Much financial aid was granted to the agricultural sector. This choice was controversial and highly politicized given the country's recent history of the politically connected corruptly accessing state resources through the agricultural sector. There is also little basis for the view that those in the agricultural sector were *particularly* negatively affected by the pandemic and its associated restrictions, especially given that the restrictions were of particularly biting force in the urban (and so overwhelmingly non-agricultural) environment. In the agricultural sector, it is politicians and the closely politically connected who tended to benefit. Indeed, the country was in the middle of a huge scandal in which it was revealed that politicians had awarded each other alleged agriculture loans under the farm mechanization program in huge amounts distributed by the RBZ which amounts were never repaid (Magaisa, 2020). Details of a more recent distribution of agricultural loans under the command agriculture scheme remain unclear; that scheme was still in operation at the time the pandemic began (Zimbabwe Democracy Institute, 2020). The persistence of the RBZ in quasi-fiscal activities—especially in this case of aid to agriculture—is especially notable given that these activities have a long and disturbing history in Zimbabwe's economy; these agriculture-dominated quasi-fiscal activities were a major factor in the shocking hyperinflation levels of the economy in 2000 to 2009, a time when the nation's inflation rate is asserted to have reached an astounding 89.7 sextillion percent in November 2008 (Hanke and Kwok, 2009), leading to the ultimate collapse of the Zimbabwean currency in February 2009.

Some of the RBZ's regulatory activity was targeted at raising foreign currency. In that respect, the RBZ allowed Money Transfer Agencies to open during the national lockdown. Once it moved away from the fixed exchange rate system, the RBZ reinstated a 30-day maximum for liquidation of surplus foreign exchange receipts from exports; failing such liquidation, the foreign exchange receipts were compulsorily released onto the auction market. The RBZ also sought to starve the foreign currency parallel market by subjecting mobile platform transactions to strong regulations including a ban on most transactions. This made everyday payments extremely difficult in the country, especially because the RBZ had also imposed strict cash withdrawal limits. The informal sector was especially hard-hit by these restrictions. These difficulties imposed upon the public in pursuit of foreign currency are cast in a particularly negative light by the corruption controversies that erupted in the misuse of such foreign currency in the purported procurement of COVID-19 supplies.

The choice to direct money to politically connected places is evident in other fiscal choices made in responding to the pandemic. The government promised a ZW$18 billion (9% of GDP) rescue package in response to the pandemic. Two details emerge here. First, agriculture received the most support, with over two-thirds of the allocation. This choice is controversial for the reasons noted above. Secondly, the ZW$1 billion devoted to the mining sector was going to be substantially available in foreign currency. Considering that the exchange rate fell from US$1:ZW$39 on 30 March 2020 to US$1:105 by 27 June 2020—and has since continued falling—the funding given to mining is, in real terms, substantially higher than initially appears. Mining is the other industry that has become very politically sensitive, as clear in the involvement of the army and political leaders in mining in the eastern and central provinces of the country in recent years (Maguwu et al., 2020). This funding choice therefore supported the strong impression that self-dealing by political actors in responding to the pandemic was a serious problem. Another basis for such concerns arose from the use of "expedited" procurement regulations. This quickly led to procurement scandals. In one widely reported case, the Minister of Health and Child Welfare was eventually removed from his post and criminally charged with flouting tender regulations and making multi-million dollar payments to a suspicious newly formed company; those payments were so controversial that they were flagged by INTERPOL (France24, 2020).

There was an allocation of ZW$0.5 billion to SMEs, some of which was to be devoted to the additional capitalization of the Small and Medium Enterprises Development Corporation (a parastatal) as well as the Women's Bank and the Empower Bank to enable them to support small businesses. This promised relief package which was targeted at SMEs was the only measure that can be deemed to have sought to benefit the self-employed. Yet means for accessing funds from the rescue package remained unclear. There was no clearly set out classification of what an SME amounts to either. There was also no indication that the government had any idea of what SMEs existed in the country; correspondence suggests that the government sought to create such a register in response to the need to distribute pandemic funding. Without a clear definition of an SME in a highly informal economy lacking unemployment insurance such that most people engage in some type of commerce to survive (meaning that the distinction between the self-employed and unemployed is particularly fluid), the distribution of such funds would really lack any principled and transparent guidance. There are suggestions of political nepotism and corruption in such access. For example, determining the list for the SMEs fell to the Ministry of Women Affairs, Community, Small and Medium Enterprises Development; the Ministry is alleged to have allowed the country's ruling party and main opposition party to compile the list of informal traders for purposes of creating a list of SME beneficiaries.

The government's actual attitude towards informal sector players seemed quite hostile. At the beginning of April, the president announced that the country's open-air agricultural markets should remain open to protect farmers' and vendors' livelihoods and ensure food supply for people in high-density areas. This was in the wake of outrage over a raid by riot police officers on Sakubva open market in the eastern city of Mutare where the officers were recorded burning food wares owned by vendors. However, this position never made it into law. Further, government policy soon moved to the destruction of places where informal sector workers ply their trade as the government specifically resolved that local authorities ought to take advantage of the lockdown to clean up and renovate small and medium enterprise and informal traders' workspaces. Though framed as "cleaning", this has historically been a process of bulldozing and other destruction of places where informal sector workers carry out their activities, areas which are often perceived as eyesores in urban areas; reports highlight that such wanton destruction of workspaces and vendors' wares without notification similarly occurred across urban centers throughout the country (ZPP, April 2020; ZPP, May 2020; Forum, 19 April 2020; Forum, 29 April 2020; Forum, 4 June 2020).

The High Court in at least two cases issued orders stopping the government from demolishing vending stalls and tuckshops during the lockdown (Kairiza, 2020; Forum, 11 May 2020; Forum, 12 May 2020).

The government persisted with a minimalist governance agenda by effectively outsourcing COVID-19 testing obligations to the private sector. Companies were only allowed to emerge from the lockdown if they were formal and could test all employees. To be defined as "formal", a company had to be recognized by the tax authorities, the local authorities (such as having a shop license) or by an employment council. The government outsourced testing by requiring that companies formalize and test all employees who were to attend the workplace for COVID-19 if they were to be allowed to reopen at the end of the initial lockdown period. This restriction was very costly to informal enterprises which could not open (though economic pressures meant that they probably needed to open more urgently than larger enterprises) and to small enterprises which could not afford the costs of testing all their employees. Private testing services were very expensive, especially in the early days of the pandemic. As of 28 June 2020, it was mainly those still classified as informal sector players who remained under lockdown. The government clearly sought to use the COVID-19 regulatory framework to force greater formality upon players in the informal economy, as also indicated in a speech by the president on 12 June 2020 in which he stated that informal sector players would be allowed to resume operations if they formally registered themselves or their enterprises. Thus, the greater level of hardship delivered by the government on the informal economy was, in fact, a result of a policy choice rather than mere oversight.

The banning of standard private transport operators also negatively impacted poorer people. People who did not own private vehicles, many of whom are self-employed or small business owners and their employees, could not return to work even if it was otherwise lawful for them to do so. Private transport operators were also deeply affected by the ban which effectively destroyed their businesses. The shortage of buses owned by ZUPCO meant that even the few employees intent on going to work spent many hours of the day waiting for transport. The ban on private transport operators raised costs for those companies that did open as many of them had to find ways to hire transport companies to ferry their workers to and from work. As noted above, an attempt by the Zimbabwe Chamber for Informal Workers Association and the Passenger Association of Zimbabwe to seek judicial remedy arguing unfair discrimination against the informal sector and private transport operators was dismissed by the courts.

The increasing breadth of sectors classified as essential services really meant that it was the limitation on public transport, the requirement of formality and the testing requirement for reopening that continued to create the public health response's required reduction in contact between people. It thus also determined who bore the brunt of the economic slowdown created by the public health restrictions; this had huge distributional implications in that it specifically hurt small businesses and poor people.

Rampaging inflation impacted informal economic actors especially negatively given the restrictions to which they were subjected as set out above. These negative effects were especially strong in urban areas where restrictions were enforced relatively rigidly and where such restrictions had great significance in terms of preventing livelihood activities. In the informal sector, failure to work due to restrictions easily brings the informally employed to the edge of starvation. Some non-governmental entities such as the Zimbabwe Human Rights NGO Forum began warning about serious mental health consequences due to the extreme vulnerability to which informal actors, particularly vendors, were being subjected (Forum, 11 April 2020; Forum, 1 May 2020). They also noted reports of increased drug abuse as inactive informal sector players got more hopeless and desperate (Forum, 11 April 2020; Forum, 1 May 2020).

Formal corporate entities had opportunities for monetary support during the pandemic, although hyperinflationary conditions mean that the amount of support may not have been as meaningful by the time it was received as it otherwise would have been. The support was channelled largely using the same means as are ordinarily employed. This is problematic as Zimbabwe already has high levels of socioeconomic inequality and depositing large chunks of resources into the same channels that created the initial inequality only exacerbated it. More generally, major concerns existed around the distribution of these resources as political patronage appeared to play a major role in the distribution process.

5 The Labour Market

The Zimbabwean economy is highly informal and the country does not provide unemployment insurance. Employees, in general, got no formalized relief in the COVID-19 response. The government did declare that it had improved public servants' terms of service. The government announced at the end of March that it would provide ZW$50 million funding for the Premier Service Medical Aid Society (PSMAS). PSMAS is a privatized former public medical aid society which continues to provide medical aid cover for most civil servants. The government also awarded a 50% salary increment to all civil servants and granted them a flat non-taxable COVID-19 allowance of "US" $75 per month for the months of June, July, and August. Given the aforementioned inflation rates, the Zimbabwean dollar increment was of little significance. The "US$" component of the increment became controversial as it became clear that it was not convertible into any actual US currency and had limited usage; for example, it could not be withdrawn in cash in actual US dollars, it could only be withdrawn at obviously low official conversion rates, and it could not be used in online transactions (Women's Institute for Leadership Development, 2020). The government also asserted that it would provide a tax-free risk allowance and comprehensive medical, accident, and death insurance for all government employees working on the frontlines in the battle against COVID-19 as well as recruit an additional 4000 health workers. In a tacit acknowledgment of the reality that its Zimbabwean dollar increments were of little real value given hyperinflation, the government also promised to work on a wage packet including significant non-monetary benefits. The inadequacy of the increments in the inflationary environment produced industrial action in a pandemic, as public sector medical doctors and nurses went on strike over the poor conditions of service and lack of necessary PPE for their jobs, which industrial action was met with violence by the riot police (Reuters, 2020). Doctors also filed suit in the courts demanding PPE and other protective measures as they dealt with the COVID-19 response.

Although there was no relief specific to the unemployed, some relief was announced for those who were classified as SMEs—a matter discussed above—and for those deemed to be vulnerable. No classification criteria of "vulnerability" were set out. At the end of March, there was an initial plan for social welfare payments to 1 million households under a cash transfer program in respect of which the Minister of Finance pledged

ZWL$200 million per month for April, May, and June. In May, ZW$2.4 billion was set aside for a food grant for 1 million vulnerable households for 8 months; these 1 million were to include 200,000 micro-enterprise owners whose businesses were deemed to have been disrupted by the lockdown. Determining the list of the "vulnerable" fell to the Ministry of Public Service, Labor and Social Welfare. The Social Welfare Assistance Act does provide for monetary payments to "destitute or indigent persons" based on an assessment of the persons' financial circumstances by the Director of Social Welfare or someone acting in their stead. There is little clarity as to how the vulnerability determination was actually made. Government officials asserted that payments to beneficiaries were made through mobile money transfers (Mugabe, 2020). The Deputy Minister of Public Service, Labor and Social Welfare stated that the government had determined the vulnerable from phone numbers on the country's largest mobile phone network (AllAfrica, 2020). He later clarified that the government had also considered phone numbers on the second largest mobile phone network (Mugabe, 2020). It is unclear how screening through either or both of these phone networks can produce a meaningful screening mechanism for vulnerability. On the contrary, it seems certain that such a process would be arbitrary, would be open to corruption, and would certainly exclude the most vulnerable. The Minister of Finance then asserted that he had used a "sophisticated algorithm system" to determine the beneficiaries of the funds (Kunambura, 2020). He has never explained the algorithm system. Widespread reports also highlight that ruling party officials and members took over the process of resource distribution and carried it out along partisan lines, including in some cases hijacking donor-funded programs (Forum, 12 April 2020; Forum, 8–9 May 2020; Forum, 27 May 2020; ZPP, April 2020; ZPP, May 2020).

On 12 June, the Minister of Public Service, Labor and Social Welfare announced that the National Social Security Authority (NSSA), which runs the civil services' pension scheme, would set up a National Unemployment Benefit Scheme to facilitate the distribution of aid to unemployed persons in dealing with difficulties brought on by the pandemic (Sunday Mail, 2020). If done, this could mark a departure from the small government neoliberal ideas that currently hold sway.

One area in which benefits may have been spread more liberally is in the deferral of rent in respect of residential accommodation for April,

May, and June and deferral of mortgage payments for the months of April, May, and June. Such payments are to be paid after the month of June in installments allowing each deferred month's rental/mortgage payment to be paid over 3 months. Rent and mortgage increases during the lockdown period were also outlawed, notwithstanding the terms of the rent or mortgage agreement. This is significant, given the effects of hyperinflation.

In many ways, the Zimbabwean government stayed within neoliberalism's camp with little attention to the protection of employees. Given the amounts made available through the RBZ and through fiscal policy, it is notable that company receipt of government largesse was not made dependent on retaining employees. There were no COVID-19-related changes to labor laws to make it easier to cut wages or lay off workers. Companies however did cut wages and lay off workers under the pre-existing regime which already allowed companies to cut wages subject to certain labor participation procedural safeguards and to lay off workers subject only to certain termination payments. Whether some of the more extreme wage-cutting and termination decisions will be held lawful will depend on whether employees challenge them before the courts and what the courts eventually decide. Zimbabwean courts have staunchly followed currency nominalism such that hyperinflation will mean that the delay within the court system alone will make it unworthwhile to challenge employment decisions in many cases.

Informal economy workers constitute a very vulnerable group of workers in Zimbabwe. They received no protection save to the extent that they found themselves fitted into the "vulnerable" category, however actually defined, or managed to access some SME funds. The little relief from the difficulties brought on by the pandemic that employees, the informally employed and the unemployed received was undermined by the deteriorating economic conditions, particularly by hyperinflation. The absence of an operational unemployment insurance system showed itself to be an especially costly failing during the pandemic. The situation was also particularly difficult for the informally employed as attempts to force them into formality during a pandemic—a process which demands substantial resources from them—potentially pushed them to the edge of penury.

6 Conclusion

Much of the pandemic response was through executive regulation, often in the application of broad empowering statutes. Many elements of the COVID-19 policy response appeared to have little rooting in their purported justification, that is, mitigating the effects of COVID-19. Nothing in COVID-19 gave cogent justification for the introduction of a public transport monopoly or the return to dollarization. Lockdown measures appear to have been used to clamp down on political dissent. The decision not to hold by-elections due to COVID-19 concerns while at the same time continuing the constitutional amendment process also suggested that the asserted COVID-19 concerns were merely pretextual. RBZ activity raised similar concerns. Distributional choices were made that did not seem to be targeted to the actual impacts of COVID-19 and the restrictions introduced to combat it, for example, the significant privileging of agriculture in the response seemed to have little basis in the actual impacts of the pandemic. There were virtually no new measures in the means by which economic relief was provided. The approach was largely an infusion of larger amounts of resources into the same inequitable systems as applied before the pandemic. The measures were thus biased towards formal sector businesses and the politically connected. Individuals without political connections were effectively ignored and restrictions on activity to curb the pandemic were openly applied harshly on the informal economy, notwithstanding that the country's economic activity is heavily tilted towards the informal economy. This all served to follow-up the punch delivered by the pandemic on the poorest in society with a punch delivered by the policy purportedly introduced to combat the pandemic. The government focused on enforcement with relatively minimal attention to welfare needs. In the absence of any pre-existing unemployment benefits scheme, there were no pre-existing conditions for receiving unemployment benefits. The conditions for access to funding related to possibilities from the nebulous and ill-defined classifications as "SMEs" and/or as "vulnerable". Widespread reports suggest that distribution was politicized, with ruling party officials and supporters being the main beneficiaries of the funds. The hyperinflationary environment during this period means that the relief probably did not achieve very much.

What was achieved is that the government maintained a small-government socio-economic mission in which it palmed off substantial responsibility for the pandemic response to the private sector. Government only became stronger in terms of entrenching itself politically, distributing resources into the inequitable channels that had sustained it thus far, and providing opportunities for the politically connected to capture a growing share of national resources.

References

AllAfrica. (2020) Zimbabwe: 800,000 Social welfare beneficiaries picked from Econet users—Minister, 24 April. https://allafrica.com/stories/202004240252.html.

Anti-Corruption Trust of Southern Africa (ACT-SA). (2020) Draft Report: Corruption threatening the gains made against fighting the Coronavirus (Covid-19) in Zimbabwe, (26 May).

BBC. (2020) Coronavirus: Zimbabwe arrests 100,000 for "violations" of measures, 19 July. https://www.bbc.com/news/world-africa-53462259.

Brett, M., and Winter, S. (2003) Origins of the Zimbabwe crisis, Focus 30—Second Quarter 2003. https://hsf.org.za/publications/focus/issue-30-second-quarter-2003/origins-of-the-zimbabwe-crisis.

Chimhangwa, K. (2020) Zimbabwe citizens demand accountability from government over debt in a landmark high court ruling, 22 December. https://www.opendemocracy.net/en/oureconomy/zimbabwe-citizens-demand-accountability-government-over-debt-landmark-high-court-ruling/.

Economic Intelligence Unit. (2015) Zimbabwe: Informal employment dominates. http://country.eiu.com/article.aspx?articleid=453276029&Country=Zimbabwe&topic=Economy.

Economic Intelligence Unit. (2020) Opposition members expelled from Zimbabwe's parliament, 22 March. http://country.eiu.com/article.aspx?articleid=1450844928&Country=Zimbabwe&topic=Politics&subtopic_3.

France24. (2020) Zimbabwe health minister charged over virus kit scandal, 20 June. https://www.france24.com/en/20200620-zimbabwe-health-minister-charged-over-virus-kit-scandal.

Hanke S., and Kwok, A. (2009) On the Measurement of Zimbabwe's Hyperinflation, Cato Journal, 29 (2).

Kairiza, T. (2020) Zimbabwe: Vendors' stalls demolitions illegal, 30 April. https://allafrica.com/stories/202005010298.html.

Karombo, T. (2020a) Khupe recalls 9 more MDC Alliance lawmakers as court ruling awaited, 23 June. https://www.zimlive.com/2020/06/23/khupe-recalls-9-more-mdc-alliance-lawmakers-as-court-ruling-awaited/.

Karombo, T. (2020b) Zimbabwe telcos link up on COVID-19 hotline, 23 April. https://Www.Itweb.Co.Za/. https://itweb.africa/content/6GxRKMYJXy8qb3Wj.
Kunambura, A. (2020) Transparency a pipedream as Ncube throws algorithm farce, 30 April 2020. https://www.theindependent.co.zw/2020/04/30/transparency-a-pipedream-as-ncube-throws-algorithm-farce/.
Mackworth-Young, C. R. S., Chingono, R., Mavodza, C., McHugh, G., Tembo, M., Dziva Chikwari, C., Weiss, H. A., Rusakaniko, S., Ruzario, S., Bernays, S., and Ferrand, R. A. (2020) 'Here, we cannot practice what is preached': early qualitative learning from community perspectives on Zimbabwe's response to COVID-19, 20 April. http://dx.doi.org/10.2471/BLT.20.260224.
Magaisa, A. (2020) Exclusive: Beneficiaries of the RBZ farm mechanisation scheme, 18 July. https://www.newzimbabwe.com/exclusive-beneficiaries-of-the-rbz-farm-mechanisation-scheme/.
Maguwu, F., Mlevu, S., Nhachi, T. O., and Nyapokoto, H. (2020) From blood diamonds to blood gold—A report on machete violence in Zimbabwe's ASM gold sector, Center for Natural Resources Governance, ISSUE 01 (Thursday 30 July 2020).
Mavhunga, C. (2020a) Rights groups welcome court ban on brutal Zimbabwe COVID-19 lockdown, 15 April. https://www.voanews.com/a/africa_rights-groups-welcome-court-ban-brutal-zimbabwe-covid-19-lockdown/6187599.html.
Mavhunga, B. C. (2020b) Zimbabwean sues government to end lockdown over alleged abuse. Voice of America, 10 April. https://www.voanews.com/science-health/coronavirus-outbreak/zimbabwean-sues-government-end-lockdown-over-alleged-abuse.
Medina, L., and Schneider, F. (2017) Shadow economies around the world: What did we learn over the last 20 years? IMF Working Paper, WP/18/17.
Ministry of Finance and Economic Development. (2020) Details on the COVID-19 economic recovery and stimulus package: A ZW$18 billion package (9% of GOP), 4 May.
Mugabe, T. (2020) Covid-19 relief cash transfers start today as virus cases rise to 18, 15 April. https://www.herald.co.zw/covid-19-relief-cash-transfers-start-today-1-coronavirus-confirmed-cases-rise-to-18/.
Muñoz, S. (2007) Central Bank quasi-Fiscal losses and high inflation in Zimbabwe: A note, IMF Working Papers, Volume 2007: Issue 098.
Mutsaka, F. (2020) Nearly 2 dozen escape from virus quarantine in Zimbabwe, 20 May. https://apnews.com/article/0a79dff43fac66bc2ecfe5abc6ea30cf.
Narula. (2020) Policy opportunities and challenges from the covid-19 pandemic for economies with large informal sectors. Journal of International Business Policy 3, 302–310.

Ndebele, L. (2020) Journalist is first person in Zimbabwe to die from Covid-19, 23 March. https://www.timeslive.co.za/news/africa/2020-03-23-journalist-is-first-person-in-zimbabwe-to-die-from-covid-19/.

NewZimbabwe. (2020) Khupe Recalls Khumalo, Hwende, Mutseyami, Timveous from parliament, 5 May. https://www.newzimbabwe.com/breaking-khupe-recalls-khumalo-hwende-mutseyami-timveous-from-parliament/.

Reuters. (2020) Nurses in Zimbabwe arrested as they protest over pay, 6 July. https://www.reuters.com/article/us-health-zimbabwe-protests/nurses-in-zimbabwe-arrested-as-they-protest-over-pay-idUSKBN2471LN.

Sunday Mail. (2020) Unemployment benefit scheme in pipeline, 14 June. https://www.sundaymail.co.zw/unemployment-benefit-scheme-in-pipeline.

The Independent. (2020) Who is responsible? 5 June. https://www.theindependent.co.zw/2020/06/05/who-is-responsible/.

Vainio. (2012) Market-based and rights-based approaches to the informal economy: A comparative analysis of the policy implications, Nordiska Afrikainstitutet

Veritas BILL WATCH 12/2020 (7 April 2020).

Veritas BILL WATCH 16/2020 (16 April 2020).

Women's Institute for Leadership Development. (2020) COVID-19 Allowance—Unfolding dilemma, 5 August. https://kubatana.net/2020/08/05/covid-19-allowance-unfolding-dilemma/.

World Bank data. (2020) https://data.worldbank.org/country/ZW.

Zimbabwe Democracy Institute. (2020) Command Agriculture: Post-Mugabe Authoritarian Consolidation.

Zimbabwe Human Rights NGO Forum, Zimbabwe COVID-19 Lockdown Monitoring Report (Daily reports). https://www.hrforumzim.org/.

Zimbabwe Peace Project Monthly Monitoring Report, March 2020.

Zimbabwe Peace Project Monthly Monitoring Report, April 2020.

Zimbabwe Peace Project Monthly Monitoring Report, May 2020.

Zimbabwe Peace Project Monthly Monitoring Report, June 2020.

ZimEye. (2020) "This Is Ridiculous," Chamisa says on Coronavirus return of US dollar in Zimbabwe, 27 March. https://www.zimeye.net/2020/03/27/this-is-ridiculous-chamisa-says-on-coronavirus-return-of-us-dollar-in-zimbabwe/.

ZIMSTAT. (2019) Labour force and child labour survey. https://www.zimstat.co.zw/wp-content/uploads/publications/Economic/Employment/Labour-Force-Report-2019.pdf.

ZIMSTAT. (2020) Monthly Consumer Price Index. https://www.zimstat.co.zw/cpi/.

Regulations

Civil Protection (Declaration of State of Disaster Rural and Urban Areas of Zimbabwe) (COVID-19) Notice, SI 76 of 2020.

Exchange Control (Exclusive Use of Zimbabwe Dollar for Domestic Transactions) (Amendment) Regulations, SI 85 of 2020 Presidential Powers (Temporary Measures) (Deferral of Rent and Mortgage Payments During National Lockdown) Regulations, SI 96 of 2020 (Consolidated).

Letter from Ministry of Women Affairs, Community Small and Medium Enterprises Development to "SME and Informal Sector Associations" (1 April 2020).

Letter from Ministry of Local Government and Public Works to "All Town Clerks/Secretaries and Chief Executive Officers", ref: "SMEs and informal traders workspace" (8 April 2020).

Movement for Democratic Change and Ors v Mashavira and Ors SC 56/2020 (issued 31 March 2020).

Policy Announcements, Correspondence and Court Judgments.

Presidential Powers (Temporary Measures) (Deferral of Rent and Mortgage Payments During National Lockdown) Regulations, SI 96 of 2020 (Consolidated).

Presidential Powers (Temporary Measures) (Deferral of Rent and Mortgage Payments During National Lockdown) (Amendment) Regulations, 2020 (No. 2) (SI 135 of 2020).

Press Statement: Parliament and COVID-19 Response (30 April 2020).

Press Statement on Economic Mitigatory Measures to Contain the Impact of Corona Virus 2019 (COVID-19) (30 March 2020, Ministry of Finance and Economic Development).

Press Statement: Payment of Civil Service Covid-19 Allowances and Salary Review (17 June 2020, Ministry of Finance and Economic Development).

Public Health (COVID-19 Prevention, Containment and Treatment) Regulations, SI 77 of 2020 (Consolidated).

Public Health (COVID-19 Prevention, Containment and Treatment) (National Lockdown) Order, SI 83 of 2020 (Consolidated).

Public Health (COVID-19 Prevention, Containment and Treatment) (National Lockdown) (Amendment) Order, SI 110 of 2020.

Public Health (Standards for Personal Protective Apparel, Materials and Equipment) Regulations, 2020.

RBZ Press Statement: Resolutions of the Monetary Policy Committee Meeting held on 24 April 2020 (29 April 2020).

RBZ Press Statement: Resolutions of the Monetary Policy Committee Meeting held on 22 May 2020 (8 June 2020).

RBZ Press Statement: Interventions in Response to the Financial Vulnerabilities Caused by the Covid-19 Pandemic (26 March 2020).

RBZ Press Statement: On the Suspension of Monetary Transactions on Phone Based Mobile Money Platforms (27 June 2020).
RBZ Press Statement: On Provision of International Remittance Services by Money Transfer Agencies During the National Covid-19 Lockdown Period (6 April 2020).
Statement by the Zimbabwe stock exchange limited: Deferment of Publication of Issuers' 31 December 2019 Financial Statements and Statutory Shareholders' Meetings—Measures on Covid-19 (24 March 2020).
Statement by the Zimbabwe stock exchange limited: Deferment of Publication of Stockbrokers' 2019b Financial Statements in Light of the Covid-9 Pandemic (01 April 2020).
Statement by the Zimbabwe stock exchange limited Re: Convening of Annual General and Extraordinary General Meetings by Listed Companies in Light of the Covid-19 Pandemic (27 May 2020).
Zimbabwe Chamber for Informal Workers and Ors v the Minister of Health and Child Welfare and Ors HH 334/2020.
ZIMRA Public Notice Number 22 of 2020: Submission of Income Tax Returns (ITF 12C, ITF1, CGT1) for Tax Year Ended 31st December 2019 [Given Outbreak Covid-19 and the Declared National Lock Down].
ZSE Press Statement: Donation of ZSE Trading Levies to Aid the Fight Against the Covid-19 Pandemic (24 April 2020).
ZSE Public Notice: Zimbabwe Stock Exchange Limited (ZSE) Response to the Extension of Lockdown (21 April 2020).
ZSE Public Notice: Zimbabwe Stock Exchange Limited's ("ZSE") Response to Covid-19 Virus (24 March 2020).
ZSE Public Notice: Zimbabwe Stock Exchange Limited's ("ZSE") Response to the Lockdown (1 April 2020).

First 100 days of Brazilian COVID-19 Policy

Tiago Couto Porto, Alexandre San Martim Portes, Mariella Pittari, and João Victor R. Longi

1 Introduction

The beginning of the COVID-19 pandemic initiated a global cascade of policy responses for the disruptions it created. In Brazil, these disruptions took place amidst intense economic and political turmoil. Since 2015, the Brazilian economy had been struggling to recover from the economic crisis that began during President Dilma's administration and

T. C. Porto (✉)
Getulio Vargas Foundation of São Paulo, São Paulo, Brazil
e-mail: tiago.porto@fgv.br

A. S. M. Portes · M. Pittari
University of Turin, Torino, Italy
e-mail: alexandre.sanmartimportes@anu.edu.au

M. Pittari
e-mail: mariella.pittari@unito.it

J. V. R. Longi
Mediterranea International Centre for Human Rights Research MICHR, Reggio Di Calabria, Italy
e-mail: joaovrlonghi@yahoo.com.br

A. Stojanović et al. (eds.), *The First 100 Days of Covid-19*,
https://doi.org/10.1007/978-981-19-6325-4_14

was reinforced by the contested Impeachment process that put an end to her government in 2016. The crisis was further aggravated by President Temer's politically fragile interim government (2016–2018), which was teeming with corruption scandals, and bet on fiscal economic reforms to circumvent the economic depression. The political scenario was of utmost polarization, with the massive spread of fake news and institutional conflicts between the executive, the legislative, and the judiciary. In this context of political instability and considerable rise in inequality and poverty, Brazil elected in 2018 the extreme-right leader Jair Messias Bolsonaro to become the president of the country.

In the first 100 days of the pandemic, Bolsonaro neglected the seriousness of the pandemic, opposed isolation measures, disseminated fake news about the efficacy of drugs—such as chloroquine—and hampered the vaccine acquisition (Oliva, 2021; Adamo Idoeta, 2021). In addition, he attacked Brazil's democratic institutions, criticizing the Brazilian Supreme Court (STF) and ministers and confronting journalists (Soares, 2021). This political turmoil created by the President arguably hampered appropriate responses to the pandemic.

Even though the scenario described is worrisome, it could have been far worse without resistance movements and solid and institutionalized public policies. For instance, the STF prevented Bolsonaro's attempts to curtail state governors' autonomy to implement any measures to tackle the crisis.[1] Moreover, the Supreme Court openly condemned the dissemination of fake news by President Bolsonaro and his allies.[2] Similarly, the Brazilian Congress also had a very crucial role in guaranteeing a reasonable value (R$600.00) for the Emergency Social Aid, a federal government program to ensure a minimum condition of living for different social groups.[3]

The Brazilian universal health care, the "Unified Health System" (Sistema Único de Saúde—SUS), developed after the re-democratization of 1988, prevented the country from greater disaster resulting from the world's highest number of COVID-19 cases and hospitalizations, by guaranteeing treatment for the entire population even in the most alarming moments, with few exceptions. Finally, civil society organizations in the surveillance and security area seized the window of opportunity brought by the COVID-19 and accelerated the constitutionalizing of personal data protection.

This chapter develops a descriptive and multidisciplinary analysis of how the COVID pandemic has reinforced, attenuated, or changed the trajectories of crucial Brazilian public policies while reflecting on possible challenges and expectations for the post-pandemic age. In particular, the focus on economic, political, and health issues revealed, on the one hand, the importance of the welfare apparatus and democratic institutions built after the military dictatorship, and, on the other hand, the inefficacy of those in political and economic power that neglect the role of science, state institutions, and public policies.

2 Democracy and Civil Activism

In 2020, Brazilians were celebrating Carnival while fears of an ongoing pandemic were spreading across the globe and countries were enacting measures at an unprecedented pace to contain the spread of the infection. From the WHO declaration of Covid-19 as a pandemic on 11 March 2020 (Cucinotta and Vanelli, 2020), jurisdictions felt encouraged to design a strategy to fight the virus, deploying available devices more suited to a warlike scenario (Abriani et al., 2020). Indeed, the war discourse conformed to the necessary mobilization measures adopted by the government. Furthermore, those provisions were already present in most constitutional documents invoking an abnormal state of emergency to cope with events, therefore materializing as the appropriate venue to pursue.

In the Brazilian case, it is necessary to emphasize the recent dictatorial past, marked by the closing of Congress and the ease with which the military regime circumvented constitutional mechanisms that protect the existence of democracy (Silva, 1984). To avoid the repetition of an escalation towards authoritarianism, the still in force 1988 Constitution sets forth a chapter dedicated to solving a constitutional crisis, an essential element for understanding how the three branches of power dialogued with the Constitution during the pandemic period (Bonavides and Andrade, 2003).

The activation of the state of emergency varies according to the level of threat imposed on constitutional normality (Ackerman, 2008), considering that the constitutional system of crises serves to restore disruptures in constitutional normalcy.[4]

Primarily, the recognition of a state of crisis aims to defend the state and democratic institutions. After Brazil endured decades of dictatorship, initiated in 1964 and ended with the promulgation of 1988's Constitution, constituents ensured that the system was prompt to impose restrictions of fundamental rights only as *ultima ratio* and submitted to following judicial review (Gilmar and Branco, 2018).

The state of emergency and siege are manifestations in scale following the need to impose an exceptional regime (Cogliolo, 1917). Rights such as assembly or free circulation might be curbed depending on the needs as essential features for exercising the state of defense and siege are also the exceptionality and limited duration.

As discussed in this chapter, constitutional devices were put in operation since the beginning of the pandemic, unleashing budgetary expenses, authorizing monthly payments for those deprived of income, and creating channels to implement a nationwide mobilization. This section aims to investigate the occurrences of the state of exception during the pandemic. Although a state of calamity was formally declared, thus avoiding constitutional prohibitions arising from the state of defense or siege, many of the measures adopted tangibly cross the point of undecidability[5] between rules and the exception.

2.1 From the State of Emerging to the State of Calamity: Internal Legislative Measures

Brazilian President Bolsonaro with message No. 93, March 2020 addressed the Congress declaring a state of calamity in March 2020. Consequently, and according to the provisions setting forth that the Federal Union is empowered to plan and promote permanent defense against public calamities,[6] the Brazilian Congress enacted legislative decree 06/2020 aiming to address the Covid-19 emergency.

The main effect of the legislative decree proclaiming the state of calamity was to remove the limits of spending placed by budgetary commands according to the fiscal responsibility law.[7]

It is worth noting that the state of emergency precedes the state of calamity. While the Health Minister issued the state of emergency through an ordinance, the state of calamity required the President of the Republic and Congress's participation, considering the fiscal effects arising from the declaration of a state of public calamity.[8] However, the worsening of the state of calamity has led the government to adopt more limiting measures.[9] Thus, as stated above, the consequences deriving from the decree proclaiming the state of defense and siege have further limited fundamental freedoms, even though they failed in sufficiently addressing the sanitary issue at stake. Additionally, prolonging of the state of emergency raised the risk of possible constitutional amendments or reforms jeopardizing basic guarantees.

At the federative level, because of the need to address the pandemic in specific ways, states have invoked the necessity for centralized executive power to act and manage the covid emergency in order to limit the spread of infections among federative states. For instance, states such as São Paulo, which have seen higher population flows than other states, would have required anticipatory measures to be enforced in order to limit the spread of the virus at an earlier stage.

Relevant in the analysis of the interactions between the federative and central dimension is also a decision of the Brazilian Constitutional Court, that was appealed to decide on the constitutionality of Presidential Provisory Measure 926/2020 (ADI 6341). The Provisory Measure challenged before the Supreme Court argued that the measure was limiting the federative autonomy of states, by suppressing the joint competence to deal with public health.[10] Consequently, the Court declared the unconstitutionality for the Union to enact policies disregarding federative states' entitlement to regulate sanitary policies.

2.2 Reasons Why the State of Calamity (Decree 7.257/2010) Was Declared Instead of the State of Defense or Siege

The Minister of Health was the first to inaugurate the state of emergency through Ordinance n. 188. However, the pandemic's unfolding required the adoption of other measures to be requested by the President of the Republic, with authorization from the National Congress.

Hence, on March 18, 2020, President Bolsonaro made a statement requesting Congress to allow the spending beyond the constraints contained in the Fiscal Responsibility Law.[11] Following the President's request, the National Congress expressly recognized the existence of the state of public calamity, providing the Union greater flexibility to achieve budgetary pursuits.[12]

This possibility is provided by Article 167, paragraph third of the Brazilian Constitution, which establishes that the primary purpose of approving the state of calamity is to release additional credit, liberating resources to cover unforeseeable expenses. By recognizing the calamity, the Union is thus permitted to spend beyond the previously approved annual budget and released from the need to forecast revenues to be raised through taxes. According to Legislative Decree 06/2020, the state of calamity was supposed to last until December 31, 2020, since the unleashing of budgetary expenses required the identification of an expiration date, in conformity to the law 13.979/2020. During this period, the country faced resistance from the President in complying with the emergency guidelines. President Bolsonaro's presidency was marked by a vocal encouragement for reopening the country and constant denial of the threats posed by the virus. Nonetheless, despite presidential skepticism on the risks offered by the increasing infection rate, both the Congress and the Executive were keen to pass reforms despite the high societal disapproval, taking advantage of the emergency situation to pass unpopular laws.

Those clashes of approach directly impacted the federative harmony among states and the Union due to the fact that opposition to governors handling the crisis generated profound constitutional disputes (HORTA, 1958). For instance, as mentioned in the previous paragraph, Provisional Measure 926 modified the discipline about the competence given to the states of the Federation to contain the spread of the disease, demanding direct Supreme Court intervention to solve the hostility arising among federative entities.

Indeed, Brazil lacked an articulated effort to adequately address the pandemic, using social demobilization to retrench rights. Instead of political alliances combining efforts to mitigate the effects of the skyrocketing rate of infections, political parties used the pandemic as a battleground for political gain. The government pushed for privatization of water and basic sanitation, the release of the Amazon rainforest for land grabbing, and the dismantling of labor rights under the excuse of preserving jobs, whereas the opposing political parties, while vocal in public, did not activate necessary mechanisms to prevent spurious coalitions.[13]

Moreover, the unambiguous transfer of public funds from the state to financial institutions through the Constitutional "War" Reform (*Emenda Constitucional* 106/2020), allowed the Brazilian President and Congress to waive trillions from federal funds to private parties, explicitly giving away public money in the exclusive benefit of financial institutions.

Nevertheless, the Executive agenda did not stop with the Constitutional Reform. The Executive achieved much of its aspirations while engaging with the Centrão (the center-right political party that controls Congress) to approve controversial legislation towards disputed political priorities, such as granting Brazilian public assets to private parties. In this scenario, the Covid pandemic triggered the acceleration of bills pushing for privatization in various areas, releasing electricity, water, and crucial oil drilling plants from public control.

Through the enactment of Law 14026/2020, the promotion of sanitation discourse enabled the pricing of water resources.[14] On the same path, Bill 191/2020, aiming to liberate native land for mining, was first discussed in the House of Representatives and was then introduced when covid-19 dissemination took over the public debate.[15]

Bill 2633/2020, initiated in May 2020 and still under parliamentary discussion, aims to grant immunity to those who participate in the land grabbing and deforestation campaigns, releasing environmental offenders from responsibilization for the practice.[16]

Those three main axes reflect the scenario that Brazilians faced in the first 100 days of the pandemic.

The list of rights under attack or threat was extensive: (i) Passing constitutional Reform aiming to transfer private assets to the Central Bank without further accountability; (ii) Undermining rights of indigenous populations; (iii) Exempting large corporations to mine in protected areas; (iv) Allowing land grabbing; (v) Privatizing access to water; (vi) Deepening of the privatization of national resources—only to bring about situations in which democratic normality was eroded in favor of a small fraction of the privileged class; (vii) Insufficient protection of food security; and (viii) Exempting public officials for errors committed in the management of Covid-19 (ADI 6421).

Because this comprehensive list of legislative novelties was adopted during compromised legislative debates, it follows that many of those legislative changes had to be challenged before the STF on their constitutional grounds.

The STF had a crucial role in balancing the clashes of branches in this period. When tensions among states and the Federal Union escalated, the Supreme Court decided that states could not block the circulation of goods and persons among federative units, given the importance of ensuring the supply of products during the pandemic. Action 6343 allowed states to apply pandemic mitigation policies. Also, striking down Provisional Measure 966 as unconstitutional, the Court nullified the Executive's exemption of public authorities from liability.[17]

The STF held that the criteria established were not compatible with the Constitution. The Republic Federal Supreme Court. It has already rendered more than 4000 decisions related to the pandemic. However, despite the activism and speed in granting injunctions, other problems started to gain relevancy in the crisis.

Nonetheless, the Supreme Court's activism came at a cost. Non-elected justices assumed an increasingly political role, dramatically affecting the balance of power with political institutions. For this reason, when the Court struck down presidential ambitions, the Executive threatened over-packing the Court to reduce the justice's power by diluting the weight of their opinions among the President's appointees. However, such a move is unfeasible given Supreme Court's composition constitutional nature. The pandemic proved the existence of frictions among powers that ultimately undermined the importance and harmony of the institutions.

Another important measure to be mentioned in the context of this analysis is President enacted Decree 10.277.2020. This decree established a committee composed of the Federal Government's highest-level representatives (the Crisis Committee), whose main objective was coordinating operations and monitoring the actions adopted by public and private actors concerning Covid-19. Moreover, in June 2020 a resolution was issued by the Crisis Committee addressing the supervision and monitoring of the impacts of Covid-19. The Working Group's purpose was to maintain the President informed during the pandemic. However, besides being a committee composed predominantly of allies, it did not have any binding force capable of compelling the President to shift government policy.

The pandemic was a large-scale test on the government's capacity to react before unforeseeable events. It served to question grounded achievements in science and technology, given that a considerable period of uncertainty passed before governments could put into practice effective solutions.

3 Surveillance and Security

The Brazilian 1988 Constitution contains a robust list of individual and collective rights and guarantees. However, the history of authoritarianism combined with profound social inequality in the country can make the constitutional text distant from reality even in times of "institutional normality". In addition, the Constitution mandates that a certain level of cooperative federalism should be achieved especially in relation to the implementation of social rights such as health, education, housing, and food. However, as noted earlier, the implementation of policies addressing the consequences and impact of the COVID pandemic in Brazil was marked by the total absence of the federal government's leadership. Mass disinformation campaigns, justified through a rhetorical and denialist discourse, contributed to the clumsy and disconnected response to the pandemic in Brazil.

On enforcement measures and *restrictions* on rights, the issue of personal data is notable, especially in the state of São Paulo. According to Bioni et al. (2020), two significant measures adopted in this field were the Intelligent Monitoring System (SIMI), a partnership between the Government of São Paulo and mobile phone companies to share aggregated data in the form of heat maps, and the Social Isolation Index, developed by a Brazilian startup using aggregated data from geolocation.[18]

A recent scenario brought up the Brazilian General Data Protection Law (LGPD)—Law No. 13,709 of August 14, 2018—and one of the most disturbing issues concerns the practice called *profiling*.[19] The term has great importance because it reflects an inexorable facet of the use of algorithms that, used in the processes of processing *large data collections (Big Data)*, provide the design of the "behavioral profile" of the individual, which begins to be analyzed and objectified from these projections.

The main impacts of the pandemic at this point were the risks of increasing algorithmic discrimination, a violation of the fundamental right to privacy[20] with the need for urgent countermeasures to be adopted to such practices, to the extent that we are all living in a *goldfish bowl*.[21]

Population's control based on data surveillance[22] is something that has started to be increasingly used also in Brazil. An example can be found in the state of São Paulo. In this state, a partnership between the state government and telephone companies Vivo, Claro, Oi, and TIM began to feed a system called Simi-SP, under the following justification: "With Simi-SP, the Government of São Paulo can consult georeferenced information on urban mobility in real-time in the municipalities of São Paulo. To ensure the privacy of each citizen, monitoring is done based on collective data collected in clusters from 30,000 people".[23]

After the announcement of the measure adopted by the São Paulo government, the Ministry of Science, Technology, Innovations and Communications (MCTIC) and a fifth company (Algar Telecom) joined the four operators mentioned. The aim of Simi-SP was to get information from transmission towers, which can identify people's movement and that allow the monitoring of data of 220 million mobile devices.[24,25] In relation to this project and emphasizing the importance of regulatory frameworks for the protection of personal data, Danilo Doneda argues that:

> Since data protection is aimed at the protection of citizens, its discipline includes devices capable of legitimizing the use of your personal data in situations in which your interest or that of society is a priority, as occurs in a situation like the one we are going through. (...) However, the legitimation for the use of this data in emergency situations is in no way a blank letter provided by data protection laws for the unrestricted use of personal data: as in other situations, its processing must respect individual rights and guarantees (...), the processing shall be allowed only for the strict purpose of containing the emergency, risks must be minimized through the use of a minimum set of data possible, anonymization and pseudonymization shall take pace where possible and necessary security measures shall be used.[26]

There is no doubt about the relevance of data processing—even if anonymized—during a pandemic. Data can help ensure state control over the movement of people, especially in regions of higher risk, such as neighborhoods where many elderly people live or in the vicinity of hospitals or nursing homes, and even in areas prone to agglomerations, such as parks, public squares, subway and bus stations, and supermarkets.

What cannot be accepted is the non-transparent, broad, and criteria-based use that, although disclosed—such as, in the case of the State of São Paulo, the containment of only agglomerations with more than 30,000 people—are not easily auditable. And this concern has been signaled by doctrine for years.

The risk that profiling measures can pose has been captured in Bentham's panopticon,[27] which as described by Miran Božovič can be described as follows: "personal experience, media stories and increased invasion and overlap of surveillance in the era of combating terrorism and preventing health care are likely to promote increasing recognition of the potentially implicit interconnectivity, agility and impact of surveillance systems on someone's life".[28]

Especially in times of confinement and social isolation due to a pandemic, it becomes essential to clarify which are the impacts of the measures and technological instruments adopted for data collection and processing. The informed self-determination,[29] is concrete evidence of the need for normative effectiveness in order to prevent an unwanted scenario of data hyper-surveillance.

More than ever before, a data protection framework with emphasis on fundamental rights to privacy, freedom, and intimacy is crucial to uncovering abuses and excesses practiced in data collection and processing.

4 Challenges and Constraints on the Brazilian Economy

4.1 *Pre-COVID-19 Economic Policies*

The outbreak of the COVID-19 forced a significant shift in the direction of economic policies in Brazil. While economic policies in the last six years were directed to reduce the scope of the state in the economy, the advent of the coronavirus—and a significant pressure and demand from society—forced the government to place the State again as the central economic actor.

Since 2015 the country has been applying orthodox economic policies, and after 2016, the country has implemented several liberal reforms. The economic platform of the previous president Michel Temer and of President Jair Bolsonaro were centred on neoliberal concepts and recommendations in which economic growth would be restored through liberal reforms, that would increase the confidence of agents and stimulate private spending by households and companies.

In 2017 the first reform was implemented. It consisted of a ceiling for the public expenditure (named *Teto de Gastos*) requiring that public spending is adjusted only by the previous year inflation, therefore freezing in real terms government expenditure for 20 years.[30] The second, the labour reform implemented in November 2017, aimed to make the labour market flexible by allowing temporary and intermittent contracts and 12-h working days, among others. The third, the pension reform, effective in November 2019, raised the minimum retirement age and extended the minimum contribution period, among other things.

Frustrating the expectation of those in favor of the reforms, the principal economic indicators have worsened after those policies had been implemented. The country's growth rates have remained low. After the economic crisis of 2015–2016, in which the economy has observed a negative growth rate of 3.4% on average, the period of 2017–2019 remained semi-stagnant, growing at an average rate of 1.5% per year.[31] Public debt did not stop rising after the reforms. Central government gross public debt was 65.5% in December 2015 and reached 77.03% in March 2020. Social inequality has worsened in the period. The Gini index raised from 51.9 to 53.4 between 2015 and 2019. Within the same period, the extreme poverty and poverty gap index has increased from 3.2% to 4.6% (at 1.90 USD a day) and from 6.9% to 8.1% (at 5.50 USD per day),[32] respectively.

The economic scenario of Brazil before the outbreak of the pandemic was, thus, extremely challenging and problematic. The pandemic has pushed governments worldwide to step in and actively engage in rescuing the economy. Brazil's case is no different. However, the government did not endogenously decide to tackle the economic challenges of the pandemic but only implemented the most significant economic policies after strong pressure from the population, economic actors, congress, governors, majors, and from the supreme court. Consequently, the ultra-liberal economic minister—Paulo Guedes—and the liberal president of the Central Bank of Brazil—Roberto Campos—have implemented a substantial amount (in both absolute and relative terms) of non-conventional fiscal and monetary policies, respectively, to circumvent the crisis.

4.2 *The Big Shift: Economic Policies to Tackle Coronavirus Crisis*

According to the fiscal monitor of the International Monetary Fund (IMF), Brazil has been one of the developing countries that have implemented the largest amount on fiscal measures as a percentage of GDP in 2020. On the one hand, the economic policies implemented seemed effective in softening the economic and social impacts of the crisis, in terms of a growth slowdown, income inequality, employment, etc. On the other hand, important policies took time to be implemented and/or have been implemented only after great pressure from different actors.

In general, in an environment of anti-science and denial of the severity of the health crisis, economic policies implemented during the COVID-19 crisis have been efficient compared to many other public policies implemented by the government (health, educational, environmental, etc.). However, Bolsonaro's and Paulo Guedes' rhetoric that there is a dichotomy between saving the economy or the health crisis is symbolic to illustrate that all the economic effort was not sufficient to hinder the widespread of the virus and the paramount number of deaths in the country.

As we have briefly described, the economic scenario was already problematic before the advent of the coronavirus crisis and previous reforms have restricted the scope for state action. Therefore, the economic policies implemented during the crisis were only possible due to the State of Public Calamity decreed by Congress on March 20 and the approval of the Constitutional Amendment Project (PEC) "War Budget" on May 7. Summarily, while the former was important to allow the government to miss fiscal targets set by the Fiscal Responsibility Law and the Budget Guidelines Law, the latter authorized the Brazilian Central Bank (BCB) to buy national treasure bonds and private bonds to cope with pandemic spending.

The first round of policies implemented in March 2020 had no fiscal impact and constituted mainly of anticipation of expenses or deferral of revenues. They included anticipating salary bonuses for workers and two installments of the 13th wage payments to retirees, postponing the payment of company tax contributions and, reducing by up to 95% employers' social security contributions for companies with up to 100 employees affected by the pandemic, etc. Initial policies also included the enlargement of Bolsa Familia resources and the provision of R$ 16 billion in financial aid to states and municipalities.[33]

Those policies were clearly insufficient to circumvent the crisis and after significant pressure from the population and the congress, the government implemented a set of fiscal measures that have been crucial to soften the impact of the health crisis on the economy and society. They consisted of (i) social protection measures such as the Emergency Aid Program; (ii) assistance to states and municipalities; (iii) measures to direct combat the coronavirus crisis; (iv) employment protection measures; and (v) company relief measures.

The main measure—in terms of importance and the amount of resources—has been the Emergency Aid Program. It consisted of three-month installments of special social aid of BRL 600.00 to persons over 18 years old whose monthly family income did not exceed three minimum wages or ½ (half) minimum wage per capita. Later, the aid was extended for two more installments. According to Paiva et al. (2021) the aid reached about 67 million beneficiaries in more than 40 million families and is composed of almost 130 million people, which corresponds to 60% of the population. Nonetheless, it is important to mention that the original program sent by the government consisted of the aid of BRL 200.00 and the congress amplified it to reach the amount of BRL 600.00.

This program accounted for more than 50% of all economic policies implemented in 2020 (Soares and Orair, 2021).

Some studies have been showing that the Emergency Aid Program was very effective as a contra-cyclical measure as well as a policy to reduce inequality and poverty rates (Barbosa and Prates, 2020; Paula, 2021). Using data from PNAD COVID, Duque (2020) shows that within the first four months of the social aid program the percentage of the population living below the poverty line decreased from 23.72% to 18.41%, and the percentage of the population living below the extreme poverty line dropped from 4.18% to 2.29%. In the same line, data from PNAD COVID-19 also shows that the Emergency Aid has contributed to reducing income inequality, as the average effective income has risen sharply at the bottom of the income deciles. Gonçalves et al. (2021) have shown that the percentage variation of the difference between the average effective income before and after the Emergency Social Aid drops progressively as the average effective income grows. For example, the first and most poor decile of the population had an increase of 76.2% in their average effective income after accounting for the social aid, while the 10th decile had an increase of 0.7%.

However, the positive impact of the emergency aid on reducing income inequality and poverty rates were not sufficient to neutralize the very unequal impact of the pandemic on the Brazilian population according to race, region, and income. Pires et al. (2021) created an index of "Social Risk Factors to Covid" and have shown that the aid helped to neutralize short term wage disparities but were insufficient to neutralize multi-dimensional structural inequalities and that racial, regional, and income inequalities have been exacerbated by the pandemic.

In addition to the fiscal measures succinctly described above, it is important to discuss briefly the monetary policies implemented by BCB. Firstly, the BCB has reduced its Policy Rate from 4.25 at the beginning of the COVID-19 to 2.25 on 17 June 2020, reaching the historical minimum at the time. Secondly, the BCB announced in March 2020 the largest package of liquidity expansion measures in Brazilian history (R$ 1.2 tr, 16.5% of GDP). However, as of August 2020 only 25.36% were indeed implemented. According to the BCB the main policies can be divided into two subcategories: measures for the release of liquidity and measures for the release of capital.

The former included lessening in reserve requirements by reducing the rate on term deposits from 31 to 25% and later to 17% and the creation of the Term Deposit with Special Guarantees (DPGE), allowing financial institutions to capture deposits guaranteed by the Credit Guarantee Fund (FGC). The latter included a reduction of the capital requirement for credit operations to small and medium enterprises (SME) and the creation of a specific line of credit for financing the floating capital of SME.

Paula (2021) describes and analyzes the monetary policies implemented by the BCB with great detail and has shown that initially—from April 2020 to June 2020—the policies implemented were important to prevent a liquidity crisis but had a limited effect on credit supply. Providing the financial system with liquidity did not guarantee that the resources reached the enterprises and citizens in the first moment, and indeed, credit only reached SME by means of the use of guarantee funds such as the Guarantee Funds for Investment (FGI) and the Operation Guarantee Fund (FGO).

All in all, the government and BCB have implemented substantial non-traditional fiscal and monetary policies that although came with some delay and after pressure from congress and population, were still effective in softening economic crisis and social collapse. However, the country faces a difficult scenario of Stag-inflation, and as indicated by the official budget guidelines and projections, the plan is to restore rigid fiscal consolidation that is incapable to absorb expenses transmitted from the pandemic period. In fact, there is no evidence that the current government is looking (or ever looked) to the COVID-19 crisis as a window of opportunity to combine the conjuncture struggles with structural challenges, such as the strengthening of the health system (including the health industrial complex), the increase of social protection coverage and the search for inclusive and sustainable growth.

5 The Labor Market

The COVID-19 pandemic has had an enormous impact on the labor market in all parts of the world. Lockdowns and social distancing measures have profoundly affected the number of jobs available and have arguably permanently shaped how and where people work. In Brazil, the inherent inequality that characterizes the country's labor market aggravated the effects of these transformations. This section explains the state of the Brazilian labor market prior to the pandemic, the significant impacts that it generated, and the government's responses to address those impacts.

5.1 The Brazilian Labor Market Pre-COVID-19

As discussed in the previous section, the Brazilian economy already presented before the pandemic several challenges that directly impacted the labour market. As the solid economic growth that the country experienced in the 2000s waned, the unemployment rate became a key concern for the Brazilian government throughout the 2010s. In 2014, when Former President of Brazil, Dilma Rousseff was re-elected, the unemployment rate fluctuated around 7%. In 2017, in contrast, this rate reached 14% (IBGE, 2021). This significant growth in the number of unemployed people had profound impacts on people's livelihoods and labor conditions.

One of the main characteristics of the Brazilian labor market, similar to other middle and low-income countries, is informality. Informal workers do not have formal contracts with their employers and, therefore, no access to the social welfare system connected to the formal labor market. Even though the favorable economic scenario in the 2000s created a significant amount of jobs and reduced informality, informal work became prominent once again as the economic activity decreased (Mazano et al., 2021). Data from 2019 shows that 41.6% of workers were informal. The rate of informality varies significantly depending on other characteristics of the worker. For instance, the informality rate among people who have not completed elementary school was 62.4%, while among workers who finished university, it was 21.9%. People of color also had a higher rate of informality (47.4%) in comparison to their white counterparts (34.5%) (Campos, 2020).

Leite (2020) highlighted that informality is not a novel phenomenon in Brazil. On the contrary, it has been part of the structural inequalities that characterize the Brazilian labor market. However, informality became even more relevant to the Brazilian economy with the rise of the "gig economy". As shown by Manzano and Krein (2020), there has been a significant increase in informal workers using ride and delivery apps. In 2020, before the pandemic, it was estimated that 13% of the adult population had already worked using such platforms (Guimarães, 2021).

Finally, another crucial element to understand the Brazilian labour market is the regulatory reform that changed several aspects of the Labor Law. In 2016, the growing economic crisis and political instability culminated in the impeachment of Dilma Rousseff. As a result, Michel Temer came to power with a strong neoliberal agenda. As mentioned in section four, one of the most crucial points of this agenda was the reform of the Brazilian Labor Law. For the government, creating a new Labor Law (Law 13.467/2017) represented the cornerstone for a speedy economic recovery since it would make work relations more flexible, benefiting both employers and employees. However, the legislative negotiations were contentious due to the possible deleterious implications that this reform would cause for workers.

Research shows that the reform did not accomplish its goals. Between 2015 and 2017, unemployment maintained a relatively stable rate of around 11% and 13% and informality grew from 46.3% to 50.8% (Manzano et al., 2021). These data also suggest that unemployment was still a significant issue for the economy, and the existing jobs were increasingly becoming more informal and precarious.

Based on this brief background, it is possible to argue that the Brazilian labour market underwent important transformations in the past decade. The high rates of unemployment and informality combined with more flexible work relations created a challenging context for Brazilian workers. The pandemic's beginning represented a severe impact on this already difficult scenario. As with other parts of the world, the pandemic aggravated this scenario by imposing social distance measures and reducing economic activity in general. The first 100 days of the pandemic had a significant impact on the country's economy and labor market. Data shows, for instance, that unemployment grew to almost 15% (IBGE, 2021). In addition, workers' income was severely affected by the reduction of economic activity and the regulatory measures outlined below.

5.2 *Regulatory Responses During the Pandemic*

Like other governments globally, the Brazilian government tried to provide rapid regulatory responses to the pandemic, especially concerning work conditions and income maintenance. On 22 March 2020, Provisory Measure 927 (MP 927), one of the first measures to fight the effects of COVID, was adopted. The main objective of this measure was the creation of alternatives that employers could adopt to protect the existing jobs and workers' income. This measure provides the adoption of different instruments, such as remote working, the advancement of individual vacations, collective leave period, and the usage of "time banking". These flexibilities were released as a Provisory Measure, which suggests that they were designed for a scenario where the pandemic would last for only a few months.

One relevant aspect of this measure is that it contained a provision that allowed the unilateral suspension of a contract by the employer for up to four months, with no guarantee of income for the employee in this period. After a strong reaction from workers' unions and other social movements, this mechanism was removed (Scherer and Marcolino, 2020), showing these organizations' active role during the pandemic. In addition, it is noteworthy that the goal of this measure was to maintain formal jobs during the first months of the pandemic; therefore, it did not apply to informal workers. MP 927 was not transformed into law or renewed, expiring in June 2020.

The second relevant labor market regulation was MP 936, enacted in April 2020. It created the Emergency Employment and Income Maintenance Program to provide formal workers with financial compensation in case of temporary suspension of their work contract or the reduction of work hours. This measure was mainly designed to allow employers to reduce their financial commitments with their staff, transferring part of these commitments to the state. The main goal of this measure was to alleviate the financial constraints faced by employers and guarantee the maintenance of the work contract during its suspension or the reduction of working hours. Therefore, to be eligible for this benefit, the employer cannot permanently terminate the contract with their workers, except in legally foreseen cases as determined by MP 944. MP 936 was converted into Law 14,020 in July 2020.

MP 963, in contrast to MP 927, created a more robust instrument to promote more flexibility during the pandemic and ensure that employees would not completely lose their income. The income of workers was, nonetheless, deeply affected by the pandemic. Scherer and Marcolino (2020) describe that this instrument foresees the payment of 100% of the salary only in the case of the minimum wage. The higher the worker's income, the lower the benefit received compared to the salary. The authors also highlight that the role of unions in the negotiation of work hours reduction is limited, which can cause deleterious effects for workers. In this sense, even though unions had a crucial role during the pandemic, the regulatory measures adopted in this period gave them a more peripheral role.

In 2020, more than 20 million agreements between employers and employees were registered, affecting almost 10 million workers. Table 1 shows the number of agreements registered for the measure's first four months, divided into economic sectors (Ministério da Economia, 2022).

It is clear from this table that the secondary and tertiary sectors were the most affected by the pandemic.

Finally, it is essential to mention the Emergency Aid Program cited in section four again. The main difference between this programme and these other measures is that it targets the unemployed, self-employed, and informal workers. The Emergency Aid Program encompasses a much larger number of workers than the current legislation regulating unemployment aid, which considers only formal workers. Nevertheless, the regulation still neglects the so-called "gig workers", including app drivers, waiters, tourism guides, and domestic workers. The Government rejected a law proposal to provide such workers with social benefits (Verdélio, 2020).

6 Health Care

6.1 *Health Care Infrastructure: COVID-19 as the Opportunity to Reconcile Social (Universal Health Care) and Economic (Health Industrial Complex) Goals*

Bolsonaro's government became famous as the most anti-scientist and negationist president worldwide. He has denied the gravity of the pandemic crisis, he has been against vaccination and social isolation measures, he has propelled the population to use remedies that have been proved to be ineffective to deal with the coronavirus—such as the hydroxychloroquine. Bolsonaro has changed the health minister four times since the outbreak of the coronavirus crisis due to his disapproval of pro-science statements by the respective ministers.[34] Therefore, as could be projected in such a scenario, the crisis in Brazil has been severe and the country sadly achieved one of the highest positions in the rank of lives lost to covid, both in absolute and relative terms.

However, the collapse could have been much larger if there were not resilient and consolidated health and vaccination policies in the country. Brazil is famous for having the largest health care and vaccination system in the world. The Federal Constitution of 1988 defined health as everyone's right and duty of the State. The main institution to put into practice this normative goal is the Unified Health System (SUS), which follows the guidelines of decentralization, comprehensive care, and popular participation and respects the principles of universality, integrality, and equality established in the Constitution itself, became the largest public health

Table 1 Agreements between employers and employees divided by sector

Sector	*April*	*May*	*June*	*July*
Agriculture	15,796 (0.27%)	12,988 (0.38%)	6289 (0.2%)	7808 (0.25%)
Commercial	1,618,181 (27.28%)	786,978 (22.75%)	764,020 (24.87%)	780,799 (24.93%)
Construction	160,115 (2.70%)	97,578 (2.82%)	59,405 (1.93%)	61,913 (1.98%)
Industry	1,315,215 (22.17%)	932,370 (26.95%)	675,432 (21.98%)	509,433 (16.26%)
Not informed	53,858 (0.91%)	31,173 (0.9%)	17,040 (0.55%)	24,051 (0.77%)
Services	2,769,119 (46.68%)	1,598,633 (46.21%)	1,550,401 (50.46%)	1,748,231 (55.81%)
Total	5,932,284	3,459,720	3,072,587	3,132,235

Source Ministry of Economy (2022)

system in the world, serving about 190 million people, 80% of whom depend exclusively on the system for health care.[35]

No less important is the Brazilian National Immunization Program (PNI), which has been developed since 1973 and is the largest in the world offering 45 different immunobiological to the entire population. According to the Ministry of Health, PNI has vaccines for more than 30 diseases, makes available about 300 million doses annually, and has about 38 thousand vaccination rooms distributed throughout the country.[36]

Nonetheless, as expected in public policies of such dimension and complexity, both the SUS and PNI face different challenges. It is common knowledge that they face underfunding that had become more severe after the liberal fiscal reforms discussed in Sect. 2.1. Rossi and David (2021) show that the growth rate of public spending with health care has been reducing; it grew at an annual average of 5.4% between 2000 and 2012 and at an annual average of 1.0% between 2014 and 2019.

The authors also show throughout simulations the inadequacy of the last fiscal reform—PEC95 of the spending ceiling (*Teto de Gastos*)—to the financing needs of the health system in the country, which triggered a decrease in per capita expenditure in health care. In addition, the increase of the health care system since the 1988 Constitution has been accompanied by an increase in imports and the formation of growing trade deficits, bringing key external vulnerabilities to the system that had been exacerbated by the coronavirus crisis.

In general, the SUS and the PNI have shown important resilience in the coronavirus crisis, even though the system had passed through very difficult moments in which the UTI occupation was totally full and/or even operating on excess capacity. That is not surprising as Brazil is one of the countries that performed worst in terms of COVID cases and deaths. For example, the seven days moving average ratio of new deaths per one million inhabitants in Brazil reached 4.73 on the 100th day after the first death, while it was 0.57 in Argentina and 0.92 in France.[37] It seems to be the case that actions of temporary governments could be terrible enough to make the work of solid institutions very difficult. The study of Touchton et al. (2021) corroborates this argument by empirically showing that opposition governors implemented earlier and more strict sanitary measures than those supporting the Bolsonaro administration.

The COVID-19 crisis demanded coordinated actions between states municipalities and federal government, and between public agencies and private companies. In the absence of a unified federal response, Touchton et al. (2021) show that the States' response was neither homogeneous nor synchronized and that, on average, the social distancing measures were implemented only 45 days after the first case in the country. Indeed, the supreme court had to decentralize decision-making about isolation measures due to the absence of the federal government in acting.

The purchase of personal protective equipment (PPE), testing, and medical equipment was also decentralized, bringing enormous challenges for the acquisition and importation of these products in a context of very tough international competition. Export restrictions were imposed on products essential to the fight against Covid-19, which exposed and accentuated the social and economic vulnerability of the least developed countries and populations (Gadelha et al., 2021). The country faced a shortage of ventilators and a shortage of anesthetics for the intubation of patients. There was no effective policy to test the population. In fact, Brazil's testing rate is only half of the world average and ten times lower than that of developed countries.[38]

During the initial phase of the crisis, vaccination was still a wishful mystery, however, most of the problems related to the health system faced in the first one hundred days are similar to those confronted in the vaccination production latter one: the importance of central coordination, the vulnerability of production structure in the segment and the dependence on imports.

The country had been building important institutional mechanisms to develop its health industrial complex, such as the interministerial "Health Industrial Complex Executive Group (Gecis)" and the Partnerships for Productive Development (PDP) For example, it was the technological capacity of Fiocruz in biopharmaceuticals and Butantan in viral vaccines, built on complex technologies obtained by the PDP instrument that prepared the country to produce vaccines for COVID. However, this coordination and policies had been abandoned by the last two governments, which condemned the development of structures and technological capacity that needs long-term strategies and public policies. That's the reason Gadelha et al. (2021) and Gadelha (2006) urges for the discussion about the possibility of linking the guarantee of universal access to health to a more egalitarian development pattern and argue in favour of the establishment of a structural link between innovation and universal access in the context of the SUS.

Brazil is a very unequal country, and the guarantee of universal health care and the SUS is a very important triumph of the democratic period. Nevertheless, the pandemic has exacerbated the structural inequalities in the country. Rocha et al. (2021) have shown that the existing socioeconomic inequalities (instead of age and other comorbidities) have affected the course of the epidemic with a disproportionate adverse burden on states and municipalities with high socioeconomic vulnerability. Increasing the financing capacity of the system and amplifying the scope of health policies to also embrace the possibility of linking economic and social development throughout a consolidated Health Industrial Complex seems urgent to promote equitable development. Unfortunately, the present government and the last liberal economic reforms are signalizing the opposite direction.

7 Conclusion

The outbreak of the COVID pandemic reinforced multiple trends in the Brazilian economy and democracy that culminated in the current scenario of "stagflation" with an unprecedented level of unemployment, the resurgence of extreme poverty, instability of the democratic institutions, and accumulation of a paramount number of lives lost to the disease.

As examined in this chapter, the Brazilian government's responses to the COVID-19 pandemic went beyond addressing the health crisis or preoccupations with the financial support of companies and households. Instead, the government showed efforts to approve legislation that, under the scrutiny of public debate, would not stand.

Despite Bolsonaro's constant attacks on Brazilian democratic institutions, the beginning of the pandemic initiated strong societal mobilization in various political domains. Civil society organizations and states were crucial actors in the compliance with the measures to contain the spread of the virus and protect the most vulnerable population. In addition, as mentioned above, the Supreme Court had a notable role in balancing power disputes and ensuring constitutional obedience. Moreover, the slow-paced legislative process allowed the society to have enough time to grow awareness of political schemes and prevent some bills from turning into laws after the harshest pandemic periods are gone.

Nonetheless, the outbreak of the COVID-19 forced a significant shift in the direction of economic policies in Brazil. The government and BCB have implemented substantial non-traditional fiscal and monetary policies that, although came with some delay and after pressure from congress and population, were still effective in softening economic crisis and social collapse. However, these economic measures have not been enough to reduce the exacerbation of the structural inequalities of the country caused by the pandemic. Moreover, there is no evidence that the current government is using the COVID-19 crisis as a window of opportunity to overcome structural challenges, such as the strengthening of the health system (including the health industrial complex), the increase of social protection coverage and the search for inclusive and sustainable growth. In fact, the guidelines and projections is that the plan is to restore rigid fiscal consolidation that is incapable to absorb expenses transmitted from the pandemic period.

In the first 100 days of the pandemic, Brazil showed the dangerous consequences of a negligent government. The lack of coordinated actions between the federal government and states in addition to the politicization of the pandemic only aggravated the health and economic crises. Moreover, the case of Brazil shows how structural inequality permeated policy responses, deepening the gap between the rich and poor. It is expected that these first 100 days will strongly influence the 2022 elections and future policy-making decisions.

Notes

1. SUPREMO TRIBUNAL FEDERAL. (2022). ADI 6855, Available at: *Portal.Stf.Jus.Br*. https://portal.stf.jus.br/processos/detalhe.asp?incidente=6187929, accessed on April 28.
2. A crucial tool for searching Supreme Court decisions regarding Covid-19 policies are available at: Resumo COVID ADI. (2022). Retrieved 28 April, from https://portal.stf.jus.br/textos/verTexto.asp?servico=resumocovid&pagina=resumocovid_adi.
3. Different legislative documents addressed how vulnerable groups would receive government subsidies during the pandemic, see Ordinary Law 13,982, available at: http://www.planalto.gov.br/ccivil_03/_ato2019-2022/2020/lei/l13982.htm, retrieved 28 April 2022.
4. See Hur, Domênico Uhng, José Manuel Sabucedo Cameselle, and Mónica Alzate. (2021). "Bolsonaro e Covid-19: negacionismo, militarismo e neoliberalismo." Revista Psicología Política 21(51): 550–569.
5. A term that finds translation in Agamben's work on monastic life as a hybrid state that does not satisfy a juridical or a moral commandment. See AGAMBEN, Giorgio. (2017). Homo Sacer IV, 1. The Highest

Poverty: "Monastic Rules and Form-of-Life. In The Omnibus Homo Sacer, Stanford: at University Press, pp. 917–1010.

6. Article 21, item X and XVIII, of the 1988's Brazilian Constitution.
7. Budgetary responsibility law establishes limits on public expenditures addressed to the Union, municipalities and states that compose the Brazilian Federation. See CONGRESSO NACIONAL. (2022) Lei Complementar 101. available at: *Planalto.Gov.Br*. http://www.planalto.gov.br/ccivil_03/leis/lcp/lcp101.htm, accessed on April 28.
8. One of the essential aspects of the declaration resonates with public spending, as demonstrated in the following Supreme Court's holding decided in a case initiated to prevent Executive cutting on a massive welfare program entitled Bolsa Família. See ACO 3359 MC-Ref, Relatora: MARCO AURÉLIO, Tribunal Pleno, julgado em 05/08/2020, PROCESSO ELETRÔNICO DJe-215 DIVULG 27–08-2020 PUBLIC 28–08-2020. *Pesquisa de jurisprudência - STF* (2022). Available at: https://jurisprudencia.stf.jus.br/pages/search/sjur429900/false, accessed on 2 May 2022.
9. Those limiting measures the President can proclaim encompasses defence, siege, or federal intervention (art. 49, IV, Brazilian Constitution).
10. Articles 23, II, and 198, I of the Constitution of the Republic.
11. According to article 65 of the Fiscal Responsibility Law.
12. Legislative Decree 06/2020.
13. Those issues listed below follow a path corresponding to the Coup d'État unfolding consequences after former President Dilma's impeachment. See Santana, Carlos Henrique Vieira. (2018). "The geopolitics of the Brazilian coup d'état and its consequences." *Transcience* 9(1): 75–110.
14. L14026. Planalto.Gov.Br, 2022, http://www.planalto.gov.br/ccivil_03/_ato2019-2022/2020/lei/l14026.htm, accessed 28 April 2022.
15. See Câmara dos Deputados. PL 191/2020. Available at: https://www.camara.leg.br/propostas-legislativas/2236765, accessed 28 April 2022.
16. See Portal da Câmara dos Deputados. Projeto de lei 2633/2020. Available at Camara.Leg.Br. https://www.camara.leg.br/proposicoesWeb/fichadetramitacao?idProposicao=2252589, accessed 28 April 2022.
17. Action 6421 filed before the Supreme Court discussed the President's possibility of overcoming a constitutional provision concerning the civil responsibility of public agents. Supremo Tribunal Federal. Available at: https://portal.stf.jus.br/processos/detalhe.asp?incidente=5912207, accessed 28 April 2022. for a comprehensive compilation of cases decided by the Court during the pandemic, see (2022) *Stf.jus.br*. Available at: https://www.stf.jus.br/repositorio/cms/portalStfInternacional/portalStfAgenda_en_us/anexo/case_law_compilation_covid19.pdf, accessed 2 May 2022.

18. Zanatta, R., Bioni, B., Keller, C., & Favaro, I. (2020). The Data and the Virus. *Revista Brasileira De Direitos Fundamentais & Justiça*, *14*(1), 231–256. https://doi.org/10.30899/dfj.v14i1.1031. p. 238.
19. HEUSI, Tálita Rodrigues. (2016) Perfil criminal como prova pericial no Brasil. *Brazilian Journal of Forensic Sciences, Medical Law and Bioethics*, Itajaí, 5(3), 232–250.
20. STAPLES, William G. 2007. *Encyclopedia of privacy*. Westport: Greenwood Press, 93. Comments: "*Key issues in the debate over the authority to violate personal privacy concern racial or ethnic profiling, wiretapping, monitoring of personal communications* via *cellular telephones, access to personal records that show the reading habits of private citizens, monitoring of electronic mail and other Internet use, monitoring of personal movement* via *the Global Positioning System (GPS), and the use of radio frequency identification (RFID) chips to track the movement of pets, personal goods, and shipped items, among others*".
21. FROOMKIN, A. Michael. (2000). The death of privacy? *Stanford Law Review*, Stanford, v. 32, 1461–1544, p. 1465. Diz: "*That surveillance technologies threaten privacy may not be breaking news, but the extent to which these technologies will soon allow watchers to permeate modem life still has the power to shock. Nor is it news that the potential effect of citizen profiling is vastly increased by the power of information processing and the linking of distributed databases. We are still in the early days of data mining, consumer profiling, and DNA databasing, to name only a few. The cumulative and accelerating effect of these developments, however, has the potential to transform modem life in all industrialized countries. Unless something happens to counter these developments, it seems likely that soon all but the most radical privacy freaks may live in the informational equivalent of a goldfish bowl*".
22. CLARKE, Roger A. (1988). *Information technology and dataveillance. Communications of the ACM*, Nova Iorque, 31(5), 498–512.
23. More details at: https://www.saopaulo.sp.gov.br/noticias-coronavirus/governo-de-sp-apresenta-sistema-de-monitoramento-inteligente-contra-coronavirus/, accessed 17 March 2020.
24. MAGENTA, Matheus. (2020) Coronavírus: governo brasileiro vai monitorar celulares para conter pandemia. *BBC News Brasil*, 3 abr. Disponível em: https://www.bbc.com/portuguese/brasil-52154128. Acesso em: 17 abr. The data which were reported as "a layer above personal data" were anonymized.
25. ROMANI, Bruno. (2020). Uso de dados de localização no combate à covid-19 pode ameaçar privacidade. *O Estado de S. Paulo*, 12 abr. Disponível em: https://link.estadao.com.br/noticias/cultura-digital,uso-de-dados-de-localizacao-no-combate-a-covid-19-pode-ameacar-privacida de,70003268063, accessed 17 March 2020. Defines anonymized data to LGPD, art. 5. ... *omissis*... III—anonymised data: data relating to

a holder who cannot be identified, considering the use of reasonable technical means available at the time of its treatment.

26. DONEDA, Danilo. (2020) A proteção de dados em tempos de coronavírus: a LGPD será um elemento fundamental para a reestruturação que advirá após a crise. *Jota*, 25 mar. Disponível em: https://www.jota.info/opiniao-e-analise/artigos/a-protecao-de-dados-em-tempos-de-coronavirus-25032020. Acesso em: 10 abr. 2020.
27. O BENTHAM, Jeremy. (1995) Panopticon letters. *In:* BOŽOVIČ, Miran (Ed.). *Jeremy Bentham*: the panopticon writings. Londres: Verso, p. 29.
28. LOS, Maria. (2006). Looking into the future: surveillance, globalization and the totalitarian potential. *In:* LYON, David (Ed.). *Theorizing surveillance*: the panopticon and beyond. Portland: Willan Publishing, 81.
29. Article 2, item II, Brazilian Law protection personal data).
30. Indeed, the growth of the country's population would represent a decrease in real public expenditure per capita.
31. Calculus based on The World Bank Open Data (https://data.worldbank.org/).
32. Calculus based on The World Bank Open Data (https://data.worldbank.org/).
33. It is possible to track the timeline of the economic policies implemented by the Ministry of Economics at https://www.gov.br/economia/pt-br/centrais-de-conteudo/publicacoes/boletins/covid-19/timeline?b_start:int=30.
34. https://www.nytimes.com/2020/05/15/world/americas/brazil-health-minister-bolsonaro.html.
35. Figures extracted from the National Health Council: http://www.conselho.saude.gov.br/web_sus20anos/sus.html.
36. https://portal.fiocruz.br/noticia/programa-nacional-de-imunizacoes-comemora-48-anos.
37. Calculus based on data from World Health Organization (WHO).
38. https://noticias.uol.com.br/colunas/jamil-chade/2022/01/28/brasil-so-testa-058-a-cada-mil-habitantes-por-dia-metade-da-media-mundial.htm.

References

Abriani, N., Caselli, G. C., Celotto, A., Marzio, F., Masini, S. and Tremonti, G. (2020) Il Diritto e l'eccezione: Stress Economico in Tempi di Emergenza. Roma: Donzelli editore.

Ackerman, B. (2008) Before the Next Attack. New Haven: Yale University Press.

Adamo Idoeta, P. (2021) A história de Bolsonaro com a hidroxicloroquina em 6 pontos: de tuítes de Trump à CPI da Covid. BBC News Brasil, https://www.bbc.com/portuguese/brasil-57166743, accessed 13 May 2022.

Agamben, G. (2017) Homo Sacer IV. The Highest Poverty: Monastic Rules and Form-of-Life. Stanford: Stanford University Press.

Barbosa, R. and Prates, I. (2020) Efeitos do Desemprego, do Auxílio Emergencial e do Programa Emergencial de Preservação do Emprego e da Renda (MP 936): Sobre a Renda, a Pobreza e a Desigualdade Durante e Depois da Pandemia. Mercado de Trabalho 69, https://doi.org/10.38116/bmt69/notastecnicas2

Bonavides, P. and Andrade, P. (2003) História constitucional do Brasil. Porto: Universidade Portucalense.

Campos, A. (2020) IBGE: informalidade atinge 41,6% dos trabalhadores no país em 2019. Agência Brasil. https://agenciabrasil.ebc.com.br/economia/noticia/2020-11/ibge-informalidade-atinge-416-dos-trabalhadores-no-pais-em-2019, accessed 13 May 2022.

Clarke, R. A. (1988) Information technology and dataveillance. Communications of the ACM 31(5): 498–512.

Cogliolo, P. (1917) Legislazione di Guerra nel Diritto Civile e Commerciale con una parte speciale sopra la colpa, i danni, la forza maggiore. Raccolta completa di tutti i decreti-legge in rapporto al Diritto Privato. Seconda edizione. Torino: Unione Tipografico-editrice Torinese.

Cucinotta, M. and Vanelli, D. (2020) WHO Declares COVID-19 a pandemic. Acta Bio-Medica: Atenei Parmensis 91(1): 157–160.

Duque, D. (2020) Auxílio Emergencial Para de Crescer em Agosto, e Pobreza Cai de Novo. Blog do Ibre, https://blogdoibre.fgv.br/Posts/Auxilio-Emergencial-Para-de-Crescer-Em-Agosto-e-Pobreza-Cai-Denovo-Com-Reducao-Do-Beneficio, accessed 13 May 2022.

Froomkin, A. M. (2000) The death of privacy? Stanford Law Review 32: 1461–1544.

Gadelha, C. A. (2006) Desenvolvimento, Complexo Industrial Da Saúde e Política Industrial. Revista de Saúde Pública 40 (spe): 11–23.

Gadelha, C. A., Kamia F. D., Moreira, J., Montenegro K., Safatle, L. and Nascimento, M. (2021) Dinâmica Global, Impasses Do SUS e o CEIS Como Saída Estruturante Da Crise. Cadernos Do Desenvolvimento 16(28): 281–302.

Gonçalves, R., Nascimento, J. C., Oliveira, A. A., Michelman, C., Guidolin, A. P. and Melo, G. (2021) Impactos Do Auxílio Emergencial Na Renda e No Índice de Gini. Nota de Conjuntura 16. https://www.eco.unicamp.br/covid19/nota-impactos-do-auxilio-emergencial-na-renda-e-no-indice-de-gini, accessed 13 May 2022.

Guimarães, F. (2021) Cerca de 11,4 milhões de brasileiros dependem de aplicativos para ter uma renda. CNN Brasil. https://www.cnnbrasil.com.br/business/cerca-de-11-4-milhoes-de-brasileiros-dependem-de-aplicativos-para-ter-uma-renda/, accessed 13 May 2022.

Heusi, T. R. (2016) Perfil criminal como prova pericial no Brasil. Brazilian Journal of Forensic Sciences, Medical Law and Bioethics 5(3): 232–250.

Horta, R. M. (1958) Perspectivas do federalismo brasileiro, Vol. 2. Universidade de Minas Gerais.

Hur, D. U., Sabucedo Cameselle, J. M. and Alzate, M. (2021) Bolsonaro e Covid-19: negacionismo, militarismo e neoliberalismo. Revista Psicología Política 21(51): 550–569.

Instituto Brasileiro de Geografia e Estatística. (2021) Pesquisa Nacional por Amostra de Domicílios Contínua – PNAD Contínua, https://www.ibge.gov.br/estatisticas/sociais/trabalho/9171-pesquisa-nacional-por-amostra-de-domicilios-continua-mensal.html?edicao=32820&t=series-historicas, accessed 13 May 2022.

Leite, K. (2020) A Esperada Pandemia E Suas Implicações Para O Mundo Do Trabalho. Psicologia & Sociedade, 32. https://doi.org/10.1590/1807-0310/2020v32240215

Los, M. (2006) Looking into the future: surveillance, globalization and the totalitarian potential. In: D. Lyon (Ed.) Theorizing Surveillance: The Panopticon and Beyond. Portland: Willan Publishing, p. 81.

Manzano, M. and Krein, A. (2020) A pandemia e o trabalho de motoristas e de entregadores por aplicativos no Brasil. Campinas: Cesit/Unicamp.

Manzano, M., Krein, J. D. and Abílio, L. C. (2021) The Dynamics of Labor Informality in Brazil, 2003–2019. Global Labour Journal 12(3): 227–243. https://doi.org/10.15173/glj.v12i3.4434.

Ministry of Economy. (2022) Painel de Informações sobre o Benefício Emergencial de Preservação do Emprego e da Renda (Bem). https://app.powerbi.com/view?r=eyJrIjoiMGUxYTljODgtNjkzYy00YmJmLWExMzEtMWU4YzNmNThhOWNiIiwidCI6IjNlYzkyOTY5LTVhNTEtNGYxOC04YWM5LWVmOThmYmFmYTk3OCJ9, accessed 13 May 2022.

O Bentham, J. (1995) Panopticon letters. In: M. Božovič (Ed.) Jeremy Bentham: The Panopticon Writings. Londres: Verso.

Oliva, G. (2021) 251 mil mortes por covid: Relembre as falas de Bolsonaro sobre a pandemia. Poder 360, https://www.poder360.com.br/governo/251-mil-mortes-por-covid-relembre-as-falas-de-bolsonaro-sobre-a-pandemia, accessed 13 May 2022.

Paiva, L. H., Bartholo, L., De Souza, P. H. and Orair, R. O. (2021) A Reformulação Das Transferências de Renda No Brasil: Simulações e Desafios. IPEA Texto para Discussão 2701.

Paula, L. F. (2021) The COVID-19 crisis and counter-cyclical policies in Brazil. European Journal of Economics and Economic Policies 18(2): 177–197. https://doi.org/10.4337/ejeep.2021.02.06.

Pires, L. N., de Carvalho, L. B. and Rawet, E. L. (2021) Multi-Dimensional Inequality and Covid-19 in Brazil. Investigación Económica 80(315): 33–58.

Rocha, R., Atun, R., Massuda, A., Rache, B., Spinola, P., Nunes, L., Lago, M. and Castro, M. (2021) Effect of socioeconomic inequalities and vulnerabilities on health-system preparedness and response to COVID-19 in Brazil: a comprehensive analysis. The Lancet Global Health 9(6): 782–792. https://doi.org/10.1016/S2214-109X(21)00081-4.

Rossi, P. and David, G. (2021) Execução Orçamentária Na Pandemia e o Futuro Do Financiamento Público Da Saúde. Cadernos Do Desenvolvimento 16(28): 267–280.

Santana, C. (2018) The geopolitics of the Brazilian coup d'état and its consequences. Transcience 9(1): 75–110.

Scherer, C. and Marcolino, A. (2020) O Programa Emergencial de Manutenção do Emprego e da Renda diante dos impactos da Covid-19. Revista Ciências do Trabalho 17.

Silva, J. (1984) Curso de direito constitucional positivo. Sao Paulo: Malheiros Editores.

Soares, F. V. and Orair, R. O. (2021) Política Fiscal e Proteção Social na Resposta à COVID-19: Da Resposta Emergencial à Recuperação Econômica. Revista Tempo Do Mundo 26: 67–102. https://doi.org/10.38116/rtm26art2.

Soares, I. (2021) Bolsonaro volta a atacar jornalistas: "Ridículo, nasça de novo". Correio Braziliense, https://www.correiobraziliense.com.br/politica/2021/06/4933688-bolsonaro-volta-a-atacar-jornalistas-ridiculo-nasca-de-novo.html, accessed 13 May 2022.

Staples, W. G. (2007) Encyclopedia of Privacy. Westport: Greenwood Press.

Supremo Tribunal Federal. (2020) Tramitação da ADI 6341. http://portal.stf.jus.br/processos/detalhe.asp?incidente=5880765, accessed February 25 2022.

Touchton, M., Knaul, F. M., Arreola-Ornelas, H., Porteny, T., Sánchez, M., Méndez, O. and Faganello, M. (2021) A Partisan Pandemic: State Government Public Health Policies to Combat COVID-19 in Brazil. BMJ Global Health 6(6): e005223. https://doi.org/10.1136/BMJGH-2021-005223.

Verdélio A. (2020) Guedes confirma prorrogação do auxílio emergencial por dois meses. Agência Brasil. https://agenciabrasil.ebc.com.br/economia/noticia/2020-06/guedes-confirma-prorrogacao-do-auxilio-emergencial-por-dois-meses, accessed 13 May 2022.

Zanatta, R., Bioni, B., Keller, C. and Favaro, I. (2020) The Data and the Virus. Revista Brasileira De Direitos Fundamentals & Justiça 14(1): 231–256. https://doi.org/10.30899/dfj.v14i1.1031.

The Deepening of an Economic and Political Crisis: The First 100 Days of COVID-19 in Chile

Javiera Rojas, Luis Cortés, José Ledesma, and Javiera Toro

1 Introduction

Since the end of the Military Dictatorship on 11 March 1990, Chile experienced constant economic growth during the early 1990s and after a brief interruption following the impact of the Asian crisis. The increase in economic growth was mainly driven by the appropriation of extraordinary income in the form of land rent[1] from mining; as well as rent from the agrarian, forestry, and fishing sectors, though in smaller portions (Rivas and Kornblihtt, 2017; Rivas and Seiffer, 2021). This process of growth through rent seeking was directed by political personnel linked to the

J. Rojas (✉)
University of Buenos Aires, Buenos Aires, Argentina
e-mail: jrojas@campus.ungs.edu.ar

L. Cortés
Freie Universität Berlin, Berlin, Germany

J. Ledesma · J. Toro
University of Chile, Santiago, Chile
e-mail: jose.ledesma@ug.uchile.cl

A. Stojanović et al. (eds.), *The First 100 Days of Covid-19*,
https://doi.org/10.1007/978-981-19-6325-4_15

forces that drove the plebiscite to end the Military Dictatorship that had administered the Chilean State for 17 years. Over the next 30 years after the end of the Military Dictatorship, a series of focalized policies of state subsidies were enforced that enabled a fragmented reproduction of the Chilean working class, as a consequence of a national industry which was destroyed during the decade of the 1980s towards a reorganization of the production around natural resource exports (Díaz, 1989; Moguillansky, 1990).

However, in contrast with these previous decades, during the last years of the 2010s the reproduction of the working class showed a relative stagnation in terms of salary and quality of life, driven by the fall of the copper price and the subsequent depreciation of the local currency, which had a general effect in the profitability of the capitals in the entire economy. This general crisis led to the outbreak of the "October Revolt" of 2019, a mass mobilization process that started in October 2019 triggered by a hike in the price of public transport price in Santiago, which involved mass working-class demonstrations and daily street confrontations with police forces to demand better living conditions. The response by the government of Sebastián Piñera was militarized repression in the streets, which extended the unrest into a generalized critique of the 30 yearspost-dictatorship system and precipitated the fall of Sebastián Piñera's government into a deep political crisis. This culminated in a parliamentary agreement to draft a new political Constitution to replace the 1980 Constitution, which has been in place since the Pinochet dictatorship. The civil unrest, however, continued even after this event.

The impact of the COVID-19 pandemic and the response adopted by the government administration and the Chilean working class is linked to this social, political, and economic crisis. The balance of political forces between the government, the institutional opposition and the millions of non-institutionalized groups and spontaneous demonstrators in the streets that crafted the agreement for a new Constitution was radically transformed by the pandemic, giving grounds for the government to: enforce an economic adjustment program; implement martial law restricting free movement; and engage in a tug-of-war over the constituent process.

As we will show, the emergency pandemic measures enforced by the government during the initial shockwave of COVID-19, between May 2020 and the first weeks of July of 2020, had a continuity with its pre-pandemic program. This could be effectively implemented with limited effective opposition by the parliament given the extraordinary constitutional emergency powers, and by the mass demonstrations that were limited by the pandemic situation. All of this while the government still maintained a very high disapproval rating (González, 2020). For the former, we will specially highlight the more relevant policy areas: economic growth, employment and pensions and social security.

After contextualizing the outbreak of the COVID-19 pandemic in Chile, the rest of the chapter is structured as follows: In the second section, we provide a more specific historical narrative of the October Revolt and how it relates to the prior years of institutional development, in order to provide background to the policy decisions that were made and how they were perceived by the population. In the third section, we provide an account of the forms in which the necessities of state-controlled surveillance were an instrument against the mass mobilizations, while facing strong questioning by the public and by scientific organizations. In the fourth section, we consider the continuity between the adjustment economic policies adopted by Sebastian Piñera's administration pre and post pandemic, to show that there was a continuity between both as part of a longer profitability crisis of the local capital. As such, we will show how a strong emphasis was put over currency stability and Small and medium-sized enterprises (SME) liquidity over worker's welfare. In the fifth section, we focus on the labor policy objectives along this trajectory showing how they were a part of the economic policies to subsidize local capital, cheapening salary and layoff costs through spending from the social security funds. In the sixth section we consider the specific dynamic of the private pension system before and after the pandemic, and we explain how it was dismantled to finance workers' subsistence had an important political weight over the discussions between "neoliberal" versus "statist" alternatives.

We conclude by summarizing the different forms in which policy making reflected the same approach used before the COVID-19 pandemic, as the expression of an economic, political, and social crisis that took several years in the making. In this context, the catastrophe allowed the State to enforce economic adjustment and political control policies that would have been impossible under other conditions. Thus, it was a deepening of the same contradictions that triggered the October Revolt and not a radical shift from them.

2 Democracy and Civil Activism

2.1 State of the Nation Pre-COVID-19

When the Covid-19 pandemic reached Chile, the country was in a deep political and social crisis due to a loss of legitimacy and trust in the political, social, and economic system, that had been on the rise over the past 30 years. Since the early 2000s, there has been growing social mobilization against the dictatorial legacy raised by different sectors such as: students; native peoples; environmental and feminist movements; which finally converged in the October Revolt.

As a result of these mobilizations, at the beginning of 2020 the country was on the verge of a constituent plebiscite, resulting from a parliamentary agreement between the main opposition parties and the right-wing government parties (Cámara de Diputados, 2019). This was a historic milestone for social movements and left-wing sectors that sought to end the dictatorial Constitution in force since 1980.

For this reason, a large part of the Chilean population was mobilized and politically active prior to the arrival of the pandemic, as public confidence in the government of President Sebastián Piñera was already at rock bottom (González, 2020). Broadly speaking, the politically active population acted through two forms of organizations. Firstly, through groups which had an institutional perspective and demands that existed prior to the Revolt, which included the Communist Party and the new left wing political parties associated with the *Frente Amplio* coalition (*Revolución Democrática*, *Convergencia Social*, *Comunes* and *Partido Liberal*). Secondly, through organizations that raised specific interests or demands such as trade union federations like the Central Unitaria de Trabajadores (or CUT, by its Spanish acronym); as well as organizations with specific demands such as No + AFP (pensions) or the Chilean Confederation of Student Federations (CONFECH). However, a big part of the activism came from small, grassroots, independent organizations outside the institutional framework: territorial assemblies and town councils, along with assistance and solidarity organizations: professional assistance brigades (medical, legal, etc.) against state repression, the so-called "front line" which organized the direct struggle with *Carabineros* (Chilean police), etc. All these groups defined themselves in open rejection and opposition to political parties and the State apparatus, remaining sometimes just as small local organizations, or coordinating as federations or as larger networks. Many organizations also existed on a spectrum between these two.[2]

However, the pandemic changed the existing balance of power, allowing the government to intervene in economic adjustment measures and apply martial law restricting free movement. Furthermore, it was necessary to reschedule the constituent plebiscite (Reyes et al., 2020).[3]

2.2 Democracy and Legal Challenges in a Post Pandemic Age

In Chile, there are mainly three statutes that provide extraordinary powers to the administrative authority and the armed forces. All of them were used as a response to the pandemic.

Firstly, on 8 February 2020, a Health Alert was issued by executive decision (Decree No. 4/2020). It granted the Health Authority (that is: the Health Minister, his local representatives (SEREMIs, Secretarios Regionales Ministeriales) and the Director of the Institute of Public Health, in accordance with article 5 of the Sanitary Code) extraordinary powers to carry out public health actions (Abujatum et al., 2020). Initially, the Health Alert was issued for one year, but it has been successively extended and is now in force until 31 March 2021 by Decrees No. 1/2020, 24/2021, 39/2012 and 52/2021.

The law that allows the issuing of a Health Alert (Sanitary Code Art. 36) does not specify which are the "extraordinary powers" that are given to the Health Authority; therefore, the content of this emergency statute has been defined by the Chilean institutions in the administrative decisions adopted in periods of emergency. This wide administrative discretion comes from the medical and scientific consensus that influenced the institutional design built during the twentieth century in response to pandemics and natural tragedies (López and Beltrán, 2013).

Secondly, on 18 March 2020, a state of emergency called "Constitutional State of Catastrophe" was declared by the President in all 16 regions of the country (Supreme Decree No. 104/2020). This is an exclusive presidential prerogative (Constitution Art. 41) that has to be reported to the National Congress.[4] The State of Catastrophe was issued at first by a term of 90 days, extended for an additional term of 90 days (Decree No. 269/2020) (Ministerio del Interior y Seguridad Pública, 2020).[5]

The State of Catastrophe gives the President powers to restrict freedoms of movement and assembly, as well as to requisition assets, limit property rights and adopt extraordinary administrative measures (Constitution Art. 43). Under this statute, the President must name a military chief—Chief of National Defense—for each disaster area, to whom he may delegate his exceptional powers (Organic Act of Exception States Art. 6).

According to the State of Catastrophe, Chiefs of National Defense took command of both armed forces and police forces in each region, for the purposes of ensuring public order and to face the effects of the catastrophe. These military chiefs have powers to control entrance and exit and traffic in each region, and also to dictate measures to protect public services, mining operations, and industries, among others. They can also order the storage of food reserves and goods, control the entry and exit of such goods from the region they command and distribute them among the population. As well, they can dictate instructions regarding the catastrophe to any official of the state, public companies, or municipalities.

The third emergency law used to confront the pandemic was the Earthquake and Catastrophe Act, when the President declared a Disaster Area on 23 March 2020 (Supreme Decree No. 107/2020) in all the 346 communes—or *comunas* in Spanish, the smallest local structure in Chile—of the country. This gave the local authorities flexibility on financial and administrative rules. The declaration of Disaster Area was initially issued for twelve months, but was later extended for six additional months (Supreme Decree No. 76/2021).

The application of these three emergency statutes was exclusively through Government decisions, subject only to an *ex ante* legality check by an autonomous government body called the General Comptroller of the Republic (CGR, *Contraloría General de la República*).[6]

Despite the above, the main exceptional powers attributed to the executive branch have its legal ground in the Health Alert Decree, and they are taken by the Health Ministry without any type of legal control (exempt resolutions, *resoluciones exentas*). Indeed, since 30 September 2021, when the Constitutional State of Catastrophe ceased, the curfew and quarantine measures were ended, but there were still several restrictions to movement and freedom of assembly in place.

During the pandemic, the powers granted by Decree No. 4/2020 were expanded through ten decrees issued during the past two years: Decrees No. 6/2020, 10/2020, 18/2020, 19/2020, 21/2020, 23/2020, 24/2020, 28/2020, 12/2021, and 38/2021. These included the power to impose the use of masks and other elements of protection, close shops, and workplaces, suspend schools and massive events, impose isolation measures, prohibit entry into the country of foreigners, and close internal borders. Likewise, the Health Ministry could impose limitations on the private sector, with price fixation to medicines and health supplies, the control of hoarding and taking control of private health facilities. In the public health system, there was administrative easing to contract and public procurement rules. Control of these measures is carried out by the military and police forces under each Chief of National Defense. Enforcement relies on a combination of purposes imposed by the health authority and criminal action, which can lead to imprisonment, especially in cases of recidivism.

According to these powers, a national curfew was in force from 22 March 2020 to 30 September 2021. Additionally, massive quarantines and serious restrictions on freedoms of movement and assembly were decreed. Since July 2020, a gradual strategy was applied to respond to the health situation of each area of the country ("*Plan Paso a Paso*", Step by Step Plan).[7]

Due to the centralization of political power, the decision-making in the pandemic response had fallen on the national Government and was not consulted with local authorities. However, the political conflict between the national Government and some mayors was relevant before the pandemic. When the Government was being criticized for delaying isolation measures, the decision of some mayors to suspend schools and close shopping centers (even this last measure was out of their competence in accordance to Opinion No. 8935/20 of the Comptroller), forced the national Government to decree the suspension of classes nationwide and quarantines in some territories (Caro and Fernández, 2020).

As seen, the Health Authority has wide powers for taking measures that restrict personal rights and freedoms to control the pandemic. Regarding judicial control, the Supreme Court has sustained an extreme administrative deference to authority, based on article 45 of the Constitution that prevents courts from qualifying the foundations of the state of exception. These decisions have been criticized because they are founded in a misconception that overlooks the fact that most measures are not founded in the Constitutional State of Catastrophe. Instead, they are decisions of the Health Authority under the Health Alert (Cordero, 2020). During 2021, the Supreme Court kept this broad deference and low control of the legality of the Health Authority decisions. However, it exercised control in some exceptional cases. In particular, in the face of unequal treatment in economic matters and in cases related to freedom of worship (Cordero, 2021).

From a social perspective, at first, the State of Catastrophe was not popularly opposed. On the contrary, the Government was strongly criticized by civil society for not adopting measures in a timely manner (El Mostrador, 2020e). Even some judicial actions were held to require the authorities to establish quarantines (Figueroa, 2020). When the Government announced an early "safe return" plan to reopen public services, public official's union strongly opposed (Navarrete, 2020). Nevertheless, in working class neighborhoods mobility never decreased as expected due to the continuity of many industries and the need to work for many informal workers (ISCI, 2020).

The limits of the government's relief policies were the starting point for the collective action during this period, in order to supply indispensable necessities which were not covered by the State. Thus, a series of collective initiatives were organized such as *ollas comunes* (self-managed community food services), collective goods purchases, donation centres and sanitation brigades. All these instances acted independently from the government, grouped under broader organizations of a territorial nature throughout the country which started during the October revolt. Given the expansion of activities associated with reproduction, together with the growing number of women leaving the labor market in this context, it is not surprising that the presence of women was now predominant here (Cisternas, 2020).

It was because of this precariousness that in mid-May 2020, protests reappeared in popular neighborhoods. These protests were not against the extraordinary measures, but against poverty and hunger (BBC Mundo, 2020), demanding greater economic relief measures to be able to implement social distancing and isolation (Cooperativa, 2020; Delgado, 2020; El Desconcierto, 2020b; Zamorano, 2020).

With the extension of the sanitary restrictions—especially the wide-nation curfew—questions began to arise regarding the authoritarian drift of the Government during COVID-19 crisis (El Mostrador, 2020a). Significant restrictions on rights of movement and assembly are generally accepted as necessary to control the pandemic. However, COVID-19 crisis coincided with a serious human rights crisis since the social outbreak of October 2019 (Arellano et al., 2019). With the return of popular protests, police repression increased. Thus, the COVID-19 pandemic was an opportunity for the government to increase the military presence and to expand its repressive agenda.

Regarding women rights, quarantines brought an increase in domestic violence without sufficient protection measures. Also, an increase in abuse was reported against highly vulnerable groups, such as domestic workers, migrant women and Mapuche women (Presidencia del Senado, 2020), as well as sex workers (Freixas, 2020). Also, the prison situation—already below human rights standards– worsened due to the absence of measures to control the spread of Covid (El Mostrador, 2020b).

Likewise, an authoritarian deepening in national governance has been noted. The Government intended to fast track an intelligence Bill that increased the Executive's repressive powers and would allow armed forces to take control of public order (El Mostrador, 2020c). Moreover, during the pandemic military presence has increased in Biobío and Araucanía, where the Mapuche people have been in a long struggle with the State and forest industry (Fuentes, 2020; Resumen, 2020; El Mostrador, 2022).

Ultimately, as a consequence of the economic crisis, the social crisis caused by the State's inability to ensure minimum fundamental rights—such as health, housing, and food—has deepened (Aylwin and Morales, 2020; Fries, 2020; Said and Astudillo, 2020), as discussed below.

3 Surveillance and Security

3.1 *Pre-COVID-19 Surveillance and Security*

Chile was already in a big political crisis since the October revolt. A raise in the public transport fare of the capital announced by Sebastian Piñera's administration escalated into a series of student demonstrations through mass payment evasion of the transport fare by jumping over the turnstiles in the subway Stations. The Executive ordered a mass occupation by the militarized police units (*Fuerzas Especiales*), which in turn triggered a mass response by the Santiago working class that eventually extended to the whole country. The government, in turn, answered with a country-wide Martial Law and lockdown enforced by military troops, which was heavily rejected and actively resisted by the population as it brought to memory the times of Pinochet's Military Dictatorship. The military troops had to be withdrawn shortly after, and from that day forward the Chilean security forces had been overrun. Street confrontations between citizens and the Chilean police were a daily occurrence, which also resulted in the occupation by protestors of the central urban spaces such as Plaza de la Dignidad (formerly known as Plaza Baquedano).

In contrast with the above, the restriction of free movement, the closing of working places and the lockdown of international borders would be heavily resisted by Sebastian Piñera's administration, as these were obstacles to an open border economy and free trade policies. This explains why until patient zero had been detected in Chile (3 March), the only measure taken by the government against limiting the spread of the virus was a mandatory declaration of one's health condition as a requirement to enter the country (27 February).

3.2 Surveillance and Militarization as a Political Tool

The first measure that was imposed to restrict movement was a lockdown of international borders, enforced since 17 March. Along with this, the first restrictions were imposed over the right of reunion: first were for public or private events with more than 200 people (16 March), and then up to a 50 people limit (24 March). Also, since 20 March the government mandated the shutdown of theaters, cinemas, pubs, discotheques, cabarets, gyms open to the public and restaurants and similar establishments (Resolution No. 200 of the Undersecretary of Public Health).

On 23 March a national curfew was announced, which imposed a restriction of movement between 10 p.m. and 5 a.m. Lockdowns were later introduced, which were all-day movement restrictions declared only for specific territories. The specific territory affected could have been a region (the main territory division), an urban space, a commune (district), or even a part of a commune, which created logistical problems for commutation and public transport routes, especially in cases of big cities. In any case, even general lockdowns were always more permissive than curfews, so on the same day different lockdown regimes could coexist. The complexity of this general lockdown strategy was referred to by the government as "dynamic lockdowns" and was criticized as one of the main flaws of the government's strategy to face the pandemic. The first lockdown of this kind in continental territory was declared on 22 March, and the most important one, affecting the city of Santiago as a whole, was enforced on 15 May.

This general lockdown strategy was also complemented with sanitary customs and cordons. Sanitary customs ("Aduanas Sanitarias") were checkpoints that controlled the movement of the population in highways to prevent the circulation of infected people and the enforcement of general measures. These measures were usual in the first phases of the spread. However, due to the reticence from the government to implement a general lockdown, the sanitary customs were replaced with sanitary cordons ("Cordones sanitarios") which entailed: border controls around cities that forbid the population from going in or out of specific territories. The sanitary cordons were widely used to prevent the movement of the population during holidays such as Holy week.

However, the attitude against government action was ambivalent in this sense. Despite some reluctance to comply with the restrictions, the Chilean working class also mobilized to demand stronger restrictions to movement and the closing of workplaces, especially in sectors where home office was not possible. The first organized responses came from workers of the retail sector, which on 17 March began to organize a series of protests calling for the closure of shopping centers. This was followed by protests in regions calling for the imposition of strict sanitary checkpoints, particularly in towns and cities with a high rotation of workers from mining and salmon farming industries, as well as in territories that normally receive a high influx of tourists, such as in several coastal towns that barricaded before the *semana santa* holidays on 21 March (Cerda, Reyes and Navarrete, 2020), or later in the island of Chiloé (25 March).

Prison inmates were another active actor during this period. As a result of the lack of sanitary measures and the transfer of prisoners to other areas of the country, there were riots in prisons at the beginning of the pandemic, and violent clashes between prisoners for fear of contagion (La Tercera, 2020). A specific organization of prisoners tied to the October Revolt, *Coordinadora por la Libertad de los Prisionerxs Políticxs 18 de Octubre*,[8] were one of the main activists in this matter, issuing several statements regarding the conditions in prisons for political prisoners and other inmates, organizing national and international events in solidarity and has also established solidarity networks with other prison organizations (Izquierda, 2020).

Along with these, general rules for confinement were also set in place, which were systematized in Resolution No. 403 of the Undersecretary of Public Health on 28 May, and general mask use in closed spaces was enforced on 16 April (Resolution 282 of the same organism). Along with these general rules, people over 75 years old were also compelled to strict quarantines throughout the whole territory from 13 May.

Regarding surveillance, the governmental strategy was expanding the testing capacity of the country, getting to have by far the best testing capacity of Latin America and a standard capacity compared with OECD countries (Ritchie et al., 2020). Notwithstanding the latter, the traceability failures hugely undermined this (Sepúlveda and Miranda, 2020), as the government enabled a Contact Center with the duty of tracking by phone infected and suspicious people and warning those who enter in either of these categories, in order to initiate a confinement. However, the Center was severely understaffed. At first authorities never clarified how many people they had hired for the task (Miranda, 2020), and only on 17 July they indicated they had 2600 tracers (Sandoval, 2020), far below the 9000 suggested by experts in June (Villa, 2020).

While the government tried to present the testing capacity as a big success, the system as a whole had a huge transparency problem, having no clear surveillance strategy publicized by the government. This was denounced by civil society organizations, mainly scientific guilds, and health professional unions, which had a strong support of the citizens (Piérola, 2020). From the beginning of the health crisis these organizations played a fundamental role in the public sphere, particularly the *Colegio Médico*, as a dissident organization which confronts the government by engaging in discussions from a technical perspective, requesting, among other measures, full lockdown (The Clinic, 2020). As such, Dr. Izkia Siches who was one of the main spokespersons for the opposition, even started receiving death threats (CNN Chile, 2020b). Among her most important proposals, was a sanitary plan that would start in full lockdown, and later implement gradual stages of social distancing and reopening of the economy, along with an economic proposal to alleviate the crisis (Colmed, 2020).

This secrecy of the government exploded on 13 June, when a prestigious journalism media outlet revealed that the government had been reporting two different death counts: one to the Chilean public, and a different one (which almost doubled the former) to the WHO (Sepúlveda, 2020). This manipulation caused a political crisis, the resignation of the Minister of Health and a redefinition of the whole strategy. After this, the government agreed to deliver the data according to the WHO standards: on 17 June, the government announced the aggregation of 31,412 infected that were not previously included into the total count (which implied a rise of 14%), and on 20 June, 3069 deaths that were not previously reported were also added (which represented a 43% increase in the total deaths).

The government was unable to enhance further surveillance mechanisms (such as the use of mobile phone data), as this decision required a political and social consensus about the use of the data which the government alone could never obtain. Attempts like the request of some mayors to the central government to have the personal data of infected and confined (name and address) people to help them, were stopped for infringing the Protection of Personal Life Act (Law No. 19,628) and the Bill of Rights Regarding Healthcare (Law No. 20,584).

4 Challenges and Constraints on the Chilean Economy

4.1 *Pre-COVID-19 Economic Policy*

Chile experienced a strong industrial reorganization driven by the transformations in the international division of labor throughout the second part of twentieth century. In South America this process developed as a sustained deindustrialization, given that it was progressively more difficult to maintain the Import substitution industrialization policies that shaped these countries from 1930 to 1970.[9] Particularly, in Chile this process destroyed the national industry, by reorganizing the production around natural resource exports, which essentially changed the capital's demand for labor force, maintaining an important number of unskilled labour, but also increasing the quantity of a more highly skilled working class (Robbins, 1994). This also means that most of the industrial goods for consumption are imported. Since the end of Pinochet's Dictatorship, the Chilean economy has enjoyed a relatively stable development based on the extraordinary rent of their natural resources—mainly copper, but also fisheries, forestries and the production of export fruits and vegetables—which allowed an overvalued currency that cheapened imports and capital goods. The existence of a local commercial and industrial capital depended in part on the institutions that maintained these conditions. As such, the Chilean Central Bank has an economic and political autonomy granted by the Constitution which secures the stability of the currency and the exchange rate with the dollar, while the country also has free trade agreements with most of the world, which secure low import costs.

However, as it was already mentioned, the local capital was facing a steady medium-term profitability and productivity crisis. Although the frequency with which companies were going out of business accelerated since 2018—when longstanding traditional industries that survived the 80's industrial reconfigurations went broke, such as Pastas Suazo, Guante and Gacel shoe manufacturers, and a Maersk Container Industry San Antonio (MCIS) went out of business—this trend only accelerated before the pandemic.

The policies adopted by the government during that period were subsidies to small and medium capitals through (i) low cost credits financed by the State, (ii) granting longer deadlines and waiving the payment of certain taxes, and (iii) giving subsidies for the payment of low wage the workers' salaries (this was presented as a mandatory minimum salary which would be partially funded by the government). This was announced through an *Agenda de protección del empleo, reactivación económica, reconstrucción y apoyo a las MiPymes* ("Pro-Employment & Economic Recovery Plan") of USD5.5 billion as an answer to the economic crisis that, according to the government, was caused by the October revolt. When the Covid-19 pandemic arrived, Chile already had two months of negative GDP growth and downward growth prospects.

4.2 Post COVID-19 Economic Prospects

The direct impact of the pandemic was directly reflected in the cost of consumer goods and in the output of industrial production, resulting in a drop in GDP of 7%, as estimated in the last Monetary Policy Report of the Central Bank of Chile in 2020 (Banco Central, 2020a), which was assessed as the worst drop in GDP in 38 years since the foreign bank debt crisis of 1982. At the same time, real unemployment, which considers unemployed workers, reached in June 1.5 million workers: almost 16% of the resident workforce (Cárdenas, 2020).

To confront the crisis the government announced two economic emergency plans, which would be financed by the issue of public debt, and with the use of the *Fondo de Estabilización Económica y Social* ("Economic and Social Stabilization Fund"), which is a sovereign fund that amounts to around 7% of Chile's GDP. The first of these plans, in early March for US$ 11.75 billion[10] (almost 5% of Chile's GDP) established three main policy areas: the protection of jobs and income, injection of liquidity for companies (with special emphasis on small ones), and support for vulnerable families. The second plan announced on 8 April 2020, would inject an additional US$ 5 billion into the initial plan, incorporating relief measures for groups not contemplated in the initial plan, such as informal workers, and enabling a credit line with state guarantee for companies and SMEs for US$ 24 billion (Nogales, 2020). It is important to note that the nature of the measures of these plans followed a continuity with the one presented as a response to the October revolt.

One of the first priorities of these plans was the injection of liquidity to companies. In that sense, several measures were contemplated: (i) a *Línea de Crédito COVID* ("COVID Credit Line") to ensure access to emergency credits through a government guarantee of up to 85% of the total amount; (ii) a capital injection to Banco Estado[11] to finance cheap credits and funds for SMEs[12]; (iii) a postponement in the payment of the first-category tax (income tax) and the payment of VAT that is retained by the final seller was postponed for three months, to alleviate the tax burden on small and medium-sized companies; (iv) *Ley de Protección al Empleo* ("Employment Protection Act"), that would allow for the complete or partial suspension of employment contracts, whose salaries will be paid completely or partially by the Unemployment Insurance funds.[13]

The Central Bank complemented these government's measures by lowering the interest rate, making it exceptionally low compared to the immediate previous period. Thus, at the beginning of 2019 the Monetary Policy Rate (MPR) stood at 3%, in July 2019 it dropped to 2.5%, and in November 2019 to 1.75%; while in March 2020 it dropped to 1.38% and from April to date it fell again to 0.5% (Banco Central, 2020b). This determined a decrease in the interbank interest rate and the interest of short and medium term bonds in Chilean pesos, thus falling even to negative rates in the case of bonds in re-adjustable units (such as the Chilean *Unidad de Fomento* or UF).

Another measure adopted by the Central Bank was to maintain the exchange rate intervention programme implemented since the October revolt. To this end, it sold US$ 20 billion in the market in order to alleviate the pressure on the Chilean peso (El Mostrador, 2020d). In addition, the Central Bank made deposits in order to ensure the financial liquidity of private banks and other institutions (e.g. savings cooperatives), to help finance loans to final consumers.

Direct financial aid to workers was small in the first 100 days of the pandemic. The government implemented specific measures since April targeting "vulnerable families" (Ministerio de Desarrollo Social, 2018), thus focusing on the economically precarious population, instead of providing an universal relief package. Among the measures that stand out are: (i) an emergency family income (*Ingreso Familiar de Emergencia* or IFE) for families who have seen their income reduced, provided by the government. This focused in 80% of the most vulnerable population in the country, according to the government (Gobierno de Chile, 2020a); (ii) suspension of shutting down of basic services (electricity, gas, and running water) on non-payment grounds for the lowest 40% of the most vulnerable families (Nogales, 2020), and; (iii) payment of a Covid-19 subsidy amounting to US$ 63 to vulnerable families.

In addition to this direct subsidy, the Congress also approved a Law that allowed the withdrawal of 10% of the pension fund savings from the *Administradoras de Fondos de Pensiones* (APF), a private and individual account pension savings system. Law No. 21,248 was a constitutional reform (as this withdrawal was restricted by constitutional norms), and was heavily opposed by the government administration, which led it to a new political crisis, as many of its parliamentarians also voted for the withdrawal pressured by the mass spontaneous and labor union (port workers, specially) demonstrations for it (El Desconcierto, 2020a).

Thus, the emergency mechanisms were financed either by indebtedness or savings of the State, when they focused capitals or were small subsidies by poor families; or were financed by funds in social security systems financed by workers. It is important, however, to compare their weight. The AFP withdrawal was by far the biggest emergency measure, representing 6.09% of the Chilean PIB, and it was financed by worker's savings. On the other spectrum, the *Banco Estado* credits for SMEs financed by the State represented 3.52% of the PIB (Montt et al., 2020).

5 The Labor Market

5.1 Pre-COVID-19 Unemployment

The current legal framework for labor relations was imposed as part of a set of profound economic and legal reforms during the 1970s by the Military Dictatorship, which was the institutional expression of an authoritarian industrial reorganization process (Díaz, 1989). These reforms, enforced under strong political persecution and while collective bargaining by trade unions was forbidden, were a reaction to the economic crisis of the previous cycle and meant profound changes in

State administration, along with the privatization of public companies. As described by Coloma and Rojas (2000): "the objective of these reforms was essentially to complement the adjustment required by other structural reforms and to introduce flexibility in the labor market, in order to promote greater efficiency and reduce the high unemployment rates that rose to double-digit levels".

Once the democratic regime arrived, changes were introduced that sought to contribute to strengthen collective bargaining and protect workers'rights, within a framework of labor flexibility. However, the collective bargaining standards that existed before the military dictatorship were never fully restored. During the 2000s, there were no major labor reforms, although some changes were introduced, mainly linked to the legalization of subcontracting and the expansion of individual rights (Rojas, 2007).

With the arrival of the 2009 financial crisis, Latin American economies reversed a growth process of several consecutive years, negatively impacting the region in the flow and price of exports, increased public debt to finance public spending, remittances, and capital flows (CEPAL, 2010). This also meant high inflation and unemployment rates for most countries. Notwithstanding the above, in relative terms the region had more elements to face the crisis, with a lower fiscal deficit that allowed it to take on debt and compensate for the adverse effects through public spending.

The case of Chile in this context was considered exemplary, as it had a better regulated and capitalized banking system (Montt et al., 2020), having moderate and brief consequences compared to previous crises, with a smaller contraction of GDP and a faster recovery. However, the labor market was particularly affected and had a much slower recovery. This recovery slowed down especially during the 2010s. In this sense, "the regional GDP evidenced the effects of lower international prices of the primary products it exports, by registering a deceleration in 2014 (0.9%) and a contraction in 2015 (–0.5%) and 2016 (–0.9%). This led to an increase in the Latin American unemployment rate, which went from 6.1% in 2014, to 6.6% and 7.9%, in 2015 and 2016, respectively. The increase of 1.3 percentage points between 2015 and 2016 represented the largest increase in the regional unemployment rate in more than two decades for a single year" (OIT, 2018).

According to available data, one of the most relevant characteristics of unemployment in Chile corresponds to underemployment: part-time workers that aim to work more hours, but due to labor market impediments are unable to do so. When considering the category of underemployed as part of the unemployed, the latter category reaches approximately one and a half million people (Montt et al., 2020).

The Chilean economic slowdown has been also manifesting in the composition of employment during the 2010 decade. First, there was an increase in self-employment in relation to total employment (Villanueva and Espinoza, 2021), growing from being 16.5% of the total employed labour force in 2013 to 18.9% in 2017 (Szederkenyi and Vergara, 2017). Likewise, private salaried employment grew in a limited way (1.1% on average), with the main sustainer of hiring being public salaried employment (4.3%). Likewise, informality rose sharply especially between 2017 and 2019, reaching 28.7% of informal workers.

The increase in the unemployment rate, the presence of informal employment and the creation of precarious jobs have characterized Chilean employment during the last years. Total employment in the economy grew on average almost 2% per year during 2014–2019. The economic sectors that explain this growth are mainly the Hotel and Restaurant activities that account for 17% of such growth, trade (16%), construction (10%), and education and health services (28%) (Villanueva and Espinoza, 2021). Thus, the economic sectors that have sustained job creation in recent times were the most impacted ones by the pandemic.

5.2 *The Future of the Chilean Labor Market*

As previously mentioned, the measures taken by the government were focused mostly on protecting companies. Its implementation of relief towards workers was organized through the social stratification made according to the type of contract a worker had and to the amount of income each family receives.

For contracted workers, several legal reforms were implemented to ensure the continuity of the work process where it was possible. First, the pandemic was used as an excuse for the accelerated approval of the telework bill (Law No. 21,220), which was being discussed prior to the pandemic (Gutiérrez, 2020; Ugarte, 2020). This reform established the conditions under which this activity would be developed, but left the determination of the form and times in which the worker would render the services to the negotiation of the parties in the work contract, thus being able to modify already existing work contracts or renegotiate new ones according to the employer's needs. Although the norm recognized a "right of disconnection", it left a high margin of autonomy to the parties of the labour relationship, which would result in unfair situations for the worker. For example, critics have indicated that the law does not recognize overtime for workers outside the working day, as it is considered in Chilean labor law (CUT, 2021). Thus, as it did not set contractual limits to the employers, the reform allowed for precarious working conditions for workers in these areas.

Secondly, Law No. 21,218 was also approved, which created a state subsidy to supplement the wages of lower-income workers, guaranteeing a monthly minimum wage of US$ 455 (Ministerio de Desarrollo Social, 2020). Through this Bill, presented after the October revolt but approved and implemented in May 2020, the government legally recognized a raise in the cost of the labour power but at the same time paid for it partially, reducing the effective wage costs of companies.

In case the company could not continue with its functions for sanitary or economic reasons, Law No. 21,227: *Ley de Protección al Empleo.* This Law allows for (i) the suspension of work contracts in non-essential activities, freezing the payment of wages by the employers, or (ii) the reduction of working hours with an income that would complement the wage reduction for the worker. In both cases, partial or complete wages were paid by Unemployment Insurance funds, which are mainly financed by the worker's salary.[14] This was one of the most used mechanisms during the first months of the pandemic.[15]

Self-employed and informal workers were not recognized as workers for relief measures, as they did not have an employment contract. As such, they could only apply for the already mentioned subsidies for vulnerable families.

In terms of benefits for mothers, they were extended or transformed to fit the current pandemic situation. As such, a postnatal leave already existed for women who were mothers while working, consisting of a subsidy paid by the State that lasts 12 weeks from delivery, extendable for a further 12 weeks. Because of the pandemic this benefit could be extended up to 90 days more (Law No. 21,247). Also, the obligation of providing a nursery service for companies that had more than 20 women employed was changed to a bonus equivalent to the cost of the nursery, in accordance with Opinion No. 1884/14 of 2020 of the Directorate of Labour.

However, no institutional measures could contain the impact the COVID-19 would have in the local labor market. In this sense, Latin America and the Caribbean was the region with the greatest loss of working hours worldwide (in relation to total hours worked in 2019) with a reduction of 16% per year versus a global loss of 8.8% (Montt et al., 2020). In Chile this appeared as the most serious and generalized crisis in the labor market that the country has ever suffered: almost two million jobs were destroyed in Chile between the last quarter of 2019 and the second quarter of 2020 (Villanueva and Espinoza, 2021), without considering the number absent workers or workers with reduced working hours to whom the Employment Protection Law was applied (es they were considered employed).

In relation to the types of work affected, the sharp fall during the pandemic in self-employment and informal wage earners stands out, affecting the poorest and most vulnerable workers (Villanueva and Espinoza, 2021). This implied a drop in the wage mass from US$ 6.87 billion in 2019 to US$ 6.1 billion in 2020. The loss of jobs and labor income during the crisis implied an increase in poverty rates from 8.6% in 2017 to 10.8% in 2020 according to the CASEN survey, which implies that 540,000 persons fell below the poverty line due to the economic and health crisis. This strong fall in living standards explains the mass hunger protests that exploded during May, that drove into several other mass demonstrations that ended with the approval of the AFP withdrawal Bill by the Congress.

Thus, the pandemic hit an already unstable Chilean labor market. The measures implemented by the government focused mainly on the protection of companies and on the stabilization of the currency exchange rate and the interest rate, leaving the workers to finance their own subsistence through social security mechanisms (with the exception of very punctual subsidies). As most of the workers were not covered by these social security institutions, this provoked a sharp drop in living standards for a big part of the Chilean population.

6 Pensions

6.1 Pre-COVID-19 Individual Savings Pension Funds System

Within the package of reforms promoted by the military dictatorship was the creation of the current Chilean pension system, whose center would be individual capitalization of savings: the system offers each member a benefit according to his or her contributions to the system, plus what the private fund managers (*Aseguradoras de Fondos de Pensiones*, AFP) are able to obtain from their investment in the capital market (Uthoff, 2001). Thus, this system would provide funding for local and regional capitals while at the same time withdrawing governmental spending from the pension system. This individual logic is the current basis of the Chilean social security system.

The percentage of workers covered by the individually funded pillar of the AFP—the basis of the individual capitalization system—was approximately 55% in 2005. The workers who contributed mandatorily to the AFPs were salaried workers, including agricultural workers, domestic workers and employees of micro companies who are obligatorily covered by this pillar. Since 2019, self-employed workers have also been incorporated. According to the Pensions Superintendence, "the coverage of the new system, like the old one, is around 55% of the workforce. In that system, people had access to pensions whose level was determined by the benefits granted by each fund" (Berstein et al., 2005).

The first generation that contributed during their complete working life in the AFP system began to retire between 2015 and 2019. In relation to the amount obtained by retirees, 50% of the 984 thousand retirees who received an old-age pension obtained less than US$ 257, which was less than the minimum wage. Likewise, 50% of the 127 thousand people who retired during 2019, through their savings and the profitability obtained by the AFPs, were only able to finance a pension of less than US$ 62 (Gálvez and Kremerman, 2020).

The above situation has led to the growth of demands associated with the end of the AFP system, which is seen as one of the main pillars of the Dictatorial reforms. Such demands have entailed broad mobilizations carried out between 2017 and 2018 and occupied a central part of the October revolt. The central idea is to end the AFPs as the center of social security, even though there is no consensus on the form the new system should take, or what the exact status of the ownership of pension funds would be.

However, no profound changes have been introduced to the AFP system. A “solidarity pillar” was implemented aimed at increasing pension financing through subsidies provided by the State to the AFPs, but this operates in a focalized form depending on socioeconomic conditions. Aside from this, since its creation no relevant reform has touched the AFP system.

6.2 *Post Pandemic Age Pensions*

On 13 May a Bill was introduced by a transversal group of opposition representatives to enable a withdrawal of up to 150 U.F. from the individual pillar of the AFP as an emergency relief measure. The original project also established that the government would issue a bond at the end of the withdrawal process that would restore the money to the individual pension accounts that would have done the withdrawal. It is important to mention that the bill’s mechanism was not entirely new: a similar Bill to withdraw a portion of the pension savings was presented in 2002 by the right wing party Renovación Nacional, justifying this due to “the desirability of financing consumption through the use of savings funds rather than through increased public spending” (República de Chile, 2002). However, its implications would be different as the political climate had drastically changed.

This relief measure was strongly criticized as regressive, as it financed the crisis through savings in social security institutions and would benefit formal workers more as they paid contributions to the system and had more savings (López, 2020). This was also reinforced by the fact that the government would not issue bonds to restore the withdrawals, as it was taken out by the government during the discussion of the Bill. Nevertheless, the project gained political traction, as the relief measures organized by the government had been insufficient and had driven an important part of the Chilean working class into deep financial distress or poverty, as it was already shown. As such, the “hunger strikes” of mid-May were followed by similar mass protests at the beginning of July, where protesters barricaded main arteries of several cities and engaged in direct confrontations with the police to exercise pressure to approve the withdrawal of funds from the AFP private pension system (El Desconcierto, 2020c).

In spite of the regressiveness of the measure and that the Bill indicated clearly that it would be an emergency withdrawal based on the current contingency, several political groups that promoted it insisted on indicating that it was a "first step" in the collapse of the private pension system and especially an important strike against the AFPs (ANEF, 2020). Moving in the same logic, the business associations answered that precisely the withdrawal of these funds would open the possibility of withdrawing all the funds, thereby destroying the current pension system (CNN Chile, 2020a).[16] The issue thus reflected a continuity with the demands that emerged during the October revolt: to strengthen the State apparatus in mediating the reproduction of the working class, in opposition to the failure of the market as a mechanism for the organization of life. However, the AFP withdrawal also reinforced the perception that a property right existed over individual pension funds, thus jeopardizing the possibility of future expropriation policies for a pension system organized over solidarity principles.

According to the Pensions Superintendence, 11,107,715 applications were accepted with an average of US$ 1680. In total, US$ 18,668 million were withdrawn from the AFP system.[17] This measure did reinforce and not counter the tendencies of the governmental policies, however, as it financed the crisis through social security systems rather than State expenditure.

7 Conclusion

The COVID-19 pandemic response in Chile continued the policy trends that were present throughout the economic and political crisis that exploded in the October Revolt. On the one hand, the militarization of the public space as a measure of political control against civil unrest was deepened and legitimized because of the sanitary situation. Along with this, an aid program was implemented that focused on reducing costs for local capital through social security spending, while refraining from acting through direct subsidies or bailouts to companies. The extraordinary circumstances allowed the government to enforce their program, even though they had a strong social and institutional opposition, and they could eventually pass an important relief measure such as the withdrawal of pension funds from the private administrators. It is however questionable how far this measure moved from the governmental policies.

This article attempted to contribute to the analysis of potential post-pandemic trajectories that these policies will adopt in different areas such as economy, labor, and security, and a special emphasis was put on the pension system as it centered the discussion over the current economic and political system. In this sense, one of the absentees was the constitutional change revindication, whose plebiscite was delayed on sanitary grounds and the whole discussion was put on hold to resolve the more pressing issues of the first months of the pandemic. However, this demand would come again to the front after the entrance plebiscite on October 25th, 2021, where the approval for a new Constitution won with 78.28% of the votes. In spite of its absence, several of the discussions around the implementation of lockdowns or the enforcement of relief measures moved implicitly through the same coordinates, with the withdrawal of the pension funds from the AFP a particularly important example of this. This shows yet another aspect of the Chilean case: the relief for workers was implemented and planned as a measure to support local capitals. The implementation of emergency measures depended strongly on the social security funds and was planned mainly as a mechanism to save layoff costs, while the State expenditure concentrated on liquidity measures for capitals. Even in a political measure supported by the political opposition and by demonstrations on the street, this tendency was reinforced and not countered.

Notes

1. Chile has marked its historical development in the export of raw materials to the world market. The production of these goods under preferential conditions marks the cycles of expansion and growth and contraction in relation to the price prevailing in the world market (Rivas and Seiffer, 2021). The relationship between land rent, land appropriation mechanisms and the determination of social life can be further explored in (Iñigo Carrera, 2013, 2017).
2. For example, many of the grassroot organizations are integrated by activists that may participate in Nueva Mayoría, Communist Party, and Frente Amplio political parties. Conversely, many broad organizations and federations of smaller organizations define themselves as "social movements" (Coordinadora Feminista 8M, No + AFP), and participate in institutional instances and are disputed by political parties too.
3. The constituent plebiscite was held on 25 October 2020, with massive citizen participation. Constituent delegates were elected on May 15 and 16, 2021, in an unprecedented two-day election. Currently, the Constituent Convention has been working for six months, the New

Constitution proposal is expected for early July, and it has to be approved in a new national plebiscite.

4. After 180 days of this state of emergency, the National Congress has the power to cancel it if the reasons for the state of emergency cease to exist.
5. This was finally in force until 30 September 2021, after four extensions, in accordance with Supreme Decrees No. 400/2020, 646/2020, 72/2021, and 153/2021.
6. In Chilean law, as a general rule, administrative acts are subject to *ex ante* control by the CGR. This is a legality check, which verifies the conformity of administrative acts with the law (OECD, 2014).
7. With the vaccination process, the plan has been updated, conditioning the mobility restrictions and the control of place capacities in compliance with the vaccination schedule.
8. The organization's demands are related to imprisoned and detained protesters during the October revolt protests. They consider themselves political prisoners, as they were detained and retained for minor unrelated felonies and extralimiting preventive criminal measures (such as preventive custody) as a form of political punishment.
9. The development of microelectronics, transport, and telecommunications that widened the already large productivity gaps between national industries and its domestic market, as opposed to those with the capacity to produce for the global market (Charnock and Starosta, 2016).
10. Calculated with a 1 USD = 784 CLP exchange rate (July 2020).
11. Banco Estado is the state company whose sole and specific line of business is to provide commercial banking services throughout the national territory, in addition to administering the single fiscal budgetary account, which is the bank account of the Chilean treasury, and being the instrument of the state to grant credits and guarantees to small capital through the Small Business Guarantee Fond (FOGAPE).
12. The credit was set up to ensure access to new loans for SMEs, to flexibilize already existing loans, to allow repurchases of credits, and to create a credit guarantee fund to secure all these policies.
13. The government injected US$ 2000 million in to the solidarity fund of Unemployment Insurance to support lost work income (Gobierno de Chile, 2020b). This only covered cases where workers had saved insufficient funds in their individual accounts of the Unemployment Insurance.
14. Seguro de Cesantía ("Unemployment Insurance") has two components: an individual savings system (cuenta individual) that is complemented with a solidarity fund (fondo solidario). If workers do not have enough funds in their individual accounts, they are paid a lower amount by the solidarity fund. The worker contributes to his individual account of 0.6% of

his taxable wage, while the employer deposits 1.6% into the worker's individual account (however, this amount can be discounted by the employer if a worker is fired with severance pay). Along with this, the employer also pays 0.8% of the worker's salary, which goes into the solidarity fund.

15. During April, Ley de Protección al Empleo received more than 500,000 applications from more than 70,000 companies, of which 394,000 were approved. By the second week of May, this number grew to 86,000 companies, equivalent to 593,000 workers of which 503,000 were approved. Most of these applications were made in the Metropolitan Region (66%), and 52% correspond to micro and small businesses (Superintendencia de Pensiones, 2020). The most affected economic sectors were commerce (with 24% of the total applications) followed by accommodation and food services (20%) and finally construction (15%).
16. This particular example is illustrative, because a similar Bill to withdraw a portion of the pension savings was presented in 2002 by the right wing party Renovación Nacional, justifying this due to "the desirability of financing consumption through the use of savings funds rather than through increased public spending" (República de Chile, 2002).
17. Two more withdrawals were later also approved by the government. The second withdrawal had a similar total amount of US$ 15,442 million.

References

Abujatum, J. et al. (2020) Gobernanza en la Gestión de Emergencia frente al "COVID-19": Marco normativo. Roles, atribuciones e instancias de coordinación [Governance in Emergency Management against 'COVID-19': Regulatory framework. Roles, attributions and instances of coordination]. Biblioteca del Congreso Nacional de Chile.

ANEF. (2020) 'Aprobar el camino a la Dignidad - Carta al Director (Publicado en El Mercurio)', ANEF - Agrupación Nacional de Empleados Fiscales, 15 July. Available at: http://anef.cl/comunicaciones/aprobar-el-camino-a-la-dignidad-carta-al-director-publicado-en-el-mercurio/. Accessed 19 July 2020.

Arellano, F. et al. (2019) 'El "Nunca Más" que nunca fue: análisis de los cuatro informes sobre Derechos Humanos tras el 18/O', CIPER Académico, 20 December. Available at: https://www.ciperchile.cl/2019/12/20/el-nunca-mas-que-nunca-fue-analisis-de-los-cuatro-informes-sobre-derechos-humanos-tras-el-18-o/.

Aylwin, J., and Morales, R. (2020) 'Empresas y derechos humanos en Chile en tiempos de COVID-19', Observatorio Ciudadano, 9 June. Available at: https://observatorio.cl/empresas-y-derechos-humanos-en-chile-en-tiempos-de-covid-19/.

Banco Central. (2020a) 'Informe de Política Monetaria marzo 2020'. Banco Central. Available at: https://www.bcentral.cl/contenido/-/detalle/informe-de-politica-monetaria-marzo-2020.

Banco Central. (2020b) 'Medidas del Banco Central de Chile para enfrentar el COVID-19'. Available at: https://www.bcentral.cl/documents/33528/2233873/Recuadro_medidas_banco_central.pdf/5544322b-dbb1-d08f-7008-ef4f3e4d8c51?t=1585737242190.

BBC Mundo. (2020) 'Coronavirus en Chile: las imágenes de las protestas en Santiago por la difícil situación económica creada en Chile por la pandemia de covid-19', 19 May. Available at: https://www.bbc.com/mundo/noticias-america-latina-52717413.

Berstein, S., Larraín, G., and Pino, F. (2005) 'Cobertura, densidad y pensiones en Chile: Proyecciones a 20 años plazo'. Superintendencia de Administradoras de Fondos de Pensiones. Available at: https://repec.spensiones.cl/repec/3_doctrabajos/12_2005_cobertura_densidad_pensiones_chile.pdf.

Cámara de Diputados. (2019) 'Firman acuerdo por la Paz Social y nueva Constitución'. Available at: https://www.camara.cl/prensa/sala_de_prensa_detalle.aspx?prmid=138442.

Cárdenas, R. (2020) 'Desempleo llega a su mayor nivel en 16 años y Covid destruye 1.5 millones de puestos de trabajo'. La Tercera, 30 June. Available at: https://www.latercera.com/pulso/noticia/desocupacion-llega-a-su-mayor-nivel-en-16-anos-y-covid-destruye-15-millones-de-empleos/EFI52PEMMZG73KHSBMCS5FXBJI/.

Caro, I., and Fernández, O. (2020) 'Gobierno y alcaldes acuerdan suspensión de clases [Government and mayors agree to suspension of classes]'. La Tercera, 15 March. Available at: https://www.latercera.com/nacional/noticia/gobierno-y-alcaldes-acuerdan-suspension-de-clases/2WIV4W4ZOBCUTPGZVNTDWOJ2UE/.

CEPAL. (2010) 'Panorama Social de América Latina 2009'. Santiago de Chile: CEPAL. Available at: https://www.cepal.org/es/publicaciones/1232-panorama-social-america-latina-2009.

Cerda, L., Reyes, R., and Navarrete, J. M. (2020) 'Vecinos Del Litoral Central Impiden Con Barricadas El Acceso a Turistas y Alcaldes Decretan Cierre de Comunas Para Evitar Propagación de Covid-19'.

Charnock, G., and Starosta, G. (2016) 'The New International Division of Labour: Global Transformation and Uneven Development'. London: Palgrave Macmillan.

Cisternas, M. (2020) 'Otra Vez Las Mujeres: Las Ollas Comunes Contra La Desesperación En Tiempos de Crisis « Diario y Radio U Chile'. Dario UChile [Preprint].

CNN Chile. (2020a) '"Aún es tiempo de rectificar el rumbo", el llamado del gran empresariado a no aprobar el retiro de fondos de las AFP'. CNN Chile, 13

July. Available at: https://www.cnnchile.com/economia/llamado-gran-empresariado-retiro-fondos-afp_20200713/. Accessed 19 July 2020a.
CNN Chile. (2020b) 'Colegio Médico Interpondrá Querella Tras Amenaza de Muerte y Violación a Izkia Siches'. CNN Chile [Preprint].
Colmed. (2020) 'Colmed convoca a destacados economistas para realizar propuesta de apoyo social en el contexto de la pandemia'. Colegio Médico de Chile [Preprint].
Coloma, F., and Rojas, P. (2000) 'Evolución del Mercado Laboral en Chile: Reformas y Resultados'. In La Transformación Económica de Chile. Santiago de Chile: Universitaria, p. 714. Available at: https://www.cepchile.cl/cep/site/artic/20160304/asocfile/20160304093219/12_coloma.pdf.
Cooperativa. (2020) '"No damos abasto": Vecinos de La Pintana protestaron por falta de ayuda económica'. cooperativa.cl [Preprint].
Cordero, L. (2020) 'Delimitando la revisión judicial en la emergencia [Delimiting judicial review in emergency]'. El Mercurio Legal, 28 May. Available at: https://www.elmercurio.com/legal/movil/detalle.aspx?Id=908493&Path=/0D/DC/.
Cordero, L. (2021) 'El 2021 en la Tercera Sala de la Corte Suprema: revisión judicial en tiempos de cambio [2021 in the Third Chamber of the Supreme Court: judicial review in times of change]'. El Mercurio Legal, 30 December. Available at: https://www.elmercurio.com/legal/Registro/Login.aspx?urlBack=/Legal/Noticias/Analisis-Juridico/2021/12/30/tercera-sala-corte-suprema-2021.aspx.
CUT. (2021) 'CUT: reformular el Teletrabajo, reconocer a los trabajadores de plataformas digitales y evitar la concentración de la riqueza'. 30 March. Available at: https://cut.cl/cutchile/2021/03/30/cut-propuestas-al-senado-para-reformular-el-teletrabajo-reconocer-a-los-trabajadores-de-plataformas-digitales-y-evitar-la-concentracion-de-la-riqueza/.
Delgado, F. (2020) 'Vecinos de La Pintana Protestan Con Barricadas Por Falta de Ayuda En Medio de Pandemia'. Bio Bio Chile [Preprint].
Díaz, Á. (1989) 'La Reestructuración Industrial Autoritaria En Chile'. Revista Proposiciones, 17, pp. 14–35.
El Desconcierto. (2020a) 'Trabajadores portuarios anuncia paralización para presionar votación del 10%'. 15 July. Available at: https://www.eldesconcierto.cl/2020/07/15/trabajadores-portuarios-anuncia-paralizacion-para-presionar-votacion-del-10/. Accessed 26 July 2020.
El Desconcierto. (2020b) 'Vecinos de El Bosque se enfrentan a Carabineros tras protestar por falta de ayuda y alimentos'. El Desconcierto, 18 May. Available at: https://www.eldesconcierto.cl/2020/05/18/videos-vecinos-de-el-bosque-se-enfrentan-a-carabineros-tras-protestar-por-falta-de-ayuda-y-alimentos/. Accessed 19 July 2020.

El Desconcierto. (2020c) 'VIDEOS | 34 años después: Pese a la cuarentena, manifestaciones se toman la capital rememorando las históricas protestas del 2 y 3 de julio de 1986'. El Desconcierto, 3 July. Available at: https://www.eldesconcierto.cl/2020/07/03/videos-34-anos-despues-pese-a-la-cuarentena-manifestaciones-se-toman-la-capital-rememorando-las-historicas-protestas-del-2-y-3-de-julio-de-1986/. Accessed 19 July 2020.

El Mostrador. (2020a) 'Carmen Frei, Maya Fernández, Carmen Hertz y Beatriz Sánchez denuncian la "arremetida autoritaria" de Piñera: "Hay un riesgo a nuestra democracia"'. 29 June. Available at: https://www.elmostrador.cl/noticias/pais/2020/06/29/carmen-frei-maya-fernandez-carmen-hertz-y-beatriz-sanchez-denuncian-la-arremetida-autoritaria-de-pinera-hay-un-riesgo-a-nuestra-democracia/.

El Mostrador. (2020b) 'Colmed advierte que el coronavirus en las cárceles está "fuera de control" y podría agravar el problema de salud pública'. 2 June. Available at: https://www.elmostrador.cl/dia/2020/06/02/colmed-advierte-que-el-coronavirus-en-las-carceles-esta-fuera-de-control-y-advierten-que-podria-agravar-el-problema-de-salud-publica/.

El Mostrador. (2020c) 'Ley de Inteligencia entre gallos y medianoche: cuestionan apuro del Gobierno por aprobarla en plena pandemia y advierten intento velado de neutralizar protesta social'. 2 June. Available at: https://www.elmostrador.cl/noticias/pais/2020/06/02/ley-de-inteligencia-entre-gallos-y-medianoche-cuestionan-apuro-del-gobierno-por-aprobarla-en-plena-pandemia-y-advierten-intento-velado-de-neutralizar-protesta-social/.

El Mostrador. (2020d) 'Lunes negro: Banco Central admite "una situación externa delicada" y anuncia que el "programa de intervención cambiaria puede reactivarse"'. El Mostrador, 9 March. Available at: https://www.elmostrador.cl/dia/2020/03/09/lunes-negro-banco-central-admite-una-situacion-externa-delicada-y-anuncia-que-el-programa-de-intervencion-cambiaria-puede-reactivarse/.

El Mostrador. (2020e) 'Presidenta del Colegio Médico golpea la mesa y acusa "total falta de transparencia" en el manejo del Gobierno en la crisis del coronavirus [President of the College of Physicians slams the table and accuses "total lack of transparency" in the government's handling of the coronavirus crisis]'. 20 March. Available at: https://www.elmostrador.cl/noticias/pais/2020/03/20/presidenta-del-colegio-medico-golpea-la-mesa-y-acusa-total-falta-de-transparencia-en-el-manejo-del-gobierno-en-la-crisis-del-coronavirus/.

El Mostrador. (2022) 'Senado aprueba por sexta vez prórroga del Estado de Excepción en La Araucanía y Biobío'. 4 January. Available at: https://www.elmostrador.cl/dia/2022/01/04/senado-aprueba-por-sexta-vez-prorroga-del-estado-de-excepcion-en-la-araucania-y-biobio/.

Figueroa, N. (2020) 'Los 26 recursos de protección que presionan al gobierno para que declare cuarentena nacional [The 26 remedy of protection that pressure the government to declare a national quarantine]'. El Desconcierto, 24 March. Available at: https://www.eldesconcierto.cl/2020/03/24/los-26-recursos-de-proteccion-que-presionan-al-gobierno-para-que-declare-cuarentena-nacional/.

Freixas, M. (2020) 'Ser trabajadora sexual en tiempos de COVID-19: "A nosotras no nos va a matar el virus, sino este sistema"'. El Desconcierto, 10 April. Available at: https://www.eldesconcierto.cl/nacional/2020/04/10/ser-trabajadora-sexual-en-tiempos-de-covid-19-a-nosotras-no-nos-va-a-matar-el-virus-sino-este-sistema.html.

Fries, L. (2020) 'La pandemia ahonda la crisis de derechos humanos'. Cooperativa, 15 July. Available at: https://opinion.cooperativa.cl/opinion/derechos-humanos/la-pandemia-ahonda-la-crisis-de-derechos-humanos/2020-07-15/094722.html.

Fuentes, C. (2020) 'La nueva conquista de la Araucanía'. CIPER Académico, 24 June. Available at: https://www.ciperchile.cl/2020/06/24/la-nueva-conquista-de-la-araucania/.

Gálvez, R., and Kremerman, M. (2020) 'Pensiones bajo el m´ınimo: Los montos de las pensiones que paga el sistema de capitalizaci´on individual en Chile. Documento de Trabajo 2020'. Fundación Sol. Available at: https://fundacionsol.cl/cl_luzit_herramientas/static/wp-content/uploads/2020/06/PBM2020-1.pdf.

Gobierno de Chile. (2020a) 'Presidente Piñera anuncia segunda etapa de plan económico de emergencia: "Nuestra principal prioridad es cuidar la salud, la vida, los ingresos y los trabajos de las familias"'. 8 April. Available at: https://prensa.presidencia.cl/comunicado.aspx?id=149692.

Gobierno de Chile. (2020b) 'Presidente presenta plan económico de emergencia por US$11.750 millones para proteger el empleo y a las pymes: "Necesitamos unidad"'. 19 March. Available at: https://prensa.presidencia.cl/comunicado.aspx?id=148684.

González, T. (2020) 'Histórico: Encuesta CEP sitúa a Piñera como el Presidente de más baja aprobación en 30 años'. Diario UChile, 16 January. Available at: https://radio.uchile.cl/2020/01/16/historico-encuesta-cep-situa-a-pinera-como-el-presidente-de-mas-baja-aprobacion-en-30-anos/. Accessed 19 July 2020.

Gutiérrez, F. (2020) 'La promesa engañosa de la ley de teletrabajo'. CIPER Académico, 17 April. Available at: https://www.ciperchile.cl/2020/04/17/la-promesa-enganosa-de-la-ley-de-teletrabajo/.

Iñigo Carrera, J. (2013) 'El Capital: razón histórica, sujeto revolucionario y conciencia'. Buenos Aires. Argentina: Imago Mundi. Available at: https://cicpint.org/es/inigo-carrera-juan-2003-el-capital-razon-historica-sujeto-revolucionario-y-conciencia-imago-mundi/. Accessed 1 October 2020.

Iñigo Carrera, J. (2017) 'La renta de la tierra. Formas, fuentes y apropiación. Imago Mundi'. Available at: https://cicpint.org/es/inigo-carrera-j-2017-la-renta-de-la-tierra-formas-fuentes-y-apropiacion-imago-mundi-2/. Accessed 5 May 2020.

ISCI. (2020) 'Estudio de la U. de Chile: movilidad en la Región Metropolitana bajó sólo un 35% promedio durante primer mes de cuarentena masiva'. Instituto Ssistemas Complejos de Ingeniería, 22 June. Available at: https://isci.cl/covid19/estudio-de-la-u-de-chile-movilidad-en-la-region-metropolitana-bajo-solo-un-35-promedio-durante-primer-mes-de-cuarentena-masiva/.

Izquierda, L. (2020) 'Declaración de Coordinadora 18 de Octubre por la Libertad de lxs Prisionerxs Políticxs de Tarapacá frente a la pandemia del COVID19'. La Izquierda Diario - Red internacional [Preprint].

La Tercera. (2020) 'Reos de cárcel de Puente Alto intentan motín con toma de rehenes a gendarmes'. La Tercera, 22 April. Available at: https://www.latercera.com/nacional/noticia/reos-de-carcel-de-puente-alto-intentan-motin-con-toma-de-rehenes-a-gendarmes/.

López, F. (2020) 'Retiro del 10%: Limitaciones de un proyecto regresivo'. CIPER, 14 July. Available at: https://www.ciperchile.cl/2020/07/14/retiro-del-10-limitaciones-de-un-proyecto-regresivo/.

López, M., and Beltrán, M. (2013) 'Chile entre pandemias: la influenza de 1918, globalización y la nueva medicina [Chile between pandemics: the 1918 influenza, globalization and the new medicine]'. Revista Chilena de Infectología, 30(2). http://dx.doi.org/10.4067/S0716-10182013000200012.

Ministerio de Desarrollo Social. (2018) 'Informe de desarrollo social 2018'. Ministerio de Desarrollo Social y Familia. Available at: http://www.desarrollosocialyfamilia.gob.cl/storage/docs/Informe_de_Desarrollo_Social_2018.pdf.

Ministerio de Desarrollo Social. (2020) 'Ley 21218. Crea un subsidio para alcanzar un ingreso mínimo garantizado'. Available at: https://www.bcn.cl/leychile/navegar?idNorma=1144041.

Ministerio del Interior y Seguridad Pública. (2020) 'Decreto 269 Prorroga Declaración de Estado de Excepción Constitucional de Catástrofe, Por Calamidad Pública, En El Territorio de Chile, Por el lapso que indica'. Available at: https://www.bcn.cl/leychile/navegar?idNorma=1146700.

Miranda, B. (2020) 'Las razones por las que Mañalich perdió la "batalla de Santiago": movilidad descontrolada y pérdida de la trazabilidad'. CIPER, 16 June. Available at: https://www.ciperchile.cl/2020/06/16/las-razones-por-las-que-manalich-perdio-la-batalla-de-santiago-movilidad-descontrolada-y-perdida-de-la-trazabilidad/.

Moguillansky, G. (1990) 'La inversión en Chile: ¿el fin de un ciclo de expansión? Santiago de Chile: CEPAL'. Fondo de Cultura Económica. Available at: https://www.cepal.org/es/publicaciones/2084-la-inversion-chile-fin-un-ciclo-expansion. Accessed 26 July 2020.

Montt, G. et al. (2020) 'Panorama laboral en tiempos de la COVID-19. Chile: Impacto de la COVID-19 sobre los mercados de trabajo y la generación de ingresos'. Organización Internacional del Trabajo (OIT). Available at: https://www.ilo.org/wcmsp5/groups/public/---americas/---ro-lima/---sro-santiago/documents/publication/wcms_761863.pdf.

Navarrete, J. (2020) 'Senadores de oposición piden retiro de circular sobre retorno de funcionarios y llaman a diálogo con Anef y comité asesor tras explicaciones de ministros [Opposition senators demand the withdrawal of the circular about return of officials and call for dialogue with Anef and the advisory committee after explanations from ministers]'. 20 April. Available at: https://www.latercera.com/politica/noticia/senadores-de-oposicion-piden-retiro-de-circular-sobre-retorno-de-funcionarios-y-llaman-a-dialogo-con-anef-y-comite-asesor-tras-explicaciones-de-ministros/IRGNYQKUINCEPBYIGM3ABKRSS4/.

Nogales, D. (2020) 'Segunda parte del plan económico de emergencia contempla fondo de US$ 2.000 millones para los más vulnerables y grandes líneas de crédito para los "empresarios que lo requieran"'. La Tercera, 8 April. Available at: https://www.latercera.com/pulso/noticia/pinera-anuncia-el-plan-economico-de-emergencia-crea-nuevo-fondo-de-us-2000-millones-para-los-mas-vulnerables-y-grandes-lineas-de-credito-para-empresas/F265Z3OR4ND7BNPOYRKJNFIYCQ/.

OECD. (2014) 'Chile's Supreme Audit Institution Enhancing Strategic Agility and Public Trust'. OECD. Available at: https://www.oecd-ilibrary.org/governance/chile-s-supreme-audit-._9789264207561-en.

OIT. (2018) 'El mercado laboral en Chile: Una mirada de mediano plazo. Informe 2017'. Informes Técnicos 4. Organización Internacional del Trabajo (OIT). Available at: https://www.ilo.org/wcmsp5/groups/public/---americas/---ro-lima/---sro-santiago/documents/publication/wcms_632360.pdf.

Piérola, G. (2020) '"No enterarse por la prensa": la petición de la Mesa Social Covid al Presidente'. Pauta, 5 May. Available at: https://www.pauta.cl/politica/mesa-social-covid-19-le-pide-informacion-al-presidente-de-la-republica.

Presidencia del Senado. (2020) 'Agenda género COVID19. Hacer política pública con una mirada de género en situaciones de crisis'. Santiago. Available at: https://www.senado.cl/senado/site/mm/20200623/asocfile/20200623134514/agenda_g__nero_covid_22_de_junio_1.pdf.

República de Chile. (2002) 'Cámara de Diputados. Legislatura 347, ordinaria. Sesión 30, en miércoles 14 de agosto de 2002'. Available at: https://www.camara.cl/verDoc.aspx?prmID=4943%20&prmTIPO=TEXTOSESION.

Resumen. (2020) 'Militarización de territorio mapuche aumenta en plena pandemia'. Resumen Diario, 24 June. Available at: https://resumen.cl/articulos/militarizacion-de-territorio-mapuche-y-el-pais-aumentan-en-plena-pandemia?fbclid=IwAR0B5OzxA_PxHlP1YvyeEc7XQ48BYaXqPlZTRzy3L_zmsXvYmU6gW1NtNmE.

Reyes, C. et al. (2020) 'Partidos logran acuerdo y definen el 25 de octubre como nueva fecha para el plebiscito [Parties reach agreement and define October 25 as the new date for the plebiscite]'. La Tercera, 19 March. Available at: https://www.latercera.com/politica/noticia/partidos-logran-acuerdo-y-definen-el-25-de-octubre-como-nueva-fecha-para-el-plebiscito/FAC4P5KE4ZC3DCORJCBNA52BJY/.

Ritchie, H., Mathieu, E., Rodés-Guirao, L., Appel, C., Giattino, C., Ortiz-Ospina, E., Hasell, J., MacDonald, B., Beltekian, D., Dattani, S., and Roser, M. (2020) 'Coronavirus (COVID-19) Testing'. University of Oxford. https://ourworldindata.org/coronavirus-testing.

Rivas, G., and Kornblihtt, J. (2017) 'Notas Preliminares Sobre La Magnitud de La Renta de La Tierra Minera y Su Apropiación En Chile (1997–2012)'. In Jornada; X Jornadas de Economía Crítica. Buenos Aires, Argentina.

Rivas, G., and Seiffer, T. (2021) 'Sobre el origen y desarrollo de la conciencia política del movimiento estudiantil universitario chileno. De su conciencia anarquista a su antineoliberalismo. 1906-2012'. Anuario Del Conflicto Social, 12. https://doi.org/10.1344/ACS%20ACS%202021.12.12.

Robbins, D. (1994) 'Relative wage structure in Chile, 1957–1992: Changes in the structure of demand for schooling'. Estudios de Economía, 21(3), pp. 49–78.

Rojas, I. (2007) 'Las reformas laborales al modelo normativo de negociación colectiva del Plan Laboral'. Revista Ius et Praxis, 13(2), pp. 195–221. https://dx.doi.org/10.4067/S0718-00122007000200009.

Said, C., and Astudillo, D. (2020) 'Aumentan familias albergadas en campamentos por "pandemia social"'. La Tercera, 10 July. Available at: https://www.latercera.com/nacional/noticia/aumentan-familias-albergadas-en-campamentos-por-pandemia-social/GUBKYTQKFVF43FMM2PTPOJJONM/.

Sandoval, G. (2020) 'Paula Daza, subsecretaria de Salud Pública: "Queremos que los casos de Covid-19 investigados sean más del 90%"'. La Tercera, 17 July. Available at: https://www.latercera.com/nacional/noticia/paula-daza-subsecretaria-de-salud-publica-queremos-que-el-porcentaje-de-casos-investigados-sea-mas-del-90/AVVK5U2K4JDTZDPXPHH7HITV4M/.

Sepúlveda, N. (2020) 'Minsal reporta a la OMS una cifra de fallecidos más alta que la informada a diario en Chile'. CIPER, 13 June. Available at: https://www.ciperchile.cl/2020/06/13/minsal-reporta-a-la-oms-una-cifra-de-fallecidos-mas-alta-que-la-informada-a-diario-en-chile/.

Sepúlveda, N., and Miranda, B. (2020) 'Falla pieza clave para contener el virus: acta interna del Minsal revela graves problemas en la trazabilidad de casos'. CIPER, 29 May. Available at: https://ciperchile.cl/2020/05/29/falla-piezaclave-para-contener-el-virus-acta-interna-del-minsal-revela-graves-problemas-en-latrazabilidad-de-casos/.

Superintendencia de Pensiones. (2020) 'Ficha Estadística Semanal Ley de Protección al Empleo y Ley del Seguro de Cesantía'. Available at: http://www.spensiones.cl/portal/institucional/594/articles-13937_recurso_1.pdf.

Szederkenyi, F., and Vergara, R. (2017) 'Evolución del empleo en Chile: Asalariados y cuenta propia'. Centro de Estudios Públicos (CEP). Available at: https://www.cepchile.cl/cep/site/docs/20170605/20170605170421/pder457_fszederkenyi_rvergara.pdf.

The Clinic. (2020) 'Colegio Médico llama a "extremar medidas" por coronavirus: solicitaron suspender clases en colegios y universidades'. The Clinic, 14 March. Available at: https://www.theclinic.cl/2020/03/14/colegio-medico-llama-a-extremar-medidas-por-coronavirus-solicitaron-suspender-clases-en-colegios-y-universidades/. Accessed 19 July 2020.

Ugarte, J. L. (2020) 'Nueva ley de teletrabajo: legislar para una minoría'. Available at: http://rhmanagement.cl/legislar-para-una-minoria/.

Uthoff, A. (2001) 'La reforma del sistema de pensiones en Chile: desafíos pendientes'. 112. Santiago de Chile: CEPAL-ECLAC. Available at: https://repositorio.cepal.org/handle/11362/5090.

Villa, C. (2020) 'Colegio Médico y propuesta de nueve mil trazadores: "No es necesario que lo haga un profesional de salud"'. Diario UChile, 1 July. Available at: https://radio.uchile.cl/2020/07/01/colegio-medico-y-propuesta-de-nueve-mil-de-trazadores-no-es-necesario-que-lo-haga-un-profesional-de-salud/.

Villanueva, F., and Espinoza, S. (2021) 'Empleo en Chile: antes, durante y después de la pandemia'. CIPER, 12 November. Available at: https://www.ciperchile.cl/2021/11/12/empleo-en-chile-antes-durante-y-despues-de-la-pandemia/.

Zamorano, E. (2020) 'Protestas en Santiago centro ante el coronavirus: Barricadas en Diagonal Paraguay y proyectan "hambre" en edificio Telefónica'. ADN, 18 May. Available at: https://www.adnradio.cl/nacional/2020/05/18/protestas-en-santiago-centro-ante-el-coronavirus-barricadas-en-diagonal-paraguay-y-proyectan-hambre-en-edificio-telefonica.html. Accessed 19 July 2020.

Reinforcement of Economic Inequality and Extra Economic Power—Law and Political Economy of the US Pandemic Policy Response

Aleksandar Stojanović, Lauren Sweger-Hollingsworth, and Dashiell Anderson

1 Introduction

The first detected case of COVID-19 in the United States appeared on 20 January 2020 (Foertsch et al., 2020). By the end of March, lockdowns had been put in place across the country while vaccines became available in December 2020. Initial measures varied and were not particularly strict. State-level economic re-openings in May 2020 and lack of widespread

A. Stojanović (✉)
New York University in Shanghai, Shanghai, China
e-mail: as14902@nyu.edu

L. Sweger-Hollingsworth · D. Anderson
New School for Social Research, New York, NY, USA
e-mail: swegl427@newschool.edu

D. Anderson
University of Leeds, Leeds, UK
e-mail: bnda@leeds.ac.uk

A. Stojanović et al. (eds.), *The First 100 Days of Covid-19*,
https://doi.org/10.1007/978-981-19-6325-4_16

mask orders throughout the first 100 days of the pandemic resulted in a sharp rise in cases across most of the continental United States as the virus spread from Northeastern states that were first affected. At the time of writing (May 2022), the United States has surpassed one million pandemic-related deaths, and the total number of reported cases since the start of COVID-19 is above 83 million. The COVID-19 pandemic ranks first on the list of disasters in the United States by death toll. The United States has seen the largest number of deaths of any country in the world and is among twenty countries with the highest number of pandemic-related deaths per capita worldwide. In contrast, the economic effects of the pandemic seem not to have been as severe, at least on an apparent level. Despite initial hardship in the financial sector and the real economy, the United States has experienced the so-called v-shaped recovery.

Existing literature on the US Covid-19 policy response focuses on different reasons behind its' shortcomings mainly highlighting the political basis of differences in response, compliance, and the effects of the policy. Alexander et al. (2022) argue that policy suffered from a variety of problems. They can be divided into "technical" such as delays, slowness, and general lack of resources on the one hand and "political" such as the lack of clear policy direction and weak compliance. The literature follows this divide. Many authors focus on ineffectiveness of the policy. Social distancing requirements faced weak compliance (Masters et al., 2020) due to the lack of legal obligations, absence of surveillance (Kugler et al., 2020), and a general lack of capacity on data collection in support of the policy (Galaitsi et al., 2021). In addition, Schuchat (2020) documents the government's inability to stop large scale importation of goods and mass gatherings. Other authors focus on differences and disagreements that plagued the policy process. Bergquist et al. (2020) analyze the diversity of responses across states, focusing on the decentralized and federalist nature of the US COVID-19 policy. A significant part of the literature links this diversity to the politicization of the COVID-19 response and some of the contributions link compliance with that aspect as well. Baccini and Brodeur (2021) and Andersen (2020) document the political polarity in COVID-19 compliance, while Grossman et al. (2020) show that democrat-leaning areas were more likely to reduce mobility and follow social distancing guidelines. In addition, Kerr et al. (2021) show that these constituencies were generally more on board with preventative COVID-19 measures. The discussion of the politicization of the pandemic response goes beyond the issue of compliance. Xu and Basu (2020) trace the correlation between social distancing ability and income levels and find that richer individuals have the ability to socially distance themselves much easier than poorer individuals. Weill et al. (2020) consider public health surveillance and potential human rights violations associated with "punitive enforcement of public health measures", while Hastings et al. (2021) document racially imbalanced health effects of COVID-19 due to structural problems. Finally, Santis (2020) discusses the Trump administration's abuse of the state of exception to push a radical neoliberal agenda.

In order to contextualize the US pandemic response, it is important to consider how the pandemic was part of the interplay between a multiplicity of different crises that include "skyrocketing economic inequality, an increasingly destabilizing and extractive system of global finance, dramatic shifts in the character of work and economic production, a crisis of social reproduction, the ongoing disregard of Black and brown lives, the rise of new authoritarianisms [...] and, of course, looming above all, the existential threat of global climate change" (Harris and Varellas, 2020). Many of these crisis phenomena can be observed worldwide, but a particularly strict neoliberal law and policy direction that the US elites have propagated and followed since the 1980s can be identified as one of the main roots of the limited capacity to deal with the above-mentioned predicament. Neoliberalism is particularly hard to define (Thorsen and Lie, 2006), as it relies upon a diversified discursive strategy (Mirowski and Plehwe, 2015) and an interplay between domestic and international dimensions (Slobodian, 2018). The specificity of neoliberal law and policy can be traced to the denial of the fact that the markets are governed (Vogel, 2021). This leads to the normalization of "decentralized, self-regulatory infrastructures in a wide range of legal fields" (Zumbansen, 2021: 462). We can summarize neoliberal strategy in two steps. First, any attempt to embed markets within a wider set of institutions that ensure the primacy of societal equity and political governance over economic processes is criticized as self-defeating, inherently flawed, and economically suboptimal. This opens the space for structuring markets with the end of a highly unequal distribution of economic benefits and further concentration of power under the guise of respect for individual freedom and private property. Letting private entities participate in markets "freely" enables the price mechanism to establish the most efficient arrangement for the allocation of goods. In this context, financial markets are seen as a fundamental channel for the price mechanism to connect the future and the present of consumer preferences and entrepreneurial activity (Hayek, 1945).

Having in mind the significance of the state of emergency for the establishment of legal order and power formations, this article discusses the legal and political-economic aspects of the first 100 days of the pandemic policy response. We attempt to understand to what extent this policy has affected the general trajectory of neoliberal legal-economic transformation in the United States. In contrast to the dominant account of the failure in managing the health crisis and the success in managing the economic crisis, we show that the US policy response to the pandemic resulted in an increase of inequality, a reinforcement of the existing economic power formation and the introduction of novel practices in exerting extra-economic power. Declarations of emergencies within individual states often granted excessive power to state governors and unchecked decision-making influence to experts. The pandemic allowed for an unprecedented rise in the surveillance of private citizens, by state and local governments as well as employers. State governments often outsourced the implementation of surveillance and control measures to the private sector. Some of these measures continue to persist long after the retraction of the emergency conditions, with a potential to become a part of a "new normal" in the management of employees. The economic policy was the main US policy tool used by the federal government to tackle the pandemic and it was used in a manner reflective of existing power structures. While poverty, income inequality, gender, and racial gaps increased, big business and the financial sector captured most of the benefits brought about by the policy.

The rest of the article proceeds as follows: In the second section, we focus on the state of emergency and its implementation; In the third section, we turn to surveillance measures, compliance, and data use; In the fourth section we discuss economic policy response; and Section 5 concludes.

2 The State of Emergency and Its Implementation

Although President Trump and his cabinet made frequent statements once the COVID-19 pandemic began to escalate rapidly, their direct extra-economic policy aimed at tackling the spread of the virus, ultimately often failed to materialize from their rhetoric. General confusion and a lack of unified leadership from the federal government resulted from the executive office's flow of inconsistent, contradictory, and oftentimes false or misleading information (Holmes, 2020). In fact, with respect to the virus, Trump later revealed that he sought "to always play it down" (Summers, 2020). For instance, the president remarked on 4 July 2020 that "we have tested almost 40 million people. By doing so, we show cases, 99% of which are totally harmless" (Holmes, 2020). Conversely, officials like doctor Anthony Fauci, the director of the National Institute of Allergy and Infectious Diseases and a member of the White House COVID-19 taskforce, urged that the country "should be overly aggressive" as it would be better to "get criticized for overreacting", imploring all states to issue stay-at-home orders on 2 April 2020 (Doherty, 2022). Yet, the serious concerns voiced by Dr. Fauci and US national health administrations never translated into federal regulations to control the spread and remained simply as federal guidelines and suggestions.

Since the federal government (and the Trump administration specifically) played such a limited role in pandemic-era extra-economic policy, significant policy efforts to directly tackle the spread of the virus occurred on the state level. As we have already mentioned, this led to significant diversity in terms of how the pandemic was handled. In this section, we compare the emergency legal frameworks and their implementations across states, focusing on the states of emergency across the tri-state area (New York, New Jersey, and Connecticut) as well as Pennsylvania and Massachusetts. In order to get a better understanding of policy diversity, we contrast these to the state of emergency implementation in Wisconsin. Many policy actions occurred practically simultaneously across the northeastern states of the United States, with state governments largely following the policy path of New York and working in coordination with one another (Foertsch et al., 2020: 1). Coastal states with democrat-led state governments such as Oregon, Washington, and California acted similarly to New York in responding to the virus. Thus, New York state serves as a good representation for such approaches to COVID-19 policy-making. Alternatively, states with strong republican-majority governments took very limited action towards the virus, representing the other extreme. However, the political context of Wisconsin demonstrated important differences, illustrating the decentralized and uncoordinated responses to the COVID-19 pandemic, which were typical across many states in the United States. States with mixed party majorities within their governments, like Wisconsin, illustrated inconsistencies and erratic evolutions in their COVID-related policy. Hence, Wisconsin is a good example of this type of policy path.

2.1 Legal Framework

The US government is modeled as a federalist system of representative democracy. Possessing three theoretically coequal branches, the legislative, executive, and judiciary, this structure aims to create a check on the balance of power in the federal government. Under the US Constitution "executive Power" is "vested in a President of the United States" (United States Const. art. II sec. 1). In times of emergency, specific expanded powers have been conferred to the US President under the National Emergencies Act (1976) and the Public Health Service Act (1944), among others (Brennan Center for Justice, 2019). Similarly, the governments of the states that compose the United States are constructed after the federalist system and allow similar extensions of power in cases of emergencies. In general, the invocation of a state of emergency allows for the expansion of executive powers for the purpose of confronting a crisis. Executive powers are added to the legal framework of a state to ensure coverage for gaps in legislation in times of crises or to make up for responses that would be inadequate from local governments (Foertsch et al., 2020: 4).

Emergency provisions can also be found at the level of state law. In New York, for instance, the governor's ability to declare a state of emergency is vaguely implied by the state's constitution, which vests "executive power…in the governor" (New York Const. art. IV sec. 1). However, the executive's power in declaring a state of emergency is defined more clearly under New York's Executive Law. When the governor declares "a disaster emergency by executive order", the public must be notified of the emergency and "appropriate protective actions" must be carried out, with the governor given "authority to direct that other actions be taken" by other offices (Executive Law of New York art. 2-B sec. 28). Under the law, the emergency order cannot remain in effect above six months, but the "governor may issue additional orders to extend the state disaster emergency" as long as the additional periods do not exceed six months. Furthermore, the governor has the ability to "request for federal assistance" and release resources from "the governmental emergency fund or such other funds as may be available". Lastly, the legislature has the ability to terminate a "state disaster emergency" at any time by a concurrent resolution.

Similar laws relating to emergency powers can be found in state-level legislation across the United States. The constitution of the state of Wisconsin, for example, does not mention a specific provision on the declaration of states of emergency, but does permit the executive particular expanded powers in the case of a public health crisis (Jackson, 2020: 2). In the Wisconsin constitution, the governor has the "the power to convene the legislature" when confronted with "danger from the prevalence of a contagious disease" (Wisconsin Const. art. V sec. 4). The governor has the power to enact executive orders, an undefined power based loosely on the executive power, and the ability to "transact all necessary business with the officers of the government, civil and military" (Wisconsin Const. art. V sec. 1 and sec. 4). In addition, under the state's Emergency Management Statute, the governor may declare a "Public Health Emergency", granting emergency power to the state health department for a 60-day period, without conferring additional executive powers (Wisconsin State Statutes chapter 323 subchapter II 323.10). Similarly to New York and Wisconsin, state law in Connecticut allows the governor to state a Declaration of Public Health and Civil Preparedness, while the governor of Massachusetts can institute a state of emergency through executive order (Foertsch et al., 2020: 4).

2.2 *Stages, Targets, and Institutions*

Some state governors fully utilized expanded powers in declaring states of emergency—a sharp contrast to the actions taken by the presidential office. In responding to COVID-19, the office of the executive at the federal level made only a handful of regulatory contributions. After many states had already issued emergency declarations and congress had been working on legislation to contain the virus and offer relief, the president signed into law the first COVID-19 relief Bill of a series on 18 March 2020 (Fitzgerald, 2020: 1). This Bill, HR 6201, authorized funding for increased testing in individual states. A few days later, on March 22nd, the administration authorized FEMA (the Federal Emergency Management Agency) to fund US National Guard units in testing operations. With this action, National Guard units would be deployed to individual states with exceptionally large coronavirus outbreaks to assist in testing. Next, on April 1st, a mandatory two-week lockdown was instituted across federal prisons to prevent the virus from spreading in the facilities. Over a month later, on 11 May 2020, the US government implored states to test all residents and staff of nursing homes. By June 24th, the administration announced its plans to reduce support at testing sites, urging state governments to take their place. Additionally, for the first time, on July 21st, the president asked citizens to wear masks when social distancing could not be maintained. From the above stages of the federal response to the pandemic, it is clear that individual states had to play significantly more active roles in producing and enforcing COVID-19 policy if they wanted to aggressively confront the virus.

Although the New York state government began making preparations for the virus at an earlier point, New York and Wisconsin issued states of emergency for COVID-19 within less than a week of one another (Foertsch et al., 2020; Jackson, 2020). On 24 January 2020, New York began testing for possible cases and the state government encouraged health precautions (Foertsch et al., 2020: 1). By the beginning of February, a public health hotline was created for questions regarding COVID. New York had its first confirmed case of the virus on March 1st and the following day would mark the continuous flow of new legislation addressing the health crisis (Foertsch et al., 2020: 1–2). New York's governor at the time, Andrew Cuomo, was a Democrat and the majority of state's legislature was in the democratic party as well (Foertsch et al., 2020: 3). As such, COVID-related policy passed rapidly through the state's government and was set into motion, facing little to no friction. In contrast, Wisconsin did not begin preparations for the impending pandemic until nearly a month after the state's first confirmed case of the virus on 5 February 2020 (Jackson, 2020: 1). The state began testing on the 2nd of March and issued a declaration of a health emergency 10 days later on 12 March 2020. Much of the legislation related to COVID-19 that followed was issued through the office of the governor in the form of an executive order. Unlike New York, the legislative and executive branches of the state's government were of opposing parties and, thus, cooperation on regulation was limited (Jackson, 2020: 2).

Once the state of emergency was declared in New York on 7 March 2020, government measures to combat the virus became increasingly extensive and restrictive (Foertsch et al., 2020: 1–2). As March progressed, residents of New York saw the cancelation of large events, limitations on smaller events and social gatherings, bars and restaurants moved to takeout and delivery, increases in hospital capacities and medical equipment, closures of non-essential businesses, social distancing and self-quarantine, and the delay of a primary election. In the four months that followed, public mask-wearing was made mandatory; the role of the health department expanded; relief was given to renters, homeowners, and the unemployed; and plans were made for multi-stage re-openings. Furthermore, inter-state coordination on COVID-19 measures began in the tri-state area on March 16th, with four other neighboring states also in collaboration for re-opening.

At the onset of the COVID-19 crisis, the governor of Wisconsin, Tony Evers, issued a declaration of health emergency on 12 March 2020 (Jackson, 2020: 1). That month, all schools were closed, gatherings were restricted to less than 10 people, unemployment requirements were reduced, the "Safer at Home" order was issued, and evictions and foreclosures were suspended, among other measures. The next month, the governor suspended in-person voting—a measure overturned by the state supreme court—and economic relief was sent out for employers and employees. That month, a reopening plan was also announced. In May, the Wisconsin Supreme Court would also strike down the governor's "Safer at Home" order.

As we saw above, the US federal government played a relatively imperceptible role in COVID-related regulations, largely leaving state governments to implement controls on their own. In this way, no policy on the federal level had a direct impact on individuals in terms of regulation of the virus (Fitzgerald, 2020: 2). The Whitehouse Coronavirus Taskforce, composed of members of the White House, FEMA, and the Center for Disease Control (CDC), offered guidelines and recommendations for individuals, businesses, and states, but no control mandates. Action from the federal level was chiefly in the form of suggestions, with general recommendations for people to avoid bars, restaurants, and unnecessary travel, and to cap social gatherings at nine people. In addition to issuing general guidelines and assistance for testing in individual states, the federal government offered some incentives for good practices. For instance, a set of relief measures passed by the federal government in March aimed to ensure that small businesses were capable of granting leaves of absence or sick leave to their employees so that infected individuals would not be required to work (Fitzgerald, 2020: 3). Furthermore, the federal government passed additional relief funds to incentivize employers to keep employees working from home. Yet, no punitive measures were instituted at the federal level for noncompliance. Thus, measures of control were left to states and businesses.

Wisconsin and New York, along with all states in the United States, implemented policies to help stop the spread of COVID-19, but the extent and length of these policies remained highly dependent upon the political makeup of state governments. Both New York and Wisconsin enforced public health measures through local and state law enforcement. However, New York additionally asked its residents to police one another by reporting misdeeds to authorities. In addition, cooperation with the instituted policies as well as their enforcement relied upon the political leanings of individual citizens and local officials

In New York, New Rochelle was the first majorly affected area by the virus. On 10 March 2020, the governor ordered all of the town's churches, schools, and large gatherings to close for two weeks and deployed the national guard to the area (Foertsch et al., 2020: 1). Two days later, the governor made a state-wide order to cancel all gatherings greater than 500 people and limit gatherings of less than 500 by 50%. Limits were also placed on nursing home visitations at this time. Shortly thereafter, the workforce of the local government was reduced by 50%, social gatherings were reduced to a 50-person maximum, restaurants and bars were ordered to move to takeout and delivery, and gyms, movie theaters, and casinos were closed. By March 18th, the governor ordered employers to half in-office personnel with the exception of essential services and, two days later, non-essential businesses had to close as mandated by the "New York on PAUSE" executive order (Foertsch et al., 2020: 2). The last major restriction on the public was an executive order delaying the primary election to June 23rd.

For the month following governor Evers' declaration of a health emergency, Wisconsinites experienced a number of restrictions like those of New York. On 13 March 2020, all Wisconsin schools were closed. Four days later, public gatherings were restricted to less than 10 people and the governor issued the "Safer at Home" order after a week which directed the health department to prohibit nonessential travel, among other things (Jackson, 2020: 1, 3). What's more, the governor suspended in-person voting and extended mail-in voting on April 6th, an order later overturned by the Wisconsin Supreme Court.

It remains clear in the case of New York that the public's rights took the backseat to the health and safety of the public (Foertsch et al.,

2020: 5). Technically, the right of "free exercise and enjoyment of religious... worship" and the right of peaceful assembly to petition the government were perhaps infringed upon by social gathering restrictions (New York Const. art I). Yet, aside from mandatory curfews, the protests against police brutality were not disbanded and no closures of places of worship were mandated (Foertsch et al., 2020: 5–6). Furthermore, by enacting statutes, issuing orders, and lifting restrictions and regulations, the government of New York, in some cases, preserved several rights that would have been lost under the state of emergency.

In Wisconsin, the violation of the public's rights is less clear. However, the declaration of a public health emergency implies a prioritization of public health over rights. An infringement upon the constitutional rights of Wisconsinites may have occurred with the "Safer at Home" order and the closure of schools (Jackson, 2020: 4). These actions may have violated the right to peaceably assemble and rights pertaining to public schools and school children (Wisconsin Const. art. I sec. 23 and sec. 24).

The majority of the above actions could not have been carried out unless through a major centralization of power. In New York, this centralization began before the disaster declaration. Four days prior to the New York governor's declaration of emergency, the legislature passed into law an expansion of executive power and a 40-million-dollar appropriation (Foertsch et al., 2020: 1, 7). Once the declaration of emergency did occur, the result was a significant centralization of power (Foertsch et al., 2020: 6). In the northeastern United States, much of this centralization removed the short-term need for legislature's involvement and allowed the executive to alter existing statutes. For instance, the declaration of emergency in Connecticut even permits the governor to suspend existing laws. With the state judiciary remaining the only check on these powers, power was incredibly centralized during COVID-19 because state's supreme court largely functioned on a limited basis. Furthermore, the homogeneity of political party affiliation in Northeastern governments also eased the way for COVID-19 policy. Taking New York as an example, the state's legislature further expanded governor Cuomo's reach by amending laws relating to executive power and more clearly defining the types of emergencies that allow the expansion of this power (Foertsch et al., 2020: 7). During the crisis, the New York legislature also passed several laws reinforcing the governor's mandates. Interestingly, the Connecticut Legislature was on recess from April to August of 2020, essentially suspending the representative and democratic elements of the government.

In Wisconsin, the executive branch faced harsh resistance from other branches of government, illustrating a divergence from the experiences of the Northeast. The existing statutes and constitution of Wisconsin remain vague in dividing responsibility in the instance of an emergency (Jackson, 2020: 4). In the short term, the governor acquires significant power. The governor's ability to declare a health emergency and issue executive orders may allow increased power, but, in the medium-term, other branches can contest these actions. Therefore, the state's legislature held more direct responsibility in addressing the crisis through normal, democratic means. However, the declaration of a public health emergency, as in the case of COVID, gives crucial emergency powers to the state's Department of Health Services: a non-elected, administrative branch of the government (Jackson, 2020: 2). As will be investigated below, the role of expertise in the pandemic response lent power to individuals outside of the representative and democratic context.

The advice of experts was a main driver of governmental policy and served as its justification. In both Wisconsin and New York, as well as other states, experts were given wide-reaching power in creating and shaping COVID-19 policy as well. The role of experts in this capacity represents a step outside the legally established functions of democratically elected representatives. In New York, the volume of statutory changes and attention to detail implies the governor's close work with the state's department of health and illustrates the state's coherence to the reports and guidelines of the WHO, CDC, and US Health and Human Services (Foertsch et al., 2020: 8). Governor Cuomo routinely granted power to experts, allowing them to act on their own decisions.

Instead of granting the executive office expanded powers, a declaration of a public health emergency in Wisconsin places emergency powers in the hands of the Department of Health Services (DHS) for a 60-day period (Jackson, 2020: 2). When governor Evers declared a health crisis, the DHS was tasked as the "lead agency" in responding to the crisis (Wisconsin Executive Order #72). The Wisconsin DHS was granted the power to "take all necessary and appropriate measures to prevent and respond" to matters relating to COVID-19 and the agency was also given the ability to suspend administrative rules if the DHS Secretary "determines that compliance with that rule would prevent, hinder, or delay necessary actions". Under these circumstances, local governments were essentially powerless against the state government and especially the DHS (Jackson, 2020: 5). The DHS was instrumental to Wisconsin's governor in crafting pandemic-era executive orders and the public health and medical experts of the DHS and CDC were frequently cited for justifications. This emphasizes the role of expertise in COVID-19 policy, illustrating the significant power and influence held by non-elected individuals and entities.

2.3 *Exceptions and the Aftermath*

The policies enacted to respond to the pandemic have had a lasting impact in New York, but this has not been the case in Wisconsin. After the short-term surge in power, no new legislation or executive orders have been put into place Wisconsin (Jackson, 2020: 6). The "Safer at Home" order was struck down by the Wisconsin Supreme Court in May, less than two months after it had been issued, and the declaration of a health emergency limited the powers of the DHS once the 60-day duration passed. On the other hand, New York and the northeastern United States in general have experienced longer-lasting effects of the COVID-era policies. This can be seen most clearly in the region's attempts at reopening, as any uptick in cases led to pauses in the lifting of restrictions or a reversion to the circumstances of states of emergency. Policy in the Northeast is still very much influenced by the reports of the CDC, US Department of Health and Human Services, and state health departments. In Massachusetts for instance, rises in COVID-19 cases stopped the state's reopening at the second phase out of four in July 2020 (Foertsch et al., 2020: 10). Similarly, surges in the rate of infection led to a pause in reopening in Connecticut, also causing a stop halfway through the phases of reopening. Furthermore, one can see the residuals of pandemic-era regulation in the continuing virus monitoring practices of states—a topic which is the focus of the following section.

The government responses to COVID-19 across the United States were ripe with contradiction. United States' historical values of the balance of power and representation by democratically elected individuals were not consistent with the approach to the pandemic—primarily on the state level. There was a clear contradiction between the notion of balance of powers and the emergency powers given to state governors and other public entities in the case of an emergency. For instance, power in the state governments of New York and Wisconsin was quickly thrown out of balance in the early days of the pandemic. Even prior to Governor Cuomo's issuance of a state of emergency, the legislature of New York conferred greater power to the executive's office. Even though the members of the state government who passed this action were democratically elected, it still remains a violation of the traditional balance of powers. In other states in the northeastern United States, balances of power were disrupted by the long recesses taken by state legislatures and supreme courts. Furthermore, the reliance upon and decision-making abilities of experts is in conflict with the tenet of democratically elected representatives of the public. We saw a strong reliance on experts in both Wisconsin and New York and the declaration of emergency in Wisconsin constitutionally gave the DHS expanded powers in confronting the virus and the ability to remove possible obstacles. In the United States, the rights of citizens, balances of power, and representative democratic principles all saw contradictions throughout the COVID-19 crisis. Further contradictions were apparent regarding the economic policy response discussed below.

3 Surveillance, Compliance, and Data Use

Since the extra-economic policy measures of the US federal government during the outbreak of COVID-19 were limited and the Trump administration took a hands-off approach to the crisis, this section centers on surveillance and control on the state level and among individual businesses. The state of New York had arguably the most extensive measures on control and surveillance during the pandemic and, therefore, it serves as a vital case to analyze in this regard.

3.1 Legal Framework, Surveillance Practices Before the Pandemic

In the United States, the laws that regulate surveillance, restrictions of movement, and the use of personal data implemented during the COVID-19 pandemic are difficult to pinpoint and not related in any direct manner. However, the 4th and 5th Amendments of the US constitution, the Health Insurance Portability and Accountability Act (HIPAA), and the USA PATRIOT Act, along with earlier national security acts, vaguely sketch a legal framework for these practices. Under the US constitution, the 4th Amendment hints at an individual's right to privacy, but by no means states it explicitly. The 4th Amendment gives US citizens the right "to be secure in their persons, houses, papers, and effects, against unreasonable searches and seizures" (United States Const. Amendment IV). Under this amendment, search and seizure shall only occur with the issuance of a warrant substantiated by probable cause and describing precisely "the place to be searched, and the persons or things to be seized". In addition, the 5th Amendment states that a citizen shall not "be deprived of life, liberty, or property, without due process of law" (United States Const. Amendment V). The mention of liberty particularly in this amendment is relevant to this topic's discussion. Next, HIPAA outlines some privacy measures related to personal medical information. It is difficult to assess the level of confidentiality used by states and private companies in handling COVID-19 testing information during the period. Hence, there may be questions surrounding the data collected by states and municipalities related to COVID-19 testing and if it was stored and transferred in a manner consistent with HIPAA. Finally, the USA PATRIOT Act, or the Uniting and Strengthening America by Providing Appropriate Tools Required to Intercept and Obstruct Terrorism Act of 2001, was signed into law after the attacks on September 11th. This act expanded the surveillance abilities of the US federal government for the purpose of national security. The Patriot Act may have allowed greater surveillance and data tracking to occur during COVID-19 than would have been permissible without the act. Since the pandemic presented such a unique situation, there was no strict legal framework that outlined protocols for surveillance, personal data use, or control of movement: governments had to improvise.

With the rapid and continuous technological advances of modern history, employers' methods of controlling and surveilling employees and their work have become incredibly sophisticated. Before the start of the pandemic, employers had already begun using technology to monitor actions on employees' computers, but this monitoring would quickly progress as work-from-home measures were instituted due to the pandemic. For decades, employers have used technology such as video surveillance and ID cards for security, safety, and loss prevention, in addition to monitoring employees' work-hour emails and other specific activities (Blumenfeld et al., 2020). The surveillance tools which existed before the pandemic focused on particular employee activities, operating in isolation. However, with the arrival of the pandemic, monitoring technology evolved to surveil employees 24/7 across their activities.

3.2 *Surveillance Practice and Data Use During the Pandemic*

Two days after the first COVID-19 case was discovered in New York, Governor Cuomo signed an emergency management authorization into law (Foertsch and Scott, 2020: 1). This Bill was crafted by the state legislature to confer broad powers to the executive's office in issuing directives. One week later, on 10 March 2020, the governor instituted a containment zone surrounding the highly infected town of New Rochelle. At this point, contact tracing was put into effect. However, no executive orders or laws were passed to initiate the practice. On the 29th of March, a fine for the violation of social distancing standards was established (Foertsch and Scott, 2020: 2). Shortly thereafter, New York created its own COVID-19 data tracking website and the fine for social distancing violations was doubled. In mid-April, Governor Cuomo and the governor of New Jersey issued mandatory mask orders for those who could not maintain a safe distance in public. In May, over three thousand contact tracers were hired and Cuomo announced that the mandates would be fully enforced through June. In addition, random inspections would be conducted by public agencies to ensure that businesses would open safely and follow proper guidelines.

For the most part, business operated as usual until mid-March, as the COVID-19 virus had not become prevalent enough across the United States to cause significant and widespread alarm. Prior to mandated closures, some businesses voluntarily reduced office capacities or asked employees to work remotely (if this was an option). Additionally, many businesses chose to intensify cleaning practices within their facilities to place customers and employees at ease, but there was no clear incentive to significantly disrupt regular operations. However, once closures began, the doors to business shuttered rapidly. In New York, for instance, it started with the mandated closures of casinos, gyms, and movie theaters on March 16th (Foertsch et al., 2020: 1–2). Two days later, amusement parks, indoor malls, and bowling alleys were directed to close and in-office personnel was required to decrease by 50%. A few days after that, tattoo parlors, barbershops, nail salons, and hair salons were ordered to close, along with all other non-essential businesses. By mid-April, New York required employers to supply masks to employees who work with the public and, in general, mandated everyone to wear masks in public. On May 15th, the state began gradually reopening. In the states like New

York, which took aggressive actions to fight the pandemic, private business was obligated to follow COVID-19 directives or face financial or legal penalties. Businesses which were allowed to remain open through the pandemic and those which reopened later on were ordered by the state to ensure that their employees and customers followed COVID-19 safety protocols. We analyze enforcement of these rules in-depth below.

At the federal level, the US government exercised minimal power or guidance with respect to surveillance or control in the containment of COVID. Besides the general recommendations, handful of incentivizing measures, and temporary assistance in testing from the federal level, COVID-19 was controlled entirely by the state and local governments. In fact, there remained no direct impact on individuals in terms of surveillance or management measures from the federal government (Fitzgerald, 2020: 2). With the lack of federal guidance, local and state governments put into action their own surveillance techniques and methods of enforcement—that is, if they elected to do so independently. The enforcement of and voluntary participation in the control and surveillance of the virus in the United States were shown by a patchwork of local and state policies and a fragmentary social response (Fitzgerald, 2020: 2). Without federally mandated measures for COVID-19 prevention, stay-at-home orders, mask mandates, and business closures and operational regulations often occurred at the local level. However, due to the nature of decentralized power in the United States and the politicization of the virus, local and state responses were immensely varied. In some cases, local and state health departments organized teams of private citizens to assist in contact tracing (Fitzgerald, 2020: 4). In other cases, contact tracing was practically nonexistent. Control methods of the virus remained highly dependent upon the state and locality, and any move to enforce protective equipment usage, restrict movement, or limit business operations faced protest and criticism.

New York and the northeastern states in general aimed to produce unified strategies for countering the virus. For instance, New York and Massachusetts enforced social distancing measures through fines (Foertsch and Scott, 2020: 3). New York began with a fine, which it later doubled, whereas Massachusetts set fines for social distancing violations and added possible prison time. In contrast, Connecticut mandated masks and social distancing, but did not enforce the mandates with fines. Although regulations were established for individual noncompliance, the New York government more strictly enforced its pandemic mandates with respect to businesses (Foertsch and Scott, 2020: 4). Generally, individual citizens did not have to fear recourse for noncompliance in their everyday lives. However, individuals were policed more indirectly by the state through data tracking and contact tracing, while also facing surveillance from their employers in the new work-from-home and "essential worker" settings.

New York and Connecticut remain important examples of COVID-19 surveillance methods through their use of contact tracing and data tracking. New York state's health department collected information on each infected patient, while the infection control coordinator kept a "tally of patients through contact tracing" (Foertsch and Scott, 2020: 4). People known as contact tracers would reach out to COVID-positive patients in order to identify and alert individuals who may have been exposed to the virus. The state hired and trained contact tracers "to work with state-of-the-art software to gather information on the spread of the infection" (Foertsch and Scott, 2020: 4). What's more, the particular software implemented by the New York state government was "known to tap into cellular mobile networks using device location data to pinpoint specific individuals" and individuals "who could have been in close contact with them"—and all of this could be done "*without need of a warrant issued by a judge*" (Foertsch and Scott, 2020: 4). Similarly, the government of Connecticut initiated the "ContaCT" programme, using a software system for monitoring those affected by the virus. When an individual tested positive for COVID-19 in the state, they were asked to isolate and contacted by public health professionals to fill out a survey (Foertsch and Scott, 2020: 5). This questionnaire aimed to collect basic information on symptoms, the ability to self-isolate", assess "unmet needs (such as access to food, housing, and healthcare, etc.)", and "to connect people who are being asked to isolate with the resources needed to be successful" (Foertsch and Scott, 2020: 5). In addition, Massachusetts initiated contact tracing, primarily carried out through cell phone data and volunteered information (Foertsch and Scott, 2020: 6).

Aside from contact tracing, to limit the spread of COVID-19, states intensified testing practices, enacted quarantine controls, placed restrictions on travelers, and tested new methods for the identification of those infected. Once testing began, the northeastern states sought to ramp up testing as much as possible (Foertsch and Scott, 2020: 5). Programs of hyperlocal testing started in areas where positivity was high, but the rate of testing was low. As touched on previously, the New York state government placed a quarantine control into effect over New Rochelle—an early hotspot for the disease—and this control was also implemented on other occasions in New York City. Furthermore, measures were also adopted mandating individuals to quarantine if traveling to northeastern states from states with high rates of infection. Thermal scanners were also used to detect infected individuals in public and private places, with Connecticut even using thermal imaging drones for the detection of COVID-19 in several locations around the state. The overarching justification for these measures was, of course, to stop the spread of the virus. However, state governments offered numerous explanations to justify and legitimize such practices.

Data collection, restriction of movement, tracking practices, and other COVID-related measures were primarily justified as necessary to slow the spread of the virus and to facilitate the return to more normal conditions. State governments also partnered with educational, research, and philanthropic entities to further justify their surveillance initiatives. For example, the state government of New York partnered with Johns Hopkins Bloomberg School of Public Health, Bloomberg Philanthropies, and Vital Strategies in creating the "NYS Contact Tracing Program" which they described as "a nation-leading initiative to help slow the spread of COVID-19 and make it safer to begin to return to normal" (Foertsch and Scott, 2020: 4). Similarly, Connecticut provided the rationale for its ContaCT program as helping to "combat COVID-19" and enabling "the safe re-opening of the state" (Foertsch and Scott, 2020: 4). Moreover, the New York Department of Health connected with independent authorities and federal agencies to lend legitimacy to its contact tracing and other pandemic-related regulations, such as Johns Hopkins, Doctor Anthony Fauci, and the CDC (Foertsch and Scott, 2020: 7). New York and Connecticut both ensured the safe handling of the gathered information and assured their citizens that such programs remained the "best chance to protect [their] families, friends, co-workers, and broader communities" (Foertsch and Scott, 2020: 5). Similar moral overtones are apparent in the Connecticut state government's statement that completing the tracing questionnaires "is one way you can continue to do your part and help U.S. fight COVID-19" (Foertsch and Scott, 2020: 5). Ethical appeals were not only used as justification for surveillance, but used as means of enforcing pandemic measures as well.

In the private sector, both "frontline" and work-from-home employees were required to follow novel measures in the redefined workplaces (Aloisi and De Stefano, 2022: 5). The majority of these precautionary measures were packaged as state-of the-art applications and hi-tech solutions to protect the health workers and the public, but turned into devices to monitor performance (Aloisi and De Stefano, 2022: 6). For workers performing manual-types of labor, remote work was obviously not an option. These on-site workers were typically asked by their employers to install applications or new software on their personal devices for safety purposes—and most employees were not in a position to decline. Such applications were aimed at tracking the health of workers and ensuring that hygienic, protective, and safe-distancing standards were followed. The new software gathered biometric and location data, while sending workers notifications and functioning as passports to the worksites. Those who could transfer to the work-from-home setting faced similar intrusions from employers.

In a nearly overnight fashion, large masses of the population began teleworking at the start of the pandemic (Aloisi and De Stefano, 2022: 7). Since the health of the public and employees is not a critical issue in remote work, employers had minimal need for the tracking of health data. Thus, new technology was used to blatantly gather data, without any pretense of pandemic safety. Out of concerns for slacking productivity in the new work setting, demand surged for monitoring software promising to maintain the focus of employees (Aloisi and De Stefano, 2022: 9). New workplace surveillance software such as Activtrack, Time-Doctor, Sneek, Interguard, and OccupEye monitored every action of employees. For instance, applications would inform managers if individual employees were distracting themselves with online browsing or social media, while other software would flag sets certain behaviors. In other cases, software would take intermittent screenshots of employees' personal computer screens, create timelines of their bandwidth utilization and search histories, and record the length of time they stepped away from their workstations—with some software even possessing facial recognition capabilities. Even seemingly innocuous applications like Microsoft 365 aggregated wide-ranging data points on workers, organizing them into simple graphs and charts bound for the curious gazes of managers.

The main purpose of these surveillance measures was to support the enforcement of pandemic-related rules. The enforcement was in turn executed by the institutions of the state and by the businesses.

In the northeastern United States, COVID-19 surveillance practices were enforced through various institutions, both public and private, and with varying methods of enforcement. Since state governments were primarily responsible for pandemic policy and the governors' offices held emergency powers to enact such policies, COVID-19 measures were typically enforced through this executive power—unless other actors were tasked with enforcement by the executive (Foertsch and Scott, 2020: 3). In enforcing the compliance of businesses, several public agencies conducted random inspections upon reopening (Foertsch and Scott, 2020: 2). These agencies provided support and guidance for best practices and reviewed the safety plans of the businesses. In New York City, rules were enforced over businesses as required, with issuances of court summonses for repeat violators or especially atrocious cases. For initial breaks with pandemic safety protocols, businesses would face non-monetary orders and educational campaigns. Following this, violations would be handed down by inspectors, with first-time violators incurring a $5000 fine and a stop-work order and subsequent violations fined at $10,000. Furthermore, a New York state executive order empowered local officials to shut down violating businesses and revoke their liquor licenses (Foertsch and Scott, 2020: 3). When Governor Cuomo believed that safety measure enforcement was not occurring on a sufficient basis and that citizens' compliance was slipping, he announced the creation of a new enforcement department of the state to fortify local efforts. In enforcing individual compliance, other methods and actors came into play.

In some cases, state enforcement over individual action was nonexistent, whereas in other cases, individuals were served court orders for noncompliance. In a particular instance, citizens of Rockland County, New York were handed subpoenas to compel them to comply with local officials investigating a cluster of new cases (Foertsch and Scott, 2020: 3). In other circumstances, local governments turned to court summons or subpoenas in order to impose mask-wearing, social distancing measures, and contract tracing. However, most public safety measures were voluntary and received compliance due to the idle threat of enforcement, as police officers arbitrarily ensured compliance in typical public enforcement situations (Foertsch and Scott, 2020: 7). Since measures were generally treated as voluntary, state governments would most commonly just urge citizens to follow safety guidelines and participate in tracking. States frequently used language to draw on citizens' morality and personal responsibility, using statements like "to do your part and help U.S. fight COVID-19" (Foertsch and Scott, 2020: 5). In other instances, governors called individuals who did not wear masks "disrespectful" (Foertsch and

Scott, 2020: 7). Without direct enforcement upon the public from state and municipal officials, enforcing the compliance of individuals largely took the form of hollow threats and moral appeals. In any case, state governments of the United States leaned heavily on private businesses for enforcement of pandemic directives, with the average individual principally experiencing COVID-19 safety enforcement in private businesses, specifically from the employees of these businesses.

When the governors of New Jersey and New York issued executive orders requiring the use of masks when a distance of six feet could not be maintained, businesses were obligated to enforce this order (Foertsch and Scott, 2020: 2). Business owners (and, thus, their employees) were compelled to impose public mask-wearing and social distancing on their premises. In fact, one executive order from Governor Cuomo specifically held bars responsible for policing the sidewalk spaces in front of their establishments (Foertsch and Scott, 2020: 3). On top of ensuring mask-wearing and social distancing, it was common practice for private businesses to resort to using thermal scanners for the detection of infected individuals, both employees and customers. One result of the state's lack of direct enforcement over citizens was the regular harassment workers would face from customers. Without the state directly enforcing COVID-19 safety measures and expecting private businesses to fill this role, regular employees who directly interacted with the public had to become police. The result of this was countless instances of physical and verbal violence from customers directed at employees of private businesses. Other non-state actors, such as non-profits were also involved in surveillance and enforcement. As previously noted, Bloomberg Philanthropies was a partner in New York's contract tracing program (Foertsch and Scott, 2020: 7). Plus, other compliance measures have been outsourced to non-state entities to assist in hard-to-reach areas, like the testing of immigrant populations, for example. Furthermore, New York State issued guidelines that allowed employers to take invasive measures against their employees on the grounds of cybersecurity (Foertsch and Scott, 2020: 6). These guidelines permitted employers to place supervisor oversight or so-called "compensating controls" on individuals' personal mobile devices, possibly making them download forced management and security software or preventing them from deleting sensitive information. Besides the enforcement responsibilities placed on the private sector from the state, private entities independently elected to surveil and enforce individual action. In the name of maintaining productivity and ensuring the health of employees and the public, employers initiated programs of worker surveillance. Due to the precarity of the job market during the pandemic, workers were not in a position to refuse such measures. Employers clearly had incredible leverage in these situations.

3.3 *Surveillance and Data Use After the Pandemic*

Since the federal government offered such a limited response to the pandemic and the actions it did take were restricted to the very short term, one is hard-pressed to find any lasting impacts on surveillance and data usage following the pandemic at this level. Anything relating to sweeping federal action virtually ended when the Trump administration announced its wind-down of support for testing sites on 24 June 2020 (Fitzgerald, 2020: 1). Some sections of the administrative branch, such as the CDC and Health and Human Services, continued to track the progression of the disease and offered guidelines to individuals and states, but these actions have little to no direct impact on American society at large. As the CDC was able to operate largely independently from political commentaries, it remained a trusted resource on control and surveillance measures for COVID-19 for some state governments (Fitzgerald, 2020: 4). Federal support for testing and CDC studies on the virus were the only practices relating to surveillance and data collection that occurred at a national level, leaving essentially no direct federal impact on the American public. Any lasting impacts from pandemic-era measures primarily function at the state and private levels and remain dependent upon the extent of a state's response to the virus and employers' affinities for technology.

Since the federal government played no specific role in COVID-19 surveillance, the surveillance techniques which did exist in the United States were entirely the products of state and local governments (Fitzgerald, 2020: 3). Thus, any residuals of these measures remaining after the pandemic can be found at the state level. Furthermore, continued surveillance of the virus was justified when it came to reopening, as data on COVID-19 in local populations determined if reopening would continue, pause, or revert back to earlier stages of the shutdown. For instance, when planning for a staged reopening, the New York governor cited a lack of enforcement and insufficient compliance as reasons for reevaluating indoor dining (Foertsch and Scott, 2020:

3). A few days later, Cuomo commented that "citizen compliance" was "slipping" and he considered a pause on rolling back particular safety measures unless the public took existing measures seriously (Foertsch and Scott, 2020: 4). Unless it has been otherwise stated, one cannot be sure how long the surveillance practices will last. Some governors are allowed to alter existing statutes under their emergency powers, while also possessing the ability to renew the state of emergency as they see fit. On the state level, the direct consent of citizens was not involved in the implementation of surveillance techniques and methods of enforcement due to the nature of executive emergency power (Foertsch and Scott, 2020: 6). Many of the above practices were implemented without legal proceedings and, although surveillance measures were presented as voluntary, the enforcement actions taken by the states illustrate a different story. In order to reopen states and protect the public against COVID, surveillance and personal data usage may last indefinitely within certain states.

In similar instances with state level pandemic measures, measures taken by private businesses may last indefinitely, with many emergency provisions already becoming structural workplace features (Aloisi and De Stefano, 2022: 2). In addition, the crisis circumstances of the pandemic and its effect on the workplace allowed employers and tech companies to treat employees as "guinea pigs" for testing out new productivity-enhancing and surveillance technologies to remain in the post-COVID-19 world (Aloisi and De Stefano, 2022: 6). The surveillance and control technologies implemented during the pandemic were also found to have increased the workload of employees (Aloisi and De Stefano, 2022: 7). What had initially appeared to be a modern, flexible environment that allowed workers greater agency ended up making work hours longer and workers permanently available to their employers. In a country where a worker's free time has been continually subject to an ever-engulfing work culture, the necessities of pandemic-era only intensified this culture. Family and leisure time have been further encroached upon and the lines demarcating personal life and work life were further blurred. The temporary technological and organizational necessities of the pandemic have become the new modes of operating.

One can only imagine the situation of the US federal government partnering with big tech to monitor and control COVID-19 and its possible results. The surveillance and control experiences of parts of Europe may offer essential insights into these possibilities. Nevertheless, the lack of legislation protecting the privacy of US citizens compared to citizens of the European Union would have resulted in marked differences. With the United States being the home of some of the most recognizable names in big tech, such as Facebook, Microsoft, and Apple, there would be no shortage of available technologies to aid in the surveillance and control of the coronavirus. Above, we already saw the liberties given to New York's private sector by the state government in allowing the use of invasive software and its partnerships with large companies for other matters. If this took place on a national level, it may have allowed the social circumstances warned about by Orwell and paved the way for a social organization modeled after Bentham's panopticon. With such nightmarish conditions, the American public could face endless monitoring by a combination of the federal government and Silicon Valley.

4 Economic Policy

The COVID-19 pandemic created a novel type of challenge for US economic policy. It brought about significant financial turbulence and a crisis of the real economy at the same time. Unlike the crisis beforehand, the pandemic disrupted the ordinary operation of the economy—9-to-5 in person jobs, quick and accessible consumer markets, and dependable supply chains. The two main questions that arose for the policy makers were how "the entire monetary and financial system could be directed toward supporting markets and livelihoods", and "who was [to be] supported and how" (Tooze, 2021: 28–29).

4.1 Economic Policy Before the Pandemic

In "normal" times, the monetary and fiscal policy followed a countercyclical rationale. Figure 1 provides a depiction of the US business cycle, based on the fluctuation of unemployment. On average, the cycles have become longer, and the cycle before the pandemic was particularly long as the economy began growing back in 2010 after the 2008 crisis recovery.

In the context of the business cycle, the uptake in fiscal spending (expansionary fiscal policy) and relaxation of lending conditions would be implemented in periods of economic slowdown, the spending would be limited and lending would tighten in the periods of overheating (Fig. 2). In the years leading up to the 2020 COVID-19 crisis, as low unemployment indicated that the economy was overheating, the financial architecture in place was going through a monetary contraction that

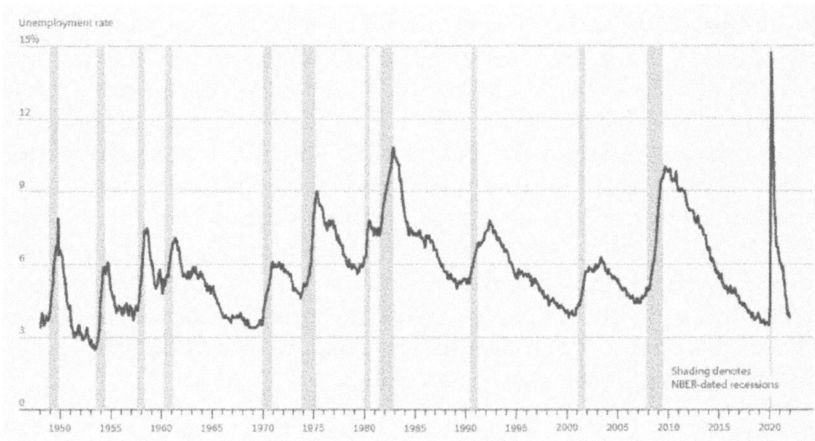

Fig. 1 US business cycle (*Source* FREDD)

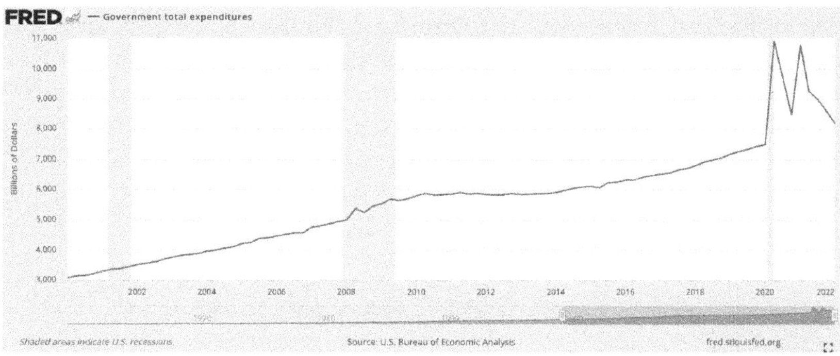

Fig. 2 Fiscal policy (*Source* FRED)

was supposed to discourage unsustainable investment. This can be clearly seen in the case of rising rates on borrowing in the interbank market that the Fed influences through a variety of tools, as shown in Fig. 3. There we also see the Fed's 2019 interest rate cut that came in anticipation of the pandemic. After a long period of monetary tightening, this had been the first interest rate cut since 2008. Figure 2 shows the fiscal side—the recessionary periods entail minor uptakes in fiscal spending, with spending growing at a steady pace since the beginning of 2016.

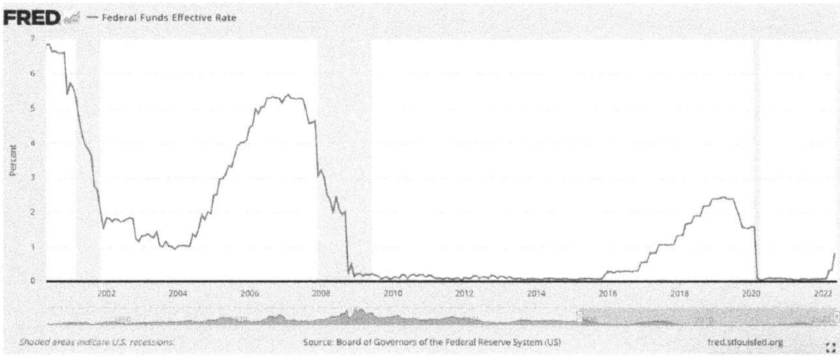

Fig. 3 Monetary policy (*Source* FRED)

Furthermore, due to the experience of the 2008 crisis, monetary policy has evolved as "the Fed [had] embarked along a path of backstopping financial markets through asset purchases and other facilities devoted to liquidity provision ...[that involved] securities purchasing through quantitative easing, repo operations, supporting money market mutual funds, international swap lines, etc." (Klingler et al., 2020: 2, see Mehrling [2010]). Figure 4 shows that, from that point on, the Fed's asset purchase program was not only backstopping banks through purchases of public debt and reserve lending but also non-bank financial institutions and corporations as it began buying private debt.

Though downturns and slowdowns have been a regular occurrence, economic expansion is considered to be the natural state of the US market economy. With that idea in mind, despite the relative monetary tightening ahead of 2020, businesses were supported through tax cuts. President Trump's Tax Cuts and Jobs Act in 2017 cut the corporate tax rate drastically from 35 to 21%, which would supposedly increase corporations' after-tax investment returns and therefore drive corporations to invest further into development projects and job-creating economic sectors. Figure 5 shows the impact of this legislation in the period before the 2020 crisis. Beyond explicit support, the US government has helped currently dominant corporate entities in the early stages

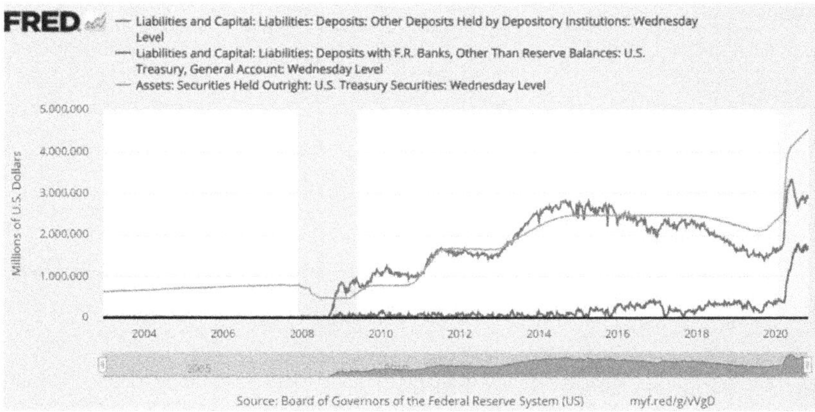

Fig. 4 Fed balance sheet (*Source* FRED)

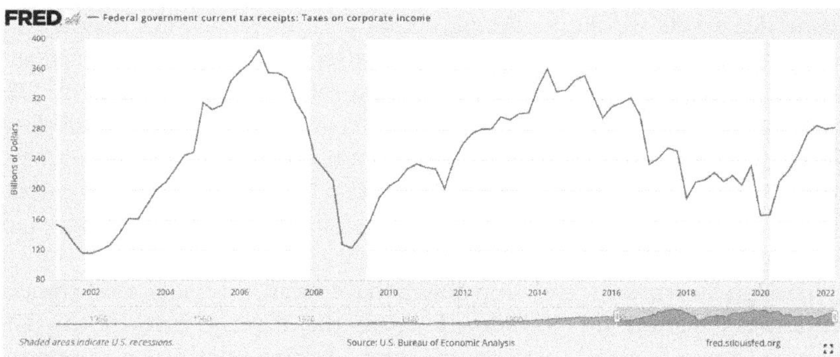

Fig. 5 Federal tax receipts (*Source* FRED)

through targeted spending via grants and contracts. As Marianna Mazzucato (2010) famously pointed out, this type of support has led to major technological breakthroughs (which are the foundation of US corporate success) such as: GPS, touch screens and the Internet, which were advanced by the Defense Department's battery technologies and solar panels developed on a grant from the US Department of Energy; search engine algorithms that were created with the help of the National Science Foundation innovations; and many modern drugs that were developed through research from the National Institute for Health.

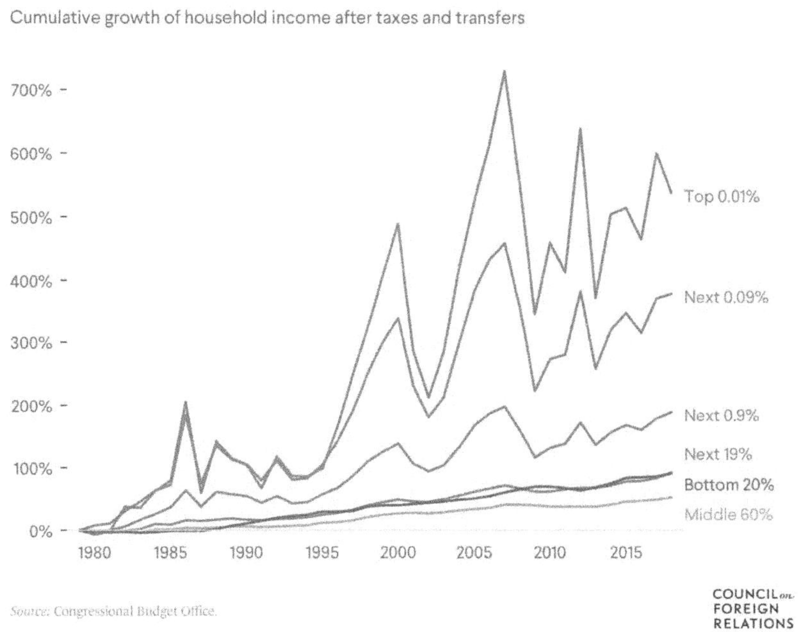

Fig. 6 Income inequality (*Source* CFR)

In contrast to these measures put in place to support big businesses and financial institutions, very little has been done for small, medium business and labor. The political justification of this unequal treatment is based on the idea that big businesses and their lenders are responsible for the majority of American jobs, and therefore, through a "trickle-down" (or "Reagonomics") assumption of economic functioning, warrant more direct financial assistance than small businesses. This approach has led to a significant and rising income inequality (Fig. 6) and racial wealth gap (Fig. 7).

4.2 Economic Policy During the Pandemic

The pandemic brought about significant challenges in the US financial system and the real economy at the same time. Unemployment rose from around 3% to just below 15% (see Fig. 1). Different sectors were hit

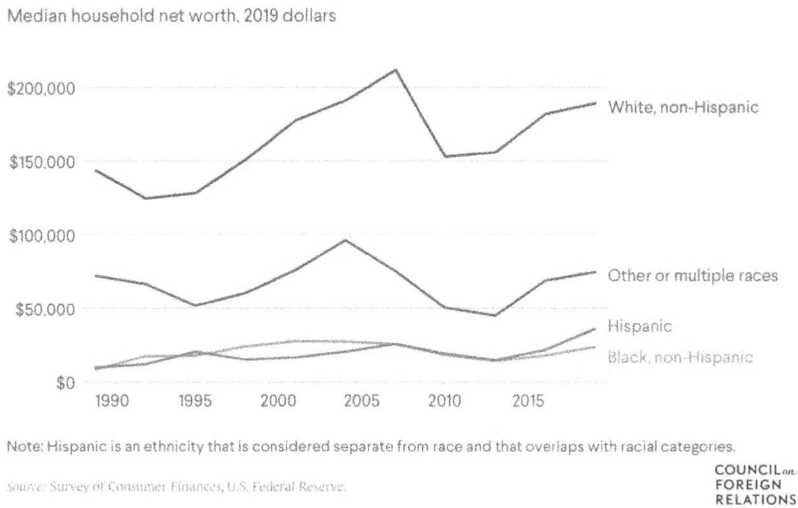

Fig. 7 Racial wealth gap (*Source* CFR)

unequally, with leisure and hospitality losing over 8 million jobs in March and April, followed by retail, professional and business services, and education and health (Manning, 2020). Other hard-hit sectors include oil, real estate, manufacturing, and food industries. Manning (2020) documents unequal harm across communities:

> African American owned businesses have been disproportionately impacted, shuttering at a rate of 41% (roughly 440,000 enterprises), compared to 17% of white-owned businesses; sole proprietorships have been severely impacted and faced major barriers to federal support; Native American tribes' tax base was cut to zero when the pandemic forced all tribal businesses to close, and they did not have the tax base that non-tribal regions do to assist with important health and safety resources, let alone business relief; and entrepreneurs in the informal economy such as undocumented food vendors or sex workers, many of whom watched their income evaporate with the onset of COVID-19, are ineligible for government business support.

New York data is also telling of the unequal harm experienced across communities. According to the survey performed by a group of CUNY researchers (CUNY SPH, 2020), 41% of the city's Hispanic community "either they or a household member lost their job in the last two weeks", as compared to 24% of Caucasian and Asian respondents, and 15% of African American respondents. Also 34% of NYC households with annual income under $50,000 reported losing a job, compared to 28% of respondents with income between $50,000–$100,000 and 16% of those with income over $100,000. Finally, 32% of respondents who did not have a college degree lost a job. (Quoted based on Doyran, 2020.)

Initially in February 2020, in anticipation of the incoming slowdown, investors fled for safer assets, causing a selloff in the stock market and a correlative rise in the fixed income market. This improved borrowing conditions faced by firms, and was thus supposed to help the economy overcome the upcoming challenges. However, in early March, investors started doubting the safety of corporate bonds and even treasuries - typically considered to be the safest asset in the market - and began a bond selloff (see Fig. 8) in order to develop positions in cash. This made interest rates go up, thus impeding real economy borrowing. As Tooze (2021: 123) succinctly stated historically, "only "Black Monday" in October 1987 and the darkest days of 1929 were worse" (Fig. 9)

The initial response to the ensuing economic crisis in 2020 was largely reflective of the response to the 2008 crisis, including "the twin arms of Congressional stimulus legislation... and... the vastly expanded money-printing operations effected through the Fed and the Treasury" (Klingler et al., 2020: 2). The timely manner in which the Fed initiated its monetary policy measures and the Congressional stimulus legislation was

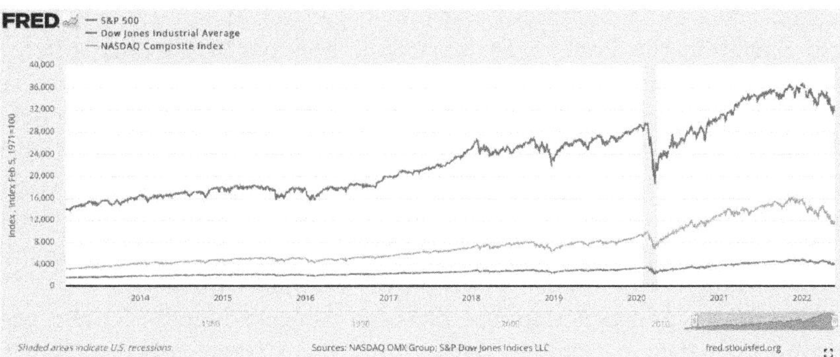

Fig. 8 Stock market performance (*Source* FRED)

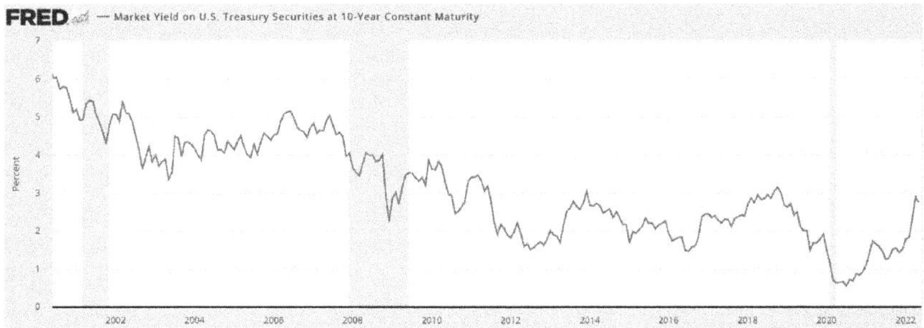

Fig. 9 Treasury market performance (*Source* FRED)

engendered by a relatively slow and lackluster implementation of monetary and fiscal responses in 2008. Taking lessons from 2008, the Fed acted in anticipation of the incoming shutdown of the real economy and correlative financial turbulence.

This initially consisted of cutting the target federal funds rate on March 3 in order to not stifle reserve trading among commercial banks. This was followed by large-scale asset purchases and further lowering the interest rates all the way to zero on March 15. That way the Fed hoped to encourage bank lending and corporate bond issuance that companies could reach for in the case of need to revive their cash flows. Additionally, the Fed took "a combination of re-instituted facilities from the past together with certain newly instituted/expanded ones" in order to combine conventional and unconventional liquidity provision measures that were "more open-ended than after 2007" (Klingler et al., 2020: 2).

The Fed's more significant activities began on March 17 by putting into operation the Primary Dealer Credit Facility (PDCF) that offered overnight loans to banks and financial institutions and the Commercial Paper Funding Facility (CPFF) which bought unsecured, short-term debt obligations issued by corporations. Six days later the Primary Market Corporate Credit Facility (PMCCF) was set up in order to purchase corporate bonds from investment grade corporations, and the Secondary Market Corporate Credit Facility (SMCCF) to purchase corporate bonds and exchange-traded funds (ETFs) on the secondary market.

The most significant response measure came on March 27 (and was expanded further in April) in the form of The Coronavirus Aid, Relief, and Economic Security Act (The CARES Act). As "Of the $2.3 Trillion dollars earmarked by this Bill, it provides $377 billion in small business loans, and $500 billion in loans for distressed companies put into the Economic Stabilization Fund, commonly referred to as the Main Street Lending Program". The CARES act was also intended to specifically support small businesses and NGOs as well as labor, through $20 billion for Economic Injury Disaster Loans (EIDL), $669 billion for Paycheck Protection Program (PPP), tax benefits to businesses that allowed them to defer social security tax payments for up to 2 years, Employee Retention Tax Credit, increased tax deduction for net operating losses for 2018, 2019, and 2020, and increased limits of tax-deductible charitable donations from 10 to 25% of income. As Manning (2020) clarifies, the CARES act "is the biggest economic relief package in U.S. history, equaling 10% of U.S. GDP (compare, for example, to the stimulus package passed in 2009 of $831 Billion)".

In addition to monetary expansion, expansionary fiscal policies were enacted by federal government entities including the Internal Revenue Service (IRS) and the Small Business Administration (SBA). This included the increase of fiscal spending through business loans and payments to individuals as well as through tax cuts, all of which were not particularly egalitarian in terms of distribution. Whether through stimulus checks, direct credit provisions to businesses, or implementing tax policy, fiscal policy was massively unequal among economic players. For instance, of the tax cuts that were included in the CARES Act, which totaled a sum of $650 billion, "less than 3% were targeted to families earning less than $100,000" (Klingler et al., 2020: 3).

The support for businesses and the support for labor from the Fed and in the Congressional stimulus legislation was unequal. Support for large and small businesses severely outweighed the support for labor. And within the support for businesses, large businesses were often given more support through monetary and fiscal policy than small businesses. While the stimulus package passed by Congress and signed by President Trump consisted of several components, large business loans accounted for the largest share (see the CARES act). $500 billion of the $2 trillion CARES Act was allocated to the Treasury's Economic Stabilization Fund (ESF) "to provide loans, loan guarantees or other investments" to large businesses and airlines (Klingler et al., 2020: 7). Furthermore, the CARES aid package faced widespread public criticism upon its major distributional inequities (Manning, 2020). In fact, $104 million in federal aid in PPP loans was dispensed to 41 large companies with plentiful cash reserves (Manning, 2020). Among these receiving companies, the biotech firm Athersys Inc., reported itself to have no significant impacts on business from the pandemic (Manning, 2020). In addition to the fund and loan distribution to small businesses being unequal to that of big businesses, the agencies often failed to meet the promise of paying out the PPP loans in a timely manner. Such distribution problems did not exist to the same degree for large businesses, which further showed the imbalance of support—both in funds and in distribution—for large businesses and small businesses.

Aside from the monetary and fiscal policy measures that were implemented and that would provide indirect support, the Congressional stimulus package did very little to assist and support workers directly. Economic impact payments (EIPs) were distributed by the Internal Revenue Service (IRS) as part of the CARES Act in the form of direct stimulus payments to individuals and families. This included a one-time payment of $1200 per adult and $500 per child, which were based on 2019 income tax returns. The total cost for stimulus payments was around $250–$300 billion. Besides this, financial assistance for labour was structured in a way that required mediation and oversight by the private sector, and in particular, big businesses. For instance, the Treasury's investment in Payroll Support Programs for private businesses as a way of mitigating newly unemployed workers and declining worker wages ultimately showed the federal government's overreliance on creating worker-protection incentives for the private sector rather than supporting workers directly. Unlike in the case of the support for business, further reauthorization of the few labor supporting measures, including stimulus checks for individuals, enhanced unemployment benefits, a period of rent freezes, and a moratorium on foreclosures and evictions in federally funded housing, faced great difficulties (Klingler et al., 2020: 3).

Further complication arose in relation to the way in which these fiscal and monetary measures were distributed among the states. Under Title V of the CARES Act, "the law directs the Treasury to distribute the $150 billion of the Coronavirus Relief Fund to governments in states, territories, and tribal areas" (Klingler et al., 2020: 9). The way in which these funds were distributed among states and localities were based on population and the local significance of public health emergencies, available funding for PPE, ability for local overtime pay and the level of local testing capacity. All states were guaranteed a minimum of $1.25 billion, and additionally, all counties with more than 500,000 residents and cities with more than 250,000 residents were guaranteed a certain amount of funding. For instance, the state of New York was given just over $7.5 billion, with about 70% of this given to the state government and the remaining 30% given to local governments. In comparison, the state of Connecticut was given $1.38 billion, with $622 million of that sum that could be used by local governments. The CARES Act additionally established the Municipal Liquidity Facility (MLF), which allowed both cities and states to borrow up to $500 billion. However, due to the penalty rate associated with borrowing from the MLF, very few state governments showed interest in borrowing. Additionally, by declaring a state of emergency, local governments were able to push back the deadline for filing taxes. Nevertheless, workers were by and large not given the tax breaks and tax cuts as large businesses, and were mostly still required to file their taxes in the Summer 2020.

4.3 Economic Policy After the Pandemic

Two years after COVID-19's emergence, though still recognized as a problem, it is no longer being considered the threat that it was in 2020. Economies around the world have almost entirely reopened, and the COVID-19 narrative has shifted to something "we all must live with". With this declaration, many of the monetary and fiscal policy measures that were introduced in 2020 are now gone. In certain ways, monetary policy, fiscal policy, and the everyday functioning of the economy have returned to pre-pandemic operation.

Considering general macroeconomic parameters, US economic policy seems to have been successful. The financial turbulence veined soon after the Fed engaged with markets more actively and a v-shaped recovery ensued, as can be seen in Fig. 10.

What is of particular interest is the economic trajectory of the financial sector (Fig. 11) and specifically of the non-banking financial institutions (Fig. 12) throughout the pandemic. Despite short term turbulence, the financial sector has in fact grown during the pandemic. Its capacity to capture the benefits of pandemic relief policy is quite stunning.

It is clear that these apparent successes entailed an enormous expansion of the Fed's balance sheet which implies a correlative expansion of supply in means of payment throughout the economy. This helped bridge the gaps in financial markets and allowed the real economy to pick up pace in the short term. However, the implicit expectations of growth based

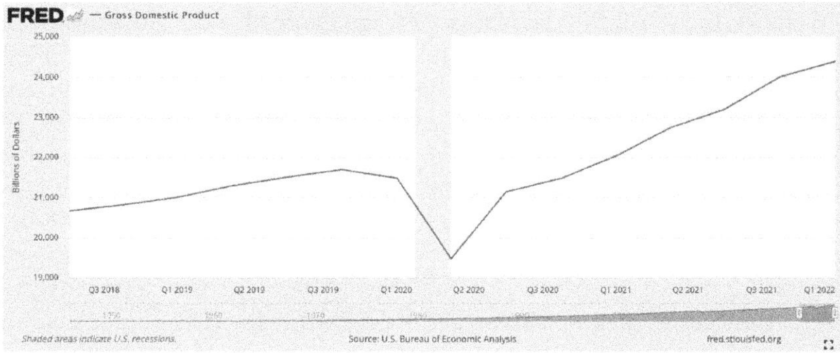

Fig. 10 GDP recovery (*Source* FRED)

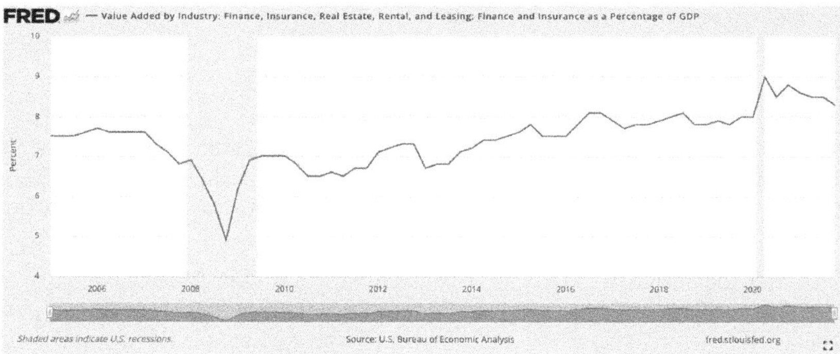

Fig. 11 Expansion of the financial sector (*Source* FRED)

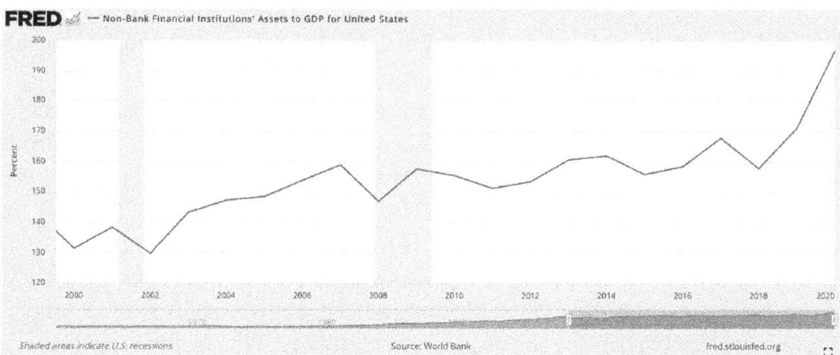

Fig. 12 Non-banking financial institutions (*Source* FRED)

on the lending that has occurred in this period now face a reality check. Even before the distortions occurring in the commodities markets due to the current geopolitical crisis, the economy had been facing challenges in the capacity of the supply chain to meet the surging demand after the lockdowns ended, overheating in the labor market, rising inflation and a significant downward correction in the stock market due to necessary monetary tightening.

As people returned to work and as private businesses found ways to adjust their business model to fit the minimal COVID-19 restrictions in place (such as allowing workers to permanently or mostly move to working online), the Paycheck Protection Program (PPP) officially ended on May 31, 2021. Some existing PPP loan borrowers are still eligible to apply for additional PPP loan forgiveness. The US Small Business Administration (SBA) continues to offer additional economic relief in the form of Second Draw PPP loans and the possibility for EIDL increases. On the labor side, there has been virtually no direct assistance over the last 2 years outside of minimal changes to unemployment benefits and three installments of stimulus checks. Virtually all rental assistance and rent freezes have ended since the state of New York's COVID-19 Emergency Eviction and Foreclosure Prevention Act of 2020 officially ended in January 2022.

However, the COVID-19 crisis, due to its longevity (it is still going on in 2022 at the time of writing), has required more and longer assistance to the working class. Only two months after the first confirmed COVID-19 case in the United States, Congress was discussing an additional $3 trillion HEROES Act that would provide additional support to workers in the form of more "direct stimulus checks, mortgage and debt relief, student loan forgiveness, payroll tax cut, hazard pay, unemployment benefits extension for six more months, housing and food assistance, and nearly $1 trillion for state and local governments to pay workers" (Klingler et al., 2020: 12). While some of these happened and some did not, the lesson was simple: workers were the center of the US economy, even if they were not treated equally to private capital.

The CARES Act and various other federal and state economic recovery programs did not provide virtually any commitment to distributional justice. Even Jerome Powell, the Chair of the Federal Reserve, "acknowledged the disproportionate impact of the employment situation on communities of color", and stressed that "the rise in joblessness has been especially severe for lower-wage workers, for women, and for African

Americans and Hispanics" (Klingler et al., 2020: 9). As it turns out, "many minority-owned business owners, mostly women and African Americans, did not receive any loans" (Ibid). Further public criticism of federal aid has arisen from the exclusion of assistance to undocumented workers and the informal sector (Manning, 2020). Particularly, sex workers and food and construction work have been shut out of assistance (Manning, 2020). California set aside $75 million for undocumented workers, but only 150,000 workers (5% of the total estimated undocumented workers of the state) received $1000 per family in aid or $500 per individual (Manning, 2020). A great disparity is apparent when one considers the millions available to citizens, green card holders, and visa holders in the form of SBA loans (Manning, 2020).

Another sign of distributional bias can be found in the state of New York. For the first series of PPP loans, approximately 81,000 of New York's small business were approved for loans, amounting to $20.3 billion (Doyran, 2020). Yet, this federal program meant for the bolstering of small businesses was also approved for over 200 publicly traded companies—more than 16 of which were located in New York (Doyran, 2020). In the next series of federal assistance, New York state received $17.6 billion in PPP loans for 164,271 recipients (Doyran, 2020). Of these loans, funds were allocated to publicly traded companies which included "a luxury cruise company, affiliated with National Geographic, a film distribution company that provides content to Netflix and Hulu, a mid-size battery manufacturer with over 500 employees and a financial management firm serving wealthy individuals" (Doyran, 2020).

In general, economic policy did not stop the pandemic from disproportionately harming vulnerable communities, and the elites largely captured beneficial effects, based on their race, gender, and relationship to large publicly traded corporations. For instance, the combined wealth of billionaires in the United States rose by 70.3% from March 2020 to October 2021—an increase of $2.071 trillion (https://inequality.org). The five richest people in the country (Bill Gates, Larry Page, Jeff Bezos, Mark Zuckerberg, and Elon Musk) saw their combined wealth increase by 123% in the same period, from $349 billion to a staggering $779 billion (inequality.org). As for the further enrichment of shareholders and top executives, in the third quarter of 2021, American corporation's after-tax profits broke a record $2.5 trillion (inequality.org). What's more, of the largest 100 low-wage employers, CEO pay jumped by an average of 15%

in 2020. These executives acquired huge bonuses, while their workers' median pay stagnated (inequality.org).

The further entrenchment of inequality in America from COVID-19 is indisputable. While the wealthy took on major gains, US poverty increased in 2020 and unemployment skyrocketed from the economic effects of the pandemic (Delavega, 2021). According to the country's Census Bureau, the "share of Americans living below the poverty line increased by 1 percentage point, to 11.4%" (Delavega, 2021). Those in the lowest income brackets faced much greater economic setbacks from the crisis and also encountered greater difficulty in bouncing back. Americans of colour confronted greater hardship than their white counterparts. For example, white unemployment was at 12.4%, while Hispanic, Black, and Asian unemployment was at 17.6, 16.8, and 15.0%, respectively, as of May 2020 (Wilson, 2020). Furthermore, disparities occurred between genders, as 54% of overall job loss was shouldered by women (Madgavkar et al., 2020).

5 Conclusion

Dominant commentary on the US pandemic response entails criticism of the government's activity in curtailing the spread of the virus and the ensuing health crisis, and praise for the quick and effective economic support offered throughout the economy. In the sections above, we tried to show how the pandemic resulted in an increase of inequality, a reinforcement of both economic power formation and the introduction of novel practices in the exertion of extra-economic power. Neoliberal direction of US policy over the past decades has led to rising inequality as well as an increase in the racial and gender wealth gap. It has also led to an expansion of the role of big corporate actors and the financial sector in the economy, and a retraction of the public sector outside of the domain of the military and police. While generally devised in continuation of the neoliberal policy direction pursued previously, the pandemic policy reinforced the implicit division of responsibility between the state and federal levels. While economic support was delegated to the federal level, the management of the "non-economic" dimension of the pandemic was entrusted to states.

State-level approaches to the health crisis lacked robust obligatory rules. Instead they appealed to financial and moral criteria, outsourcing surveillance and enforcement measures to the private sector. This effectively framed the issue as an alternative between a questionable use of emergency power and an absence of democratic checks on expertise on the one hand, and the complete lack of support and guidance on the other.

Federal level approach exerted technocratic efficiency with an appearance of bipartisanship and neutrality as it was exclusively focused on economic outcomes. It still allowed for the pandemic to exacerbate existing inequalities and economic hardship on the least affluent and reinforced the essential role of the large corporations and in particular of the financial sector.

By way of conclusion it is interesting to consider how neoliberal policy concealed and obscured the possibility of a solitary-based response by emphasizing the presumably natural and procedural interplay between state and federal level responsibilities. At the federal level, unequal financial support was provided through the technocratic practices of central bank policy. Based on US global monetary dominance that allows the creation of dollar liquidity and incurring significant amounts of public debt, it was able to preserve the current mechanism of US (and global) capital accumulation. At the same time, federal level policy intended to represent "the will of the people" was limited in going anywhere beyond this. No capacity to politically agree at a societal level on specific rules, rights, and obligations that all citizens would adopt in solidarity in order to confront a common threat could effectively be reached. That problem was taken up at the state level. However, as this process was not backed by an attempt to create a society-wide protection of people's wellbeing and to ensure their subsistence, it devolved into partisan-based conflict lacking the capacity to bring the community together. Furthermore, because no public self-obligation could be reached, the strategy implied putting the private sector center stage so that surveillance and necessary obligations could be imposed as part of the employment contract. In this sense, the process was plagued not by politicization but by subsumption under a fetishized capitalist fiction of political process that had nothing to do with community participation and economic solidarity.

References

Alexander, M., et al. (2022). United States response to the COVID-19 pandemic, January–November 2020. Health Economics, Policy and Law, 17(1): 62–75.

Aloisi, A., and De Stefano, V. (2022). Essential jobs, remote work and digital surveillance: addressing the COVID-19 panopticon. International Labour Review, 161(2): 1–26, https://onlinelibrary.wiley.com/doi/epdf/https://doi.org/10.1111/ilr.12219, accessed 28 May 2022.

Andersen, M. (2020). Early evidence on social distancing in response to COVID-19 in the United States. Available at SSRN 3569368.

Baccini, L., and Brodeur, A. (2021). Explaining governors' response to the COVID-19 pandemic in the United States. American Politics Research, 49(2): 215–220.

Bergquist, S., et al. (2020). COVID-19 pandemic in the United States. Health Policy and Technology, 9(4): 623–638.

Blumenfeld, S., et al. (2020). COVID-19 and employee surveillance. Centre for Labor, Employment, and Work, https://www.wgtn.ac.nz/clew/news/a-question-of-trust-should-bosses-be-able-to-spy-on-workers,-even-when-they-work-from-home, accessed 5 May 2022.

Brennan Center for Justice. (2019). Emergency powers and their use, New York University School of Law, https://www.brennancenter.org/sites/default/files/legislation/Emergency%20Powers_Printv2.pdf, accessed 28 May 2022.

CUNY, SPH. (2020). CUNY New York City COVID-19 Survey Week 2: Job loss in NYC disproportionately impacts Hispanics and lower income city residents. Available at https://sph.cuny.edu/research/covid-19-tracking-survey/week-2

Delavega, E. (2021). COVID-19: this is how many americans now live below the poverty line. World Economic Forum, 21 September 2021, https://www.weforum.org/agenda/2021/09/poverty-america-united-states-covid-coronavirus-pandemic, accessed 28 May 2022.

Doherty, E. (2022). A timeline of Fauci's predictions about the COVID-19 pandemic. Axios, 27 April 2022, https://www.axios.com/covid-timeline-told-through-fauci-predictions-d696e20d-507b-4956-8baa-2ec46e7044d1.html, accessed 3 May 2020.

Doyran, M. A. (2020). Law and economics of COVID19, business relief and protection jurisdiction: New York state, http://globalresponsescovid19.com/reports/Business%20Relief%20and%20Protection_New%20York%20State%20Doyran.pdf, accessed 28 May 2022.

Fitzgerald, H. (2020). Surveillance and compliance, jurisdiction: USA, http://globalresponsescovid19.com/reports/Surveillance%20and%20Compliance_USA%20Fitzgerald.pdf, accessed 28 May 2022.

Foertsch, S., and Scott, C. (2020). Surveillance and compliance, jurisdiction: United States of America, northeast, http://globalresponsescovid19.com/reports/2%20North%20East%20Foertsch.pdf, accessed 28 May 2022.
Foertsch, S., et al. (2020). State of exception, jurisdiction: United States of America, northeast region, http://globalresponsescovid19.com/reports/State%20of%20Exception_North%20East%20Jackson%20and%20Foertsch.pdf, accessed 28 May 2022.
Galaitsi, S. E., et al. (2021). The challenges of data usage for the United States' COVID-19 response. International Journal of Information Management 59: 1–9.
Grossman, G., et al. (2020). Political partisanship influences behavioral responses to governors' recommendations for COVID-19 prevention in the United States. Proceedings of the National Academy of Sciences, 117(39): 24144–24153.
Harris, A., and Varellas, J. J. (2020). Law and political economy in a time of accelerating crises. Journal of Law and Political Economy, 1(1).
Hastings, C., et al. (2021). Intersections of treatment, surveillance, and criminal law responses to HIV and COVID-19, American Journal of Public Health, 111(7): 1252–1254.
Hayek, F. A. (1945). The use of knowledge in society. The American Economic Review, 35(4): 519–530.
Holmes, O. (2020). What Donald Trump has said about covid-19 – a recap. The Guardian, 2 October 2020, https://www.theguardian.com/us-news/2020/oct/02/what-donald-trump-has-said-about-covid-19-a-recap, accessed: 3 May 2022.
Inequality.org. (2022). Inequality and covid-19, https://inequality.org/facts/inequality-and-covid-19/, accessed 28 May 2022.
Jackson, H. (2020). State of exception, jurisdiction: Wisconsin, http://globalresponsescovid19.com/reports/State%20of%20Exception_Wisconsin%20Jackson.pdf, accessed 28 May 2022.
Kerr, J., et al. (2021), Political polarization on COVID-19 pandemic response in the United States, Personality and Individual Differences, 179: 110892, ISSN 0191-8869, https://doi.org/10.1016/j.paid.2021.110892.
Klingler, D., et al. (2020). Informative report on question 3: legal-financial architecture, http://globalresponsescovid19.com/reports/Legal-Financial%20Architecture_USA%20Klingler%20Chaudhry%20Chappe.pdf, accessed 28 May 2022.
Kugler, M. B., et al. (2020). American law enforcement responses to COVID-19.
Madgavkar, A., et al. (2020). COVID-19 and gender equality: countering the regressive effects. McKinsey Global Institute, 15 July

2020, https://www.mckinsey.com/featured-insights/future-of-work/covid-19-and-gender-equality-countering-the-regressive-effects, accessed 28 May 2022.

Manning, F. T. C. (2020). Global responses to COVID-19 informative report, business relief and protection, jurisdiction: USA, http://globalresponsescovid19.com/reports/Business%20Relief%20and%20Protections_USA%20Manning.pdf, accessed 28 May 2022.

Masters, N. B., et al. (2020). Social distancing in response to the novel coronavirus (COVID-19) in the United States. PLoS One, 15(9): e0239025.

Mazzuccato, M. (2010). The entrepreneurial state: debunking public vs. private sector myths. The Anthem press.

Mehrling, P. (2010). The New Lombard Street. The New Lombard Street. Princeton University Press.

Mirowski, P., and Plehwe D. (eds.). (2015). The road from Mont Pèlerin: The making of the neoliberal thought collective, with a new preface. Harvard University Press.

Santis, E. L. (2020). From the leader's lips, to the public's ears: The state of exception, administrative evil, and the enemy in President Trump's rhetoric during COVID-19. Administrative Theory & Praxis, 42(4): 558–570.

Schuchat, A., (2020). Public health response to the initiation and spread of pandemic COVID-19 in the United States: February 24–April 21. Morbidity and Mortality Weekly Report, 69(18): 551.

Slobodian, Q. (2018). Globalists. In Globalists. Harvard University Press.

Summers, J. (2020). Timeline: how Trump has downplayed the coronavirus pandemic, NPR, 2 October 2020, https://www.npr.org/sections/latest-updates-trump-covid-19-results/2020/10/02/919432383/how-trump-has-downplayed-the-coronavirus-pandemic?t=1651592341502, accessed 3 May 2022.

Thorsen, D. E., and Lie, A. (2006). What is neoliberalism, Oslo, University of Oslo, Department of Political Science, Manuscript: 1–21.

Tooze, A. (2021). Shutdown: How Covid shook the world's economy. Penguin.

Vogel, S. K. (2021). The Regulatory Roots of Inequality in America. Journal of Law and Political Economy, 1(2).

Weill, J. et al. (2020). Social distancing responses to COVID-19 emergency declarations strongly differentiated by income. Proceedings of the National Academy of Sciences, 117(33): 19658–19660.

Wilson, V. (2020). Inequities exposed: How COVID-19 widened racial inequities in education, health, and the workforce – Testimony before the U.S. House of Representatives Committee on Education and Labor. Economic Policy Institute, 22 June 2020, https://www.epi.org/publication/covid-19-inequities-wilson-testimony/, accessed 28 May 2022.

Xu, H. D., and Basu, R. (2020). How the United States Flunked the COVID-19 test: some observations and several lessons. The American Review of Public Administration, 50(6–7): 568–576.
Zumbansen, P. (2021). Economic law: anatomy and crisis. Journal of Law and Political Economy.

Appendix: Law and Economics of COVID-19 Questionnaire

Questionnaire

Report Writing Instructions
Please closely follow these general instructions on structure of the report.

- Format
  - 2000 words long (excluding regulatory timeline, bibliography, and footnotes), descriptive, factual, directly responding to one questionnaire entry.
  - The structure will involve a regulatory timeline, introduction, body, and conclusion.

  1. Regulatory Timeline
     - Provide a list of policy measures relevant to the question addressed in your report according to the date of their enactment (if they are not available indicate an approximate time point).
  2. Introduction
     - Begin by introducing basic information and data analytics of relevant trends in the jurisdiction for the specific entry (will be specified below).
     - Signal when the pandemic begun to spread in the jurisdiction—please indicate dates when the first cases were reported and when the first policy measure was adopted.

A. Stojanović et al. (eds.), *The First 100 Days of Covid-19*,
https://doi.org/10.1007/978-981-19-6325-4

    - Signal how far in dealing with pandemic the jurisdiction is at the time of writing.
    - Include measures taken until June 27, 2020—these measures are the topic of the report; they are to be described in the body. All that happens afterwards should be disregarded (in the exceptional case that you consider that report needs to include later measures, please consult with the regional coordinator).
  3. Body
    - The body should strictly follow the structure indicated in the questionnaire entry—use provided titles for the sections and indicate what question you are answering by putting the number at the beginning of the paragraph: "[1]", "[2]", "[3]", etc.
    - Provide detailed answer to all questions.
    - Refer to local (e.g. Region/city-level) policy efforts, practices, and initiatives examples for all jurisdictions.
  4. Conclusion
    - This is the short analytical part of the report.
    - Shortly summarize the information provided and discuss the leading question of the entry.
- Leading question: each entry will have a leading question that will focus on a critical diagnosis of the efforts in the specific regulatory domain.
- Writing style
  - Please bear in mind that the reader is not familiar with your jurisdiction and include any relevant baseline information contextualizing the addressed issue.
  - Use direct writing style with short sentences (no more than two lines).
  - Exclude any information or consideration unnecessary for answering the questions of the specific questionnaire entry.
  - Follow APA style of citation.
  - The main text needs to be fully accessible without consultation of additional materials and information in the footnotes.
  - Footnotes can only address necessary issues.
  - Strictly avoid any form of plagiarism—in particular, no direct copying of internet text is allowed.

- Please quote relevant expressions used by policy makers to justify the adoption of the measures.
- Acknowledgement availability of used documentation.
- Refer to personal experience only when necessary and no other sources are available, and signal reliance on them clearly at every occasion.
- Closely follow the specific instructions indicated at the beginning of the entry.

• Methodology

- Present information in absolute terms and in relation to the context (national average, median, influential precedent, etc.).
- Include debate around law/policy and not just law/policy itself.

    Go beyond black letter of law/policy.
    Consider debate among legislators.
    Acknowledge justification of the measures adopted and of those that were not.

- Consult reports published on the web relevant for the jurisdiction/ questionnaire entry.
- Include influential public opinions/interventions.
- Include oficial policy documentation, speech material, and media material.

(1) State of Exception

**Specific Instructions*

• In answering the following questions please include basic information on the form of government, legislative procedure, and potential electoral procedures of the jurisdiction and ruling party/coalition (date of coming into power, proportion of support in the elected body)

**Leading Question*

• *How has the establishment of state of emergency (or lack thereof) determined the character of regulatory measures taken in response to the pandemic?*

1. Regulatory Timeline

   Please include, among others, main relevant data on spread, intensity, and timing of the pandemic numbers and timeline in terms of population and healthcare system (expenditure per person, etc.).

   Please report main dates related to adoption of emergency measures (e.g. proposal, adoption, and end).
2. Introduction

   Please provide a short introductory explanation on the political situation and division of power in the jurisdiction at the time when the pandemic begun to affect the situation as well as the content demanded in the general instructions above.
3. Body

   3.1 Division of Power
   1. Has a state of emergency been proclaimed in the jurisdiction? When and on the basis of what procedure?
   2. Who activated the "state of emergency" or similar extraordinary response? What kind of controls are established in order to limit the extraordinary powers attributed to the executive branch of government? (for example is there a previous or subsequent control of the Parliament?)
   3. What was the normative justification for the adoption of the state of exception? (please quote relevant expressions used by policy makers)
   4. What powers does the state of emergency grant to the executive branch of government?
   5. What kind of prerogatives and powers are allowed or attributed to the executive branch or other authorities according to the "state of emergency" procedure?
   6. How long is the state of emergency going to last (or has lasted) according to the legal instrument which declared it? Is it possible for it to be extended?
   7. Has there been any political or popular resistance to the adoption of the State of emergency or other relevant measures (where the State of emergency has not been proclaimed)?
   8. Do you have the impression Governments have prioritized health at the expense of other rights (e.g., privacy and data protection, labour rights)?
   9. What rights have been disregarded during the pandemic?

In cases, where the State of emergency has not been proclaimed...

1. If the state of emergency has not been proclaimed, are there any norms or rules that allow/have allowed the government to change/adapt existing rules?
2. In cases, where the State of emergency has not been proclaimed, how long are the measures taken intended to last (are there measures that are supposed to remain in effect after the crisis)? Did the measures already (or will) have an extension?
3. In cases where no state of emergency has been proclaimed, was any public body or authority given discretionary powers to deal with the covid-19? Which ones? On which legal basis and procedure?
4. In cases where no state of emergency has been proclaimed, were any measures justified by using an "emergency justification".

3.2 Competences

1. What are the competences attributed to the different levels of government? What is the relationship between competences among different levels of government involved? Are there possible mechanisms of "centralization" of the powers, allowing the State to interfere and restrict the other level of government's competences? Are there any measures that have removed existing competences?
2. In particular, are there any conflicts between authorities of different levels (e.g. national and regional) in the process of adoption of measures to address the pandemic? How is this affecting the general response to the spread of the virus in the jurisdiction? Has there been any discussion on how the measures align (or not) with constitutional provisions?
3. How have the elected bodies (e.g. parliament, senate) been involved in the decision making process during the crisis? Have the functioning of elected bodies been suspended? What kind of instruments have been used to guarantee the functioning of the elected bodies (for example electronic vote, video-sessions, reduction of the Parliaments' members physically participating in the elected bodies' sessions?

4. What role has been played by the judiciary? Are there any interesting or relevant Courts' decisions related to the legitimacy of Government's decisions? In particular, are there any decisions from the Constitutional Court?

3.3 Role of Expertise

1. What has been the role of expertise (medical expertise) and political authority in making these decisions? Did government officials refer to scientific/expert theories and evidence? Was there any criticism on their way of interpreting this content?
2. Did the Government establish a specific task force or group of experts? If yes, what tasks have been attributed to them (e.g. a prior evaluation of the Government decisions or the study of specific guidelines used by the Government as a basis for political choices)?
3. How, when and at which conditions the limitations imposed by public authorities have been modified or cancelled, considering the development of the health crisis? Is there a monitoring system collecting the epidemiologic data, used by public authorities in order to evaluate the necessity of a return to more restrictive measures?

4. Conclusion

Shortly summarize the information provided and discuss the leading question of the entry.

(2) Surveillance and Compliance

**Leading Question*
What has been the interplay between enforcement of rules, use of surveillance techniques and citizens' compliance in relation to rules adopted to tackle the pandemic?

1. Regulatory Timeline

- Please include, among others, dates on measures that affected individual as well as introduction of specific enforcement practices and surveillance techniques.

2. Introduction

    - Please provide a short introductory explanation on the rule of law, enforcement practices, surveillance techniques, and level of compliance in the jurisdiction at the time when the pandemic begun to affect the situation as well as the content demanded in the general instructions above.

3. Body

    3.1 Enforcement

    1. What specific measures dealing with the pandemic affect the individual: curfew, lockdown (of what degree, spatial magnitude) confinement, social distancing, forced use of masks/globes? Please describe them.
    2. In which practices citizens voluntarily engage, and which are strictly enforced by the Government? Is there a grey space in-between? Despite the mandatory measures imposed by the government, is there any resistance or lack of capacity of the population to comply with them? What are the causes? How were mandatory measures justified by policy makers? (quote significant expressions).
    3. How does the Government ensure compliance with the measures? Has the Government introduced criminal or administrative measures aiming at punishing people not respecting the restrictions imposed? Which measures and what sanctions have been imposed? How strict is the enforcement of those measures?

    3.2 Surveillance

    1. What specific surveillance techniques have been implemented? Identify the different types of measures used by the Government:
        - Contract tracing or other technologies (thermal scanner technologies in public places)
        - Symptom monitoring (for example the use of telemedicine or e-health systems)
        - Quarantine control
        - Extent of testing; any formal programmes?
        - Use of cell phones and/or GPS systems?
        - Displacement monitoring

2. How were surveillance techniques put into effect? Describe the practical process of implementation of those measures in detail. Which executive bodies or authorities were involved in the implementation? Has any part of the activity outsourced to the private parties?
3. Who was in charge of ensuring compliance with those measures? Which techniques or procedures were implemented for this purpose? (e.g. self-authorization)
4. Were citizens involved in the enforcement of the rules and surveillance of others' compliance?
5. Were specific non-governmental or private actors involved in surveillance and enforcement?
6. Have there been any informal social surveillance/ enforcement measures (e.g. naming and shaming practices)?
7. Have there been any privacy concerns with respect to the measures taken by the Government? Briefly describe the relevant laws regulating these technologies and privacy issues.
8. Have independent authorities been involved in the decision making process, controlling the legitimacy or the correct employment of these techniques and technologies in particular?
9. Are there studies, authorities, or forms of control over the effectiveness and efficacy of the measures adopted to stop or to control the spread of the virus?

4. Conclusion

- Shortly summarize the information provided and discuss the leading question of the entry.

(3) Legal-Financial Architecture

**Specific Instructions*

- In answering the following questions distinguish between liquidity measures (keep payments from freezing, and fire sales from occurring) and measures addressing solvency, (support for "essential" or "important" businesses like airlines).
- In answering the following questions identify if authorities are working under existing frameworks, or if new ones were adopted—how are these measures coordinated internationally.

- In answering the following questions please distinguish direct cash grants, financial interventions by the central bank or government guarantees.

**Leading Question*
Which monetary, fiscal, insurance (in particular regarding Included provisions on the occurrence of pandemic), solvency, and tax relief measures were adopted?

1. Regulatory Timeline
   - Please include, among others, dates and timeline on monetary, fiscal, insurance (in particular regarding included provisions on the occurrence of pandemic), solvency, and tax relief measures.
2. Introduction
   - Please provide a short introductory explanation monetary, fiscal, insurance (in particular regarding included provisions on the occurrence of pandemic), solvency, and taxation policy in the jurisdiction at the time when the pandemic began to affect the situation as well as the content demanded in the general instructions above.
3. Body

   3.1 General Fiscal Policy
   1. What are the current measures taken by the central bank to tackle the economic effects of the pandemic? Please describe both the monetary policy (including different assets purchase programmes and related measures) and supervision/prudential domains (with regard to measures such as relaxation of capital requirements, use of buffers)
   2. In what form was liquidity provided to individuals and companies?
   3. What are distributional characteristics of these measures (e.g. do they target the poor or vulnerable in a specific way)? What groups have preferential treatment and of what kind?

4. How are fiscal measures (economic relief packages) being financed? Printing currency, grants and loans from multinational institutions, redistribution of revenue expenditure, etc.?
5. What are the conditions of repayment? Is it expected or explicitly proclaimed that the current rise in debt will be followed by measures of financial discipline in cases of inability to meet debtors' conditions ?
6. What are central banks buying—Government debt? Business debt? Are they buying commercial paper (so that wages are being paid)?
7. In which currency is debt being held?
8. Which are the procedures to be followed by citizens to gain access to State direct payments/benefits? Were there any issues in having access to them (e.g. overloaded site on the day of the opening)?
9. Are there specific groups of the population that do not have access to the relief measures (e.g. undocumented migrants, citizens outside of the country, etc.)?

3.2 Specific Financial Issues and Relief

1. How is COVID-19 impacting insurance payments?
2. Have any types of housing relief been adopted? If yes, for how long and which are the procedures to be followed to have access to it?
3. Which types of tax relief have been adopted? For how long? At which level (e.g. national, state, regional, local)? Have States provided clarification on the application of doubt tax treaties in relation to both individuals and companies (e.g. on residence status or permanent establishment)?
4. Has there already been any proposals of possible tax policies to be implemented after the pandemic?

4. Conclusion

- Shortly summarize the information provided and discuss the leading question of the entry

(4) Employee Relief and Protection of Work

**Specific Instructions*

- In answering the following questions please distinguish between general and sector-specific tendencies among sectors of economy when answering the questions;
- In answering the following questions please distinguish between employees under different labour contracts and conditions of labour;
- In answering the following questions please focus on types of unequal treatment across sectors and individuals in different labour conditions.

**Leading Question*

In what form and to what extent has the relief and protection been offered to employees and unemployed in the economy?

1. Regulatory Timeline

    - Please include, among others, dates and timeline on adoption and implementation of measures of employee relief and protection of labour across sectors as well as the unemployed?

2. Introduction

    - Please provide an overview of conditions of labour across sectors and contract types as well as the conditions of unemployed—consider both legal (level of protection) and economic conditions (income, etc.).

3. Body

    3.1 Employees, Self-Employed and Unemployed

    1. What are the differences in the way that relief is offered to employees, self-employed and the unemployed?
    2. In particular among the employees, how are the informally employed being treated?
    3. What is the definition of unemployment that is operative in the measures targeting relevant segments of the population? Is unemployment defined as widely as possible or are there limitations and some social groups are excluded as they dont

fit the definition? If so, which groups and how big a segment of the population do they cover?
4. How are the conditions for receiving unemployment benefits set up? Have these conditions been modified in light of the current crisis?

3.2 Specific Issues in Employment Relationship

1. Is company borrowing or tax relief dependent on keeping employees?
2. Are companies cutting wages and performing collective dismissals? Is the state compensating for the percentage of the wage that has been cut?
3. Have there been practices of making specific offers (carrot or stick type) to workers in order to keep them working? Have there been ways to receive higher monetary compensation in return for willingness to put health at risk? Has there been any legal/policy action against that?
4. Has there been any complaints by the labour force on employer treatment in relation to COVID-19?
5. Is labour inspection active or affected anyhow during the pandemic?

3.3 Vulnerable Groups and Essential Workers

1. Who are the vulnerable groups of workers within your jurisdiction framework and have they been treated with any measures?
2. Are the workers in the informal economy facing extreme vulnerability and specific risks (for example undocumented migrant workers, etc,. depending on the country)?
3. Are there any groups among the self-employed (gig workers in cases when they are considered self-employed, owners of small (for example family) business), that have been particularly vulnerable in the current situation and what measures have been applied to them?
4. Have there been official declarations of particular worker categories as key or essential workers? What worker categories have been declared essential?
5. Is there a child care provision for essential workers?

3.4 Insurance and Health
1. Have there been any changes to conditions of workers in medical insurance and workers medical protection? How is COVID-19 Impacting Insurance Payments?
2. What are the extra health and safety measures for people working during the pandemic (health care, grocery workers, cleaners, food processing)?
3. Were those measures state, regional, local, or workplace level initiatives?
4. Are mass accommodation facilities (especially in the case of migrant workers) being utilized? Do they provide significantly worse conditions than regular accomodation?

3.5 Social Dialogue
1. Have any bottom-up labour initiatives emerged during the pandemics? On what motive, with which demands?
2. Have unions been involved or vocal? Have the unions and employers associations been involved in discussions with the government around any of the above mentioned state interventions or any other Covid 19 policies or anti-crisis measures which may impact workers or employers? Did any political parties take stands with regard to these issues?

4. Conclusion

- Shortly summarize the information provided and discuss the leading question of the entry.

(5) Business Relief and Protection

**Specific Instructions*
- In answering the following questions please distinguish between general and sector-specific tendencies;
- In answering the following questions please focus on types of unequal treatment across, small vs large companies, corporate vs non-corporate sector, financial vs non-financial sector companies (in particular, venture capital companies), public vs private sector companies.

**Leading Question*
In what form and to what extent has support been provided to companies across different sectors of the economy?

1. Regulatory Timeline
   - Please include, among others, dates and timeline on adoption and implementation of measures of business relief and protection across sectors.
2. Introduction
   - Please provide an overview of general economic conditions and nature of companies across different sectors of the economy.
3. Body
   1. Which measures have been adopted for economically sustaining companies?
   2. Which were the procedures to follow and requirements to fulfill to have access to those benefits? e.g. businesses/beneficial owners must not be resident in tax havens.
   3. Was there any public criticism of the form of cooperation between the state and business sector (and some of its specific parts) related to the measures that have been adopted ?
   4. Have countries openly asked their citizens to support domestic industries to overcome the economic crisis?
   5. Have any measures been taken against distress sales of domestic companies through the FDI route. What changes were made to contain such sales?
   6. How did adopted measures differ across different industrial sectors? Were ad hoc targeted measures adopted for selected sectors? On which criterion was the selection made? For example, vulnerability (airlines).
   7. How did adopted measures differ across the private and public sector?
   8. How did adopted measures differ across different scales (e.g. SMEs vs big corporate actors)?
   9. Which measures were taken for adopting security/health COVID-19 protection and how they influenced businesses? Were there any winners and losers?

10. Is there a differentiation between “essential” and “not essential” business? What are the consequences for companies that fall into one of these categories or the other?
    - lockdown and reopenings: for how long, modalities and for which sectors
    - “smart-working”: modalities and for which sectors
    - production conversion according to States’ needs, e.g. masks, ventilators, etc.
11. Were businesses provided with supplies necessary to operate during COVID-19?
12. Were businesses granted funds for expenses aimed at covering the costs of necessary supplies for working under security conditions? Which procedure has been adopted for granting those benefits?
13. Were there any environmental and other Corporate Social Responsibility (CSR) concerns taken into account? How limited were the adopted relevant measures in the context of objective challenges in these domains—such as for example climate change?
14. Are out-of-Court procedures promoted in your jurisdictions? If YES please describe
15. Is there any provision of compulsory bankruptcy in your jurisdiction? If YES please explain
16. Which policy responses have been adopted in the area of international investment? (e.g. Investment incentives seek to enhance production in the health sector, Acquiring shares in crisis-affected companies, foreign investment screening, Instrumentalizing intellectual property)
17. Has there been any mention of legal action on the part of companies that would involve the activation of private resolution mechanisms?

4. Conclusion

- Shortly summarize the information provided and discuss the leading question of the entry.

(6) Alternatives

**General Question*
What has been the reaction and which were the main alternative proposals being made by social movements, activists groups, and civil society in response to COVID-19 crisis in your jurisdiction?

1. Regulatory Timeline
   - Please include, among others, dates and timeline on responses (in particular, protests) and public appearance of main alternative proposals.
2. Introduction
   - Please provide an overview of the relationship between different stakeholders in the jurisdiction—including social movements, civil society, activist groups, and other social organizations.
3. Body
   1. What are the *main* alternative proposals being made by social movements, activists groups, and civil society in response to COVID-19 crisis in your jurisdiction?
   2. What issues and demands we see arising from the Covid crisis that can be expected to be carried forward in the post-pandemic context?
   3. How are people seeing the role of the state and its different branches?

   3.1 Forms of Reaction
      1. What role the organization of social solidarity and mutual aid have played in their local or regional response to the crisis?
      2. Have there been strikes, protests, or actions of organized resistance? Have other forms of protest/resistance been utilized? By whom? For what reason? How were they addressed by the state/police? How much popular support did they attract?

3. Has the reaction taken the form of political or popular resistance?

3.2 Actors and Vulnerable Groups

1. Which specific actors have been involved in these alternative proposals and forms of reaction? Comment on relevant distinctions and groups mentioned below
2. Which groups were particularly affected by the pandemic? Were they recipients of support or special support by the government? Comment on relevant distinctions and groups mentioned below
    - Rural vs urban population
    - Political parties
    - Indigenous peoples
    - Ethnic minorities
    - Religious groups

3.3 Proposals

1. Please analyse the alternative proposals put forward across different sectors: health, housing, labour, inequality, poverty, food provisioning, and others.
2. Have there been calls for expropriation of private productive assets?
3. Have there been calls for people's bailout, i.e. devolving ownership of productive assets to workers?
4. Have there been calls for rent strike?

4. Conclusion

- Shortly summarize the information provided and discuss the leading question of the entry.

Index

A. Stojanović et al. (eds.), *The First 100 Days of Covid-19*, https://doi.org/10.1007/978-981-19-6325-4

D

F

G

H

N

O

Q

R

S

T

www.ingramcontent.com/pod-product-compliance
Ingram Content Group UK Ltd.
Pitfield, Milton Keynes, MK11 3LW, UK
UKHW020833290926
15470UKWH00004B/1320
* 9 7 8 9 8 1 1 9 6 3 2 4 7 *